IISS

GW00362615

THE MILITARY BALANCE

1995–1996

Published by  Oxford University Press for

**THE INTERNATIONAL
INSTITUTE FOR
STRATEGIC STUDIES**

23 Tavistock Street
London WC2E 7NQ

THE MILITARY BALANCE 1995–1996

Published by Oxford University Press for
The International Institute for Strategic Studies
23 Tavistock Street, London WC2E 7NQ

Director:	Dr John Chipman
Assistant Director for Information:	Col. Andrew Duncan
Information Officers:	
Ground Forces:	Phillip Mitchell
Aerospace:	Wg Cdr Kenneth Petrie RAF
Naval Forces:	Lt Cdr John Downing RN
Defence Economist:	Digby Waller
Editorial:	Rachel Neaman
Production:	Denise Fouché
	Rosalind Winton
Cover Design:	Denise Fouché

This publication has been prepared by the Director of the Institute and his Staff, who accept full responsibility for its contents. These do not, and indeed cannot, represent a consensus of views among the world-wide membership of the Institute.

First published October 1995

ISBN   0-19-828055-6
ISSN   0459-7222

The Military Balance (ISSN 0459 7222) is published annually by Oxford University Press, Walton Street, Oxford OX2 6DP, UK. The 1995 annual subscription rate is: UK £37; overseas $US59.

Payment is required with all orders and subscriptions are accepted and entered by the volume (one issue). Prices include air-speeded delivery to Australia, Canada, India, Japan, New Zealand and the USA. Delivery elsewhere is by surface mail. Air-mail rates are available on request. Payment may be made by cheque or Eurocheque (payable to Oxford University Press), National Girobank (account 500 1056), credit card (Access, Mastercard, Visa, American Express, Diners' Club), direct debit (please send for details) or UNESCO coupons. Bankers: Barclays Bank plc, PO Box 333, Oxford, UK, code 20-65-18, account 00715654. Claims for non-receipt must be made within four months of dispatch/order (whichever is later).

Please send subscription orders to the Journals Subscription Department, Oxford University Press, Walton Street, Oxford, OX2 6DP, UK. Tel: +44 (0) 1865 267907. Fax: +44 (0) 1865 267773.

In North America *The Military Balance* is distributed by Virgin Mailing and Distribution, 10 Camptown Road, Irvington, NJ 07111-1105, USA. Second-class postage paid at Newark, NJ, and additional entry points.

US POSTMASTER: Send address corrections to *The Military Balance*, c/o Virgin Mailing and Distribution, 10 Camptown Road, Irvington, NJ 07111-1105, USA.

Printed in Great Britain by Bell & Bain Ltd, Glasgow.

CONTENTS

THE MILITARY BALANCE 1995–1996
LAYOUT AND PRINCIPLES OF COMPILATION

The Military Balance is updated each year to provide a timely, quantitative assessment of the military forces and defence expenditures of over 160 countries. The current volume contains data as of 1 June 1995 (although any significant developments that occurred in June and July are also reported). This chapter explains how *The Military Balance* is structured and outlines the general principles of compilation. The format for country entries remains the same as in the 1994–95 edition.

The break-up of the Soviet Union has necessitated a re-evaluation of the way in which *The Military Balance* divides the world into geographical sections. Russia is both a European and an Asian state and is given a separate section in the book. *The Military Balance* assumes that Russia has taken on all former USSR overseas deployments unless there is specific evidence to the contrary. All the strategic nuclear forces of the former Soviet Union are shown in the Russian section. Those forces still located in other former Soviet republics are listed again in the relevant country entry. Information regarding European security arrangements, such as the Western European Union, Partnership for Peace and the Stability Pact will be found in the NATO section. The section on 'Non-NATO Europe' includes the Baltic states, Belarus, Ukraine, Moldova and the three Transcaucasian republics (Azerbaijan, Armenia and Georgia). The latter have been included in Europe as signatories of the Conventional Armed Forces in Europe (CFE) Treaty. Bosnia-Herzegovina, Croatia, the Former Yugoslav Republic of Macedonia (FYROM) and Slovenia are listed as independent, while Serbia and Montenegro are shown in a single entry as the follow-on states to the Federal Republic of Yugoslavia. There are two Asian sections. 'Central and Southern Asia' covers the five Central Asian republics of the former Soviet Union (Kazakhstan, Kyrgyzstan, Tajikistan, Turkmenistan and Uzbekistan), Afghanistan, Bangladesh, India, Myanmar (Burma), Nepal, Pakistan and Sri Lanka. The remaining Asian countries are in the 'East Asia and Australasia' section (with China no longer receiving individual-section status). The innovation, introduced last year, of grouping countries in some regional sections into sub-sections has been discontinued. In all sections countries are listed alphabetically throughout.

GENERAL ARRANGEMENT

There are two parts to *The Military Balance*. The first comprises national entries grouped by region; the Index on page 12 gives the page reference for each national entry. Regional groupings are preceded by a short introduction describing the strategic issues facing the region, and significant changes in the defence postures, economic status and military-aid arrangements of the countries concerned. Inclusion of a country or state in no way implies legal recognition or IISS approval of it.

The second part contains more general analysis and tables, and includes three descriptive essays. The first examines developments in the field of Weapons of Mass Destruction (WMD): progress towards implementing the Strategic Arms Reduction Talks (START I) Treaty; the assistance being provided for the elimination of the former Soviet Union's nuclear weapons; the nuclear test moratorium; targeting; the future of the Nuclear Non-Proliferation Treaty (NPT); the possibility of a fissile-material production ban; progress towards a Comprehensive Test Ban Treaty (CTBT); North Korea and proliferation; and developments in the Chemical Weapons Convention (CWC) and the Missile Technology Control Regime (MTCR). The second essay covers all other aspects of arms control including: the CFE Treaty two years after its entry into force; the new United Nations (UN) Register of Conventional Weapons; and the Organisation for Security and Cooperation in Europe (OSCE). The third describes how the IISS estimates and interprets data on defence expenditure. There is also a summary of the composition of all UN and other peacekeeping forces, together with a short description of their missions. In the 1993–94 edition of *The Military Balance*, a 'Reader Reaction Questionnaire' was enclosed. The main recommendations of readers who returned the questionnaire are set out in this edition.

A list of all the abbreviations and symbols used is printed on a card which can be detached from the book for easier use. A loose wall-map is provided which covers the Middle East. The main map, which shows the deployment of key offensive weapons including surface-to-surface missiles, is surrounded by large-scale maps of potential flashpoints.

ABBREVIATIONS AND DEFINITIONS

Abbreviations are used throughout because of space constraints and to avoid repetition. The abbreviation may have both singular or plural meanings, for example, 'elm' = 'element' or 'elements'. The qualification 'some' means *up to*, while 'about' means *the total could be higher than given*. In financial data, the $ sign refers to US dollars unless otherwise stated; the term billion (bn) signifies 1,000 million (m). Footnotes particular to a country entry or table are indicated by letters, while those which apply throughout the book are marked by symbols (i.e., * for training aircraft counted by the IISS as combat capable, and † where serviceability of equipment is in doubt).

NATIONAL ENTRIES

Information on each country is given in as standard a format as the available information permits: economic and demographic data; military data, including manpower, length of conscript service, outline organisation, number of formations and units; and an inventory of the major equipment of each service, followed where applicable by a description of their deployment. Details of national forces stationed abroad and of foreign stationed forces are also given.

GENERAL MILITARY DATA

Manpower

The 'Active' total comprises all servicemen and women on full-time duty (including conscripts and long-term assignments from the Reserves). Under the heading 'Terms of Service', only the length of conscript service is shown; where service is voluntary, there is no entry.

In *The Military Balance* the term 'Reserve' is used to describe formations and units not fully manned or operational in peacetime, but which can be mobilised by recalling reservists in an emergency. Unless otherwise indicated, the 'Reserves' entry includes all reservists committed to rejoining the armed forces in an emergency, except when national reserve service obligations following conscription last almost a lifetime. *The Military Balance* estimates of effective reservist strengths are based on the numbers available within five years of completing full-time service, unless there is good evidence that obligations are enforced for longer. Some countries have more than one category of Reserves, often kept at varying degrees of readiness; where possible these differences are denoted using the national descriptive title, but always under the heading of 'Reserves' to distinguish them from full-time active forces.

Other Forces

Many countries maintain paramilitary forces whose training, organisation, equipment and control suggest they may be usable in support, or in lieu, of regular military forces. These are listed, and their roles described, after the military forces of each country; their manpower is not normally included in the Armed Forces totals at the start of each entry. Home Guard units are counted as paramilitary. Where paramilitary groups are not on full-time active duty, the suffix (R) is added after the title to indicate that they have reserve status. When internal opposition forces are armed and appear to pose a significant threat to the security of a state, their details are listed separately after national paramilitary forces.

Equipment

Quantities are shown by function and type and represent what are believed to be total holdings, including active and reserve operational and training units and 'in store' stocks. Inventory totals for missile systems (e.g., SSM, SAM, ATGW, etc.) relate to launchers and not to missiles.

Stocks of equipment held in reserve and not assigned to either active or reserve units are listed as 'in store'. However, aircraft in excess of unit establishment holdings, held to allow for repair and modification or immediate replacement, are not shown 'in store'. This accounts for apparent disparities between unit strengths and aircraft inventory strength.

Operational Deployments

The Military Balance does not normally list short-term operational deployments, particularly where military operations are in progress. An exception to this rule is made in the case of peacekeeping operations. The contribution or deployment of forces on operations are normally covered in the text preceding each regional section.

GROUND FORCES

The national designation is normally used for army formations. The term 'regiment' can be misleading. In some cases it is essentially a brigade of all arms; in others, a grouping of battalions of a single arm; and lastly (the UK and French usage) a battalion-sized unit. The sense intended is indicated. Where there is no standard organisation the intermediate levels of command are shown as headquarters (HQs), followed by the total numbers of units which could be allocated between them. Where a unit's title overstates its real capability, the title is in inverted commas, and an estimate of the comparable NATO unit size is in parentheses: 'bde' (coy).

Equipment

The Military Balance uses the same definitions as those agreed to at the CFE negotiations. These are:

Battle Tank (MBT): An armoured tracked combat vehicle weighing at least 16.5 metric tonnes unladen, may be armed with a 360° traverse gun of at least 75mm calibre. Any new wheeled combat vehicles entering service which meet these criteria will be considered battle tanks.
Armoured Combat Vehicles (ACV): a self-propelled vehicle with armoured protection and cross-country capability. ACVs include the following:
    Armoured Personnel Carrier (APC): A lightly armoured combat vehicle designed and equipped to transport an infantry squad, armed with integral/organic weapons of less than 20mm calibre. Versions of APC converted for other uses (such as weapons platforms, command posts, communications terminals) which do not allow infantry to be transported are considered 'look-alikes' and are not regarded as treaty-limited equipment (TLE), but are subject to verification.
    Armoured Infantry Fighting Vehicle (AIFV): An armoured combat vehicle designed and equipped to transport an infantry squad, armed with an integral/organic cannon of at least 20mm calibre. There are also AIFV 'look-alikes'.
    Heavy Armoured Combat Vehicle (HACV): An armoured combat vehicle weighing more than six metric tonnes unladen, with an integral/organic direct-fire gun of at least 75mm (which does not fall within the definitions of APC, AIFV or MBT). *The Military Balance*

does not list HACV separately, but under their equipment type (light tank, recce or assault gun), and where appropriate annotates them as HACV.

Artillery: Systems with calibres of 100mm and above, capable of engaging ground targets by delivering primarily indirect fire, namely guns, howitzers, gun/howitzers, multiple-rocket launchers (MRL) and mortars.

Weapons with bores of less than 14.5mm are not listed, nor, for major armies, are hand-held ATK weapons.

Military Formation Strengths

The manpower strength, equipment holdings and organisation of formations such as brigades and divisions differ widely from state to state. Where possible, the normal composition of formations is given in parentheses. It should be noted that where divisions and brigades are listed, only separate brigades are counted and not those included in divisions. The table which showed the manpower and equipment strength of divisions has been discontinued as these are being restructured in most countries following the end of the Cold War.

NAVAL FORCES

Categorisation is based partly on operational role, partly on weapon fit and partly on displacement. Ship classes are identified by the name of the first ship of that class, except where a class is recognised by another name (e.g., *Krivak, Kotlin*, etc.). Where the class is based on a foreign design, the original class name is added in parentheses.

Each class of vessel is given an acronym designator based on the NATO system. All designators are included in the list of abbreviations on the perforated card at the back of the book.

The term 'ship' refers to vessels of over both 1,000 tonnes full-load displacement and 60 metres overall length; vessels of lesser displacement, but of 16m or more overall length, are termed 'craft'. Vessels of less than 16m overall length are not included.

The term 'commissioning' has different meanings in a number of navies. In *The Military Balance* the term is used to mean that a ship has completed fitting out, initial sea trials, and has a naval crew; operational training may not have been completed, but in all other respects the ship is available for service. 'Decommissioning' means that a ship has been removed from operational duty and the bulk of its naval crew transferred. De-storing and dismantling of weapons may not have started. Where known, ships in long refit are shown as such.

Classifications and Definitions

To aid comparison between fleets, naval entries have been subdivided into the following categories, which do not necessarily agree with national categorisation:

Submarines: Those with submarine-launched ballistic missiles (SLBM) are listed separately under 'Strategic Nuclear Forces'.

Principal Surface Combatants: These include all surface ships with both 1,000 tonnes full-load displacement and a weapons system other than for self-protection. They comprise aircraft carriers (with a flight-deck extending beyond two-thirds of the vessel's length); cruisers (over 8,000 tonnes) and destroyers (less than 8,000 tonnes), both of which normally have an anti-air-warfare role and may also have an anti-submarine capability; and frigates (less than 8,000 tonnes) which normally have an anti-submarine role.

Patrol and Coastal Combatants: These are ships and craft whose primary role relates to the protection of the sea approaches and coastline of a state. Included are: corvettes (600–1,000 tonnes carrying weapons systems other than for self-protection); missile craft (with permanently fitted missile-launcher ramps and control equipment); and torpedo craft (with an anti-surface-ship capability). Ships and craft which fall outside these definitions are classified as 'patrol'.

Mine Warfare: This category covers surface vessels configured primarily for mine-laying or mine countermeasures (which can be minehunters, mine-sweepers or dual-capable vessels).

A further classification divides both coastal and patrol combatants and mine-warfare vessels into: offshore (over 600 tonnes); coastal (300–600 tonnes); and inshore (less than 300 tonnes).

Amphibious: Ships specifically procured and employed to disembark troops and their equipment over unprepared beachheads or directly to support amphibious operations are listed. Vessels with an amphibious capability, but which are known not to be assigned to amphibious duties, are not included. Amphibious craft are listed at the end of each entry.

Support and Miscellaneous: This category of essentially non-military vessels provides some indication of the operational sustainability and outreach of the navy concerned.

Weapons Systems: Weapons are listed in the order in which they contribute to the ship's primary operational role. After the word 'plus' are added significant weapons relating to the ship's secondary role. Self-defence weapons are not listed. To merit inclusion, a SAM system must have an anti-missile range of 10km or more, and guns must be of 70mm bore or greater.

Aircraft: The CFE definition of combat aircraft does not cover maritime aircraft. All armed aircraft, including anti-submarine-warfare and some maritime-reconnaissance aircraft, are included as combat aircraft in naval inventories.

Organisations: Naval groupings such as fleets and squadrons are often temporary and changeable; organisation is only shown where it is meaningful.

AIR FORCES

The following remarks refer to aviation units forming an integral part of ground forces, naval forces and (where applicable) marines, as well as to separate air forces.

The term 'combat aircraft' comprises aircraft normally equipped to deliver ordnance in air-to-air or air-to-surface combat. The 'combat' totals include aircraft in operational conversion units (OCU) whose main role is weapons training, and training aircraft of the same type as those in front-line squadrons that are assumed to be available for operations at short notice. (Training aircraft considered to be combat-capable are marked by an asterisk: *.) Where armed maritime aircraft are held by air forces, these are not included in combat aircraft totals, whereas they are in separate naval aviation listings. Air force operational groupings are shown where known. Squadron aircraft strengths vary; attempts have been made to separate total holdings from reported establishment strength.

The number of aircraft categories listed is kept to a minimum. 'Fighter' denotes aircraft with the capability (weapons, avionics, performance) for aerial combat. Dual-capable aircraft are shown as FGA, fighter and so on, according to the role in which they are deployed. Different countries often use the same basic aircraft in different roles; the key to determining these roles lies mainly in air-crew training. For bombers, 'long-range' means having an unrefuelled radius of action of over 5,000km, 'medium-range' 1,000–5,000km and 'short-range' less than 1,000km; light bombers are those with a payload of under 10,000kg (no greater than the payload of many FGA).

The CFE Treaty lists three types of helicopters: attack (equipped to employ anti-armour, air-to-ground or air-to-air guided weapons by means of an integrated fire control and aiming system); combat support (which may or may not be armed with self-defence or area-suppression weapons, but do not have a control and guidance system); and unarmed transport helicopters. *The Military Balance* uses the term 'attack' in the CFE sense, and the term 'assault' to describe armed helicopters used to deliver infantry or other troops on the battlefield. Except in the case of CFE signatories, *The Military Balance* continues to employ the term 'armed helicopters' to cover those equipped to deliver ordnance, including ASW ordnance.

ECONOMIC AND DEMOGRAPHIC DATA

Defence economic data are provided in the first section under individual country entries, and in the second section under Tables and Analyses. The intention is to give a concise measure wherever possible of the defence effort and military potential of a country expressed in terms of defence expenditure, economic performance and demography. A more detailed explanation of the IISS methodology is given in *The Military Balance 1994–1995* on pages 278–85.

Defence Expenditure

Where possible, the data shown under individual country entries include both past (expenditure) and planned (budgetary) figures denominated at current prices in both national currencies and $ at average market or, as appropriate, official exchange rates. In the case of convertible currencies, the use of average annual exchange rates can exceptionally give rise to a misleading indication of real budget increases or declines when a currency revaluation or devaluation has occurred. In these cases, defence budgets are converted at the average monthly exchange rate applicable at the time of budget publication. Final defence outlays are, however, always converted at annual rates. In the case of inconvertible currencies, a purchasing-power-parity (PPP) $ exchange rate has been used in several clearly marked country entries where the use of exchange rates is considered to be misleading. Available data for the two most recent years (usually 1993 and 1994) and the latest defence budgetary data for the current financial year (as at 30 June 1995) are generally cited. In some cases, substantial discrepancies can occur in the official defence budget and actual military expenditure because of falsification by the government concerned. In these instances the IISS provides its own estimates of real military outlays based on NATO definitions of military expenditure, and these are clearly marked 'ε'.

For NATO member-states, both national and NATO accounts of defence spending are provided. NATO defines defence expenditure as all spending on national military forces, including pensions, host-government expenses for other NATO forces stationed in the country, allocated NATO common funding costs covering the three separate military, civilian staff and infrastructure accounts, foreign military assistance, and expenditure on paramilitary forces where these have a military role. NATO figures for the military expenditures of member-states are often larger than the official defence budgets and outlays of the countries concerned.

Under individual country entries, data on foreign military assistance (FMA) refer to that supplied by the US unless otherwise specified. US foreign military assistance covers: grants and loans for equipment purchases (Foreign Military Financing — FMF); International Military Education and Training (IMET) funds; voluntary peacekeeping operations; Emergency Drawdown Authorities (EDA) funds to provide defence services in response to military emergencies or to provide assistance for international narcotics control, disaster relief and refugee containment; and the Excess Defence Articles fund for the sale or transfer of surplus equipment. The terminology of US military aid will change in 1995, with FMF being termed Military Assistance (MA) and IMET becoming Direct Training (DT). Individual details of US support for narcotics (Narcs) interdiction and control are provided. Financial data on military assistance supplied by nations other than the US are identified where these are available. FMA grants have not been included in the defence expenditure of recipient countries.

Economic Performance

Each country entry includes the following economic performance indicators for the latest two years available: nominal gross domestic product (GDP) at current market prices denominated in both the national currency and $ at average annual exchange rates, or exceptionally at a weighted average exchange rate in cases where currency revaluation or devaluation has occurred during the year; real GDP growth; annual inflation measured by the consumer price index; and either one of two measures of debt. In the case of Organisation for Economic Cooperation and Development (OECD) countries, the measure used is gross public debt as a proportion of GDP; and for all other countries, including those with former communist economies in transition, it is gross public- and private-sector foreign debt denominated in $. Average annual market exchange rates of the national currency with the $ or, where necessary, official exchange rates, are provided. In a few cases where currency exchange-rate distortions result in a misleading figure, PPP measures have been calculated. Otherwise, the UN System of National Accounts has been used for the primary economic indicators. The GDP per capita indicator has been derived from PPP figures published by the World Bank. These estimates do not therefore make use of official or market exchange rates, and often differ (in some cases substantially) from calculations derived from these exchange rates. In general, the economic data cited in *The Military Balance* are sourced from the publications of the International Monetary Fund (IMF) or other multilateral organisations, and readers should note that these data are subject to year-on-year changes which are also reflected in the figures given. For that small group of countries for which data from the IMF or other multilateral organisations are unavailable, and for which no reliable official figures exist, the IISS calculates its best estimates based on the available public sources.

Demography

Population aggregates are based on the most recent official census data. In the absence of recent official census information, the source for demographic data is *World Population Projections* published by the World Bank. Disaggregated demographic data for three age groups (13–17, 18–22 and 23–32) of both sexes are provided as an indication of the numbers potentially available for military service. Information on ethnic and religious minorities is provided under the country entries for those cases where a related security problem exists, or in the IISS view may potentially exist.

Sources

International Financial Statistics (IMF)
Government Financial Statistics Yearbook (IMF)
World Economic Outlook (IMF)
Economic Reviews on the Economy of the Former USSR (IMF)
OECD Economic Outlook (OECD)
World Tables (World Bank)
World Debt Tables (World Bank)
World Development Report (World Bank)
World Population Projections (World Bank)
Penn World Table (Mark 5.5) (National Bureau of Economic Research)
Human Development Report (UN)
Economic Survey of Europe (UN)
Economic Panorama of Latin America (UN)
Economic and Social Progress in Latin America (Inter-American Development Bank)
Key Indicators (Asian Development Bank)
Asian Development Outlook (Asian Development Bank)
African Development Report (African Development Bank)
Les Etats d'Afrique, de l'océan Indien et des Caraïbes (La Ministère de la Coopération, France)
World Military Expenditures and Arms Transfers (US ACDA)
Military Expenditure Register (UN Centre for Disarmament Affairs)
The SIPRI Yearbook (SIPRI)
Russian Economic Monitor (PLANECON)

WARNING

The Military Balance is a quantitative assessment of the personnel strengths and equipment holdings of the world's armed forces. It is in no way an assessment of their capabilities. It does not attempt to evaluate the quality of units or equipment, nor the impact of geography, doctrine, military technology, deployment, training, logistic support, morale, leadership, tactical or strategic initiative, terrain, weather, political will or support from alliance partners.

The Institute is in no position to evaluate and compare directly the performance of items of equipment. Those who wish to do so can use the data provided to construct their own force comparisons. As essays in many past editions of *The Military Balance* have made clear, however, such comparisons are replete with difficulties, and their validity and utility must be suspect.

The Military Balance provides the actual numbers of nuclear and conventional forces and weapons based on the most accurate data available, or, failing that, on the best estimate that can be made with a reasonable degree of confidence — this is not the number that would be assumed for verification purposes in arms-control agreements, although it is attempted to provide this information as well.

The data presented each year in *The Military Balance* reflects judgements based on information available to the Director and Staff of the Institute at the time the book is compiled. Information may differ from previous editions for a variety of reasons, generally as a result of substantive changes in national forces, but in some cases as a result of IISS reassessment of the evidence supporting past entries. Inevitably, over the course of time it has become apparent that some information presented in earlier versions was erroneous, or insufficiently supported by reliable evidence. Hence, it is not always possible to construct valid time-series comparisons from information given in successive editions, although in the text which introduces each regional section an attempt is made to distinguish between new acquisitions and revised assessments.

CONCLUSION

The Institute owes no allegiance to any government, group of governments, or any political or other organisation. Its assessments are its own, based on the material available to it from a wide variety of sources. The cooperation of all governments has been sought and, in many cases, received. Not all countries have been equally cooperative, and some of the figures have necessarily been estimated. Pains are taken to ensure that these estimates are as professional and free from bias as possible. The Institute owes a considerable debt to a number of its own Members and consultants who have helped in compiling and checking material. The Director and Staff of the Institute assume full responsibility for the facts and judgements contained in this study. They welcome comments and suggestions on the data presented, since they seek to make them as accurate as possible.

Readers may use items of information from *The Military Balance* as required, without applying for permission from the Institute, on condition that the IISS and *The Military Balance* are cited as the source in any published work. However, applications to reproduce major portions of *The Military Balance* must be addressed to the Deputy Head of Journals, Oxford University Press, Walton Street, Oxford OX2 6DP, UK, prior to publication.

October 1995

INDEX OF COUNTRIES

The United States

Defence and Security Policy

Over the last 12 months the armed forces have faced a serious funding problem. This has become particularly apparent in differences within the Clinton Administration and between the Administration and Congress regarding the United Nations. Although some UN operations – those concerning Iraq and the Gulf states – have continued unimpeded, the controversy over policy towards the former Yugoslavia and payment of UN dues has grown extensively.

UN Funding

The US has long sought to have its share of UN costs – 25% of all UN costs, and 31.7% of peacekeeping costs – reduced. On 16 February 1995, the House of Representatives passed the National Security Revitalization Act which includes a measure requiring the Administration to deduct from its annual UN peacekeeping assessment all costs incurred in direct or indirect support of UN missions. These could amount to as much as the whole US share of UN peacekeeping costs. The bill also prohibits placing US troops under foreign command and bars the use of Department of Defense (DoD) funds for non-defence programmes. In another move, the Senate Foreign Relations Committee approved legislation calling for up to 50% of US contributions to be withheld. Similar legislation is passing through the House of Representatives. Current reports state that the US is roughly $1 billion in arrears to the UN. This arrears, together with those of other countries behind in their payment, in turn means that the UN is often unable to reimburse nations for their contribution to peacekeeping.

Iran and Iraq

The US policy of 'dual containment' has been successful in maintaining UN-imposed sanctions on Iraq despite pressure from certain member-countries for these to be relaxed. Operations *Southern Watch* and *Provide Comfort/Poised Hammer*, enforcing air-exclusion zones over southern Iraq and Kurdish northern Iraq respectively, are still in place. The attempt to isolate Iran has been less successful. The US decision taken at the end of April 1995 to impose a total trade embargo on Iran has not been followed by other Western countries, despite US pleas that they should do so. US accusations of Iran's unwarranted behaviour are not always supported by hard evidence.

Gulf Security

The US Administration continues to bolster the security capability of the Gulf Cooperation Council (GCC) states. In October 1994, when Iraq moved two Republican Guard divisions south towards the Kuwaiti border, the US promptly moved ground and extra air forces to the region. Improvements to US force readiness, equipment prepositioning and transportation assets ensured that this was completed in three days; a similar deployment in 1990 would have taken three weeks. The US now maintains an equipment stockpile for an armoured brigade in Kuwait, an agreement has been reached to locate a second in Qatar, and the site for a third is under discussion with several other Gulf states. The US Navy maintains a strong presence in the Persian Gulf, which can be quickly reinforced by other naval forces in the region. In July, the US 5th Fleet was established to take charge of naval operations in the Gulf, the Arabian Sea and the Indian Ocean. A number of joint exercises have been held by US and GCC forces.

Operations in the Former Yugoslavia

While the US provides a battalion group (UNPREDEP) for the UN in the former Yugoslav Republic of Macedonia (FYROM), an air movements unit in Croatia (UNCRO), and a large number of the aircraft involved in *Operation Deny Flight* (enforcing the UN ban on flights over

Bosnia-Herzegovina, providing protective air cover for the UN Protection Force (UNPROFOR), and conducting air strikes at the UN's request against those threatening the safe areas) and *Operation Provide Promise* (airlifting aid to Sarajevo), there are no US ground forces in Bosnia. This has led to differences of opinion – not only between the US and its European allies, but more significantly between the US Congress and the Administration – over the use of air-power and the UN arms embargo imposed on all the former Yugoslavia. In November 1994, the US withdrew its contribution to the naval operation enforcing the arms embargo on Bosnia when the newly elected Republican majority in Congress ordered funds for the operation to be cut off as the Bosnian Serbs would not accept the international peace plan. However, US naval ships continue to take part in the economic blockade of Serbia and Montenegro, and to enforce the arms embargo on other former Yugoslav republics. Since then, the Republican majority in Congress has attempted to persuade the Administration to deliver arms to the Bosnian government and to take a much stronger line with the Bosnian Serbs, including greatly increasing the use of air-power. On 8 June 1995, the House of Representatives added a clause to Bill HR1651, which is designed to cut foreign aid by $1bn, requiring the US to ignore the UN arms embargo on Bosnia. On 26 July, the Senate passed by 62 votes to 29 a bill proposed by Senator Bob Dole requiring the President to end the arms embargo either when requested to do so by the Bosnian government, or if the UN withdrew from Bosnia. This would only be implemented 12 weeks after a Bosnian government request for a UN withdrawal or when a withdrawal had been completed. The House of Representatives passed a similar bill by 298 votes to 128. President Clinton vetoed both bills on 11 August 1995. It is still unclear under what circumstances US ground forces might be employed in Bosnia (for example, to assist in the redeployment of UN troops and/or the withdrawal of UNPROFOR) and Congress is opposed to any further commitment of ground forces.

Military Operations Other Than War

A number of other operations have been undertaken by the US. In September 1994, after the military rulers in Haiti had agreed to resign by 15 October, US forces began their deployment to Haiti at the head of a multinational force authorised by UN Security Council Resolution 940. The deployed strength of the US force reached some 16,000 at its peak before it handed over responsibility to the UN Mission in Haiti (UNMIH) on 31 March 1995. The first commander of UNMIH is a US general officer and some 2,400 US troops remained in Haiti as part of UNMIH.

A US Marine Corps force deployed offshore from Mogadishu to cover the final stages of the UN withdrawal from Somalia. Part of the force landed on 28 February to cover the beachhead area and left without serious engagement on 2 March. In addition to their normal armament, it was revealed that the Marines would be carrying non-lethal weapons such as sticky foam guns, doughnut guns (firing rubber discs) and shells which release a shower of stinging pellets (bean-bags).

Nuclear Developments

At their September 1994 summit in Washington, US President Bill Clinton and Russian President Boris Yeltsin declared that they would work to ensure an indefinite extension of the Nuclear Non-Proliferation Treaty (NPT), conclude a Comprehensive Test Ban Treaty (CTBT), and achieve global prohibition on the production of fissile material for nuclear weapons. They confirmed their intention to seek early ratification of the Strategic Arms Reduction Talks (START II) Treaty and, once ratified, the US and Russia would deactivate all delivery means reduced under the Treaty by removing nuclear warheads or otherwise rendering them non-operational. They also pledged to proceed with planning for START III negotiations. At the Budapest summit in December 1994, the START I Treaty came into force following Ukraine's accession to the NPT as a non-nuclear state (Belarus acceded in February 1993 and Kazakhstan in December 1993).

At their summit meeting in Moscow on 10 May 1995, Clinton and Yeltsin:

- pledged to cooperate in meeting threats of nuclear proliferation and to improve methods of securing nuclear weapons and fuel against theft.

- agreed to ban the use in weapons, pending completion of a treaty agreed by all five nuclear-armed nations on nuclear safety, of nuclear material taken from dismantled warheads, civil programmes or newly produced material.
- promised regularly to exchange information on aggregate stockpiles of nuclear warheads and fissile material and to arrange reciprocal monitoring of fissile material removed from dismantled warheads.

They also reached basic agreement on a Statement of Principles to resolve their differences over theatre missile defence (TMD), on the rapid ratification of START II in 1995, and to preserve the NPT. When shown intelligence concerning Iran's nuclear-weapons ambitions, Yeltsin agreed not to provide Iran with a centrifuge system to enrich nuclear material, but did not agree to halt the sale of two light-water nuclear reactors to Iran. This matter was referred to US Vice-President Al Gore and Russian Prime Minister Viktor Chernomyrdin, whose Committee on Economic and Technological Cooperation has been meeting at six-monthly intervals and which has successfully resolved a number of bilateral disagreements over non-proliferation policy.

In November 1994, the US finished buying and transporting some 600kg of weapons-grade uranium from Kazakhstan, a process begun in August 1993. The Kazakhstan government received compensation of between $10 and $20 million, partly in cash and partly in assistance.

In March 1995, to help achieve the indefinite extension of the NPT, President Clinton announced that the US would withdraw 200 tons of plutonium and highly enriched uranium (HEU) from the weapons stockpile. He invited Russia to take similar action.

Following France's decision to renew nuclear testing in June, it was revealed that the Pentagon was also proposing to resume nuclear tests, but only of weapons with under a 500 ton yield. Resuming nuclear testing was opposed by both the US Department of Energy (which manufactures nuclear warheads) and the Arms Control and Disarmament Agency. The White House has since made clear that testing will not be resumed, and that it supports a CTBT with no loopholes for small-scale tests.

Strategic Forces

The *Nuclear Posture Review* (NPR), approved by President Clinton in September 1994, reviews US nuclear doctrine, force structure, command and control, operations, supporting infrastructure, safety, security and arms control. Five basic themes emerged from the *Review*:

- nuclear weapons play a smaller role in US security than at any other time in the nuclear age;
- the US requires a much smaller nuclear arsenal than it currently has;
- the US must provide a hedge against the uncertainty of the future;
- the US does not have a national deterrent posture, but rather an international posture which should be maintained;
- the US will continue to set the highest standards of stewardship.

The recommended force posture, confirmed in the annual *Report to the President and the Congress*, while not altering the number of warheads the US plans to retain under START II, did identify ways of reducing the delivery means necessary to carry them. The planned force will now comprise:

- 14 *Trident* SSBN (four fewer than previously planned), each carrying 24 D-5 SLBM each with five warheads.
- 66 B-52 bombers (28 less than previously planned) armed with AGM-86B ALCM and AGM-129 advanced cruise missiles (B-52H bombers count as 20 warheads under START II).
- 20 B-2 bombers armed with gravity bombs and short-range attack missiles (counted as 16 warheads each).
- 450/500 *Minuteman* III ICBM each carrying a single warhead.

This force level is considered sufficient to:

- deter a hostile Russian government;
- maintain a reserve force capable of deterring other nuclear powers;

- allow for weapons on systems not available due to maintenance.

The NPR also recommended preserving options for uploading and reconstituting nuclear forces, should this be thought necessary. The *Bulletin of Atomic Scientists* has suggested that this could include as many as 1,000 W78 warheads (to upload *Minuteman* III ICBM from one to three warheads), 1,000 W76 warheads (to upload *Trident* D-5 SLBM from five to eight warheads) and 1,500 warheads for bombers (including B-1 which is being given a conventional role).

As far as non-strategic nuclear forces are concerned, the NPR recommended:

- eliminating the option to deploy nuclear weapons on carrier-based aircraft;
- eliminating the option to arm surface ships with *Tomahawk* SLBM, but to retain the option to do so on attack submarines;
- retaining the commitment to NATO of dual-capable aircraft and the deployment of nuclear-gravity bombs in Europe.

The US has continued to take nuclear weapons out of service. No *Minuteman* II ICBM are operational, but because not all silos have yet been destroyed, a number of these remain START-countable. A total of 41 ICBM launch silos at Whiteman and Ellsworth Air Force Bases had been destroyed by December 1994. The number of deployed *Minuteman* III has increased by four to 533. Two more *Ohio*-class SSBN armed with *Trident* D-5 SLBM have been commissioned – one in July 1994 and one in July 1995 – bringing the total number operational to 16. Three older SSBN armed with *Trident* C-4 SLBM have been decommissioned giving a total of seven decommissioned SSBN remaining START-countable. A further seven B-2 bombers have been completed and four brought into squadron service. The B-1 force, which is to have a purely conventional role, is still START-countable as the rerolling of bombers is not permitted by START I; they will be removed from accountability once START II comes into force. 195 B-52 bombers have now been eliminated and only 148 B-52G bombers remain at the elimination site at Davis-Monthan AFB, Arizona.

Ballistic Missile Defence

US priorities for developing Ballistic Missile Defence (BMD) are, first, to provide protection for deployed US forces and their regional allies (Theater Missile Defense (TMD)) and, second, to maintain the potential, through research and development, for a national missile defence capability to counter future threats to the US. Currently 15 countries (excluding East European and former Soviet states) hold surface-to-surface missiles. A number of these countries are actively hoping to acquire or develop missiles with longer ranges and improved accuracy.

TMD is likely to be introduced in three phases. The first phase consists of low-cost, short-term improvements to existing systems. These include:

- *Talon Shield*/Joint Tactical Ground System (JTAGS). The early-warning element of TMD using data from intelligence satellites with upgraded processing hardware will improve the timeliness and accuracy of warning which is passed by an Attack and Launch Early Reporting to Theatre (ALERT) squadron (activated by the Air Force in October 1994) via the *Talon Shield* system to a deployed tactical mobile satellite ground station (JTAGS) in theatre.
- US Marine Corps HAWK Air Defence System. Improvements to the HAWK radar (TPS-59), the command, control and communications elements, and the missile's fuse and warhead, give the system a credible TMD capability. About one-third (one battery) of the Marine Corps HAWK inventory has this capability now and all will be modified by the end of fiscal year (FY) 1996.
- *Patriot*. Improvements (PAC-2) have been introduced to *Patriot* providing the system with an enhanced-guidance missile and allowing missiles to be launched up to 12km away from the radar. These are a temporary measure until PAC-3 becomes available in FY1998.

The second phase will introduce three core TMD systems.

- *Patriot* improvements (PAC-3). The Extended Range Interceptor (ERINT) has been chosen as the PAC-3 missile. By June 1994 three successful ERINT tests had been conducted. It is forecast that PAC-3 will allow engagement of 'stealth' targets, produce a more lethal 'hit-to-kill' intercept and will be a generally more reliable system.

- *Navy Area Defence.* Naval TMD will be based on the *Aegis* weapons system with which 38 cruisers and destroyers are already equipped. TMD will be provided by an improved *Standard* missile (II Block IVA) with an upgraded aiming system and an infra-red seeker. An unsuccessful test was carried out at the end of March 1995.
- Theater High-Altitude Area Defense (THAAD). THAAD is designed to provide a far wider defence capability in terms of both altitude (60 miles) and range. THAAD is an army-developed system and its total cost, which could amount to $8.5bn, has been criticised by both the Navy and the Air Force. The system would provide over 100 launchers with 1,400 missiles. Despite the lack of agreement on what constitutes TMD as opposed to anti-ballistic missiles (ABM), the Clinton Administration notified Russia that THAAD testing would begin in early 1995. One successful test flight (without attempting to engage a target) was carried out in April 1995. THAAD could be already in service as early as the year 2000.

The third phase, known as Advanced Concepts Programs, will consider the following systems:

- Medium Extended Air Defense System (formerly Corps Surface-to-Air Missile).
- Navy Theater-wide Defense System.
- Boost Phase Interception (BPI).

Conventional Forces

Ground Forces

There have been few changes to the US Army order of battle. Two independent armoured and two infantry (theater defense) brigades have been inactivated, and two mechanised divisions await inactivation later this year. A reorganisation is under way which will give the remaining ten divisions three active brigades each; the third brigade of divisions in Germany, Hawaii and South Korea will be located in the US. There will no longer be reserve 'round-out' (or third) brigades, but there will be 'round-up' (beyond the third) permanently affiliated to active divisions for training and support. There have been no major changes in the Army National Guard (ARNG), but the number of independent battalions has changed. In a number of states, independent battalions have been grouped together and given honorific brigade designations. Army Reserve (AR) units, which now only have a combat support or service support role, have been grouped into ten Reserve Support Commands and three smaller Reserve Support Groups. There is no change to the command arrangement for AR units in Europe, the Caribbean and the Pacific. In sum, the Army will be reduced by two divisional HQ and three brigades. The division based in South Korea has been redesignated a mechanised division.

Active Army manpower has been reduced by some 27,000, ARNG strength by 19,000 and that of Standing Reservists (who receive annual training) by 18,000. There has been little equipment procurement over the last 12 months. Purchases include 38 more *Fuchs* Chemical Defence reconnaissance vehicles; 90 more *Bradley* fighting vehicles; 120 M-119 towed 105mm guns; and 160 more MLRS (now all 700 MLRS are ATACMS-capable (135km-range missile system)). No new main battle tanks have been acquired and over 2,200 older models (M-48, M-60) have been disposed of. Disposal of M-110 203mm SP has also continued.

There has been a very large reduction in the number of heavy equipment positioned in Europe as stockpiles were disposed of and the size of the force reduced. Table 1 shows the numbers of Conventional Forces in Europe (CFE) Treaty Limited Equipment in Europe now, compared with when the Treaty was signed in November 1990.

The Army is following the Marine Corps by establishing its own prepositioned afloat stockpiles carrying both unit equipment packs and considerable logistic stocks. Elements were already successfully employed in the rapid deployment to Kuwait in October 1994, and to the port of Mombasa to support the humanitarian operation in Rwanda. A brigade with prepositioned equipment can be operational within six days, while airlifting an entire brigade would take up to 28 days and cost over $300m more. Army strategic mobility will be greatly increased when the requirement for additional roll-on roll-off shipping is met and the C-17 *Globemaster* production programme is completed.

Table 1:   CFE Treaty Limited Equipment in Europe, 1990 and 1995

	1990	1995
Tanks	5,904	1,192
ACVs	5,747	1,860
Artillery	2,601	998
Attack Helicopters	243[a]	114

[a] Increased to 349 when the Treaty came into force in July 1992.

To meet its long-term needs, the US Army has begun a complete programme of redesign from the front-line back to the arms industry called 'Force XX1'. Key elements include improving the use of information technology and the handling of large quantities of automatically collected real-time information. To this end the Army Digitization Office has been established to develop a master plan. A major experiment ('Army Warfighting Experiment: *Desert Hammer IV*') held in April 1994 validated the view that digitisation increases lethality and survivability and allows the tempo of operations to be increased. As a result, the Army plans to digitise one brigade during 1996 and a division and a corps by 2000. The Army is also heavily dependent on space assets for communications, intelligence and navigation. Two new weapons systems are considered essential to modernisation. The first is the RAH-66 *Comanche* armed reconnaissance helicopter designed to operate round the clock in all conditions of weather and battlefield obscurants. The second is the Advance Field Artillery System, a 155mm self-propelled howitzer employing liquid propellant, automated ammunition handling and advanced fire control, all contributing major improvements to operational capability. Directly linked to the system is the Future Armoured Resupply Vehicle for the resupply of both fuel and ammunition.

Air Force

While active Air Force manpower strength has been reduced by some 34,000, that of the Air Force Reserve (AFR) and Air National Guard (ANG) has been maintained. Reorganisation has eliminated one numbered Air Force HQ and 14 aircraft wings, but only one active tactical fighter squadron has been deactivated. Two transport squadrons are now equipped with C-17A strategic transport aircraft and nine more aircraft have entered squadron service, bringing the total operational to 20 (it is planned to buy a total of 120). Five Air Force and two AFR transport squadrons have been deactivated. The Air Force has deactivated four tanker squadrons, but the ANG and AFR have formed three more tanker squadrons each. The AFR has deactivated three FGA squadrons and the ANG three FGA, three reconnaissance and six air-defence fighter squadrons. About 100 F-15 and nearly 600 F-16 have been taken from the Air Force inventory and the DoD hopes to sell these to provide funds for other Air Force procurement.

Naval Forces

Four more improved *Los Angeles*-class SSGN have been commissioned in the last 12 months. Two *Los Angeles*-class SSN and five *Sturgeon*-class SSN have decommissioned. The first *Seawolf*-class SSN was named on 24 June 1995, and is scheduled to commission in mid-1996. There has been no change to the carrier fleet except that the USS *Enterprise* has completed its long refit. Two cruisers, the last *Truxton*-class and the last *Belknap*-class, have been retired. Five more *Arleigh Burke*-class destroyers have been commissioned and two *Oliver Hazard Perry*-class frigates from the Naval Reserve Fleet will decommission by the end of September 1995. After a Congressional delay in 1994, the *Newport*-class of Landing Ship Tank has been disposed of, with seven sold or leased to five other navies. A fourth *Wasp*-class Landing Ship Assault has been commissioned.

Naval manpower has been reduced by nearly 40,000, of which 6,000 have come from Naval Aviation. Two naval air wings have been deactivated, as have nine carrier-borne aircraft squadrons. The last two squadrons equipped with F/A-18A have been re-equipped with F/A-18C/N and numbers of F-14, A-4 and A-6 aircraft have been reduced. There are now two Marine Corps aviation squadrons based on carriers. In February 1995, the Navy formed a new Destroyer Squadron to command naval forces in the Persian Gulf in the absence of a carrier battle group. The Maritime Prepositioning Squadron (MPS-1), normally stationed on the US east coast, has been deployed to the Mediterranean.

During the year, the Naval Reserve's contribution will be greatly increased when the aircraft-carrier *Kennedy* (currently in long refit), USS *Inchon* (the first mine-control ship), four mine countermeasure ships and eleven coastal minehunters are transferred to the Reserve.

Defence Spending

Fiscal Year 1995

The US government's request for national defence for FY1995 was $263.7bn. By October 1994, the beginning of the new fiscal year, Congress had approved a Budget Authority of $263.5bn, leaving the Administration's request for an additional $300m for contingencies involving peacekeeping operations (PKO) unresolved. Supplementary funds of $299m to cover DoD costs in Rwanda and Cuba in FY1994 were also approved. Congress made little change to the total requested by the Administration, but took the opportunity to reallocate funds, as is its custom. An extra $125m was made available to the B-2 bomber programme to avoid the closure of the production line, and the pay rise to military personnel was increased from 1.6% to 2.6%.

However, the Administration's future planning received considerable criticism from Congress. In presenting the 1995–99 Future Years' Defense Program (FYDP) of $1,295bn, the government acknowledged that its proposed defence budgets were projected to be about $20bn below the level required by the 1993 *Bottom-Up Review*. In contrast, a study by the government's spending watchdog, the General Accounting Office (GAO), estimated the shortfall at some $150bn. The perceived funding inadequacies have also sparked off another debate over the extent to which the government was creating 'hollow' armed forces. The two controversies caused some quick recalculations. The DoD adjusted its estimate of the potential cost overrun to $49bn and announced the cancellation of the TSSAM missile, together with delays to several other programmes that would save some $8bn. In December 1994, the Administration announced that a further $25bn was to be added to the FYDP largely to improve the quality of life of military personnel and fund their pay increase. By February 1995, the DoD was able to claim that the shortfall had been eliminated entirely by a combination of new and lower-inflation estimates ($12bn) and an increased net saving of $12bn from lower-priority programmes.

In February 1995, the Administration requested a further $2.6bn in supplementary funding for FY1995, largely to reimburse the DoD for contingency costs arising from operations in Haiti and the former Yugoslavia and the deployment of reinforcements to Kuwait. The cost of the Haiti operation alone has amounted to $1bn since October 1994. Failing reimbursement, the Administration claimed that the funds would have to be taken from other areas of the DoD's Operations and Maintenance (O&M) budget – something that would adversely affect readiness. The request was partially offset by $703m in unspecified rescissions from the defence budget. With its new Republican leadership, Congress reacted by approving a larger supplementary authorisation of $3.1bn, but at the same time offset the supplementary funding by cutting lower-priority funding and the so-called 'non-defense programs'. This resulted in the O&M budget being reimbursed $2.7bn for PKOs and $360m for the Kuwait deployment, while cuts include $300m from the environmental clean-up programme (under the O&M heading), $300m from the Technology

Reinvestment Project and $225m from the military science and technology budget (these last two from Research and Development (R&D)). The question of PKO contingency funds is a point of contention between the government and Congress. Although Presidential Decision Directive (PDD) 25 of May 1994 established a strict set of criteria for US PKO participation, and also clarified the financing arrangements, Congress' usual stance has been that contingency operations should be absorbed by the DoD without recourse to supplementary funding and that deficit pressures forcing Congress to mandate supplementary funding should be fully offset with rescissions from other areas of defence spending. The increase in PKOs and the growing aversion within Congress to their funding have sharpened the differences between the executive, the DoD and the legislature over the issue of contingency funds.

Table 2:   Department of Defence Budget Authority, FY1993–96 (current year $ billion)

	FY1993	FY1994	FY1995	Request FY1996
Military Personnel	76.0	71.4	70.6	68.7
Operations and Maintenance	89.2	88.3	94.4	91.9
Procurement	52.8	44.1	44.6	39.4
Research and Development	37.8	34.6	35.4	34.3
Military Construction	4.6	6.0	5.5	6.6
Family Housing	3.9	3.5	3.4	4.1
Other	3.0	3.4	-1.3	0.9
Total	267.3	251.3	252.6	245.9
Real year-on change (%)	-5.8	-8.4	-1.9	-5.3

Fiscal Year 1996

For FY1996, the government has requested $257.8bn for national defence – about 5% less than for 1995 in real terms. This was made conditional on Congressional approval of supplementary funding for FY1995, granted in April. Since late 1994, the Republican-led Congress raised the prospect of a defence budget request that was 'dead on arrival', following reports of an initiative to hold defence spending at around $270bn a year in real terms for the rest of the decade, thereby adding about $50bn to the government's plans. The Administration's priorities for 1996 are, first, to enhance operational readiness and, second, to improve quality of life for personnel through increased pay and better housing. To help balance the $2bn extra involved in setting these targets, the DoD is seeking to cut procurement spending from $44bn in 1995 to some $39.4bn, said to be its lowest level in real terms since 1950, and representing the largest decline among the major functional categories of the defence budget. R&D and procurement spending are dominated by a small number of expensive programmes. BMD at $2.9bn is close to the 1995 level, but fails to accommodate the Republican *Contract with America* proposal which seeks a spending increase in continental US BMD. The FYDP 1997–2001 amounts to $1,342bn, with the government claiming to have eliminated any funding shortfall that may have existed earlier. Defense Secretary William Perry described spending priorities in terms of 'people come first', but also stated that 'recapitalisation' – modernising weapons and equipment – will start from 1997 when the procurement budget is set to rise after a decade of real decline. According to this plan, procurement will increase by almost 50% in real terms over the period 1997–2001.

   The US Army is allocated $59.3bn (24%) in the proposed DoD budget for 1996 ($246bn). Manpower is planned to reduce to 495,000 active personnel during the year, and thereafter to decline by a further 20,000 by the end of 1998. The priority for 1996 remains readiness, with consequent emphasis on O&M funding. As a result, there will be cuts in several equipment-modernisation programmes if the Administration's request is approved by Congress. Funding for the Family of Medium Tactical Vehicles (FMTV) programme will end, and spending on RAH-

66 *Comanche* attack helicopters will be cut to $199m, providing for the construction of two prototypes, but no production orders. The future of the *Comanche* programme thus remains uncertain, although it has so far escaped the fate of outright cancellation which seemed possible in late 1994. In 1996, orders will be placed for the first 18 upgrades of AH-64 *Apache* attack helicopters to *Longbow* standard, together with orders for the *Hellfire Longbow* missiles. Under present plans, the last batch of 60 UH-60 *Blackhawk* transport helicopters will also be ordered in 1996. The UH-60 has been in continuous production for the US Army since 1978. Other expensive programmes involve upgrades for the M-1 *Abrams* main battle tank, the *Bradley* infantry fighting vehicle and the 155mm M-109 SP gun *Paladin*, and the purchase of nearly 20,000 SINCGARS radio sets and 557 *Javelin* 'fire-and-forget' anti-tank weapons.

Table 3:   Department of Defense and Coast Guard Budget Authority by Service, 1993–99 (current year $ billion)

	FY1993	FY1994	FY1995	Request FY1996
Army	64.8	62.5	62.7	59.3
% DoD Total	24.2	24.9	24.8	24.1
Navy/Marine Corps	83.2	78.1	78.2	75.6
% DoD Total	31.1	31.1	30.9	30.7
Air Force	79.2	74.6	74.4	72.6
% DoD Total	29.3	29.7	29.5	29.5
Defence Agencies	40.3	6.3	37.3	38.6
% DoD Total	15.1	14.4	14.8	15.7
DoD Total	267.5	251.5	252.6	246.1
Coast Guard	3.7	3.7	3.8	3.8

The US Navy would obtain the largest funding ($75.6bn) and retain the largest individual share (31%) of the DoD budget. In the 1996 request, two more DDG-51 *Aegis* destroyers would be funded ($2.6bn), while some $1.5bn would be put towards the third SSN-23 *Seawolf* attack submarine and a further $1.2bn for the development of the successor New Attack Submarine. The last batch of 12 F/A-18 C/D *Hornet* fighters would be purchased, and initial funds provided for the first of the E/F variant, which would be ordered in 1997. After prolonged uncertainty, it looks as if the US Navy will order the V-22 *Osprey* tilt-rotor aircraft for the Marine Corps, as purchasing orders covering long-lead items for four aircraft are included in the $810m funds for the programme (Congress has long supported the *Osprey* programme against DoD advice). Refuelling and overhaul funds for the nuclear-powered aircraft carrier USS *Nimitz* amount to $222m for 1996 and a further $317m for 1997. *Trident* D-5 SLBM procurement will be cut from 18 ($742m) to six ($518m). 164 *Tomahawk* SLCM have been requested at a cost of $162m with a further $141m for *Tomahawk* R&D. Four re-manufactured AV-8B II+ *Harriers* will be ordered for the Marine Corps at a cost of $170m, and production of the upgraded Group II variant of the EC-2 AEW aircraft continues with a request for three ($214m).

The 1996 Air Force request amounts to $72.6bn – 30% of the DoD budget. In keeping with the overall DoD philosophy for 1996, the funding priorities mostly support the readiness and quality of life functions. The request for 8 C-17s ($2.5bn) consumes 39% of the entire Air Force procurement budget, while the R&D budget continues to be dominated by the F-22 ($2.1bn or 17%). The Air Force now intends to buy 442 F-22s instead of its original target of 648, and orders for the first four are expected in 1998. R&D funding of the Air Force/Navy Joint Advanced Strike Technology (JAST) programme, consolidated with the ASTOVL *Harrier* replacement programme in 1994, receives a total of $300m. The UK also joined this programme in April 1995. Procurement of 2 more E-8 JSTARS, together with further R&D, accounts for $662m; B-1 bomber upgrades call for $174m; and the purchase of 291 AMRAAM (air-to-air missiles) for $233m.

Most of the question marks in the Administration's 1996 budget request concern strategic systems – BMD and the B-2 programme – and the so-called 'non-defense programs' funded by the DoD. In 1996, BMD is set to receive some $2.9bn – down from the 1995 request for $3.3bn but about the same as the actual budget authorisation. The shift towards procurement ($454m from $271m) continues in conjunction with the Pentagon's Ballistic Missile Defense Organisation (BMDO) plans to spend nearly $1.4bn by the year 2000 on anti-missile defence systems. Despite pressure from the new Republican-led Congress to elevate the importance of BMD for the continental US, the BMDO's funding plans continue to attach less importance to US territorial defence ($371m in 1996 rising to $400m in 1997). Current B-2 funding covers the purchase of 20 aircraft with production scheduled to end this year. Negotiations between the DoD and the manufacturer on further purchases appear to have stalled over cost. The 1996 request includes incremental procurement funds of $280m and further R&D funding for $624m. This year Congress added $125m for the B-2 production base, and there may be further changes to the Administration's request, as indicated by the House of Representatives adding funding for two additional B-2, though this may not survive the authorisation process.

Defence programmes with longer-term and wider security objectives are especially vulnerable to cuts, as Congress seeks to address the perceived bias against procurement and defence-specific R&D. Particular criticism within Congress has been directed at the former Soviet Union Cooperative Threat Reduction Program (Nunn–Lugar) and the Technology Reinvestment Project. The Clinton Administration has requested $6.2bn ($6.3bn in 1995) for the Department of Energy's nuclear-related Environmental Management Program, while $2.1bn is allocated for the DoD environmental clean-up (about $200m less than for 1995), $500m for the Technology Reinvestment Project, and $400m of Nunn–Lugar funds for demilitarisation in the former Soviet Union – both of the latter at the same levels as in 1995, although each has been the focus of retroactive cuts by Congress.

US foreign military assistance (FMA) is funded under the International Security Assistance budget rather than by the DoD. The Administration's 1996 request for FMA (inclusive of economic aid promoting peace) is $6.6bn ($6.4bn in 1995), most of which goes to the Middle East. The two major recipients remain Israel ($3.1bn) and Egypt ($2.1bn), with the appropriations steady at 1995 levels. Jordan, which received $7m in 1995, will receive $30m. The budget will also maintain aid to Turkey and Greece at the same 10:7 ratio as in previous years.

To conclude, although the US was slower in reducing its defence expenditure than was typically the case among NATO member-states during the latter phases of the Cold War, the rate of decline in US defence spending since 1990 has been relatively fast, the more so if the extraordinary expenditure incurred as a result of the Gulf War in 1990–91 is discounted. The bare statistics suffice to prove the point. In 1996, defence will account for a projected 3.5% of gross domestic product (GDP), and this proportion will decline further to 2.9% in 2000. By comparison, defence accounted for 5.4% of GDP in 1990 and 6.4% of GDP in 1985.

Table 4:   Selected Budgets, 1988–98 (current year $ billion)

Early each calendar year the US government presents its defence budget to Congress for the next fiscal year which begins on 1 October of the same calendar year. It also presents its Future Years Defense Program which covers the next fiscal year plus the following five years. Until approved by Congress, the Budget is referred to as the Budget Request. After approval it becomes the Budget Authority (BA). Since the Budget Authority does not confine the spending of funds to the fiscal year in question, Congress also approves Budget Appropriations which help determine spending levels in the fiscal year under consideration. 'Outlay' represents actual expenditures incurred in the course of the fiscal year. The government also estimates outlays each year for scrutiny by Congress. In any given year, the outlay usually differs from Budget Authority and Budget Appropriation – because budget authorisation involves year-on-year rolling expenditure particularly in the areas of procurement and construction, and because contingencies may arise which require unforeseen spending.

FY 1 Oct– 30 Sept	National Defense Budget Function		Department of Defense		Atomic Energy Defense Activities	Inter- national Security Assistance	Veterans Admin- istration	Total Federal Government Exp	Total Federal Budget Deficit
	(BA)	(outlay)	(BA)	(outlay)	(outlay)	(outlay)	(outlay)	(outlay)	(outlay)
1988	292.0	290.4	283.8	281.9	7.9	4.5	29.3	1,064.1	155.2
1989	299.6	303.6	290.8	294.9	8.1	1.5	30.0	1,143.2	152.5
1990	303.3	299.3	293.0	289.8	9.0	8.7	29.0	1,252.7	221.4
1991	296.2	296.7	283.5	285.8	10.0	9.8	31.2	1,323.4	269.2
1992	287.7	286.1	274.8	274.7	10.6	7.5	33.9	1,380.9	290.4
1993	281.1	283.9	267.2	271.4	11.0	7.6	35.5	1,408.7	255.1
1994	263.3	278.8	251.4	265.8	11.9	6.6	37.4	1,460.9	203.2
1995	263.5	270.6	252.6	259.1	10.5	5.9	38.2	1,538.9	192.5
1996[R]	257.8	260.9	246.0	249.5	10.8	5.5	38.0	1,612.1	196.7
1997[P]	253.4	257.0	242.8	246.1	10.3	5.3	39.5	1,684.7	213.1
1998[P]	259.6	254.5	249.7	244.2	9.7	5.2	39.7	1,745.2	196.4

[R] = Request   [P] = Projection

Note: The National Defense Budget Function subsumes funding for the Department of Defense, the Department of Energy Atomic Energy Defense Activities and some smaller support agencies. It does not include funding for International Security Assistance (under International Affairs), Veterans Administration, US Coast Guard (Department of Transportation), nor the National Aeronautics and Space Administration (NASA). Funding for civil projects administered by the DoD (such as Army Corps of Engineers projects) is excluded from the National Defense Budget Function and DoD figures cited here.

THE UNITED STATES

GDP	1993: $6,343.3bn: (per capita $24,800)
	1994: $6,736.9bn: (per capita $25,400)
Growth	1993: 3.0%	1994: 4.1%
Inflation	1993: 3.0%	1994: 2.5%
Publ debt	1993: 63.9%	1994: 64.2%
Def bdgt	1994: BA $263.3bn, Outlay$278.8bn
	1995: BA $263.5bn, Outlay$270.6bn
Request	1996: BA $257.8bn, Outlay$260.9bn
NATO defn	1993: $297.6bn	1994: $286.4bn

Population: 263,119,000

	13–17	*18–22*	*23–32*
Men	9,141,000	9,195,000	20,346,000
Women	8,693,000	8,744,000	19,710,000

TOTAL ARMED FORCES:

ACTIVE: 1,547,300 (192,900 women, excl Coast Guard).
RESERVES: 2,045,000 (total incl Standby and Retired Reserve).
READY RESERVE: 1,794,100 Selected Reserve and Individual Ready Reserve to augment active units and provide reserve formations and units.
NATIONAL GUARD: 502,600. Army (ARNG) 387,000; Air Force (ANG) 115,600.
RESERVE: 1,291,500. Army 654,000; Navy 340,500; Marines 108,600; Air Force 188,400.
STANDBY RESERVE: 29,500. Trained individuals for mob: Army 1,100; Navy 16,800; Marines 300; Air Force 11,300.
RETIRED RESERVE: 221,400. Trained individuals to augment support and training facilities: Army 131,000; Navy 28,800; Marines 7,200; Air Force 54,400.

US STRATEGIC COMMAND (US STRATCOM):
HQ Offutt Air Force Base, NE (manpower incl in Navy and Air Force totals).

NAVY: 384 SLBM in 16 SSBN:
(Plus 16 *Poseidon*-C3 and 96 *Trident*-C4 START-accountable launchers in 7 non-op SSBN incl 2 dry deck shelters.)
SSBN: 16 *Ohio:*
8 (SSBN-734) with 24 UGM-133A *Trident* D-5 (192 msl) (SSBN 741 commissioned in July 1995).
8 (SSBN-726) (includes 1 in refit) with 24 UGM-93A *Trident* C-4 (192 msl).

AIR FORCE:
ICBM (Air Force Space Command (AFSPC)): 597:
2 strategic msl wings, 2 gp (1 test wing with 13 test silo launchers):
14 *Minuteman* II (LGM-30F) (not op).
533 *Minuteman* III (LGM-30G).
50 *Peacekeeper* (MX; LGM-118A) in mod *Minuteman* silos.
AC (Air Combat Command (ACC)): 195 hy bbr (346 START-countable):
OP: 12 bbr sqn (B-1B: 5; B-2A: 1; B-52: 6):

5 (1 ANG (not yet op)) with 93 B-1B.
6 (1 AFR) with 93 B-52H (with AGM-86B ALCM).
1 with 6 B-2A (plus 3 at production site).
FLIGHT TEST CENTRE: 9: 1 B-52, 2 B-1, 6 B-2A (not START-countable).
AWAITING CONVERSION/ELIMINATION: 148 B-52G (87 ALCM-capable).

STRATEGIC RECCE/INTELLIGENCE COLLECTION (SATELLITES):
IMAGERY: KH-11: 160–400 mile polar orbit, digital imagery (perhaps 3 op).
KH-12 (*Ikon*): 1 launched 1989. AFP-731: optical-imaging satellite with sensors operating in several wavebands. 203km orbit, at approx 60° inclination; to replace KH-11. *Lacrosse* radar-imaging satellite.
OCEAN SURVEILLANCE (OSUS): 4 satellite clusters to detect ships by infra-red and radar.
NAVIGATIONAL SATELLITE TIMING AND RANGING (NAVSTAR): 24 satellites, components of global positioning system.
ELINT/COMINT: 2 *Chalet* (*Vortex*), 2 *Magnum*, 2 *Jumpseat*; 'Ferrets' (radar-monitoring satellites).
NUCLEAR DETONATION DETECTION SYSTEM: detects and evaluates nuclear detonations. Sensors to be deployed in NAVSTAR satellites.

STRATEGIC DEFENCES:
US Space Command (HQ: Peterson AFB, CO).
North American Aerospace Defense Command (NORAD), a combined US–Canadian org (HQ: Peterson AFB, CO).
US Strategic Command (HQ: Offutt AFB, NE).
EARLY WARNING:
DEFENSE SUPPORT PROGRAM (DSP): infra-red surveillance and warning system. Approved constellation: 3 op satellites and 1 op on-orbit spare.
BALLISTIC-MISSILE EARLY-WARNING SYSTEM (BMEWS): 3 stations: Clear (AK); Thule (Greenland); Fylingdales Moor (UK). Primary mission to track ICBM and SLBM. Also used to track satellites.
SPACETRACK: USAF radars Pirinçlik (Turkey), Eglin (FL), Cavalier AFS (ND), Clear, Thule and Fylingdales, Beale AFB (CA), Cape Cod (MA), Robins AFB (GA), Eldorado AFS (TX); optical tracking systems in New Mexico, San Vito (Italy), Maui (HI), Diego Garcia (Indian Ocean).
USN SPACE SURVEILLANCE SYSTEM (NAVSPASUR): 3 transmitting, 6 receiving-site field stations in south-east US.
PERIMETER ACQUISITION RADAR ATTACK CHARACTERISATION SYSTEM (PARCS): 1 north-facing phased-array system at Cavalier AFS (ND); 2,800km range.
PAVE PAWS: phased-array radars in Massachusetts, Georgia, Texas, California; 5,500km range.

MISCELLANEOUS DETECTION AND TRACKING RADARS: US Army: Kwajalein Atoll (Pacific). USAF: Ascension Island (Atlantic), Antigua (Caribbean), Kaena Point (HI), MIT Lincoln Laboratory (MA).
GROUND-BASED ELECTRO-OPTICAL DEEP SPACE SURVEILLANCE SYSTEM (GEODSS): Socorro (NM), Taegu (S. Korea), Maui (Hawaii), Diego Garcia (Indian Ocean).
AIR DEFENCE:
RADARS:
OVER-THE-HORIZON-BACKSCATTER RADAR (OTH-B): 1 in Maine (mothballed), 1 in Mountain Home AFB (mothballed). Range 500nm (minimum) to 3,000nm.
NORTH WARNING SYSTEM: to replace DEW line. 15 automated long-range (200nm) radar stations. 40 short-range (110–150km) stations.
DEW LINE: system deactivated.
AC: ANG: 90: 6 sqn:
3 with 45 F-15A/B.
3 with 40 F-16A/B.
Augmentation: ac on call from Navy, Marine Corps and Air Force.
AAM: *Sidewinder*, *Sparrow*, AMRAAM.

ARMY: 524,900 (69,800 women).
3 Army HQ, 4 Corps HQ (1 AB).
3 armd div (3 bde HQ, 5 tk, 4 mech inf, 3 SP arty, 1 MLRS, 1 AD bn; 1 avn bde) (incl 1 ARNG bde in 1 div).
5 mech div (3 bde HQ, 4 tk, 5 mech inf, 3 SP arty; 1 MLRS, 1 AD bn; 1 avn bde) (incl 1 ARNG bde in 3 div).
2 lt inf div (3 bde HQ, 9 inf, 3 arty, 1 AD bn; 1 avn bde) (incl 1 ARNG, 1 AR bde in 1 div).
1 air aslt div (3 bde HQ, 9 air aslt, 3 arty bn; avn bde (7 hel bn: 3 ATK, 2 aslt, 1 comd, 1 med tpt)).
1 AB div (3 bde HQ, 9 AB, 1 lt tk, 3 arty, 1 AD, 1 cbt avn bn).
1 inf, 1 AB bn gp.
7 avn bde (1 army, 4 corps, 2 trg).
2 armd cav regt.
7 arty bde.
1 theatre AD comd.
9 *Patriot* SAM bn: 5 with 6 bty, 2 with 4 bty, 2 with 3 bty.
3 *Avenger* SAM bn.
READY RESERVE:
ARMY NATIONAL GUARD (ARNG): 387,000 (31,000 women): capable after mob of manning 8 div (3 armd, 1 mech, 3 inf (2 cadre), 1 lt inf); 20 indep bde (5 armd, 6 mech, 9 inf (3 lt)) incl 5 'Roundout' (1 armd, 3 mech, 1 lt inf) for Regular Army div; 1 armd cav regt; 1 inf gp (Arctic recce: 4 scout bn); 16 fd arty bde HQ. Indep bn: 4 tk, 2 mech, 63 arty, 16 avn, 21 AD (4 I HAWK, 7 *Chaparral*, 1 *Patriot*, 1 *Avenger*, 8 *Stinger* SP (div)), 53 engr.
ARMY RESERVE (AR): 654,000 (119,000 women): 9 trg div, 5 exercise div, 16 cbt spt/log bde. (Of these 242,000 Standing Reservists receive regular trg and have mob assignment. The remainder receive no trg, but

as former active-duty soldiers could be recalled in an emergency.)

EQPT:

MBT: some 12,245: 500 M-48A5, 749 M-60/-60A1/A2, 3,548 M-60A3, 7,448 M-1 *Abrams* incl M-1A1, M-1A2.

LT TK: 123 M-551 *Sheridan*.

RECCE: 93 *Fuchs*.

AIFV: 6,724 M-2/-3 *Bradley*.

APC: 4,650 M-577, 19,213 M-113 incl variants.

TOTAL ARTY: 8,624:

TOWED ARTY: 2,851: **105mm:** 782 M-101, 510 M-102, 420 M-119; **155mm:** 419 M-114, 720 M-198.

SP ARTY: 3,159: **155mm:** 2,460 M-109A1/A2/A6; **203mm:** 699 M-110A1/A2.

MRL: 227mm: 700 MLRS (all ATACMS-capable).

MOR: 1,914: **107mm:** 1,851 (incl SP); **120mm:** 63.

ATGW: 9,569 *TOW*, (2,311 *Hummer*, 534 M-901, 6,724 M-2/M-3 *Bradley*), 24,398 *Dragon*.

RL: 84mm: AT-4.

RCL: 84 mm: 27 *Carl Gustav*.

AD GUNS: 20mm: 118 M-167 *Vulcan*, 211 M-163 SP.

SAM: FIM-92A *Stinger*, 584 *Avenger* (veh-mounted *Stinger*), 73 M-54, 356 M-48 SP *Chaparral*, 462 I HAWK, 416 *Patriot*.

SURV: Ground: AN/TPQ-36 (arty), AN/TPQ-37 (arty), AN/TRQ-32 (COMINT), AN/TSQ-138 (COMINT), AN/TLQ-17A (EW). **Airborne:** 4 *Guardrail* (RC-12D/H/K, RU-21H ac), 4 EO-5ARL (DHC-7), 35 OV/RV-1D.

AMPH: 40 ships:

5 *Frank Besson* LST: capacity 32 tk.

35 *Runnymede* LCU: capacity 7 tk.

Plus craft: some 124 LCM, 26 ACV.

UAV: 5 *Pioneer*, 16 *Hunter*.

AC: 361, incl 23 OV-1D, 46 RC-12D/G/H/K, 8 RU-21, 12 RV-1D, 132 C-12D/-F, 23 C-23A/B, 11 C-26, 91 U-21, 6 UV-18A, 2 UV-20A, 3 T-34, 2 O-2, 2 C-182.

HEL: some 7,227 (1,595 armed): 601 AH-1S, 747 AH-64A, 53 AH-6/MH-6, 2,104 UH-1 (being replaced), 1,240 UH/MH-60A, 66 EH-60A (ECM), 469 CH/MH-47, 47 OH-6A, 1,349 OH-58A/C, 469 OH-58D (incl 194 armed), 82 TH-67 *Creek*.

NAVY (USN): 441,800 (51,800 women): 4 Fleets: 2nd (Atlantic), 3rd (Pacific), 5th (Indian Ocean, Persian Gulf, Red Sea) 6th (Mediterranean), 7th (W. Pacific), plus Military Sealift Command.

SUBMARINES: 100:

STRATEGIC SUBMARINES: 16 (see p. 23):

TAC SUBMARINES: 82 (incl about 8 in refit).

SSGN: 29:

21 imp *Los Angeles* (SSN-751) with 12 x *Tomahawk* SLCM (VLS), 533mm TT (Mk 48 HWT, *Harpoon, Tomahawk*).

8 mod *Los Angeles* (SSN-719) with 12 x *Tomahawk* SLCM (VLS); plus 533mm TT (Mk 48 HWT,

Harpoon, Tomahawk).

SSN: 53:

28 *Los Angeles* (SSN-688) with Mk 48 HWT, plus *Harpoon, Tomahawk* SLCM.

23 *Sturgeon* (SSN-637) with Mk 48 HWT; plus *Harpoon*, 21 with *Tomahawk* SLCM. (Incl 10 capable of special ops.)

1 *Permit* (SSN-594) with Mk 48 HWT, plus *Harpoon*.

1 *Narwhal* (SSN-671) with Mk 48 HWT, *Harpoon, Tomahawk*.

OTHER ROLES: 2 ex-SSBN (SSBN 642 and 645) (special ops).

PRINCIPAL SURFACE COMBATANTS: 137:

AC CARRIERS: 12 (incl 1 in long refit/refuel):

CVN: 7 *Nimitz* (CVN-68) (96/102,000t).

CV: 5:

3 *Kitty Hawk* (CV-63) (81,000t).

1 *Kennedy* (CV-67) (in long refit).

1 *Forrestal* (CV-59) (79,250/81,100t).

AIR WING: 13 (11 active, 2 reserve). The average mix of type and numbers of ac assigned to an Air Wing is:

2 ftr sqn with 18 F-14A

2 FGA/ftr sqn with 20 F/A-18, 1 med with 14 A-6E.

2 ASW sqn: **ac:** 1 with 6 S-3B; **hel:** 1 with 8 H-60.

2 ECM sqn with 4 EA-6B, 2 ES-3.

1 AEW sqn with 4 E-2C.

2 ECM sqn, 1 with 4 EA-6, 1 with 2 ES-3.

1 spt sqn with C-2.

CRUISERS: 32:

CGN: 5:

2 *Virginia* (CGN-38) with 2 x 2 SM-2 MR SAM/ASROC SUGW; plus 2 x 4 *Tomahawk* SLCM, 2 x 4 *Harpoon*, SH-2F hel (Mk 46 LWT), 2 x 3 ASTT, 2 x 127mm guns.

2 *California* (CGN-36) with 2 x SM-2 MR; plus 2 x 4 *Harpoon*, 1 x 8 ASROC, 2 x 3 ASTT, 2 x 127mm guns.

1 *Bainbridge* (CGN-25) with 2 x 2 SM-2 ER, plus 2 x 4 *Harpoon*, 1 x 8 ASROC, 2 x 3 ASTT.

CG: 27 *Ticonderoga* (CG-47 *Aegis*):

5 Baseline 1 (CG-47–51) with 2 x 2 SM-2 MR/ASROC; plus 2 x 4 *Harpoon*, 2 x 1 127mm guns, 2 x 3 ASTT, 2 x SH-2F or SH-60B hel.

22 Baseline 2/3 (CG-52) with 2 x VLS Mk 41 (61 tubes each) for combination of SM-2 ER, and *Tomahawk*. Other weapons as Baseline 1.

DESTROYERS: 46 (incl some 6 in refit):

DDG: 15:

11 *Arleigh Burke* (DDG-51 *Aegis*) with 2 x VLS Mk 41 (32 tubes fwd, 64 tubes aft) for combination of *Tomahawk*, SM-2 ER and ASROC; plus 2 x 4 *Harpoon*, 1 x 127mm gun, 2 x 3 ASTT, 1 x SH-60B hel.

4 *Kidd* (DDG-993) with 2 x 2 SM-2 MR/ASROC; plus 2 x 3 ASTT, 2 x SH-2F hel, 2 x 4 *Harpoon*, 2 x 127mm guns.

DD: 31 *Spruance* (DD-963) (ASW):

7 with 1 x 8 ASROC, 2 x 3 ASTT, 1 x SH-2F hel; plus

2 x 4 *Harpoon*, 2 x 127mm guns, 2 x 4 *Tomahawk*.
24 with 1 x VLS Mk 41 (*Tomahawk*), 2 x 3 ASTT, 1 x
SH-60B hel; plus 2 x 127mm guns, 2 x 4 *Harpoon*.

FRIGATES: 49 (incl some 5 in refit):

FFG: 49 *Oliver Hazard Perry* (FFG-7) (16 in NRF)
all with 2 x 3 ASTT; 24 with 2 x SH-60B hel; 27 with
2 x SH-2F hel; all plus 1 x SM-1 MR/*Harpoon*.

PATROL AND COASTAL COMBATANTS: 21:
Note: mainly responsibility of Coast Guard.

PATROL, COASTAL: 9 *Cyclone* PFC with SEAL team.

PATROL, INSHORE: 12⟨.

MINE WARFARE: 16:

MINELAYERS: none dedicated, but mines can be laid
from attack submarines, aircraft and surface ships.

MCM: 16:
2 *Osprey* (MHC-51) MHC.
14 *Avenger* (MCM-1) MCO.

AMPH: 41:

COMD: 2 *Blue Ridge*: capacity 700 tps.

LHA: 9:
4 *Wasp*: capacity 1,892 tps, 60 tk; with 6 AV-8B ac, 12
CH-46E, 4 CH-53E, 4 UH-1N, 4 AH-1W hel; plus 3
LCAC.
5 *Tarawa*: capacity 1,713 tps, 100 tk, 4 LCU or 1 LCAC,
6 AV-8B ac, 12 CH-46E, 4 CH-53E, 4 UH-1N, 4 AH-
1T/W hel.

LPH: 2 *Iwo Jima*, capacity 1,489 tps, 12 CH-46E, 4
CH-53E, 4 UH-1N hel, 4 AH-1T/W.

LPD: 11 *Austin:* capacity 788 tps, 4 tk.

LSD: 15:
8 *Whidbey Island* with 4 LCAC: capacity 450 tps, 40 tk.
2 *Harpers Ferry* with 4 LCAC: capacity 500 tps 40tk.
5 *Anchorage* with 3 LCAC: capacity 302 tps, 38 tk.

LST: 2 *Newport*: capacity 347 tps, 10 tk.

CRAFT: 114:
77 LCAC: capacity 1 MBT.
About 37 LCU-1610: capacity 3 MBT.
Numerous LCVP, LCU, LCM.

SPT AND MISC: 114:

UNDER WAY SPT: 44:

AO: 19:
5 *Cimarron*, 1 *Wichita*, 13 *Henry Kaiser* (MSC).

AOE: 7:
3 *Supply*, 4 *Sacramento*.

AE: 10:
2 *Kilauea* (MSC), 8 *Butte*.

AF: 8:
5 *Mars* (MSC), 3 *Sirius* (MSC).

MAINT AND LOG: 38:
4 AD, 6 AS, 10 AT (7 MSC), 11 AOT (MSC), 2 AH
(MSC), 5 salvage/rescue.

SPECIAL PURPOSES: 8:
2 comd, 6 technical spt (4 MSC).

SURVEY AND RESEARCH: 24:
6 *Stalwart* AGOS (towed array) (MSC).
5 AGOR (2 MSC), 9 AGHS (MSC).
4 *Victorious* AGOS (SWATH) (MSC).

MILITARY SEALIFT:
Mil Sealift Comd (MSC) operates 123 ships, incl 53
Naval Fleet Auxiliary Force ships deployed in direct fleet
spt and special mission ships for survey, range and
research activities incl in those listed under Spt and Misc.
Other assets are:

MSC ACTIVE FORCE: 58:

OPERATING VESSELS: 26:
12 dry cargo (3 *Ro-Ro*, 1 *Combo*, 8 freighters, 2 other),
14 tkr.

AFLOAT PREPOSITIONING FORCE: 32:
13 maritime prepositioning ships (MPS) (in 3 sqn each
to spt an MEB), 19 prepositioned ships (MPS) (16 cargo
ships and 3 tankers). Based in Diego Garcia and Guam.

MSC STANDBY FORCE: 12:
1 sqn of 8 fast sealift ships (30 kt *Ro-Ro* at 4 days'
readiness), 2 avn log spt ships, 2 hospital ships.

ADDITIONAL MILITARY SEALIFT:

READY RESERVE FORCE: 77:
70 dry cargo ships, 5 tankers, 2 troopships (at 4–20 days'
readiness, maintained by Dept of Transportation).

NATIONAL DEFENCE RESERVE FLEET (NDRF): 46:
30 dry cargo, 13 tankers, 3 troopships.

NAVY RESERVE:

CBT SPT FORCES: 4:
2 MCM-1, 1 MCS, 1 MHC-51.

NAVAL RESERVE SURFACE FORCES: 16 FFGs crewed
by 70% active USN and 30% reserve.

AUGMENT FORCES: 28 MIUW units and 12 cargo
handling bn.

NAVAL INACTIVE FLEET: about 116: includes
about 21 'mothballed' USN ships, incl 2 CV, about 25
dry cargo ships, 10 tankers and some 60 Victory WW II
cargo ships (60–90 days' reactivation, but many ships
are very old and of doubtful serviceability). 89 ships
awaiting scrap/sale.

NAVAL AVIATION: ε80,110, incl 11 carrier air
wings. Flying hours: F-14, 248; F-18, 257; A-6, 264.

AC:

FTR: 15 sqn: 8 with F-14A, 4 with F-14B, 3 with F-14D.

FGA/ATTACK: 28 sqn:
6 with A-6E.
22 with F/A-18C/N.

ELINT: 4 sqn:
2 with EP-3, 2 with ES-3A.

ECM: 10 sqn with EA-6B.

MR: 13 land-based sqn: 2 with P-3CII, 11 with P-3CIII.

ASW: 10 sqn with S-3B.

AEW: 11 sqn with E-2C.

COMD: 2 sqn with E-6A (TACAMO).

OTHER: 5 sqn:
1 with C-130F, 1 with LC-130, 3 with C-2A.

TRG: 18 sqn:

5 'Aggressor' with F-5E/F, A-4, F-16N.
13 trg with T-2C, T-34C, T-44, T-45A.
HEL:
ASW: 20 sqn:
10 with SH-60B (LAMPS Mk III).
10 with SH-60F/HH-60H.
MCM: 2 sqn with MH-53E/CH-53E.
MISC: 5 sqn with CH-46, 1 with CH-53E.
TRG: 2 sqn with TH-57B/C.

NAVY RESERVE:
FTR ATTACK: 2 sqn with F-18.
FTR: 1 sqn with F-14.
AEW: 1 sqn with E-2C.
ECM: 1 sqn with EA-6B.
MPA: 9 sqn with P-3B/C.
FLEET LOG SPT: 1 wing with 11 sqn with C-9B/DC-9, 3 sqn with C-130T.
HEL: 1 wing with 3 ASW sqn with SH-2G and SH-3H, 2 HCS sqn with HH-60H.
EQPT (incl NR): 1634 cbt ac; 301 armed hel.
AC:
F-14: 361*. **-A:** 233 (ftr, incl 48 NR) plus 12 in store; **-B plus:** 77 (ftr); **-D:** 51 (ftr). **F/A-18:** 777*. **-A:** 274 (FGA, incl 36 NR); **-B:** 33 (trg); **-C:** 344 (FGA); **-D:** 126 (trg). **F-5E/F:** 32* (trg). **F-16:** 11*. **-N:** 9 (trg); **TF-16N:** 2 (trg). **A-4:** 74* (trg). **TA-:** 74; **4F/J:** (trg) (plus 68; **TA-F/J:** 58 in store). **A-6:** 245. **E:** 127* (FGA, incl 20 NR); **EA-6B:** 118 (ECM, incl 4 NR plus 25 in store). **E-2:** 93. **-C:** 91 (AEW, incl 10 NR) (plus 7 in store); **TE-2C:** 2 (trg). **P-3:** 285. **-C:** 252* (MR incl 72, NR); **EP-3:** 12 (ELINT); **RP-3A/D:** 5 (survey); **U/VP-3A:** 5 (VIP); **TP-3A:** 11 (trg) (plus 6 **P-3** in store). **S-3** 141. **-A:** 1 (ASW) (plus 16 in store); **-B:** 119 (ASW); **ES-3A:** 16 (ECM); **-US-3A:** 5 (tpt). **C-130:** 22. **-T:** 12 (tpt NR); **-LC-130F/R:** 4 (Antarctic); **-TC-130G/Q:** 2 (tpt/trg) **EC-130Q:** 4 (CMD) (1 **TC-130G/Q** and **3-F** in store). **CT-39:** 9 (misc). **C-2A:** 38 (tpt). **C-9B:** 19 (tpt). **DC-9:** 10 (tpt). **C-20:** 7 (**-D:** 2 VIP, **-G:** 5 (tpt)). **UC-12:** 85. **-B:** 65; **-F:** 10; **-M:** 10. **NU-1B:** 1 (utl). **U-6A:** 2 (utl). **T-2B/C:** 111 (trg) (plus 23 in store). **T-39D/N:** 17 (trg). **TA-7C:** 3 (trg) (plus 2 in store). **T-44:** 57 (trg). **T-45:** 44 (trg). **T-34C:** 272 (plus 42 in store). **TC-4C:** 3 (trg).
HEL:
HH-1N: 37 (utl) plus 6 in store. **CH-53E:** 11 (tpt). **SH-60:** 235. **-B:** 158 (ASW); **-F:** 7 (ASW). **HH-60H:** 20 (cbt spt). **SH-2F/G:** 26 (ASW) plus 23 in store. **SH-3H:** 40 (ASW/SAR). **CH-46D:** 28 (tpt, trg). **UH/HH-46D:** 47 (utl). **TH-57:** 129. **-B:** 48 (trg); **-C:** 81 (trg) (plus B-2, C-6 in store). **VH-3A:** 4 (VIP).
MSL:
AAM: AIM-120 AMRAAM, AIM-7 *Sparrow*, AIM-54A/C *Phoenix*, AIM-9 *Sidewinder*.
ASM: AGM-45 *Shrike*, AGM-88A *HARM* (anti-radiation); AGM-84 *Harpoon*, AGM-119 *Penguin* Mk-3.

MARINE CORPS: 171,900 (7,600 women).
GROUND: 3 div:

1 with 3 inf regt (10bn), 1 tk, 2 lt armd recce (LAV-25), 1 aslt amph, 1 cbt engr bn, 1 arty regt (4 bn).
1 with 3 inf regt (8 bn), 1 tk, 1 lt armd recce (LAV-25), 1 aslt amph, 1 cbt engr bn, 1 arty regt (4 bn).
1 with 2 inf regt (6 bn), 1 arty regt (2 bn), 1 cbt engr, 1 recce coy.
3 Force Service Support Groups.
1 bn Marine Corps Security Force (Atlantic and Pacific).
Marine Security Guard bn (1 HQ, 7 region coy).
RESERVES (MCR):
1 div (3 inf (9 bn), 1 arty regt (5 bn); 2 tk, 1 lt armd inf (LAV-25), 1 aslt amph, 1 recce, 1 cbt engr bn)
1 Force Service Spt Gp.
EQPT:
MBT: 271 M-1A1 *Abrams* (plus 151 M-60A1 in store).
LAV: 423 LAV-25 (**25mm** gun), 240 LAV (variants, excl ATGW).
AAV: 1,322 AAV-7A1 (all roles).
TOWED ARTY: 155mm: 584 M-198.
MOR: 81mm: 656.
ATGW: 1,300 *TOW*, 1,978 *Dragon*, 95 LAV-*TOW*.
RL: 84mm: 1,300 AT-4.
RCL: 83mm: 1,919.

AVIATION: 35,260 (1,240 women); 3 active air wings. Flying hours cbt aircrew: 231.
AIR WING (no standard org, but a notional wing is shown below): **ac:** 166 fixed-wing; **hel:** 155: **ac:** 48 F/A-18A/C, 36 F/A-18D, 60 AV-8B, 10 EA-6B, 12 KC-130; **hel:** 12 CH-53D, 32 CH-53E, 30 AH-1W, 21 UH-1N, 60 CH-46E.
AC:
FTR/ATTACK: 10 sqn with F-18A/C.
FGA: 7 sqn with AV-8B.
ECM: 4 sqn with 20 EA-6B.
COMD: 6 sqn with 72 F/A-18D.
TKR: 3 sqn with KC-130F/R.
TRG: 3 sqn.
HEL: 34 sqn:
ARMED: 6 lt attack/utl with 84 AH-1W and 63 UH-1N.
TPT: 19 **med** sqn with 180 CH-46E and 32 CH-53D; 6 **hy** sqn with 96 CH-53E.
TRG: 3 sqn.
SAM: 3+ bn:
1 bn (3 bty) with phase III I HAWK.
2+ bn (5 bty) with *Stinger* and *Avenger*.
UAV: *Pioneer*.

RESERVES: 5,300 (300 women) (MCR); 1 air wg.
AC:
FTR/ATTACK: 5 sqn with 60 F-18A.
FGA: 1 sqn with 12 A-4M.
1 *Aggressor* sqn with 12 F5-E, 1 F5-F.
TKR: 2 tkr/tpt sqn with 24 KC-130T.
HEL:
ARMED: 2 attack/utl sqn with 36 AH-1W, 18 UH-1N.
TPT: 6 sqn:

4 **med** with 24 CH-46E, 2 **hy** with 16 RH-53A.
SAM: 1 bn (3 bty) with I HAWK, 1 bn (2 bty) with *Stinger* and *Avenger*.
EQPT (incl MCR): 478 cbt ac; 189 armed hel.
AC:
F-18A/-B/-C/-D: 262 (FGA incl 48 MCR, 34* trg). **AV-8B:** 216. 184 (FGA), 17* (trg); **TAV-8B:** 15* (trg). **EA-6B:** 25 (ECM). **F-5E/F:** 13 (trg, MCR). **KC-130:** 68. **-F:** 30 (OCU); **-R:** 14; **-T:** 24 (tkr, MRC).
HEL:
AH-1W: 140 incl 96* (armed, 30 MCR, 18 trg) (plus 43 in store). **UH-1N:** 93* (incl 18 MCR, 12 trg). **CH-46D/E:** 230 (tpt, incl 24 MCR, 6 HMX, 20 trg). **CH-53A/-D/-E:** 159 (tpt, incl 20 trg), plus 17 in store. **RH-53D:** 16 (MCR) plus 1 in store. **VH-60A:** 8 (VIP tpt). **VH-3D:** 11 (VIP tpt).
MSL:
SAM: 60 phase III I HAWK launcher, 1,929 *Stinger*, 235 *Avenger*.
AAM: *Sparrow, Sidewinder*.
ASM: *Maverick*.

COAST GUARD 37,300 (includes 3,000 women).
By law a branch of the Armed Forces; in peacetime operates under, and is funded by, the Department of Transportation. Bdgt are not incl in the figures at p. 23:
Bdgt   1992: BA $3.6bn
           1993: BA $3.7bn
           1994: request $3.8bn
PATROL VESSELS: 137:
OFFSHORE: 51:
12 *Hamilton* high-endurance with HH-65A LAMPS *Dolphin* hel, 2 x 3 ASTT, 4 with 1 x 76mm gun, 3 with *Harpoon* SSM (4 in refit).
13 *Bear* med-endurance with 1 x 76mm gun, HH-65A hel.
20 *Reliance* med-endurance with 1 x 3 inch gun, hel deck (excl 2 undergoing modernisation).
2 *Vindicator* (*USN Stalwart*) med-endurance cutter.
4 other med-endurance cutters.
INSHORE: 86:
49 *Farallon*, 37 *Point Hope*⟨.
SPT AND OTHER: 12:
2 icebreakers, 9 icebreaking tugs, 1 trg.
AVN: ac: 41 HU-25, 30 HC-130H, 2 RG-8A; **hel:** 39 HH-60J, 94 HH-65A.

COAST GUARD RESERVE: 8,000.

AIR FORCE: 408,700 (63,700 women).
Air Combat Comd (ACC): 5 air force (incl 1 ICBM), 23 ac wg. **Air Mobility Comd** (AMC): 2 air force, 10 ac wg. Flying hours: ftr 238, bbr 238.
TAC: 52 tac ftr sqn (sqn may be 12 to 24 ac):
13 with F-15.
7 with F-15E.
21 with F-16C/D (incl 3 AD).
3 with F-111.
5 with A-10.
1 *Wild Weasel* with F-4G.
2 with F-117.
SPT:
RECCE: 3 sqn with U-2R and RC-135.
AEW: 1 Airborne Warning and Control wing; 6 sqn (incl 1 trg) with E-3.
EW: 2 sqn with EC-130, 1 sqn with EF-111.
FAC: 7 tac air control sqn, mixed A-10A/OA-10A.
TRG: 36 sqn:
1 *Aggressor* sqn with F-16.
35 trg sqn with **ac:** F-15, F-16, T-37, T-38, AT-38, T-1A, -3A, C-5, -130, -141; **hel:** HH-53, -60, U/TH-1.
TPT: 40 sqn:
15 strategic: 4 with C-5, 9 with C-141, 2 with C-17.
10 tac airlift with C-130.
Units with C-135, VC-137, C-9, C-12, C-20, C-21.
TKR: 25 sqn:
21 with KC-135, 4 with KC-10A.
SAR: 9 sqn (incl STRATCOM msl spt), HH-3, HH-60 hel, HC-130N/P.
MEDICAL: 3 medical evacuation sqn with C-9A.
WEATHER RECCE: WC-135.
TRIALS: weapons trg units with **ac:** A-10, F-4, F-15, F-16, F-111, T-38, C-141; **hel:** UH-1.

RESERVES:
AIR NATIONAL GUARD (ANG): 115,580 (15,950 women).
BBR: 1 sqn with B-1B.
FTR: 6 AD sqn.
FGA: 36 sqn:
5 with A-10, OA-10.
25 with F-16 (incl 3 AD).
6 with F-15A/B (incl 3 AD).
RECCE: 1 sqn with RF-4C.
EW: 1 sqn with EC-130E.
TPT: 25 sqn:
20 tac (1 trg) with C-130E/H.
3 strategic: 1 with C-5, 2 with C-141B.
TKR: 20 sqn with KC-135E/R.
SPECIAL OPS: 1 sqn (AFSOC) with EC-130E.
SAR: 3 sqn with **ac:** HC-130; **hel:** HH-60.
TRG: 7 sqn.
AIR FORCE RESERVE (AFR): 78,700 (15,450 women).
21 wings, 60 sqn (39 with ac).
BBR: 1 sqn with B-52H.
FGA: 10 sqn:
7 with F-16 (3 F-16C/D; 4 F-16A/B).
3 (incl 1 trg) with A-10.
TPT: 18 sqn:
6 strategic: 2 with C-5A, 4 with C-141B.
11 tac with 7 C-130H, 4 C-130E.
1 weather recce with WC-130E/H.
TKR: 6 sqn with KC-135E/R (2 KC-135R, 4 KC-135E).
SPECIAL OPS: 1 sqn (AFSOC/AFR) with AC-130A

and HC-130.

SAR: 3 sqn (ACC) with **ac:** HC-130H; **hel:** HH-60.

ASSOCIATE: 21 sqn (personnel only):
4 sqn for C-5, 11 for C-141, 1 aero-medical for C-9, 1 C-17A, 4 sqn for KC-10.

EQPT:

LONG-RANGE STRIKE/ATTACK: 204 cbt ac (plus 148 awaiting elimination).

B-52: 94. **-H:** 94 strike (with AGM-86 ALCM, 1 test) plus 148-G at elimination site. **B-1B:** 95 (2 test). **B-2A:** 15 (6 test, 3 at production site).

RECCE: U-2R/RT: 37; RC-135: 19; SR-71: 3.

COMD: E-3B/C: 34. E-4B: 4. EC-135: 15.

TAC: 2,655 cbt ac (incl ANG, AFR plus 854 in store); no armed hel: **F-4:** 122. **-E:** 20 (FGA); **-G:** 54; **RF-4C:** 48 (plus 280 in store (incl 64 RF-4C)). **F-15:** 726. **-A/B/C/D:** 414 (ftr incl 146 ANG); 108 (OCU, test); **-E:** 204 (FGA); (plus 55 F-15A/B in store). **F-16:** 1,253. **-A:** 166 (incl 137 ANG, 14 AFR); **-B:** 48 (incl 31 ANG, 1 AFR); **-C:** 903 (incl 310 ANG, 70 AFR); **-D:** 136 (incl 23 ANG, 5 AFR); (plus 347 F- 16A/B in store). **F-111E/F:** 95 (FGA) (incl 23 OCU); plus 3 in store. **EF-111A:** 40 (ECM). **F-117:** 52. 41 (FGA), 10* (trg), plus 1 test. **A-10A:** 213 (FGA, incl 69 ANG, 41 AFR); plus 169 in store. **OA-10A:** 167* (FAC incl 47 ANG, 27 AFR). **EC-18B/D:** 6 (Advanced Range Instrumentation). **E-8A/C:** 3 (JSTARS ac). **WC-135B:** 2 (weather recce). **OC-135:** 3 ('Open Skies' Treaty). **AC-130:** 27. **-A:** 6* (special ops, AFR); **-H/U:** 21* (special ops, USAF). **HC-130N/P:** 58 (28 special ops; 30 SAR incl 11 ANG, 12 AFR); **EC-130E/H:** 27 (special ops incl 6 SOF); **MC-130E/H:** 38 (special ops); **WC-130E/H:** 12 (weather recce, AFR). **OA-37B:** 1 (test, plus 13 in store).

TPT:

C-5: 126. **-A:** 74 (strategic tpt; incl 13 ANG, 30 AFR); -**B:** 50, **-C:** 2. **C-141B:** 184 (173 strategic tpt, 11 OCU, incl 16 ANG, 40 AFR); plus 18 in store. **C-130:** 529. 498 (tac tpt, incl 188 ANG, 110 AFR); 31 (trg, incl 9 ANG); plus 31 in store. **C-135A/B/C/E:** 6. **VC-137B/C:** 7 (VIP tpt). **C-9A/C:** 23. **C-12:** 75 (liaison). **C-17A:** 22 (2 test, 20 strategic tpt). **C-20:** 13. **-A:** 3, **-B:** 6, **-C:** 3, **-D:** 1. **C-21:** 79. **C-22B:** 4 (ANG). **C-23A:** 3. **VC-25A:** 2. **C-26A/B:** 33 (ANG); **VC-26C:** 1. **C-27A:** 10 (tpt). **T-43A:** 2 (tpt ANG).

TKR:

KC-135: 551 (293 USAF, 201 ANG, 57 AFR); plus 21 in store. **KC-10A:** 59 tkr/tpt.

TRG:

T-3A: 91. **T-37B:** 487 (plus 69 in store). **T-38:** 497 (plus 142 in store). **T-39:** 6. **T-41D/C:** 3. **T-43A:** 12. **TC-135S:** 1. **TC-135W:** 1. **UV-18B:** 2. **Schweizer 2-37:** 18. **T-1A:** 80, **TG-7A:** 9.

HEL:

MH-53-J: 41 *Pave Low* (special ops). **MH-60G:** 13 (incl 10 AFR). **HH-1H:** 21. **UH-1N:** 66.

MSL:

AAM: AIM-9P/L/M *Sidewinder*, AIM-7E/F/M *Sparrow*, AIM 120, A/B AMRAAM.

ASM: AGM-69A SRAM; AGM-86B ALCM; AGM-65A/ B/D/G *Maverick*; AGM-88A/B *HARM*; AGM-84A *Harpoon*; AGM-86C ALCM; AGM-142A/B/C/D *HAVE NAP*.

CIVIL RESERVE AIR FLEET (CRAF): 353 commercial ac (numbers fluctuate):

LONG-RANGE: 314:
154 passenger (Boeing 747, L-1011, DC-8/-10, B-757, B-767, A-310, MD-11).
160 cargo (Boeing 707, 747, DC-8/-10, MD-11).

SHORT-RANGE: 39 (Boeing 727, 737, 767, L-100, DC-9, MD-80) (30 passenger, 9 cargo).

SPECIAL OPERATIONS FORCES:

Units only listed – manpower and eqpt shown in relevant single-service section.

ARMY: (15,000):
5 SF gp (each 3 bn).
1 Ranger inf regt (3 bn).
1 special ops avn regt (3 bn).
1 Psychological Ops gp (5 bn).
1 Civil Affairs bn (5 coy).
1 sigs, 1 spt bn.

RESERVES: (2,800 ARNG, 9,400 AR):
2 ARNG SF gp (6 bn).
12 AR Civil Affairs HQ (3 comd, 9 bde).
2 AR Psychological Ops gp.
24 AR Civil Affairs 'bn' (coy).

NAVY: (4,000):
2 Naval Special Warfare Command (incl 1 trg).
2 Naval Special Warfare gp.
5 Naval Special Warfare units.
6 Sea–Air–Land (SEAL) teams.
2 SEAL delivery veh teams.
3 Special Boat sqn.
6 Dry deck shelters (DDS).

RESERVES: (1,400):
5 Naval Special Warfare gp det.
4 Naval Special Warfare unit det (incl 1 comd).
7 SEAL team det (incl 1 veh).
2 Special Boat unit.
1 engr spt unit.
2 cbt spt special hel sqn.

AIR FORCE: (6,000): (AFRES 1,110) (ANG 825).
1 air force HQ, 1 wing, 3 groups, 13 sqn:
  4 with MC-130, 2 with AC-130, 3 with HC-130, 3 with MH-53 hel, 1 with MH-60 hel.

RESERVES: (1,110):
1 wing, 1 group, 2 sqn (AFSOC):
  1 with 6 AC-130A plus 4 HC-130 (AFR).
  1 with 6 EC-130E (ANG).

DEPLOYMENT:

Commanders' NATO appointments also shown (e.g., COMEUCOM is also SACEUR).

EUROPEAN COMMAND (EUCOM): some 139,200, incl Mediterranean 6th Fleet: HQ Stuttgart-Vaihingen (Commander is SACEUR).
ARMY: HQ US Army Europe (USAREUR),Heidelberg.
NAVY: HQ US Navy Europe (USNAVEUR), London (Commander is also CINCAFSOUTH).
AIR FORCE: HQ US Air Force Europe (USAFE), Ramstein (Commander is COMAIRCENT).
GERMANY:
ARMY: 70,500.
V Corps with 1 armd, (-)1 mech inf div, (-)1 arty, 1 AD (1 *Patriot* (6 bty), 1 *Avenger* bn), 1 engr, 2 avn bde. Prepositioned eqpt (POMCUS) for 4 armd/mech bde. Approx 57% stored in Ge.
EQPT (incl POMCUS in Ge, Be and Nl):
some 1,070 MBT, 810 AIFV, 782 APC, 886 arty/MRL/mor, 114 atk hel.
AIR FORCE: 16,100, 96 cbt ac.
2 air force HQ: USAFE and 17th Air Force.
1 ftr wing: 4 sqn (2 with 48 F-16C/D, 1 with 24 F-15C/D, 1 with 18 A-10 and 6 OA-10).
1 airlift wing: incl 16 C-130E and 4 C-9A.
BELGIUM:
ARMY: 1,000. Approx 22% of POMCUS.
NAVY: 100.
AIR FORCE: 430.
GREECE:
ARMY: 18.
NAVY: 275. Base facilities at Soudha Bay, Makri (Crete).
AIR FORCE: 260; air base gp. Facilities at Iraklion (Crete).
ITALY:
ARMY: 2,850. HQ Vicenza. 1 inf bn gp, 1 arty bty. Eqpt for Theater Reserve Unit/Army Readiness Package South (TRU/ARPS), incl 122 MBT, 165 AIFV, 103 APC, 64 arty/MLRS/mor.
NAVY: 7,140. HQ Gaeta; bases at Naples, La Maddalena, 1 MR sqn with 9 P-3C at Sigonella.
AIR FORCE: 4,900; 1 AF HQ, 1 ftr wg, 2 sqn with 36 F-16C/D.
LUXEMBOURG:
ARMY: Approx 21% of POMCUS.
MEDITERRANEAN:
NAVY: some 16,500 (incl 2,300 Marines). 6th Fleet: typically 4 SSN, 1 CVBG (1 CV, 6 surface combatants, 2 fast spt ships), 1 URG (4 spt ships, 2 escorts). MPS-1 (4 ships with eqpt for 1 MEB).
MARINES: some 2,300: 1 MEU (SOC) embarked aboard amph ready gp ships.
NETHERLANDS:
ARMY: 450. Approx 7% of POMCUS.
AIR FORCE: 250.
NORWAY: prepositioning for 1 MEB (24 arty, no aviation assets). Army prepositioning 24 SP arty.
AIR FORCE: 60.
PORTUGAL (for Azores, see Atlantic Command):
NAVY: 55.
AIR FORCE: 950.

SPAIN:
NAVY: 2,900; base at Rota.
1 MR sqn with 9 P-3C.
AIR FORCE: 230.
TURKEY:
ARMY: 250.
NAVY: 30, spt facilities at Izmir and Ankara.
AIR FORCE: 2,670, facilities at Incirlik. 1 wg, 2 air base gps (ac on det only). 6 F-15, 18 F-16, 3 EF-111, 5 KC-135, 3 E-3B/C, 2 C-12, 2 HC-130. Installations for SIGINT, space tracking and seismic monitoring.
UNITED KINGDOM:
NAVY: 1,950. HQ London, admin and spt facilities, 1 SEAL det.
AIR FORCE: 9,500:
1 air force HQ: 1 ftr wing, 66 cbt ac, 2 sqn with 48 F-15E, 1 sqn with 18 F-15C/D.
1 special ops gp with 3 sqns: 1 with 5 MH-53J, 1 with 4 HC-130, 1 with 4 MC-130H.
1 air refuelling wg with 9 KC-135.
PACIFIC COMMAND (USPACOM): HQ: Hawaii.
ALASKA:
ARMY: 9,600; 1 lt inf bde.
AIR FORCE: 10,000. 1 air force HQ; 5 sqn (2 with 36 F-15C/D, 1 with 18 F-15E, 1 with 18 F-16C/D, 1 with 6 A-10, 60A-10).
HAWAII:
ARMY: 24,600. HQ US Army Pacific (USARPAC). 1 lt inf div (2 lt inf bde); 1 ARNG inf bde.
AIR FORCE: 4,400. HQ Pacific Air Forces (PACAF). 1 air base wg with 2 C-135B/C, 1 gp with 18 F-15A/B, 4 C-130H and 8 KC-135R (ANG), 1 comd/control sqn with 2 EC-135.
NAVY: 19,500. HQ US Pacific Fleet. Homeport for some 17 submarines, 16 PSC and 10 spt and misc ships.
MARINES: 3,900. HQ Marine Forces Pacific, 1 MEB.
SINGAPORE:
NAVY: about 100, log facilities.
AIR FORCE: 40 det spt sqn.
JAPAN:
ARMY: 2,000.
1 corps HQ, base and spt units.
AIR FORCE: 15,200. 1 air force HQ: 102 cbt ac. 2 ftr wings (5 sqn) with **ac:** 54 F-15C/D, 48 F-16, 2 C-21A; **hel:** 3 UH-1N hel.
1 sqn with 2 E-3 AWACS.
1 wg with 16 C-130E/H.
1 sqn with 15 KC-135 tkr.
1 SAR sqn with 8 HH-60.
1 special ops gp with 5 HC-130N/P and 4 MC-130E.
NAVY: 7,300. Bases: Yokosuka (HQ 7th Fleet): homeport for 1 CV, 8 surface combatants; Sasebo: homeport for 3 submarines, 3 amph ships.
MARINES: 21,000; 1 MEF.
SOUTH KOREA:
ARMY: 27,500. 1 Army HQ (UN command). 1 inf div (2 bde, (6 bn)), 2 SP arty, 1 MLRS, 1 AD bn.

AIR FORCE: 8,950. 1 air force HQ: 2 ftr wings, 90 cbt ac.
3 sqn with 72 F-16.
1 tac control sqn with 6 A-10, 12 OA-10.
1 special ops sqn, 5 MH-53J.
1 recce sqn with 3 U-2, 2 C-12.
GUAM:
AIR FORCE: 2,200. 1 air force HQ.
NAVY: 4,600, MPS-3 (4 ships with eqpt for 1 MEB).
Naval air station, comms and spt facilities.
AUSTRALIA:
AIR FORCE: 230.
NAVY: some 100. Comms facility at NW Cape, SEWS/
SIGINT station at Pine Gap, and SEWS station at Nurrungar.
DIEGO GARCIA:
NAVY: 900, MPS-2 (5 ships with eqpt for 1 MEB).
Naval air station, spt facilities.
US WEST COAST:
MARINES: 1 MEF.
AT SEA:
PACIFIC FLEET: (HQ Pearl Harbor). **Main base:** Pearl
Harbor. **Other bases:** Bangor (WA); San Diego and Long
Beach (CA).
Submarines: 7 *Ohio* SSBN, 5 SSGN, 27 SSN.
Surface Combatants: 6 CV/CVN, 29 CG/CGN, 2 DDG,
    15 DD, 12 FFG, 4 FF.
Amph: 1 comd, 3 LHA, 3 LPH, 7 LPD, 6 LSD, 6 LST,
    2 LKA.
Surface Combatants divided between two fleets:
3rd Fleet (HQ San Diego): covers Eastern and Central
    Pacific, Aleutians, Bering Sea, etc. Typically 4 CVBG,
    4 URG. Amph gp.
7th Fleet (HQ Yokosuka, Japan): covers Western Pacific,
    Japan, Philippines, ANZUS responsibilities, Indian
    Ocean. Typically 1 CVBG, 1 URG, amph ready gp (1
    MEU embarked).
CENTRAL COMMAND (USCENTCOM): comds
all deployed forces in its region.
HQ USCENTCOM: MacDill AFB, FL.
ARMY: 2,050.
AT SEA:
5th Fleet. Average Composition of US Naval Forces
deployed in Indian Ocean, Persian Gulf, Red Sea: 1
CVBG (1 CV/CVN, 2 CG/CGN, 2 FFG, 1 AO/AOE/AE,
2 SSN). (Forces provided from Atlantic and Pacific.)
KUWAIT:
ARMY: prepositioned eqpt for 1 armd bde (2 tk, 1
mech bn, 1 arty bn).
QATAR:
ARMY: prepositioned eqpt for 1 armd bde (forming).
SAUDI ARABIA:
AIR FORCE: units on rotational detachment, numbers
vary (incl: F-15, F-16, F-117, C-130, KC-135, U-2, E-3).
SOUTHERN COMMAND (USSOUTHCOM):
HQ USSOUTHCOM: Quarry Heights, Panama.
PANAMA:
ARMY: HQ US Army South, Fort Clayton, Panama: 6,300.
1 inf bde (1 inf bn), 1 avn bde.

NAVY: HQ US Naval Forces Southern Command, Fort
Amador, Panama: 700. Special boat unit, fleet spt.
MARINES: 120.
AIR FORCE: 2,000. 1 air div: 2 C-130, 1 C-21, 9 C-27,
1 CT-43.
HONDURAS:
ARMY: 150.
AIR FORCE: 50.
ATLANTIC COMMAND (USACOM):
HQ: Norfolk, VA (CINC has op control of all CONUS-
based army and air forces).
US EAST COAST:
MARINES: 1 MEF.
BERMUDA:
NAVY: 800.
CUBA:
NAVY: 1,900 (Guantánamo).
MARINES: 650 (Guantánamo).
ICELAND:
NAVY: 1,450. 1 MR sqn with 6 P-3, 1 UP-3.
AIR FORCE: 1,000. 4 F-15C/D, 1 KC-135, 1 HC-130,
4 HH-60G.
MARINES: 80.
PORTUGAL (AZORES):
NAVY: 10. Limited facilities at Lajes.
AIR FORCE: 950. Periodic SAR detachments to spt space
shuttle ops.
UNITED KINGDOM:
NAVY: 150. Comms and int facilities, Edzell, Thurso.
AT SEA:
ATLANTIC FLEET: (HQ: Norfolk, VA). Other main bases:
Groton (CT); Charleston (SC); King's Bay (GA);
Mayport (FL).
Submarines: 7 *Ohio*, 3 other SSBN, 16 SSGN, 35 SSN.
Surface Combatants: 6 CV/CVN, 23 CG/CGN, 5 DDG,
    16 DD, 23 FFG, 4 FF. Amph: 1 LCC, 2 LHA, 4
    LPH, 6 LPD, 5 LSD, 6 LST, 1 LKA.
Surface Forces divided into two fleets:
2nd Fleet (HQ: Norfolk): covers Atlantic.
Typically 4–5 CVBG, amph gp, 4 URG.
6th Fleet (HQ: Gaeta, Italy): Mediterranean. Under op
comd of EUCOM (see entry for typical force levels).

CONTINENTAL UNITED STATES
(CONUS): major units/formations only listed.
ARMY (USACOM): 113,800 provides general
reserve of cbt-ready ground forces for other comd.
Active: 2 Army HQ, 3 Corps HQ (1 AB), 2 armd, 3
    mech, 1 lt inf, 1 AB, 1 air aslt div; 2 armd, 6
    arty bde; 2 armd cav regt, 8 AD bn (2 *Avenger*,
    6 *Patriot*).
Reserve: ARNG: 3 armd, 1 mech, 3 inf, 1 lt inf div;
    20 indep bde, 1 armd cav regt. AR: 1 lt inf bde.

US STRATEGIC COMMAND (USSTRATCOM):
see entry on p. 23.

AIR COMBAT COMMAND (ACC): responsible for provision of strategic AD units and of cbt-ready Air Force units for rapid deployment.

US SPECIAL OPERATIONS COMMAND (USSOCOM): HQ MacDill AFB, FL. Comd all active, reserve and National Guard special ops forces of all services based in CONUS. See p. 29.

US TRANSPORTATION COMMAND (USTRANSCOM): responsible for providing all common-user airlift, sealift and land transportation to deploy and maintain US forces on a global basis.

AIR MOBILITY COMMAND (AMC): responsible for providing strategic, tac and special op airlift, aeromedical evacuation, SAR and weather recce.

MILITARY SEALIFT COMMAND: see p. 26.

FORCES ABROAD:
UN AND PEACEKEEPING:
BOSNIA (UNPROFOR): 3. **CROATIA** (UNCRO): 345. **EGYPT** (MFO): 1,000; 1 inf bn. **GEORGIA** (UNOMIG): 3 Obs. **GERMANY** (*Provide Promise*): C-130. **HAITI** (UNMIH): 2,400, plus 47 staff. **IRAQ/KUWAIT** (UNIKOM): 15 Obs. **ITALY** (*Deny Flight*): USAF: 2,000: 8 F-15E, 12 F-16C, 8 OA-10, 4 AC-130, 3 EC-130, 10 KC-135, 6 EF-111A. USMC: 12 F/A-18D. USN: 1 CV/CVN, 18 F/A-18C, 6 EA-6B. **ADRIATIC** (*Sharp Guard*): 1 DDG, 2 FFG, 1 PCC. **MEDITERRANEAN:** 1 CVBG, 1 amph ready gp (with MEU embarked), P-3C ac. **FYROM** (UNPREDEP): 546; inf bn, incl 3 UH-60 hel. **MIDDLE EAST** (UNTSO): 15 Obs. **WESTERN SAHARA** (MINURSO): 30 Obs. **SAUDI ARABIA** (*Southern Watch*): USAF units on rotation, numbers vary (incl F-15, F-16, F-117, C-130, KC-135, E-3). **TURKEY** (*Provide Comfort*): Army (1,560); Air Force (1,400). 1 tac, 1 Air Base GP with 18 F-16, 6 F-15C, 3 EF-111, 5 KC-135, 2 E3B/C, 2 C-12, 2 HC-130.

PARAMILITARY:
CIVIL AIR PATROL (CAP): 51,000 (17,500 cadets); HQ, 8 geographical regions, 52 wings, 1,700 units, 530 CAP ac, plus 4,450 private ac.

NATO

In almost every NATO member-state, military manpower and defence spending have been reduced in the last 12 months; by 1 January 1995, nearly all had reduced their holdings of Treaty Limited Equipment (TLE) to below their Conventional Forces in Europe (CFE) Treaty entitlement.

Partnership for Peace

NATO's Partnership for Peace (PFP) programme was developed to improve cooperation between NATO states and other European states. Invitations to join were issued on 14 January 1994, and by 13 July, 22 states, including Russia, had joined. Since then, four more states – Armenia, Austria, Belarus and Malta – have joined. By the end of May 1995, 19 had submitted Presentation Documents (setting out the scope of cooperation activities sought) and 12 Partnership Programmes had been agreed with a further eight still under negotiation.

The most important PFP development has been Russia's successful involvement. Although Russia signed the PFP in June 1994 and submitted a Presentation Document in July, Foreign Minister Andrei Kozyrev, contrary to expectation, did not sign Russia's Partnership Programme in December. He objected to the NATO Council's Work Plan for Dialogue, Partnership and Cooperation agreed upon the day before as well as to plans for NATO enlargement, particularly the drafting of a timetable for enlargement.

On 31 May 1995 at the next meeting of the North Atlantic Cooperation Council (NACC), Kozyrev accepted both Russia's Partnership Programme and a document on what is described as broader and more intense dialogue between NATO and Russia. The key recommendations were:

- Improving information sharing on European politico-security issues (including basic security information, military doctrine and strategies, conflict prevention, resolution and crisis management, conversion of defence industry and transparency of defence budgets).
- Increasing political consultation on matters such as weapons proliferation, nuclear safety and specific crises in Europe.
- Cooperating in areas such as peacekeeping, ecological security, civil science and technological policy and humanitarian matters.

On 17 July, the first meeting took place between NATO ambassadors and a high-level Russian delegation headed by its Ambassador to NATO, Vitaly Churkin. He proposed sending military and civil representatives to NATO Headquarters to facilitate direct contacts and creating a 'hot-line' for communication between NATO HQ and Moscow. NATO asked the Russian government to do more to change the image of NATO as an enemy military alliance held by the Russian people.

Three PFP exercises took place in 1994 and 11 are scheduled for 1995. A great many other activities, such as conferences and workshops, visits, exchange appointments and attendance on training courses, are taking place under the PFP mantle.

NATO Enlargement

The North Atlantic Council (NAC) decided in December 1994 to initiate an examination to determine how NATO will enlarge, the principles to guide the process and the implications of membership. They directed the Council in Permanent Session to make an extensive study. The Council was careful to assert that it would be premature to discuss the time-frame for enlargement or which particular countries would be invited to join NATO. Nevertheless, many assumed that the study would spell out the rules for eligibility for membership. (The criteria for membership was discussed in the 4 May 1995 issue of the IISS publication *Strategic Comments*.) The US appears to be the keenest NATO member on enlargement. It had been thought that Germany also favoured early enlargement, but Chancellor Helmut Kohl warned against 'building new walls' across Europe and unnecessarily antagonising Russia. He saw the question of enlargement as going hand in hand with membership of the European Union (EU). The UK parliamentary Defence Committee, in its report published on 1 August, also warned against too rapid enlargement and recommended that it should be gradual and cautious. It firmly believed that there should be no membership of the Western European Union (WEU) without NATO membership, nor any differentiation between the Visegrad Four and Bulgaria and Romania.

The European Pillar

Western European Union
On 1 January 1995, Austria, Finland and Sweden joined the European Union and now have observer status in the WEU. In March 1995, Greece deposited its instrument of ratification and so became a full member of the WEU. At the WEU Council of Ministers meeting on 14 November 1994, the Council postponed establishing a European Armaments Agency, discussed the Permanent Council's 'Preliminary Conclusions on the Formulation of a Common European Defence Policy', and tasked the Permanent Council to elaborate further on the operational role of the WEU.

Eurocorps
There have been no changes to the organisation or role of the Eurocorps in the last 12 months. It held a major exercise from 7 to 17 November 1994 and eight command post and troop exercises are planned for 1995. Eurocorps is expected to be declared operational on 1 October 1995.

Southern European Multinational Forces
France, Italy and Spain have agreed to establish two new multinational military forces. The European Force (EUROFOR) will be a 10,000–15,000-strong division with light armour, capable of rapid deployment. There will be a multinational HQ in Florence, but contingents will remain in their own countries. The European Maritime Force (EUROMARFOR) will be a non-permanent naval and air task force, probably including an aircraft carrier and an amphibious landing force. The forces are to be set up in autumn 1995. Portugal asked to join and its offer has been accepted. Both forces have been placed at the WEU's disposal for peacekeeping and humanitarian relief operations, and would also be available to NATO in the event of a main defence requirement.

Hélios *Satellite Programme*
The French-built military reconnaissance satellite *Hélios* 1A was launched on 7 July 1995 and placed in quasi-polar orbit. A resolution of one metre is claimed for its imagery, but its sensors only have a daylight and fair-weather capability. The cost of the operation has been borne by France (79%), Italy (14%) and Spain (7%). A second satellite, *Hélios* 2, is under development for launching in 2001. *Hélios* 2, while having a night capability, will still not see through cloud. Expense is a worrying factor for future developments and it is hoped that Germany can be persuaded to join the programme, but it will probably only do so if a significant proportion of contracts went to German companies. The rationale behind the *Hélios* and other European programmes is to end reliance on the US for overhead imagery which is not always made available.

Turkey and the Kurds

The civil war in south-eastern Turkey has continued unabated. The Turkish Army made two substantial incursions into Iraq in their efforts to neutralise Kurdistan Worker's Party (PKK) guerrillas who were seeking sanctuary there. The first, on 20 March 1995, involved some 35,000 troops backed by tanks, artillery, helicopters and aircraft and penetrated some 40km into Iraq. Turkey claimed that between 2,400 and 2,800 Kurdish guerrillas were based across the border. Turkish forces withdrew by 4 May, claiming to have destroyed the PKK infrastructure and to have killed 555 PKK men for the loss of 61 soldiers. The second incursion took place on 6 July, lasted only five days and involved some 3,000 troops. 167 PKK men and 26 Turkish soldiers were killed.

Greece and Turkey

On 4 March 1995, after Greece had lifted its veto, the EU reached agreement with Turkey on a custom's union. In return, Greece received a promise that the EU would open negotiations on Cypriot membership within six months of the conclusion of the 1996 EU Inter-Governmental Conference. On 1 June 1995 Greece ratified the UN Convention on the Law of the Sea which allows it to extend its territorial waters from six to 12 miles. The Turkish parliament reacted by declaring that Turkey's vital interests in the Aegean made the extension of Greek territorial waters unacceptable and granted the government all powers deemed necessary to defend the country's interests. However, the Law of the Sea Convention addresses the question of conflicting claims and a number of tribunals are empowered to arbitrate.

Anglo-French Cooperation

The formation of the Combined Air Forces Group was announced at the Anglo-French summit meeting on 18 November 1994. The Groups's main objective is to strengthen the capabilities of the two air forces to undertake humanitarian and peace-support operations. The group will comprise a planning cell of some ten officers co-located with HQ Allied Forces North-West Europe at High Wycombe (UK). Unlike Eurocorps, the Group will have no permanently allocated air forces.

Nuclear Developments

The **UK** has decommissioned a second (of four) *Polaris* SLBM armed ballistic-missile submarine (SSBN). The first *Vanguard*-class SSBN, armed with 16 *Trident* D-5 SLBM, started its first operational patrol in December 1994. The second was accepted by the Navy in January 1995. It was announced in April 1995 that all free-fall WE-177 nuclear bombs would be withdrawn by 1998 and not, as originally scheduled, in 2003. The nuclear sub-strategic role will then be taken on by single-warhead *Trident* SLBM. The third *Vanguard*-class SSBN will be operational by 1998. It is understood that the US will deliver seven D-5 SLBM annually until 1999. The UK also announced in April that it had ceased production of weapons-grade fissile material.

Shortly after his election in May 1995 as President of **France**, Jacques Chirac announced that France would resume nuclear testing at the Mururoa Pacific test site in September 1995. A total of eight tests were planned after which France would sign the Comprehensive Test Ban Treaty (CTBT). The reason for France's renewed testing has been given as the need to validate the new TN-75 warhead for the M-45 SLBM (and M-5 SLBM) (one test), to verify whether nuclear triggers are still exploding as predicted (two tests) and to calibrate data for simulation technology (four tests). France is also developing a new air-delivered stand-off nuclear weapon, *Air-Sol Longue Portée* (ASLP), also requiring a new type of warhead, to be tested presumably by simulation. The French simulation plan, Préparation à la Limitation des Essais Nucléaires (PALEN), is said to be based on the use of computers, such as the Cray T3D and Cray T3E employing a technique known as 'massively parallel architecture' x-ray accelerators and megajoule lasers. The total cost of the project could be some $3 billion. The testing announcement has produced strong negative reactions, particularly from Pacific Rim countries. Less commented on was France's subsequent announcement of a study on whether the intermediate-range ballistic missile (IRBM) site on the plain of Albion, where France has 18 S-3D silo-based missiles, should be closed. The M-5 SLBM design would have allowed it also to replace the S-3D should that have been considered necessary. The two squadrons of *Mirage* bombers previously considered to be strategic forces are now classified as 'pre-strategic' forces.

Conventional Military Developments and Plans

Belgium no longer employs conscription and has reduced its armed forces from 63,000 to 47,000 with the largest reduction of 18,000 being in the Army. Large quantities of armaments are for sale, including 155 *Leopard* tanks, 130 *Scorpion* light tanks, 60 155mm SP M109 howitzers, 24 HAWK

SAM launchers and 40 F-16 FGA aircraft. 25 *Mirage* 5 fighters have been sold to Chile with delivery to be completed in November 1995. The Navy has acquired four more mine countermeasures ships: two US *Aggressive*-class (*van Haverbeke*), and two more *Aster* (tripartite)-class.

The **Canadian** Army has disbanded its only parachute unit following revelations about its conduct in Somalia, but a parachuting capability will be maintained in some infantry battalions. The last squadron of CF-5 (F-5) fighters has been disbanded and the aircraft put in store. The Air Force has acquired five KC-130 in flight refuelling tankers and nine C-146 Bell medium helicopters to replace three older types. The Navy has commissioned a seventh *Halifax*-class frigate and two more will be commissioned this autumn.

The **Danish** Army has been reduced in strength by 5,500. Fifty-six M-113A2 APCs mounting a 25mm gun have been acquired and 24 RF-35 reconnaissance aircraft have been eliminated. The Navy has commissioned two *Flyvefisken*-class (Stanflex 300) fast patrol craft.

The **French** Army has acquired 14 more MLRS and its first *Leclerc* tank regiment will be operational by the end of 1995; 42 tanks out of 134 ordered have been delivered so far. *Leclerc* tanks are also being manufactured for the UAE. The Navy has retired two frigates, one *Tourville*-class and one *Commandant Rivière*-class, and has commissioned the first of three *Flamant*-class coastal patrol craft. The Air Force has disbanded two fighter squadrons and eliminated some 80 combat aircraft. An air-launched cruise missile, *Apaché*, is being developed. There will be three versions of it, one with a 400km range, one for airfield runway attack and one for hard target attack.

All of the **German** armed services have reduced their manpower; the Army by 14,000, the Air Force by 7,600 and the Navy by 1,600. The Navy has commissioned one *Brandenburg*-class guided-missile frigate. The Army has now disposed of all of its former East German Army equipments, except for 45 Mi-24 attack helicopters. From 1996–2000, the German Army will implement a reorganisation aimed at reducing manpower (by 24,400) and improving readiness. The resulting organisation will be complex – all the more so since some decisions over manning, status and command structure have not yet been taken. At the higher-corps level there is little change and three Corps remain: I Corps is a truly joint German–Netherlands formation commanding both German and Dutch units in peacetime; II Corps, while German in peacetime, becomes a US–German Corps in war (as does the US V Corps); IV Corps remains a national corps. At the divisional level where Divisional HQs are also Military District HQs, one division, the 14th, will lose its district responsibilities which will be taken on by 6th Division HQ in Kiel which will then no longer have an operational role. 14th Division will come under NATO's LANDJUT command in war. There are no other changes to divisional affiliations (to ARRC, Eurocorps or the V US Corps). The Air-mobile Forces Command (KLK) established to command crisis-reaction forces (KRK) carries the alternative title of 4th Division. In future there will be five categories of brigade. KRK-roled brigades, which have three manoeuvre battalions, will be fully manned in peacetime and by volunteers (conscript volunteers will be required to serve between 12 and 23 months). There will be six such brigades: two tank, one airborne, one light infantry (located in former East Germany), one air-mechanised (still forming, to include an attack helicopter unit) and the Franco-German brigade. In future, new recruit intakes for these brigades will be trained in other units to enhance readiness. The second tier of four brigades will also have three battalions each and be fully manned in peacetime. They and all other brigades have a main defence force (HVK) role. To avoid creating first- and second-class formations, it is likely that some battalions in these four brigades (one tank, one armoured infantry, one airborne and one mountain) will be KRK-roled with a similar number of battalions in KRK brigades HVK-roled. The third category comprises four mainly active brigades of three battalions; these brigades will also hold and maintain the equipment for four mobilisation brigades which would form the fifth category if mobilised. The fourth category of brigade (eight tank and armoured infantry) will remain on their current organisation of two tank and two armoured infantry battalions of which one of each type is manned in peacetime while the other would be mobilised and manned by reserves. In all there will be 22 peacetime brigades compared with the current 24. Finally, a Special Forces regiment is being formed by concentrating the Long-Range Reconnaissance Companies and other elements of the airborne brigades together under the HQ of 25 Airborne Brigade which will be disbanded.

The **Greek** Army has eliminated over 500 tanks (300 M-47, 220 M-48) and acquired 80 more *Leopard* tanks. It also acquired 120 more SP *TOW*. The Air Force has ordered 60 *Alphajet* FGA aircraft from Germany.

Italian Army manpower has been reduced by 15% to some 30,000 men. While 70 M-60 tanks have been eliminated, a further 54 *Leopard* tanks have been acquired. There have also been small increases in the numbers of artillery, including 4 more MLRS. Air Force manpower has been reduced by 5,500. 24 *Tornado* F-3 fighters are being leased from the UK, of which 12 will have been delivered by December 1995. The Navy has commissioned one more *Pelosi*-class and retired one *Toti*-class submarine. One *De Cristofaro*-class frigate has been retired and the last of the class will also be retired in late 1995. The three *Lupo*-class frigates, built originally for Iraq but never delivered, have been taken over by the Italian Navy.

The **Netherlands** is ending conscription in January 1997. The US AH-64 *Apache* attack helicopter has been chosen for the Netherlands air-mobile brigade; 30 have been ordered for delivery in 1997 and 1998, and until then 12 will be lent by the US. The Joint Belgian and Netherlands Naval Command will become operational on 1 January 1996.

Fresh information has allowed the organisation of the **Portuguese** Army to be better understood. Only two formations at brigade level remain: a composite brigade with tanks, APC mounted infantry and artillery and an airborne brigade. The remainder of the Army are deployed in low-strength regiments directly under Military District command.

The **Spanish** Army has been reorganised. Divisions, with the exception of the mechanised division (which now includes an armoured brigade), have been disbanded and replaced by one mountain and three cadre light-infantry brigades. The General Reserve Force has also been broken up and a Rapid Reaction Force (FAR) created with the airborne, air-portable and newly formed Spanish Legion brigades. Army aviation assets have also been formed into a brigade. Some 340 M-47 tanks have been eliminated and 108 *Leopard* 2 tanks are being leased from the German Army with delivery starting soon. A Memorandum of Understanding has been signed for Spain jointly to produce 200 *Leopard* tanks with Germany. 100 BTR-70 wheeled APCs have been acquired for the Spanish unit with UNPROFOR in Bosnia-Herzegovina, as have 18 more *Mistral* SAM launchers (though not for use in Bosnia). The Air Force has bought a total of 18 *Mirage* F-1 fighters from France and Qatar. The Navy has commissioned one US *Perry*-class (*Santa Maria*) frigate and two US *Newport*-class (*Hernán Cortés*) tank landing ships (LST).

Turkey has increased the length of conscription service again to up to 18 months. This has allowed the Army to increase its manpower by some 7,000. While 640 tanks (mainly M-47 and M-48) have been eliminated, Army acquisitions include 75 155mm M-114 towed artillery and 25 107mm MRL. Over 200 combat aircraft have been disposed of, including all F-104 (89), and over 100 F-5, including 20 RF-5A reconnaissance aircraft. The Air Force has added eight F-16 fighters and formed an additional air-defence squadron. The first two, of an order for seven, KC-135R in-flight refuelling tankers have been delivered. The Navy has commissioned one *Preveze*-class (German Type 209/1400) submarine and one *Barbados*-class (German MEKO 200) frigate.

The **UK** has announced that its Joint Force Headquarters will assume command of overseas operations from 1 April 1996 after its staff has assembled and validated its capabilities. The Army has established a new Headquarters, Land Command, which assumed command of all army formations and units, including those in Germany and elsewhere overseas. District boundaries have been adjusted and three District HQs renamed 'regenerative divisions'. Some 300 FV-432 APCs have been eliminated, as have 50 M109A1 155mm SP guns which have been replaced by 50 more AS-90 155mm SP guns. 30 more *Starstreak* SAM firing units have also been acquired. The cease-fire in Northern Ireland has allowed two roulement battalions to be withdrawn from the province. Although overall aircraft numbers remain much the same, the Air Force has 23 more combat aircraft (ten *Tornado* and 13 *Harrier*) in squadron service. The Navy has retired the last two

Upholder-class submarines and paid off one *Broadsword*-class and the last *Leander*-class frigate. A tenth *Norfolk*-class (Type 23) frigate has been commissioned. In March, orders were placed for 22 utility EH-101 and eight *Chinook* transport helicopters for the Air Force. In July, the decision on the Army's new attack helicopter was finally taken and 67 AH-64*Apache* helicopters have been ordered from the UK company, Westland. The UK has completed its feasibility studies into arming nuclear-attack submarines with conventionally armed *Tomahawk* cruise missiles and has formally applied to the US government to purchase an unstated quantity to enter into service in 1998.

Aircraft Collaborative Projects

Eurofighter 2000

Germany, Italy, Spain and the UK signed a 'Memorandum of Understanding' (MOU) in July 1995 setting out the revised development programme for the Eurofighter. The first two aircraft flew in 1994 while the third development aircraft, the first to be powered by the new *Eurojet* EJ200 engine designed specifically for Eurofighter, flew for the first time on 4 June 1995. The flight testing programme is going well and the Eurofighter is on course to enter into service in 2000. There is some concern over the apparent development budget over-spend.

Future Large Aircraft

The UK decision to order only 25 C-130J transport aircraft, five less than planned, released funds which allowed the UK to rejoin the Future Large Aircraft (FLA) project. Differences over the type of engine and cabin size have been resolved and the full feasibility study completed on schedule. The aircraft will be powered by four turbo-jet engines and have a four-metre cabin width. The first test flight is due to take place in December 2000 with aircraft coming into service in 2002.

Defence Procurement

The end of the Cold War has brought great pressure for NATO governments to cut defence expenditures. Procurement, inclusive of research and development (R&D) and in-service support, accounts for 30–40% of NATO defence spending, and has been the target for large cuts throughout the Alliance. Governments have generally achieved their immediate aims either by delaying and cancelling programmes, or by reducing the unit quantities ordered (which normally has the effect of increasing unit costs). These changes have induced a wave of mergers and acquisitions in national defence industries, with firms seeking to consolidate their defence business by further concentration and specialisation. Governments have encouraged the consolidation of national defence industries, but so far continue to protect them because of their strategic and wider economic significance. But pressure to cut defence expenditures is certain to remain, so procurement reform is increasingly essential. Although over-capacity is as much a feature of the US as of the European defence industry, the urgency for reform is felt most keenly in Europe, partly because cuts in demand threaten industrial efficiency, and because of the ongoing process of European integration.

The principal policy forum for European procurement issues is the Western European Armaments Group (WEAG), formed as part of the WEU in 1992 to promote cooperation in European defence procurement. The European Commission (EC) has no responsibility in matters concerning defence procurement under Article 223 of the Treaty of Rome. But since the WEU has a double function *vis-à-vis* both NATO and the EU, the EC also seeks to influence the policy debate within the WEAG, and can also claim to represent the new EU members which currently belong neither to NATO nor to the WEU.

Confronted by the need for reform in European defence procurement, three policy options have emerged in the policy debate and these are subject to increasingly vigorous bargaining within the WEAG in the run-up to the EU's Inter-Governmental Conference in 1996.

The first option, usually most identified with France and Germany, is to establish a centralised European Armaments Agency that would be ultimately responsible for the coordination and control of all European defence procurement and would exercise a preferential European purchasing policy. Advocates argue that the wealth and continuing integration of Western Europe means it now possesses the economic resources to reduce its dependence on the US. Furthermore, a 'buy-European' policy is justified in so far as it mirrors the 'buy-American' prejudice of the US. Concentration of R&D resources and larger-scale production made possible by European preference would improve the efficiency and international competitiveness of European industry *vis-à-vis* the US, and help to improve the balance of payments. Frustrated by the lack of a European consensus, France and Germany announced in mid-1993 that they intended to establish a joint armaments agency, which might serve as the forerunner of a larger European organisation, and which is planned to be in place by the end of 1995. In late 1994, the two countries formally invited their European partners to join them.

Current Trends in NATO and Other Western European Defence Procurement

	GDP 1994 $bn	Def Bdgt 1994 $m	Def bdgt 1995 $m	R&D 1994 $m	% def bdgt	R&D 1995 $m	% def bdgt	Proc 1994 $m	% def bdgt	Proc 1995 $m	% def bdgt
Belgium	228	3,948	4,572	2	0.0	2	0.0	282	7.1	286	6.3
Denmark	146	2,762	3,107	0	0.0	0	0.0	387	14.0	435	14.0
France	1,329	35,897	40,541	5,818	16.2	6,754	16.7	8,528	23.8	9,679	23.9
Germany	1,835	29,087	34,023	1,553	5.3	1,974	5.8	3,417	11.7	3,962	11.6
Greece	76	3,051	3,382	16	0.5	17	0.5	744	24.4	825	24.4
Italy	1,018	16,229	16,038	561	3.5	568	3.5	2,808	17.3	2,775	17.3
Luxembourg	11	111	131	0	0.0	0	0.0	3	2.8	4	2.8
Netherlands	330	7,473	8,557	75	1.0	86	1.0	1,375	18.4	1,575	18.4
Norway	110	3,382	3,772	147	4.4	165	4.4	789	23.3	798	21.2
Portugal	88	1,387	1,689	0	0.0	0	0.0	112	8.1	137	8.1
Spain	483	6,190	7,033	249	4.0	288	4.1	720	11.6	984	14.0
Turkey	170	5,380	6,239	5	0.1	7	0.1	1,960	36.4	2,479	39.7
UK	1,023	34,112	34,481	3,481	10.2	3,736	10.8	10,127	29.7	10,585	30.7
NATO Europe	6,846	149,009	163,565	11,907	8.0	13,597	8.3	31,253	21.0	34,524	21.1
Austria	197	1,763	2,044	0	0.0	0	0.0	361	20.5	408	20.0
Finland	98	1,966	2,115	8	0.4	10	0.5	703	35.7	572	27.1
Ireland	52	624	701	0	0.0	0	0.0	25	4.0	24	3.4
Sweden	197	4,939	5,590	85	1.7	73	1.3	2,110	42.7	2,333	41.7
Switzerland	260	4,238	4,977	88	2.1	99	2.0	1,690	39.9	2,107	42.3
Non-NATO Europe	803	13,530	15,427	180	1.3	182	1.2	4,888	36.1	5,445	35.3
US	6,737	251,400	252,600	34,600	13.8	35,400	14.0	44,100	17.5	44,600	17.7
Canada	549	8,454	8,142	183	2.2	141	1.7	2,195	26.0	2,238	27.5
Totals											
US/Canada	7,286	259,854	260,742	34,783	13.4	35,541	13.6	46,295	17.8	46,838	18.0
Europe	7,649	162,539	178,992	12,088	7.4	13,779	7.7	36,141	22.2	39,969	22.3

Note: Except in the UK case, defence procurement budgets exclude expenditure on equipment in-service support and supplies of other logistic *materiel* which form part of the O&M budget. If included in the procurement, these expenditures would add an estimated 10–20% to the total, thus adding significantly to the overall market value.
Source: National governments.

The second option, promoted by the EC, is more radical than the first. Like the latter, it involves the creation of a centralised European procurement agency and an internal defence market. An essential difference is that competition would determine the structure of European industry. It follows that, according to this view, there is no role for the traditional protectionist policies of national governments to support indigenous industries and their insistence on the principle of *juste retour* as a condition for joining European collaborative procurement programmes.

The third policy option, promoted by the UK, seeks to balance the strategic and economic benefits of European collaboration – perceived as strengthening the European pillar of NATO – with the need to sustain a strong and competitive transatlantic defence market incorporating both the US and Canada in the wider interests of the Alliance which relies heavily on the US for the more expensive military technologies. Advocates stress the need for rationalisation of European NATO defence procurement by further efficiency improvements in the management of collaborative programmes on a project-by-project basis, but oppose all-inclusive centralisation and protectionism. In line with this policy, both the UK and Italy indicated in early 1995 that they intended to join the new Franco-German agency, suggesting that it assume management responsibility for the large Eurofighter and Horizon frigate programmes. Critics of the Franco-German and EC proposals also point to the recurring failure of many European collaborative programmes to meet performance, schedule and cost targets – citing government indecision and poor project management as two primary factors – and claiming that more centralisation and anti-competitive policies would not improve industrial performance. Furthermore, they argue that state control of defence industries (particularly in France and Italy) often mitigates against efficient transnational consolidation, and that there is a stronger case for a transatlantic defence industrial structure incorporating efficiency-enhancing transnational mergers and acquisitions – giving European defence industries continuing access to US equity capital and technology transfer. Finally, the critics point to the likely costs of the two anti-competitive European policy options. If there is not to be a net loss in defence industrial capacity arising from exclusion of the US, spending on defence procurement (particularly R&D) will have to rise to perhaps double its present levels, for which there is currently little political will. Any decline in defence industrial capacity will inevitably lead to a reduced defence capability. At the same time, this would also drive another damaging wedge between the European NATO partners and the US.

BELGIUM

GDP	1993: fr 7,285bn ($210.57bn):		
	per capita $18,400		
	1994: fr 7,621bn ($227.79bn):		
	per capita $18,800		
Growth	1993: -1.7%	1994: 2.3%	
Inflation	1993: 2.8%	1994: 2.4%	
Publ debt	1993: 141.3%	1994: 140.1%	
Def exp	1993: fr 129.6bn ($3.75bn)		
	1994: fr 132.1bn ($3.95bn)		
Def bdgt	1995: fr 99.97bn ($3.45bn)		
	1996: fr 99.89bn ($3.44bn)		
NATO defn	1993: fr 129.6bn ($3.75bn)		
	1994: fr 132.1bn ($3.95bn)		
$1 = fr	1993: 34.6	1994: 33.5	
	1995: 29.0		

fr = Belgian franc

Population: 10,071,000

	13–17	18–22	23–32
Men	311,200	329,400	758,800
Women	298,200	317,800	735,400

TOTAL ARMED FORCES:
ACTIVE: 47,200 (incl 2,000 Medical Service, 3,000 women).
RESERVES: 275,700: Army 190,000; Navy 12,000; Air Force 37,700; Medical Service 36,000. With service in past 3 years: 112,500.

ARMY: 30,100 (incl 1,600 women).
Intervention Force HQ.
1 mech div with 3 mech inf bde (each 1 tk, 2 mech inf, 1 SP arty bn), 1 recce, 1 arty bn, 1 AD arty unit (2 bde at 70% cbt str) (Eurocorps).
1 para-cdo bde (1 para, 1 cdo, 1 Atk/recce bn, 1 arty, 1 AD bty).
1 lt avn gp (2 Atk, 1 tpt bn).
RESERVES:
Territorial Defence: 9 province regt, 2 engr bn.
EQPT:
MBT: 132 *Leopard* 1A5, 202 *Leopard* 1A1 (23 in store, 155 for sale).
LT TK: 132 *Scorpion* (all for sale).
RECCE: 153 *Scimitar* (33 in store).
AIFV: 236 YPR-765 (41 in store) (plus 278 'look-

alikes' (55 in store, 14 for sale)).
APC: 163 M-113 (plus 164 'look-alikes') (133/92 in store), 198 *Spartan* (plus 112 'look-alikes') (25 in store, 150 for sale).
TOTAL ARTY: 308:
TOWED ARTY: 105mm: 18 M-101 (10 in store).
SP ARTY: 198: **105mm:** 20 M-108 (all for sale); **155mm:** 41 M-109A3 (all for sale), 127 M-109A2 (12 in store); **203mm:** 10 M-110 (all for sale).
MOR: 107mm: 90 M-30 (incl 35 SP; 48 for sale); **120mm:** 2 (for sale) plus **81mm:** 285.
ATGW: 420 *Milan* (incl 222 YPR-765 (45 in store, 4 for sale), 56 M-113 (13 in store)), 22 *Striker* (in store).
AD GUNS: 35mm: 54 *Gepard* SP (all for sale).
SAM: 118 *Mistral*.
AC: 10 BN-2A *Islander*.
HEL: 80:
ASLT: 46 A-109 (8 in store).
SPT: 32 SA-318 (16 in store).
UAV: 10 *Epervier*.

NAVY: 2,800 (incl 300 women).
Under integrated op comd with Netherlands from 1 Jan 1996 (less SS).
BASES: Ostend, Zeebrugge.
FF: 2 *Wielingen* with 2 x dual role (Fr L-5 HWT), 1 x 6 ASW mor; plus 4 x MM-38 *Exocet* SSM, 1 x 100mm gun and 1 x 8 *Sea Sparrow* SAM.
MCM: 11:
4 *Van Haverbeke* (US *Aggressive* MSO) (incl 1 used for trials).
7 *Aster* (tripartite) MHC.
SPT AND MISC: 4:
2 log spt/comd with hel deck, 1 research/survey, 1 sail training.
ADDITIONAL IN STORE: 1 FF, 2 MSO, 1 MHC, 1 log spt.
HEL: 3 SA-316B.

AIR FORCE: 12,300 (incl 850 women). Flying hours: 165.
FGA: 4 sqn with F-16A/B.
FTR: 2 sqn with F-16A/B.
TPT: 2 sqn:
1 with 12 C-130H.
1 with 2 Boeing 727QC, 3 HS-748, 5 *Merlin* IIIA, 2 *Falcon* 20, 1 *Falcon* 900.
TRG: 4 sqn:
2 with 5, *Alpha Jet*, 1 with SF-260, 1 with CM-170.
SAR: 1 sqn with *Sea King* Mk 48.
EQPT: 133 cbt ac (plus 71 in store), no armed hel.
AC: F-16: 133: **-A:** 113; **-B:** 20, plus 43 in store. **C-130:** 12 (tpt). **Boeing 727QC:** 2 (tpt). *HS-748:* 3 (tpt). *Falcon 20:* 2 (vip), *Falcon 900B:* 1. **SW 111** *Merlin:* 5 (vip, Photo, cal). **CM-170:** 11 (trg, liaison). **SF-260:** 36 (trg). *Alpha Jet:* 31 (trg).
HEL: *Sea King:* 5 (SAR).

IN STORE: *Mirage* 5: 28 (-BA: 13; -BR: 12; -BD: 3).
MSL:
AAM: AIM-9 *Sidewinder*.
SAM: 24 *Mistral*.

FORCES ABROAD:
GERMANY: 4,250; 1 Force HQ, 1 mech inf bde.
UN AND PEACEKEEPING:
BOSNIA (UNPROFOR): 94; 1 tpt coy plus 8 Obs.
CROATIA (UNCRO): 777; 1 inf bn, plus 6 Obs.
INDIA/PAKISTAN (UNMOGIP): 1 Obs. **FYROM** (UNPREDEP): 1 Obs. **MIDDLE EAST** (UNTSO): 6 Obs. **WESTERN SAHARA** (MINURSO): 1 Obs.

FOREIGN FORCES:
NATO: HQ NATO Brussels; HQ SHAPE Mons.
WEU: Military Planning Cell.
US: some 1,500: Army 1,000; Navy 100; Air Force 400.

CANADA

GDP	1993: $C 712.86bn ($551.63bn):	
	per capita $20,500	
	1994: $C 750.05bn ($548.37bn):	
	per capita $21,400	
Growth	1993: 2.2%	1994: 4.5%
Inflation	1993: 1.8%	1994: 0.2%
Publ debt	1993: 94.0%	1994: 94.6%
Def exp	1993: $C 12.31bn ($9.54bn)	
Def bdgt	1994: $C 11.55bn ($8.45bn)	
	1995: $C 11.08bn ($8.14bn)	
NATO defn	1993: $C 13.29bn ($10.30bn)	
	1994: $C 12.97bn ($9.49bn)	
$ 1 = $C	1993: 1.29	1994: 1.37
	1995: 1.36	

$C = Canadian dollar

Population: 28,130,000

	13–17	*18–22*	*23–32*
Men	956,600	959,800	2,219,800
Women	914,600	926,400	2,172,400

Canadian Armed Forces are unified and org in functional comds. Mob Comd commands land combat forces and has op control of TAC; Maritime Comd commands all naval forces incl op control maritime air. Air Comd commands all air forces. This entry is set out in the traditional single service manner.

TOTAL ARMED FORCES:
ACTIVE: 70,500 (8,700 women); of the total str

some 23,100 are not identified by service.

RESERVES: Primary 37,650: Army (Militia) (incl comms) 29,400; Navy 6,500; Air Force 1,750. Supplementary 19,000.

ARMY (Land Forces): 20,300.

1 Task Force HQ.
3 mech inf bde gp, each with 1 armd regt, 3 inf bn (1 mech), 1 arty, 1 engr regt, 1 AD bty.
1 indep AD regt.
1 indep engr spt regt.
RESERVES: Militia: 28,400; 18 armd, 19 arty, 51 inf, 12 engr, 20 spt bn level units, 13 med coy. **Canadian Rangers:** 3,100; 109 patrols.
EQPT:
MBT: 114 *Leopard* C-1.
RECCE: 174 *Lynx* (in store), 195 *Cougar*.
APC: 1,858: 1,329 M-113 A2 (82 in store), 61 M-577, 269 *Grizzly*, 199 *Bison*.
TOWED ARTY: 288: **105mm:** 38 Model 44 (L-5) pack (in store), 193 C1/C3 (M-101); **155mm:** 57 M-114 (in store).
SP ARTY: **155mm:** 76 M-109.
MOR: **81mm:** 167.
ATGW: 150 *TOW* (incl 72 TUA M-113 SP).
RL: 100 *Eryx*.
RCL: **84mm:** 1,040 *Carl Gustav*.
AD GUNS: **35mm:** 20 GDF-005; **40mm:** 57 L40/60 (in store).
SAM: 34 ADATS, 96 *Javelin, Starburst*.
UAV: CL-89 (AN/USD-501).

NAVY (Maritime Forces): 10,000.

SS: 3 *Ojibwa* (UK *Oberon*) SS with Mk 48 HWT (equipped for, but not with, *Harpoon* USGW).
PRINCIPAL SURFACE COMBATANTS: 16:
DDG: 4 *Iroquois* ex-FFH (incl 1 in conversion refit) with 1 x Mk-41 VLS for 29 SM-2 MR, 2 CH-124 *Sea King* ASW hel (Mk 46 LWT), 2 x 3 ASTT, plus 1 x 76mm gun.
FRIGATES: 12:
FFH: 9:
7 *Halifax* with 1 CH-124A *Sea King* ASW hel (Mk 46 LWT), 2 x 2 ASTT; plus 2 x 4 *Harpoon* and 2 x 8 *Sea Sparrow* SAM (incl 2 commissioning autumn 1995).
2 *Annapolis* with 1 *Sea King* hel, 2 x 3 ASTT, 1 x 3 ASW mot; plus 2 x 76mm gun.
FF: 3 improved *Restigouche* with 1 x 8 *ASROC*, 2 x 3 ASTT, 1 x 3 ASW mor, plus 2 x 76mm gun.
PATROL AND COASTAL COMBATANTS: 12:
6 *Fundy* (ex-MSC) PCC (trg).
5 *Porte St Jean* PCC, 1 PCI((reserve trg).
MCM: 2 *Anticosti* MSO (converted offshore spt vessels) (reserve trg).
SPT AND MISC: 8:
2 *Protecteur* AO with 3 *Sea King*, 1 *Provider* AO with 2 *Sea King*, 1 AOT, 2 AGOR, 1 diving spt, 1 *Riverton* spt.

DEPLOYMENT AND BASES:

ATLANTIC: Halifax (National and Marlant HQ. Commander Marlant is also COMCANLANT): 3 SS, 2 DDG, 6 FFH, 2 FF, 2 AO, 1 AGOR; 2 MR plus 1 MR (trg) sqn with CP-140 and 3 CP-140A, 1 ASW and 1 ASW (trg) hel sqn with 26 CH-125 hel.
PACIFIC: Esquimalt (HQ): 1 DDG, 3 FFH, 1 FF, 6 PCC, 1 AO, 1 AGOR; 1 MR sqn with 4 CP-140 and 1 ASW hel sqn with 6 CH-124 hel.
RESERVES: 4,500 in 24 div: patrol craft, coastal def, MCM, Naval Control of Shipping, augmentation of regular units.

AIR FORCE: 17,100 (women 5,000). Flying hours: 210.

FTR GROUP:
FTR: 5 sqn (1 trg) with CF-18.
EW: 2 sqn with CECC-144 (CL-601), CT-133, CH-118.
EARLY WARNING: Canadian NORAD Regional HQ at North Bay. 47 North Warning radar sites: 11 long-range, 36 short-range; Region Op Control Centre (ROCC) (2 Sector Op Control Centres (SOCC)). 4 Coastal Radars and 2 Transportable Radars. Canadian Component – NATO Airborne Early Warning (NAEW).
MARITIME AIR GROUP:
MR: 4 sqn (1 trg) with CP-140 *Aurora*.
ASW: 3 hel sqn (1 trg) with CH-124, *Sea King*.
TAC AIR GROUP (TAG):
HEL: 3 sqn with CH-135 (1 trg), 4 reserve sqn with CH-136, 1 test sqn with CH-135 and CH-136.
AIR TPT GROUP:
TPT: 6 sqn:
4 (1 trg) with CC-130E/H *Hercules*, KCC-130 (tkr).
1 with CC-137 (Boeing 707), CC-150 (AIRBUS A-310).
1 with CC-109, CC-144.
SAR: 4 tpt/SAR sqn (1 with twinned reserve sqn) with **ac:** CC-115, CC-130, CC-138; **hel:** CH-113/-113A.
TRG (reports direct to HQ Air Comd):
2 flying schools with **ac:** CT-114; **hel:** CH-139.
1 Air Navigation Trg sqn with CC-142 (DHC-8).
1 demonstration sqn with CT-114.
EQPT: 140 (incl 18 MR) cbt ac, 88 in store: 30 armed hel.
AC: CF-18: 122: **-A:** 83; **-B:** 39. **CP-140:** 18 (MR). **CP-140A:** 3 (environmental patrol). **CC-130E/H:** 30 (tpt). **KCC-130:** 5 (tkr). **CC-137:** 5 (3 tpt, 2 tkr/ tpt). **CC-150:** 5. **CC-109:** 7 (tpt). **CC/E-144:** 16 (6 EW trg, 3 coastal patrol, 7 VIP/tpt). **CC-138:** 7 (SAR/tpt). **CC-115:** 10 (SAR/tpt). **CT-133:** 50 (EW trg/tpt plus 9 in store). **CT-114:** 108 (trg). **CC/T-142:** 6 (2 tpt, 4 trg). **IN STORE:** 88 CF-5.
HEL: CH-124: 30 (ASW, afloat). CH-135: 43 (36 tac, 7 SAR/liaison). **CH-136:** 40. **CH-113:** 14 (SAR/tpt). **CH-118:** 4 (liaison). **CH-138:** 14 (trg). **CH-146:** 9.

FORCES ABROAD:
NORWAY: prepositioned TLE: 6 arty, 14 ACV.
UN AND PEACEKEEPING:
ADRIATIC *(Sharp Guard):* 1 FFH. **BOSNIA** (UNPROFOR): 825; 1 inf bn gp, 1 engr sqn, 6 Obs; CC-130 relief missions. **CROATIA** (UNCRO): 1,206; 1 inf bn, 1 log bn, plus 7 Obs and 3 civ pol. **CYPRUS** (UNFICYP): 2. **EGYPT** (MFO): 28. **HAITI** (UNMIH): 500 (incl 450 Air Force), 8 hel plus 100 civ pol. **IRAQ/ KUWAIT** (UNIKOM): 5 Obs. **FYROM** (UNPREDEP): 1 Obs. **MIDDLE EAST** (UNTSO): 14 Obs. **RWANDA** (UNAMIR): 105 plus 18 Obs; CC-130 relief missions. **SYRIA/ISRAEL** (UNDOF): 214; log unit.

PARAMILITARY:
The Canadian Coast Guard (CCG) is to merge with the Department of Fisheries and Oceans (DFO-78 ships and vessels) by 1 April 1996.
COAST GUARD: 5,200 (civilian-manned); some 83 vessels including: 1 cable ship, 1 hy, 5 med and 11 lt icebreakers; 13 navaids and SAR vessels; 3 hovercraft; plus **ac:** 1 DC-3; **hel:** 1 S-61, 5 Bell 206L, 16 BO-104.

DENMARK

GDP	1993: kr 873.2bn ($134.67bn):
	per capita $19,100
	1994: kr 929.3bn ($146.09bn):
	per capita $19,900

Growth	1993: 1.5%	1994: 4.4%
Inflation	1993: 1.3%	1994: 2.0 %
Publ debt	1993: 66.8%	1994: 68.7%
Def exp	1993: kr 16.67bn ($2.57bn)	
Def bdgt	1994: kr 17.57bn ($2.76bn)	
	1995: kr 17.09bn ($3.11bn)	
NATO defn	1993: kr 17.39bn ($2.68bn)	
	1994: kr 17.43bn ($2.74bn)	
$1 = kr	1993: 6.48	1994: 6.36
	1995: 5.50	

kr = Danish kroner

Population: 5,214,000

	13–17	18–22	23–32
Men	153,000	178,600	404,800
Women	147,400	172,600	390,200

TOTAL ARMED FORCES:
ACTIVE: 33,100 (8,300 conscripts, 900 women).
Terms of service: 4–12 months (up to 24 months in certain ranks).
RESERVES: 72,200: Army 56,200; Navy 5,000; Air Force 11,000. Home Guard *(Hjemmevaernet)* (volunteers to age 50): Army 53,000; Naval 4,200; Air Force 8,000.

ARMY: 19,100 (7,100 conscripts, 400 women).
2 Force HQ.
1 op comd, 1 land comd (east).
1 mech inf div (3 mech inf bde, 1 recce, 1 mech inf, 1 AD, 1 engr bn, div arty (reserve)).
1 mech inf bde with 2 mech inf, 1 tk, 1 arty bn.
1 rapid reaction bde with 2 mech inf, 1 tk, 1 arty bn (20% active cbt str).
1 recce, 1 indep AD, 1 indep engr bn.
Army avn.
RESERVES:
5 regt cbt gp (incl mot inf, arty bn).
1 arty comd, 1 arty, 1 AD, 2 engr bn.
7 mil region (regt cbt gp or 1–2 inf bn).
EQPT:
MBT: 411: 230 *Leopard* 1A5 (58 in store), 128 *Centurion* (58 in store), 53 M-41DK-1.
AIFV: 56 M-113A2 (with **25mm** gun).
APC: 273 M-113 (581 incl variants).
TOTAL ARTY: 553:
TOWED ARTY: 317: **105mm:** 184 M-101; **155mm:** 24 M-59, 97 M-114/39; **203mm:** 12 M-115.
SP ARTY: **155mm:** 76 M-109.
MOR: **120mm:** 160 Brandt; plus **81mm:** 422 (incl 55 SP).
ATGW: 140 *TOW* (incl 56 SP).
RCL: **84mm:** 1,125 *Carl Gustav*; **106mm:** 158 M-40.
AD GUNS: **40mm:** 36 L/60.
SAM: *Stinger.*
SURV: *Green Archer.*
ATTACK HEL: 12 AS-550C2.
SPT HEL: 13 Hughes 500M/OH-6.

NAVY: 6,000 (incl 700 conscripts, 200 women).
BASES: Korsør, Frederikshavn.
SS: 5:
3 *Tumleren* (mod No *Kobben*) SSC with Sw FFV Type 61 HWT.
2 *Narhvalen*, SSC with FFV Type 61 HWT.
FF: 3 *Niels Juel* with 2 x 4 *Harpoon* SSM and 1 x 8 *Sea Sparrow* SAM, 1 x 76mm gun.
PATROL AND COASTAL COMBATANTS: 39:
MSL CRAFT: 10 *Willemoes* PFM with 2 x 4 *Harpoon*, 2 or 4 x 533mm TT, 1 x 76mm gun.
PATROL CRAFT: 29:
OFFSHORE: 5:
1 *Beskytteren*, 4 *Thetis* PCO all with 1 *Lynx* hel.
COASTAL: 15:
12 *Flyvefisken* (Stanflex 300) PFC.
3 *Agdlek* PCC.
INSHORE: 9 *Barsø.*
MINE WARFARE: 9:
MINELAYERS: 6:
4 *Falster* (400 mines), 2 *Lindormen* (50 mines).

MCM: 3:
2 *Alssund* (US MSC-128) MSC.
1 *Flyvefisken* (SF300) MHC.
SPT AND MISC: 8:
2 AOT (small), 4 icebreakers (civilian-manned), 1 tpt,
1 Royal Yacht.
HEL: 8 *Lynx* (up to 4 embarked).

COASTAL DEFENCE: 1 coastal fortress; 150mm guns; 40mm AA guns. Coastal radar. 2 mobile coastal missile batteries: 2 x 8 *Harpoon* (not fully op until 1995).

RESERVES (Home Guard): 37 inshore patrol craft.

AIR FORCE: 8,000 (550 conscripts, 300 women).
Flying hours: 180.
TAC AIR COMD:
FGA/FTR: 4 sqn with F-16A/B.
TPT: 1 sqn with C-130H, *Gulfstream* III.
SAR: 1 sqn with S-61A hel.
TRG: 1 flying school with SAAB T-17.
AIR DEFENCE GROUP:
AD: 2 SAM bn: 8 bty with 36 I HAWK, 160 40mm L/60, 32 40mm/L70.
CONTROL/REPORTING GROUP: 5 radar stations, one in the Faroe Islands.
EQPT: 66 cbt ac, no armed hel.
AC: F-16A/B: 66 (FGA/ftr) (**-A:** 52; **-B:** 14). **C-130H:** 3 (tpt). *Gulfstream* III: 3 (tpt). **SAAB T-17:** 28.
HEL: S-61: 8 (SAR).
MSL:
ASM: AGM-12 *Bullpup*.
AAM: AIM-9 *Sidewinder*.
SAM: 36 I HAWK.

FORCES ABROAD:
ICELAND: Navy: 30; 1 PC-3.
UN AND PEACEKEEPING:
BOSNIA (UNPROFOR): 285; elm Nordic bn incl 1 tk sqn (10 Leopard MBT), HQ Coy plus 9 Obs and 5 civ pol. Aircrew with NATO E-3A operations. Air Force personnel in tac air control parties (TACP). **CROATIA** (UNCRO): 960; 1 inf bn, plus 3 Obs and 15 civ pol. **GEORGIA** (UNOMIG): 6 Obs. **INDIA/PAKISTAN** (UNMOGIP): 6 Obs. **IRAQ/KUWAIT** (UNIKOM): 44; spt tps, plus 6 Obs. **FYROM** (UNPREDEP): 45 plus 3 Obs. **MIDDLE EAST** (UNTSO): 11 Obs. **TAJIKISTAN** (UNMOT): 4 Obs.

FOREIGN FORCES:
NATO: HQ Allied Forces Baltic Approaches (BALTAP).

FRANCE

GDP	1993: fr 7,082.8bn ($1,250.67bn): per capita $19,500	
	1994: fr 7,308.3bn ($1,329.3bn): per capita $19,900	
Growth	1993: -1.5%	1994: 2.7%
Inflation	1993: 2.1%	1994: 1.7%
Publ debt	1993: 52.9%	1994: 56.8%
Def exp	1993: fr 193.8bn ($34.2bn)	
	1994: fr 199.3bn ($35.9bn)	
Def bdgt[a]	1995: fr 202.3bn ($40.5bn)	
NATO defn	1993: fr 241.2bn ($42.6bn)	
	1994: fr 243.7bn ($43.9bn)	
$1 = fr	1993: 5.66	1994: 5.55
	1995: 4.99	

fr = franc

[a] 1995 def bdgt reduced to fr 193.9bn in June following fr 8.4bn cut in procurement.

Population: 58,125,000

	13–17	18–22	23–32
Men	1,938,800	2,080,200	4,408,800
Women	1,850,600	1,984,800	4,276,400

TOTAL ARMED FORCES:
ACTIVE: some 409,000 (17,000 women, 189,200 conscripts; 5,200 Central Staff, 8,600 (2,300 conscripts) *Service de santé*, 400 *Service des essences* not listed). *Terms of service:* 10 months (can be voluntarily extended to 12–24 months).
RESERVES: earmarked for mob: 337,000; Army 240,000, Navy 27,000, Air Force 70,000. Potential: 1,229,500; Army 915,000, Navy 135,000, Air Force 179,500.

STRATEGIC NUCLEAR FORCES:
(17,000; some 1,700 Army; 5,000 Navy; 9,700 Air Force; 600 Gendarmerie).
NAVY: 80 SLBM in 5 SSBN.
SSBN: 5 mod *Le Redoutable* with 16 M-4/TN-70 or -71; plus SM-39 *Exocet* USGW and 4 x 533mm HWT (F17.2).
AIR FORCE:
IRBM: 18 SSBS S-3D/TN-61 msl in 2 sqn.
BBR: 2 sqn with 15 *Mirage* IVP (*ASMP*: Air-Sol, *Moyenne-Portée* nuclear ASM), plus 3 in store.
TRG: 1 *Mystère-Falcon 20P*, 1 *Alpha Jet*.
TKR: 2 sqn with 11 C-135FR.

'PRE-STRATEGIC' NUCLEAR FORCES:
ARMY: 15 *Hadès* SSM launchers (in store).
NAVY: 38 *Super Etendard* strike ac (ASMP); plus

19 in store.

AIR FORCE: 3 sqn with 45 *Mirage* 2000 (ASMP).
TRG: 3 *Mystère-Falcon* 20 SNA.
Eqpt also listed with service sections.

ARMY: 241,400 (8,600 women, 136,800

conscripts). Note: regt are normally of bn size.

1 Int and EW bde.
1 corps with 3 armd, 1 mtn inf div (55,100).
Summary of div cbt units:
7 armd regt.
8 arty regt.
6 mech inf regt.
4 recce sqn.
4 mot inf regt.
3 ATK sqn.
3 mtn inf regt.
Corps units: 1 armd recce, 1 mot inf, 1 arty bde (1 MLRS,
   2 *Roland* SAM (each of 4 bty), 1 HAWK SAM regt),
   2 cbt hel regt (94 hel: 26 SA-330, 48 SA-342 *HOT*
   ATK, 20 SA-341 gunships), 1 engr bde (4 regt).
1 armd div (in Eurocorps): 3 armd, 2 mech inf, 2 arty,
   1 *Roland* SAM, 1 engr regt.
1 Fr/Ge bde (2,100: Fr units incl 1 lt armd, 1 mot inf
   regt; 1 recce sqn).
Rapid Action Force (FAR: 42,500):
1 para div: 6 para inf, 1 armd cavalry, 1 arty, 1 engr regt.
1 air-portable marine div: 2 inf, 2 lt armd, 1 arty, 1 engr
   regt.
1 lt armd div: 2 armd cavalry, 2 APC inf, 1 arty, 1 engr
   regt.
1 air-mobile div: 1 inf, 3 cbt, 1 spt hel regt (total
   234 hel: 62 SA-330, 90 SA-342/*HOT*, 20 AS-532,
   62 SA-341 (20 gun, 42 recce/liaison)).
Corps units: 1 arty bde (1 MLRS, 1 *Roland* SAM, 1
   HAWK SAM regt), 1 engr regt.
Territorial def forces incl spt of UN missions: 7 regt.
FOREIGN LEGION: (8,500); 1 armd, 1 para, 6
inf, 1 engr regt (incl in units listed above).
MARINES: (31,000, incl 13,000 conscripts, mainly
overseas enlisted): 1 div (see FAR above), 4 regt in
France (see div cbt units above), 11 regt overseas.
Special Operations Forces (units see also above):
1 Marine inf regt (para), 1 AB regt, 2 hel units (EW,
   special ops).
RESERVES: Indiv reinforcements for 1 corps
(incl Eurocorps) and FAR (92,000).
Territorial def forces: 65 regt.
EQPT:
MBT: 974 AMX-30 (658 -B2), 42 *Leclerc*.
RECCE: 325 AMX-10RC, 192 ERC-90F4 *Sagaie*, 570
AML-60/-90 (perhaps 300 in store), 694 VBL M-11.
AIFV: 713 AMX-10P/PC.
APC: 3,975 VAB (incl variants).
TOTAL ARTY: 1,479:

TOWED ARTY: 395: **105mm:** 146 HM-2; **155mm:**
144 BF-50, 105 TR-F-1.
SP ARTY: 413: **105mm:** 37 AU-50; **155mm:** 253 AU-
F-1, 123 F-3.
MRL: **380mm:** 55 MLRS.
MOR: 616: **120mm:** 366 RT-F1, 250 M-51.
ATGW: 150 *Eryx*, 1,455 *Milan*, *HOT* (incl 135 VAB SP).
RL: **89mm:** 11,200; **112mm:** 10,800 *APILAS*.
AD GUNS: 1,152: **20mm:** 9 53T1, 781 53T2; **30mm:**
362 towed.
SAM: 511: 69 HAWK, 177 *Roland* I/II, 265 *Mistral*.
SURV: STENTOR (veh), RASIT-B/-E (veh, arty),
RATAC (veh, arty).
AC: 2 Cessna *Caravan* II , 5 PC-6.
HEL: 645:
ATTACK: 373: 83 SA-341F/M, 154 SA-342M, 136 *Alouette*.
RECCE: 2 AS-532 *Horizon*.
SPT: 270: 22 AS-532, 12 AS-555, 132 SA-330, 74
SA-341F/M, 30 SA-342M.
UAV: CL-89 (AN/USD-501), CL-289 (AN/USD-502),
MART Mk II, *Crecerelle* (replacing MARE).

NAVY: 64,200 (incl 8,100 Naval Air, 3,900

Marines, 2,400 women, 18,600 conscripts).
COMMANDS: 1 strategic sub (ALFOST), 2 home
(CECLANT, CECMED); 2 overseas: Indian Ocean
(ALINDIEN), Pacific Ocean (ALPACI).
BASES: France: Cherbourg, Brest (HQ), Lorient, Toulon
(HQ). **Overseas:** Papeete (HQ) (Tahiti), La Réunion;
Noumea (New Caledonia); Fort de France (Martinique).
SUBMARINES: 18:
STRATEGIC SUBMARINES: 5 SSBN (see above).
TAC SUBMARINES: 13:
SSN: 6 *Rubis* ASW/ASUW with F-17 HWT, L-5
LWT and SM-39 *Exocet* USGW.
SS: 7:
4 *Agosta* with F-17 HWT and L-5 LWT; plus *Exocet*
   USGW.
3 *Daphné*, with E-15 HWT and L-5 LWT (plus 5 in store).
PRINCIPAL SURFACE COMBATANTS: 42:
CARRIERS: 2 *Clémenceau* CVS (33,300t), capacity 40 ac
(typically 2 flt with 16 *Super Etendard*, 1 with 6 *Alizé*; 1 det
with 2 *Etendard* IVP, 2 *Super Frelon*, 2 *Dauphin* hel).
CRUISERS: 1 *Jeanne d'Arc* CCH (trg/ASW) with 6
MM-38 *Exocet* SSM, 2 x 2 100mm guns, capacity 8
x SA-319B hel.
DDG: 4:
2 *Cassard* with 1 x 1 *Standard* SM-1 MR; plus 8 x
   MM-40 *Exocet*, 1 x 100mm gun, 2 x ASTT, 1 *Lynx*
   hel (ASW/OTHT).
2 *Suffren* with 1 x 2 *Masurca* SAM; plus 1 *Malafon*
   SUGW, 4 ASTT, 4 MM-38 *Exocet*, 2 x 100mm guns.
FF: 35:
6 *Floréal* with 2 MM-38 *Exocet*, 1 AS-365 hel and
   1 x 100mm gun.
7 *Georges Leygues* with 2 *Lynx* hel (Mk 46 LWT), 2

x ASTT; plus 5 with 8 MM-40, 2 with 4 MM-38 *Exocet*, all with 1 x 100mm gun.

2 *Tourville* with 2 x *Lynx* hel, 1 *Malafon* SUGW, 2 x ASTT; plus 6 x MM-38 *Exocet*, 2 x 100mm guns.

1 *Aconit* with *Malafon*, 2 x ASTT; plus 8 MM-38 *Exocet*, 2 x 100mm guns.

1 *Commandant Rivière* with 2 x 3 ASTT, 1 x 12 ASW mor; plus 3 with 4 x MM-38 *Exocet*, all with 2 x 100mm guns.

17 *D'Estienne d'Orves* with 4 x ASTT, 1 x 6 ASW mor; plus 6 with 2 x MM-38, 6 with 4 x MM-40 *Exocet*, all with 1 x 100mm gun.

1 *La Fayette* with 8 x MM-40 Exocet, CN-2 SAM, 1 x 100mm gun, 1 x *Panther* hel.

PATROL AND COASTAL COMBATANTS: 23:
PATROL, OFFSHORE: 1 *Albatross* PCO (Public Service Force).
PATROL, COASTAL: 22:
11 *L'Audacieuse*.
8 *Léopard* PCC (trg).
1 *Flamant* PCC.
1 *Sterne*, 1 *Grebe* PCC (Public Service Force).
PATROL, INSHORE: 2 *Athos* PCI.
Plus 4 *Patra* PCI, 1 *La Combattante* PCI, 5 PCI⟨ (manned by Gendarmarie Maritime).
MINE WARFARE: 21:
MINELAYERS: nil, but submarines and *Thetis* (trials ship) have capability.
MCM: 21:
9 *Eridan* tripartite MHC.
5 *Circé* MHC.
4 *Vulcain* MCM diver spt.
3 *Antares* (route survey/trg).
AMPH: 9:
1 *Foudre* LPD, capacity 450 tps, 30 tk, 4 *Super Puma* hel, 2 CDIC LCT or 10 LCM.
2 *Ouragan* LPD: capacity 350 tps, 25 tk, 2 *Super Frelon* hel.
1 *Bougainville* LSD: capacity 500 tps, 6 tk, 2 AS-332 hel (assigned to spt DIRCEN nuclear test centre South Pacific).
5 *Champlain* LSM (*BATRAL*): capacity 140 tps, tk.
Plus craft: 6 LCT, 24 LCM.
SPT AND MISC: 39:
UNDER WAY SPT: 5 *Durance* AO with 1 SA-319 hel.
MAINT AND LOG: 21:
1 AOT, 1 *Jules Verne* AR with 2 SA-319 hel, 4 *Rhin* depot/spt, 1 *Rance* med and trg spt, all with hel; 8 tpt, 6 ocean tugs (3 civil charter).
SPECIAL PURPOSES: 7:
5 trial ships, 2 *Glycine* trg.
SURVEY/RESEARCH: 6:
5 AGHS, 1 AGOR.

NAVAL AIR: (8,100, incl 650 women, 500 conscripts).
Flying hours for *Etendard* and *Crusader* aircrew: 190.
NUCLEAR STRIKE: 2 flt with *Super Etendard* (ASMP nuc ASM).
FTR: 1 fleet with F-8E (FN) *Crusader*.
ASW: 2 fleet with *Alizé*.
MR: 6 fleet:
1 with *Atlantic*, 3 with *Atlantic*-2, 2 with *Gardian*.
RECCE: 1 fleet, with *Etendard* IV P-PM.
OCU: *Alizé*.
TRG: 5 units with N-262 *Frégate*, EMB-121 *Xingu*, MS-760 *Paris*, *Falcon* 10MER, *Rallye* 880, CAP 10.
MISC: 4 comms/liaison units (1 VIP) with *Falcon* 10MER, N-262, EMB 121, *Xingu*.
1 trial unit with *Atlantique* 2, MS-760 *Paris*.
2 lt ac units with 12 *Rallye* 880, 6 CAP-10.
ASW: 2 sqn with *Lynx*.
COMMANDOS: 2 aslt sqn with SA-321.
TRG: SA-316.
MISC: 2 comms/SAR units with SE-313B, SA-316B, SA-319B, 1 trials unit with SA-319, *Lynx*, SA-321.
EQPT: 84 cbt ac (plus 36 in store); 40 armed hel (plus 15 in store).
AC: *Super Etendard*: 32 (strike); plus 22 in store. Total of 48 to be mod for *ASMP*. ***Etendard*:** IV P-PM: 8 (recce); plus 1 in store. ***Crusader*:** 12 (ftr); plus 4 in store. ***Alizé*:** 18 (AEW); plus 6 in store. ***Atlantic*:** 7 (MR). ***Atlantique* 2:** 20 (MR) plus 3 in store. ***Gardian*:** 5 (MR). ***Nord 262*:** 24 (9 MR trg, 15 misc). ***Xingu*:** 18 (8 trg, 10 misc). ***Rallye* 880:** 14 (4 trg, 10 misc). ***CAP-10*:** 8 (misc). ***MS-760*:** 6 (trg). ***Falcon* 10MER:** 5 (3 trg, 2 misc).
HEL: *Lynx*: 25 (ASW) plus 9 in store. ***SA-321*:** 12 (ASW); plus 4 in store. ***SA-313*:** 10 (2 trg, 8 misc). ***SA-316/-319*:** 30; ***AS-365*:** 7 (SAR); ***AS-565SA*:** 3 plus 2 in store.
MSL:
ASM: *Exocet* AM-39.
AAM: R-550 *Magic* 2, AIM-9 *Sidewinder*.

MARINES: (3,900).
COMMANDO UNITS: (400). 4 aslt gp.
1 attack swimmer unit.
NAVAL BASE PROTECTION: (2,300).
FUSILIERS-MARIN: (1,200).
PUBLIC SERVICE FORCE: naval personnel, performing general coast guard, fishery, SAR, anti-pollution and traffic surv duties: 1 *Albatros*, 1 *Sterne*, 1 *Grebe*, 1 *Flamant* PCC, **ac:** 4 N-262; **hel:** 4 SA-365 (ships incl in naval patrol and coastal totals). Comd exercised through 'Maritime Prefectures' (Premar): **Manche** (Cherbourg), **Atlantique** (Brest), **Méditerranée** (Toulon).

AIR FORCE: 89,200 (6,000 women, 33,800 conscripts, incl strategic and pre-strategic forces).
AIR DEFENCE COMMAND (CASSIC):
CONTROL: automatic *STRIDA* II, 10 radar stations, 1 wing with 4 E3F.
SAM: 16 sqn:
12 (1 trg) with 24 *Crotale* bty (48 fire, 24 radar units).

4 *Mistral*.
AA GUNS: 300 bty (**20mm**).

AIR COMBAT COMMAND (CFAC):

Average annual flying hours for fighter/FGA pilots: 180.
9 wings, 23 sqn.
FTR: 4 wings, 7 sqn:
1 with *Mirage* F-IC; 6 with *Mirage* 2000C/B.
FGA: 9 sqn:
1 with *Mirage* 2000N.
2 with *Mirage* 2000D.
4 with *Jaguar* A.
2 with *Mirage* F1-CT.
RECCE: 2 sqn with *Mirage* F-1CR.
TRG: 1 OCU sqn with *Jaguar* A/E.
1 OCU sqn with F1-C/B,
1 OCU sqn with *Mirage* 2000/BC.
EW: 1 with C-160 ELINT/ESM.
HEL: 1 sqn with SA-313, SA-319.

AIR MOBILITY COMMAND (CFAP):

TPT: 18 sqn:
1 hy with DC-8F, A310-300.
5 tac with C-160/-160NG/C-130H.
12 lt tpt/trg/SAR with C-160, DH-6, CN235, *Falcon* 20, *Falcon* 50, *Falcon* 900, MS-760, TBM-700, N-262.
TRG: 1 OCU with N-262, C-160.
EW: 1 sqn with DC-8 ELINT.
HEL: 7 sqn with AS-332, AS-355, SA-313/-319, SA-350.
TRG: 1 OCU with SA-313/-319, SA-330.

AIR EDUCATION AND TRAINING

COMMAND (CEAA): (5,000).
TRG: *Alpha Jet*, CAP-10B/-20, CM-170, EMB-121, TB-30.
EQPT: 682 cbt ac, no armed hel.
AC: *Mirage*: 410: **F-1B:** 17 (OCU); **F-1C:** 44 (ftr); **F-1CT:** 44 (FGA); **F-1CR:** 51 (recce); **MIVP:** 18 (bbr); **-M-2000B/C:** 135 (109 -C, 26 -B); **-M-2000N:** 72; **-M-2000D:** 29. *Jaguar:* 115: **-A:** 93 (strike, FGA, trg); **-E:** 22* (trg). *Alpha Jet:* 157* (trg). **E-3F:** 4 (AEW). **A 310-300:** 2. **DC-8:** 4. **C-130:** 12: **-H:** 3 (tpt); **-H-30:** 9 (tpt). **C-135F/FR:** 11 (tkr). **C-160:** 74 (2 *Gabriel* ELINT/ESM, 4 *Astarte* comms, 40 tac tpt, 8 OCU, 20 -NG tac tpt) of which 14 tkr). **CN-235M:** 8 (tpt). **N-262:** 24 (21 lt tpt, 2 trg, 1 trials). *Falcon:* 19: **-20:** 13 (7 tpt, 6 misc); **-50:** 4 (tpt); **-900:** 2 (tpt). **MS-760:** 25 (misc). **DHC-6:** 10 (tpt). **EMB-121:** 25 (trg). **TB-30:** 148 (trg). **CAP-10/20/23:** 9 (trg). **TBM-700:** 12 (trg). *Tucano:* 16 (trg).
HEL: SA-313: 6 (OCU) (*Alouette* II). **SA-319:** 14 (12 tpt, 2 OCU) (*Alouette* III). **SA-330:** 29 (26 tpt, 3 OCU) (*Puma*). **SA-365:** 3 (tpt) (*Cougar*). **AS-332:** 7 (tpt) (*Super Puma*). **AS-350:** 6 (*Ecureuil*). **AS-355:** 39 (30 tpt, 9 OCU) (*Fennec*).
MSL:
ASM: AS-30/-30L, Martel AS-37.
AAM: Super 530F/D, R-550 Magic 1/II.

DEPLOYMENT:
NAVY:

Atlantic Fleet: (HQ, Brest): 5 SSBN, 6 SS, 6 ASW FF, 10 FF, 1 AO, 1 ML, 12 MHC, 1 AGOS, 1 clearance diving ship, plus craft.
Channel Flotilla: (HQ, Cherbourg): 1 clearance diving ship plus craft.
Mediterranean Fleet: (HQ, Toulon): 6 SSN, 1 SS, 2 CV, 4 DDG, 7 FF, 5 ASW ships, 2 MCMV, 3 amph, 3 AO, 1 LSM, 1 AH, 1 AGOR, 2 clearance diving ships.

FORCES ABROAD:

GERMANY: 15,000; Eurocorps with 1 armd div; Gendarmerie (260).
ANTILLES (HQ Fort de France): 5,000; 3 marine inf regt (incl 2 SMA), 1 marine inf bn, 1 air tpt unit: **ac:** 2 C-160; **hel:** 2 SA-330, 1 SA-319.
FRENCH GUIANA AND WEST INDIES (HQ Cayenne): 3,600; 2 marine inf (incl 1 SMA), 1 Foreign Legion regt, 1 spt bn, 6 ships (incl 1 FF and 2 amph), 1 *Atlantic* ac, 1 air tpt unit: **hel:** 4 SA-330, 3 AS-355; Gendarmerie (1,400).
INDIAN OCEAN (Mayotte, La Réunion): 4,000; 2 Marine inf (incl 1 SMA) regt, 1 spt bn, 1 Foreign Legion coy, 1 air tpt unit: **ac:** 2 C-160; **hel:** 2 SA 355; Gendarmerie (700).
NAVY: Indian Ocean Squadron, Comd ALINDIEN (HQ afloat): (1,400); 3 FF, 2 patrol combatants, 2 amph, 3 spt (1 comd), reinforcement 1 FF, 1 *Atlantic* ac.
NEW CALEDONIA (HQ Nouméa): 3,900; 1 Marine inf regt, 1 spt bn; some 14 AML recce, 5 105mm arty; 1 air tpt unit, det: **ac:** 2 C-160; **hel:** 2 AS-355, 6 SA-330; Navy: 1 FF, 2 patrol combatants, 1 survey, 1 amp, 1 spt, 2 *Guardian* MR ac, Gendarmerie (1,100).
POLYNESIA (HQ Papeete): 3,800 (incl Centre d'Expérimentations du Pacifique); 1 Marine inf regt, 1 air tpt unit, 2 SE-210, 3 AS-332; Gendarmerie (350): Navy: 2 FF, 3 patrol combatants, 1 amph, 1 survey, 5 spt, 3 *Guardian* MR ac.
CENTRAL AFRICAN REPUBLIC: 1,300; **Garrison:** 1 bn gp incl 1 motor coy; 1 pl AML armd cars (6); spt coy with O-1E lt ac, 120mm mor, *Milan* ATGW. **From France:** 1 AML armd car sqn and 1 tp (12 AML), 2 inf coy, 1 arty bty (105mm), 1 avn det (4 SA-330 **hel**); air elm with **ac:** 5 *Jaguar*, 2 C-160.
CHAD: 800; 2 inf coy, 1 AML sqn (-); 2 C-160 ac.
CÔTE D'IVOIRE: 700; 1 marine inf bn (14 AML-60/-90); 1 AS-355 hel.
DJIBOUTI: 3,900; 1 marine inf(-), 1 Foreign Legion regt(-); 36 ERC-90 recce, 5 155mm arty, 16 AA arty; 3 amph craft, 1 sqn with **ac:** 10 *Mirage* F-1C, 1 C-160 **hel:** 3 SA-319.
GABON: 600; 1 marine inf bn (9 AML-60); **ac:** 1 C-160; **hel:** 1 SA-355.
SENEGAL: 1,500; 1 marine inf bn (14 AML-60/-90); 1 *Atlantic* MR; **ac:** 1 C-160 tpt; **hel:** 1 SA-319.

UN AND PEACEKEEPING:

ANGOLA: (UNAVEM III): 8 Obs. **ADRIATIC:** (*Sharp Guard*). 1 FF and *Atlantic* MPA ac. **BOSNIA**

(UNPROFOR): 3,826; 3 inf, 1 engr bn, 1 spt unit, 1 ALAT hel sqn (5 AS-332, 4 SA-316); plus 5 Obs, 1 civ pol. **CROATIA** (UNCRO): 839; 1 log bn; plus 4 Observers, 11 civ pol. **EGYPT** (MFO): 17; incl 1 DHC-6. **FORMER YUGOSLAVIA** (*Provide Promise*): 1 C-130. **GEORGIA** (UNOMIG): 5 Obs. **HAITI** (UNMIH): 2 Obs, plus 95 civ pol. **IRAQ/KUWAIT** (UNIKOM): 15 Obs. **ITALY** (*Deny Flight*): 7 *Mirage* 2000C, 4 *Mirage* F1-CR, 6 *Mirage*, 2000KD, 5 *Jaguar*, 6 *Super Etendard*, 1 C-135, 1 E-3F, 1 N-262, 1 C-135 (tkr), 1 E-3F (AEW). **LEBANON** (UNIFIL): 264; elm 1 log bn; Gendarmerie (11). **FYROM**: (UNPREDEP): 1 Obs. **MIDDLE EAST** (UNTSO): 14 Obs. **SAUDI ARABIA** (*Southern Watch*): 170; 6 *Mirage* 2000C, 1 C-135, 1 N-262. **TURKEY** (*Provide Comfort*): 150; 5 *Jaguar*, 1 KC-135FR. **WESTERN SAHARA** (MINURSO): 27 Obs (Gendarmerie).

PARAMILITARY:

GENDARMERIE: 93,400 (2,600 women, 11,900 conscripts, 1,200 civilians); incl: **Territorial** (59,300); **Mobile** (17,100); **Schools** (5,800); **Overseas** (3,200); **Maritime, Air** (personnel drawn from other Dept.); **Republican Guard, Air tpt, Arsenals** (5,000); **Administration** (3,000). **Reserves** (139,000).
EQPT: 121 AML, 28 VBC-90 armd cars; 33 AMX-VTT, 155 VBRG-170 APC; 278 81mm mor; 10 PCIs (listed under Navy), plus 11 other patrol craft and 4 tugs. **ac:** 6 Cessna 206C; **hel:** 3 SA-316, 9 SA-319, 29 AS-350.

GERMANY

GDP	1993	DM 2,853.7bn ($1,726.1bn):
		per capita $20,800
	1994:	DM 2,977.7bn ($1,834.9bn):
		per capita $21,100

Growth	1993: -1.7%	1994: 2.3%
Inflation	1993: 4.1%	1994: 3.0%
Publ debt	1993: 54.6%	1994: 58.7%
Def exp	1993: DM 50.3bn ($30.42bn)	
	1994: DM 47.2bn ($29.09bn)	
Def bdgt	1995: DM 47.9bn ($34.02bn)	
	1996ε: DM 47.9bn ($31.93bn)	
NATO defn	1993: DM 60.6bn ($36.5bn)	
	1994: DM 58.1bn ($35.8bn)	
$1 = DM	1993: 1.65	1994: 1.62
	1995: 1.41	
DM = Deutschmark		

Population 81,109,000

	13–17	18–22	23–32
Men	2,224,600	2,324,400	6,649,400
Women	2,106,800	2,238,600	6,350,000

TOTAL ARMED FORCES:
ACTIVE: 339,900 (137,300 conscripts; 2,100 active Reserve trg posts, all Services).
Terms of service: 12 months.
RESERVES: 414,700 (men to age 45, officers/NCO to 60): Army 337,100, Navy 12,600, Air Force 65,000.

ARMY: 234,000 (112,800 conscripts).
(Military District Command = MDC).
ARMY FORCES COMMAND:
1 air-mobile force (div) HQ with 3 AB bde.
1 army avn bde (156 UH-1D, 96 CH-53, 87 BO-105 hel).
1 SIGINT/ELINT bde.
1 spt bde.
CORPS COMMANDS:
I Ge/Nl Corps:
  2 MDC/armd div.
  1 MDC/armd inf div (for LANDJUT).
II Corps: 2 MDC/armd div; 1 MDC/mtn div.
IV Corps: 2 MDC/armd inf div.
(The 8 MDC/div comd and control 6 armd, 1 Military Region Comd (MRC)/armd, 6 armd inf, 6 MRC/armd inf, 1 mtn bde and the Ge elements of the Ge/Fr bde, of which 7 plus the Ge/Fr bde are fully manned, the remainder being mixed active and reserve units, all train their own recruits. The MDC divs also command and control 39 MRC. One armed div has been earmarked for the EUROCORPS.)
(For cbt spt a total of 8 recce bn, 6 arty regt (each 24 FH-70, 8 110mm MRL, 18 MRLS), 2 arty regt (each 24 M-109, 8 110mm MRL, 18 MRLS), and 7 AD regt (each 42 Gepard) are available.)
Corps Units: 2 armd recce bn, 3 AD regt (each 42 *Roland*), 3 ATGW hel regt (each 60 BO-105 hel).
EQPT:
MBT: 2,695: 731 *Leopard* 1A5, 1,964 *Leopard* 2 (225 to be upgraded) (plus some *Leopard* 1A1/A3 in store awaiting disposal).
RECCE: 515: 409 SPz-2 *Luchs*, 106 TPz-1 *Fuchs* (NBC).
AIFV: 2,443: 2,100 *Marder* A2/A3, 343 *Wiesel* (210-TOW, 133-20mm gun).
APC: 4,037: 913 TPz-1 *Fuchs* (incl 102 EW variant), 2,900 M-113 (incl 322 arty obs), 224 M-577.
TOTAL ARTY: 2,228:
TOWED ARTY: 370: **105mm:** 19 M-56, 141 M-101; **155mm:** 210 FH-70.
SP ARTY: 592: **155mm:** 577 M-109A3G; **203mm:** 15 M-110.
MRL: 339: **110mm:** 185 *LARS*; **227mm:** 154 MLRS.
MOR: 927: **120mm:** 391 Brandt, 99 Tampella, 437 Tampella on M-113.
ATGW: 2,462: 1,964 *Milan*, 98 *TOW*, 258 RJPz-(*HOT*) *Jaguar* 1, 142 RJPz-(*TOW*) SP.
ATK GUNS: 90mm: 8 JPz-4-5 SP.
AD GUNS: 2,093: **20mm:** 1,766 Rh 202 towed; **35mm:** 327 *Gepard* SP.
SAM: 1,511: 142 *Roland* SP, 233 *Stinger*, 1,100

Strela, 36 *Igla*.
SURV: *Green Archer* (mor), RASIT (veh, arty), RATAC (veh, arty).
HEL: 653:
ATTACK: 205 PAH-1 (BO-105 with HOT).
SPT: 448: 177 UH-1D, 110 CH-53G, 97 BO-105M, 64 *Alouette*.
UAV: CL-289 (AN/USD-502).
MARINE (River Engineers): 24 LCM, 24 PCI (river).
EQPT OF FORMER GDR ARMY (in store):
ATTACK HEL: 45 Mi-24.

NAVY: 28,500 (incl 4,500 Naval Air, 5,800 conscripts and 330 women).
Fleet Command organised into 7 type comds: Frigate; Patrol Boat; MCMV; Submarine; Support Flotillas; Naval Air; Naval Comms and Electronics.
BASES: Glücksburg (Maritime HQ) and five main bases: Wilhelmshaven, Kiel, Olpenitz, Eckernförde and Warnemünde. Other bases with limited support facilities: Baltic: Flensburg, Neustadt; North Sea: Emden.
SS: 20:
18 Type 206/206A SSC with *Seeaal* DM2 533mm HWT (12 conversions to T-206A complete).
2 Type 205 SSC with DM3 HWT.
PRINCIPAL SURFACE COMBATANTS: 13:
DDG: 3 *Lütjens* (mod US *Adams*) with 1 x 1 SM-1 MR SAM/*Harpoon* SSM launcher, 2 x 127mm guns; plus 1 x 8 *ASROC* (Mk 46 LWT), 2 x 3 ASTT.
FRIGATES: 10:
FF: 8 *Bremen* with 2 *Lynx* hel (ASW/OTHT), 2 x 2 ASTT; plus 2 x 4 *Harpoon*.
FFG: 2 *Brandenburg* with 4 x MM-38 Exocet, 1 x VLS Mk-41 SAM, 2 x RAM, 21 Mk-49 SAM, 1 x 76mm gun, 4 x 324mm TT, 2 x *Lynx* hel.
PATROL AND COASTAL COMBATANTS: 36:
MSL CRAFT: 36:
10 *Albatros* (Type 143) PFM with 2 x 2 *Exocet*, and 2 x 533mm TT.
10 *Gepard* (T-143A) PFM with 2 x 2 *Exocet*.
16 *Tiger* (Type 148) PFM with 2 x 2 *Exocet*.
MCM: 42:
10 *Hameln* (T-343) comb ML/MCC.
6 *Lindau Troika* MSC control and guidance, each with 3 unmanned sweep craft.
10 converted *Lindau* (T-331) MHC.
10 *Frankenthal* (T-332) MHC.
5 *Frauenlob* MSI.
1 MCM diver spt ship.
AMPH: craft only: some 8 LCU/LCM.
SPT AND MISC: 42:
UNDER WAY SPT: 2 *Spessart* AO.
MAINT AND LOG: 26:
6 *Elbe* spt, 4 small (2,000t) AOT, 4 *Lüneburg* log spt, 2 AE, 8 tugs, 2 icebreakers (civil).

SPECIAL PURPOSE: 10:
3 AGI, 2 trials, 3 multi-purpose (T-748), 2 trg.
RESEARCH AND SURVEY: 4:
1 AGOR, 3 AGHS (civil-manned for Ministry of Transport).

NAVAL AIR: (4,500).
Flying hours for *Tornado* aircrew: 150.
3 wings, 7 sqn.
1 wing with *Tornado*.
1 MR/ASW wing with *Atlantic*, *Lynx*.
1 SAR/liaison wing with Do-28, *Sea King*.
FGA/RECCE: 2 sqn with *Tornado*.
TRG: 1 sqn with *Tornado*.
MR/ELINT: 1 sqn with *Atlantic*.
LIAISON: 1 sqn with Do-28/Do-228.
ASW: 1 sqn with *Sea Lynx* Mk 88 hel.
SAR: 1 sqn with *Sea King* Mk 41 hel.
TPT: 1 sqn with Mi-8.
EQPT: 54 cbt ac, 17 armed hel.
AC: *Tornado*: 54. *Atlantic*: 16 (12 MR, 4 ELINT). **Do-28:** 1 (environmental monitoring). **Do-228: LM:** 1 (environmental monitoring).
HEL: *Sea Lynx* Mk 88: 17 (ASW). *Sea King* Mk 41: 22 (SAR).
MSL:
ASM: *Kormoran*, *Sea Skua*.
AAM: AIM-9 *Sidewinder*.

AIR FORCE: 75,300 (18,700 conscripts).
Flying hours: 150.
AIR FORCE COMMAND: 2 TAC cmds, 4 air div.
FGA: 4 wings with *Tornado*; 8 sqn.
FTR: 3 wg with F-4F (6 sqn); 1 wg with 1 sqn MiG-29.
RECCE: 1 wing with *Tornado*.
ECR: 1 wing with 2 sqn *Tornado*.
SAM: 6 groups (each 6 sqn) *Patriot*; 6 groups (each 6 sqn) HAWK; 14 sqn *Roland*.
RADAR: 2 tac Air Control regts.
7 sites; 10 remote radar posts.
TPT COMMAND (GAFTC):
TPT: 3 wings: 4 sqn with Transall C-160, incl 1 (OCU) with C-160, 4 sqn (incl 1 OCU) with Bell UH-1D, 1 special air mission wing with Boeing 707-320C, Tu-154, Airbus A-310, VFW-614, CL-601, L-410S (VIP); Mi-8S (VIP).
TRG: 1 sqn with UH-1D.
FGA: OCU 1 det (Cottesmore, UK) with 18 *Tornado*.
FTR: OCU (Holoman AFB, New Mexico) with 24 F-4E (17 F-4E leased from USAF).
TRG: NATO joint pilot trg (Sheppard AFB, Texas) with 35 T-37B, 41 T-38A; primary trg sqn with Beech *Bonanza*.
EQPT: 488 cbt ac (25 trg (overseas)); no attack hel.
AC: F-4: 157: **-F:** 150 (FGA, ftr); **-E:** 7 (OCU, in US).
Tornado: 273 (192 FGA, 35* ECR, 28* OCU, 18* in trinational trg sqn (in UK)). **MiG-29:** 24: 20 (ftr), **-UB:** 4 *(trg). *Alpha Jet:* 34* (trg); plus 72 in store. **Transall C-**

160: 85 (tpt, trg). **Boeing 707:** 4 (VIP). **A-310:** 3 (VIP, tpt). **CL-601:** 7 (VIP). **HFB-320:** 4 (in store). **L-410-S:** 4 (VIP). **T-37B:** 35. **T-38A:** 41. **Tu-154:** 2 (tpt). **VFW-614:** 3 (VIP). **HEL: UH-1D:** 104 (100 SAR, tpt, liaison; 4 VIP). **Mi-8S:** 6 (VIP).
MSL:
ASM: AGM-65 *Maverick,* AGM-88 HARM.
AAM: AIM-9*Sidewinder*, AA-8*Aphid*, AA-10*Alamo*, AA-11 *Archer*.
SAM: 216 HAWK launchers; 95 *Roland* launchers. 288 *Patriot* launchers.
FORMER GDR AIR FORCE (not being operated): **FTR: ac:** 23 MiG-21; 10 MiG-23; 5 Su-22 3 MiG-15, 6 MiG-17 (all TLE will be disposed of in accordance with CFE).
HEL: 1 Mi-8.

FORCES ABROAD:
NAVY: 1 DD/FF with STANAVFORLANT.
1 DD/FF with STANAVFORMED.
1 MCMV with STANAVFORCHAN.
3 MPA in ELMAS/Sardinia.
AIR FORCE: US: 450 flying trg at Sheppard and Holman AFB; UK: OCU at RAF Cottesmore.
UN AND PEACEKEEPING:
ADRIATIC (*Sharp Guard*): 1 DDG, 1 FFG with STANAVFORLANT and STANAVFORMED, 3 *Atlantic* MPA ac. **GEORGIA** (UNOMIG): 10 Obs. **IRAQ** (UNSCOM): 44; **ac:** 2 C-160; **hel:** 3 CH-53. **RWANDA** (UNAMIR): 8 civ pol. **FORMER YUGOSLAVIA** (*Provide Promise*): 1 C-160 (Falconara, Italy). **ITALY:** 12 *Tornado* (8 ECR, 4 Recce) in direct support of Rapid Reaction Forces. **WESTERN SAHARA** (MINURSO): 5 civ pol.

PARAMILITARY:
FEDERAL BORDER GUARD (Ministry of Interior): 24,500; 5 comd (constitutionally has no cbt status). Eqpt: 108 TM-170 APC; hel: 32 SA-318C, 13 UH-1D, 8 Bell 212, 22 SA-330, 3 SA-332L.
COAST GUARD: 550; some 14 PCI, 1 inshore tug, plus boats.

FOREIGN FORCES:
NATO: HQ Allied Land Forces Central Europe (LANDCENT).
HQ Allied Rapid Reaction Corps (ARRC).
HQ Allied Air Forces Central Europe (AIRCENT).
HQ Allied Land Forces Jutland and Schleswig-Holstein (LANDJUT).
Allied Rapid Reaction Force Air Staff.
HQ Multi-National Division (Central) (MND(C)).
HQ Allied Command Europe Mobile Force (AMF).

Airborne Early Warning Force: 18 E-3A *Sentry*
BELGIUM: 4,250; 1 Force HQ, 1 mech inf bde.
FRANCE: 15,000; 1 armd div (Eurocorps).
NETHERLANDS: 3,000; 1 lt bde.
UK: 28,600 Army: 23,600: 1 corps HQ (multinational), 1 armd div, 2 armd recce, 3 MLRS, 2 AD, 1 engr regt. Air Force Group HQ (5,000); 2 air bases, 6 ac sqn, 1 hel sqn; **ac:** 52 *Tornado* GR1, 26 *Harrier*; **hel:** 5 *Chinook*, 5 *Puma*, 1 *Gazelle*.
US: 86,600; 1 army HQ, 1 corps HQ; 1 armd, 1 mech div; Army 70,500, HQ USAFE; Air Force 16,200, HQ 17th Air Force, 1 tac ftr wing with 4 sqn FGA/ftr, 1 cbt spt wing, 1 air control wing, 1 tac airlift wing. 1 air base wing, 48 F-16C/D, 24 F-15C/D, 18 A-10, 6 OA-10, 16 C-130E, 9 C-9A.

GREECE

| GDP | 1993: dr 17,760.4bn ($73.11bn): per capita $8,200 |
| | 1994: dr 18,362.6bn ($75.69bn): per capita $8,300 |

Growth	1993: -0.5%		1994: 1.5%
Inflation	1993: 14.5%		1994: 10.9%
Publ debt	1993: 92.7%		1994: 87.9%
Def exp	1993: dr 723.5bn ($3.16bn)		
	1994: dr 740.2bn ($3.05bn)		
Def bdgt	1995: dr 772bn ($3.38bn)		
NATO defn	1993: dr 933bn ($4.07bn)		
	1994: dr 1,052bn ($4.34bn)		
FMA	1994: $315.1m (FMF, IMET)		
	1995: $255.2m (FMF, IMET)		
	1996: $315.0m (FMF, IMET)		
$1 = dr	1993: 229		1994: 243
	1995: 228		

dr = drachma

Population:[a] 10,455,000 (Muslim 1%)

	13–17	18–22	23–32
Men	373,400	385,000	827,200
Women	349,400	365,800	782,000

[a] ε300,000 Albanian illegal immigrants and temporary workers lived in Greece in 1994.

TOTAL ARMED FORCES:
ACTIVE: 171,300 (114,000 conscripts, 5,600 women).
Terms of service: Army up to 19 months, Navy up to 23 months, Air Force up to 21 months.
RESERVES: some 291,000 (to age 50): Army some 235,000 (Field Army 200,000, Territorial Army/National Guard 35,000); Navy about 24,000; Air Force about 32,000.

ARMY: 125,000 (98,000 conscripts, 2,900 women).
FIELD ARMY: (89,000); 3 Military Regions.
1 Army, 4 corps HQ.
2 div HQ (1 armd, 1 mech).
9 inf div (3 inf, 1 arty regt, 1 armd bn) 2 Cat A, 3 Cat B, 4 Cat C.
5 indep armd bde (each 2 armd, 1 mech inf, 1 SP arty bn) Cat A.
2 indep mech bde (2 mech, 1 armd, 1 SP arty bn), Cat A.
2 inf bde.
1 marine bde (3 inf, 1 lt arty bn, 1 armd sqn) Cat A.
1 cdo, 1 raider regt.
4 recce bn.
2 army avn bn.
10 fd arty bn.
1 indep avn coy.
8 AD arty bn.
2 SAM bn with I HAWK.
Units are manned at 3 different levels: Cat A 85% fully ready; Cat B 60% ready in 24 hours; Cat C 20% ready in 48 hours.
TERRITORIAL DEFENCE: (36,000).
Higher Mil Comd of Interior and Islands HQ.
4 Mil Comd HQ (incl Athens).
1 inf div.
4 AD arty bn.
2 inf regt.
1 army avn bn.
1 para regt.
8 fd arty bn.
RESERVES (National Guard): 34,000; internal security role.
EQPT:
MBT: 2,268: 89 M-47 (in store), 998 M-48 (102, 45 A2, 137 A3, 714 A5), 671 M-60 (359 A1, 312 A3), 154 AMX-30 (in store), 356 *Leopard* (170 1A4, 109 1A3).
RECCE: 48 M-8.
AIFV: 96 AMX-10P, 500 BMP-1.
APC: 2,072: 245 *Leonidas*, 365 M-59, 1,462 M-113.
TOTAL ARTY: 2,168:
TOWED ARTY: 830: **105mm:** 18 M-56, 461 M-101; **140mm:** 2 5.5-in; **155mm:** 268 M-114; **203mm:** 81 M-115.
SP ARTY: 415: **105mm:** 73 M-52; **155mm:** 16 M-44A1, 133 M-109A1/A2, **175mm:** 12 M-107; **203mm:** 181 M-110A2.
MRL: **122mm:** 150 RM-70.
MOR: **107mm:** 773 M-30 (incl 168 SP); plus **81mm:** 690.
ATGW: 290 *Milan*, 300 *TOW* (incl 156 SP).
RL: **64mm:** RPG-18.
RCL: **90mm:** 1,346 EM-67; **106mm:** 1,313 M-40A1.
AD GUNS: **20mm:** 101 Rh-202 twin; **23mm:** 300 ZU-23-2; **40mm:** 227 M-1, 95 M-42A twin SP.
SAM: 42 I HAWK, 12 SA-8B.
SURV: AN/TPQ-36 (arty, mor).
AC: 1 *Aero Commander*, 1 *Super King Air*, 47 U-17A.
HEL: 9 CH-47D (1 in store), 111 UH-1D/H/AB-205A, 17 AH-1P, 1 AB-212, 14 AB-206, 14 Bell 47G, 19 Hughes 300C.

NAVY: 19,500 (1,600 conscripts, 1,600 women).
BASES: Salamis, Patras, Soudha Bay.
SS: 8 *Glavkos* (Ge T-209/1100) with 533mm TT (1 with *Harpoon* USGW).
PRINCIPAL SURFACE COMBATANTS: 13:
DD: 4 *Kimon* (US *Adams*) (US lease) with 1 x SM-1; plus 1 x 8 ASROC, 2 x 3 ASTT, 2 x 127mm guns, 4 *Harpoon* SSM.
FF: 9:
1 *Hydra* (MEKO 200) with 2 x 3 ASTT; plus 2 x 4 *Harpoon* SSM and 1 x 127mm gun (1 SH-60 hel, 1 DC).
5 *Elli* (Nl *Kortenaer*) with 2 AB-212 hel, 2 x 3 ASTT; plus 2 x 4 *Harpoon*.
3 *Makedonia* (ex-US *Knox*) (US lease) with 1 x 8 ASROC, 4 x ASTT; plus *Harpoon* (from *ASROC* launcher), 1 x 127mm gun.
PATROL AND COASTAL COMBATANTS: 42:
CORVETTES: 5 *Niki* (ex-Ge *Thetis*) (ASW) with 1 x 4 ASW RL, 4 x 533mm TT.
MSL CRAFT: 18:
14 *Laskos* (Fr *La Combattante* II/III) PFM, 8 with 4 x MM-38 *Exocet*, 6 with 6 *Penguin* 2 SSM, all with 2 x 533mm TT.
2 *I. Votis* (Fr *La Combattante* IIA) PFM with 2 x 2 MM-38 *Exocet*.
2 *Stamou*, with 4 x SS-12 SSM.
TORPEDO CRAFT: 10:
6 *Hesperos* (Ge *Jaguar*) PFT with 4 x 533mm TT.
4 No '*Nasty*' PFT with 4 x 533mm TT.
PATROL CRAFT: 9:
COASTAL: 4:
2 *Armatolos* (Dk *Osprey*) PCC, 2 *Pirpolitis* PCC.
INSHORE: 5:
2 *Tolmi*, 3 PCI.
MINE WARFARE: 16:
MINELAYERS: 2 *Aktion* (US LSM-1) (100–130 mines).
MCM: 14:
9 *Alkyon* (US MSC-294) MSC.
5 *Atalanti* (US *Adjutant*) MSC.
AMPH: 10:
1 *Samos* LST with hel deck: capacity 300 tps, 16 tk.
1 *Nafkratoussa* (US *Cabildo*) LSD: capacity 200 tps, 18 tk, 1 hel.
2 *Inouse* (US *County*) LST: capacity 400 tps, 18 tk.
4 *Ikaria* (US LST-510): capacity 200 tps, 16 tk.
2 *Ipopliarhos Grigoropoulos* (US LSM-1) LSM, capacity 50 tps, 4 tk.
Plus about 65 craft: 2 LCT, 8 LCU, 13 LCM, some 42 LCVP.
SPT AND MISC: 14:
2 AOT, 4 AOT (small), 1 *Axios* (ex-Ge *Lüneburg*) log spt, 1 AE, 5 AGHS, 1 trg.

NAVAL AIR: 16 armed hel.

ASW: 1 hel div: 2 sqn with 9 AB-212 (ASW), 2 AB-212 (EW), 2 SA-319 (ASW), 5 S-70B (ASW).

AIR FORCE: 26,800 (14,400 conscripts, 1,100 women).

TAC AIR FORCE: 8 cbt wings, 1 tpt wing.
FGA: 7 sqn:
2 with A-7H.
1 with F-16.
3 with A-7E.
1 with F-4E.
FTR: 10 sqn:
2 with *Mirage* F-1CG.
2 with F-5A/B.
1 with NF-5A/B, RF-5A.
1 with F-16 C/D.
2 with *Mirage* 2000 EG/BG.
2 with F-4E.
RECCE: 1 sqn with RF-4E.
MR: 1 sqn with HU-16B.
TPT: 3 sqn with C-130H/B, YS-11, C-47, Do-28, *Gulfstream.*
LIAISON: 4 T-33A.
HEL: 2 sqn with AB-205A, Bell 47G, AB-212.
AD: 1 bn with *Nike Hercules* SAM (36 launchers).
12 bty with *Skyguard/Sparrow* SAM, twin 35mm guns.

AIR TRG COMMAND:
TRG: 4 sqn:
1 with T-41A; 1 with T-37B/C; 2 with T-2E.
EQPT: 351 cbt ac, incl 2 MR (101 in store), no armed hel.
AC: A-7: 92: **-H:** 38 (FGA) (plus 5 in store); **TA-7H:** 7 (FGA); **A-7E:** 40 (plus 15 in store); **A-7K:** 7. **F-5:** 88: **-A:** 63 (plus 10 in store); **-B:** 7, plus 1 in store; **NF-5A:** 11; **NF-5B:** 1; **RF-5A:** 6 (plus 3 in store). **F-4:** 72: **-E:** 52, plus 19 in store; **RF-4E:** 20 (recce), plus 7 in store. **F-16:** 35: **-C:** 29 (FGA/ftr), plus 3 in store; **-D:** 6. *Mirage* **F-1: CG:** 26 (ftr), plus 3 in store. *Mirage* **2000:** 36: **-EG:** 32, plus 2 in store (ftr); **BG:** 4* (trg). **F104G:** 20 in store; **RF-104G:** 6 in store; **TF-104G:** 4 in store. **HU-16B:** 2 (MR), plus 3 in store. **C-47:** 4 (tpt). **C-130H:** 10 (tpt). **C-130B:** 7 (tpt). **CL-215:** 10 (tpt, fire-fighting). **Do-28:** 12 (lt tpt). *Gulfstream* **I:** 1 (VIP tpt). **T-2:** 36* (trg). **T-33A:** 30 (liaison). **T-37B/C:** 29 (trg). **T-41D:** 19 (trg). **YS-11-200:** 6 (tpt).
HEL: AB-205A: 14 (tpt). **AB-206:** 1, **AB-212:** 4 (VIP, tpt). **Bell 47G:** 5 (liaison).
MSL:
ASM: AGM-12 *Bullpup*, AGM-65 *Maverick.*
AAM: AIM-7 *Sparrow*, AIM-9 *Sidewinder*, R-550 *Magic.*
SAM: 36 *Nike Hercules,* 40 *Sparrow.*

FORCES ABROAD:
CYPRUS: 2,250; 2 inf bn and officers/NCO seconded to Greek-Cypriot forces.
UN AND PEACEKEEPING:
ADRIATIC (*Sharp Guard*): 1 FFG. **GEORGIA** (UNOMIG): 5 Obs. **IRAQ/KUWAIT** (UNIKOM): 7 Obs.

PARAMILITARY:
GENDARMERIE: 26,500; MOWAG *Roland*, 15 UR-416 APC, 6 NH-300 hel.
COAST GUARD AND CUSTOMS: 4,000; some 100 patrol craft, 2 Cessna *Cutlass*, 2 TB-20 *Trinidad* ac.

FOREIGN FORCES:
US: 550: Navy facilities at Soudha Bay; 2 air base gp.

ICELAND

GDP	1993: K 410.98bn ($6.08bn):	
	per capita $16,900	
	1994: K 433.29bn ($6.19bn):	
	per capita $17,200	
Growth	1993: 1.1%	1994: 3.2%
Inflation	1993: 4.1%	1994: 1.6%
Publ debt	1993: 55%	1994: 48%
Sy bdgt[a]	1993: K 5.49bn ($81m)	
	1994: K 6.03bn ($86m)	
	1995: K 5.78bn ($91m)	
$1 = K	1993: 67.6	1994: 69.9
	1995: 63.8	

K = kronur

[a] Iceland has no Armed Forces. Sy bdgt is for public order and safety.

Population: 270,000

	13–17	18–22	23–32
Men	11,000	11,000	22,000
Women	10,000	10,000	20,600

ARMED FORCES: none.

PARAMILITARY: 130.
COAST GUARD: 130.
BASE: Reykjavik.
PATROL CRAFT: 4:
3 PCO: 2 *Aegir* with hel, 1 *Odinn* with hel deck.
1 PCI⟨.
AVN: 1 F-27 ac, 1 SA-360.

FOREIGN FORCES:
NATO: Island Commander Iceland (ISCOMICE, responsible to CINCEASTLANT).
US: 2,500. Navy: 1,450: MR: 1 sqn with 6 P-3C, 1 UP-3. Marines: 50. Air Force: 1,000: 4 F-15C/D, 1 HC-130, 1 KC-135, 4 HH-60G.
NETHERLANDS: Navy: 20: 1 P-3C.

ITALY

GDP	1993: L 1,550,200bn ($985.1bn):	
	per capita $18,000	
	1994: L 1,641,100bn ($1,017.8bn):	
	per capita $18,400	
Growth	1993: -1.2%	1994: 2.2%
Inflation	1993: 4.5%	1994: 4.0%
Publ debt	1993: 120.2%	1994: 122.6%
Def exp	1993: L 25,965bn ($16.5bn)	
Def bdgt	1994: L 26,167bn ($16.2bn)	
	1995: L 26,500bn ($16.0bn)	
NATO defn	1993: L 32,364bn ($20.6bn)	
	1994: L 34,179bn ($21.2bn)	
$1 = L	1993: 1,574	1994: 1,612
	1995: 1,652	
L = lira		

Population: 57,867,000

	13–17	18–22	23–32
Men	1,748,000	2,102,400	4,751,200
Women	1,662,400	2,011,200	4,616,400

TOTAL ARMED FORCES:

ACTIVE: 328,700 (174,700 conscripts; 22,100 Central Staff, 19,800 in centrally controlled formations/units). *Terms of service:* all services 12 months.

RESERVES: 584,000. Army 520,000 (obligation to age 45), immediate mob 240,000; Navy 36,000 (to age 39 for men, variable for officers to 73); Air Force 28,000 (to age 25 or 45 (specialists)).

ARMY: 175,000 (ε131,600 conscripts).

FIELD ARMY:

(Note: regt are normally of bn size.)

3 Corps HQ (1 mtn):
  1 with 1 mech, 1 armd bde, 1 armd cav regt, 1 arty, 1 AA regt, 1 avn regt.
  1 with 2 mech, 1 armd, 1 armd cav bde, 1 amph, 4 arty, 1 avn regt.
  1 with 4 mtn bde, 1 avn, 1 armd cav, 2 hy arty, 1 AA regt.
1 AD comd: 4 HAWK SAM, 3 AAA regt.
1 avn gp (1 sqn AB-412, 2 sqn CH-47, 1 flt Do-228).

TERRITORIAL DEFENCE:

7 Military Regions.
8 indep mech, 1 AB bde (incl 1 SF bn, 1 avn sqn).
Rapid Intervention Force (*FIR*) formed from 1 mech, 1 AB bde (see above), plus 1 Marine bn (see Navy), 1 hel unit (Army), 1 air tpt unit (Air Force).
5 armd cav regt.
1 inf regt.
4 engr regt.
5 avn units.

RESERVES: on mob: 1 armd, 1 mech, 1 mtn bde.

EQPT:

MBT: 1,319: 167 M-60A1 (in store), 910 *Leopard*, 242 *Centauro* B-1.
APC: 1,180 M-113, 1,792 VCC1/-2, 44 Fiat 6614, 15 LVTP-7.
TOTAL ARTY: 1,946:
TOWED ARTY: 945: **105mm:** 347 Model 56 pack (233 in store); **155mm:** 164 FH-70, 423 M-114 (in store); **203mm:** 11 M-115.
SP ARTY: 286: **155mm:** 260 M-109G/-L; **203mm:** 26 M-110A2.
MRL: 227mm: 22 MLRS.
MOR: 120mm: 693 (389 in store); plus **81mm:** 1,205 (381 in store).
ATGW: 326 *TOW* (incl 270 SP), 804 *Milan*.
RL: 1,000 *APILAS*.
RCL: 80mm: 720 *Folgore*.
AD GUNS: 25mm: 213 SIDAM SP; **40mm:** 234.
SAM: 126 HAWK, 145 *Stinger*.
AC: 33: 30 SM-1019, 3 Do-228.
HEL: 27 A-109, 28 A-129, 91 AB-205A, 102 AB-206 (obs), 14 AB-212, 23 AB-412, 34 CH-47C.
UAV: CL-89 (AN/USD-501), *Mirach* 20/-150.

NAVY: 44,000 (incl 1,560 Naval Air, 1,500 Marines and 17,600 conscripts).
Comds: 1 Fleet Commander CINCNAV (also NATO COMEDCENT); 6 Area Commands: Upper Tyrrhenian; Adriatic; Lower Tyrrhenian; Ionian and Strait of Otranto; Sicily; and Sardinia.
BASES: La Spezia (HQ), Taranto (HQ), Ancona (HQ), Brindisi, Augusta, Messina (HQ), La Maddalena (HQ), Cagliari, Naples (HQ), Venice (HQ).
SS: 9:
  4 *Pelosi* (imp *Sauro*) with Type 184 HWT (4 by September 1994).
  4 *Sauro* with Type 184 HWT (includes 2 non-op, undergoing modernisation).
  1 *Toti* SSC with Type 184 HWT.
PRINCIPAL SURFACE COMBATANTS: 32:
CARRIERS: 1 *G. Garibaldi* CVV with 16 SH-3 *Sea King* hel, 3 AV-8B (plus 2 trg) V/STOL ac, 4 *Teseo* SSM, 2 x 3 ASTT.
CRUISERS: 1 *Vittorio Veneto* CGH with 1 x 2 SM-1 ER SAM, 6 AB-212 ASW hel (Mk 46 LWT); plus 4 *Teseo* SSM, 2 x 3 ASTT.
DD: 4:
  2 *Luigi Durand de la Penne* (ex-*Animoso*) DDGH with 1 x SM-1 MR SAM, 2 x 4 *Teseo* SSM, plus 2 x AB-312 hel, 1 x 127mm gun, 2 x 3 ASTT.
  2 *Audace* DDGH, with 1 x SM-1 MR SAM, 4 *Teseo* SSM, plus 2 x AB-212 hel, 1 x 127mm gun, 2 x 3 ASTT.
FF: 26:
  8 *Maestrale* FFH with 2 AB-212 hel, 2 x 533mm DP

TT; plus 4 *Teseo* SSM, 1 x 127mm gun.
4 *Lupo* FFH with 1 AB-212 hel, 2 x 3 ASTT; plus 8 *Teseo* SSM, 1 x 127mm gun.
3 *Lupo* FF built for Iraq. Not fitted to full Navy standards (4th to be delivered in early 1996).
2 *Alpino* FFH with 1 AB-212 hel, 2 x 3 ASTT, 1 x ASW mor.
8 *Minerva* FF with 2 x 3 ASTT.
1 *De Cristofaro* FF with 2 x 3 ASTT, 1 ASW mor (paying off late 1995).

PATROL AND COASTAL COMBATANTS: 16:
MSL CRAFT: 6 *Sparviero* PHM with 2 *Teseo* SSM.
PATROL, OFFSHORE: 6:
4 *Cassiopea* with 1 AB-212 hel.
2 *Storione* (US *Aggressive*) ex-MSO.
PATROL, COASTAL: 4 *Bambu* (ex-MSC) PCC assigned MFO.

MINE WARFARE: 13:
MCM: 13:
10 *Lerici* MHC.
3 *Castagno* (US *Adjutant*) MHC.

AMPH: 3 *San Giorgio* LPD: capacity 350 tps, 30 trucks, 2 SH-3D or CH-47 hel, 7 craft.
Plus some 30 craft: about 3 LCU, 10 LCM and 20 LCVP.

SPT AND MISC: 42:
2 *Stromboli* AO, 8 tugs, 9 coastal tugs, 6 water tkr, 4 trials, 2 trg, 3 AGOR, 6 tpt, 2 salvage.

SPECIAL FORCES (Special Forces Comd – COMSUBIN):
3 gp; 1 underwater ops; 1 school; 1 research.

MARINES (San Marco gp): (1,500).
1 bn gp.
1 trg gp.
1 log gp.
EQPT: 30 VCC-1, 10 LVTP-7 APC, 16 81mm mor, 8 106mm RCL, 6 *Milan* ATGW.

NAVAL AIR: (1,600); 7 cbt ac, 74 armed hel.
FGA: 5 AV-8B II, plus, 2* TAV-8B.
ASW: 5 hel sqn with 30 SH-3D, 54 AB-212.
ASM: *Marte* Mk 2.

AIR FORCE: 67,800 (25,500 conscripts).
FGA: 8 sqn:
4 with *Tornado*.
1 with G-91Y.
3 with AMX.
CAS: 1 lt attack sqn with MB-339.
FTR: 8 sqn:
7 with F-104 ASA.
1 with *Tornado* F-3.
RECCE: 2 sqn with AMX.
MR: 2 sqn with *Atlantic* (Navy-assigned).
EW: 1 ECM/recce sqn with G-222VS, PD-808.
CALIBRATION: 1 navigation-aid calibration sqn with

G-222RM, PD-808, MB-339.
TPT: 3 sqn:
2 with G-222; 1 with C-130H.
TKR: 1 sqn with 707-320.
LIAISON: 2 sqn with **ac:** *Gulfstream* III, *Falcon* 50, DC-9; **hel:** SH-3D.
TRG: 1 OCU with TF-104G; 1 det (Cottesmore, UK) with *Tornado*; 5 sqn with **ac:** G-91T, MB-339A, SF-260M; **hel:** NH-500.
SAR: 1 sqn and 3 det with HH-3F.
6 det with AB-212.
AD: 8 SAM sqn with *Nike Hercules*.
12 SAM sqn with *Spada*.
EQPT: 369 cbt ac (plus 87 in store), no armed hel.
AC: *Tornado*: 82: **GRA:** 70 (66 FGA, 4* in tri-national sqn) plus 21 in store. **F-3:** 12. **F-104:** 112: **-ASA:** 99, plus 41 in store; **TF104G:** 13, plus 9 in store. **AMX:** 67: 65 (FGA); **-T:** 2* (trg). **G-91:** 58: **-Y:** 15; **-T:** 43; plus 7 in store. **MB-339:** 78 (13 tac, 60 (incl 50*) trg, 5 calibration), plus 9 in store. *Atlantic:* 18 (MR). **Boeing-707-320:** 2 (tkr/tpt). **C-130H:** 12 (tpt). **G-222:** 45 (40 tpt, 4 calibration), **-GE:** 1 (ECM). **DC9-32:** 2 (VIP). *Gulfstream* III: 2 (VIP). *Falcon* 50: 4 (VIP). **P-166:** 14 (**-M:** 8; **-DL3:** 6 liaison and trg). **P-180:** 5 (liaison); **PD-808:** 18 (ECM, calibration, VIP tpt); **SF-260M:** 39 (trg). **SIAI-208:** 36 (liaison). **HEL: HH-3F:** 33 (SAR). **SH-3D:** 2 (liaison). **AB-212:** 36 (SAR). **AB-47G:** 6 (trg). **NH-500D:** 53 (trg).
MSL:
ASM: AGM-88 HARM.
AAM: AIM-7E *Sparrow*, AIM-9B/L *Sidewinder*, *Aspide*.
SAM: 96 *Nike Hercules*, 7 bty *Spada*, ASPIDE.

FORCES ABROAD:
GERMANY: 93; Air Force, NAEW Force.
MALTA: 16; Air Force with 1 AB-212.
UK: 21; tri-national *Tornado* sqn with 4 ac.
US: 26 flying trg.
UN AND PEACEKEEPING:
ADRIATIC (*Sharp Guard*): 2 FFG. **EGYPT** (MFO): 82; 3 PCC. **INDIA/PAKISTAN** (UNMOGIP): 7 Obs. **IRAQ** (UNSCOM): 1 Obs. **IRAQ/KUWAIT** (UNIKOM): 6 Obs. **LEBANON** (UNIFIL): 44; hel unit. **MIDDLE EAST** (UNTSO): 8 Obs. **WESTERN SAHARA** (MINURSO): 6 Obs.

PARAMILITARY:
CARABINIERI (Ministry of Defence): 111,800: Territorial: 5 bde, 17 regt, 96 gp; Trg: 1 bde; Mobile def: 2 bde, 1 cav regt, 1 special ops gp, 13 mobile bn, 1 AB bn, avn and naval units.
EQPT: 48 Fiat 6616 armd cars; 40 VCC2, 91 M-113 APC; 24 A-109, 4 AB-205, 40 AB-206, 17 AB-412 hel.
PUBLIC SECURITY GUARD (Ministry of Interior): 80,400: 11 mobile units; 40 Fiat 6614 APC, **ac:** 3 P-64B, 5 P-68; **hel:** 12 A-109, 20 AB-206, 9 AB-212.

FINANCE GUARDS (Treasury Department): 64,100; 14 Zones, 20 Legions, 128 gps; **ac:** 5 P-166-DL3; **hel:** 15 A-109, 66 Breda-Nardi NH-500M/MC/MD; 3 PCI, 65; plus about 300 boats.
HARBOUR CONTROL (*Capitanerie di Porto*) (subordinated to Navy in emergencies): some 12 PCI, 130+ boats.

FOREIGN FORCES:
NATO: HQ Allied Forces Southern Europe (AFSOUTH). HQ 5 Allied Tactical Air Force (5 ATAF).
US: 12,700: Army (2,800); 1 AB bn gp; Navy (6,800); Air Force (3,200); 2 ftr sqn with 36 F-16C/D.
OPERATION DENY FLIGHT: France (7 *Mirage* 2000C, 4 *Mirage* F1-CR, 4 *Mirage* F-1CT (on call), 6 *Mirage* 2000KD, 6 *Super Etendard*, 5 *Jaguar*, 1 E-3F, 1 C-135), NATO (8 E-3A), Netherlands (12 F-16), Spain (8 F/A-18, 2 KC-130 (tkr), 1 CASA 212 (spt ac)), Turkey (8 F-16), UK (6 *Tornado* F-3, 8 *Harrier* GR-7, 6 *Sea Harrier*, 2 K-1 *Tristar* (tkr), 3 E-3D *Sentry*), US (8 F-15E, 12 F/A-18D (USMC), 12 F-16C (USAF), 12 F/A-18C (USN), 8 OA-10 (USAF), 6 A-6E (USN), 3 EC-130, 4 AC-130, 10 KC-135, 6 EF-111A (USAF), 12 EA-6B/E (USN). (Numbers as of 3 August 1995.)
Note: Germany provides 12 *Tornado* (8 ECR, 4 recce) in direct support of Rapid Reaction Forces.
OPERATION SHARP GUARD: Canada 1 FFH, France 1 FF, Germany 1 DDG, 1 FFG, Greece 1 FFG, Italy 2 FFG, Netherlands 1 FF, 1 FFG, Portugal 1 FF, Spain 1 FF, 1 FFG, Turkey 1 FFG, UK 1 DDG, 1 FFG, USA 1 DDG, 2 FFG, 1 PCC. Maritime aircraft from France (*Atlantic* ac), Germany (*Atlantic* ac), Italy (*Atlantic, 8 Tornado*), Netherlands (P-3C ac), Portugal (P-3P ac), Spain (P-3B ac), UK (*Nimrod* ac), US (P-3C ac). (Numbers as of 3 August 1995.)
UNHCR OPERATIONS: Canada (1 C-130), Germany (1 MD-16), UK (1 C-130), UN (1 IL), US (C-130).

LUXEMBOURG

GDP	1993: fr 347.6bn ($10.1bn)		
	per capita $20,900		
	1994: fr 355.3bn ($10.6bn)		
	per capita $21,200		
Growth	1993: 1.7%	1994: 2.7%	
Inflation	1993: 3.6%	1994: 2.2%	
Publ debt	1993: 3.0%	1994: 3.1%	
Def exp	1993: fr 3.4bn ($98m)		
Def bdgt	1994: fr 3.7bn ($111m)		
	1995: Fr 3.8bn ($114m)		
NATO defn	1993: fr 3.7bn ($108m)		
	1994: fr 4.1bn ($124m)		
$1 = fr	1993: 34.6	1994: 33.5	
	1995: 31.6		

fr = Luxembourg franc

Population: 406,000 (119,700 foreign citizens)

	13–17	*18–22*	*23–32*
Men	12,000	12,000	31,000
Women	11,400	12,200	30,400

TOTAL ARMED FORCES:
ACTIVE: 800.

ARMY: 800.
1 lt inf bn.
EQPT:
APC: 5 *Commando*.
MOR: 81mm: 6.
ATGW: *TOW* some 6 SP (*Hummer*).
RL: *LAW.*

AIR FORCE: (none, but for legal purposes NATO's E-3A AEW ac have Luxembourg registration).
1 sqn with 18 E-3A *Sentry* (NATO Standard), 2 Boeing 707 (trg).

PARAMILITARY:
GENDARMERIE: 560.

NETHERLANDS

GDP	1993: gld 574.3bn ($309.2bn):	
	per capita $18,000	
	1994: gld 600.3bn ($329.8bn):	
	per capita $18,300	
Growth	1993: 0.4%	1994: 2.5%
Inflation	1993: 2.1%	1994: 2.8%
Publ debt	1993: 78.5%	1994: 79.0%
Def exp	1993: gld 14.09bn ($7.58bn)	
Def bdgt	1994: gld 13.50bn ($7.42bn)	
	1995: gld 13.51bn ($8.56bn)	
NATO defn	1993: gld 14.1bn ($7.6bn)	
	1994: gld 12.9bn ($7.1bn)	
$1 = gld	1993: 1.86	1994: 1.82
	1995: 1.58	

gld = guilder

Population: 15,446,000

	13–17	*18–22*	*23–32*
Men	444,800	511,600	1,281,800
Women	425,800	488,200	1,215,200

TOTAL ARMED FORCES:
ACTIVE: 74,400 (incl 3,600 Royal Military

Constabulary, 800 Inter-Service Organisation, 2,600 women, 27,700 conscripts).

Terms of service: 9 months.

RESERVES: 130,600 (men to age 35, NCO to 40, officers to 45): Army 111,600 (some – at the end of their conscription period – on short leave, immediate recall); Navy some 9,000 (7,000 on immediate recall); Air Force 10,000 (immediate recall).

ARMY: 43,200 (24,700 conscripts).

1 Corps HQ (Ge/Nl), 1 mech div HQ.
3 mech inf bde (2 cadre).
1 lt bde.
1 air-mobile bde (3 inf bn).
1 fd arty, 1 AD gp.
1 engr gp.
Summary of combat arm units:
11 armd inf bn.
12 arty bn.
3 air-mobile bn.
2 AD bn.
8 tk bn.
2 MLRS bty.
4 recce bn.

RESERVES: (cadre bde and corps tps completed by call-up of reservists).
National Comd incl Territorial Comd: 3 inf, 1 SF, 2 engr bn spt units, could be mob for territorial defence.
Home Guard: 3 sectors; lt inf weapons.

EQPT:
MBT: 740: 296 *Leopard* 1A4 (in store), 444 *Leopard* 2.
AIFV: 717 YPR-765.
APC: 142 M-113, 1,055 YPR-765, 61 YP-408 (in store).
TOTAL ARTY: 581:
TOWED ARTY: 116: **105mm:** 9 M-101 (in store); **155mm:** 107 M-114 (incl 77 -114/39).
SP ARTY: 284: **155mm:** 221 M-109A3; **203mm:** 63 M-110 (in store).
MRL: 227mm: 22 MLRS.
MOR: 159: **107mm:** 21 M-30 (in store); **120mm:** 138 (incl 65 in store).
ATGW: 753 (incl 135 in store): 427 *Dragon*, 326 (incl 304 YPR-765) *TOW*.
RL: 84mm: *Carl Gustav*, AT-4.
RCL: 106mm: 185 M-40 (in store).
AD GUNS: 35mm: 95 *Gepard* SP; **40mm:** 131 L/70 towed.
SAM: 324 *Stinger*.
SURV: AN/TPQ-36 (arty, mor).
MARINE: 1 tk tpt, 3 coastal, 3 river patrol boats.

NAVY: 14,300 (incl 1,100 Naval Air, 2,900

Marines, 1,000 conscripts and 950 women).
Under integrated op comd with Belgium from 1 Jan 1996 (less SS).

BASES: Netherlands: Den Helder (HQ); Vlissingen.
Overseas: Willemstad (Curaçao), Oranjestad (Aruba).
SS: 4 *Zeeleeuw* with Mk 48 HWT; plus *Harpoon* USGW.
PRINCIPAL SURFACE COMBATANTS: 18:
DESTROYERS: 4 DDG (Nl desig = FFG):
2 *Tromp* with 1 SM-1 MR SAM; plus 2 x 4 *Harpoon* SSM, 1 x 2 120mm guns, 1 *Lynx* hel (ASW/OTHT), 2 x 3 ASTT (Mk 46 LWT).
2 *Van Heemskerck* with 1 SM-1 MR SAM; plus 2 x 4 *Harpoon*, 2 x 2 ASTT.
FF: 14:
7 *Karel Doorman* FF with 2 x 4 *Harpoon* SSM, plus 2 x 2 ASTT; 1 *Lynx* (ASW/OTHT) hel.
7 *Kortenaer* FF with 2 *Lynx* (ASW/OTHT) hel, 2 x 2 ASTT; plus 2 x 4 *Harpoon*.
MINE WARFARE: 12:
MINELAYERS: none, but *Mercuur*, listed under spt and misc, has capability.
MCM: 12:
10 *Alkmaar* (tripartite) MHC (plus 5 in reserve).
2 *Dokkum* MSC (plus 4 in reserve).
AMPH: craft only: about 12 LCA.
SPT AND MISC: 12:
1 *Amsterdam* AOR (4 *Lynx* or 3 NH-90 or 2 EH-101 hel), 1 *Mercuur* torpedo tender, 2 trg, 1 aux, 4 *Cerberus* div spt, 3 Survey.

NAVAL AIR: (1,100).
MR: 1 sqn with F-27M (see Air Force).
MR/ASW: 2 sqn with P-3C.
ASW/SAR: 2 sqn with *Lynx* hel.
EQPT: 13 cbt ac, 22 armed hel.
AC: P-3C: 13 (MR).
HEL: *Lynx*: 22 (ASW, SAR).

MARINES: (2,900).
3 Marine bn (1 cadre); 1 spt bn.
RESERVES: 1 marine bn.
EQPT:
MOR: 120mm: 14 (2 in store).
ATGW: *Dragon*.
SAM: *Stinger*.

AIR FORCE: 12,500 (2,000 conscripts).

FTR/FGA: 7 sqn with F-16A/B (1 sqn is tac trg, evaluation and standardisation sqn).
FTR/RECCE: 1 sqn with F-16A.
MR: 2 F-27M (assigned to Navy).
TPT: 1 sqn with F-27, C-130H-30, DC-10-30.
TRG: 1 sqn with PC-7.
HEL: 4 sqn, 3 with SA-316, 1 with BO-105.
SAR: 1 fleet with SA-316.
AD: 8 bty with HAWK SAM (4 in Ge).
4 bty with *Patriot* SAM (in Ge).
EQPT: 183 cbt ac, 31 armed hel.

AC: F-16: 183: **-A:** 148 (121 FGA/ftr, 19 recce, 8* trg); **-B:** 35. **F-27:** 14 (12 tpt, 2 MR). **C-130H-30:** 2. **DC-10-30:** 2 (tkr/trans). **PC-7:** 10 (trg).
HEL: AB-412 SP: 3 (SAR). **SA-316:** 59 (31 armed). **BO-105:** 24.
MSL:
AAM: AIM-9/L/N *Sidewinder*.
SAM: 48 HAWK, 5 *Patriot*, 100 *Stinger*.
AD GUNS: 25 VL 4/41 *Flycatcher* radar, 75 L/70 40mm systems.

FORCES ABROAD:
GERMANY: 3,000; 1 lt bde (1 armd inf, 1 tk bn), plus spt elms.
ICELAND: Navy: 30; 1 P-3C.
NETHERLANDS ANTILLES: Navy: 20; 1 frigate, 1 amph cbt det, 1 MR det with 2 F-27MPA ac, 1 P-3C.
UN AND PEACEKEEPING:
ADRIATIC (*Sharp Guard*): 1 FF, 1 FFG, 1 P-3C ac.
ANGOLA (UNAVEM III): 15 Obs, plus 10 civ pol.
BOSNIA (UNPROFOR): 1,508; elm 1 air mob bde, 1 tpt bn plus 23 Obs and 2 civ pol. **CROATIA** (UNCRO): 125; elm 1 sigs bn, plus 25 Obs and 7 civ pol. **HAITI** (UNMIH): 146. **ITALY:** 360: *Deny Flight*: 12 F-16. Aircrew in NATO E-3 Force. **FYROM** (UNPREDEP): 1 civ pol. **MIDDLE EAST** (UNTSO): 14 Obs.

PARAMILITARY:
ROYAL MILITARY CONSTABULARY
(*Koninklijke Marechaussee*): 3,600 (500 conscripts); 3 'div' comprising 10 districts with 72 'bde'.

FOREIGN FORCES:
NATO: HQ Allied Forces Central Europe.
US: 700: Army (450); Air Force (250).

NORWAY

GDP	1993: kr 739.5bn ($103.5bn):	
	per capita $18,700	
	1994: kr 774.2bn ($109.7bn):	
	per capita $19,500	
Growth	1993: 2.3%	1994: 5.1%
Inflation	1993: 2.3%	1994: 1.5%
Publ debt	1993: 50.7%	1994: 47.7%
Def exp	1994: kr 22.75bn ($3.21bn)	
	1994: kr 23.87bn ($3.38bn)	
Def bdgt	1995: kr 23.71bn ($3.77bn)	
	1996ε: kr 23.48bn ($3.73bn)	
NATO defn	1993: kr 22.93bn ($3.23bn)	
	1994: kr 24.17bn ($3.42bn)	
$1 = kr	1993: 7.09	1994: 7.06
	1995: 6.29	

kr = kroner

Population: 4,353,000

	13–17	*18–22*	*23–32*
Men	137,600	155,600	346,400
Women	129,000	147,200	324,000

TOTAL ARMED FORCES:
ACTIVE: 30,000 (incl recalled reservists, 400 Joint Services org, 600 Home Guard permanent staff, and 16,900 conscripts).
Terms of service: Army, Navy, Air Force, 12 months, plus 4–5 refresher trg periods.
RESERVES: 255,000 mobilisable in 24–72 hours; obligation to 44 (conscripts remain with fd army units to age 35; officers to age 55; regulars: 60): Army 108,000; Navy 33,000; Air Force: 34,400; Home Guard: some 79,000.

ARMY: 14,700 (incl 9,200 conscripts).
2 Commands, 4 district comd, 1 div HQ, 14 territorial comd.
North Norway:
   1 bde gp: 1 inf, 1 tk, 1 SP arty, 1 engr bn, 1 AD bty, spt units.
South Norway:
   2 inf bn (incl Royal Guard).
Indep units.
RESERVES: cadre units for mob: 3 mech, 3 inf bde, 20 inf, 3 arty bn; 50–60 indep inf coy, tk sqn, arty bty, engr coy, sigs units.
LAND HOME GUARD: 71,000.
18 districts each divided into 2–6 sub-districts and some 465 sub-units (pl).
EQPT:
MBT: 170 *Leopard* (-1A5NO: 111; -1A1NO: 59) (plus 38 M-48A5 in store awaiting disposal).
AIFV: 53 NM-135 (M-113/**20mm**).
APC: 170 M-113 (incl variants).
TOTAL ARTY: 402:
TOWED ARTY: 276: **105mm:** 228 M-101 (incl 156 in store); **155mm:** 48 M-114.
SP ARTY: 155mm: 126 M-109A3GN SP.
MOR: 81mm: 456 (40 SP incl 28 M-106A1, 12 M-125A2).
ATGW: 320 *TOW*-1/-2 incl 97 NM-142 (M-113/*TOW*-2).
RCL: 84mm: 2,517 *Carl Gustav*.
AD GUNS: 20mm: 252 Rh-202.
SAM: 300 RBS-70.
SURV: *Cymberline* (mor).

NAVY: 6,400 (incl 1,000 Coastal Arty, 600 Coast Guard and 3,600 conscripts).

2 Operational Comds: COMNAVSONOR and
COMNAVNON with 7 regional Naval districts.
BASES: Horten, Haakonsvern (Bergen), Ramsund,
Olavsvern (Tromsø).
SS: 12:
6 *Ula* SS with Ge *Seeal* DM2A3 HWT.
6 *Kobben* SSC (with Swe T-612) HWT (to be replaced
   with TP-613 for 1995-1997).
FF: 4 *Oslo* with 2 x 3 ASTT, 1 x 6 *Terne* ASW RL;
plus 4 x *Penguin* 1 SSM, *Sea Sparrow*.
PATROL AND COASTAL COMBATANTS: 30:
MSL CRAFT: 30:
14 *Hauk* PFM with 6 x *Penguin* 1, 2 x (Swe TP-613) HWT.
10 *Storm* PFM with 6 x *Penguin* 1.
6 *Snøgg* PFM with 4 x *Penguin* 1, 4 x 533mm TT.
MINE WARFARE: 12:
MINELAYERS: 2 *Vidar*, coastal (300–400 mines).
Note: amph craft also fitted for minelaying.
MCM: 10:
3 *Sauda* MSC, 1 *Tana* MHC, 4 *Oksoy* MHC.
2 diver spt.
AMPH: craft only: 5 LCT.
SPT AND MISC: 5:
1 *Horten* sub/patrol craft depot ship.
1 *Marjata* AGOR (civ manned).
1 *Valkyrien* Torpedo recovery.
1 *Sverdrup* II.
1 Royal Yacht.
ADDITIONAL IN STORE: 1 *Sauda* MSC.
NAVAL HOME GUARD: 6,000; on mob assigned to 7
naval/coastal defence comd.
Some 400 fishing craft.
COASTAL DEFENCE: 26 fortresses: 75mm; 105mm;
120mm; 127mm; 150mm guns. 7 cable mine and 4
torpedo bty.

COAST GUARD: (680):
PATROL, OFFSHORE: 12:
3 *Nordkapp* with 1 x *Lynx* hel (SAR/recce), fitted for
   6 *Penguin* Mk 2 SSM.
1 *Nornen*, 1 *Farm*, 7 chartered (partly civ manned).
AVN: ac: 2 P-3N *Orion*; **hel:** 6 *Lynx* (Air Force-manned).

AIR FORCE: 7,900 (4,100 conscripts). Flying
hours: 180.
FGA: 4 sqn with F-16A/B.
FTR: 1 trg sqn with F-5A/B.
MR: 1 sqn with P-3C/N *Orion* (2 assigned to Coast Guard).
TPT: 2 sqn:
1 with C-130 and *Falcon* 20C (CAL, ECM).
1 with DHC-6.
TRG: MFI-15.
SAR: 1 sqn with *Sea King* Mk 43B.
TAC HEL: 2 sqn with Bell-412SP.
SAM: 4 bty *NOAH* (Norwegian adapted HAWK), 2

bty NASAMS (Norwegian advanced SAM) (1995–
98), 4 bty *NOAH* to be converted to NASAMS).
AAA: 10 bty RB-70.
COAST GUARD: 1 sqn with 6 *Lynx* Mk 86, 2 P-3N *Orion*.
EQPT: 80 cbt ac (incl 4 MR), no armed hel.
AC: F-5A/B: 15 (ftr/trg). **F-16:** 59; **-A:** 48 (FGA); **-B:** 11
(FGA). **P-3:** 6*: **-C:** 4 (MR); **-N:** 2 (Coast Guard). **C-130H:**
6 (tpt). *Falcon* **20C:** 3 (EW/tpt Cal). **DHC-6:** 3 (tpt). **MFI-
15:** 17 (trg).
HEL: Bell 412 SP: 18 (tpt). *Sea King* **Mk 43B:** 10 (SAR).
Lynx **Mk 86:** 6 (Coast Guard).
MSL:
ASM: *Penguin* Mk-3.
AAM: AIM-9L/N *Sidewinder*.

AA HOME GUARD (on mob under comd of Air
Force): 2,000; 2 bn (9 bty) AA 20mm NM45.

FORCES ABROAD:
UN AND PEACEKEEPING:
ANGOLA (UNAVEM III): 4 Obs. **BOSNIA** (UNPRO-
FOR): some 654; log bn, incl hel unit with 4 Bell-412SP,
fd hospital plus 15 Obs and 5 civ pol. **CROATIA**
(UNCRO): 112, plus 20 Obs, 12 civ pol. **EGYPT** (MFO):
4 Staff Officers. **LEBANON** (UNIFIL): 828; 1 inf bn, 1
service coy, plus HQ personnel. **FYROM** (UNPREDEP):
46 (elm Nordic bn) plus 4 Obs. **MIDDLE EAST** (UNTSO):
16 Obs. **WESTERN SAHARA** (MINURSO): 2 civ pol.

FOREIGN FORCES:
US: prepositioned eqpt for 1 MEB.
CANADA: prepositioned 6 arty, 14 ACV.
NATO: HQ Allied Forces North Europe (HQ North).

PORTUGAL

GDP	1993: esc 13,775bn ($85.67bn):			
	per capita $8,800			
	1994: esc 14,608bn ($88.01bn):			
	per capita $8,900			
Growth	1993: -1.2%		1994: 1.2%	
Inflation	1993: 6.5%		1994: 5.3%	
Publ debt	1993: 58.4%		1994: 63.5%	
Def exp	1993: esc 352.5bn ($2.19bn)			
Def bdgt	1994: esc 250.6bn ($1.51bn)			
	1995: esc 271.8bn ($1.60bn)			
NATO defn	1993: esc 352.5bn ($2.19bn)			
	1994: esc 378.7bn ($2.28bn)			
FMA	1994: $81.5m (FMF, IMET)			
	1995: $0.5m (IMET)			
	1996: $0.8m (IMET)			
$1 = esc	1993: 161		1994: 166	
	1995: 148			
esc = escudo				

Population: 9,869,000

	13–17	18–22	23–32
Men	376,400	407,800	821,400
Women	357,600	392,600	806,800

TOTAL ARMED FORCES:

ACTIVE: 54,200 (17,600 conscripts; 4,300 Central Staff, 400 in centrally controlled formations/units).
Terms of service: Army: 4–8 months; Navy and Air Force: 4–18 months.
RESERVES: 210,000 (all services) (obligation to age 35).

ARMY: 29,700 (15,000 conscripts).
3 Military Districts, 2 Military Comds.
1 composite bde (1 mech, 2 mot inf, 1 tk, 1 fd arty bn).
1 AB bde.
2 armd cav regt.
1 tk regt.
2 engr regt.
11 inf regt incl 3 garrison.
2 fd, 1 AD, 1 coast arty regt.
1 MP regt.
EQPT:
MBT: 198: 24 M-47, 86 M-48A5, 88 M-60A3.
RECCE: 29 *Saladin*, 40 AML-60, 15 V-150, 21 EBR-75, 8 ULTRAV M-11, 30 *Ferret* Mk 4.
APC: 350: 249 M-113, 65 V-200 *Chaimite*, 2 EBR, 22 YP 408, 12 *Condor*.
TOTAL ARTY: 318:
TOWED ARTY: 168: **105mm:** 54 M-101, 24 M-56; **140mm:** 50 5.5-in; **155mm:** 40 M-114A1.
SP ARTY: 155mm: 6 M-109A2.
MOR: 144: **107mm:** 62 M-30 (incl 14 SP); **120mm:** 82 Tampella; **81mm:** some.
COASTAL ARTY: 27: **150mm:** 15; **152mm:** 6; **234mm:** 6.
RCL: 84mm: *Carl Gustav*.
ATGW: 51 *TOW* (incl 18 M-113, 4 M-901), 65 *Milan* (incl 6 ULTRAV M-11).
RCL: 90mm: 112; **106mm:** 128 M-40.
AD GUNS: 105, incl **20mm:** M-163A1 *Vulcan* SP; **40mm:** L/60.
SAM: 12 *Blowpipe*, 5 *Chaparral*.
DEPLOYMENT:
Azores and Madeira: 2,000; 3 garrison inf regt, 2 coast arty bn, 2 AA bty.

NAVY: ε12,500 (incl 2,100 Marines and 800 conscripts).
1 Naval area Comd, with 5 Subordinate one Comds (Azores, Madeira, North Continental, Centre Continental and South Continental).
BASES: Lisbon (Alfeite), Portimão (HQ Continental Comd), Ponta Delgada (HQ Azores), Funchal (HQ Madeira).

SS: 3 *Albacora* (Fr *Daphné*) SS with EL-5 HWT.
FF: 11:
3 *Vasco Da Gama* (Meko 200) with 2 x 3 ASTT (US Mk-46), plus 2 x 4 *Harpoon* SSM, 1 x 8 *Sea Sparrow* SAM, 1 x 100mm gun (with 2 x *Super Lynx* hel in some).
4 *Commandante João Belo* (Fr *Cdt Rivière*) with 2 x 3 ASTT, 1 x 4 ASW mor; plus 3 x 100mm gun.
4 *Baptista de Andrade* with 2 x 3 ASTT; plus 1 x 100mm gun.
PATROL AND COASTAL COMBATANTS: 30:
PATROL, OFFSHORE: 6 *João Coutinho* PCO, hel deck.
PATROL, COASTAL: 10 *Cacine*.
PATROL, INSHORE: 13:
5 *Argos*, 8⟨.
RIVERINE: 1 *Rio Minho*⟨.
AMPH: craft only: 3 LCU, about 7 LCM.
SPT AND MISC: 14:
1 Berrio (UK Green Rover) AO, 9 AGHS, 2 trg, 1 ocean trg, 1 div spt.

MARINES: (2,100).
3 bn (2 lt inf, 1 police), spt units.
EQPT: 4 V-200 *Chaimite* APC, 36 **120mm** mor.

AIR FORCE: 7,300 (1,800 conscripts).
1 operational air command (COFA).
FGA: 5 sqn:
2 with A-7P.
1 with F-16A/B.
2 with Alpha Jets.
SURVEY: 1 sqn with C-212.
MR: 1 sqn with P-3P.
TPT: 4 sqn:
1 with C-130.
1 with C-212.
1 with *Falcon* 20 and *Falcon* 50.
1 with SA-316 hel.
SAR: 2 sqn:
1 with SA-330 hel; 1 with SA-330 hel and C-212.
LIAISON: 1 sqn with Reims-Cessna FTB-337G.
TRG: 1 sqn with SOCATA TB-30 *Epsilon*.
EQPT: 97 cbt ac, plus 6 MR ac, no attack hel.
AC: *Alpha Jet:* 40 (FGA trg), plus 10 in store. **A-7:** 37: **-7P:** 31 (FGA); **TA-7P:** 6* (trg). **F-16A/B:** 20. **P-3P:** 6 (MR). **C-130H:** 6 (SAR, tpt). **C-212:** 22: **-A:** 18 (12 tpt/SAR, 1 Nav trg, 2 ECM trg, 3 fisheries protection); **-B:** 4 (survey). **Cessna 337:** 12 (liaison). ***Falcon* 20:** 1 (tpt, calibration). ***Falcon* 50:** 3 (tpt). ***Epsilon:*** 16 (trg).
HEL: SA-330: 10 (SAR/tpt). **SA-316:** 21 (trg, utl).

FORCES ABROAD:
UN AND PEACEKEEPING:
ADRIATIC (Sharp Guard): 1 FF.
ANGOLA (UNAVEM III): 121 plus 8 Obs, 1 civ pol.

BOSNIA (UNPROFOR): 5 Obs, 4 civ pol.
CROATIA (UNCRO): 7 Obs, 26 civ pol.

PARAMILITARY:
NATIONAL REPUBLICAN GUARD: 20,900;
Commando Mk III APC, 7 SA-313 hel.
PUBLIC SECURITY POLICE: 20,000.
BORDER SECURITY GUARD: 8,900.

FOREIGN FORCES:
NATO: HQ IBERLANT area at Lisbon (Oeiras).
US: 1,155: Navy (55); Air (1,100) (incl Azores).

SPAIN

GDP	1993:	pts 60,904bn ($478.4bn):
	per capita $13,400	
	1994:	pts 64,673bn ($482.8bn):
	per capita $13,900	

Growth	1993: -1.1%	1994: 2.0%
Inflation	1993: 4.6%	1994: 4.8%
Publ debt	1993: 59.4%	1994: 63.5%
Def exp	1993: pts 895.1bn ($7.03bn)	
	1994: pts 829.3bn ($6.19bn)	
Def bdgt[a]	1994: pts 805.5bn ($6.01bn)	
	1995: pts 812.1bn ($6.59bn)	
NATO defn	1993: pts 1,055bn ($8.29bn)	
	1994: pts 1,021bn ($7.62bn)	
FMA	1994: $0.05m (IMET)	
	1995: $0.05m (IMET)	
	1996: $0.05m (IMET)	
$1 = pts	1993: 127	1994: 134
	1995: 123	

pts = peseta

[a] 1995 def bdgt reduced from pts 866.5bn ($7.03bn) in Jan 1995.

Population: 39,144,000

	13–17	18–22	23–32
Men	1,476,400	1,653,800	3,340,400
Women	1,391,400	1,564,800	3,209,200

TOTAL ARMED FORCES:
ACTIVE: 206,000 (126,000 conscripts (to be reduced), some 200 women).
Terms of service: 9 months.
RESERVES: Army 420,000; Navy 10,000; Air Force 8,000.

ARMY: 144,700 (97,000 conscripts).
8 Regional Operational Commands incl 2 overseas: 1 mech div (with 1 armd, 2 mech bde).
2 armd cav bde (1 cadre).
1 mtn bde.
3 lt inf bde (cadre).
1 air-portable bde.
1 AB bde.
Spanish Legion:
    1 bde (forming – to be 3 lt inf, 1 arty, 1 engr bn, 1 atk coy).
    2 regt (each with 1 mech, 1 mot bn, 1 atk coy).
3 island garrison (Canary, Balearic Islands, Ceuta and Melilla).
1 arty bde; 1 AD regt.
1 engr bde.
1 Army Avn bde (1 attack, 1 tpt hel bn, 4 utl units).
1 AD comd: 6 AD regt incl 1 HAWK SAM, 1 composite *Aspide*/35mm, 1 *Roland* bn.
1 Coast Arty Comd (6 mixed arty regt; 1 coast arty gp).
3 special ops bn.
Rapid Action Force (FAR) formed from 1 Spanish Legion, 1 AB and 1 air-portable bde (see above).

EQPT:
MBT: 668: 210 AMX-30 (150 EM2, 60 ER1), 164 M-48A5E, 294 M-60 (-A1: 50; -A3: 244), some *Leopard* 2 (being delivered).
RECCE: 340 BMR-VEC (100-**90mm**, 208-**25mm**, 32-**20mm** gun).
APC: 2,092: 1,313 M-113 (incl variants), 679 BMR-600, 100 BTR-70 (UNPROFOR).
TOTAL ARTY: 1,292:
TOWED ARTY: 633: **105mm:** 282 M-26, 170 M-56 pack; **122mm:** 73 122/46; **155mm:** 84 M-114; **203mm:** 24 M-115.
SP ARTY: 180: **105mm:** 48 M-108; **155mm:** 96 M-109A1; **203mm:** 36 M-110A2.
MRL: **140mm:** 14 *Teruel.*
MOR: **120mm:** 465 (incl 19 2SP); plus **81mm:** 1,314 (incl 187 SP).
COASTAL ARTY: 71: **6-in:** 52; **305mm:** 16; **381mm:** 3.
ATGW: 442 *Milan*, 28 *HOT*, some *TOW* (being delivered).
RCL: **106mm:** 638.
AD GUNS: **20mm:** 329 GAI-BO1; **35mm:** 92 GDF-002 twin; **40mm:** 274 L/70.
SAM: 24 I HAWK, 18 *Roland*, 13 *Skyguard/Aspide*, 90 *Mistral.*
HEL: 176 (28 attack): 53 HU-10B, 70 HA/HR-15 (31 with **20mm** guns, 28 with *HOT*, 9 trg), 6 HU-18, 11 HR-12B, 18 HT-21, 18 HT-17.
SURV: 2 AN/TPQ-36 (arty, mor).

DEPLOYMENT:
CEUTA AND MELILLA: 10,000; 2 armd cav, 2 Spanish Legion, 2 mot inf, 2 arty regt; 2 lt AD bn, 2 engr, 1 coast arty gp.
BALEARIC ISLANDS: 2,500; 1 mot inf regt: 2 mot inf bn, 1 mixed arty regt: 2 fd arty; 1 engr bn, 1 special ops coy.

CANARY ISLANDS: 6,500; 2 inf regt; 1 Spanish Legion, 2 mixed arty regt, 2 engr bn, 2 special ops coy.

NAVY: 31,900 (incl 1,000 Naval Air, 7,000 Marines and 16,900 conscripts) plus 8,550 civilians.
5 Comds (Fleet, plus 4 Naval Zones: Cantabrian, Strait (of Gibraltar), Mediterranean and Canary (Islands)).
BASES: El Ferrol (La Coruña) (Cantabrian HQ), San Fernando (Cadiz) (Strait HQ), Rota (Cadiz) (Fleet HQ), Cartagena (Murcia) (Mediterranean HQ), Las Palmas (Canary Islands HQ), Palma de Mallorca and Mahón (Menorca).
SS: 8:
4 *Galerna* (Fr *Agosta*) with F-17 and L-5 HWT.
4 *Delfin* (Fr *Daphné*) with F-17 and L-5 HWT.
PRINCIPAL SURFACE COMBATANTS: 18:
CARRIERS: 1 (CVV) *Príncipe de Asturias* (16,200t); air gp: typically 6 to 10 AV-8S/EAV-8B FGA, 4 to 6 SH-3D ASW hel, 2 SH-3D AEW hel, 2 utl hel.
FRIGATES: 17
FFG: 11 (AAW/ASW):
6 *Santa Maria* (US *Perry*) with 1 x 1 SM-1 MR SAM/*Harpoon* SSM launcher, 2 x SH-60B hel, 2 x 3 ASTT; plus 1 x 76mm gun.
5 *Baleares* with 1 x 1 SM-1 MR SAM, 1 x 8 *ASROC*, 4 x 324mm and 2 x 484mm ASTT; plus 2 x 4 *Harpoon*, 1 x 127mm gun.
FF: 6 *Descubierta* with 2 x 3 ASTT, 1 x 2 ASW RL; plus 2 x 2 *Harpoon* SSM.
PATROL AND COASTAL COMBATANTS: 31:
PATROL, OFFSHORE: 5:
4 *Serviola*, 1 *Chilreu*.
PATROL, COASTAL: 10 *Anaga* PCC.
PATROL, INSHORE: 16:
6 *Barceló* PFI; 10 PCI⟨.
MINE WARFARE: 12:
MCM: 12:
4 *Guadalete* (US *Aggressive*) MSO.
8 *Júcar* (US *Adjutant*) MSC.
AMPH: 4:
2 *Castilla* (US *Paul Revere*) amph tpt, capacity: 1,600 tps; plus some 15 amph craft.
2 *Hernán Cortés* (US *Newport*) LST, capacity: 400 troops, 500t vehicles, 3 LCVPs, 1 LCPL.
Plus 13 craft: 3 LCT, 2 LCU, 8 LCM.
SPT AND MISC: 33:
2 AO, 5 ocean tugs, 3 diver spt, 2 tpt/spt, 3 water carriers, 6 AGHS, 1 AGOR, 1 sub salvage, 1 AK, 5 trg craft, 4 sail trg.

NAVAL AIR: (1,000 (300 conscripts)).
FGA: 2 sqn:
1 with AV-8S *Matador* (*Harrier*), TAV-8S.
1 with AV-8B.
LIAISON: 1 sqn with 3 *Citation* II.
HEL: 4 sqn:
ASW: 2 sqn:
1 with SH-3D/G *Sea King* (mod to SH-3H standard).
1 with SH-60B (LAMPS-III fit).
AEW: 1 fleet with SH-3D (*Searchwater* radar).
COMD/TPT: 1 sqn with AB-212.
TRG: 1 sqn with Hughes 500.
EQPT: 20 cbt ac, 25 armed hel.
AC: EAV-8B: 10; **AV-8S:** 8; **TAV-8S:** 2 (trg). *Citation* II: 3 (liaison).
HEL: AB-212: 10 (ASW/SAR). **SH-3D:** 12 (9 -H ASW, 3 -D AEW). **Hughes 500:** 10 (trg). **SH-60B:** 6 (ASW).

MARINES: (7,000 (3,550 conscripts)).
1 marine regt (3,500); 2 inf, 1 spt bn; 3 arty bty.
5 marine garrison gp.
EQPT:
MBT: 16 M-60A3.
AFV: 17 *Scorpion* lt tk, 19 LVTP-7 AAV, 28 BLR APC.
TOWED ARTY: **105mm:** 12 Oto Melara M-56 pack.
SP ARTY: **155mm:** 6 M-109A.
ATGW: 12 *TOW*, 18 *Dragon*.
RL: **90mm:** C-90C.
RCL: **106mm:** 54.
SAM: 12 *Mistral*.

AIR FORCE: 29,400 (12,100 conscripts).
Flying hours: EF-18/*Mirage* F-1: 180; F-5: 165.
CENTRAL AIR COMMAND (MACEN): 4 wings.
FTR: 3 sqn:
2 with EF-18 (F-18 *Hornet*), 1 with RF-4C.
TPT: 7 sqn:
2 with C-212.
1 with Boeing 707.
2 with CN-235.
1 with *Falcon* (20, 50, 900).
1 with AS-332 (tpt).
SPT: 4 sqn:
1 with CL-215.
1 with C-212 (EW) and *Falcon* 20.
1 with C-212, AS-332 (SAR).
1 with C-212 and Cessna *Citation*.
TRG: 4 sqn:
1 with C-212.
1 with Beech (*Baron*).
1 with C-101.
1 with Beech (*Bonanza*).
EASTERN AIR COMD (MALEV): 2 wings.
FTR: 3 sqn:
2 with EF-18 (F-18 *Hornet*), 1 with *Mirage* F1.
TPT: 2 sqn:
1 with C-130H, 1 tkr/tpt with KC-130H.
SPT: 1 sqn with **ac:** C-212 (SAR); **hel:** AS-332 .
GIBRALTAR STRAIT AIR COMD (MAEST): 4 wings.
FTR: 2 sqn with *Mirage* F-1 CE/BE.

FGA: 3 sqn:
2 with F-5B; 1 with C-101.
MR: 1 sqn with P-3A/B.
TRG: 6 sqn:
2 hel sqn with AB-205, *Hughes* 300C, S-76C.
1 with C-212; 1 with E-26 (*Tamiz*); 1 with C-101; 1 with
   C-212 and *Bonanza*.
CANARY ISLANDS, AIR COMD (MACAN): 1 wing.
FGA: 1 sqn with *Mirage* F-1EE.
TPT: 1 sqn with C-212.
SAR: 1 sqn with **ac:** F-27; **hel:** AS-332 (SAR).
LOG SPT COMD (MALOG):
1 trials sqn with C-101, C-212, E-26.
EQPT: 161 cbt ac, no armed hel.
AC: EF-18 A/B: 69 (ftr, OCU). **F-5B:** 22 (FGA). *Mirage:*
62: **F-1CF/-BE/-EE. RF-4C:** 8* (recce). **P-3:** 7: **-A:** 2 (MR);
-B: 5 (MR). **Boeing 707:** 3 (tkr/tpt). **C-130:** 12: **-H:** 7 (tpt);
KC-130H: 5 (tkr). **C-212:** 76 (32 tpt, 9 SAR, 6 recce, 25
trg, 2 EW, 2 trials). **Cessna** *Citation:* 2 (recce). **C-101:** 81
(trg). **CL-215:** 21 (spt). *Falcon 20:* 5 (3 VIP tpt , 2 EW);
Falcon 50: 1 (VIP tpt); *Falcon 900:* 2 (VIP tpt). **F-27:** 3
(SAR). **E-26:** 39 (trg). **CN-235:** 20 (18 tpt, 2 VIP tpt). **E-
20** (*Baron*): 5 trg; **E-24** (*Bonanza*): 27 trg.
HEL: SA-330: 5 (SAR), **AS-332:** 16 (10 SAR, 6 tpt),
Hughes 300C: 15 (trg), **S-76C:** 8 (trg).
MSL:
AAM: AIM-7 *Sparrow,* AIM-9 *Sidewinder.*
ASM: *Maverick, Harpoon, HARM.*

FORCES ABROAD:
UN AND PEACEKEEPING:
ADRIATIC (*Sharp Guard*): 1 FF, 1 FFG, ac. 1 P-3B.
BOSNIA (UNPROFOR): 1,438; 1 inf bn gp, 12 Obs.
CROATIA (UNCRO): 6 Obs. **ITALY** (*Deny Flight*)
280: 8 F/A-18, 2 KC-130 (tkr), 1 CASA-212 (spt ac).
FYROM (UNPREDEP): 1 Obs.

PARAMILITARY:
GUARDIA CIVIL: 75,000 (2,200 conscripts); 9 re-
gions, 19 inf *tercios* (regt) with 56 rural bn, 6 traffic
security gp, 6 rural special ops gp, 1 special sy bn; 22
BLR APC, 18 Bo-105, 5 BK-117 hel.
GUARDIA CIVIL DEL MAR: (550); about 19
PCI and PCI⟨.

FOREIGN FORCES:
US: 4,900: Navy (4,500); Air Force (400).

TURKEY

GDP   1993: TL 1,937,742bn ($176.4bn):
              per capita $4,800
              1994: TL 5,039,804bn ($170.2bn):

per capita $4,500

Growth	1993:	7.5%	1994:	-5.4%
Inflation	1993:	66.1%	1994:	106.3%
Debt	1993:	$67.4bn	1994:	$64.8bn
Def exp	1993:	TL 77,834bn ($7.09bn)		
	1994:	TL 159,456bn ($5.39bn)		
Def bdgt	1995:	TL 264,198bn ($6.24bn)		
	1996ε:	TL 412,376bn ($7.50bn)		
NATO defn	1993:	TL 77,834bn ($7.09bn)		
	1994:	TL 159,456bn ($5.39bn)		
FMA[a]	1994:	$451.4m (FMF, IMET, Narcs)		
	1995:	$365.9m (FMF, IMET, Narcs)		
	1996:	$451.4m (FMF, IMET, Narcs)		
$1 = TL	1993:	10,985	1994:	29,609
	1995:	42,306		

TL = Turkish lira

[a] Under a 1991 agreement also involving the US, Saudi Arabia,
Kuwait and the UAE, Turkey is to receive $3.5bn over 5 years
for its spt of the Coalition Forces in the Gulf War. The first tranche
of $1.2bn was released in Oct 1994.

Population: 61,284,000 (Kurds 17%)

	13–17	18–22	23–32
Men	3,272,200	3,268,000	5,375,800
Women	3,099,400	3,051,800	5,159,000

TOTAL ARMED FORCES:
ACTIVE: 507,800 (415,200 conscripts).
Terms of service: 18 months.
RESERVES: 378,700 to age 41 (all): Army
258,700; Navy 55,000; Air Force 65,000.

ARMY: 400,000 (352,000 conscripts).
4 army HQ: 9 corps HQ.
1 mech div (1 mech, 1 armd bde).
1 mech div HQ.
1 inf div.
14 armd bde (each 2 armd, 2 mech inf, 2 arty bn).
17 mech bde (each 2 armd, 2 mech inf, 1 arty bn).
9 inf bde (each 4 inf, 1 arty bn).
4 cdo bde (each 4 cdo bn).
1 inf regt.
1 Presidential Guard regt.
5 border def regt.
26 border def bn.
RESERVES:
4 coastal def regt.
23 coastal def bn.
EQPT:
RECCE: some *Akrep*.
AIFV: 135 AIFV.
APC: 3,576: 286 IAPC, 2,815 M-113/-A1/-A2, 475 AWC.
TOTAL ARTY: 4,341:
TOWED ARTY: 1,618: **105mm:** 640 M-101A1;

150mm: 128 Skoda; **155mm:** 517 M-114A1\A2, 171 M-59; **203mm:** 162 M-115.
SP ARTY: 820: **105mm:** 362 M-52A1, 26 M-108; **155mm:** 4 M-44A1, 164 M-44T1; **175mm:** 36 M-107; **203mm:** 9 M-55, 219 M-110A2.
MRL: 60: **107mm:** 48; **227mm:** 12 MLRS.
MOR: 1,843: **107mm:** 1,265 M-30 (some SP); **120mm:** 578; plus **81mm:** 3,792 incl SP.
ATGW: 943: 186 Cobra, 365 TOW SP, 392 Milan.
RL: M-72.
RCL: 57mm: 923 M-18; **75mm:** 617; **106mm:** 2,329 M-40A1.
AD GUNS: 1,664: **20mm:** 439 GAI-DO1; **35mm:** 120 GDF-003; **40mm:** 803 L60/70, 40 T-1, 262 M-42A1.
SAM: 108 *Stinger*, 789 *Redeye*.
SURV: AN/TPQ-36 (arty, mor).
AC: 168: 3 Cessna 421, 34 Citabria, 4 B-200, 4 T-42A, 98 U-17B, 25 T-41D.
ATTACK HEL: 38 AH-1W/P.
SPT HEL: 221: 10 S-70A, 12 AB-204B, 64 AB-205A, 2 AB-212, 28 H-300C, 3 OH-58B, 94 UH-1H, 8 R-22B.
UAV: CL-89 (AN/USD-501), GNAT 750.

NAVY: 51,000 (incl 3,100 Marines and 34,500 conscripts).

BASES: Ankara (Navy HQ and COMEDNOREAST), Gölcük (HQ Fleet), Istanbul (HQ Northern area and Bosphorus), Izmir (HQ Southern area and Aegean), Eregli (HQ Black Sea), Iskenderun, Aksaz Bay, Mersin (HQ Mediterranean).
SS: 16:
6 *Atilay* (Ge Type 209/1200) with SST-4 HWT.
7 *Canakkale/Burakreis*† (plus 2 non-op) (US *Guppy*) with Mk 37 HWT.
2 *Hizirreis* (US *Tang*) with Mk 37 HWT.
1 *Preveze* (Ge Type 209/1400).
PRINCIPAL SURFACE COMBATANTS: 21:
DD: 5:
3 *Yücetepe* (US *Gearing*) (ASW/ASUW) with 2 x 3 ASTT (Mk 46 LWT); 1 with 1 x 8 *ASROC*, 2 with *Harpoon* SSM, all with 2 x 2 127mm guns.
2 *Alcitepe* (US *Carpenter*) with 1 x 8 ASROC, 2 x 3 ASTT, 1 x 2 127mm guns.
FF: 16:
4 *Yavuz* (Ge *MEKO* 200) with 1 x AB-212 hel (ASW/OTHT), 2 x 3 ASTT; plus 2 x 4 *Harpoon* SSM, 1 x 127mm gun.
1 *Gemlik* (Ge T-120 *Köln*) with 4 x 533mm ASTT, 2 x 4 ASW mor; plus 2 x 100mm gun.
2 *Berk* with 2 x 3 ASTT, 2 Mk 11 *Hedgehog*.
8 *Muavenet* (US *Knox*-class) with 1 x 8 ASROC, 4 x ASTT; plus *Harpoon* (from *ASROC* launcher), 1 x 127mm gun.
1 *Barbados* (MOD Ge MEKO 200) with 1 x AB-212 hel.
PATROL AND COASTAL COMBATANTS: 44:
MSL CRAFT: 17:

8 *Dogan* (Ge Lürssen-57) PFM with 2 x 4 *Harpoon* SSM.
8 *Kartal* (Ge *Jaguar*) PFM with 4 x *Penguin* 2 SSM, 2 x 533mm TT.
1 *Yildiz* with 2 x 4 *Harpoon* SSM, 1 x 76mm gun.
PATROL CRAFT: 27:
PATROL, COASTAL: 10:
1 *Girne* PFC, 6 *Sultanhisar* PCC, 3 *Trabzon* PCC.
PATROL, INSHORE: 17:
1 *Bora* (US *Asheville*) PFI, 12 AB-25 PCI, 4 AB-21.
MINE WARFARE: 23:
MINELAYERS: 2:
1 *Nusret* (400 mines).
1 *Mersin* (US LSM) coastal (400 mines).
Note: *Gelibolu* FF, *Bayraktar*, *Sarucabey* and *Çakabey* LST have minelaying capability.
MCM: 21:
11 *Seymen* (US *Adjutant*) MSC.
6 *Karamürsel* (Ge *Vegesack*) MSC.
4 *Foça* (US *Cape*) MSI.
AMPH: 8:
1 *Osman Gazi*: capacity 980 tps, 17 tk, 4 LCVP.
2 *Ertugal* (US *Terrebonne Parish*): capacity 400 tps, 18 tk.
2 *Bayraktar* (US LST-512): capacity 200 tps, 16 tk.
2 *Sarucabey*: capacity 600 tps, 11 tk.
1 *Çakabey*: capacity 400 tps, 9 tk.
Plus about 59 craft: 35 LCT, 2 LCU, 22 LCM.
SPT AND MISC: 27:
1 *Akar* AO, 5 spt tankers, 2 Ge *Rhein* plus 3 other depot ships, 3 salvage/rescue, 2 survey, 3 tpt, 5 tugs, 2 repair, 1 div spt.

NAVAL AVIATION: 9 cbt ac, 14 armed hel.
ASW: 1 sqn with **ac:** 9 S-2A/E/TS-2A *Tracker* (Air Force aircraft, Air Force and Navy crews); **hel:** 3 AB-204AS, 14* AB-212 ASW.

MARINES: (3,100); 1 regt.
HQ, 3 bn, 1 arty bn (18 guns), spt units.

AIR FORCE: 56,800 (28,700 conscripts).
2 tac air forces, 1 tpt, 1 air trg comd, 1 air log comd.
Flying hours: 180.
FGA: 13 sqn:
3 (1 OCU) with F-5A/B.
4 (1 OCU) with F-4E.
6 (1 OCU) with F-16C/D.
FTR: 5 sqn:
2 with F-4E.
3 with F-16C/D.
RECCE: 2 sqn with RF-4E.
ASW: 1 sqn with S-2A/E *Tracker* (see Navy).
TPT: 5 sqn:
1 with C-130B/E.
1 with C-160D.

2 with CN-235.

1 VIP tpt unit with *Gulfstream, Citation* and CN 235.
TKR: 2 KC-135R.
LIAISON: 10 base fleet with **ac:** T-33; **hel:** UH-1H.
TRG: 4 sqn:
1 with T-41; 1 with SF-260D, 1 with T-37; 1 trg
school with **ac:** T-38, CN-235; **hel:** UH-1H.
SAM: 4 sqn with *Nike Hercules*; 2 sqn *Rapier*.
EQPT: 447 cbt ac, no attack hel.
AC: F-16C/D: 146: **-C:** 122; **-D:** 24. **F-5:** 108: **A/B:** 64,
NF-5A/B: 44 (FGA). **F-4E:** 184: 96 FGA, 48 ftr; **RF-4E:**
40 (recce). **S-2A/E *Tracker*:** 9*. **C-130:** 13 (tpt). **KC-
135R:** 2, **C-160D:** 19 (tpt). *Citation*: 2 (VIP): **CN-235:**
22 (tpt). **SF-260D:** 39 (trg). **T-33:** 34 (trg). **T-37:** 62 trg.
T-38: 70 (trg). **T-41:** 28 (trg).
HEL: UH-1H: 21 (tpt, liaison, base flt, trg schools).
SAM: 92 *Nike Hercules*, 24 *Rapier*.

FORCES ABROAD:
CYPRUS: 30,000; 1 corps; 235 M-48A5 MBT; 57
M-113, 50 M-59 APC; 126 105mm, 36 155mm, 8
203mm towed; 18 105mm, 6 155mm SP; 102 107mm
mor; 84 40mm AA guns; 8 ac, 13 hel.
UN AND PEACEKEEPING:
ADRIATIC (*Sharp Guard*): 1 FFG. **BOSNIA** (UN-
PROFOR): 1,469; 1 inf bn gp. **GEORGIA**
(UNOMIG): 5 Obs. **IRAQ/KUWAIT** (UNIKOM): 6
Obs. **ITALY** (*Deny Flight*): 170, 8 F-16 C.

PARAMILITARY:
GENDARMERIE/NATIONAL GUARD
(Ministry of Interior, Ministry of Defence in war):
180,000 active, 50,000 reserve.
EQPT: 302 BTR-60, 141 BTR-80, 34 UR-416, 25
Condor APC; **ac:** 0-1E; **hel:** 36 S-70A, 10 AB-206A.
COAST GUARD: 2,200 (incl 1,400 conscripts),
36 PCI, 16 PCI⟨, plus boats, 2 tpt.

OPPOSITION:
KURDISTAN WORKERS PARTY (PKK):
ε10,000 plus 50,000 spt militia.

FOREIGN FORCES:
NATO: HQ Allied Land Forces South Eastern Eu-
rope (LANDSOUTHEAST).
HQ 6 Allied Tactical Air Force (6 ATAF).
OPERATION PROVIDE COMFORT:
FRANCE: Air (150); 5 *Jaguar*, 1 KC-135.
UK: Air (260); 6 *Tornado*, 2 VC-10 (tkr).
US: 2,900; Army (200). Air (2,700); 1 wing, 2 air
base gp with 18 F-16, 6 F-15C, 3 EF-111, 5 KC-135,
3 E-3B/C, 2 C-12, 2 HC-130 (ac on det only).

UNITED KINGDOM

GDP	1993: £630.8bn ($947.5bn):		
	per capita $17,300		
	1994: £668.1bn ($1,023.3bn):		
	per capita $17,900		
Growth	1993: 2.2%	1994: 3.8%	
Inflation	1993: 1.6%	1994: 2.5%	
Publ debt	1993: 47.4%	1994: 51.6%	
Def exp	1993: £23.42bn ($35.18bn)		
	1994: £22.77bn ($34.88bn)		
Def bdgt	1995: £21.72bn ($34.48bn)		
	1996: £21.92 ($34.80bn)		
NATO defn	1993: £23.34bn ($35.06bn)		
	1994: £22.71bn ($34.79bn)		
$1 = £1	1993: 0.67	1994: 0.65	
	1995: 0.63		

£ = pound sterling

Population: 58,288,000 (Northern Ireland 1,600,000:
Protestant 56%, Roman Catholic 41%).

	13–17	18–22	23–32
Men	1,797,200	1,905,200	4,587,000
Women	1,709,800	1,814,600	4,421,000

TOTAL ARMED FORCES:
ACTIVE: 236,900 (incl 16,500 women and some
5,200 enlisted outside the UK).
RESERVES: Army: 260,300: Regular 195,300;
Territorial Army (TA) 59,700; Royal Irish Regt (Home
Service) 5,300 (3,050 full time); Navy/Marines: 25,800:
Regular Reserve 22,100, Volunteers and Auxiliary forces
3,700. Air Force: 46,800: Regular 45,500; Volunteers
and Auxiliary Forces 1,300.

STRATEGIC FORCES: (1,900).
SLBM: 48 msl in 3 SSBN:
2 *Resolution* SSBN each with 16 *Polaris* A-3TK SLBM.
1 *Vanguard* SSBN with 16 *Trident* (D5) will not deploy
with more than 96 warheads (plus 1 *Vanguard* SSBN
undergoing fleet trials; op date early 1996).
EARLY WARNING:
Ballistic-Missile Early-Warning System (BMEWS)
station at Fylingdales.

ARMY: 116,000 (incl 6,600 women and 4,450 enlisted
outside the UK, of whom some 4,400 are Gurkhas).
(Note: regt are normally of bn size.)
1 Land Comd HQ.
3 Military Districts, 3 (regenerative) div HQ (former
mil districts), 1 UK Spt Comd Germany (UKSCG).
1 armd div with 3 armd bde, 3 arty, 4 engr, 1 avn, 1 AD regt.

1 div with 2 mech (*Warrior/Saxon*), 1 AB bde, 3 arty, 2 engr, 1 avn, 1 AD regt.

UKSCG tps: 2 armd recce, 3 MLRS, 2 AD, 1 engr regt (EOD).

1 air-mobile bde.

13 inf bde HQ (3 control ops in N. Ireland, remainder mixed regular and TA for trg/administrative purposes only).

Summary of combat arm units:

9 armd regt (incl 1 trg regt).

2 armd recce regt.

4 mech inf bn (*Saxon*).

8 armd inf bn (*Warrior*).

26 inf bn (incl 3 Gurkha).

3 AB bn (2 only in para role).

1 SF (SAS) regt.

12 arty regt (3 MLRS, 5 SP, 3 fd (1 cdo, 1 AB, 1 air-mobile), 1 trg).

4 AD regt (2 *Rapier*, 2 *Javelin*).

10 engr regt (incl 1 Gurkha, 1 amph, 5 armd).

5 avn regt (2 atk, 2 air mobile, 1 general).

6 Home Service inf bn (N. Ireland only, some part-time).

RESERVES:

Territorial Army: 1 armd recce, 4 lt recce regt, 36 inf bn, 2 SF (SAS), 3 fd, 3 AD, 9 engr, 1 avn regt; Hong Kong Regiment; Gibraltar Regiment.

EQPT:

MBT: ε20 *Challenger* 2, 426 *Challenger*, 60 *Chieftain* (plus 412 in store).

LT TK: 13 *Scorpion* (plus 194 in store).

RECCE: some 314 *Scimitar*, 11 *Fuchs*.

AIFV: some 786 *Warrior* (incl 'look-alikes'), 11 AFV 432 *Rarden*.

APC: 3,101: 1,709 AFV 432 (incl 'look-alikes'), 628 FV 103 *Spartan*, 664 *Saxon*, 54 *Saracen*, 46 *Humber* (in store).

TOTAL ARTY: 568:

TOWED ARTY: 286: **105mm:** 210 L-118; **140mm:** 5 5.5-in; **155mm:** 71 FH-70.

SP ARTY: 218: **155mm:** 39 M-109A1, 179 AS-90 (plus 16 **105mm** *Abbot* in store).

MRL: 227mm: 64 MLRS.

MOR: 81mm: 543 (incl 110 SP).

ATGW: 811 *Milan* (incl 72 FV 103 *Spartan* SP), 58 *Swingfire* (FV 102 *Striker* SP), *TOW*.

RCL: 84mm: *Carl Gustav*.

SAM: 70 *Starstreak*, some 382 *Javelin* and *Starburst*; 74 *Rapier* (some 24 SP).

SURV: 43 *Cymbeline* (mor).

AC: 6 BN-2, 21 *Chipmunk* trg.

ATTACK HEL: 69 *Scout*, 169 SA-341, 126 *Lynx* AH-1/-7/-9.

UAV: CL-89 (AN/USD-501).

LANDING CRAFT: 2 *Ardennes*, 9 *Arromanches* log; 4 *Avon*, LCVP; 3 tugs, 28 other service vessels.

NAVY (RN): 50,500 (inclε7,100 Fleet Air Arm, 7,300

Marines, 3,800 women and 275 enlisted outside the UK).

ROYAL FLEET AUXILIARY (RFA): (2,100 civilians) mans major spt vessels.

ROYAL MARITIME AUXILIARY SERVICE (RMAS): (400 civilians) provides harbour/coastal services.

RESERVES: Navy/Marines: 25,800: Regular Reserve, 22,100, Volunteer and Auxiliary Forces, 3,700.

BASES: UK: Northwood (HQ Fleet, CINCEASTLANT), Devonport (HQ), Faslane, Portland, Portsmouth, Rosyth (HQ). Overseas: Gibraltar, Hong Kong.

SUBMARINES: 16:

STRATEGIC SUBMARINES: 3 SSBN (see p. 64).

TAC SUBMARINES: 12:

SSN: 12:

7 *Trafalgar*, 5 *Swiftsure* with *Spearfish* or Mk 24 HWT and *Harpoon* USGW.

PRINCIPAL SURFACE COMBATANTS: 38:

CARRIERS: 3 *Invincible* CVV each with **ac:** 8 *Sea Harrier* V/STOL; **hel:** 12 *Sea King*: up to 9 ASW, 3 AEW; plus 1 x 2 *Sea Dart* SAM (includes 1 *Invincible* at extended readiness).

DDG: 12 *Birmingham* with 1 x 2 *Sea Dart* SAM; plus 1 *Lynx* hel, 2 x 3 ASTT, 1 x 114mm gun (3 in refit).

FF: 23 (incl 1 in refit):

4 *Cornwall* (Type 22 Batch 3) with 1 *Sea King* or 2 *Lynx* hel (*Sting Ray* LWT), 2 x 3 ASTT; plus 2 x 4 *Harpoon* SSM, 1 x 114mm gun.

9 *Broadsword* (Type 22 Batch 1/2) with 2 *Lynx* hel (2 with 1 x *Sea King*), 2 x 3 ASTT; plus 4 x MM-38 *Exocet* SSM (4 Batch 1 trg).

10 *Norfolk* (Type 23) with 1 x *Lynx* hel, 2 x 2 ASTT, plus 2 x 4 *Harpoon* SSM, 1 x 114mm gun.

PATROL AND COASTAL COMBATANTS: 33:

PATROL, OFFSHORE: 17 PCO:

1 *Endurance*, 2 *Castle*, 6 *Island*, 3 *Peacock*, 5 *River*.

PATROL, INSHORE: 16 PCI:

2 *Kingfisher*, 12 *Archer* (incl 4 trg), 2 *Ranger*.

MINE WARFARE: 19:

MINELAYER: no dedicated minelayer, but all submarines have limited minelaying capability.

MCM: 19:

14 *Hunt* MCO.

5 *Sandown* MHC.

AMPH: 7:

2 *Fearless* LPD (incl 1 in extended readiness) with 4 LCU, 4 LCVP; capacity 400 tps, 15 tk, 3 hel.

1 *Sir Galahad*, 4 *Sir Lancelot* LST: capacity 340 tps, 16 tk (*Sir G.* 18), 1 hel (RFA manned).

Plus 32 craft: 15 LCU, 17 LCVP.

Note: see Army for additional amph lift capability.

SPT AND MISC: 28:

UNDER WAY SPT: 10:

2 *Fort Victoria* AOE.

2 *Olwen*, 3 *Green Rover* AO, 2 *Fort Grange* AF, 1 *Rescource* AO.

Rescource AO.
MAINT AND LOG: 10:
1 AR, 4 AO, 2 AE, 3 AT.
SPECIAL PURPOSE: 3:
1 Royal Yacht, 1 *Endurance*, 1 avn trg ship.
SURVEY: 5:
2 *Bulldog*, 1 *Roebuck* 1 *Herald*, 1 *Gleaner*.

FLEET AIR ARM: (7,150 (450 women)).
A typical CVS air group consists of 8 *Harrier*, 9 *Sea King* (ASW), 3 *Sea King* (AEW). Flying hours for *Sea Harrier* pilots: 180.
FTR/ATK: 3 ac sqn with *Sea Harrier* FRS-1/ F/A2 plus 1 trg sqn with *Harrier* T-4.
ASW: 5 hel sqn with *Sea King* HAS-5/6.
ASW/ATK: 2 sqn with *Lynx* HAS-3 HMA8 (in indep fleets).
AEW: 1 hel sqn with *Sea King* AEW-2.
COMMANDO SPT: 3 hel sqn with *Sea King* HC-4.
SAR: 1 hel sqn with *Sea King* MK-4.
1 hel sqn with *Sea King* MK-5.
TRG: 2 sqn: 1 **ac** with *Jetstream*; 1 **hel** with SA-341 *Gazelle* HT-2.
FLEET SPT: *Hawk*, *Mystère-Falcon* 20 (civil registration), 1 Cessna *Conquest* (civil registration), 1 Beech *Baron* (civil registration) (op under contract).
TPT: *Jetstream*.
EQPT: 22 cbt ac, 110 armed hel.
AC: *Sea Harrier: FRS-1/F-A2:* 18 plus 15 in store. **T-4N:** 4* (trg) plus 4 in store. **Hawk:** 12 (spt) (plus 3 in store). ***Mystère-Falcon* 20:** 13 (spt). **Jetstream:** 17: **T-2:** 12 (trg) (plus 2 in store); **T-3:** 3 (trg).
HEL: *Sea King:* 98. **HAS-6:** *60, plus 10 in store; **HC-4:** 29, plus 7 in store (cdo); **AEW-2:** 9, plus 1 in store. ***Lynx* HAS-3:** *50, plus 26 in store. ***Gazelle* HT-2/-3:** 20 (trg plus 4 in store).
MSL:
ASM: *Sea Skua, Sea Eagle*.
AAM: AIM-9 *Sidewinder*.

MARINES: (7,300).
1 cdo bde: 3 cdo; 1 cdo arty regt (Army) + 1 bty (TA); 2 cdo engr sqn (1 Army, 1 TA), 1 log regt (joint service); 1 lt hel sqn.
1 mtn and arctic warfare cadre.
Special Boat Service (SF): HQ: 5 sqn.
2 aslt sqn.
1 gp (*Commachio*).
EQPT:
MOR: 81mm.
ATGW: *Milan*.
SAM: *Javelin, Blowpipe*.
HEL: 9 SA-341 (*Gazelle*); plus 3 in store, 6 *Lynx* AH-1.
AMPH: 16 RRC, 2 LCU, 4 LCVP, 4 LACV.

AIR FORCE (RAF): 70,400 (incl 6,100 women).

Flying hours: 220.
FGA/BBR: 6 (nuclear-capable) sqn:
4 with *Tornado* GR-1.
2 with *Tornado* GR-1B (maritime attack).
FGA: 5 sqn:
3 with *Harrier*; GR-7.
2 with *Jaguar*.
FTR: 6 sqn, plus 1 flt:
6 with *Tornado* F-3 (1 flt in the Falklands).
RECCE: 2 sqn with *Tornado* GR-1A; 1 sqn photo-recce unit with *Canberra* PR-9; 1 sqn with *Jaguar*.
MR: 3 sqn with *Nimrod* MR-2.
AEW: 1 sqn with *Sentry* E-3D.
ELINT: 1 ELINT with *Nimrod* R-1.
TKR: 2 sqn:
1 with VC-10 K-2/-3/-4.
1 with *Tristar* K-1/KC-1/-2 (tkr/tpt).
TPT: 5 sqn:
1 strategic with VC-10 C-1/C-1K.
4 tac with *Hercules* C-1/-1K/-1P/-3P.
LIAISON: 1 comms VIP sqn with **ac:** HS-125, BAe 146; **hel:** Wessex, SA-341 (*Gazelle*).
CALIBRATION: 2 sqn:
1 with *Andover* E-3; 1 target facility with *Hawk*.
OCU: 7: *Tornado* GR-1, *Tornado* F-3, *Jaguar* GR-1A/T2A, *Harrier* GR-7/-T10, *Hercules*, SA-330/CH-47. 1 wpn conversion unit with *Tornado* GR-1.
TRG: *Hawk* T-1/-1A/-1W, *Jetstream* T-1, *Bulldog* T-1, *Chipmunk* T-10, HS-125 *Dominie* T-1, *Tucano* T-1.
TAC HEL: 7 sqn:
1 with CH-47.
1 with CH-47 and SA-330 (*Puma*).
2 with *Wessex* HC-2.
2 with SA-330 (*Puma*).
1 with CH-47 and *Sea King* HAR3.
SAR: 2 hel sqn; 6 flt:
1 with *Wessex* HC-2, 5 with *Sea King* HAR-3.
TRG: *Wessex*, SA-341 *Sea King*.
EQPT: 559 cbt ac, incl 26 MR (plus 58 in store), no armed hel.
AC: *Tornado:* 315: **GR-1:** 115; **GR-1A:** 26; **GR-1B:** 26; **F-3:** 148; plus 21 GR-1 in store. **Jaguar:** 69: **GR-1A/-B:** 54; **T-2A/B:** 15 (plus 16 in store). **Harrier:** 93: **GR-7:** 70; **GR-3:** 2, **GR-5:** 6, **T-4:** 9, **T-10:** 6 (plus 11 **GR-7** in store). **Hawk: T-1/1-A-W:** 106 (*56 (T1-A) tac weapons unit *Sidewinder*-capable), 50 trg. **Canberra:** 9: **T-4:** 2, **PR-7:** 2, **PR-9:** 5. **Nimrod:** 28: **R-1:** 2 (ECM); **MR-2:** 26* (MR); plus 4 in store. **Sentry (E-3D):** 7 (AEW). **Tristar:** 9: **K-1:** 2 (tkr/tpt); **KC-1:** 4 (tkr/cgo); **C-2:** 3 (tpt). **VC-10:** 25: **C-1/C-1K:** 13 (strategic tpt to be mod to tkr/tpt); **K-2:** 5 (tkr); **K-3:** 4 (tkr); **K-4:** 3. **Hercules:** 61: **C-1:** 26; **C-1K:** 5 (tkr); **C-3:** 29; **W-2:** 1. **Andover:** 4. **HS-125:** 27: **T-1:** 19 (trg); **CC-2/-3:** 8 (liaison). **Islander CC-MK2:** 2. **BAe-146:** 3 (VIP tpt). **Tucano:** 82 (trg), plus 47 in store. **Jetstream:** 11 (trg). **Bulldog:** 115 (trg). **Chipmunk:** 56 (trg).
HEL: Wessex: 59. **CH-47:** 31. **SA-330:** 42. **Sea King:** 19. **SA-341** (*Gazelle*): 29.

ASM: *Martel*, AGM-84D-1 *Harpoon*, *Sea Eagle*.
AAM: AIM-9G *Sidewinder*, *Sky Flash*.
ARM: ALARM.

ROYAL AIR FORCE REGIMENT:

3 fd sqn (with 81mm mortars), 5 SAM sqn with 52 *Rapier*.
RESERVES (Royal Auxiliary Air Force Regiment): 5 fd def sqn.

DEPLOYMENT:
ARMY:
Land Command.
Reinforcements for ARRC (declared to LANDCENT).
Active: 1 div, 1 air-mobile bde.
Additional TA units incl 8 inf bn, 2 SAS, 3 AD regt.
Allied Command Europe Mobile Force (*Land*)
   (AMF(L)): UK contribution: 1 inf bn, 1 arty bty, 1 sigs sqn.
HQ Northern Ireland (some 10,500, plus 5,300 Home Service); 3 inf bde HQ, up to 12 major units in inf role (6 resident, 4 roulement inf bn), 1 engr, 1 avn regt, 6 Home Service inf bn.
Remainder of Army regular and TA units for Home Defence.
NAVY:
FLEET (CinC is also CINCEASTLANT and COMNAVNORTHWEST): Regular Forces, with the exception of most Patrol and Coastal Combatants, Mine Warfare and Support Forces, are declared to EASTLANT.
MARINES: 1 cdo bde (declared to SACLANT).
AIR FORCE:
STRIKE COMD: commands all combat air operations other than for Cyprus, Falklands and Hong Kong: 5 Groups: No. 1 (Strike, Attack), No. 2 (Strike, Attack; based in Germany), No. 11 (Air Defence), No. 18 (Maritime), No. 38 (Transport/AAR).
LOG COMD: supply and maint spt of other comds.
PERSONNEL AND TRG COMD: flying and ground trg.

FORCES ABROAD:
ANTARCTICA: 1 ice patrol ship (in seasonal summer).
ASCENSION ISLAND: RAF some 100.
BRUNEI: Army: some 900; 1 Gurkha inf bn, 1 hel flt (3 hel).
CANADA: Army: trg and liaison unit; RAF: 100; routine training deployment of *Tornado* GR1, *Harrier*, *Jaguar*.
CYPRUS: 3,800.
Army: 2,400; 2 inf bn, 1 engr spt sqn, 1 hel flt.
RAF: 1,400; 1 hel sqn (*Wessex*), routine trg deployment of *Tornado* ac, 1 sqn RAF regt field sqn.
FALKLAND ISLANDS: 2,000. Army: 1 inf coy gp, 1 engr sqn (fd, plant); RN: 1 DD/FF, 1 PCO, 1 AO, 1 AR; RAF: 100. 1 *Tornado* F-3 flt, 2 *Hercules* C-1K, 2 *Sea King* HAR-3, 2 CH-47 hel, 1 sqn RAF regt (*Rapier* SAM).
GERMANY: 28,600: Army: 23,600: 1 corps HQ (multinational), 1 armd div, 2 armd recce, 3 MLRS, 2

AD, 1 engr regt (declared to LANDCENT); RAF (No. 2 GP RAF): 5,000; 6 ac sqn, 4 *Tornado*, 2 *Harrier*, 1 hel sqn (SA-330 (*Puma*)//CH-47 (*Chinook*) tpt), RAF regt; 2 *Rapier* SAM sqn, 1 fd sqn (declared to AIRCENT).
GIBRALTAR: 600: Army: 50; Gibraltar regt (400); Navy/Marines: 400; 2 PCI, Marine det, 2 twin *Exocet* launchers (coastal defence), base unit; RAF: 150; periodic ac det.
HONG KONG: some 900. Army: 500; 1 Gurkha inf bn, 1 Gurkha engr sqn, 3 small landing craft, 3 other vessels; Navy/Marines: 180 (plus 240 locally enlisted); 3 *Peacock* PCC (12 patrol boats in local service); RAF: 200; 1 *Wessex* hel sqn (with 4 *Wessex* HC2). Reserves: Hong Kong regt (1,200).
INDIAN OCEAN (*Armilla Patrol*): 2 DD/FF, 1 spt ship.
Diego Garcia: 1 naval party, 1 Marine det.
NEPAL: Army: 1,200 (Gurkha trg org).
WEST INDIES (see also Belize): 1 DD/FF, 1 AO.
MILITARY ADVISERS: 455 in 30 countries.

UN AND PEACEKEEPING:
ADRIATIC (*Sharp Guard*): 1 DDG, 1 FFG (resubordinated from STANAVFORMED and STANAVFORLANT. Also available for WEU tasking). 3–4 spt ships; UK task group Adriatic: 1 CVV (6 Harriers for spt to *Deny Flight*, 7 ASW *Sea Kings* for spt to *Sharp Guard*), 1 DD/FF, 1 AO, 1 AR. RAF: 60: 2 *Nimrod* ac. **ANGOLA** (UNAVEM III): 649: 1 log bn. **BOSNIA** (UNPROFOR): 4,440; elm 1 air-mobile bde plus 1 armd inf, 1 mech inf bn gp, 1 engr regt, 2 armd recce sqn, 1 log bn gp, 2 arty bty, 1 arty loc bty, 1 armd engr sqn, 13 Obs; 4 Royal Naval *Sea King* H-C4 hel. **CROATIA** (UNCRO): 6 Obs. **CYPRUS** (UNFICYP): 364; 1 inf bn(-), 1 hel flt, engr spt (incl spt for UNIFIL). **FORMER YUGOSLAVIA** (*Provide Promise*): RAF: 20; 1 C-130 ac. **GEORGIA** (UNOMIG): 10 Obs. **IRAQ/KUWAIT** (UNIKOM): 15 Obs. **ITALY** (*Deny Flight*): 540; 6 *Tornado* F3, 2 K-1 *Tristar* (tkr), 2 E-3D *Sentry*; 8 *Harrier* GR-7, 6 *Sea Harrier*. **RWANDA** (UNAMIR): 1. **SAUDI ARABIA** (*Southern Watch*): 310; 6 *Tornado* GR-1A, 1 VC-10 (tkr). **TURKEY** (*Provide Comfort*): RAF: 7330; 6 *Tornado*, 1 VC-10 tkr.

FOREIGN FORCES:
US: 11,500: Navy (2,000); Air (9,500): 1 Air Force HQ, 66 cbt ac, 2 sqn with 48 F-15E, 1 sqn with 18 F-15C/D. 1 Special Ops Gp, 3 sqn with 5 MH-53J, 4 HC-130, 4 MC-130H, 1 air refuelling wg with 9 KC-135.
GERMANY/ITALY: tri-national *Tornado* trg sqn.
NATO: HQ Allied Forces North-west Europe (AFNORTHWEST).
HQ Allied Naval Forces North-west Europe (NAV NORTHWEST).
HQ Allied Air Forces North-west Europe (AIR NORTH WEST).
HQ Eastern Atlantic Area (EASTLANT).

Non-NATO Europe

Most international attention has focused on the conflict in the former Yugoslavia which intensified during the year and risked further expansion following Croatia's successful recovery of Krajina in August 1995. However, there was some improvement in the situation in the Caucasus and useful negotiations took place between Russia and the Baltic states to stabilise the situation there.

Transcaucasus

The cease-fire agreed to in May 1994 has held firm, but Armenia and Azerbaijan are no closer to a political settlement nor have they authorised the deployment of the peacekeeping force being set up by the Organisation for Security and Cooperation in Europe (OSCE). Plans for deploying the force to Nagorno-Karabakh are well advanced and a number of reconnaissance visits have taken place. Both sides have exchanged all prisoners of war. Details of the planned OSCE mission are given at page 306.

The Baltic States

Russian forces have now completed their withdrawal from the Baltic states with the exception of the technicians manning the early-warning radar station at Skrunda, Latvia, due to close in 2000. The new radar station there was demolished on 4 May 1995. Lithuania and Russia have reached a new agreement over Russian transit rights to Kaliningrad, and Estonia and Russia have settled the issue of paying social guarantees to the 10,000 Russian pensioners there.

Moldova

In October 1994, the withdrawal by October 1997 of the Russian 14th Army was agreed. The disposal of very large quantities of obsolete ammunition located in Dniestr remains a major problem and environmental groups are opposing any destruction bar a small amount each day.

Former Yugoslavia

UN Forces

UNSC Resolutions 981–983 were adopted on 31 March 1995 which, in addition to extending the UN force mandate in the former Yugoslavia to 30 November 1995, altered the name of the force in Croatia to the United Nations Confidence Restoration Operation in Croatia (UNCRO) and the force in the former Yugoslav republic of Macedonia (FYROM) to the United Nations Preventive Deployment Force (UNPREDEP). All three forces will continue to be controlled from the United Nations Peace Force Headquarters (UNPF HQ) in Zagreb.

Croatia

On 2 December 1994, Croatia and the Krajina Serbs agreed on a number of economic issues, including the Serb commitment to open the stretches of the Zagreb–Belgrade motorway that run through Serb-controlled territory. On 1 May 1995, Croatia successfully attacked western Slavonia and recovered UN Sector West, taken by the Serbs in 1991. On 22 July, Presidents Alija Izetbegovic of Bosnia-Herzegovina and Franjo Tudjman of Croatia signed an agreement on cooperation, including in the military sphere. Within a week Croatian troops had begun an offensive from the Bosnian town of Livno and quickly took the towns of Glamoc on the Split–Banja Luka road and Bosanska Grahovo on the road leading to Bihac which controls the main route from Knin to Serb-held areas in northern Bosnia and on to Serbia. Krajina Serb and Croatian government representatives met UN negotiator Thorvald Stoltenberg in Geneva on 3 August. Early on 4 August the Croats mounted a major offensive on Krajina preceded by heavy shelling of Knin, which resulted in the recapture of the territory and the movement of at least 150,000 Serbian refugees into Bosnia and Serbia.

Bosnia-Herzegovina

In July 1994, the five-member Contact Group presented a new set of peace proposals and a map showing the local control that would be granted to each faction. This allotted 51% of territory to the Bosnian–Croat Federation and 49% to the Bosnian Serbs. The plan and the map were presented on a 'take it or leave it' basis. The Bosnian government accepted, but the Bosnian Serbs did not, despite provisions for the Serbs to secede, following a referendum, after two years.

In late October 1994, the Bosnian Army Corps based in Bihac launched an offensive which caught the Serbs by surprise and led to the capture of some 60 square miles south and east of Bihac. At the same time, a joint Bosnian–Bosnian Croat attack was launched, recapturing the town of Kupres, originally mainly Croat-inhabited. The Serbs did not wait long before reacting to this loss and by mid-November had recovered virtually all lost territory and, aided by the Krajina Serbs, were threatening the Bihac safe area. On 18 and 19 November aircraft from the Ubdina airfield in Krajina attacked Bihac. The UN Security Council authorised air attacks against targets in Krajina and NATO attacked Udbina on 21 November. The next day NATO aircraft were attacked by Serbian surface-to-air missiles which were, in their turn, attacked on 23 November. Since then NATO has declined to mount air strikes or air drops of supplies to Bihac unless they are permitted to take out Serb air defences beforehand. So far the UN has withheld this permission. After these attacks, the Serbs held UN troops hostage at weapons-monitoring sites until mid-December.

On 18 December, former US President Jimmy Carter visited Sarajevo and Pale and brokered a cease-fire which came into effect for four months on 24 December. The UN appealed for 6,500 more troops to assist in monitoring the cease-fire, but few were contributed.

Throughout the past 12 months, aid convoys have been routinely obstructed and those crossing the Mount Igman track into Sarajevo have been fired upon. In addition, Sarajevo airport has been closed to aid flights since 8 April 1995. The question of whether to lift the arms embargo has been on the political agenda in Washington throughout this period. In November 1994, the US Congress ordered that funds for the US contribution to maintain the arms embargo against Bosnia be cut off. However, US naval ships still take part in *Operation Sharp Guard*, but only to enforce the arms embargo on the other republics of the former Yugoslavia and to enforce the economic blockade of Serbia and Montenegro. On 26 July, with a majority of 62 to 29, the US Senate passed a bill, presented by Senator Bob Dole, for the US to end the arms embargo against Bosnia. However, the bill stipulated that Bosnia-Herzegovina must request both the end of the embargo and the withdrawal of UN troops from Bosnia, and that the UN must decide to withdraw before the embargo was terminated. On 1 August, the US House of Representatives passed a similar bill by 298 votes to 128. President Bill Clinton has vetoed the bill despite its more than two-thirds majority, which would allow the veto to be overridden if none of the votes are changed. Serious consideration has been given to a UN withdrawal for some time and a NATO plan has been developed and approved to provide military support should the withdrawal be obstructed by force. The US is committed to providing up to 25,000 troops for such an operation.

On 24 May, the UN Protection Force (UNPROFOR) Commander, General Rupert Smith, issued an ultimatum to the Bosnian Serbs to return all heavy weapons removed from UN-monitored sites by noon on 25 May or face air-strikes. The Serbs failed to comply with the ultimatum and NATO aircraft attacked an ammunition dump close to Pale on 25 and 26 May. The Serbs reacted by taking over 300 UN troops hostage and used some as 'human shields' at likely targets for further air attack. This massive hostage taking led France and the UK to announce that they would immediately send reinforcements to render UNPROFOR less vulnerable. Perhaps unwisely, the force was called the Rapid Reaction Force. The British first sent two batteries of light artillery and a squadron of armoured engineers. The rest of the reinforcements took longer to arrive as, first, the UN Security Council had to authorise the increase in forces and, second, the British, who were sending large numbers of helicopters, needed to arrange to lease and prepare ground for a helicopter base from the Croatian government. On 6 July 1995, while the Rapid Reaction Force was still assembling, the Serbs launched an attack on the most exposed of the UN 'safe areas', Srebrenica, and captured the town on 11 July. Virtually straight after this, another safe area, Zepa, came under attack and although much smaller than Srebrenica managed to hold out until 22 July. On 21 July, the second London Conference was held. It had been preceded by several days of talks between officials and two meetings of the French, British and US Chiefs of Staff. The Conference concentrated on the remaining eastern Bosnian enclave, Gorazde, and decided that any Serb move to attack this would be met by the immediate and substantial use of air-power. On 23 July, a group of senior generals from France, the UK and the US delivered an ultimatum to General Ratko Mladic, the Bosnian-Serb commander, at Belgrade airport.

On 23 July, Serbian artillery attacked a UN convoy on Mount Igman and a UN barracks in Sarajevo, killing a French soldier on each occasion. Elements of the Rapid Reaction Force, including the British artillery, were despatched to Mount Igman where they took up positions, not to protect Sarajevo, but to return any fire directed at the UN or its convoys.

Serbia

Considerable political faith has been placed in Serbian President Slobodan Milosevic's ability to pressurise the Bosnian Serbs into more reasonable behaviour. Some consider this faith misplaced. Despite many meetings with the Contact Group and with the UN and European Union (EU) negotiators Thorvald Stoltenberg and Carl Bildt. Milosevic has, so far, failed to recognise either the state of Bosnia-Herzegovina or Croatia.

Nuclear Developments

In **Ukraine**, the Verkhovna Rada adopted the law on its accession to the Nuclear Non-Proliferation Treaty (NPT) in November 1994. On 5 December at Budapest, after receiving formal assurances from Russia, the UK and the US, President Leonid Kuchma signed the instruments of ratification, and the Strategic Arms Reduction Talks (START) Treaty came into force.

The process of removing nuclear weapons from Belarus and Ukraine, begun in early 1994, has continued. All SS-25 road-mobile ICBM in **Belarus** were scheduled to have been transferred to Russia by 25 July 1995, but on 6 July, when 18 SS-25 still remained, Belarus President Aleksandr Lukashenka was said to have halted the process on the grounds that it was unnecessary as the two states might shortly be unified. It now emerges that Lukashenka was misquoted; there is no Belarussian intention to retain nuclear weapons. The original date for the completion of SS-25 withdrawal was Autumn 1996 but this was brought forward by the Russians. **Ukraine** has returned over 400 nuclear warheads to Russia, but, by 13 July, had not received all of the fuel for its nuclear power stations that had been agreed at the Moscow summit in January 1994. This problem has now been settled. Forty SS-19 ICBM have been eliminated. Russia is negotiating to buy the 19 Tu-160 *Blackjack* and 25 Tu-95 *Bear* H strategic bombers held by Ukraine.

Conventional Force Developments

Baltic States

In **Estonia,** armed-forces manpower has increased by 1,000 to 3,500. A Navy, separate from the Maritime Border Guard, has been formed and its craft split between the two. The Navy has up to eight patrol craft with up to six *Osa*-class PFM acquired in the last 12 months, two mine countermeasures ships and three support ships. The **Latvian** Army has been supplied by the Czech Republic with towed artillery and air-defence guns. **Lithuania** is forming a navy modelled on the US Coast Guard and has acquired three *Osa*-class PFM, one Swedish *Victoria*-class and one SK 21 PCI. The Baltic states are cooperating in the peacekeeping field.

Transcaucasus

The **Armenian** Army has formed seven more independent motor rifle regiments, one with a training role. It has also formed a *Spetsnaz* (SF) regiment and four surface-to-air missile units.

Equipment holdings are virtually unchanged. Fresh information has allowed a revision of the armed forces in **Azerbaijan**. Manpower is now some 21,000 stronger than previously listed, all in the army. Two more motor rifle brigades have been formed. Equipment increases (over previous assessments) include 50 tanks, 130 infantry fighting vehicles and 12 Mi-24 attack helicopters. Most artillery types show a small decrease, presumably from battle casualties, but the overall total is maintained by the addition of 32 more 120mm PM-38 mortars. Information is now available on the ships acquired from the Black Sea Fleet by Georgia. They include two *Grisha*-class frigates, one *Turya* torpedo craft and 12 patrol craft (9 *Stenka* PFC, 3 *Muravey* PHT).

Belarus and Ukraine

In **Belarus**, army manpower strength has been reduced by 7,500, whilst that of the Air Force has increased by 1,200. There are now 9,000 men and 3,500 women serving on contract engagements. In February 1995, President Aleksandr Lukashenka suspended the elimination of Conventional Forces in Europe (CFE) Treaty limited equipment on the grounds that Belarus could not afford the economic cost. Nevertheless some 760 tanks, 350 infantry fighting vehicles and about 50 aircraft have been eliminated in the last 12 months.

In **Ukraine** the overall strength of the armed forces has dropped by some 65,000. Ground-force manpower is some 96,000 fewer while the Air Force has 5,000 more men and centrally controlled staffs and units 24,000 more. The bulk of the attack helicopter force has been resubordinated to the Army from the Air Force and most army corps have an attack helicopter regiment under their command. Army corps also have a surface-to-surface missile brigade. Weapons holdings have also been reduced significantly as CFE treaty limited equipment is eliminated, including 600 tanks (T-54, T-55) and 400 APCs (BTR-60, BTR-70). The Air Force has disbanded one bomber division and only keeps 26 Tu-22M in squadron service, and six fighter regiments have been disbanded. Agreement has finally been reached on the division of the Black Sea Fleet. Although the Fleet's assets were to be divided equally, Ukraine is selling some 63% of its share of the Fleet's ships to Russia. The Ukrainian Navy has commissioned a *Krivak* III-class frigate.

Former Warsaw Pact Countries

The Military Balance 1994–1995 incorrectly stated the organisation of the Bulgarian Army in respect of one military district/army. Instead of only having one tank brigade, it also commands a motor rifle division and a regional training centre. Nearly 200 T-34 tanks, over 50 Su-100 assault guns, and 135 elderly artillery pieces had been eliminated by 1 January 1995. The Air Force has also eliminated 20 MiG-21 fighters.

The **Czech** Army is being reorganised on a brigade basis. The two Corps HQ remain, but the five divisions have been disbanded. They and the independent mechanised brigade have been replaced by six strong mechanised brigades and a seventh brigade is planned. The war establishment of each brigade is planned to be four mechanised battalions (with both tanks and AIFVs), two artillery, one anti-tank, one air-defence, one reconnaissance and one engineer battalion. Two brigades are fully formed but two of their battalions have a training role. Two other brigades are kept on a mobilisation only basis. Tank numbers have been reduced by over 400, and artillery by over 500, but the number of AIFVs has increased, mainly because the BPzV was shown as a reconnaissance vehicle and not as an AIFV last year. Manpower has been reduced by about 23,000.

The **Hungarian** Defence Minister announced in May 1995 that all *Scud* SSM taken out of service in 1991 would be destroyed. Twenty-four MiG-21 fighters have been withdrawn from squadron service and ten have been destroyed. The length of conscript service is to be reduced from 12 to nine months from February 1996. It is likely that the present four military districts will be reduced to two, one covering each side of the Danube. Russia is expected to repay its debt to Hungary by supplying more modern armoured combat vehicles, possibly the 203mm *Smersh* MRL and spares for the Air Force's MiG-29 aircraft. **Poland** is planning to introduce the PT-91 main battle tank, and 55 should be in service during 1995. The Air Force has disposed of 34 aircraft and holdings are now within the CFE limit. Production of W-3W *Sokol* attack helicopter continues, with five added to the inventory by 1 January 1995; the production rate is one per month. **Romanian** armed forces manpower has been reduced by some 8,000. 550 tanks (mainly T-34), 350 other armoured vehicles (including 90 Su-76 assault guns) and nearly 800 artillery pieces were eliminated during the last 12 months. But this still leaves 460 tanks and 860 pieces of artillery to be destroyed by mid-November under the CFE Treaty. Romania is to build 96 AH-1F *Cobra* attack helicopters under licence for delivery starting in 1999. **Slovakia** is to form a 12,000-strong national guard, organised in two brigades and five regiments. The National Guard is to be the equivalent of territorial defence troops, it will be manned by reservists. During the last 12 months Slovakia has eliminated 270 tanks, 300 armoured combat vehicles and 180 pieces of artillery. The active forces have been reorganised into two ground force corps and one air force and air-defence corps.

Neutral and Non-Aligned States

The **Austrian** armed forces have changed the terms of their conscript service. Conscripts now carry out seven (as opposed to six) months recruit training followed by 30 (formerly 60) days of reservist refresher training spread over ten (formerly 15) years. The Army has retired its 24 155mm M-114 guns and added 60 more RBS-56 *Bill* ATGW and 48 more 105mm SP *Kuerassier* anti-tank guns. Fresh information shows the armament of the ground air-defence troops as 80 *Mistral* SAM launchers, 120 20mm and 74 35mm twin anti-aircraft guns with *Skyguard* radar. The **Cypriot** Army took part in the annual student's parade marking Greece's independence day on 25 March 1995 and displayed a wide range of weapons including newly delivered *Exocet* coastal defence missiles, *Aspide* (12 launchers delivered) and *Mistral* (12 more delivered) SAM. It is reported that a transfer of 50 AMX-30 tanks from Greece was blocked by France, the original supplier.

The **Finnish** Army's organisation is now better understood. All brigades are manned by reservists, but the ten *Jaeger* and one armoured brigade have a training role in peacetime. Fresh information has allowed an understanding of the new organisation of the Swedish ground forces introduced in 1993–94. These are divided into divisions with differing numbers of brigades and defence districts organised as regiments, normally only with infantry and some artillery. All are on a reserve basis. The Army has taken delivery of 160 *Leopard* 2 tanks, 30 Stridsfordon 90 infantry fighting vehicles (50 more are due to be delivered in 1995), 360 MT-LB (formerly East German) APCs and six Hkp-9A (BO-105) anti-tank helicopters. Stridsfordon are currently developing a family of armoured vehicles. So far only the infantry fighting vehicle and anti-aircraft version are in service.

Former Yugoslavia

Despite the UN arms embargo imposed on all republics of the former Yugoslav Federal Republic, weapons are reaching all the warring parties in Croatia and Bosnia-Herzegovina, but obtaining accurate information is naturally difficult. Some indigenous production is also taking place. Croatia held an exhibition of domestic arms production in May 1995 and a military parade in June at which they displayed SAAB RBS 15 anti-ship missile and Russian SA-10 missile canisters. How much these were staged for propaganda purposes is not known. The Croats claim to be manufacturing tanks (a version of the M-84), artillery and MRL as well as many types of small arms. The Croatian Army is undoubtedly far better organised, trained and armed than it was two years ago. However, it and the Bosnian Muslim and Bosnian Croatian forces still lack heavy weaponry such as tanks, APCs and artillery when compared with Serb holdings. The Croatian Air Force has managed to acquire a further eight MiG-21 aircraft and five Mi-24 attack helicopters in the last 12 months. The Bosnian Serbs may have acquired some SA-10 SAM, but certainly not as many as the 32 launchers which they boast as having.

Defence Spending

After remaining static in 1994, regional defence spending is set for a real increase of 15% in 1995. Non-NATO **European Union** countries and **Switzerland** continue to account for over half the regional total, although their share is declining. Among the **Visegrad Four**, there are real increases in the defence budgets of **Poland**, the **Czech Republic** and **Hungary**. Defence spending in **Ukraine** and **Belarus** appears to be still in decline, due primarily to their continuing economic difficulties. In the **former Yugoslavia**, **Croatia** and, despite sanctions, **Serbia** experienced real growth for the first time since the federation collapsed, and in 1995 there are large real increases in the official defence budgets of **Croatia** (up one-quarter) and **Serbia** (up one-third).

The three most recent EU members were all experiencing the effects of the global recession when the 1994 referenda confirmed their entry. For this reason, more than the end of the Cold War, underlying levels in the defence budgets of these traditionally neutral or non-aligned countries have been stable or in gentle decline since 1992. Currency movements since 1992 have, however, reduced the dollar value of **Sweden's** defence budget by nearly $1bn, but increased that of **Switzerland** by over $1bn, although changes to these budgets when denominated in national currencies have been moderate. Both countries are currently spending at least twice as much on defence as any other in the region. **Finland's** dollar-denominated defence budget also declined by a quarter in 1993 owing to currency depreciation, but in 1995 it has nearly recovered to the 1992 level. The recent procurement budgets of these countries and those of other non-NATO EU members (**Austria** and **Ireland**) are examined in an outline study in the NATO section of the European defence procurement market.

In 1992, **Poland** was the first former communist country in Eastern Europe to register economic growth following the dismemberment of COMECON. In 1994, the economies of the **Czech Republic**, **Hungary** and **Slovakia** also started to grow again. This growth is reflected in their 1995 defence budgets. **Poland's** defence budget increases from $2.1bn to $2.6bn in current-year dollars, **Czech** defence spending is set to grow from $931m to $1,025m, and **Hungary's** defence budget increases from $556m to $641m. Three of the **Visegrad Four** thus appear to be beginning military reinvestment. In contrast, the continuing economic decline in **Ukraine** and **Belarus** is constraining defence spending. Economic difficulties have forced all former Warsaw Pact countries to prioritise manpower and operations and maintenance (O&M) spending (with the notable exception of **Ukraine** where the emphasis has been on infrastructure) at the expense of procurement and research and development (R&D).

Table 1: Structure of 1993 Defence Expenditures, Selected ex-Warsaw Pact Countries

	Poland		Czech Republic		Hungary		Ukraine		Belarus	
	$m	%	$m	%	$m	%	$m	%	$m	%
Personnel	838	38	296	37	386	53	19	2	217	33
O&M	686	31	426	53	296	41	31	4	353	53
Procurement	273	12	19	2	10	1	4	0	0	0
R&D	50	2	9	1	4	1	3	0	4	1
Infrastructure	77	4	51	6	27	4	768	93	88	13
Pensions, other	276	13	0	0	0	0	0	0	0	0
Total	2,200	100	801	100	724	100	824	100	661	100

Source: UN Centre for Disarmament Affairs.

As economic recovery and the restructuring of national defence industries gathers momentum, defence planners in former communist countries are being confronted with difficult procurement policy issues. With the effects of industrial dislocation arising from Soviet centralisation increasingly behind them, countries face the choice of whether to renew defence industrial links with Russia and other former Soviet republics; make a clean break from the past through procurement from the US, Western Europe and elsewhere; or steer a middle path by using both traditional and new defence supply sources. Whatever the decision, the expense of the most modern weapon systems may predicate either direct purchase with offsets (or as debt repayment as in the case of Russia's recent transactions with **Slovakia** and **Hungary,** and current proposals to **Bulgaria**) or, where a defence industry exists, international collaboration through licensed production and joint ventures. In some cases the national defence industries remain satisfactory as independent sources of supply for many less costly weapons and equipment. The defence industries of these former communist countries remain active in the international arms market. At present, the most successful arms exporter is the **Czech Republic**, whose military exports amounted to some $167m in 1993 and $194m in 1994 – much more than was spent on domestic procurement. By comparison Poland, as the next largest arms exporter of this group, delivered weapons and equipment worth an estimated $60m in 1993.

Table 2:   Structure of Polish and Czech Defence Budgets in 1994 and 1995 ($m)

	Poland				Czech Republic			
	1994	%	1995	%	1994	%	1995	%
Personnel	884	39	1,395	54	309	33	360	35
O&M	846	38	835	32	527	57	443	43
Procurement	380	17	227	9	55	6	148	14
R&D	50	2	53	2	29	3	37	4
Infrastructure, pensions, other	90	4	67	3	11	1	37	4
Total	2,250	100	2,577	100	931	100	1,025	100

In 1994 economic growth also resumed in the Baltic republics of **Estonia**, **Latvia** and **Lithuania. Estonia's** defence budget in 1995 is $33m, up from $25m, and that of **Latvia** $65m, about the same as last year. Military expenditures in the Baltic republics are probably larger than the defence budgets indicate, since they do not reflect the costs of paramilitary border guards and some procurement from foreign sources. These countries have also received military aid in the form of equipment and services from a variety of sources including other Nordic countries, the Czech Republic, the UK and the US. In 1995, US equipment (including communications and field equipment, and uniforms) to support the Baltic Peacekeeping Force (BALTBAT) was delivered as part of a Foreign Military Assistance (FMA) commitment.

In the Caucasus, **Armenia** resumed economic growth in 1994, whereas the economies of **Georgia** and **Azerbaijan** remained in decline. Audits of defence and security expenditure conducted by the International Monetary Fund (IMF) are now available for 1992–93 which show that these countries are gradually assuming financial responsibility for their own defence. The full extent to which they make financial contributions to support residual Russian forces is, however, unclear. **Armenia** has agreed to accept Russian military bases on its territory, and reportedly to pay the cost of servicing these bases. The budgeted cost of the OSCE planning cell for **Nagorno-Karabakh (Azerbaijan)** was about $3m in 1994. For 1995, **Georgia's** central government budget is dominated by defence (15.7%) and law enforcement (13.7%) – giving a combined security budget of $56m. The cost of **UNOMIG** in 1994 was about $11m. Russia retains a military presence in Abkhazia and South Ossetia. The Georgian government is at present linking the issue of permanent Russian bases in Georgia to a favourable resolution of the Abkhazian conflict. Russian border troops are also based in Georgia, and the government is reportedly making a financial contribution for their upkeep.

In the **former Yugoslavia,** the economies of **Croatia** and **Serbia-Montenegro** resumed growth – in the latter case despite sanctions. The possible escalation of the civil war is signalled by large increases in the defence budgets of **Croatia** (about 25% when measured in kunas but in dollar terms from $978m to $1,784m because the kuna is linked to the German mark) and **Serbia** (from $740m to $1,143m). In the case of **Bosnia,** details of military expenditures are not released by the government nor by the Bosnian Serb leadership. The war effort of the Bosnian Muslims has so far conspicuously lacked the indigenous economic and military resources available to the other conflicting parties. Apart from being the weakest (other than the FYROM) of the republics of the former Yugoslavia in economic terms, the Bosnian government had to rely at the outset of the civil war on the weaponry, equipment and stores remaining after the departure of the Yugoslav National Army. The country also contains part of the defence industry of the former Yugoslavia, some of which is in Bosnian Muslim control and reported to be functioning. Reports also suggest that the Bosnian government has received material amounts of foreign military assistance, both in cash and in kind – according to reports mainly from Turkey, Iran and Saudi Arabia – which has enabled it, along with other participants, to circumvent the UN arms embargo. The main backer of the Bosnian Serb forces appears to remain Serbia itself, reportedly payrolling the officers and providing regular support in military equipment and war *materiel* – in apparent circumvention of agreements with the UN. Serbia has also been the main supplier of the Croatian Serbs in Krajina. Serbian military expenditure is almost certainly much higher than budgeted, and probably accounts for up to one-third of gross domestic product (GDP). The cost of UNPROFOR operations in the former Yugoslavia – mainly Bosnia – was about $1.6bn in 1994, whilst the UN has estimated that some $500m in food aid was required for that year.

ALBANIA

GDP	1993ε: leke 113bn ($1.1bn): per capita $2,800 1994ε: leke 164bn ($1.6bn): per capita $3,000	
Growth	1993: 11.0%	1994: 7.4%
Inflation	1993: 85%	1994: 23%
Debt	1993: $755m	1994ε: $770m
Def exp	1993: leke 3.84bn ($37.3m)	
Def bdgt	1994ε: leke 4.58bn ($44.0m) 1995ε: leke 5.10bn ($50.4m)	
FMA	1994: $0.2m (IMET) 1995: $0.2m (IMET) 1996: $0.4m (IMET)	
$1 = leke	1993: 103 1995: 101	1994: 104

Population: 3,535,000 (Muslim 70%, Greek Orthodox 20%, Roman Catholic 10%, Greek ε3–8%)

	13–17	18–22	23–32
Men	177,000	170,600	317,600
Women	162,600	156,600	296,000

TOTAL ARMED FORCES:
ACTIVE: 73,000 (22,800 conscripts).
Terms of service: 12 months.
RESERVES: 155,000 (to age 56): Army 150,000; Navy 2,500; Air Force 2,500.

ARMY: 60,000 (incl Reserves, 20,000 conscripts).
9 inf div.[a]
EQPT:
MBT: 138 T-34, 721 T-59.
LT TK: 30 Type-62.

RECCE: 15 BRDM-1.
APC: 103 Ch Type-531.
TOWED ARTY: 122mm: 425 M-1931/37, M-30, 208 Ch Type-60; **130mm:** 100 Ch Type-59-1; **152mm:** 90 Ch Type-66.
MRL: 107mm: 270 Ch Type-63.
MOR: 82mm: 259; **120mm:** 550 M-120; **160mm:** 100 M-160.
RCL: 82mm: T-21.
ATK GUNS: 45mm: M-1942; **57mm:** M-1943; **85mm:** 61 D-44, Ch Type-56; **100mm:** 50 Type-86.
AD GUNS: 23mm: 12 ZU-23-2/ZPU-1; **37mm:** 100 M-1939; **57mm:** 82 S-60; **85mm:** 30 KS-12; **100mm:** 56 KS-19.

[a] Inf div strengths vary from 3,000 to 5,500.

NAVY: 2,500 (incl 350 Coastal Defence and ε1,000 conscripts).
BASES: Durrës, Himarë, Sarandë, Sazan Island, Shëngjin Vlorë, Orikjum.
SS:† 2 Sov *Whiskey* with 533mm TT (plus 1 trg, unserviceable).
PATROL AND COASTAL COMBATANTS:† 37–43:
TORPEDO CRAFT: 24–30 Ch *Huchuan* PHT with 2 x 533mm TT.
PATROL CRAFT: 13:
2 Sov *Kronshdat* PCO;
6 Ch *Shanghai*-II.
5 Sov Po-2 PFI.
MCM:† 6:
2 Sov T-43 (in reserve), 4 Sov T-301 MSI (2 in reserve).
SPT: 15:
2 Sov *Khobi* harbour tkr, 2 Sov *Shalanda* AK, 1 *Sekstan*, 1 *Poluchat*, 1 *Nyryat*, 1 *Toplivo*, 2 *Tugur*, 4 *Arcor* 25, 1 Po-2.

AIR FORCE: 10,000 (1,800 conscripts); 98 cbt act†, no armed hel. Flying hours: 30.
FGA: 1 air regt with 10 J-2 (MiG-15), 14 J-6 (MiG-17), 23 J-6 (MiG-19).
FTR: 2 air regt:
1 with 20 J-6 (MiG-19), 10 J-7 (MiG-21).
1 with 21 J-6 (MiG-19).
TPT: 1 sqn with 10 C-5 (An-2), 3 Il-14M, 6 Li-2 (C-47).
HEL: 1 regt with 15 Ch Z-5 (Mi-4).
TRG: 8 CJ-5, 15 MiG-15UTI, 6 Yak-11.
SAM:† some 4 SA-2 sites, 22 launchers.

FORCES ABROAD:
UN AND PEACEKEEPING:
GEORGIA (UNOMIG): 1 Obs.

PARAMILITARY: 13,500.
INTERNAL SECURITY FORCE: (5,000).
PEOPLE'S MILITIA: (3,500).
BORDER POLICE (Ministry of Public Order): (ε5,000).

ARMENIA

GDP	1993ε: r 2,032bn ($2.2bn)	
	per capita $2,300	
	1994ε: d n.k. ($2.3bn)	
	per capita $2,500	
Growth	1993ε: -14.8%	1994ε: 5.4%
Inflation	1993ε: 3,732%	1994ε: 5,268%
Debt	1993: $128m	1994: $160m
Def exp[a]	1992ε: r 1.98bn ($84m)	
	1993ε: r 57.50bn ($62m)	
Def bdgt[a]	1994ε: d n.k. ($71m)	
	1995ε: d n.k. ($77m)	
$1 = d[b]	1993: 35	1994: 220
	1995: 408	

r = Russian rouble
d = dram

[a] Excl procurement.
[b] The dram was introduced in November 1993 at a floating exchange rate with convertible currencies.

Population: 3,800,000 (Azeri 3%, Kurd 2%, Russian 2%)

	13–17	18–22	23–32
Men	178,000	155,600	273,800
Women	173,200	152,200	267,800

TOTAL ARMED FORCES: some 60,000
incl 800 MoD and comd staff.

Terms of service: conscription, 18 months.
RESERVES: some mob reported, possibly 300,000 with mil service within 15 years.

ARMY: some 51,800.
1 Army HQ.
4 MR bde; 9 (1 trg) indep MRR.
1 SF regt.
1 arty bde; 1 arty regt.
1 ATK regt.
1 tk trg sqn.
2 SAM bde, 2 SAM regt.
1 indep hel sqn.
EQPT:
MBT: 98 T-72, 30 T-55.
AIFV: 164 BMP-1/-2, BMD-1.
APC: some 56 BTR-60/-70/-80/-152, 75 MT-LB.
TOTAL ARTY: 225:
TOWED: 122mm: 59 D-30; **152mm:** 2 D-1, 34 D-20, 26 2A36.
SP: 122mm: 10 2S1; **152mm:** 28 2S3.
MRL: 122mm: 47 BM-21.
MOR: 120mm: 19 M-120.
ATK GUNS: 105: **85mm:** D-44; **100mm:** T-12.
ATGW: 18 AT-3 *Sagger*, 27 AT-6 *Spiral*.
SAM: 25 SA-2/-3, 54 SA-4, 20 SA-8, SA-13.
SURV: GS-13 (veh), *Long Trough* ((SNAR-1) arty), *Pork Trough* ((SNAR-2/-6) arty), *Small Fred/Small Yawn* (arty), *Big Fred* ((SNAR-10) veh/arty).
AC: 6 cbt: 5* Su-25, 1* MiG-25, 1 L-29.
ATTACK HEL: 7 Mi-24.
SPT HEL: 7 Mi-2, 2 Mi-9, 7 Mi-8, 5 Mi-24K/P.

PARAMILITARY:
Ministry of Interior: ε1,000; 4 bn: 34 BMP-1, 30 BTR-60/-70/-152.

FOREIGN FORCES:
RUSSIA: Army: 5,000; 1 mil base with 80 MBT, 190 APC, 100 arty. AD: 1 sqn MiG-23.

AUSTRIA

GDP	1993: OS 2,117.8bn ($182.1bn):		
	per capita $18,300		
	1994: OS 2,244.9bn ($196.5bn):		
	per capita $19,100		
Growth	1993: -0.1%	1994:	2.7%
Inflation	1993: 3.6%	1994:	3.0%
Publ Debt	1993: 58.3%	1994:	59.0%
Def exp	1993: OS 20.90bn ($1.80bn)		
	1994: OS 21.28bn ($1.86bn)		

Def bdgt	1994: OS 20.14bn ($1.76bn)	
	1995: OS 20.23bn ($2.04bn)	
	1996ε: OS 21.91bn ($2.21bn)	
$1 = OS	1993: 11.6	1994: 11.4
	1995: 9.9	
OS = Austrian schilling		

Population: 7,981,000

	13–17	18–22	23–32
Men	236,600	260,600	670,000
Women	225,400	248,600	646,400

TOTAL ARMED FORCES (Air Service

forms part of the Army):

ACTIVE: some 55,750 (incl 30,000 active and short term; ε20–30,000 conscripts; some 66,000 reservists a year undergo refresher trg, a proportion at a time).
Terms of service: 7 months recruit trg, 30 days reservist refresher trg during 10 years (or 8 months trg, no refresher); 60–90 days additional for officers, NCO and specialists.

RESERVES: 119,000 ready (72 hrs) reserves; 960,000 with reserve trg, but no commitment. Officers, NCO and specialists to age 65, remainder to age 50.

ARMY: 51,500 (22,000 conscripts).

3 Corps:
 2 each with 1 engr bn, 1 recce, 1 arty regt, 3 Provincial mil comd[a]; 10 inf regt (total).
 1 with 3 mech inf bde (1 tk, 1 mech inf, 1 SP arty bn), 1 engr, 1 recce bn, 1 arty regt, 2 Provincial mil comd[a], 7 inf regt.
1 Provincial mil comd[a] with 1 inf regt.
EQPT:
MBT: 169 M-60A3.
APC: 465 Saurer 4K4E/F (incl variants), some *Pandur* (being delivered).
TOWED ARTY: 105mm: 108 IFH (M-2A1).
SP ARTY: 155mm: 138 M-109/-A2.
FORTRESS ARTY: 155mm: 24 SFK M-2.
MOR: 81mm: 701; **107mm:** 100 M-2/M-30; **120mm:** 244 M-43.
ATGW: 179 RBS-56 *Bill*.
RCL: 2,199 incl **74mm:** *Miniman*; 84mm: *Carl Gustav*. **106mm:** 445 M-40A1.
ATK GUNS:
SP: 105mm: 282 *Kuerassier* JPz SK.
TOWED: 85mm: 206 M-52/-55.
STATIC: 90mm: 11 M-47 tk turrets; **105mm:** some 228 L7A1 (*Centurion* tk).
AD GUNS: 20mm: 558; **35mm:** 74 GDF-002 twin towed.
MARINE WING (under School of Military Engineering): 2 river patrol craft⟨; 10 unarmed boats.

[a] On mob Provincial mil comd convert to bde.

AIR FORCE: 4,250 (3,400 conscripts); 48 cbt ac, no armed hel.
1 air div HQ; 3 air regt; 3 AD regt, 1 air surv regt.
FGA: 1 wg with 24 SAAB J-35Oe.
FTR: 1 wg with 24 SAAB J-35Oe.
HEL:
LIAISON: 11 OH-58B, 11 AB-206A.
TPT: 23 AB-212; 8 AB-204 (9 in store).
SAR: 24 A-316 B *Alouette*.
TPT: 2 *Skyvan* 3M.
LIAISON: 1 15 O-1 (L-19A/E), 12 PC-6B.
TRG: 16 PC-7, 29 SAAB 105Oe.
AD: 80 *Mistral*; 120 **20mm** AA guns: 74 Twin **35mm** AA guns with *Skyguard* radars; air surv *Goldhawk* with *Selenia* MRS-403 3D radars.

FORCES ABROAD:
UN AND PEACEKEEPING:
CYPRUS (UNFICYP): 353; 1 inf bn. **GEORGIA** (UNOMIG): 4 Obs. **HAITI** (UNMIH): 20 civ pol. **IRAQ/KUWAIT** (UNIKOM): 7 Obs. **MIDDLE EAST** (UNTSO): 13 Obs. **RWANDA** (UNAMIR): 15 Obs. **SYRIA** (UNDOF): 468; 1 inf bn. **TAJIKISTAN** (UNMOT): 5 Obs. **WESTERN SAHARA** (MINURSO): 4 Obs, plus 10 civ pol.

AZERBAIJAN

GDP	1993ε: m 166bn ($3.8bn)	
	per capita $2,200	
	1994ε: m 1,674bn ($2.9bn)	
	per capita $1,700	
Growth	1993ε: -23.3%	1994ε: -21.9%
Inflation	1993ε: 1,129%	1994ε: 1,664%
Debt	1993: $36m	1994: $152m
Def exp	1992ε: m 1.64bn ($321m)	
	1993ε: m 13.29bn ($305m)	
Def bdgt	1994ε: m 145bn ($132m)	
	1995ε: m 480bn ($109m)	
$ = m[a]	1993: 93	1994: 1,100
	1995: 4,390	

m = manat

[a] The manat was introduced in August 1992 as a parallel currency to the rouble and became sole legal tender in January 1994.

Population: 7,640,000 (Russian 6%, Armenian 6%, Daghestan 3%)

	13–17	18–22	23–32
Men	372,200	326,000	601,400
Women	347,600	316,800	671,200

TOTAL ARMED FORCES:
ACTIVE: ε86,700.
Terms of service: 17 months, but can be extended for ground forces.
RESERVES: some mob 560,000 with military service within 15 years.

ARMY: 73,300.
1 tk bde.
14 MR bde (incl 2 trg, 2 with inf units only).
1 air aslt bde.
2 indep MRR.
2 mtn inf regt.
2 arty bde, 1 MRL, 1 Atk regt.
EQPT:
MBT: 325: T-72, T-55.
AIFV: 135 BMP-1, 206 BMP-2, 3 BMP-3, 78 BMD, 33 BRM-1.
APC: 379: 25 BTR-60, 118 BTR-70, 14 BTR-80, 200 MT-LB, 22 BTR-D.
TOTAL ARTY: 343:
TOWED: 122mm: 127 D-30; **152mm:** 34 D-20, 24 2A36.
SP: 122mm: 14 2S1.
COMBINED GUN/MOR: 120mm: 29 2S9.
MRL: 122mm: 63 BM-21.
MOR: 120mm: 52 PM-38.
SAM: 60+: SA-4/-8/-13.
SURV: GS-13 (veh); *Long Trough* ((SNAR-1) arty), *Pork Trough* (SNAR-2/-6) arty), *Small Fred/Small Yawn* (veh, arty), *Big Fred* ((SNAR-10) veh, arty).

NAVY: ε2,200. As a member of the CIS, Azerbaijan's naval forces operate under CIS (Russian) control.
BASE: Baku.
About 34 naval units from ex-Sov Caspian Flotilla and Border Guards, incl 2 *Petya*-II FF, 2 *Osa*-II, 10 *Stenka* PFI, 1 *Zhuk* PCI, 5 *Sonya* MSC, 4 *Yevgenya* MSI, 4 *Polnochny* LSM, 1 *Svetlyak* PCI, 2 *Yurka* MCC, 3 *Vanya* MCC.

AIR FORCE: 11,200; 46 cbt ac, 18 attack hel.
AC: 4 sqn with 30 MiG-25, 7 Su-24, 2 Su-17, 2 Su-25, 5 MiG-21, 52 L-29 (trg).
HEL: 1 sqn with 2 Mi-2, 13 Mi-8, 18* Mi-24.
SAM: 100 SA-2/-3/-5.

PARAMILITARY:
MILITIA (Ministry of Internal Affairs): 20,000+.
POPULAR FRONT (Karabakh People's Defence): ε20,000.

OPPOSITION:
Armed forces of Nagorno-Karabakh: ε20–25,000 (incl ε8,000 volunteers from Armenia). Eqpt reported incl 50+ MBT,100+ AIFV/APC, 100 arty.

BELARUS

GDP	1993ε: r11,067bn ($28bn)	
	per capita $6,300	
	1994ε: r34,975bn ($22bn)	
	per capita $5,300	
Growth	1993ε: -9.5%	1994ε: -21.7%
Inflation	1993ε: 1,188%	1994ε: 2,220%
Debt	1993: $967m	1994: $1,009m
Def exp	1993ε: r 261bn ($661m)	
Def bdgt	1994ε: r 768bn ($491m)	
	1995ε: r 892bn ($78m)	
FMA[a]	1994: $0.1m (IMET)	
	1995: $0.1m (IMET)	
	1996: $0.3m (IMET)	
$1 = r[b]	1993: 395	1994: 1,564
	1996: 11,500	

r = rubel

[a] Excl obligations 1992–94 by the US ($3.4m) under the Nunn–Lugar Cooperative Threat Reduction Programme which continues in 1995–96.
[b] The rubel became sole legal tender in November 1994.

Population: 10,372,000 (Russian 12%, Polish 4%, Ukrainian 3%)

	13–17	18–22	23–32
Men	396,200	371,000	686,600
Women	384,600	363,400	693,000

TOTAL ARMED FORCES:
ACTIVE: 98,400 incl about 1,200 MoD staff and 21,000 in centrally controlled units.
Terms of service: 18 months.
RESERVES: some 289,500 with military service within 5 years.

STRATEGIC NUCLEAR FORCES
(Russian-controlled forces on Belarus territory):
ICBM: 18:
SS-25 *Sickle* (RS-12m): 18 (mobile, single-warhead msl; 2 regt of 9).

ARMY: 50,500.
MoD tps: 2 MRD (1 trg), 1 ABD, 1 indep AB bde, 1 arty div, 2 arty, 2 MRL regt.
1 rear defence div (reserve inf units only).
1 SSM, 1 ATK, 1 *Spetsnaz*, 2 SAM bde.
3 Corps:
   1 with 3 mech, 1 SSM, 1 SAM bde, 1 arty, 1 MRL regt.

1 with 1 mech, 1 SSM, 1 SAM bde, 1 arty, 1 MRL regt.
1 with no manned cbt units.
EQPT:
MBT: 2,348: 381 T-55, 170 T-62, 1,797 T-72.
LT TK: 8 PT-76.
AIFV: 2,024: 461 BMP-1, 1,278 BMP-2, 161 BRM, 124 BMD-1.
APC: 1,014: 221 BTR-60, 415 BTR-70, 189 BTR-80, 117 BTR-D, 72 MT-LB.
TOTAL ARTY: 1,579:
TOWED: 440: **122mm:** 190 D-30; **152mm:** 6 M-1943 (D-1), 58 D-20, 136 2A65, 50 2A36.
SP: 588: **122mm:** 239 2S1; **152mm:** 168 2S3, 120 2S5; **152mm:** 13 2S19; **203mm:** 48 2S7.
COMBINED GUN/MOR: 120mm: 54 2S9.
MRL: 419: **122mm:** 275 BM-21, 11 9P138; **130mm:** 1 BM-13; **220mm:** 84 9P140; **300mm:** 48 9A52.
MOR: 120mm: 78 2S12.
ATGW: 480: AT-4 *Spigot*, AT-5 *Spandrel* (some SP), AT-6 *Spiral* (some SP), AT-7 *Saxhorn*.
SSM: 60 *Scud*, 36 *FROG/SS-21*.
SAM: 350: SA-8/-11/-12/-13.
SURV: GS-13 (arty), *Long Trough* ((SNAR-1) arty), *Pork Trough* ((SNAR-2/-6) arty), *Small Fred/Small Yawn* (veh, arty), *Big Fred* ((SNAR-10) veh, arty).

AIR FORCE: 25,700 (incl 12,000 AD); 1 air army, 349 cbt ac, 74 attack hel. Flying hours: 40.
FGA: 42 Su-24, 99 Su-25.
FTR: 45 MiG-23, 13 MiG-25, 83 MiG-29, 25 Su-27.
RECCE: 42* Su-24.
HEL:
ATTACK: 74 Mi-24.
CBT SPT: 9 Mi-24K, 10 Mi-24P, 148 Mi-8.
TPT: ac: 29 Il-76, 6 An-12, 7 An-24, 1 An-26, 1 Tu-134; **hel:** 26 Mi-2, 14 Mi-26.
AWAITING ELIMINATION: 4 MiG-23, 32 MiG-25, 4 Su-17, 1 Yak-28.

AIR DEFENCE: 12,000.
SAM: 200 SA-2/-3/-5/-10.

PARAMILITARY:
BORDER GUARDS (Ministry of Interior): 8,000.

BOSNIA-HERZEGOVINA

GDP[a]	1991ε: $14bn:
	per capita $4,500
Def exp[b]	1993ε: $875m
	1994ε: $900m

[a] There are no reliable statistics for recent economic activity.

[b] Incl Foreign Military Assistance but excl UNPROFOR. The cost of UNPROFOR in 1994 was $1.6bn.

Population: 4,383,000 (Muslim 44%, Serb 31%, Croat 17%)

	13–17	18–22	23–32
Men	187,800	171,600	357,400
Women	177,200	160,600	339,800

TOTAL ARMED FORCES:
ACTIVE: some 92,000.
RESERVES: some 100,000.

ARMY (BiH): 92,000 (incl ε40,000 reserves).
1 'Army' HQ.
6 'Corps' HQ.
2 div HQ (reported).

Some 78 inf 'bde'.	9 mot 'bde'.
Some 13 mtn 'bde'.	1 SF 'bde'.
1 recce bde.	5 territorial def 'bde'.
2 arty 'bde'.	Some 2 AD regt.

EQPT:
MBT: ε31 incl T-34, T-55.
APC: ε35.
ARTY: ε100 incl **130mm**, **203mm**.
MRL: 2 incl **262mm:** M-87 *Orkan*.
MOR: 200: **82mm; 120mm**.
ATGW: 100 AT-3 *Sagger*, Ch *Red Arrow* (TF-8) reported.
AD GUNS: 20mm, 30mm.
SAM: SA-7/-14.
HEL: 5 Mi-8/-17.
AC: 3 UTVA-75.

DEPLOYMENT (manpower incl some reserves).
1 Corps: Sarajevo (incl Goradze, Srebrenica, Zepa and Mt Igman): up to 21 inf, 8 mot, 7 mtn, 1 HVO, 2 arty bde.
2 Corps: Tuzla: up to 26 inf, 1 mot, 3 mtn, 2 HVO, 1 engr bde.
3 Corps: Zenica: and up to 16 inf, 1 armd bde.
4 Corps: Mostar/Konjic: up to 5 inf, 1 mtn.
5 Corps: Bihac: up to 8 inf (1 HVO), 1 SF bde.
7 Corps: Travnik: 5 inf, 2 mtn bde.
Abdic Faction (Bihac): 2 defected BiH bde, expanded to 6 bde.

OTHER FORCES:
CROAT (Croatian Defence Council (HVO)): ε50,000.
4 op zone (Mostar, Tomislavgrad, Vitez, Orasge).
Some 36 'bde'.
1 mixed arty 'div'.
1 MRL 'div'.
3 'extremist bde'.
1 SF 'bde'.

EQPT:
MBT: ε100, incl T-34, T-55.
AFV: ε80.
ARTY: ε200.
MRL: ε30.
MOR: ε300.
SAM: SA-7/-14/-16.
SERB (Army of the Serbian Republic of Bosnia and Herzegovina) (SRB: BH): up to 75,000.
7 'Corps' HQ.
8 armd 'bde'.   1 armd regt.
Some 62 inf 'bde'.   1 mech inf 'bde'.
1 mot inf 'bde'.   4 mtn 'bde'.
1 SF 'bde'.   1 arty 'bde'; 1 arty regt.
1 Atk, 1 AD regt.
EQPT:
MBT: ε370, incl T-34, T-55, M-84, T-72.
APC: 295.
TOWED ARTY: 700: **122mm:** D-30, M-1938 (M-30); **130mm:** M-46; **152mm:** D-20.
SP ARTY: **122mm:** 30 2S1.
MRL: **128mm:** 70 M-63; **262mm:** 6 M-87 *Orkan*.
MOR: ε900 incl **120mm**.
SSM: *Frog*-7.
AD GUNS: incl **20mm**, **23mm** incl ZSU 23-4; **30mm:** M53/59SP; **57mm:** ZSU-57-2; **90mm**.
SAM: SA-2, some SA-3/-6/-7b/-9/-14.
AC: some 20 *Galeb, Jastreb*, G-4 *Super Galeb* and *Orao*, UTVA, *Kraguj, Cessna*.
HEL: 12 Mi-8, 12 SA-341 *Gazela*.

DEPLOYMENT:

1 Krajina Corps: Banja Luka: up to 13 inf, 2 armd 'bde'; 1 Atk, 1 AD regt.
2 Krajina Corps: Bihac: 6 inf 'bde'.
3 Krajina Corps: Doboj: up to 13 inf, 2 armd, 1 SF 'bde'.
Tuzla Corps: Bijeljina: up to 8 inf, 1 armd 'bde'.
Drina Corps: 7 inf, 4 mtn, 2 armd 'bde'.
Sarajevo Corps: up to 8 inf, 1 mech, 1 mot, 1 arty 'bde'; 1 arty regt.
Herzegovina Corps: 7 inf, 1 armd 'bde'; 1 armd regt.

FOREIGN FORCES:

UNITED NATIONS (UNPROFOR): some 5,100 incl 6 inf bn for Sarajevo. Some 19,800 incl 11 inf bn (some armd recce and engr spt) for aid distribution and 'safe area' protection. See p. 303 for full details.

BULGARIA

GDP   1993: leva 286bn ($11.0bn): per capita $5,000
           1994: leva 514bn ($11.17bn): per capita $5,100

Growth	1993: -4.2%	1994: 0.2%
Inflation	1993: 72.8%	1994: 96.0%
Debt	1993: $12.25bn	1994ε:$11.34bn
Def exp	1993: leva 8.25bn ($317.1m)	
Def bdgt	1994: leva 12.92bn ($280.9m)	
	1995: leva 24.0bn ($364.0m)	
FMA	1994: $0.3m (IMET)	
	1995: $0.4m (IMET)	
	1996: $0.7m (IMET)	
$1 = leva	1993: 26	1994: 46
	1995: 66	

Population: 8,411,000 (Turk 8%, Romany 3%, Macedonian 3%)

	13–17	*18–22*	*23–32*
Men	311,800	317,800	571,800
Women	295,200	301,400	552,400

TOTAL ARMED FORCES:
ACTIVE: 101,900 (incl ε51,300 conscripts, about 22,300 centrally controlled, 3,400 MoD staff, but excl some 10,000 construction tps).
Terms of service: 18 months.
RESERVES: 303,000: Army 250,500; Navy (to age 55, officers 60 or 65) 7,500; Air Force (to age 60) 45,000.

ARMY: 51,600 (ε33,300 conscripts).
3 Military Districts/Army HQ.
1 with 1 tk bde.
1 with 1 MRD, 1 Regional Training Centre (RTC), 1 tk, 1 mech bde.
1 with 2 MRD, 2 RTC, 2 tk bde.
Army tps: 4 *Scud*, 1 SS-23, 1 SAM bde, 3 arty, 3 ATK, 3 AD arty, 1 SAM regt.
1 AB bde.
EQPT:
MBT: 1,786: 177 T-34, 1,276 T-55, 333 T-72.
ASLT GUN: 68 SU-100.
RECCE: 58 BRDM-1/-2.
AIFV: 114 BMP-23, BMP-30.
APC: 781 BTR-60, 1,113 MT-LB (plus 1,270 'look-alikes').
TOTAL ARTY: 2,052:
TOWED: 730: **100mm:** 16 M-1944 (BS-3); **122mm:** 379 M-30, 25 M-1931/37 (A-19); **130mm:** 72 M-46; **152mm:** 32 M-1937 (ML-20), 206 D-20.
SP: **122mm:** 656 2S1.
MRL: **122mm:** 222 BM-21.
MOR: 444: **120mm:** 6 M-38, 18 2B11, 61 B-24, 359 *Tundzha* SP.
SSM: launchers: 28 *FROG*-7, 36 *Scud*, 8 SS-23.
ATGW: 200 AT-3 *Sagger*.
ATK GUNS: **85mm:** 150 D-44; **100mm:** 200 T-12.
AD GUNS: 400: **23mm:** ZU-23, ZSU-23-4 SP; **57mm:**

S-60; **85mm:** KS-12; **100mm:** KS-19.
SAM: 20 SA-3, 27 SA-4, 20 SA-6.
SURV: GS-13 (veh), *Long Trough* ((SNAR-1) arty),
Pork Trough ((SNAR-2/-6) arty), *Small Fred/Small Yawn* (veh, arty), *Big Fred* ((SNAR-10) veh, arty).

NAVY: ε3,000 (ε2,000 conscripts).
BASES: Coastal: Varna (HQ), Atiya, Sozopol,
Balchik. **Danube:** Vidin (HQ).
SS: 2 *Pobeda* (Sov *Romeo*)-class with 533mm TT†.
FF: 1 *Smeli* (Sov *Koni*) with 1 x 2 SA-N-4 SAM, 2 x
12 ASW RL; plus 2 x 2 76mm guns.
PATROL AND COASTAL COMBATANTS: 23:
CORVETTES: 7:
4 *Poti* ASW with 2 x ASW RL, 4 x ASTT.
1 *Tarantul* II ASUW with 2 x 2 SS-N-2C *Styx*, 2 x 4
  SA-N-5 *Grail* SAM; plus 1 x 76mm gun.
2 *Pauk* I with 1 SA-N-5 SAM, 2 x 5 ASW RL; plus
  4 x 406mm TT.
MSL CRAFT: 6 *Osa* PFM with 4 x SS-N-2A/B *Styx* SSM.
PATROL, INSHORE: about 10 *Zhuk* PFI.
MINE WARFARE: 27:
MINELAYERS: 10 *Vydra*.
MCM: 17:
4 *Sonya* MSC.
13 MSI: 4 *Vanya*, 4 *Yevgenya*, 5 *Olya*.
AMPH: 2 Sov *Polnocny* LSM, capacity 150 tps, 6 tk.
SPT AND MISC: 7:
2 AOT, 2 AGHS, 1 AGI, 1 trg, 1 AT.

NAVAL AVIATION: 10 armed hel.
HEL: 1 SAR/ASW sqn with 9 Mi-14 (ASW), 1 Ka-25.
COASTAL ARTY: 2 regt, 20 bty.
GUNS: 100mm: ε150; **130mm:** 4 SM-4-1.
SSM: SS-C-1b *Sepal*, SSC-3 *Styx*.

NAVAL GUARD: 3 coy.

AIR FORCE: 21,600 (16,000 conscripts); 272
cbt ac, 44 attack hel. 2 air div, 1 mixed air corps.
FGA: 1 regt with 39 Su-25.
2 regt with 94 MiG-21.
1 regt with 36 MiG-23.
FTR: 4 regt with some 41 MiG-23, 20 MiG-21, 21
MiG-29.
RECCE: 1 regt, 21 Su-22.
TPT: 1 regt with 2 Tu-134, 3 An-24, 4 An-26, 5 L-
410, 3 Yak-40 (VIP).
SURVEY: 1 An-30.
HEL: 2 regt with 14 Mi-2, 7 Mi-8, 25 Mi-17, 44 Mi-
24 (attack).
TRG: 3 trg regt with 74 L-29, 35 L-39.
MSL:
ASM: AS-7 *Kerry*.

AAM: AA-2 *Atoll*, AA-7 *Apex*, AA-8 *Aphid*.
SAM: SA-2/-3/-5/-10 (20 sites, some 110 launchers).

FORCES ABROAD:
UN AND PEACEKEEPING:
ANGOLA (UNAVEM III): 10 Obs plus 10 civ pol.

PARAMILITARY:
BORDER GUARDS (Ministry of Interior): 12,000;
12 regt, some 50 craft incl about 12 Sov PO2 PCI⟨.
SECURITY POLICE: 4,000.
RAILWAY AND CONSTRUCTION TROOPS:
18,000.

CROATIA

GDP	1993ε: $10.6bn		
	per capita $5,000		
	1994ε: k 84bn ($11.0bn)		
	per capita $5,200		
Growth	1993ε: -3.2%	1994: 1.8%	
Inflation	1993ε: 1,516%	1994ε: 98%	
Debt	1993: $2.7bn	1994: $3.0bn	
Def exp	1993ε: $975m		
	1994: k 8,040m ($1,117m)		
Def bdgt	1994: k 7,040m ($978m)		
	1995: k 8,900m ($1,784m)		
FMA[a]	1995: $0.07m (IMET)		
	1996: $0.20m (IMET)		
$1 = kuna	1994: 7.20	1995: 4.99	
k = kuna[b]			

[a] The cost of UNPROFOR in 1994 was $1.6bn.
[b] The kuna was introduced in May 1994 to replace the Croatian dinar.

Population: 4,785,000 (Serb 12%, Muslim 1%, Slovene
1%) excl 386,000 refugees.

	13–17	18–22	23–32
Men	169,800	166,600	335,800
Women	160,000	158,800	324,600

TOTAL ARMED FORCES:
ACTIVE: ε105,000 (65,000 conscripts).
Terms of service: 10 months.
RESERVES: Army: 180,000; Home Def: 10,000.

ARMY: ε99,600 (ε65,000 conscripts).
6 op zone (OZ) (Zagreb, Bjelovar, Split, Osijek, Gospic,
  Karlovac).
29 inf 'bde'.
6 mech bde.

1 arty/MRL bde.
1 Atk bde.
1 AD bde.
1 SF bde (2 SF, 1 mtn, 1 amph, 1 AB bn).
1 engr bde

RESERVES: 37 Home Def regt.

EQPT:
MBT: 176: 9 T-34, 140 T-55, 27 M-84.
LT TK: 5 PT-76.
RECCE: 5 BRDM-2.
AIFV: 82 M-80.
APC: BTR-40/-50, 19 M-60 plus 22 'look-alikes', ε150 BIV (reported).
TOTAL ARTY: some 949 incl:
TOWED: 76mm: ZIS-3; **85mm; 105mm:** 29 M-56, 31 M-2A1; **122mm:** 22 M-1938, 21 D-30; **130mm:** 34 M-46; **152mm:** 15 D-20, 13 M-84.
SP: 122mm: 2 2S1.
MRL: 122mm: 19 BM-21; **128mm:** 2 M-63; **262mm:** M-87 *Orkan* reported.
MOR: 82mm; 120mm: 677 M-74/-75, 84 UBM-52.
ATGW: 152 AT-3 *Sagger*, 28 AT-4 *Spigot*.
ATK GUNS: 100mm: 70 T-12.
RL: 90mm: M-79.
AD GUNS: 600+: 14.5mm: ZPU-2/-4; **20mm:** BOV-1 SP, M-55; **30mm:** M-53/59, BOV-3SP.
SAM: SA-7, SA-9, SA-10, SA-13, SA-14.

NAVY: 1,100.
BASES: Split, Pula, Sibenik, Ploce.
Minor facilities: Lastovo, Vis.
SS: 1 *Una* SSI for SF ops.
PATROL AND COASTAL COMBATANTS: 8:
CORVETTES: 1 Krajl-class with 2 or 4 x2 Saab RBS SSM.
MSL CRAFT: 3:
1 *Rade Koncar* PFM with 2 x RBS-15.
2 *Mitar Acev* (Sov *Osa*-I) PFM with 4 x SS-N-2A.
TORPEDO CRAFT: 1 *Topcider* (Sov *Shershen*) with 4 x 533mm TT.
PATROL, INSHORE: 3 *Mirna*.
MINE WARFARE: 4:
MINELAYERS: 2 *Cetina* (*Silba*-class), 94 mines. D-3 and D-501 LCT can also lay 100 mines – see amph forces.
MCM: 2:
1 *Vukov Klanac* MHC.
1 UK *Ham* MSI.
AMPH: craft only: 5 D-3/D-501 LCT, 4 LCM and about 3 LCU.
SPT AND MISC: 5:
1 *Spasilac* salvage, 1 Sov *Moma* survey, 1 AE, 2 tugs.

MARINES: 7 indep inf coy.

COASTAL DEFENCE: some 16 coast arty bty.

AIR FORCE: ε300; 28 cbt ac, 5 armed hel.
FGA/FTR: 21 MiG-21, 6 Galeb, 1 Orao.
TPT: 2 An-2, 2 An-26, 5 UTVA.
HEL: 18 Mi-8, 5* Mi-24, 1 UH-1, MD-500.

PARAMILITARY:
POLICE: 40,000 armed.
HOS (military wing of Croatian Party of Rights (HSP)): up to 5,000 reported (deployed in Bosnia).

OTHER FORCES:
ARMY OF THE REPUBLIC OF SERB KRAJINA: 40–50,000. (Org and weaponry before the Croatian attack on Krajina on 4 August 1995.)
6 'Corps' HQ (North Dalmatia, Lika, Kordun, Banija, Baranja/East Slavonia, West Slavonia).
Some 27 'bde'.
3 mech bde.
1 arty bde.
1 ATK regt.
1 SF bde.
Irregular Units: Capt Dragan, Arkan's Tiger, White Eagle, Chetniks.
EQPT:
MBT: ε250: T-34, T-55, M-84.
AIFV: M-80.
APC: ε100, incl M-60P.
TOTAL ARTY: ε200.
TOWED: 76mm: Z1S-3; **105mm:** M-56; **122mm:** D-30, M-1931/37 (A-19); **130mm:** M-46; **155mm:** M-65.
MRL: 14 incl **128mm:** M-63.
MOR: 81mm; 82mm; 120mm: UBM-52.
ATGW: AT-3 *Sagger* incl SP (BOV-1).
RCL: 82mm: M-60; **105mm:** M-65.
ATK GUNS: 100mm: 30 T-12.
AD GUNS: 20mm: M-55/-75; **30mm:** M-53/-59; **57mm:** ZSU-57-2 SP.
AC: Some 16 *Galeb, Orao*.
HEL: some 9 SA-341 *Gazella,* Mi-8.

FOREIGN FORCES:
UNITED NATIONS (UNCRO): 17,900; 13 inf bn, plus spt units from 15 countries. See p. 303 for full details.

CYPRUS

GDP	1993: £C 3.14bn ($6.32bn): per capita $9,600
	1994ε: £C 3.37bn ($6.86bn): per capita $10,000
Growth	1993: 1.5% 1994ε: 4.6%

Inflation	1993:	4.9%	1994:	4.3%
Debt	1993:	$926m	1994:	$903m
Def exp[a]	1993:	£C 245m ($492m)		
	1994:	£C 181m ($368m)		
Def bdgt	1995:	£C 194m ($411m)		
FMA[b]	1994:	$15m (Econ aid)		
	1995:	$15m (Econ aid)		
	1996:	$15m (Econ aid)		
$1 = £C	1993:	0.50	1994:	0.49
	1995:	0.45		

£C = Cypriot pound

[a] Official out-turn in 1993 was £C 166.3m ($333m).
[b] The 1994 cost of UNFICYP was $44m.

Population: 742,000 (Turkish 18%)

	13–17	18–22	23–32
Men	29,400	26,400	57,000
Women	27,400	25,000	54,000

TOTAL ARMED FORCES:
ACTIVE: 10,000 (8,700 conscripts; 445 women).
Terms of service: conscription, 26 months, then reserve to age 50 (officers 65).
RESERVES: 88,000: 45,000 first-line (age 20–34); 43,000 second-line (age 35–50).

NATIONAL GUARD: 10,000 (8,700 conscripts).
(All units classified non-active under Vienna Document.)
2 lt inf div.
2 lt inf bde.

2 bde HQ.	1 SF bn.
1 armd bde (-).	1 ATK bn.
2 lt inf regt.	7 arty bn.

1 coastal def SSM bty with MM-40 *Exocet*.
EQPT:
MBT: 52 AMX-30B-2.
RECCE: 124 EE-9 *Cascavel*, 15 EE-3 *Jararaca*.
AIFV: 27 VAB-VCI.
APC: 92 *Leonidas*, 100 VAB (incl variants), 12 AMX-VCI (reported).
TOWED ARTY: 75mm: 4 M-116A1 pack; **88mm:** 54 25-pdr (in store); **100mm:** 10 M-1944; **105mm:** 18 M-101, 54 M-56; **155mm:** 12 TR F1.
SP: 155mm: 12 F3.
MRL: 128mm: 13 Yug M-63 (YMRL-32).
MOR: 392: **81mm:** 180 E-44, 70+ M1/M29 (in store); **107mm:** 26 M-2; **120mm:** 116 RT61.
SSM: 3 MM-40 *Exocet*.
ATGW: 45 *Milan* (15 on EE-3 *Jararaca*), 72 *HOT* (18 on VAB).
RL: 73mm: ε450 RPG-7; **112mm:** ε450 *Apilas*.
RCL: 90mm: ε220 EM-67; **106mm:** 144 M-40A1.

AD GUNS: 80: **20mm:** 36 M-55; **35mm:** 24 GDF-005 with *Skyguard*; **40mm:** 20 M-1 (in store).
SAM: 24 SA-7, 30+ *Mistral*, 12 *Aspide*.
MARITIME: 1 *Salamis* PFI (plus 11 boats).
AC: 1 BN-2A *Maritime Defender*, 2 PC-9, 1 PA-22.
HEL: 3 Bell 206, 4 SA-342 *Gazelle* (with *HOT*), 1 Bell 412, 2 Mi-2 (in store).

PARAMILITARY:
ARMED POLICE: 3,700; Shorland armd cars, 2 VAB/VTT APC, 1 Bell 412 SP hel.
MARITIME POLICE: 320; 3 PFI: 2 *Evagoras* and 1 *Kinon* PFI (plus boats).

FOREIGN FORCES:
GREECE: 950 (ELDYK) (Army); 2 inf bn, plus ε1,300 officers/NCO seconded to Greek-Cypriot National Guard.
UNITED KINGDOM (in Sovereign Base Areas): 3,900; Army: 2 inf bn, 1 armd recce sqn; Air Force: 1 hel sqn, plus ac on det.
UNITED NATIONS (UNFICYP): some 1,138; 3 inf bn (Argentina, Austria, UK), plus 35 civ pol.

'TURKISH REPUBLIC OF NORTHERN CYPRUS'

Data presented here represent the *de facto* situation on the island. This in no way implies recognition or IISS approval.

Def exp   1995: $510–540m (Turkey)

TOTAL ARMED FORCES:
ACTIVE: some 4,000.
Terms of service: conscription, 24 months, then reserve to age 50.
RESERVES: 11,000 first-line; 10,000 second-line; 5,000 third-line.

ARMY: 4,000.
7 inf bn.

MARITIME: 3 patrol boats.

FOREIGN FORCES:
TURKEY: 30,000; 1 corps, 235 M-48A5 MBT; 57 M-113, 50 M-59 APC; 126 **105mm**, 36 **155mm**, 8 **203mm** towed; 18 **105mm**, 6 **155mm** SP; 102 **107mm** mor, 84 **40mm** AA guns; 8 ac, 13 hel.

THE CZECH REPUBLIC

GDP	1993: Kc 910.6bn ($31.24bn):
	per capita $7,400
	1994: Kc 1,037.5bn ($36.04bn):
	per capita $7,700
Growth	1993: -0.3% 1994: 2.7%
Inflation	1993: 20.8% 1994: 10.0%
Debt	1993: $8.66bn 1994: $10.09bn
Def exp	1993: Kc 23.36bn ($801.2m)
Def bdgt	1994: Kc 26.79bn ($930.5m)
	1995: Kc 26.90bn ($1,025.3m)
FMA	1994: $0.5m (IMET)
	1995: $0.5m (IMET)
	1996: $0.7m (IMET)
$1 = Kc	1993: 29.2 1994: 28.8
	1995: 26.2

Kc = Czech koruna

Population: 10,374,000 (Slovak 4%, German 0.5%)

	13–17	18–22	23–32
Men	414,400	429,200	715,800
Women	396,400	411,800	688,200

TOTAL ARMED FORCES:

ACTIVE: 86,400 (incl 40,400 conscripts, about 6,800 MoD and 23,700 centrally controlled formations/units). *Terms of service:* 12 months.

ARMY: 37,400 (21,400 conscripts).

MoD tps: 1 rapid-reaction bde (2 mech, 1 AB, 1 recce, 1 arty bn), 1 SF bde, 1 ops regt, 5 civil defence regt.
2 Corps HQ.
6 mech bde (incl 1 cadre, org varies); total cbt units incl 8 mech, 4 recce, 4 arty, 2 ATK, 3 AD, 4 engr bn.
Corps tps:
  2 arty bde (each 2 bn incl 1 MRL).
  1 recce bde, 1 AD regt; 2 AD bn.
  2 engr bde, 1 op bn.

EQPT:
MBT: 1,011: 469 T-54/-55, 542 T-72M.
RECCE: some 182 BRDM, OT-65.
AIFV: 951: 129 BPZV, 621 BMP-1, 186 BMP-2, 15 BRM-1K.
APC: 550: 39 OT-62A/B, 19 OT-64A/C, 412 OT-90, 80 OT-65 plus 756 'look-alikes'.
TOTAL ARTY: 893:
TOWED: 263: **100mm:** 75 M-53; **122mm:** 25 M-1938 (M-30), 157 D-30, 2 M-1931/37; **130mm:** 2 M-46; **152mm:** 2 M-1937 (ML-20).
SP: 372: **122mm:** 98 2S1; **152mm:** 274 *Dana* (M-77).
MRL: **122mm:** 165 RM-70.
MOR: **120mm:** 93 M-1982.

SSM: 10–14: *FROG*-7, SS-21, *Scud*, SS-23.
ATGW: AT-3 *Sagger*, AT-5 *Spandrel*.
AD GUNS: **30mm:** M-53/-59; **57mm:** S-60.
SAM: SA-7, SA-9/-13.
SURV: GS-13 (veh), *Long Trough* ((SNAR-1) arty), *Pork Trough* ((SNAR-2/-6) arty), *Small Fred/Small Yawn* (veh, arty), *Big Fred* ((SNAR-10) veh arty).

AIR FORCE: 18,500 (incl AD and 3,900 conscripts); 224 cbt ac, 36 attack hel. Flying hours: 65.
FGA: 3 regt:
1 with 35 Su-22.
1 with 39 MiG-23 BN, 39 MiG-21.
1 with 25 Su-25.
FTR: 1 regt with 31 MiG-23, 10 MiG-29; 1 sqn with 27 MiG-21.
TPT: 3 regt:
2 with **ac:** 8 L-410, 4 An-24, 1 Tu-134, 1 Tu-154; **hel:** 2 Mi-2, 8 Mi-8, 1 Mi-9, 6 Mi-17.
1 with **ac:** 10 L-410, 1 Il-14, 1 An-30, 1 An-12, 4 An-26; **hel:** 2 Mi-17.
HEL: 2 regt (aslt/tpt/attack):
1 with 8 Mi-2, 7 Mi-8, 11 Mi-17, 19* Mi-24.
1 with 7 Mi-2, 13 Mi-17, 17* Mi-24.
TEST CENTRE: 7 MiG-21, 2 L-29, 2 L-39, 1 Mi-17, 1 Mi-2.
TRG: 1 regt with **ac:** *18 MiG-21 U/MF, 33 L-29, 23 L-39; **hel:** 12 Mi-12, 2 Mi-8, 9 Mi-17.
AAM: AA-2 *Atoll*, AA-7 *Apex*, AA-8 *Aphid*, AA-10 *Alamo*, AA-11 *Archer*.
SAM: 2 AD div (7 AD units), SA-2, SA-3, SA-5, SA-6.

FORCES ABROAD:
UN AND PEACEKEEPING:

BOSNIA (UNPROFOR): 11 Obs. **CROATIA** (UNCRO): 922; 1 inf bn, incl 8 Obs. **GEORGIA** (UNOMIG): 5 Obs. **LIBERIA** (UNOMIL): 16 Obs. **FYROM** (UNPREDEP): 1 Obs.

PARAMILITARY:

BORDER GUARDS: 4,000 (1,000 conscripts).
INTERNAL SECURITY FORCES: 1,600 (1,500 conscripts).

ESTONIA

GDP	1993ε: kn 26.13bn ($1.98bn):
	per capita $6,300
	1994ε: kn 27.93bn ($2.15bn):
	per capita $6,700
Growth	1993ε: -6.6% 1994ε: 6.0%
Inflation	1993ε: 89% 1994ε: 48%
Debt	1993: $155m 1994: $339m

Def exp	1993ε: kn 1,016m ($77m)	
Def bdgt	1994: kn 319.7m ($24.6m)	
	1995: kn 416.8m ($33.4m)	
FMA[a]	1994: $0.2m (IMET)	
	1995: $0.2m (IMET)	
	1996: $0.4m (IMET)	
$1 = kn	1993: 13.2	1994: 13.0
	1995: 12.5	

kn = kroon

[a]FMA also received 1992–94 from Germany, Finland, Sweden.

Population: 1,541,000 (Russian 30%, Ukrainian 3%)

	13–17	18–22	23–32
Men	58,200	54,600	106,200
Women	55,600	52,800	101,200

TOTAL ARMED FORCES:
ACTIVE: 3,500 (incl 2,650 conscripts).
Terms of service: 12 months.
RESERVES: some 6,000 militia.

ARMY: 3,300.
3 inf bn (2 more to form); 3 inf coy.
1 guard, 1 AD bn.
1 peacekeeping coy (forming).
RESERVES: Militia: 6,000 (2,000 armed): 17 League of Defence units.
EQPT:
RECCE: 7 BRDM-2.
APC: 32 BTR-60/-70/-80.
MOR: 81mm: some.
RCL: 106mm: 21.
AD GUNS: 23mm: 2.
HEL: 1 Mi-2.

NAVY: 150.
BASE: Paldiski.
PATROL CRAFT: up to 8:
Up to 6 *Osa* i PFM (armament unknown).
2 *Zhuk* PCI.
MCM: 2 *Kondor*-1 MSO†.
SPT AND MISC: 1 *Maagen* (HQ and Flagship), 1 *Mayak* AK, 1 *Akedemik Shuleykin* AGOR.

FORCES ABROAD:
UN AND PEACEKEEPING:
CROATIA (UNCRO): 32.

PARAMILITARY:
BORDER GUARD (Ministry of Interior): 2,000 (1,200 conscripts): 1 regt. Maritime elm of Border Guard

also fulfils task of Coast Guard.
BASE: Tallinn.
PATROL CRAFT: 4: 1 *Storm* PCC (unarmed), 1 *Silma* PCC, 1 *Koskelo* PCI, 1 001 PCI.
SPT AND MISC: 1 *Linda* PCO (trg).
AVN: 2 L-410 UVP-1 *Turbolet*.

FINLAND

GDP	1993: m 480.5bn ($84.11bn):	
	per capita $16,000	
	1994: m 511.6bn ($97.94bn):	
	per capita $16,900	
Growth	1993: -1.6%	1994: 3.9%
Inflation	1993: 2.1%	1994: 1.1%
Publ debt	1993: 56.2%	1994: 62.7%
Def exp	1993: m 9.75bn ($1.71bn)	
	1994: m 10.27bn ($1.97bn)	
Def bdgt	1995: m 9.14bn ($2.12bn)	
	1996ε: m 10.14bn ($2.38bn)	
$1 = m	1993: 5.7	1994: 5.2
	1995: 4.3	

m = markka

Population: 5,105,000

	13–17	18–22	23–32
Men	169,800	161,800	364,400
Women	160,000	154,000	347,600

TOTAL ARMED FORCES:
ACTIVE: 31,100 (23,900 conscripts).
Terms of service: 8–11 months (11 months for officers, NCO and soldiers with special duties). Some 30,000 a year do conscript service.
RESERVES (all services): some 700,000; some 30,000 reservists a year do refresher trg: total obligation 40 days (75 for NCO, 100 for officers) between conscript service and age 50 (NCO and officers to age 60).

Total str on mob some 500,000, with 300,000 in general forces (bde etc) and 200,000 in local defence forces (Army 460,000, Navy 12,000, Air Force 30,000), plus 200,000 unallocated as replacements etc.

ARMY: 25,700 (21,600 conscripts).
(all bdes reserve, some with peacetime trg role.)
3 Military Comd:
   1 with 5 mil provinces, 2 armd (1 trg), 3 *Jaeger* (trg),
      9 inf, 1 coastal bde (trg).
   1 with 2 mil provinces, 3 *Jaeger* (trg) bde.
   1 with 5 mil provinces, 4 *Jaeger* (trg), 5 inf bde.
Other units:
4 AD regt.
2 engr bn.

RESERVES: some 200 local defence bn and coy.
EQPT:
MBT: 70 T-55M, 162 T-72.
AIFV: 150 BMP-1, 110 BMP-2 (plus 17 'look-alikes').
APC: 110 BTR-60, 310 XA-180 *Sisu*, 220 MT-LB
(plus 12 'look-alikes').
TOWED ARTY: 105mm: 252 H 61-37; **122mm:** 468 H
63 (D-30); **130mm:** 166 K 54, **152mm:** 324 H 55 (D-
20), H 88-40, H 88-37 (ML-20), H 38 (M-10);
155mm: 36 M-74 (K-83).
SP ARTY: 122mm: 72 PsH 74 (2S1); **152mm:** 18
Telak 91 (2S5).
COASTAL ARTY: 100mm: D-10T (tank turrets);
122mm: M-60; **130mm:** 170 M-54; (static).
COASTAL SSM: 5 RBS-15.
MRL: 122mm: Rak H 76 (BM-21), Rak H 89 (RM-70).
MOR: 81mm: 880; **120mm:** 789: KRH 40, KRH 92.
ATGW: 100: incl 24 M-82 (AT-4 *Spigot*), 12 M-83
(BGM-71D *TOW* 2), M-82M (AT-5 *Spandrel*).
RL: 112mm: *APILAS*.
RCL: 55mm: M-55; **66mm:** 66 KES, 75 (M-72A3);
95mm: 100 SM-58-61.
AD GUNS: 23mm: 100+ ZU-23; **30mm; 35mm:**
GDF-005, *Marksman* GDF-005 SP; **57mm:** 12 S-60
towed, 12 ZSU-57-2 SP.
SAM: SAM-78 (SA-7), SAM-79 (SA-3), SAM-86
(SA-16), 20 SAM-90 (*Crotale* NG).

NAVY: 2,500 (1,000 conscripts).
BASES: Upinniemi (Helsinki), Turku.
4 functional sqn (msl, patrol, two mine warfare).
Approx 50% of units kept fully manned; others are
in short-notice storage, rotated regularly.
PATROL AND COASTAL COMBATANTS: 21:
CORVETTES: 2 *Turunmaa* with 1 x 120mm gun, 2 x
5 ASW RL.
MSL CRAFT: 10:
4 *Helsinki* PFM with 4 x 2 MTO-85 (Sw RBS-15SF) SSM.
2 *Tuima* (Sov *Osa*-II) with 4 MTO-66 (Sov SS-N-2B)
  SSM.
4 *Rauma* PFM with 2 x 2 and 2 x 1 MTO-85 (Sw RBS-
  15SF) SSM.
PATROL CRAFT, INSHORE: 9:
2 *Rihtniemi* with 2 ASW RL.
2 *Ruissalo* with 2 ASW RL.
5 *Nuoli* PFI .
MINE WARFARE: 14:
MINELAYERS: 8:
2 *Hämeenmaa*, 150–200 mines, plus 1 x 6 MATRA
  Mistral SAM.
1 *Pohjanmaa*, 100–150 mines; plus 1 x 120mm gun
  and 2 x 5 ASW RL
3 *Pansio* aux minelayer, 50 mines.
2 *Tuima* (ex-PFM), 20 mines.
MCM: 6 *Kuha* MSI (plus 7 *Kiiski*-class minesweepers).
AMPH: craft only: 3 *Kampela* LCU tpt, 3 *Kala* LCU.

SPT AND MISC: 14:
4 *Valas* coastal tpt (can be used for minelaying).
Plus about 10 civilian-manned ships:
  1 *Aranda* AGOR (Ministry of Trade control).
  9 icebreakers (Board of Navigation control).

AIR FORCE: 2,900 (1,300 conscripts); 108 cbt ac,
no armed hel, 3 AD areas: 3 ftr wings. Flying hours: 150.
FTR: 3 wings:
1 with 13 MiG-21bis, 10 *Hawk* Mk 51 and 51A.
2 with 39 J-35, 20 *Hawk* Mk 51 and 51A.
OCU: 4* MiG-21U/UM, 5* SAAB SK-35C.
RECCE: some *Hawk* Mk 51 and MiG-21T (incl in ftr sqn).
SURVEY: 3 *Learjet* 35A (survey, ECM trg, target-towing).
TPT: 1 ac sqn with 3 F-27; 1 **hel** fleet with 2 Hughes
500D, 7 Mi-8 (tpt/SAR).
TRG: 17 *Hawk** Mk 51, 28 L-70 *Vinka*.
LIAISON: 15 Piper (9 *Cherokee Arrow*, 6 *Chieftain*),
10 L-90 *Redigo*.
AAM: AA-2 *Atoll*, AA-8 *Aphid*, AIM-9 *Sidewinder*,
RB-27, RB-28 (*Falcon*).

FORCES ABROAD:
UN AND PEACEKEEPING:
BOSNIA (UNPROFOR): 7 Obs plus 2 civ pol.
CROATIA (UNCRO): 48; guard unit, incl 4 Obs plus
6 civ pol. **CYPRUS** (UNFICYP): 2. **INDIA/PAKISTAN**
(UNMOGIP): 7 Obs. **IRAQ/KUWAIT** (UNIKOM): 6
Obs. **LEBANON** (UNIFIL): 522; 1 inf bn. **FYROM**
(UNPREDEP): 428; 1 inf bn 1 Obs plus 1 civ pol.
MIDDLE EAST (UNTSO): 17 Obs.

PARAMILITARY:
FRONTIER GUARD (Ministry of Interior): 3,500
(on mob 24,000); 4 frontier, 3 Coast Guard districts, 1
air comd; 2 offshore, 3 coastal, 7 inshore patrol craft;
hel: 3 AS-332, 6 AB-206L, 4 AB-412; **ac:** 1 PA-NAVAJO.

GEORGIA

GDP[a]	Gc 12,681bn ($2.3bn)	
	per capita $2,300	
	1994ε: Gc n.k. ($1.5bn)	
	per capita $1,600	
Growth	1993ε: -39.2%	1994ε: -35.0%
Inflation	1993ε: 1,130%	1994ε: 7,380%
Debt	1993: $420m	1994: $654m
Def exp	1992ε: Gc 5.3bn ($111m)	
	1993ε: Gc 521bn ($94m)	
Def bdgt	1994ε: Gc n.k. ($47m)	
	1995: Gc 71,442bn ($56m)	
FMA[b]	1994: $0.06m (IMET)	

1995: $0.08m (IMET)
1996: $0.30m (IMET)
$1 = Gc[c]   1993: 29,168   1994: 650,000
1995: 1,280,000
Gc = Georgian coupon

[a] Coupon-denominated GDP excludes Abkhazia, South Ossetia and western parts of Georgia affected by war.
[b] The cost of UNOMIG in 1994 was $11m.
[c] The Georgian coupon was introduced in April 1993 and became sole legal tender in August 1993.

Population: 5,441,000 (Russian 6%, Armenian 8%, Ossetian 3%).

	13–17	18–22	23–32
Men	214,200	203,000	377,400
Women	207,400	195,200	363,200

TOTAL ARMED FORCES: n.k.

Terms of service: conscription, 2 years.
RESERVES: possibly up to 250,000 with mil service in last 15 years.

ARMY: up to 20,000 planned, 6,000 probable.

2 Corps HQ.
Some 5 bde (incl border guard, plus trg centre).
EQPT:
MBT: ε40 T-55, ε8 T-72.
AIFV/APC: 51 BMP-1, BTR.
TOWED ARTY: 60 incl: **85mm:** D-44; **100mm:** KS-19 (ground role); **122mm:** D-30.
MRL: 122mm: BM-21.

NAVY: 2,000.

PATROL AND COASTAL COMBATANTS: 15:
FF: 2 *Grisha* I/V with 2 x SA-N-4 SAM, 4 x 533mm TT.
TORPEDO CRAFT: 1 *Turya* PFT with 4 x 533mm TT.
PATROL CRAFT: 12:
9 *Stenka* PFC with 4 x 406mm TT, 1 x 76mm gun.
3 *Muravey* PHT with 2 x 406mm TT.

AIR FORCE: 1,000. Flying hours: 25.

Some 2 Su-25 ac, 1 Mi-8 hel.
AIR DEFENCE:
SAM: 75 SA-2/-3/-5.

OPPOSITION:

ABKHAZIA: ε5,0000; 50+ T-55 MBT, 80+ AIFV/APC, 80+ arty.
SOUTH OSSETIA: ε2,000; 30+ MBT, 30 AIFV/APC.

FOREIGN FORCES:

RUSSIA: Army: 22,000: 3 mil bases with 2 MRD, (200 MBT, 570 ACV, 220 arty/ MRL/mor. Air Force: 1 composite regt. Some 35 tpt ac and hel incl An-12, An-26 and Mi-8.
PEACEKEEPING: ε2,500; 1 AB regt, 2 MR bn (Russia).
UNITED NATIONS (UNOMIG): some 135 Obs from 23 countries.

HUNGARY

GDP	1993: f 3,320bn ($36.11bn):
	per capita $6,100
	1994: f 4,310bn ($40.99bn):
	per capita $6,500
Growth	1993: -2.3% 1994: 2.6%
Inflation	1993: 22.5% 1994: 18.9%
Debt	1993: $24.8bn 1994: $28.5bn
Def exp	1993: f 66.5bn ($723.2m)
Def bdgt	1994: f 58.5bn ($556.2m)
	1995: f 77.1bn ($641.0m)
FMA	1994: $0.7m (IMET)
	1995: $0.7m (IMET)
	1996: $1.0m (IMET)
$1 = f	1993: 92 1994: 105
	1995: 120

f = forint

Population: 10,206,000 (Romany 4%, German 3%, Slovak 1%, Romanian 1%)

	13–17	18–22	23–32
Men	399,400	398,200	666,600
Women	374,800	371,000	625,800

TOTAL ARMED FORCES:

ACTIVE: 70,500 (47,500 conscripts).
Terms of service: 12 months.
RESERVES: 173,000: Army 161,600; Air Force 11,400 (to age 50).

LAND FORCES: 53,700 (36,300 conscripts).

Land Forces HQ tps: 1 attack hel, 1 spt hel regt.
4 Military District Corps/HQ:
  1 with 2 tk, 2 mech bde, 1 MRL, 1 ATK, 1 AD arty, 2 engr regt, 1 recce bn.
  1 with 1 tk, 3 mech, 2 arty, 1 ATK bde, 1 ATK, 1 engr regt, 1 recce bn.
  1 with 4 mech, 1 arty, 1 AD arty, 1 engr bde, 1 engr regt, 1 air mobile (SF), 2 recce bn.
  1 (Budapest) with 2 guard, 1 engr regt, 1 rivercraft unit.
RESERVES: 2 Home Defence bde.
EQPT:

MBT: 1,016: 5 T-34 (in store), 16 T-54 (2 in store), 857 T-55 (183 in store), 138 T-72.
RECCE: 161 FUG D-442.
AIFV: 502 BMP-1, BRM-1K (11 in store).
APC: 1,096: 150 BTR-80, 916 PSZH D-944 (48 in store), 30 MT-LB (plus some 483 'look-alike' types).
TOTAL ARTY: 894:
TOWED: 532: **122mm:** 230 M-1938 (M-30) (52 in store); **152mm:** 302 D-20 (7 in store).
SP: 151: **122mm:** 151 2S1 (2 in store).
MRL: 122mm: 56 BM-21 (1 in store).
MOR: 155: **120mm:** 155 M-120 (11 in store, plus 300 awaiting export).
ATGW: 353: 117 AT-3 *Sagger*, 30 AT-4 *Spigot* (incl BRDM-2 SP), 206 AT-5 *Spandrel*.
ATK GUNS: 85mm: 162 D-44 (62 in store); **100mm:** 106 MT-12 (10 in store).
AD GUNS: 57mm: 189 S-60 (43 in store).
SAM: 244 SA-7, 60 SA-14.
SURV: GS-13 (veh), *Long Trough* ((SNAR-1) arty), *Pork Trough* ((SNAR-2/-6) veh, arty), *Small Fred/Small Yawn* (veh, arty), *Big Fred* ((SNAR-10) veh, arty).
ATTACK HEL: 39 Mi-24.
SPT HEL: 17 Mi-2. 50 Mi-8/-17.
RIVER CRAFT:
MCMV: 6 *Nestin* MSI (riverine); some 45 An-2 mine warfare/patrol boats.

AIR FORCE: 16,800 (11,200 conscripts).
AIR DEFENCE COMD: 147 cbt ac (plus 14 in store). Flying hours: 70.
FTR: 3 regt with 86 MiG-21bis/MF/UM, 12 MiG-23MF, 28 MiG-29 (plus 14 MiG-21 in store).
RECCE: 1 sqn with 14* Su-22.
TPT: 9 An-26, 3 L-410.
TRG: 7 *MiG-21U, 19 L-39, 12 Yak-52.
HEL: 16 Mi-2, 2 Mi-8/-17.
AAM: AA-2 *Atoll*.
SAM: some 14 sites, 1 bde, 3 regt with 82 SA-2/-3/-5, 18 SA-4, 40 SA-6, 45 SA-9, 4 SA-13.

FORCES ABROAD:
UN AND PEACEKEEPING:
ANGOLA (UNAVEM III): 10 Obs plus 15 civ pol.
CYPRUS (UNFICYP): 4 Obs. **EGYPT** (MFO): 41 Obs. **GEORGIA** (UNOMIG): 7 Obs. **IRAQ/KUWAIT** (UNIKOM): 7 Obs. **TAJIKISTAN** (UNMOT): 1 Obs. **WESTERN SAHARA** (MINURSO): 13 civ pol.

PARAMILITARY:
BORDER GUARDS (Ministry of Interior): 730; 24 APC.
INTERNAL SECURITY FORCES (Police): 1,800.

IRELAND

GDP	1993: £I 32.29bn ($47.37bn):
	per capita $12,600
	1994: £I 34.54bn ($51.74bn):
	per capita $13,400

Growth	1993: 4.1%	1994: 6.0%
Inflation	1993: 1.4%	1994: 2.3%
Publ debt	1993: 92.7%	1994: 87.9%
Def exp	1993: £I 389.5m ($571.5m)	
	1994: £I 415.3m ($622.1m)	
Def bdgt	1995: £I 432.7m ($700.1m)	
$1 = £I	1993: 0.68	1994: 0.67
	1995: 0.62	

£I = Irish pound

Population: 3,579,000

	13–17	18–22	23–32
Men	168,200	171,800	300,600
Women	159,200	162,800	286,800

TOTAL ARMED FORCES:
ACTIVE: 12,900 (incl 100 women).
Terms of service: voluntary, 3-year terms to age 60, officers 56–65.
RESERVES: 16,270 (obligation to age 60, officers 57–65). Army: first-line 640, second-line 15,250; Navy: 350.

ARMY: 10,900.
4 Territorial Commands.
1 inf force (2 inf bn).
4 inf bde:
2 with 2 inf bn, 1 with 3, all with 1 fd arty regt, 1 cav recce sqn, 1 engr coy.
1 with 2 inf bn, 1 armd recce sqn, 1 fd arty bty.
Army tps: 1 lt tk sqn, 1 AD regt, 1 Ranger coy.
(Total units: 11 inf bn; 1 UNIFIL bn *ad hoc* with elm from other bn, 1 tk sqn, 4 recce sqn (1 armd), 3 fd arty regt (each of 2 bty); 1 indep bty, 1 AD regt (1 regular, 3 reserve bty), 4 fd engr coy, 1 Ranger coy.)
RESERVES: 4 Army Gp (garrisons), 18 inf bn, 6 fd arty regt, 3 cav sqn, 3 engr sqn, 3 AD bty.
EQPT:
LT TK: 14 *Scorpion*.
RECCE: 19 AML-90, 32 AML-60.
APC: 60 Panhard VTT/M3, 10 *Timoney*, 2 A-180 *Sisu*.
TOWED ARTY: 88mm: 48 25-pdr; **105mm:** 12 lt.
MOR: 81mm: 400; **120mm:** 72.
ATGW: 21 *Milan*.
RCL: 84mm: 444 *Carl Gustav*; **90mm:** 96 PV-1110.
AD GUNS: 40mm: 24 L/60, 2 L/70.
SAM: 7 RBS-70.

NAVY: 1,000.
BASE: Cork.
PATROL AND COASTAL COMBATANTS: 7 PCO:
1 *Eithne* with 1 *Dauphin* hel.
3 *Emer*, 1 *Deirdre*.
2 *Orla* (UK *Peacock*).

AIR FORCE: 1,000; 20 cbt ac, 15 armed hel.
3 wings (1 trg).
COIN: 1 sqn with 6 CM-170-2 *Super Magister*.
COIN/TRG: 1 sqn with 8 SF-260WE.
MR: 2 *Super King Air* 200, 2 CN-235MP.
TPT: 1 HS-125-700B, 1 *Super King Air* 200, 1 *Gulfstream* IV.
LIAISON: 1 sqn with 6* Cessna Reims F-172H Rocket.
HEL: 3 sqn:
1 Army spt with 8 SA-316B (*Alouette* III).
1 Navy spt with 2 SA-342L (*Gazelle*).
1 SAR with 5 SA-365FI (*Dauphin*).

FORCES ABROAD:
UN AND PEACEKEEPING:
BOSNIA (UNPROFOR): 3 Obs, 1 civ pol. **CROATIA** (UNCRO): 6 Obs plus 11 civ pol. **CYPRUS** (UNFICYP): 25 plus 15 civ pol. **HAITI** (UNMIH): 2. **IRAQ/ KUWAIT** (UNIKOM): 7 Obs. **LEBANON** (UNIFIL): 647; 1 bn; 4 AML-90 armd cars, 10 *Sisu* APC, 4 120mm mor. **MIDDLE EAST** (UNTSO): 17 Obs. **WESTERN SAHARA** (MINURSO): 9 Obs plus 14 civ pol.

LATVIA

GDP	1993ε: L 1.59bn ($2.70bn)	
	per capita $3,900	
	1994ε: L 1.60bn ($2.85bn)	
	per capita $4,200	
Growth	1993ε: -14.8%	1994ε: 2.0%
Inflation	1993: 109%	1994: 36%
Debt	1993: $231m	1994: $343m
Def exp	1993ε: L 55m ($95m)	
Def bdgt	1994ε: L 36m ($64m)	
	1995: L 36m ($65m)	
FMA[a]	1994: $0.2m (IMET)	
	1995: $0.2m (IMET)	
	1996: $0.4m (IMET)	
$1 = lats[b]	1993: 0.59	1994: 0.56
	1995: 0.55	
L = lats		

[a] FMA received from Germany, Denmark and other Nordic countries, 1992–94.
[b] The lats was introduced in June 1993 ($1 = 0.68 lats) at a floating exchange rate with convertible currencies.

Population: 2,602,000 (Russian 34%, Belarussian 5%, Ukrainian 3%, Polish 2%).

	13–17	18–22	23–32
Men	97,000	87,000	174,600
Women	93,000	84,200	169,600

TOTAL ARMED FORCES:
ACTIVE: 6,950 (incl Border Guard).
Terms of service: 18 months.
RESERVES: Home Guard 18,000.

ARMY: 1,500.
1 inf bn, 1 peacekeeping coy (forming).
1 recce bn.
1 engr bn.
RESERVES: Home Guard: 5 bde each of 5–7 bn.
EQPT:
RECCE: 2 BRDM-2.
APC: 13 M-42.
TOWED ARTY: 100mm: 25 M-53; **122mm:** 20.
AD GUNS: 12.7mm.

NAVY: 1,000 (incl 350 coastal defence).
BASES: Liepaja, Riga.
PATROL CRAFT: some 14, incl 2 *Kondor*-II, with 3 x twin 20mm gun, 3 *Osa*-I PFM, 1 *Storm* PCC (unarmed) plus approx 8 craft.

COASTAL DEFENCE: 1 coastal def bn (350).

AIR FORCE: 150.
ac: 2 An-2, 1 L-410 ; **hel:** 5 Mi-2.

PARAMILITARY:
BORDER GUARD: 4,300; 1 bde (9 bn).
COAST GUARD: 3 patrol craft, 5 Sw Coast Guard PCI⟨ and 4 converted fishing boats.

LITHUANIA

GDP	1993ε: L 13.3bn ($3.4bn)	
	per capita: $3,200	
	1994ε: L 16.0bn ($3.7bn)	
	per capita: $3,300	
Growth	1993ε: -16.5%	1994ε: 1.5%
Inflation	1993ε: 410%	1994: 72%
Debt	1993: $291m	1994: $486m
Def exp	1993ε: L 505m ($130m)	
Def bdgt	1994ε: L 376m ($94m)	
	1995ε: L 468m ($116m)	

FMA[a]   1994: $0.2m (IMET)
              1995: $0.2m (IMET)
              1996: $0.4m (IMET)
$1 = L[b]   1993: 3.9   1994: 4.0
              1995: 4.0

L = litas

[a] FMA also received from Germany, Denmark and other Nordic countries.
[b] The litas was introduced in June 1993 at a floating exchange rate with convertible currencies.

Population: 3,743,000 (Russian 9%, Polish 8%, Belarussian 2%)

	13–17	18–22	23–32
Men	140,200	130,200	271,600
Women	136,000	127,800	263,000

TOTAL ARMED FORCES:
ACTIVE: ε8,900 (incl Border Guard).
Terms of service: 12 months.
RESERVES: 12,000.

ARMY: 4,300 (incl conscripts).
1 motor rifle bde (8 bn), 1 peacekeeping coy (forming).
EQPT:
RECCE: 10 BRDM-2.
APC: 10 BTR-60, 13 M-42.
RESERVES: Volunteer Home Guard Service.

NAVY: ε350.
BASE: Klaipeda.
FF: 2 Sov 2 *Grisha*-III, with 2 x 12 ASW RL, 4 x 533mm TT.
PATROL AND COASTAL COMBATANTS: about 10: 1 Sw Coast Guard PCI, plus 2 Sov *Turya* PHT (no TT), 1 GDR *Kondor*-I, 1 *Storm* PCC (unarmed), 3 *Osa* 1 PFM (armament unknown), 1 *Victoria* PCI, 1 Sk 21 PCI, plus craft.

AIR FORCE: 250: no cbt ac.
ac: 4 L-39, 2 L-410, 24 AN-2; **hel:** 3 Mi-8.

FORCES ABROAD:
UN AND PEACEKEEPING:
CROATIA (UNCRO): 33.

PARAMILITARY:
BORDER GUARD: 4,000.

Former Yugoslav Republic of
MACEDONIA

GDP	1993ε: $1.6bn:	
	per capita $3,400	
	1994ε: $1.5bn:	
	per capita $3,200	
Growth	1993ε: -15.5%	1994ε: -7.2%
Inflation	1993ε: 248%	1994ε: 55%
Debt	1993ε: $866m	1994ε: $909m
Def exp	1993ε: $30m	
Def bdgt	1994ε: $30m	
	1995ε: $34m	
FMA[a]	1995: $0.1m (IMET)	
	1996: $0.3m (IMET)	
$1 = denar	1993: n.k.	1994: n.k.
	1995: n.k.	

[a] The cost of UNPROFOR in 1994 was $1.6bn.

Population: 2,228,000 (Albanian 30%, Turkish 5%, Romany 2%, Serb 2%, Muslim 2%).

	13–17	18–22	23–32
Men	93,800	87,400	182,000
Women	85,600	80,400	162,600

TOTAL ARMED FORCES:
ACTIVE: 10,400 (8,000 conscripts).
RESERVES: 100,000 planned.

ARMY: 10,400.
3 Corps HQ (cadre).
3 indep bde (planned).
EQPT:
some T-34 tks reported, former Territorial Defence Force: mor, RCL, AD guns, man-portable SAM.

AIR FORCE: 50; no ac, only hel planned.

PARAMILITARY:
POLICE: 7,500 (some 4,500 armed).

FOREIGN FORCES:
UNITED NATIONS (UNPREDEP): some 1,150: 2 inf bn (US, Nordic), incl 24 Obs and 24 civ pol from 23 countries.

MALTA

GDP	1993: LM 938m ($2.54bn):	
	per capita: $6,900	
	1994: LM 1,000m ($2.65bn):	
	per capita $7,200	
Growth	1993: 3.8%	1994: 2.3%
Inflation	1993: 4.1%	1994: 4.2%
Debt	1993: $746.3m	1994ε:$741.8m
Def exp	1993: LM 8.8m ($23.9m)	
Def bdgt	1994: LM 10.3m ($27.3m)	
	1995ε:LM 10.5m ($30.0m)	
$1 = LM	1993: 0.37	1994: 0.38
	1995: 0.35	

LM = Maltese lira

Population: 367,000

	13–17	18–22	23–32
Men	14,600	13,800	25,600
Women	14,000	12,800	25,200

TOTAL ARMED FORCES:
ACTIVE: 1,850.

'ARMED FORCES OF MALTA': 1,850.
Comd HQ, spt tps.
No. 1 Regt (inf bn) with 3 rifle, 1 spt coy.
No. 2 Regt (composite regt):
  1 air sqn with **ac:** 5 0-1 *Bird Dog*, 1 BN-2 *Islander*;
  hel: 3 SA-316B, 2 NH-369M Hughes, 1 AB-206A,
  4 AB-47G2.
  1 maritime sqn (200) with 2 ex-GDR *Kondor*-II PCC,
  4 PCI⟨, plus boats.
  1 AD bty; **14.5mm:** 50 ZPU-4; **40mm:** 40 Bofors.
No. 3 Regt (Depot Regt) with 1 engr sqn, 1 workshop,
  1 ordnance, 1 airport coy.

FOREIGN FORCES:
ITALY: 16; Air Force, hel 1 AB-212.

MOLDOVA

GDP	1993ε: L 2.13bn ($1.2bn):	
	per capita $3,800	
	1994ε: L 3.63bn ($1.0bn):	
	per capita $3,100	
Growth	1993ε:-8.7%	1994ε:-22.1%
Inflation	1993ε:837%	1994ε:111%
Debt	1993: $289m	1994: $390m
Def exp	1993ε:L 58m ($32m)	
Def bdgt	1994: L 29m ($7m)	
	1995: L 60m ($13m)	

FMA	1994: $0.05m (IMET)	
	1995: $0.06m (IMET)	
	1996: $0.20m (IMET)	
$1 = L[a]	1993: 1.8	1994: 4.0
	1995: 4.5	

L = leu

[a] The Moldovan leu was introduced in November 1993 in place of the coupon.

Population: 4,357,000 (Ukrainian 14%, Russian 13%, Gaguaz 4%, Bulgarian 2%, Jewish 2%)

	13–17	18–22	23–32
Men	191,600	170,800	286,000
Women	187,200	165,600	299,000

TOTAL ARMED FORCES: 11,850
(11,000 conscripts).
Terms of service: up to 18 months.
RESERVES: some 66,000 with mil service within last 5 years.

ARMY: 10,550.
3 MR bde.
1 arty bde.
1 recce/assault bn.
EQPT:
AIFV: 54 BMD.
APC: 11 BTR-80, 11 BTR-D, 2 BTR-60PB, 71 TAB-71, 59 MT-LB plus 67 'look-alikes'.
TOWED ARTY: 122mm: 18 M-30; **152mm:** 32 D-20, 21 2A36.
COMBINED GUN/MOR: 120mm: 9 2S9.
MRL: 220mm: 15 9P140 *Uragan*.
MOR: 82mm: 54; **120mm:** 30 M-120.
ATGW: 70 AT-4 *Spigot*, 19 AT-5 *Spandral*, 27 AT-6 *Spiral*.
RCL: 73mm: SPG-9.
ATK GUNS: 100mm: 26 MT-12.
AD GUNS: 23mm: 30 ZU-23; **57mm:** 12 S-60.
SURV: GS-13 (arty), 1 L219/200 PARK-1 (arty), *Long Trough* ((SNAR-1) arty), *Pork Trough* ((SNAR-2/-6) veh, arty), *Small Fred/Small Yawn* (veh, arty), *Big Fred* ((SNAR-10) veh, arty).

AIR FORCE: 1,300 (incl AD).
FTR: 1 regt with 27 MiG-29.
HEL: 1 sqn with 8 Mi-8.
TPT: 1 An-24, 2 An-72, 1 Tu-134, 1 IL-18.
SAM: 1 bde with 25 SA-3/-5.

PARAMILITARY:
INTERNAL TROOPS (Ministry of Interior): 2,500.

OPON (riot police) (Ministry of Interior): 900.

OPPOSITION:
DNIESTR: 5,000; incl Republican Guard (Dniestr bn), Delta bn, ε1,000 Cossacks.

FOREIGN FORCES:
RUSSIA (14th Army): ε9,200. 1 Army HQ, 1 MRD, 1 tk bn, 1 arty regt, 1 AA bde (120 MBT, 180 ACV, 130 arty/MRL/mors) (in Dniestr).
PEACEKEEPING: 6 AB bn (Russia), 3 inf bn (Moldova), 3 bn (Dniestr).

POLAND

GDP	1993: z 155.6bn ($85.9bn):
	per capita $4,900
	1994: z 207.8bn ($91.5bn):
	per capita $5,200

Growth	1993: 3.8%	1994: 5.0%
Inflation	1993: 36.9%	1994: 33.3%
Debt	1993: $45.3bn	1994: $46.0bn
Def exp	1993: z 3.99bn ($2.2bn)
	1994: z 5.12bn ($2.3bn)
Def bdgt	1994: z 4.79bn ($2.11bn)
	1995: z 6.19bn ($2.58bn)
	1996ε: z 8.20bn ($3.04bn)
FMA	1994: $0.7m (IMET)
	1995: $1.7m (FMF, IMET)
	1996: $1.0m (IMET)
$1 = z	1993: 1.81	1994: 2.27
	1995: 2.40
z = zloty

Population: 38,492,000 (German 1%, Ukrainian 1%, Belarussian 1%)

	13–17	18–22	23–32
Men	1,677,800	1,506,400	2,624,200
Women	1,592,600	1,430,200	2,511,200

TOTAL ARMED FORCES:
ACTIVE: 278,600 (158,100 conscripts).
Terms of service: all services 18 months.
RESERVES: 465,500: Army 375,000; Navy 20,500 (to age 50); Air Force 70,000 (to age 60).

ARMY: 188,200 (incl 108,100 conscripts, 2,300 centrally controlled staffs, 27,700 trg, 19,600 log units and 3,100 Coastal Defence).
4 Military Districts/Army HQ:
  1 (Pomerania) with 2 mech, 1 coast defence div, 1 arty, 1 engr bde, 1 SSM, 1 SA-6 regt.
  1 (Silesia) with 3 mech, 1 armd cav div, 2 arty, 2 engr, 1 SA-4 bde, 2 SSM, 1 SA-6 regt.
  1 (Warsaw) with 3 mech div, 1 arty, 1 engr bde.
  1 (Krakow) with 1 air cavalry div HQ, 1 armd, 1 mech, 1 air aslt, 1 'podhale rifle' bde, 1 mech, 1 arty, 1 tpt hel regt.
Div tps: 9 SA-6/-8 regt.
RESERVES: 1 mech div.
EQPT:
MBT: 1,752: 1,035 T-55, 717 T-72.
RECCE: 464 BRDM-2.
AIFV: 1,406 BMP-1, 37 BRM-1.
APC: 110 OT-64 plus some 624 'look-alike' types.
TOTAL ARTY: 1,725:
TOWED: 554: **122mm:** 394 M-1938 (M-30); **152mm:** 160 M-1938 (ML-20).
SP: 634: **122mm:** 516 2S1; **152mm:** 110 *Dana* (M-77); **203mm:** 8 2S7.
MRL: 260: **122mm:** 230 BM-21, 30 RM-70.
MOR: 120mm: 277 M-120.
SSM: launchers: 38 *FROG*.
ATGW: 403: 263 AT-3 *Sagger*, 115 AT-4 *Spigot*, 18 AT-5 *Spandrel*, 7 AT-6 *Spiral*.
ATK GUNS: 85mm: 711 D-44.
AD GUNS: 990: **23mm:** ZU-23-2, ZSU-23-4 SP; **57mm:** S-60.
SAM: 1,290: SA-6/-7/-8/-9/-13.
HEL: 38 Mi-8/Mi-17.
SURV: GS-13 (arty), 1 L219/200 PARK-1 (arty), *Long Trough* ((SNAR-1) arty), *Pork Trough* ((SNAR-2/-6) veh, arty), *Small Fred/Small Yawn* (veh, arty), *Big Fred* ((SNAR-10) veh, arty).

NAVY: 17,800 (incl 2,800 Naval Aviation, 9,600 conscripts).
BASES: Gdynia, Hel, Swinoujscie; Kolobrzeg (border/coast guard).
SS: 3:
1 *Orzel* SS (Sov *Kilo*) with 533mm TT.
2 *Wilk* (Sov *Foxtrot*) with 533mm TT.
PRINCIPAL SURFACE COMBATANTS: 2:
DD: 1 *Warszawa* DDG (Sov mod *Kashin*) with 2 x 2 SA-N-1 *Goa* SAM, 4 x SS-N-2C *Styx* SSM, 5 x 533mm TT, 2 x ASW RL.
FF: 1 *Kaszub* with 2 x ASW RL, 4 x 533mm TT, 76mm gun.
PATROL AND COASTAL COMBATANTS: 33:
CORVETTES: 4 *Gornik* (Sov *Tarantul* I) with 2 x 2 SS-N-2C *Styx* SSM.
MSL CRAFT: 7 Sov *Osa*-I PFM with 4 SS-N-2A SSM.
PATROL CRAFT: 22:
COASTAL: 3 *Sassnitz*.
INSHORE: 8 *Obluze* PCI, 11 *Pilica* PCI⟨.
MINE WARFARE: 24:
MINELAYERS: none, but SS, *Krogulec* MSC and *Lublin* LSM have capability.

MCM: 24:
6 *Krogulec* MSC.
12 *Goplo* (*Notec*) MSI.
4 *Mamry* (*Notec*) MHI.
2 *Leniwka* MSI.
AMPH: 5 *Lublin* LSM, capacity 135 tps, 9 tk.
Plus craft: 3 *Deba* LCU (none employed in amph role).
SPT AND MISC: 17:
1 comd ship, 2 AGI, 4 spt tkr, 3 survey, 3 trg, 2 research, 2 salvage.

NAVAL AVIATION: (2,800).
35 cbt ac, 11 armed hel.
2 regt, 2 sqn.
FTR: 1 regt, 35 MiG-21 BIS/U.
1 special naval regt with 14 TS-11, 7 An-2.
1 ASW/SAR sqn with 5 Mi-2, 11 Mi-14 (ASW), 3 Mi-14 (SAR).
1 SAR/liaison sqn: 3 An-28RM, 6 W-3 Sokol.

COASTAL DEFENCE: (3,100, incl in Army total).
6 arty bn with M-1937 152mm.
3 SSM bn with SS-C-2B.

AIR FORCE: 72,600 (incl AD tps, 40,300 conscripts); 412 cbt ac (plus 20 in store), 30 attack hel.
Flying hours: 60.
FTR: 3 AD Corps: 7 regt with 216 MiG-21, 37 MiG-23, 12 MiG-29.
FGA: 2 air div, 4 regts with 16 Su-20, 103 Su-22.
RECCE: 28* MiG-21R/U.
TPT: 2 regt with 10 An-2, 1 An-12, 10 An-26, 10 Yak-40, 1 Tu-154, 2 Il-14.
HEL: armed, 30 Mi-24, 40 Mi-2URP, 10 W-3W; aslt: 68 Mi-2, 5 Mi-8.
TPT: 106 Mi-2, 5 Mi-8, 7 W-3 *Sokol*.
TRG: 191 TS-11 *Iskra*, 5 PZL I-22 *Iryda*, 24 PZL-130 *Orlik*.
IN STORE: 20 MiG-21.
AAM: AA-2 *Atoll*, AA-8 *Aphid*.
ASM: AS-7 *Kerry*.
SAM: 4 bde; 1 indep regt with 50 sites with about 232 SA-2/-3/-5.

FORCES ABROAD:
UN AND PEACEKEEPING:
ANGOLA (UNAVEM III): 7 Obs. **BOSNIA** (UNPROFOR): 12 Obs, 3 civ pol. **CROATIA** (UNCRO): 1,063; 1 inf bn, incl 16 Obs, 25 civ pol. **FORMER YUGOSLAVIA:** 2 Obs. **GEORGIA** (UNOMIG): 5 Obs. **IRAQ/KUWAIT** (UNIKOM): 6 Obs. **KOREA** (NNSC): staff. **LEBANON** (UNIFIL): 558; 1 inf bn, mil hospital. **FYROM** (UNPREDEP): 2 Obs plus 1 civ pol. **RWANDA** (UNAMIR): 2 Obs. **SYRIA** (UNDOF): 354; 1 inf bn. **TAJIKISTAN** (UNMOT): 2 Obs. **WESTERN SAHARA** (MINURSO): 2 Obs.

PARAMILITARY:
BORDER GUARDS (Ministry of Interior): 16,000; 14 Provincial Comd: 14 units.
MARITIME BORDER GUARD: about 28 patrol craft: 2 PCC, 9 PCI and 17 PCI⟨.
PREVENTION UNITS OF POLICE (OPP): 7,400 (1,400 conscripts).

ROMANIA

GDP	1993: lei 18,835bn ($24.78bn):
	per capita $2,900
	1994ε: lei 43,256bn ($26.13bn):
	per capita $3,000
Growth	1993: 1.3% 1994: 3.4%
Inflation	1993: 256% 1994: 137%
Debt	1993: $4.46bn 1994: $4.37bn
Def exp	1993: lei 421bn ($554m)
Def bdgt	1994: lei 1,260.3bn ($761.5m)
	1995: lei 1,772.7bn ($927.5m)
FMA	1994: $0.3m (IMET)
	1995: $0.5m (IMET)
	1996: $0.7m (IMET)
$1 = lei	1993: 760 1994: 1,655
	1995: 1,911

Population: 22,805,000 (Hungarian 9%)

	13–17	18–22	23–32
Men	928,400	947,200	1,733,600
Women	892,800	909,800	1,673,800

TOTAL ARMED FORCES:
ACTIVE: ε217,400 (incl ε104,700 conscripts, 9,700 MoD staff and 5,900 centrally controlled units).
Terms of service: Army, Air Force: 12 months; Navy: 18 months.
RESERVES: 427,000: Army 400,000; Navy 6,000; Air Force 21,000.

ARMY: 128,800 (ε84,700 conscripts).
4 Army Areas:
6 Corps HQ:
1 with 1 tk, 2 mech, 1 inf, 1 mtn, 1 arty, 1 ATK bde, 1 mixed AAA regt, 1 recce, 1 SSM, 2 airport gd, 2 engr bn.
1 with 2 mech, 1 mtn, 1 arty bde, 1 recce, 1 engr bn.
1 with 1 tk, 2 mech, 1 mtn, 1 ATK bde, 1 AAA regt, 1 recce bn.
1 with 2 mech, 1 mot inf, 1 mot inf, 1 mtn, 1 ATK bde, 1 recce, 1 airport gd, 1 SSM, 1 engr bn.
1 with 2 tk, 1 inf, 1 ATK bde, 1 recce, 1 engr bn.
1 with 3 mech, 1 mot inf, 1 mtn, 1 arty, 1 ATK bde, 1 arty regt, 1 recce, 1 engr bn.

Army tps: 1 tk, 1 mech, 1 mtn, 1 arty, 1 ATK, 3 AAA bde,
  1 mech, 1 arty, 4 AAA, 4 SAM, 3 engr regt.
MoD tps: 3 AB (Air Force), 1 gd bde, 2 recce bn.
Land Force tps: 2 *Scud*, 1 arty, 1 engr bde; 2 engr regt.

EQPT:
MBT: 1,843: 146 T-34, 822 T-55, 30 T-72, 620 TR-85, 225 TR-580.
ASLT GUN: 160: 94 SU-76, 66 SU-100.
RECCE: 139 BRDM-2, 8 TAB-80.
AIFV: 178 MLI-84.
APC: 2,032: 168 TAB-77, 414 TABC-79, 1,365 TAB-71, 85 MLVM, plus 976 'look-alikes'.
TOTAL ARTY: 2,341:
TOWED: 1,174: **100mm:** 132 Skoda (various models); **105mm:** 72 Schneider; **122mm:** 334 M-1938 (M-30), 12 M-1931/37 (A-19); **130mm:** 98 Gun 82; **150mm:** 6 Ceh (Model 1937); **152mm:** 81 D-20, 101 Gun-How 85, 55 Model 1938, 283 Model 81.
SP: 48: **122mm:** 6 2S1, 42 Model 89.
MRL: 311: **122mm:** 38 APR-21, 273 APR-40.
MOR: 808: **120mm:** 332 M-38, 476 Model 1982.
SSM: launchers: 13 *Scud*, 12 *FROG*.
ATGW: 534: AT-1 *Snapper*, AT-3 *Sagger* (incl BRDM-2).
ATK GUNS: 1,450: **57mm:** M-1943; **85mm:** D-44; **100mm:** 829 Gun 77, 75 Gun 75.
AD GUNS: 1,118: **30mm; 37mm; 57mm; 85mm; 100mm.**
SAM: 62 SA-6/-7.
SURV: GS-13 (arty), 1 L219/200 PARK-1 (arty), *Long Trough* ((SNAR-1) arty), *Pork Trough* ((SNAR-2/-6) veh, arty), *Small Fred/Small Yawn* ((veh, arty), *Big Fred* ((SNAR-10) veh, arty).

NAVY: ε19,000 (incl 8,000 Naval Infantry and ε10,000 conscripts). 1 maritime div, 1 patrol boat bde, 1 river bde, 1 maritime/river bde.
BASES: Coastal: Mangalia, Constanta;
Danube: Braila, Giurgiu, Tulcea.
SS: 1 Sov *Kilo* SS with 533mm TT.
PRINCIPAL SURFACE COMBATANTS: 6:
DD: 1 *Marasesti* (ex-*Muntenia*) DDG with 4 x 2 SS-N-2C *Styx* SSM, plus SA-N-5 *Grail* SAM, 2 IAR-316 hel, 2 x 3 533mm TT, RBU 6000.
FF: 5:
4 *Tetal* with 2 x ASW RL, 4 x ASTT, 1 imp *Tetal* with 2 x ASW RL, 4 x ASTT, plus 1 SA-316 hel.
PATROL AND COASTAL COMBATANTS: 77:
CORVETTES: 3 *Tarantul* I with 2 x 2 SS-N-2C *Styx*, 1 x 4 SA-N-5 *Grail* SAM; plus 1 x 76mm gun.
MSL CRAFT: 6 Sov *Osa*-I PFM with 4 x SS-N-2A *Styx*.
TORPEDO CRAFT: 32:
12 *Epitrop* PFT with 4 x 533mm TT.
20 Ch *Huchuan* PHT with 2 x 533mm TT.
PATROL CRAFT: 36:
OFFSHORE: 4 *Democratia* (GDR M-40) PCO.
INSHORE: 8:

4 Ch *Shanghai* PFI, 4 Ch *Huchuan*.
RIVERINE: 24:
some 6 *Brutar* with 1 x 100mm gun, 1 x 122mm RL, 18⟨.
MINE WARFARE: 39:
MINELAYERS: 2 *Cosar*, capacity 100 mines.
MCM: 37:
4 *Musca* MSC.
8 T.301 MSI (plus some 9 non-op).
25 VD141 MSI⟨.
SPT AND MISC: 10:
2 *Constanta* log spt with 1 *Alouette* hel, 3 spt tkr, 2 AGOR, 1 trg, 2 tugs.
HEL: 3 1AR-316, 4 Mi-14 PL.

NAVAL INFANTRY (Marines): (8,000).
2 mech, 1 mot inf, 1 arty regt, 1 airport gd, 1 ATK, 1 recce bn.
1 indep inf bn.
EQPT:
MBT: 168 TR-580.
ASLT GUN: 12 SU-76.
APC: 90 TAB-71, 33 TABC-79 plus 79 'look-alikes'.
TOTAL ARTY: 126:
TOWED: 122mm: 36 M-1938 (M-30); **152mm:** 36 Model 81.
MRL: 122mm: 18 APR-40.
MOR: 120mm: 24 Model 1982, 12 M-38.

COASTAL DEFENCE (1,000): HQ Constanta
4 sectors.
4 coastal arty bty with 32 **130mm**.
10 AA arty bty: 3 with 18 **30mm**; 5 with 30 **37mm**; 2 with 12 **57mm**.

AIR FORCE: 54,000 (incl 8,000 AB, 10,000 conscripts); 402 cbt ac, 17 attack hel.
Air Force comd: 1 Air div, 1 AD div, 3 para bde. Flying hours: 40.
FGA: 3 regt with 10 MiG-17, 75 IAR-93, 25 MiG-15, 45 MiG-21.
FTR: 4 regt with 120 MiG-21, 38 MiG-23, 18 MiG-29.
OCU: 46* MiG-21.
RECCE: 2 sqn:
1 with 12 Il-28 (recce/ECM), 1 with 11* MiG-21.
TPT: 1 regt with 8 An-24, 14 An-26, 2 Il-18, 2 Boeing 707, 2 Rombac 1-11.
SURVEY: 3 An-30.
HEL: 5 regt plus 4 sqn with:
ATTACK: 17 IAR 316 CBT.
SPT: 81 IAR-316, 69 IAR-330, 2 Mi-17, 7 Mi-8.
UTL: 4 AS-365N.
TRG: ac: 45 L-29, 32 L-39, 2 MiG-15, 14* IAR-99.
AAM: AA-2 *Atoll*, AA-7 *Apex*.
AD: 1 div: 20 SAM sites with 120 SA-2.

FORCES ABROAD:
UN AND PEACEKEEPING:
ANGOLA (UNAVEM III): 137. **KUWAIT** (UNIKOM): 7 Obs.

PARAMILITARY:
BORDER GUARDS (Ministry of Interior): 22,300 (incl conscripts: 6 bde, 7 naval gp; 33 TAB-71 APC, 18 SU-100 aslt gun, 12 M-1931/37 (A19) 122mm how, 18 M-38 120mm mor, 20 Ch *Shanghai* II PFI).
GENDARMERIE (Ministry of Interior): 10,000; 8 bde; some APC.
SECURITY GUARDS (Ministry of Interior): 46,800.

Federal Republic of Yugoslavia:

SERBIA/MONTENEGRO

GDP	1993ε: $12.3bn:
	per capita $4,000
	1994ε: $13.0bn:
	per capita $4,200

Growth	1993ε: -30.0%	1994ε: 5.5%
Inflation:	1993: hyper-inflation 1994ε: 500%	
Debt	1993ε: $6.2bn	1994ε: $6.5bn
Def exp	1993ε: n.k. ($2,800m)	
Def bdgt	1994: sd 1,000m ($741m)	
	1995: sd 1,611m ($1,143m)	
$1 = sd[a]	1994: 1.62	1995: 1.41
sd = super dinar		

[a] The super dinar was introduced in January 1994 when it was fixed at parity with the DM. Unofficial rates in mid-1995 were $=3sd.

Population: Serbia and Montenegro 10,821,000. Serbia 10,040,000 (Serb 66%, Albanian 17%, Hungarian 4%, Muslim 2%). Montenegro 782,000 (Montenegrin 62%, Muslim 15%, Serb 9%, Albanian 7%). ε2,032,000 Serbs were living in the other Yugoslav republics before the civil war began.

	13–17	18–22	23–32
Men	427,400	425,800	834,400
Women	403,200	402,800	791,800

TOTAL ARMED FORCES:
ACTIVE: 126,500 (ε60,000 conscripts).
Terms of service: 12–15 months.
RESERVES: some 400,000.

ARMY (JA): some 90,000 (ε37,000 conscripts).
3 Army, 8 Corps (incl 1 mech).

3 tk bde.	1 SF bde.
8 mech bde.	6 arty bde.
7 mot inf bde.	1 ATK arty bde.
1 AB bde.	9 AD regt.
2 Task Force.	5 SAM-6 regt.

RESERVES: 1 Task Force, 1 inf bde gp (4 bde), 22 mot inf, 10 inf, 1 mtn, 2 arty, 2 ATK arty bde; 3 arty, 2 ATK regt.
EQPT:
MBT: 639: 407 T-54/-55, some 232 M-84 (T-74; mod T-72).
RECCE: 38 BRDM-2.
AIFV: 517 M-80.
APC: 112 M-60P, BOV-VP.
TOTAL ARTY: 1,499:
TOWED: 786: **105mm:** 174 M-56; **122mm:** 168 M-1931/37, M-1938, 132 D-30; **130mm:** 180 M-46; **152mm:** 48: M-1937, D-20, M-84; **155mm:** 84: M-59, M-65.
SP: 105mm: M-7; **122mm:** 75 2S1.
MRL: 72: **128mm:** 48 M-63, 24 M-77.
MOR: 82mm: 1,700; **120mm:** 566.
ATGW: 135 AT-3 *Sagger*, incl SP (BOV-1, BRDM-1/2).
RCL: 57mm: 1,550; **82mm:** 1,000 M-60PB SP; **105mm:** 650 M-65.
ATK GUNS: 76mm: 60; **90mm:** 74 M-36B2 (incl SP); **100mm:** 130 T-12.
AD GUNS: 20mm: 475 M-55/-75, 65 BOV-3 SP triple; **30mm:** 350 M-53, M-53/-59, 8 BOV-30 SP; **57mm:** 54 ZSU-57-2 SP.
SAM: 175: SA-6/-7/-9.

NAVY: ε6,000 (incl 4,500 conscripts).
BASE: Kotor, Tivat, Bar. (Most former Yugoslav bases are now in Croatian hands.)
SS: 4:
2 *Sava* SS with 533mm TT (poss only 1 op).
2 *Heroj* SS with 533mm TT.
(Plus 5 *Una* SSI for SF ops.)
FF: 4:
2 *Kotor* with 4 x SS-N-2C *Styx* SSM, 1 x 2 SA-N-4 SAM, 2 x 12 ASW RL, 2 x 3 ASTT.
2 *Split* (Sov *Koni*) with 4 SS-N-2C, 1 x 2 SA-N-4 SAM, *Styx* SSM, 2 x 12 ASW RL.
PATROL AND COASTAL COMBATANTS: 41:
MSL CRAFT: 10:
5 *Rade Koncar* PFM with 2 x SS-N-2B *Styx* (some †).
5 *Mitar Acev* (Sov *Osa*-I) PFM with 4 x SS-N-2A.
TORPEDO CRAFT: 4 *Topcider* (Sov *Shershen*) with 4 x 533mm TT.
PATROL CRAFT: 27:
INSHORE: 6 *Mirna*.
RIVERINE: about 21⟨ (some in reserve).
MINE WARFARE: 5:

MINELAYERS: 1 *Sibla*-class, 94 mines.
D-3 and D-501 LCTs can also lay 100 mines.
MCM: 4:
2 *Vukov Klanac* MHC.
2 UK *Ham* MSI.
(Plus some 12 riverine MSI(.)
AMPH: craft only: about 18: 4 D-3/D-501 LCT, about 14 LCM.
SPT AND MISC: 5:
1 PO-91 *Lubin* tpt, 1 trg, 1 river flagship, 2 harbour tkr.

MARINES: (900).
2 marine bde (2 regt each of 2 bn).

AIR FORCE: 29,000 (3,000 conscripts); 282 cbt ac, 110 armed hel.
4 air bde, 2 hel regt.
FGA: some 80 *Jastreb*, *Super Galeb*, *Orao* 2.
FTR: 7 sqn with 87 MiG-21F/PF/M/bis, 10 MiG-21U, 16 MiG-29 (-A: 14; -UB: 2).
RECCE: 2 sqn with some 29* *Orao*, MiG-21.
ARMED HEL: some 110 Mi-8 (aslt); *Gazela*.
ASW: 1 hel sqn with 4 Mi-14, 4 Ka-25, 2 Ka-27.
TPT: 2 An-12, 15 An-26, 4 CL-215 (SAR, fire-fighting), 2 *Falcon* 50 (VIP), 2 *Learjet* 25, 6 Yak-40.
LIAISON: ac: 46 UTVA-66; **hel:** 14 *Partizan*.
TRG: ac: 60 **Super Galeb/Jastreb*, 100 UTVA; **hel:** 20 *Gazela*.
AAM: AA-2 *Atoll*, AA-8 *Aphid*, AA-10 *Alamo*, AA-11 *Archer*.
ASM: AGM-65 *Maverick*, AS-7 *Kerry*.
AD: 8 SAM bn, 8 sites with 24 SA-2, 16 SA-3. 15 regt AD arty.

SLOVAKIA

GDP	1993: Ks 340.2 bn ($11.97bn): per capita $5,500		
	1994: Ks 398.3bn ($12.85bn): per capita $5,800		
Growth	1993: -4.1%	1994: 4.8%	
Inflation	1993: 23.1%	1994: 11.7%	
Debt	1993: $3.33bn	1994: $4.28bn	
Def exp	1993: Ks 8.2bn ($273.3m)		
	1994: Ks 9.6bn ($309m)		
Def bdgt	1994: Ks 10.4bn ($335.5m)		
	1995: Ks 12.9bn ($403.1m)		
FMA	1994: $0.3m (IMET)		
	1995: $0.4m (IMET)		
	1996: $0.5m (IMET)		
$ = Ks	1993: 30.8	1994: 32.1	
	1995: 29.4		

Ks = Slovak koruna

Population: 5,414,000 (Hungarian 11%, Romany 5%, Czech 1%)

	13–17	18–22	23–32
Men	237,800	225,600	394,600
Women	229,000	218,800	384,200

TOTAL ARMED FORCES:
ACTIVE: 47,000.
Terms of service: 18 months.

ARMY: 33,000.
2 Corps HQ.
1 mech inf div.
EQPT:
MBT: 912 T-72M, T-54/-55.
RECCE: 129 BRDM, 90 OT-65.
AIFV: 476: BVP-1, BMP-2, BPZV, BRM-1K.
APC: 567: OT-90, 476 OT-64A/C.
TOTAL ARTY: 808:
TOWED: 297: **100mm:** M-53; **122mm:** M-1931/37 (A-19), M-1938, D-30.
SP: 189: **122mm** 2S1; **152mm:** *Dana* (M-77).
MRL: 243: **122mm:** RM-70; **130mm:** RM-130 (M-51).
MOR: 79: **120mm;** **240mm:** 2S4.
SSM: 9 *FROG*-7, SS-21, *Scud*, SS-23.
ATGW: AT-3 *Sagger*, AT-5 *Spandrel*.
AD GUNS: 286: **30mm:** M-53/-59, *Strop* SP; **57mm:** S-60.
SAM: 437: SA-7, SA-9/-13.
SURV: GS-13 (veh), *Long Trough* (SNAR-1), *Pork Trough* ((SNAR-2/-6) arty), *Small Fred/Small Yawn* (veh, arty), *Big Fred* (SNAR-10) veh, arty).

AIR FORCE: 14,000; 111 cbt ac (plus 30 in store), 19 attack hel.
FGA: 34, incl Su-22, Su-25.
FTR: 50 MiG-21, 15 MiG-29.
RECCE: 8 MiG-21 RF.
TPT: 16, incl An-12, An-24/-26, Tu-134, Tu-154, L410M.
TRG: some 15 L-29, 25 L-39, 4* MiG-21 U/MF.
ATTACK HEL: 19 Mi-24.
ASLT TPT: 26, incl Mi-8, Mi-17.
IN STORE: about 30 incl MiG-21, Su-7.
AAM: AA-2 *Atoll*, AA-7 *Apex*, AA-8 *Aphid*.
AD: SA-2, SA-6.

FORCES ABROAD:
UN AND PEACEKEEPING:
ANGOLA (UNAVEM III): 5 Obs. **CROATIA** (UNCRO): 589; 1 engr bn.

PARAMILITARY:

BORDER GUARDS: 600.
INTERNAL SECURITY FORCES: 250.
CIVIL DEFENCE TROOPS: 3,100.

SLOVENIA

GDP	1993: t 1,414.7bn ($13.2bn):
	per capita $6,400
	1994: t 1,779.2bn ($14.5bn):
	per capita $6,800

Growth	1993: 1.3%	1994: 5.0%
Inflation:	1993: 31.9%	1994: 19.8%
Debt	1993: $1.92bn	1994: $2.26bn
Def exp	1993ε:t 23.2bn ($205m)	
	1994ε:t 37.4bn ($290m)	
Def bdgt	1994: t 24.6bn ($191m)	
	1995ε:t 33.6bn ($298m)	
FMA	1994: $0.3m (IMET)	
	1995: $0.1m (IMET)	
	1996: $0.3m (IMET)	
$1 = t	1993: 113	1994: 129
	1995: 113	

t = tolar

Population 2,007,000 (Croat 3%, Serb 2%, Muslim 1%)

	13–17	18–22	23–32
Men	75,600	75,000	149,400
Women	71,000	71,200	149,200

TOTAL ARMED FORCES:
ACTIVE: 8,400 (5,500 conscripts).
Terms of service: 7 months.
RESERVES: 70,000 (incl 47,000 first-line reserves).

ARMY: 8,400 (5,500 conscripts).
6 Military Districts; 27 Military Regions.
7 inf 'bde' (bn).
1 SAM 'bde' (bn).
2 indep mech bn.
RESERVES: 1 special, 1 avn 'bde', 2 indep mech, 1 arty, 1 coast def, 1 ATK bn.
EQPT:
MBT: 42 M-84, 40 T-55.
RECCE: 15 BRDM-2.
AIFV: 62 M-80.
APC: 12 BOV-VP, 10 BTR-50PU.
TOWED ARTY: 105mm: 8 M-2.
SP ARTY: 122mm: 8 2S1.
MRL: 128mm: 56 M-71 (single tube), 4 M-63.
MOR: 120mm: 64 M-52.
ATGW: AT-3 *Sagger* (incl 12 BOV-1SP).
AD GUNS: 20mm: 12 SP; **30mm:** 8 SP; **57mm:** 18SP.

SAM: 9 SA-9.
AC: 3 PC-9, 3 ZUN-242, 1 LET L-410.
HEL: 1 AB-109, 2 B-206, 8 B-412.

MARITIME ELEMENT: 35 (plus 460 reservists).
BASE: Koper.
2 PCI⟨.

PARAMILITARY:
POLICE: 4,500 armed (plus 5,000 reserve); **hel:** 2 AB-206 Jet Ranger, 1 AB-109A, 1 AB-212, 1 AB-412.

SWEDEN

GDP	1993: Skr 1,442.18bn ($185.3bn):
	per capita $17,500
	1994: Skr 1,516.95bn ($196.6bn):
	per capita $18,200

Growth	1993: -2.6%	1994: 2.2%
Inflation	1993: 4.6%	1994: 2.6%
Publ Debt	1993: 74.6%	1994: 79.4%
Def exp	1993: Skr 40.93bn ($5.26bn)	
	1994: Skr 38.11bn ($4.94bn)	
Def bdgt	1995: Skr 40.75bn ($5.59bn)	
	1996ε:Skr 40.34bn ($5.53bn)	
$1 = Skr	1993: 7.78	1994: 7.72
	1995: 7.29	

Skr = Swedish kronor

Population: 8,785,000

	13–17	18–22	23–32
Men	258,200	283,200	631,000
Women	243,400	269,200	596,000

TOTAL ARMED FORCES:
ACTIVE: 64,000 (31,600 conscripts).
Terms of service: Army and Navy 7–15 months; Air Force 8–12 months.
RESERVES (obligation to age 47):[a] 729,000: Army (incl Local Defence and Home Guard) 586,000; Navy 66,000; Air Force 77,000.

[a] 48,000 reservists carry out refresher trg in 1995–96; length of trg depends on rank (officers up to 31 days, NCO and specialists, 24 days, others 17 days). Commitment is 5 exercises during reserve service period, plus mob call-outs.

ARMY: 43,500 (27,000 conscripts).
Joint: 3 joint (tri-service) comd each with: Army div and def districts, naval comd (2 in Central Joint Comd) Air Comd, logistics regt.
No active units (as defined by Vienna Document).

6 div with total of 2 armd, 4 mech, 6 inf, 4 arctic bde, 7 arty regt.
22 def districts (4 mech, 18 inf).

EQPT:
MBT: 288 *Centurion*, 260 Strv-103B, 160 Strv-121 (*Leopard* 2).
LT TK: 210 Ikv-91.
AIFV: 405 Pbv-302 plus 200 'look-alikes', 30 Strf-9040.
APC: 360 Pbv 401A (MT-LB).
TOWED ARTY: 105mm: 455 Type-40; **155mm:** 153 FH-77A/B, Type F 182.
SP ARTY: 155mm: 26 BK-1A.
MOR: 81mm: 1,000; **120mm:** 510.
ATGW: 57 *TOW* (Pvrbv 551 SP), RB-55, RB-56 *Bill*.
RL: 84mm: AT-4.
RCL: 84mm: *Carl Gustav*; **90mm:** PV-1110.
AD GUNS: 40mm: 600.
SAM: RBS-70 (incl Lvrbv SP), RB-77 (I HAWK), RBS-90.
SURV: *Green Archer* (mor).
HEL: 26 Hkp-9A ATK, 16 Hkp-3 tpt, 25 Hkp-5B trg, 19 Hkp-6A utl.

NAVY: ε9,000 (incl Coastal Defence, 320 Naval Air and ε4,100 conscripts).
BASES: Muskö, Karlskrona, Härnösand, Göteborg (spt only).
SS: 13:
4 *Västergötland* with TP-617 HWT and TP-613 and TP-43.
1 modernised *Näcken* (AIP) with TP-613 and TP-42.
2 *Näcken*.
5 *Sjöormen*, with TP-613 and TP-42.
1 *Spiggen* II (ASW target) submarine.
PATROL AND COASTAL COMBATANTS: 41:
MSL CRAFT: 34 PFM:
4 *Göteborg* with 4 x 2 RBS-15 SSM; plus 4 x 400mm TT, 4 x ASW mor.
2 *Stockholm* with 4 x 2 RBS-15 SSM (or up to 4 additional 533 TT); plus 2 x 533mm, 4 x 400mm TT, 4 x ASW mor.
16 *Hugin* with 6 RB-12 (No *Penguin*) SSM; plus 4 ASW mor.
12 *Norrköping* with 4 x 2 RBS-15 SSM or up to 6 x 533mm TT.
PATROL CRAFT: 7:
1 PCI, 6 PCI⟨.
MINE WARFARE: 29:
MINELAYERS: 3:
1 *Carlskrona* (200 mines), trg.
2 *Älvsborg* (200 mines).
(Mines can be laid by all SS classes.)
MCM: 26:
1 *Utö* MCMV spt.
7 *Landsort* MHC.

3 *Arkö* MSC.
10 MSI, 5 MSI⟨.
AMPH: craft only: 12 LCM.
SPT AND MISC: 12:
1 AGI, 1 sub rescue/salvage ship, 1 survey, 6 ice-breakers, 2 tugs, 1 SES PCI (trials).

COASTAL DEFENCE:
2 coast arty bde: 4 naval bde, 12 mobile, 53 static units, incl 2 amph defence bn, arty, barrier bn, minelayer sqn.
EQPT:
GUNS: 40mm, incl L/70 AA; **75mm, 120mm** incl CD-80*Karin* (mobile); **75mm,** 120mm*Ersta* (static).
MOR: 81mm, 120mm: 70.
SSM: RBS-17 *Hellfire*, RBS-08A, RBS-15KA, RB-52.
MINELAYERS: 9 inshore, 16 inshore⟨.
PATROL CRAFT: 18 PCI.
AMPH: 10 LCM, 80 LCU, about 60 LCA.

NAVAL AIR: (320); 1 cbt ac, 10 armed hel.
ASW: 1 C-212 ac.
HEL: 3 sqn with 10 Hkp-4B/C (ASW), 10 Hkp-6 liaison.

AIR FORCE: 11,500 (5,500 conscripts); 393 cbt ac (plus 51 in store), no armed hel.
3 Air Comd.
FGA: 4 sqn with 74 SAAB AJ-37 (plus 13 in store); incl 1 (OCU) with 15 SAAB SK-37 (plus 15 in store).
FTR: 8 sqn:
1 with 40 SAAB J-35 (plus 23 in store), 10 SAAB SK-35C.
7 with 135 SAAB JA-37.
RECCE: 2 sqn with *50 SAAB SH/SF-37.
ECM: 2 *Caravelle*, 13 SAAB J-32E.
TPT: 1 sqn with 8 C-130E/H, 3 *King Air* 200, 2 *Metro* III (VIP), 13 SK-60D/E, 1 SAAB 340B.
TRG: 25 SAAB J-32B/D/E (-E ECM trg: 13; -D target-towing: 5; -B: 7), 69 *SK-69B/C (also have lt attack/recce role), 71 SK-61.
SAR: 11 Hkp-10 (*Super Puma*), 6 Hkp-3 (Bell 204).
AAM: RB-24 (AIM-9B/3*Sidewinder*), RB-27 (*Improved Falcon*), RB-28 (*Falcon*), RB-71 (*Skyflash*), RB-74 AIM 9L (*Sidewinder*).
ASM: RB-04E, RB-05A, RB-15F, RB-75 (*Maverick*).
AD: semi-automatic control and surv system, *Stril* 60, coordinates all AD components.

FORCES ABROAD:
UN AND PEACEKEEPING:
ANGOLA (UNAVEM III): 20 Obs. **BOSNIA** (UNPROFOR): 1,121; 1 armd inf bn, 6 Obs plus 5 civ pol. **CROATIA** (UNCRO): 137; HQ coy, 11 Obs, 30 civ pol. **GEORGIA** (UNOMIG): 7 Obs. **INDIA/ PAKISTAN** (UNMOGIP): 8 Obs. **IRAQ/KUWAIT**

(UNIKOM): 6 Obs. **KOREA** (NNSC): 6 Staff. **FYROM** (UNPREDEP): 38 plus 1 Obs. **MIDDLE EAST** (UNTSO): 17 Obs.

PARAMILITARY:
COAST GUARD: (600); 1 *Gotland* PCO and 1 KBV-171 PCC (fishery protection), some 65 PCI; Air Arm: 3 C-212 MR, 1 Cessna 337G, 1 402C ac.
CIVIL DEFENCE: shelters for 6,300,000. All between age 16–25 liable for civil defence duty.
VOLUNTARY AUXILIARY ORGANISATIONS: some 35,000 volunteers.

SWITZERLAND

GDP	1993: fr 343.0bn ($232.13bn):		
	per capita $22,300		
	1994: fr 356.2bn ($260.44bn):		
	per capita $23,100		
Growth	1993: -0.9%	1994:	2.1%
Inflation	1993: 3.3%	1994:	0.8%
Publ Debt	1993: 20.2%	1994:	21.8%
Def exp	1993: fr 5.8bn ($3.9bn)		
	1994: fr 5.9bn ($4.3bn)		
Def bdgt	1995: fr 6.02bn ($5.16bn)		
	1996ε: fr 6.00bn ($5.13bn)		
$1 = fr	1993: 1.48	1994:	1.37
	1995: 1.17		

fr = Swiss franc

Population: 7,071,000

	13–17	*18–22*	*23–32*
Men	202,600	219,000	543,600
Women	194,000	211,400	534,800

TOTAL ARMED FORCES (Air Corps forms part of the Army):
ACTIVE: about 3,400 regular, plus recruits (2 intakes (1 of 11,000, 1 of 17,000) each for 15 weeks only).
Terms of service: 15 weeks compulsory recruit trg at age 19–20, followed by 10 refresher trg courses of 3 weeks over a 22-year period between ages 20–42. Some 313,100 attended trg in 1994.
RESERVES (all services): 396,300.

ARMY: 363,800 on mob.
Armed Forces Comd (All units Reserve status).
Comd tps: 2 armd bde, 2 inf, 1 arty, 1 airport, 2 engr regt.
3 fd Corps each 2 div (3 inf, 1 arty regt), 1 territorial div (5/6 regt), 1 armd bde, 1 arty, 1 engr, 1 cyclist, 1 fortress regt.

1 mtn corps with 3 mtn div (2 mtn inf, 1 arty regt), 3 fortress bde, 2 mtn inf, 2 fortress, 1 engr regt, 1 territorial div (6 regt), 2 territorial bde.
EQPT:
MBT: 117 Pz-61, 186 Pz-68, 186 Pz-68/88, 380 Pz-87 (*Leopard* 2).
AIFV: 192 M-63/73, 315 M-63/89 (all M-113 with **20mm**).
APC: 836 M-63/73 (M-113) incl variants, some *Piranha*.
TOWED ARTY: 105mm: 216 Model-35, 341 Model-46.
SP ARTY: 155mm: 558 PzHb-66/-74/-79/-88 (M-109U).
MOR: 81mm: 2,750 M-33, M-72; **120mm:** 402 M-87, 132 M-64 (M-113).
ATGW: 2,700 *Dragon,* 303 TOW-2 SP (MOWAG) *Piranha.*
RL: 83mm: 20,000 M-80.
ATK GUNS: 90mm: 850 Model-50/-57.
AD GUNS: 20mm: 1,700.
SAM: 56 B/L-84 (*Rapier*), *Stinger.*
SURV: *Green Archer* (mor).
UAV: *Scout.*
HEL: 60 *Alouette* III.
MARINE: 11 *Aquarius* patrol boats.

AIR CORPS: 32,500 on mob (incl mil airfield guard units); 153 cbt ac, no armed hel.
The Air Corps is an integral part of the Army, structured in 1 Air Force bde, 1 AD bde, 1 Air-base bde and 1 Comd-and-Control bde. Flying hours: 150-200. Reserves 50–70.
FTR: 9 sqn:
7 with 90 *Tiger* II/F-5E, 12 *Tiger* II/F-5F.
2 with 29 *Mirage* IIIS, 4 -III DS.
RECCE: 1 sqn with 18* *Mirage* IIIRS.
TPT: 1 sqn with 17 PC-6, 2 *Learjet* 36, 3 Do-27.
HEL: 3 sqn with 15 AS-332 M-1 (*Super Puma*), 12 SA-316)*Alouette* III.
TRG: 19 *Hawk* Mk 66, 38 PC-7, 12 PC-9.
ASM: AGM-65A/B *Maverick.*
AAM: AIM-9 *Sidewinder*, AIM-26 *Falcon.*
AIR DEFENCE:
1 SAM regt with 2 bn (each with 3 bty, *Bloodhound*).
1 AD bde: 1 SAM regt (3 bn, each with 2 or 3 bty: *Rapier*); 7 AD regt (each with 2 bn of 3 bty; 35mm guns, *Skyguard* fire control).

FORCES ABROAD:
UN AND PEACEKEEPING:
BOSNIA (UNPROFOR): 6 Obs. **GEORGIA** (UNOMIG): 5 Obs. **KOREA** (NNSC): 6 Staff. **MIDDLE EAST** (UNTSO): 8 Obs. **FYROM** (UNPREDEP): 1 Obs plus 6 civ pol. **TAJIKISTAN** (UNMOT): 3 Obs.

PARAMILITARY:
CIVIL DEFENCE: 480,000 (300,000 trained).

UKRAINE

GDP[a]   1993ε: krb 153,490bn ($51bn)
           per capita $4,300
           1994ε: krb 355,000bn ($39bn)
           per capita $3,400

Growth   1993ε: -17.1%   1994ε: -23.0%
Inflation 1993ε: 4,735%   1994ε: 891%
Debt   1993: $4.1bn   1994: $7.1bn
Def exp   1993ε: krb 2,500bn ($824m)
Def bdgt   1994: krb 16,823bn ($881m)
           1995ε: krb 39,215bn ($850m)
FMA[b]   1994: $0.6m (IMET)
           1995: $0.6m (IMET)
           1996: $1.0m (IMET)
$1 = krb[c] 1993: 4,532   1994ε: 19,100
           1995ε: 143,000

krb = karbovanets

[a] 1994 krb-denominated GDP for Jan–June only.
[b] Excl obligations 1992–94 by the US ($277m) under the Nunn–
Lugar Cooperative Threat Reduction programme which continues
in 1995–96.
[c] The karbovanets was introduced in November 1993.

Population: 51,932,000 (Russian 22%, Polish 4%,
Jewish 1%)

	13–17	18–22	23–32
Men	1,880,200	1,825,200	3,480,200
Women	1,820,600	1,788,800	3,453,800

TOTAL ARMED FORCES:
ACTIVE: 452,500 (excl Strategic Nuclear Forces
and Black Sea Fleet; incl 71,000 in central staffs and
units not covered below).
Terms of service: 2 years.
RESERVES: some 1m with military service
within 5 years.

STRATEGIC NUCLEAR FORCES (to be
eliminated under START):
ICBM: 136:
SS-19 *Stiletto* (RS-18): 90 (at two sites).
SS-24 *Scalpel* (RS-22): 46 (silo-based, one site co-
   located with SS-19.
BBR: 44: 20 Tu-95H16, 5 Tu-95H6 (with AS-15
ALCM), 19 Tu-160 (with AS-15 ALCM) plus 2
Tu-95A/B in store (under Ukrainian comd).

GROUND FORCES: 212,600.
MoD tps: 1 TD (trg), 1 arty bde (trg), 1 *Spetsnaz*, 1 arty,
   1 SSM, 1 ATK, 3 engr bde, 1 attack, 1 tpt hel regt.

Western Op Comd:
   Comd tps: 1 arty div (2 arty, 1 MRL, 1 ATK bde),
      1 SSM bde, 1 TD (trg), 1 engr regt.
3 Corps:
   1 with 2 MRD (1 res), 2 mech (1 res), 1 SSM, 1
      arty, 1 SAM, 1 engr bde, 1 MRL, 1 ATK, 1
      attack hel regt.
   1 with 2 mech div, 1 mech, 1 SSM, 1 arty, 1 SAM
      bde, 1 ATK (res), 1 MRL (res), 1 attack hel regt.
   1 with 1 TD, 1 ATK, 1 attack hel regt.
Southern Op Comd:
   Comd tps: 2 mech div (1 trg), 1 air-mobile div, 1 arty
      div, 1 *Spetsnaz*, 1 SSM, 2 arty (1 res), 2 SAM bde.
4 Corps:
   1 with 2 mech bde, 1 arty, 1 SAM bde, 1 ATK, 1
      MRL regt (last 4 res).
   1 with 1 TD (trg) 1 MRD (res), 1 mech div, 1 SSM,
      1 SAM bde, 1 MRL, 1 ATK (res), 1 attack hel regt.
   1 with 1 TD, 2 mech div, 1 SSM, 1 arty bde, 1
      ATK, 1 MRL, 1 attack hel regt.
   1 with 1 mech div, 1 MRL regt.

EQPT:
MBT: some 4,775 (incl some 1,800 in store): 680 T-
54/-55, 85 T-62, 2,345 T-64, 1,320 T-72, 345 T-80.
LT TK: 5 PT-76.
RECCE: some 1,500.
AIFV: some 3,400: 1,325 BMP-1, 1,460 BMP-2, 6
BMP-3, 124 BMD, 490 BRM.
APC: some 1,770: 220 BTR-60, 2,000 BTR-70, 450 BTR-
80, 40 BTR-D; plus 2,000 MT-LB, 4,700 'look-alikes'.
TOTAL ARTY: 3,685:
TOWED: 1,095: **122mm:** 400 D-30; **152mm:** 220 D-
20, 185 2A65, 290 2A36.
SP: 1,304: **122mm:** 640 2S1; **152mm:** 500 2S3, 24
2S5, 40 2S19, **203mm:** 100 2S7.
COMBINED GUN/MOR: 120mm: 64 2S9, 2 2B16.
MRL: 640: **122mm:** 375 BM-21, 25 9P138; **132mm:**
5 BM-13; **220mm:** 140 9P140; **300mm:** 95 9A52.
MOR: 580: **120mm:** 330 2S12, 250 PM-38.
SSM: 132 *Scud*, 140 *FROG*/SS-21.
ATGW: AT-4 *Spigot*, AT-5 *Spandrel*, AT-6 *Spiral*.
SAM: SA-4/-6/-8/-11/-12A/-15.
ATTACK HEL: 204 Mi-24.
SPT HEL: 14 Mi-2, 33 Mi-6, 136 Mi-8, 40 Mi-24 P-
K, 16 Mi-26.
SURV: SNAR-10 (*Big Fred*), *Small Fred* (arty).

AIR FORCE (incl Air Defence): 151,000; some 846
cbt ac, plus 380 in store (MiG-21, MiG-23, MiG-25,
MiG-27, MiG-29, Su-24, Yak-28), 24 attack hel.
2 air corps, 1 PVO army.
BBR: 1 div HQ, 2 regt with 26 Tu-22M.
FGA/BBR: 2 div HQ, 5 regt (1 trg) with 166 Su-24.
FGA: 1 regt with 34 Su-25.
FTR: 2 div, 6 PVO regt with 140 MiG-23, 73 MiG-25,

146 MiG-29, 57 Su-15, 66 Su-27.
RECCE: 4 regt (1 trg) with 17* Tu-22, 41* Su-17, 41* Su-24, 13* MiG-25.
ECM: 1 sqn with 29 Mi-8.
TPT: 174 Il-76, 100 others incl An-12.
TRG: 7 regt with 23* Tu-22M, 3* Tu-16, 430 L-39.
ATTACK HEL: 24 Mi-24.
SPT HEL: 16 Mi-6, 144 Mi-8, 8 Mi-26.
SAM: 825: SA-2/-3/-5/-10.

NAVY: ε16,000 (incl 7,000 Naval Aviation, 5,000 Coastal Defence) (planned total is probably 40,000).
BASES: Sevastopol, Odessa.
PRINCIPAL SURFACE COMBATANTS: 4:
2 *Krivak*-III PCO, 1 *Petya*-II FF, 1 *Grisha* V FF.
OTHER SURFACE SHIPS: 1 *Slavutich* (Sov *Kamchatka*) comd vessel, 1 *Krivak* III FF, some 40 coastal, inshore and riverine patrol craft, incl *Grisha* V, *Zhuk*, *Pauk* I, *Stenka*, *Muravey* and *Shemel* classes, 1 or 2 small log spt vessels; 2 large *Pomornik* hovercraft (capacity 3 tkr or 10 APC, 300 tps).

BLACK SEA FLEET: (ε48,000) (HQ Sevastopol): since August 1992 the Black Sea Fleet has been controlled *de jure*, jointly by Russia and Ukraine. In practice, this has been *de facto* Russian control. Some, mainly minor, units of the Fleet have already been transferred to Ukraine (see above, and Border Guard below) and to Georgia.

NAVAL AVIATION: (7,000): 6 regt with 63 MiG-29, 45 Su-17 (plus 41 in store), 44 Su-25, 18 Tu-16, 39 Tu-22M (Tu-16, Tu-22M also listed by Russia in CFE data).

COASTAL DEFENCE TROOPS: (5,000) (listed by both Ukraine and Russia in CFE data).
1 Coast Defence div (res).
2 marine inf regt (only 1 listed by Russia).
EQPT:
MBT: 226 T-64.
AIFV: 140 BMP-1, 150 BMD.
APC: 20 BTR-60, 260 BTR-70, 200 BTR-80.
TOWED ARTY: 72 D-30.
SP ARTY: 21 2S1.
COMBINED GUN/MOR: 24 2S9.

FORCES ABROAD:
UN AND PEACEKEEPING:
BOSNIA (UNPROFOR): 580; 1 inf bn, plus 9 civ pol. **CROATIA** (UNCRO): 499; 1 inf bn, plus 6 Obs and 13 civ pol.

PARAMILITARY FORCES: 66,000.
NATIONAL GUARD: 23,000 (to be 30,000; former MVD eqpt in service).
BORDER GUARD (incl Coast Guard): 43,000; about 40 minor units ex-Black Sea Fleet and KGB.

Russia

The Russian armed forces were still grappling with the problems of reorganisation following the break-up of the Soviet Union and withdrawal from Eastern Europe, as well as a much-reduced budget and manpower problems, when they were required to mount large-scale operations in Chechnya. The Chechen crisis only made the Russians more determined that the Conventional Forces in Europe (CFE) Treaty be reinterpreted to allow them to deploy stronger forces in the Caucasus. The prospect of NATO enlargement has also been a major concern for Russia. Elimination of strategic nuclear weapons has continued and the reduction of CFE Treaty Limited Equipment (TLE) is nearly complete.

Chechnya

Following the break-up of the Soviet Union in December 1991, the (then) Chechen-Ingush Autonomous Soviet Socialist Republic of the Russian Federation insisted on total independence, led by Air Force General Dzhokhar Dudayev, who had been elected president of the Republic in October. Although Russian President Boris Yeltsin declared a state of emergency in November 1991, this was reversed by the Supreme Soviet and the only action taken against the breakaway republic was an economic blockade. In 1994, a covert operation backed by the Russian Federal Counter-Intelligence Service (FSB), but fronted by Chechens opposed to Dudayev, began. This was still unsuccessful after reinforcement by the Russian military. During an attack on the Chechen capital, Grozny, on 26 November 1994, a number of Russian soldiers were captured and publicly paraded, much to the surprise of their divisional commander, who did not know of their secondment. It was probably this which proved the final straw for Yeltsin, who then decided on military intervention and to overthrow the Dudayev regime.

The conduct of military operations in Chechnya by the Russian armed forces has been a chapter of disaster which has led some commentators to suggest that NATO had totally misassessed the competence and capability of Soviet armed forces in the years before the break-up of the USSR. There are a number of reasons why operations were handled so badly; some of these could have been avoided, others could not.

The operation caught the Russian forces, particularly the Army, at a very bad moment. In many ways their situation was comparable to that of the British Army when it was decided to deploy an armoured division to the Persian Gulf. The British were then in the middle of the 'Options for Change' programme which included reducing the number of divisions in Germany from three to one; totally reorganising the remaining division; and a series of unit amalgamations and disbandments (most of these units were therefore well understrength as they awaited reorganisation). The changes imposed on the Russian Army by the end of the Cold War and the break-up of the Soviet Union were on a far greater scale. Thirty-seven divisions had to be withdrawn from Central Europe and the Baltic States; 57 divisions were handed over to Belarus and Ukraine; new regulations granted exemption from conscript service to thousands of students; a number of divisions were being reorganised into independent brigades or were disbanding; and thousands of tanks, ACVs and artillery were being destroyed as required by the CFE Treaty. All units were understrength, living conditions for many were deplorable and morale was understandably low.

Before the Coalition operation to retake Kuwait from Iraq in 1991, the British Army, like others, had several months in which to absorb the extra manpower every unit needed and to train together. The Russians had no such breathing space for their operation; the initial force was assembled in a matter of days and deployed into Chechnya within a week, on 11 December 1994. To make matters worse a veritable pot-pourri of units was assembled, presumably the most readily available and up to strength, from every branch of the forces: a North Caucasian-based mechanised division; airborne troops; naval infantry; and OMON and ODON Ministry of Interior troops – none of which had operated together before. As the campaign got under way more units

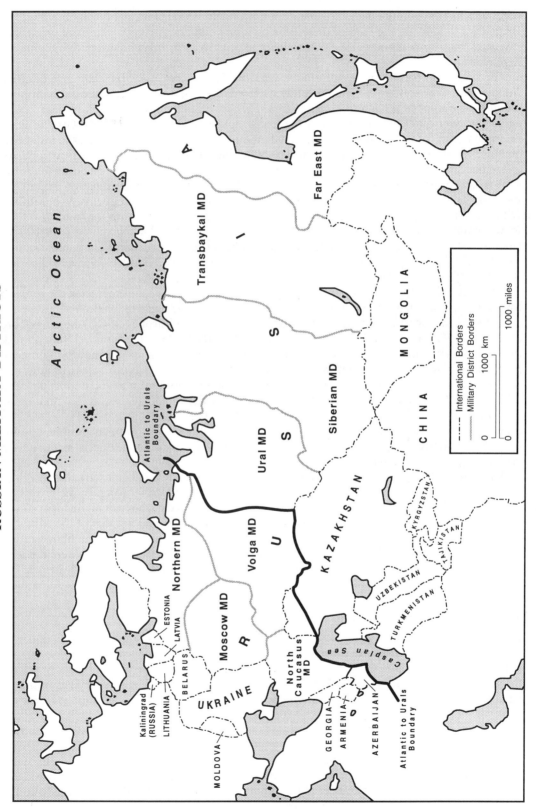

RUSSIAN MILITARY DISTRICTS

deployed, but never more than a regiment for any one division (presumably taking with it, as the British did in Kuwait, the bulk of their division's manpower). An early statement on casualties revealed that, by 6 January 1995, units from at least five military districts (MDs) had been deployed.

The operation had a number of unique features. It was the first large-scale use of Russian troops on Russian soil against Russian citizens. It was the first time Russian soldiers had operated under the cameras of the international media. This added to the political requirement to get the operation over quickly, and so led to the disastrous decision to try and take Grozny with an armoured dash for the Presidential palace when military common sense pointed to a systematic and measured street-by-street approach. The attacking forces paid dearly for this major error of judgement.

Russian commanders also badly underestimated the strength and determination of Dudayev's men. Before 1991, an armoured training centre had been based in Grozny. When this was withdrawn a deal was brokered, allowing it to leave unhindered in return for handing over half its weaponry to Chechen forces. From this the Chechens would have acquired over 100 tanks (mainly T-54), about 20 BMP infantry fighting vehicles and over 50 artillery pieces, including several BM-21 MRL. A large number of training aircraft, L-29 and L-39, were also left at Khankala (Grozny East).

Following the capture of Grozny in early February 1995, Russian forces took the remaining towns as the Chechens slowly withdrew into the hills. While fighting continued, peace talks, arranged by the Organisation for Security and Cooperation in Europe (OSCE), began but broke down on 25 May 1995. On 14 June a group of about 100 Chechen rebels raided Budennovsk in the neighbouring Stavropol Territory, eventually capturing the hospital and holding some 1,000 hostages, including hospital staff and patients. The Army made two unsuccessful attempts to recapture the hospital. Russian Prime Minister Viktor Chernomyrdin negotiated an agreement allowing the Chechens free passage back to Chechnya. They took 100 hostages with them who were then released there on 20 June. Following a cease-fire, which came into effect on 23 June, a new round of peace talks began on 28 June. On 23 July it was announced that a military agreement had been reached which covered matters such as the exchange of prisoners, 'hot-line' communications and disarmament.

The mishandling of the Chechen operations and the Budennovsk débâcle led to the resignation of several senior officers and the dismissal of others. President Yeltsin accepted the resignations of Viktor Yerin, the Interior Minister, Sergey Stephashin, Head of the Federal Security Service, and Nikolay Yegorov, Deputy Prime Minister for Nationalities, but not that of the Minister of Defence, General Pavel Grachev. It was also announced that a new Army, the 58th, was to be deployed to the Transcaucasus MD, and based at Vladikavkaz. In effect, this move creates a more senior commander with a larger staff and infrastructure than the Corps HQ already located in the MD, one of which will be absorbed into 58th Army HQ.

The CFE and the Flanks Issue

Article V of the CFE Treaty created an additional geographic zone comprising the countries and Soviet MDs on the northern and southern flanks of the two existing blocs. This zone was to be superimposed on the zones already defined in Article IV. After the break-up of the Soviet Union, the Leningrad and North Caucasus MDs formed the Russian flank zone and TLE limits were agreed with the other former Soviet Republics. There are no separate TLE limitations for the north or south flank, purely an aggregate limit for both.

Russian Defence Minister Grachev and other senior officers have complained of the restrictive effects of Article V, which was agreed to in a quite different set of circumstances. The Russians want the Treaty limits changed so that they can station more troops in the Caucasus without reducing strength on the northern flank. Officials have said that they will need around 400 tanks, 2,400 ACVs and 800 artillery pieces above what is now authorised in the flank area to confront and control potential problems in the Caucasus. The Russians also face severe accommodation problems as the bulk of their army units are required by the Treaty to be located in the Moscow and Volga MDs, and the Russians wish to spread the load into the North Caucasus, described by Grachev as the main base area for Russian Rapid Deployment Forces.

From a purely military perspective, the Russians undoubtedly have a case, as the situation has radically changed since the Treaty was first signed. However, Russia's neighbours on the southern flank are opposed to any change, although Ukraine also wants to be able to deploy more TLE in the former Odessa MD. Most signatories oppose any change before the first review conference due in May 1996 on the grounds that it could lead to the total unravelling of the Treaty. A number of suggestions have been made to the Russians on how they could use flexibility in the Treaty (such as redeploying ACVs to internal security forces and units of coastal defence and marine infantry which are not subject to Article V) to increase their strength without violating it. In July, the Russians made a further submission to the CFE Joint Consultative Group, suggesting the declaration of a zone in the Caucasus which would be excluded from the CFE (such a zone exists in Turkey in the border region with Syria and Iraq).

Most countries have already achieved, or are very close to achieving, their reduction liabilities. Russia has done so in respect of artillery and has only a further 700 other TLE left to be reduced by the November 1995 deadline. Few countries have the will or the finance to fund increases in armament procurement. It could therefore be argued that the CFE has served its purpose and is no longer necessary. But scrapping it would also lose an essential component; that of verification and transparency, essential for reducing regional tensions. It must be said that the CFE (and the OSCE Vienna Document) inspections and observation of military activities will be the only way to gain low-level intelligence on unit organisations, training standards, logistic preparations and weapon systems not covered by the CFE but held by units subject to inspection.

Kaliningrad

Concern has been expressed in some quarters about the growing military strength in the Kaliningrad region. The facts, as demonstrated by the CFE Treaty military information exchanges, show that in some categories there has been a decline in numbers. Table 1 shows the unit and weapon strength in Kaliningrad in 1990 and 1995. In 1990, Soviet forces in the three Baltic states also included two motor rifle, one airborne, one coastal defence and two training divisions and some 11 air force, air defence and naval air regiments. All have now been withdrawn.

Table 1:   Kaliningrad Unit and Weapon Strength, 1990 and 1995

	1990	1995
Tank Division	2	1[a]
Motor Rifle Division	1[b]	2
Artillery Division	1	-[c]
Airborne Brigade	1	-
Naval Infantry Brigade	1	1
Coastal Artillery Regiment	1	1
Surface-to-Surface Missile Brigades	3	1
Tanks	802	893
ACV	1,081	1,156
Artillery	677	495
Attack Helicopters	48	52
Combat Aircraft	155	32

Notes: [a] Plus one independent brigade.
           [b] Plus one redeploying from Czechoslovakia.
           [c] Three of six brigades remain.

Military Arrangements in Former Soviet Republics

On 21 October 1994, after two and a half years of negotiations, Russian Prime Minister Chernomyrdin and Moldovan Prime Minister Andrei Sangheli signed an agreement on the withdrawal of Russia's 14th Army to be completed in three years. In January 1995 the strength of the 14th Army was some 6,400, forming one understrength motor rifle division.

On 21 February 1995, Russia and Belarus signed a military cooperation agreement largely concerning the maintenance of airfields, the basing of Russian aircraft, and the mutual use and support of each others' defence enterprises. Both the anti-ballistic missile radar at Baranovichi and submarine communications centre at Vileyka will be under Russian control.

In addition to the agreement reached over the division of the Black Sea Fleet, Russia and Ukraine have agreed to cooperate in the military-industrial area. Russia has a shopping list for aircraft and aircraft spares which the Soviet Union relied on Ukrainian plants to manufacture. Payment for these items could be made in terms of energy-debt forgiveness.

In February 1995, Kazakhstan and Russia signed some 15 separate military agreements. The most important of these concerns the status of military personnel serving in the territory of the other party. Russia will be able to use firing ranges in Kazakhstan and is developing cooperation to allow unified forces to be formed in times of crisis. In a separate agreement, Russia has leased its Baikonur missile launch centre where most Soviet, and Russian, space flights have originated.

Russia continues to support the government of Tajikistan in its fight against rebels on the border with Afghanistan. The Russian Duma ratified an agreement with Estonia on social guarantees for the 10,000 Russian pensioners who live in Estonia in July 1995. The Estonian parliament has not yet ratified the agreement.

The Commonwealth of Independent States

The council of the Commonwealth of Independent States (CIS) Heads of State (also known as the Collective Security Council) met three times in the last 12 months. In October 1994 it endorsed the mandate for a peacekeeping operation in Georgia and Abkhazia and extended the period for stationing CIS peacekeeping forces in Tajikistan. In February 1995 it agreed a statement of guidelines for deepening military cooperation. There would be cooperation in three areas: the military-political sphere, including the formation of a secretariat for the Collective Security Council; armed forces training, planning and early-warning coordination; research and development, and logistic support. Agreement was also reached by all except Azerbaijan on the creation of a Joint Air Defence System. In May, seven CIS countries (Armenia, Belarus, Georgia, Kazakhstan, Kyrgyzstan, Russia and Tajikistan) signed an agreement on the protection of CIS external borders in Minsk.

Future Reorganisation

Several statements have been made forecasting further reorganisation of the armed forces over the next ten years. The most important change would be the appointment of a civilian Minister of Defence in place of the traditional general. The General Staff, which would be responsible for command and control of the forces, would then report directly to the President. The present five services would be reduced to three with the Air Force, Air Defence Force and Strategic Rocket Forces merging to form an Aerospace Force. The eight military districts would be reduced to six, and the status of the Baltic and Black Sea Fleets reduced. Manpower would be reduced to around 1.5 million initially and later to 1.2 million.

Manpower and Conscription

In April 1995, Russian military manpower problems led to the length of conscript service being increased by six months to two years from October 1995. At the same time, the rules for deferment for educational purposes were amended allowing the call-up of more students. In July, the Duma decided that conscripts who served in areas of military action should only serve for 18 months. It is not clear what constitutes an area of military action – certainly service in Chechnya and Tajikistan would qualify, but other peacekeeping tours, such as Moldova or Georgia, might not.

Accurately assessing manpower strengths is always difficult, even when much more information is publicly available. It is never certain whether statements on Russian manpower concern authorised or actual strengths. Recent statements include:

- 'The armed forces number 1,917,000' (General Pavel Grachev, *Interfax*, 6 May 1995).
- 'The armed forces were cut by 385,000 men in 1994 and would be cut by a further 217,000 in 1995' (Colonel General Mikhail Kolesnikov, *Military News*, May 1995).
- '85% of the 209,000 men needed had been drafted by 7 June 1995; 60% of these would serve in the armed forces, the remainder in the Border, Interior and Railroad forces' (Colonel General Vyacheslav Zherebtsov, *Interfax*, 7 June 1995).

(The first two statements probably refer to authorised strengths).

Manpower figures given in the CFE Treaty data of December 1994 show a drop of some 8.7% overall. These figures only include forces west of the Urals and exclude naval forces (other than those permanently land based) and Strategic Rocket Forces. Again, it is not clear if actual or authorised numbers are given.

Table 2: **Manpower 1993, 1994 and 1995 (in thousands)**

	1993	1994	1995
Ground Forces	578	448	409
Air Force and Air Defence Aviation	259	226	178
Other Air Defence Troops	205	157	149
Central Staff	5	2	2
Centrally Controlled Units	166	219	210
Land-Based Naval Units	24	18	15
Total	**1,237**	**1,070**	**963**

A growing number of soldiers are on short contracts, but there are no up-to-date figures available – the total could be as high as 300,000. There are 160,000 women now serving in the armed forces. It is planned to recall some 12,000 reserve officers for active service during 1995 and 18,000 graduates, who previously would not have expected to serve, are to be called up each year. To some extent, the shortage of manpower has been alleviated by the measures described above and the continued reduction of the number of units to be manned.

Nuclear Forces

The elimination of strategic nuclear weapons has continued both in Russia and in the nuclear-armed former Soviet Republics. In April 1995 it was reported by the Commander of Strategic Rocket Forces that all nuclear warheads in Kazakhstan had been removed from their missiles and transported back to Russia. Eighteen SS-25 ICBM remain in Belarus. These are due to be transferred to Russia by Autumn 1996, although Russia plans to complete the transfer in 1995. Belarus has confirmed that all nuclear warheads will have been transferred by the end of 1995.

The last SS-11 and SS-13 ICBM have been eliminated and only ten SS-17 remain. So far only 24 SS-18 in Russia have been eliminated, and only two of their silos destroyed (all SS-18 must be eliminated under the terms of the Strategic Arms Reduction Talks Treaty (START II)). Ten SS-19 have been eliminated and SS-25 transferred from Belarus have been deployed to Vypolzovo (an SS-17 site), Drovyanya (SS-11) and Barnaul. There has been no change to the numbers and deployment of either silo-based or train-mobile SS-24.

There have been fewer changes to the ballistic missile submarine (SSBN) force. The December 1994 Memorandum of Understanding showed 45 SSBN, with a total of 684 countable missiles. There are also two *Yankee* 1 SSBN which, although withdrawn from service, remain START-countable. SSBN are no longer based at Olen'ya in the Kola peninsula.

There has been little change to the strategic bomber force. The number of Tu-95B/G has been reduced from 45 to 24 (now all Tu-95G) and one additional Tu-160 *Blackjack* bomber has been produced. Russia is negotiating with Ukraine to buy its 46 strategic bombers (mainly *Blackjack* and *Bear* H).

The START II Treaty was presented to the Duma on 26 June for ratification.

Conventional Forces

Ground Forces

The Leningrad MD has been renamed the Northern MD. The 11th Army in Kaliningrad is directly subordinate to the General HQ of the ground forces. The 58th Army has been established in the North Caucasus MD. Most changes in the order of battle noted in the last 12 months took place east of the Urals. Ten motor rifle divisions have been disbanded, three of them converting to independent motor rifle brigades. The machine gun/artillery division in the Kuril Islands has been reduced to brigade status. Some new equipment has been produced while CFE elimination continues. West of the Urals there have been the following increases: 140 T-80 tanks, 100 BTR-80 APC, 30 BMD-3 airborne fighting vehicles, 110 2 S19 152 SP guns, 130 2 A65 152mm towed artillery and 25 9A52 300mm (*Smerch*) MRL. All these weapons feature strongly in Russian military export efforts.

Naval Forces

Over the last 12 months there has been an increase in naval activity. In the first six months of 1995 some 14 naval exercises involving over 400 submarines, surface warships and support ships have taken place. In April 1995 an exercise was held involving elements of all four fleets. Its aim appears to have been to check operational capability and mobilisation readiness. Live firing of ballistic, cruise and surface-to-air missiles has increased by 30%.

The long-standing dispute over division of the Black Sea Fleet between Russia and Ukraine and the provision of shore facilities for Russia in the Crimea appear to have been solved, although some details may not have been fully worked out yet. The Fleet's warships are to be split equally between the two navies, but Ukraine only requires some 18.3% of the whole and will hand over the other 31.7% to Russia in return for unspecified compensation. The land-based components – coastal defence forces, naval infantry and naval aviation units – are to be divided equally, based on the situation as of 3 August 1992. The division of the Fleet was agreed at a summit meeting at Sochi on 9 June 1995. This did not address the question of where the two fleets would be based, other than that Sevastopol would be the main base and headquarters of the Russian Black Sea Fleet.

Two *Akula*-class nuclear-powered submarines, a fourth Admiral *Ushakov*-class cruiser and some corvettes and torpedo craft have been commissioned in the last 12 months. One of the *Akula* which deployed to the Pacific is reliably reported to be armed with presumably a conventional version of the *Shkval* underwater missile, claimed to have a speed of 200 knots. The aircraft carrier *Gorshkov*, ten frigates, seven missile craft and about ten landing ships have been retired. Large numbers of ships decommissioned earlier are being disposed of as scrap, mainly to South Korea (which has bought two aircraft carriers), Minsk and Norovossiysk (some 50 submarines and many others). India is still believed to be negotiating to buy the last remaining aircraft carrier, the *Kuznetsov*.

The Russian Navy is much reduced, but could still pose a significant threat, particularly given the recent revelation of its 200-knot submarine-launched underwater missile, *Shkval*.

Air and Air Defence Forces

Both Air Force and Air Defence Force (PVO) manpower and aircraft strength have decreased over the last 12 months. The Long-Range Aviation Command has retired all its Tu-22 aircraft, including the reconnaissance version; it now comprises 130 Tu-26 (Tu-22m) bombers and 40 tankers (plus the strategic bomber force). Frontal Aviation has 200 fewer air-defence fighters in service, but has only marginally reduced fighter ground-attack numbers. The numbers of aircraft held in store awaiting elimination had been reduced by 500 by 1 January 1995. The Air Defence Force has merged the 6th (*St Petersburg*) and 10th (*Arkhangel*) PVO Armies, and the 4th PVO Army in the Volga MD has been reduced to Corps status. The fighter regiment based in Kaliningrad has been disbanded. Some 500 aircraft have been taken out of squadron service and most still await elimination while 500 aircraft taken out of service earlier were eliminated during 1994.

Considerable numbers of surface-to-air missiles have been retired, including some 500 SA-2, 200 SA-3 and 500 SA-5 launchers. Numbers of SA-10, which has a limited anti-ballistic missile capability, have risen by 250 to 1,750. The SA-10 is being widely marketed for export.

Defence Expenditure

In budgetary terms, 1994 seemed initially to promise a real increase in spending for the Russian military after the uncertainties of 1992 and 1993. When the Federal Budget finally became law in July 1994, after a prolonged contest between the military interest groups and the Finance Ministry, the military received some 40.6tr roubles – well short of its request for r 87.8tr – but still 21% of the Federal Budget. Not only did the defence budget increase its proportion of the Federal Budget compared to the two previous years (Table 3), but it appeared to represent a large nominal increase over the 1993 budget (three- to four-fold) and out-turn (five- to six-fold). Expectations of high price inflation undoubtedly played a part in the budget calculations, but by mid-1994 it was becoming clear that inflation was running well below 1993 levels of about 900%. In the event it fell to about 300% by the end of the year. During 1994 the Finance Ministry continued to sequester authorised budgetary funds in response to massive tax revenue shortfalls (only r 48.3tr – or 36% – of budgeted revenue was received by the Federal government in 1994), and the decline in inflation provided an additional justification for these measures. As a result, the Finance Ministry was able to claw back some of the funds committed but not released for defence, so that actual allocations to the military and defence industry fell short of authorisations by about 30% (reportedly some r 10.8tr). Between January and September 1994 the military received just r 14.6tr (about 60% of authorised funds), despite having committed procurement orders to industry. Thereafter, the government relaxed monetary policy to pay some of its debts to the military and its suppliers.

Table 3:   **Official Defence Budget and Outlay, 1992–1995 (in current roubles bn)**

	Defence budget	% Federal budget	Defence outlay	% Federal budget
1992	384.0	16.0	855.3	10.8
1993	3,115.5	16.6	7,210.0	21.0
1994	40,626.0	20.9	29,826.0	25.0
1995	48,577.0	19.6	–	–

Notes:
[a] The final adjusted value of the 1993 defence budget was r 8,327bn.
[b] 1994 data for outlay and % of Federal government expenditure are provisional.
[c] IMF data cite a provisional outlay of r 28,000bn for 1994.
Source: Official budgets, Economic Review of the Russian Federation (IMF 1994, 1995)

In contrast to last year, the 1995 defence budget implies a reduction in spending – perhaps of as much as one-third – when measured against the forecast for inflation. Much will depend on whether armed forces costs can be held down until lower inflation levels prevail. As part of the 1995 agreement with the International Monetary Fund (IMF), the government is aiming for a target inflation rate of 1% a month on average in the second part of the year, and about 140% for the year as a whole. The same programme calls for an end to Russian quotas for oil exports, which will tend to drive up the domestic costs of fuel and oil derivatives. Compared with 1994, the 1995 budget allocations appear less likely to match spending at the current level of activities, and there seems little likelihood that the target will be met. When the prolonged campaign in Chechnya is taken into account, the prospect appears remoter still. This impression is reinforced by official reports in May 1995 of the r 1.9tr cost of military operations in Chechnya for the period December 1994–March 1995, including Defence Ministry costs of more than r 1tr, the Ministry for Internal Affairs (r 412 billion), and the Ministry for Emergencies (r 115 bn).

Table 4: Main Expenditure Headings in the Official Defence Budget (current roubles bn)

	1993	%	1994	%	1995	%
Personnel, O&M	1,556.3	50.0	22,105.0	54.4	21,981.8	45.3
Procurement	569.5	18.3	8,442.0	20.8	10,275.3	21.2
R&D	224.7	7.2	2,433.0	6.0	4,935.9	10.2
Infrastructure	514.2	16.5	4,778.0	11.8	6,138.2	12.6
Pensions	171.2	5.5	1,994.0	4.9	4,014.8	8.3
Nuclear, other	79.6	2.6	874.0	2.2	1,231.0	2.5
Total	**3,115.5**	**100.0**	**40,626.0**	**100.0**	**48,577.0**	**100.0**

Note: 1993 defence budget is that announced in May 1993 which was adjusted to a final figure of r 8,327bn in late 1993.
Source: Official defence budget.

The military initially requested r 115tr and received r 48.6tr in the Federal Budget, which became law at the end of March 1995. This allocation represented some 20% of the Federal Budget – a marginal decline from the previous year (Table 3). The 1995 defence budget shows a nominal 20% increase over the 1994 budget and a 63% increase over the provisional 1994 out-turn. According to the IMF, the inflation level is likely to fall to around 140% this year, and if this forecast holds for armed forces expenses there could be a real decline in defence spending in 1995 unless the military is able to resist inflationary pressures within its own domain.

Table 5:   Estimated Unit Production of Major Weapon Systems

	1991	1992	1993	1994
Main Battle Tanks	900	500	200	40
Infantry Fighting Vehicles	3,000	750	300	400
Bombers	30	20	10	0–5
Fighters/FGA	225	150	100	50
Transport Aircraft[a]	70	60	60	35
Helicopters[a]	350	175	150	100
Submarines	6	6	4	4
Major Surface Ships	3	1	1	0
Strategic Missiles	100	65	35	25

Note: [a] Includes civilian production.
Source: UK Ministry of Defence.

Functional allocations are shown in Table 4. Spending on Personnel, Operations and Maintenance (PO&M) is set for a marginal reduction over 1994. Some savings will be effected through the reduction in manpower levels authorised in the budget law (from 1,917,400 as at 1 January 1995 to 1,469,900 (i.e., 23%) by January 1996), although an increase in pensions will offset some of the gains. The government also announced in April that the period of conscription is to be increased from 18 months to two years, and that the rules on exemptions are to be tightened considerably. This development reflects the view expressed by the Defence Ministry and the General Staff that a volunteer army remains a distant prospect; there is little doubt that the substantial incremental cost of contract service personnel has influenced this thinking. Whatever the longer-term implications of reductions in manpower, the likelihood remains that expenditure on the Chechnya campaign will overstretch the PO&M budget, in part because of increased salaries and incentives payable to servicemen, and in part because the extra costs associated with greater use of equipment, as well as equipment damage and write-offs.

As a proportion of the defence budget, allocations to Construction and Research and Development (R&D) have increased over 1994. The construction (infrastructure) budget retains its substantial share as the effort to improve service conditions for personnel continues. It accounts for some 13% of the 1995 budget – an increase over 1994 of its relative share, and a high proportion by NATO standards. Since 1990, additional funds of over $5bn from the German government have been available to support housing construction for servicemen returning from former East Germany.

A significant feature in the 1995 budget is increased spending on R&D, reflecting the consolidation of previously extra-budgetary R&D accounts into the defence vote. Whilst spending on procurement is at about the same level as last year, R&D increases its proportion of the defence fund by some two-thirds. No systematic detail in respect of individual R&D programmes nor their costs is provided by the Defence Ministry. The same applies to procurement, which has retained a similar proportion of the budget to last year. In general, although Russian procurement of major weapons systems probably remains sizeable in comparison with the major European NATO states, there is no doubt that it has fallen steeply from peak Soviet levels and is currently below US levels. In the absence of any official data on unit production quantities, UK Ministry of Defence estimates of the decline in military production of major weapons systems are shown in Table 5.

Table 6: **Other Military Expenditure in the 1995 Federal Budget (current roubles bn)**

	Total	Comment
Demilitarisation	2,404.6	Under the International Activity budget heading, to implement START and CFE Treaty commitments.
Security Services	2,547.7	Foreign Intelligence and Counter-Intelligence Services.
Internal Troops	1,441.7	
Border Troops	2,331.1	
Railway Troops	281.9	
Roadbuilding Directorate	170.6	Part of the Ministry of Defence.
Defence Conversion	2,315.4	Including r915bn expenditure and r1,400bn loans.
Subsidies to Closed		Subsidies to closed administrative regions with MoD and MINATOM establishments.
Baikonur Lease	161.0	Baikonur Space Station in Kazakhstan.
1994 Debts to Industry	3,553.4	Excluding r 1,333bn debt repaid in the defence budget.
Federal Industrial Investment	3,219.5	Estimated 25% of total industrial investment for dual-use aerospace programmes.
Civil Defence and Mobilisation	53.7	
State Emergencies	3,076.0	Contingency funds for emergency programmes, including Chechnya.
Science and Technology Budget	4,545.0	Military and dual-use components estimated at 75% of budget.
Subtotal	**27,144.8**	
Defence Budget	48,577.0	
Total Military Budget	75,721.8	
Federal Budget	248,344.3	
% Federal Budget	30.5	

Source: Federal Budget 1995.

Extra-budgetary funds for the Russian military effort present a separate issue. Under NATO definitions of military expenditure, several military-related activities are not funded by the Russian defence budget. Instead, they appear in the Federal Budget under the headings of other ministries or else lie outside the Budget altogether. From 1992–94 the sources of funds outside the Federal Budget were the Central Bank of Russia, which issued large credits to industry, and several quasi-independent trusts, principal of which were the Pensions and Social Insurance Funds and smaller funds devoted to conversion and R&D. The important feature of these trusts was that they were partly administered on a regional and local basis beyond the control of the Finance Ministry, and were independent of central government supervision. The 1995 Federal Budget Law has resulted in an important change for the Central Bank which no longer has authority to issue un-budgeted credits.

Table 6 indicates military-related expenditure excluded from the 1995 defence budget and placed elsewhere in the Federal Budget. Some budgets are listed explicitly, and pose no interpretative problems. Others, such as the science and technology budget, and the industrial capital investment budget give no clues as to their military component, which has been estimated. The IISS believes that Russia's military-related expenditure under NATO definitions but excluded from the defence budget amounts to some r 27tr (which may err on the conservative side). With these assumptions the true figure for Russia's 1995 budget comes to nearly r 76tr, or over 30% of the Federal Budget.

In such uncertain circumstances it is unsurprising that independent estimates of Russian military expenditure vary widely (Table 7). The far left column shows the official defence budget converted to dollars at the average market exchange rate for the year. IMF statistics are based on those of Goskomstat, but are adjusted. The IMF estimates defence spending as a proportion of GDP – here using a narrow definition (i.e., the defence budget outlay) of between 4 and 5%. The Stockholm International Peace Research Institute (SIPRI) adopts an intermediate position, citing a figure of over 6% of GDP after allowing for extra-budgetary expenditure. At the top end of the scale, NATO cites a figure of greater than 10% of GDP, while the US Arms Control and Disarmament Agency (ACDA) gives both a high dollar valuation and high proportion of GDP.

Table 7:   Estimates of Russian Military Expenditure

	Defence budget at market exchange rate $bn	IMF estimates of defence expenditure % of GDP	SIPRI estimates of military expenditure % of GDP	NATO estimates of military expenditure % of GDP	US ACDA estimates of military expenditure ($bn)	US ACDA estimates of military expenditure % of GDP
1991	83.9	n.a.	>10	>12	260.0	10.3
1992	9.4	4.7	>6	>10	142.3	16.7
1993	13.8	4.4	>6	>10	113.8	14.6
1994	21.7	4.5	8–10	–	–	–
1995	12.1	5.0	–	–	–	–

Note: Defence budget dollar conversions apply. Market exchange rates applicable at the time of budget finalisation.

Table 8 shows IISS estimates of Russia's military expenditure according to both official and NATO definitions, using purchasing-power parity dollar conversions instead of market exchange rates. (An explanation of purchasing-power parity methodology is given in *The Military Balance 1994–1995,* pp. 278–81.) Russia's real military expenditure for 1994–95 is likely to be in the range $100–$110bn and represents 9–10% of GDP. It may be more. This level of spending could be seen as extravagant and, given the country's economic performance, it may be unsustainable. In any case, the Russian military will be hard pressed to remain within its budget in 1995, and will inevitably call for more resources. But the government and the Duma are bound to press for further contraction in military spending, justified on economic as well as security grounds.

Taking the resource allocation trends within NATO for comparison, the Russian armed forces do not seem under-resourced. Their problems may have more to do with efficiency, disorientation, low morale and perhaps unrealistic aspirations. It is unlikely that they will need to pursue commercialisation like the Chinese, although Defence Minister Grachev is known to want the Defence Ministry to control Russian arms exports. The outcome of elections in 1995 and 1996 for the Duma and Presidency will be a further indication of Russia's intentions regarding military reform.

Table 8: **IISS Estimates of Russian Defence Spending**

	Defence Budget		Official outlay		IISS estimate of military expenditure		Military expenditure as % of GDP
	r bn	$bn	r bn	$bn	r bn	$bn	%
1992	384.0	85.9	855.0	57.4	2,086.0	140.0	11.7
1993	3,115.5	75.1	7,210.0	50.7	15,350.0	107.9	9.3
1994	40,626.0	78.5	29,826.0	48.8	66,930.0	109.6	9.6
1995	48,577.0	62.8	–	–	75,722.0	98.0	8.8

Notes: All dollar conversions are derived from purchasing-power parity estimates cited by Plan Econ. Purchasing-power parity rates calculated by the World Bank, if used in these estimates, would reduce the $ values by about half.

RUSSIA

| GDP[a] | 1993: r 162,300bn ($1,160bn): per capita $7,800 |
| | 1994: r 630,000bn ($1,120bn): per capita $7,700 |

Growth[b]	1993: -12%	1994: -15%
Inflation	1993: 896%	1994: 302%
Debt	1993: $83.7bn	1994: $95.0bn
Def exp[c]	
Def bdgt[a]	1993: r 8,327bn ($75bn)
	1994: r 40,626bn ($79bn)
	1995: r 48,577bn ($63bn)
	1996ε: r 75,000bn ($76bn)
FMA[d]	1994: $0.5m	1995: $0.7m
	1996: $1.1m
	1990–95: $5.0bn (Germany)
$1 = r	1993: 928	1994: 2,188
	1995: 4,300–4,900

r = rouble

[a] PPP est.
[b] An IMF study concludes that official figures overstate GDP decline.
[c] See separate commentary on Russian def exp.
[d] Under the US Nunn–Lugar programme, $400m to support START I implementation and demilitarisation in the FSU has been authorised each year from 1992–95. The 1996 request is also for $400m. Russia's share is approximately two-thirds of the total. Following early delays in the obligation of funds, actual obligations were reported in mid-1995 to be near the level of budget authorisations.

Population: 148,940,000 (Tatar 4%, Ukrainian 3%, Belarussian 1%, Moldovan 1%, other 10%)

	13–17	18–22	23–32
Men	5,668,000	5,282,400	10,442,800
Women	5,471,800	5,117,000	10,093,000

TOTAL ARMED FORCES:
ACTIVE: ε1,520,000 (perhaps 400,000 conscripts, 160,000 women; incl about 220,000 MoD staff, centrally controlled units for EW, trg, rear services, not incl elsewhere).
Terms of service: 2 years. Women with medical and other special skills may volunteer.
RESERVES: some 20,000,000: some 2,400,000 with service within last 5 years; Reserve obligation to age 50.

STRATEGIC NUCLEAR FORCES:
149,000 (incl 49,000 assigned from Air Force, Air Defence and Navy).

NAVY: (ε13,000). 684 msl in 45 SSBN.
SSBN: 45 (all based in Russian ports):
6 *Typhoon* with 20 SS-N-20 *Sturgeon* (120 msl).
7 *Delta*-IV with 16 SS-N-23 *Skiff* (112 msl).
13 *Delta*-III with 16 SS-N-18 *Stingray* (208 msl).
4 *Delta*-II with 16 SS-N-8 *Sawfly* (64 msl).
15 *Delta*-I with 12 SS-N-8 *Sawfly* (180 msl).
(A further 2 *Yankee*-1 remain START-countable with 32 msl.)

STRATEGIC ROCKET FORCES: (ε100,000 incl 50,000 conscripts).

5 rocket armies, org in div, regt, bn and bty, launcher gp with normally 10 silos (6 for SS-18) and one control centre; 12 SS-24 trains each 3 launchers.

ICBM: 928:

SS-17 *Spanker* (RS-16): 10 (at 1 field; mod 3/4 MIRV; all in Russia).

SS-18 *Satan* (RS-20): 222 (at 6 fields; mostly mod 4/5, 10 MIRV; 174 in Russia, 48 in Kazakhstan (without warheads).

SS-19 *Stiletto* (RS-18): 250 (at 4 fields; mostly mod 3, 6 MIRV; 160 in Russia, 90 in Ukraine).

SS-24 *Scalpel* (RS-22): 92 (10 MIRV; 10 silo, 36 train in Russia, 46 silo in Ukraine).

SS-25 *Sickle* (RS-12M): 354 (mobile, single-warhead msl; 10 bases with some 40 units of 9. 336 in Russia, 18 in Belarus).

GROUND DEFENCE: some 1,820 APC, hel declared under CFE (APC: Russia (West of Urals) 750, Ukraine 800, Belarus 270).

STRATEGIC AVIATION: (ε15,000).

Long-Range Forces (Moscow).

BBR: 95, plus 14 test ac (plus 46 in Ukraine):

24 Tu-95G (with 1 and 2 AS-4 ASM).

28 Tu-95H6 (with AS-15 ALCM) (plus 5 in Ukraine).

37 Tu-95H16 (with AS-15 ALCM) (plus 20 in Ukraine) (plus 2 Tu-95A/B in store in Ukraine).

6 Tu-160 (with AS-15 ALCM) (plus 19 in Ukraine).

Test ac: 14: 8 Tu-95, 6 Tu-160.

STRATEGIC DEFENCE: (21,000).

ABM: 100: 36 SH-11 (mod *Galosh*), 64 SH-08 *Gazelle*.

WARNING SYSTEMS:

SATELLITES: 9 with ICBM/SLBM launch detection capability. Others incl 2 photo-recce, 11 ELINT.

RADARS:

OVER-THE-HORIZON-BACKSCATTER (OTH-B): 3: 2 near Kiev and Komsomolsk (Ukraine), covering US and polar areas; 1 near Nikolayevsk-na-Amure, covering China (these sites are non-op).

LONG-RANGE EARLY-WARNING ABM-ASSOCIATED:

6 long-range phased-array systems: **Op:** Olenegorsk (Kola), Lyaki (Azerbaijan), Pechora (Urals). **Under test:** Sary-Shagan (Kazakhstan). **Under construction:** Baranovichi (Belarus), Mishelevka (Irkutsk).

11 *Hen House*-series; range 6,000km, 6 locations covering approaches from the west and south-west, north-east and south-east and (partially) south.

Engagement, guidance, battle management: 1 *Pill Box* phased-array at Pushkino (Moscow).

ARMY: ε670,000 (about 210,000 conscripts, 170,000 on contract).

8 Military Districts (MD), 1 Group of Forces.

14 Army HQ, 8 Corps HQ.

17 TD (incl 4 trg) (3 tk, 1 motor rifle, 1 arty, 1 SAM regt; 1 armd recce bn; spt units).

47 MRD (incl 6 trg) (3 motor rifle, 1 arty, 1 SAM regt; 1 indep tk, 1 ATK, 1 armd recce bn; spt units).

5 ABD (each 3 para, 1 arty regt; 1 AA bn) (plus 1 trg div; status and location unknown).

7 MG/arty div.

4 arty div incl 1 trg (no standard org: perhaps 4 bde (12 bn): 152mm SP, 152mm towed and MRL: plus ATK bde).

Some 47 arty bde/regt; no standard org: perhaps 4 bn: 2 each of 24 152mm towed guns, 2 each of 24 152mm SP guns, some only MRL.

4 hy arty bde (with 4 bn of 12 203mm 2S7 SP guns).

6 AB bde (each 4 inf bn; arty, SAM, ATK; spt tps).

1 indep tk bde.

15 indep (1 under airborne comd) MR bde (more forming).

7 (1 airborne) SF (*Spetsnaz*) bde.

24 SSM bde (incl 3 trg).

20 ATK bde/regt.

28 SAM bde/regt.

22 attack hel regt.

4 aslt tpt hel regt.

6 hel trg regt.

Other Front and Army tps: engr, pontoon-bridge, pipeline, signals, EW, CW def, tpt, supply bde/regt/bn.

EQPT (figures in parentheses are those reported to CFE on 15 December 1994):

MBT: about 19,000 (6,696), incl: T-54/-55 (412), T-62 (761), T-64A/-B (625), T-72L/-M (1,938) and T-80/-M 9 (3,144), T-90 (2), plus some 11,000 in store east of Urals (incl Kazakhstan, Uzbekistan).

LT TK: 200 PT-76 (126).

RECCE: some 2,000 BRDM-2.

AIFV: about 17,000 (7,351), incl: BMP-1 (2,241), BMP-2 (3,124), BMP-3 (28), some 1,600 BMD-1/-2/-3 (AB) (1,377), BRM (581).

APC: over 16,000, incl: BTR-50P/-60P/-70/-80/-152, BTR-D (3,530); MT-LB (798), plus 'look-alikes'.

TOTAL ARTY: 20,650 (6,240), plus some 13,000, mainly obsolete types, in store east of the Urals.

TOWED: about 9,000 (2,014), incl **122mm:** D-30 (892); **152mm:** D-20 (293), *Giatsint-B* 2A36 (430), *MSTA-B* 2A65 (281); **203mm:** B-4M.

SP: some 3,750 (2,587), incl **122mm:** *Gvozdika* 2S1 (927); **152mm:** *Acatsia* 2S3 (980), *Giatsint-S* 2S5 (398), *MSTA-S* 2S19 (282); **203mm** *Pion* 2S7 (105).

COMBINED GUN/MOR: about 400 (363): **120mm:** *Nona-S* 2S9 SP (360), *Nona-K* 2B16 (37), 2 S23 (1).

MRL: about 2,500 (913), incl: **122mm:** BM-21 (442), BM-13 (8), 9P138 (28); **220mm:** 800 (337) 9P140 *Uragan*; **300mm:** 100 (98) *Smerch* 9A52.

MOR: about 5,000 (363), incl: **120mm:** 2S12 (302), PM-38 (50); **160mm:** M-160 (2); **240mm,** *Tulpan* 2S4 SP (9).

SSM (nuclear-capable): some 600 launchers, incl *FROG* (*Luna*)/SS-21 *Scarab* (*Tochka*), Scud-B/-C mod (R-17).

ATGW: AT-2 *Swatter*, AT-3 *Sagger*, AT-4 *Spigot*, AT-5 *Spandrel*, AT-6 *Spiral*, AT-7 *Saxhorn*, AT-9, AT-10.

RL: 64mm: RPG-18; **73mm:** RPG-7/-16/-22/-26; **105mm:** RPG-27/-29.

RCL: 73mm: SPG-9; **82mm:** B-10.

ATK GUNS: 57mm: ASU-57 SP; **76mm; 85mm:** D-44/SD-44, ASU-85 SP; **100mm:** T-12/-12A/M-55 towed.

AD GUNS: 23mm: ZU-23, ZSU-23-4 SP; **37mm; 57mm:** S-60, ZSU-57-2 SP; **85mm:** M-1939; **100mm:** KS-19; **130mm:** KS-30.

SAM: 500 SA-4 A/B *Ganef* (twin) (Army/Front weapon).
400 SA-6 *Gainful* (triple) (div weapon).
400 SA-8 *Gecko* (2 triple) (div weapon).
200 SA-9 *Gaskin* (2 twin) (regt weapon).
250 SA-11 *Gadfly* (quad) (replacing SA-4/-6).
100 SA-12A/B (*Gladiator/Giant*).
350 SA-13 *Gopher* (2 twin) (replacing SA-9).
100 SA-15 (replacing SA-6/SA-8).
SA-19 (2S6 SP) (8 SAM, plus twin **30mm** gun).
SA-7, SA-14 being replaced by SA-16, SA-18 (man-portable).

HEL: some 2,600:

ATTACK: 1,000 Mi-24 (872), 4 Ka-50 *Hokum*.

TPT: some 1,300, Mi-6, Mi-8 (some armed), Mi-26 (hy).

GENERAL PURPOSE: 200, incl Mi-2, Mi-8 (comms).

AIR FORCE: 130,000 (some 40,000 conscripts); some 2,150 cbt ac. 4 comd. Force strengths vary, mostly org with div of 3 regt of 3 sqn (total 90–120 ac), indep regt (30–40 ac). Regt roles incl AD, interdiction, recce, tac air spt.

LONG-RANGE AVIATION COMD (DA):
2 div; annual flying hrs: 80.

BBR: about 130 Tu-22M-3. Plus 30 Tu-22M-2 and 90 Tu-22 (incl 30 recce) in store.

TKR: 40: 20 Mya-4, 20 Il-78.

FRONTAL AVIATION COMD (KFA):
5 air army; annual flying hrs: 40.

FGA: some 750: incl 50 MiG-27/Su-17, 500 Su-24, 200 Su-25.

FTR: some 425: incl 325 MiG-29, 100 Su-27.

RECCE: some 200: incl 50 MiG-25/Su-17, 150 Su-24.

ECM: 60 Mi-8.

TRG: 1 centre for op conversion: 170 ac, incl 110 MiG-29, 40 Su-24, 20 Su-25, 1 centre for instructor trg: 80 ac incl 20 MiG-25, 15 MiG-29, 15 Su-24, 10 Su-25, 20 Su-27.

AAM: AA-8 *Aphid*, AA-10 *Alamo*, AA-11 *Archer*.

ASM: AS-7 *Kerry*, AS-10 *Karen*, AS-11 *Kilter*, AS-12 *Kegler*, AS-13 *Kingbolt*, AS-14 *Kedge*, AS-16 *Kickback*, AS-17 *Krypton*.

MILITARY TPT AVIATION COMD (VTA):
3 div, each 3 regt, each 30 ac; some indep regt.

EQPT: some 350 ac, incl: Il-76M/MD *Candid* B (replacing An-12), An-12, An-22, An-124.

Additional long- and medium-range tpt ac in comd other than VTA: some 300: Tu-134, Tu-154, An-12, An-72, Il-18, Il-62.

Civilian Aeroflot fleet: 1,500 medium- and long-range passenger ac, incl some 350 An-12 and Il-76.

RESERVE AND TRG COMD (KPLK):
TRG: 6 schools (incl 1 for foreign students) subordinate to Air Force HQ: 1,500 ac, incl 1,000 L-39, 300 L-410/Tu-134, 80 MiG-29/Su-22/Su-24/Su-27.

RESERVES: some 100 ac, incl MiG-23, MiG-27, Su-17, Su-22.

AIR DEFENCE TROOPS (VPVO): 200,000 (60,000 conscripts); 6 Air Defence Armies: 2 indep. AD corps: air regt and indep sqn; SAM bde/regt.

AC (Aviation of Air Defence – APVO):

FTR: some 850, incl, 100 MiG-23, 425 MiG-31, 325 Su-27 (plus some 20 cbt capable MiG-23 trg variants in regts).

TRG: 1 trg school, 4 regt: 164 MiG-23, 220 L-39.

RESERVES: 350 ac, inc MiG-21, MiG-23, MiG-25, plus additional Su-15, Tu-128, MiG-23, MiG-25 awaiting elimination.

AEW AND CONTROL: 20 Il-76.

AAM: AA-6 *Acrid*, AA-7 *Apex*, AA-8 *Aphid*, AA-9 *Amos*, AA-10 *Alamo*, AA-11 *Archer*.

SAM: some 2,500 launchers in some 250 sites:

SA-2 *Guideline*: 150 (being replaced by SA-10).

SA-3 *Goa*: 100 (2 or 4 launcher rails) (being replaced by SA-10).

SA-5 *Gammon*: 500 launchers (being replaced by SA-10).

SA-10 *Grumble*: some 1,750 launchers.

CBT AC (CFE totals as at 15 December 1994 for all air forces less maritime): 3,283: **Su-15:** 128; **Su-17:** 197; **Su-22:** 63; **Su-24:** 367; **Su-25:** 201; **Su-27:** 346; **MiG-21:** 93; **MiG-23:** 635; **MiG-25:** 152; **MiG-27:** 253, **MiG-29:** 455; **MiG-31:** 234; **Tu-22:** 92; **Tu-22M:** 52; **Tu-128:** 15.

NAVY: ε200,000 (ε40,000 conscripts, ε13,000 Strategic Forces, ε30,000 Naval Aviation, ε24,000 Coastal Defence Forces).

SUBMARINES: 183:

STRATEGIC: 45 (see p. 113).

TAC: 138:

SSGN: 19:

12 *Oscar* with 24 x SS-N-19 *Shipwreck* USGW (VLS); plus T-65 HWT.

2 *Charlie*-II with 8 x SS-N-7 *Starbright* USGW; plus T-53 HWT.

1 *Echo*-II with 8 SS-N-12 *Sandbox* SSM; plus T-53 HWT.

3 *Yankee* 'Notch' with 20+ SS-N-21 *Sampson* SLCM.

1 *Yankee* (trials) with ε12 SS-NX-24 SLCM.

SSN: 49:

13 *Akula* with T-65 HWT; plus SS-N-21.

4 *Sierra* with T-65 HWT; plus SS-N-21.

26 *Victor*-III with T-65 HWT; plus SS-N-15.

2 *Victor*-II with T-53 HWT.

4 *Victor*-I with T-53 HWT.

SS: 55 (all with T-53 HWT):

24 *Kilo*, 18 *Tango*, 10 *Foxtrot, 3 Romeo*.

OTHER ROLES: 15:

SSN: 6:

3 *Uniform*, 1 *Alfa*, 1 *Echo* II experimental/trials, 2 *Yankee*.

SS: 9:

1 *Beluga*, 3 *Bravo* wpn targets, 1 *Lima*, 2 *India* rescue, 1 *X-Ray* trials, 1 *Losos* SF.

IN STORE: probably some *Foxtrot*.

PRINCIPAL SURFACE COMBATANTS: 150:

CARRIERS: 1 *Kuznetsov* CVV (67,500t) capacity 20 fixed wing ac (Su-33) and 8–10 ASW hel with 12 SS-N-19 *Shipwreck* SSM, 4 x 6 SA-N-9 SAM, 8 CADS-1, 2 RBU-12 (not fully op).

CC: 25:

CGN: 4 *Admiral Ushakov* (ex-*Kirov*) (AAW/ASUW) with 12 x 8 SA-N-6 *Grumble*, 20 SS-N-19 *Shipwreck* SSM, 3 Ka-25/-27 hel for OTHT/AEW/ASW; plus 1 with 1 x 2 130mm guns, 1 with 1 x 2 SS-N-14 *Silex* SUGW (LWT or nuc payload), 10 x 533mm TT.

CG: 21:

1 *Moskva* (CGH) (ASW) with 18 Ka-25 hel (E45-75 LWT), 1 x 2 SUW-N-1; plus 2 x 2 SA-N-3 SAM.

3 *Slava* (AAW/ASUW) with 8 x 8 SA-N-6 *Grumble*, 8 x 2 SS-N-12 *Sandbox* SSM, 1 Ka-25/-27 hel (AEW/ASW); plus 8 x 533mm TT, 1 x 2 130mm guns.

11 *Udaloy* (ASW) with 2 x 4 SS-N-14 *Silex* SUGW, 2 x 12 ASW RL, 8 x 533mm TT, 2 Ka-27 hel; plus 2 x 100mm guns.

1 *Udaloy*-II with 8 x 4 SS-N-22 *Sunburn*, 8 x SA-N-9, 2 Cads-N-1, 8 SA-N-11, 10 x 533mm TT, 2 Ka-27 hel plus 2 x 100mm guns.

4 *Nikolayev* (*Kara*) (ASW) with 2 x 4 SS-N-14 *Silex* SUGW, 10 x 533mm TT, 1 Ka-25 hel; plus 2 x 2 SA-N-3 *Goblet* (1 (*Azov*) with 3 x 8 SA-N-6, only 1 x SA-N-3 and other differences).

1 *Admiral Zozulya* (*Kresta*-I) (ASUW/ASW) with 2 x 2 SS-N-3b *Shaddock* SSM, 1 Ka-25 hel (OTHT), 10 x 533mm TT (flagship probably non-seagoing).

DDG: 22:

AAW/ASUW: 19:

17 *Sovremennyy* with 2 x 4 SS-N-22 *Sunburn* SSM, 2 x 1 SA-N-7 *Gadfly* SAM, 2 x 2 130mm guns, 1 Ka-25 (B) hel (OTHT); plus 4 x 533mm TT.

1 *Grozny* (*Kynda*) (ASUW) with 2 x 4 SS-N-3b; plus 1 x 2 SA-N-1 *Goa* SAM, 6 x 533mm TT.

1 *Sderzhannyy* (mod *Kashin*) with 4 SS-N-2C *Styx* SSM, 2 x 2 SA-N-1 SAM; plus 5 x 533mm TT.

ASW: 3 *Komsomolets Ukrainyy* (*Kashin*) with 2 x 12 ASW RL, 5 x 533mm TT; plus 2 x 2 SA-N-1 SAM (1 with trials fit 1 x SA-N-7).

FF: 102:

11 *Rezvyy* (*Krivak*-II) with 1 x 4 SS-N-14 *Silex* SUGW, 8 x 533mm TT, 2 x 12 ASW RL; plus 2 x 100mm guns.

15 *Bditelnyy* (*Krivak*-I) (weapons as *Rezvyy*, but with 2 x twin 76mm guns).

1 *Neustrashimyy* with 2 x 12 ASW RL.

(Note: frigates listed below lie between 1,000 and 1,200 tonnes full-load displacement and are not counted in official releases.)

60 *Grisha*-I, -III, -IV, -V, with 2 x 12 ASW RL, 4 x 533mm TT.

12 *Parchim*-II (ASW) with 2 x 12 ASW RL, 4 x 406mm ASTT.

3 *Petya* with ASW RL, 5 or 10 x 406mm ASTT.

PATROL AND COASTAL COMBATANTS: 143:

CORVETTES: about 80:

about 49 *Tarantul* (ASUW), 3 -I, 17–II, both with 2 x 2 SS-N-2C *Styx*; 29 -III with 2 x 2 SS-N-22 *Sunburn*.

31 *Nanuchka* (ASUW) -I, -III and -IV with 2 x 3 SS-N-9 *Siren*.

MSL CRAFT: 21:

8 *Osa* PFM with 4 x SS-N-2C.

13 *Matka* PHM with 2 x 1 SS-N-2C.

TORPEDO CRAFT: 29 *Turya* PHT with 4 x 533mm TT.

PATROL CRAFT: about 13:

OFFSHORE: about 3 T-58/-43.

COASTAL: 10:

7 *Pauk* PFC (ASW) with 2 x ASW RL, 4 x ASTT.

1 *Babochka* PHT (ASW) with 8 x ASTT.

2 *Mukha* PHT (ASW) with 8 x ASTT.

MINE WARFARE: about 188:

MINELAYERS: 3 *Pripyat* (*Alesha*), capacity 300 mines. (Note: most submarines and many surface combatants are equipped for minelaying.)

MCM: about 185:

OFFSHORE: 33:

2 *Gorya* MCO.

31 *Natya*-I and -II MSO.

COASTAL: about 87:

15 *Yurka* MSC.

2 *Andryusha* MSC (trials).

About 70 *Sonya* MSC.

INSHORE: about 65:

15 *Vanya*, about 10 MSI and 40 MSI⟨.

AMPH: 49:

LPD: 3 *Ivan Rogov* with 4–5 Ka-27 hel: capacity 520 tps, 20 tk.

LST: 29:

22 *Ropucha*: capacity 225 tps, 9 tk.

7 *Alligator*: capacity 300 tps, 20 tk.

LSM: about 17 *Polnocny* (3 types): capacity 180 tps, 6 tk (some adapted for mine warfare, but retain amph primary role).

LCM: about 14 *Ondatra*.

LCAC AND SES: about 59: incl 9 *Pomornik*, 14 *Aist*, 9 *Tsaplya*, 16 *Lebed*, 2 *Utenok*, 6 *Gus*, 2 *Orlan* and 1 *Utka* 'wing-in-ground-effect' (WIG) experimental.

Plus craft: about 80.

SPT AND MISC: about 596:

UNDER WAY SPT: 27:

1 *Berezina*, 6 *Chilikin*, 20 other AO.

MAINT AND LOG: about 230: incl some 15 AS, 38 AR, 12 general maint/spt, 20 AOT, 18 msl spt/resupply, 70 tugs, 14 special liquid carriers, 13 water carriers, 30 AK.

SPECIAL PURPOSES: about 114: incl some 40 AGI (some armed), 4 msl range instrumentation, 3 trg, about 63 icebreakers (civil-manned), 4 AH.

SURVEY/RESEARCH: about 225: incl some 40 naval, 50 civil AGOR; 90 naval, 35 civil AGHS; 10 space-associated ships (civil-manned).

MERCHANT FLEET (auxiliary/augmentation): about 2,800 ocean-going vessels (17 in Arctic service), incl 125 ramp-fitted and ro-ro, some with rails for rolling stock, 3 roll-on/float-off, 14 barge carriers, 48 passenger liners, 500 coastal and river ships.

NAVAL AVIATION: (ε30,000); some 783 cbt ac; 251 armed hel.

Four Fleet Air Forces; org in air div, each with 2–3 regt of HQ elm and 2 sqn of 9–10 ac each; recce, ASW, tpt/ utl org in indep regt or sqn.

BBR: some 100:

5 regt with some 90 Tu-22M (AS-4 ASM).

1 regt with some 10 Tu-22.

FGA: 150: 70 Su-24, 50 Su-25, 30 MiG-23/-27.

TRG: some 50: Tu-16*, Tu-26*, Tu-95*, Su-24, Su-25*, Su-27*.

ASW: ac: 151; **hel:** 238.

AC: 50 Tu-142, 36 Il-38, 65 Be-12.

HEL: 63 Mi-14, 75 Ka-25, 100 Ka-27.

MR/EW: ac: some 55; **hel:** 20.

AC: incl 14 Tu-95, 6 Tu-22, 25 Su-24, 7 An-12, 3 Il-20.

HEL: 20 Ka-25.

MCM: 25 Mi-14 hel.

CBT ASLT: 25 Ka-27 hel.

TPT: ac: 120 An-12, An-24, An-26; **hel:** 70 Mi-6/-8.

ASM: AS-4 *Kitchen*, AS-7 *Kerry*, AS-10 *Karen*, AS-11 *Kilter*, AS-12 *Kegler*, AS-13 *Kingbolt*, AS-14 *Kedge*.

COASTAL DEFENCE: ε24,000 (incl Naval Infantry, Coastal Artillery and Rocket Troops, Coastal Defence Troops).

NAVAL INFANTRY (Marines): (some 15,000).

1 inf div (7,000: 3 inf, 1 tk, 1 arty regt) (Pacific Fleet).

4 indep bde (1 reserve) (type: 3,000: 4 inf, 1 tk, 1 arty, 1 MRL, 1 ATK bn).

4 fleet SF bde: 2–3 underwater, 1 para bn, spt elm.

EQPT:

MBT: 500: T-55, T-64, T-72, 100 T-80.

LT TK: 120 PT-76.

RECCE: 60 BRDM-2/*Sagger* ATGW.

APC: some 1,500: BTR-60/-70/-80, 250 MT-LB.

SP ARTY: 122mm: 96 2S1; **152mm:** 18 2S3.

MRL: 122mm: 96 9P138.

COMBINED GUN/MOR: 120mm: 168 2S9 SP, 11 2S23 SP.

ATGW: 72 AT-3/-5.

AD GUNS: 23mm: 60 ZSU-23-4 SP.

SAM: 250 SA-7, 20 SA-8, 50 SA-9/-13.

COASTAL ARTILLERY AND ROCKET TROOPS: (4,000).

1 coastal arty div (role: protects approaches to naval bases and major ports).

EQPT:

ARTY: incl **130mm:** SM-4-1.

SSM: 40 SS-C-1b *Sepal* (similar to SS-N-3), SS-C-3, *Styx*, SS-C-4 reported.

COASTAL DEFENCE: (5,000) (all units reserve status).

2 coast defence div.

1 coast defence bde.

2 arty regt.

2 SAM regt.

EQPT:

MBT: 350 T-64.

AIFV: 450 BMP.

APC: 280 BTR-60/-70/-80, 400 MT-LB.

TOTAL ARTY: 364.

TOWED ARTY: 280: **122mm:** 140 D-30; **152mm:** 40 D-20, 50 2A65, 50 2A36.

SP ARTY: 152mm: 48 2S5.

MRL: 122mm: 36 BM-21.

NAVAL DEPLOYMENT:

NORTHERN FLEET (Arctic and Atlantic) (HQ Severomorsk):

BASES: Kola Inlet, Motovskiy Gulf, Gremikha, Polyarnyy, Litsa Gulf, Ura Guba, Severodovinsk.

SS: 109: strategic: 37 SSBN; tac: 71: 14 SSGN, 35 SSN, 22 SS; other roles: 8.

PRINCIPAL SURFACE COMBATANTS: 47: incl 1 CVV, 8 cruisers, 9 destroyers, 29 frigates.

OTHER SURFACE SHIPS: about 10 patrol and coastal combatants, 45 MCM, 10 amph, some 182 spt and misc.

NAVAL AVIATION: 200 cbt ac; 64 armed hel.

BBR: 60: 20 Tu-16, 40 Tu-22M.

FTR/FGA: 95: 8 MiG-23, 27 MiG-27, 58 Su-24/-25, 2 Su-27.

ASW: ac: 45: 5 Tu-142, 16 Il-38, 24 Be-12; **hel:** 64 (afloat): 14 Ka-25, 50 Ka-27.

MR/EW: ac: 37: 2 An-12, 20 Tu-16, 14 Tu-95, 1 Il-20. **hel:** 5 Ka-25.

MCM: 8 Mi-14 hel.

CBT ASLT HEL: 10 Ka-27.

COMMS: 6 Tu-142.

TKR: 1 Tu-16.

NAVAL INFANTRY: 2 bde (80 MBT, 130 arty).

COASTAL DEFENCE: 1 Coastal Defence (360 MT-LB, 134 arty), 1 SAM regt.

BALTIC FLEET (HQ Kaliningrad):
BASES: Kronshtadt, Baltiysk.
SS: 9: tac: 8: SS; other roles: 1 SS.
PRINCIPAL SURFACE COMBATANTS: 23: incl 3 cruisers, 2 destroyers, 18 frigates.
OTHER SURFACE SHIPS: about 65 patrol and coastal combatants, 55 MCM, 15 amph, some 102 spt and misc.
NAVAL AVIATION: 195 cbt ac, 35 armed hel.
FGA: 180: 5 regts: 26 Su-17, 72 Su-24, 28 Su-27, 70 MiG-23.
ASW: ac: 15: 15 Be-12; **hel:** 35: 3 Ka-25, 22 Ka-27, 10 Mi-14.
MR/EW: ac: 7: 1 An-12, 6 Su-24; **hel:** 5 Ka-25.
MCM: 5 Mi-14 hel.
CBT ASLT HEL: 5 Ka-29.
NAVAL INFANTRY: 1 bde, (25 MBT, 36 arty/MRL) (Kaliningrad).
COASTAL DEFENCE: 2 arty regt (133 arty).
1 SSM regt: some 8 SS-C-1b *Sepal*.

BLACK SEA FLEET: ε48,000 (incl Naval Air, Naval Infantry and Coastal Defence) (HQ Sevastopol, Ukraine). Under joint Russian/Ukrainian command for 3–5 years, then to be divided.
BASES: Sevastopol, Odessa (Ukraine).
SS: 14: tac: 10 SS; other roles: 4.
PRINCIPAL SURFACE COMBATANTS: 31: incl 1 CGH, 4 cruisers, 5 destroyers, 21 frigates.
OTHER SURFACE SHIPS: about 43 patrol and coastal combatants, 35 MCM, 10 amph, some 131 spt and misc.
NAVAL AVIATION: (7,600); 125 cbt ac; 85 armed hel.
BBR: 57: some 39 Tu-22M, 18 Tu-16.
FGA: 1 regt: 45: Su-17.
ASW: ac: 23* Be-12; **hel:** 31 Mi-14, 49 Ka-25, 5 Ka-27.
MR/EW: ac: 2 An-12, 12 Tu-16, 6 Tu-22, 1 Il-20; **hel:** 5 Ka-25.
MCM: 5 Mi-14 hel.
NAVAL INFANTRY: (2,000).
1 bde (50 MBT 218 APC, 45 arty (2S1, 2S9)).
COASTAL DEFENCE: (1,900).
1 Coastal Defence div (175 MBT (T-64), 450 AIFV (BMP-2), 72 arty (D-30)). 1 SAM regt.

CASPIAN FLOTILLA:
BASES: Astrakhan (Russia).
The Caspian Sea Flotilla has been divided between Azerbaijan (about 25%) and Russia, Kazakhstan and Turkmenistan which are operating a joint flotilla under Russian command currently based at Astrakhan.
PRINCIPAL SURFACE COMBATANTS: 2 frigates.
OTHER SURFACE SHIPS: 12 patrol and coastal combatants, 18 MCM, some 20 amph, about 10 spt.

PACIFIC FLEET (Indian Ocean): (HQ Vladivostok)
BASES: Vladivostok, Petropavlovsk, Kamchatskiy, Magadan, Sovetskaya Gavan.

SS: 51: strategic: 18 SSBN; tac: 34: (5 SSGN, 14 SSN, 15 SS); other roles: 2 SS.
PRINCIPAL SURFACE COMBATANTS: 49: incl 9 cruisers, 6 destroyers, 34 frigates.
OTHER SURFACE SHIPS: about 25 patrol and coastal combatants, 53 MCM, 14 amph, some 181 spt and misc.
NAVAL AVIATION (Pacific Fleet Air Force) (HQ Vladivostok): 170 cbt ac, 89 cbt hel.
BBR: 60: 2 regt with 60 Tu-26.
FGA: 40: 1 regt with 40 Su-17, Su-24, Su-25.
ASW: ac: 70: 20 Tu-142, 20 Il-38, 30 Be-12; **hel:** 89: afloat: 23 Ka-25, 38 Ka-27; ashore: 28 Mi-14.
MR/EW: ac: some 20 An-12, Tu-95; **hel:** 10 Ka-25.
MCM: 6 Mi-14 hel.
CBT ASLT HEL: 10 Ka-27.
COMMS: 7 Tu-142.
TKR: 2 Tu-16.
NAVAL INFANTRY: 1 div HQ, 3 inf, 1 tk and 1 arty regt:
COASTAL DEFENCE: 1 Coastal Defence div.

DEPLOYMENT:

Determining the manning state of Russian units is difficult. The following assessment is based on the latest available information. Above 75% – none reported; above 50% possibly 7 TD, 12 MRD, 5 ABD and 6 MG/Arty div. The remainder are assessed as 20–50%. All bde are maintained at or above 50%. No temporary deployments for operations in Chechnya are listed. TLE in each MD includes active and trg units and in store.

RUSSIAN MILITARY DISTRICTS:
KALININGRAD:
GROUND: 24,000: 1 Army HQ, 1 TD, 2 MRD, 1 tk, 3 arty, 1 SSM, 1 SAM bde/regt, 1 ATK, 1 attack hel regt, 870 MBT, 980 ACV, 410 arty/MRL/mor, 16 SS-21, 52 attack hel.
AD: 1 regt: 28 Su-27 (Baltic Fleet).
SAM: 75.
NORTHERN MD (HQ St Petersburg):
GROUND: 87,000: 1 Army HQ, 1 Corps HQ; 6 MRD (1 trg), 1 ABD; plus 3 indep MR bde, 6 arty bde/regt, 4 SSM, 1 AB, 1 *Spetsnaz*, 4 SAM bde, 3 ATK, 2 attack hel, 1 aslt tpt hel regt, 950 MBT, 1,600 ACV, 1,000 arty/MRL/mor, 12 Scud, 36 SS-21, 80 attack hel.
AIR: 1 hy bbr regt (20: Tu-22M), 1 air army: 1 bbr div (80: Su-24), 1 recce regt (55: MiG-25, Su-17), 1 ftr div (35 Su-27, 60 MiG-29).
AD: 7 regt: 15 MiG-25, 100 MiG-31, 90 Su-27.
SAM: 600.
MOSCOW MD (HQ Moscow):
GROUND: 116,000: 2 Army HQ, 1 Corps HQ, 5 TD (1 trg), 2 MRD, 2 ABD, plus 1 arty div (5 bde), 9 arty bde/regt, 5 ATK, 4 SSM, 4 indep MR, 2 *Spetsnaz*, 5 SAM bde, 6 attack hel, 1 aslt tpt hel regt, 2,320 MBT, 4,200 ACV, 2,950 arty/MRL/mor, 24 Scud, 18 SS-21, 230 attack hel.

AIR: 1 hy bbr regt (20: Tu-22M), 1 air army: 1 bbr div (90 Su-24), 1 ftr div (35 Su-27, 110 MiG-29), 1 FGA regt (40 Su-25), 1 recce regt (55 Su-24/MiG-25), 2 trg regt: 180 L-39. In store: 260 MiG-23, 170 MiG-27, 340 L-29.
AD: 4 regt: 60 MiG-23, 50 MiG-31, 30 Su-27 plus 190 in store.
SAM: 1,000.
VOLGA MD (HQ Kuybyshev (Samarra)):
GROUND: 68,000: 1 Army HQ, 2 TD, 2 MRD (1 trg), 1 ABD plus 1 arty bde/regt, 2 SSM, 2 SAM bde, 1 ATK, 2 attack hel, 1 aslt tpt hel, 6 hel trg regt, 1,200 MBT, 2,150 ACV, 640 arty/MRL/mor, 24 Scud, 18 SS-21, 230 attack hel.
AIR: 2 ftr trg regt: 60 MiG-29, 24 Su-17, 10 Su-25, 180 cbt ac in store.
AD: 1 PVO Corps, 2 regt: 40 MiG-23, 5 MiG-25, 25 MiG-31 plus 140 cbt ac in store.
NORTH CAUCASUS MD (HQ Rostov):
GROUND: 58,000: 1 Army HQ, 3 Corps HQ, 2 MRD, 1 ABD, 2 AB, 3 MR bde, 1 Spetsnaz, 5 arty bde, 3 SSM, 5 SAM bde, 3 ATK, 2 attack hel, 1 aslt tpt hel regt, 260 MBT, 1,200 ACV, 1,070 arty/MRL/mor, 24 Scud, 66 attack hel.
AIR: 1 Air Army: 1 bbr div (85 Su-24), 1 FGA div (110 Su-25), 1 ftr div (110 MiG-29), 1 recce regt (35 Su-24), 2 trg centres, 5 trg regt: 30 Su-22, 15 Su-24, 10 Su-25, 15 Su-27, 20 MiG-29, 410 L-39, plus 130 cbt ac in store.
AD: 1 PVO Corps, 3 regt: 5 MiG-25, 60 Su-27; 1 trg centre, 4 regt: 164 MiG-23, 220 L-39.
SAM: 150.
URAL MD (HQ Yekaterinburg):
GROUND: 2 TD (1 trg), 2 MRD, 2 arty bde/regt, 1 ATK bde. 1,200 MBT, 1,200 ACV, 750 arty/MRL/mor.
AIR: 30 Su-24.
AD: 3 regt: 40 MiG-23, 25 MiG-31, plus in store 25 MiG-23, 110 Su-15.
SAM: 100.
SIBERIAN MD (HQ Novosibirsk):
GROUND: 1 Corps HQ, 4 MRD, 1 arty div, 3 MR bde, 3 arty bde/regt, 2 SSM, 2 SAM, 1 Spetsnaz bde, 1 ATK, 1 attack hel regt, 2,000 MBT, 3,500 ACV, 2,200 arty/MRL/mor, 24 Scud, 40 attack hel.
AIR: trg units: 275 L-39.
AD: 4 regt: 140: MiG-23, MiG-31.
TRANSBAYKAL MD (HQ Chita):
GROUND: 3 Army HQ, 4 TD (1 trg), 6 MRD (1 trg), plus 2 MG/arty div, 1 arty div, 2 MR bde, 5 arty bde/regt, 3 SSM, 1 AB, 1 Spetsnaz, 2 ATK, 3 SAM bde, 2 attack hel regt, 3,000 MBT, 4,000 ACV, 4,000 arty/MRL/mor, 24 Scud, 18-SS-21, 80 attack hel.
AIR: 1 air army, bbr: 80 Su-24, ftr 30 MiG-29; 75 Su-17/24.
FAR EASTERN MD (HQ Khabarovsk):
GROUND: 4 Army, 1 Corps HQ, 3 TD (1 trg), 13 MRD (2 trg), plus 5 MG/arty div, 1 arty div, 11 arty bde/regt, 2 AB, 5 SSM, 6 SAM, 1 Spetsnaz, 3 ATK bde,

6 attack hel regt, 6,000 MBT, 8,700 ACV, 5,800 arty/MRL/mor, 60 Scud, 200 attack hel.
AIR: bbr: 120 Su-24; FGA: 100: Su-17, Su-25; ftr div: 85: MiG-29, Su-27; recce: 60: Su-17, Su-24.
AD (Transbaykal and Far Eastern MD): 200 MiG-31, Su-27.
SAM: 570.

GROUPS OF FORCES:
TRANSCAUCASUS GROUP OF FORCES (HQ Tblisi, Georgia):(31,000) (excl peacekeeping forces).
ARMENIA:
GROUND: (9,000): 1 mil base with 1 MRD(-), 80 MBT, 170 ACV, 100 arty/MRL/mors.
AD: 1 sqn MiG-23.
GEORGIA:
GROUND: (22,000): 3 mil bases with 2 MRD(-), 200 MBT, 570 ACV, 220 arty/MRL/mor.
AIR: 1 composite regt with some 35 ac: An-12, An-26; **hel:** Mi-8.

FORCES IN OTHER FORMER SOVIET REPUBLICS:
MOLDOVA (Dniestr) (14th Army): (6,400): 1 Army HQ, 1 MRD, 120 MBT, 170 ACV, 130 arty/MRL/mor.
TAJIKISTAN:
GROUND: (12,000): 1 MRD, 180 MBT, 340 ACV, 180 arty/MRL/mor.
TURKMENISTAN:
JOINT TURKMENISTAN/RUSSIAN FORCES:
GROUND: (11,000): 1 Corps HQ, 3 MRD (1 trg), 1 arty bde, 530 MBT, 1,130 ACV, 530 arty/MRL/mor.

FORCES ABROAD (other than in the former
Soviet republics or in the Group of Forces):
VIETNAM: (500); naval facility; SIGINT station.
OTHER: Cuba some 800 SIGINT andε10 mil advisers; Mongolia: ε500 SIGINT; Syria 500; Africa: 100.
PEACEKEEPING:
GEORGIA/ABKHAZIA: ε3,000; 1 AB regt, 2 MR bn. **GEORGIA/SOUTH OSSETIA:** 1 inf bn.
MOLDOVA/DNIESTR: 2 inf bn.
UNITED NATIONS:
ANGOLA (UNAVEM): 10 plus 5 Obs. **BOSNIA** (UNPROFOR): 491; 1 inf bn, 14 Obs and 3 civ pol. **CROATIA** (UNCRO): 926; 1 AB bn, 8 Obs and 20 civ pol.**GEORGIA:** (UNOMIG) 3 Obs.**HAITI:** (UNMIH): 5 civ pol. **IRAQ/KUWAIT** (UNIKOM): 14 Obs. **MIDDLE EAST** (UNTSO): 17 Obs. **FYROM** (UNPREDEP): 1 civ pol. **RWANDA** (UNAMIR): 17 Obs. **WESTERN SAHARA** (MINURSO): 30 Obs.

PARAMILITARY: 280,000.
FRONTIER FORCES (directly subordinate to the President): 100,000, 6 frontier districts, Arctic,

Kaliningrad, Moscow units.

EQPT:

1,500 ACV (incl BMP, BTR), 90 arty (incl 2S1, 2S9, 2S12).

AIR: ac: some 70 Il-76, Tu-134, An-72, An-24, An-26, Yak-40; **hel:** some 200+: Mi-8, Mi-24, Mi-26, Ku-27.

PATROL AND COASTAL COMBATANTS: about 212:

PATROL, OFFSHORE: about 23:

7 *Krivak*-III with 1 x Ka-27 hel, 1 x 100mm gun. 10 *Grisha*-II, 6 *Grisha*-III.

PATROL, COASTAL: about 32:

25 *Pauk*, 7 *Svetlyak*.

PATROL, INSHORE: about 115:

75 *Stenka*, 10 *Muravey*, 30 *Zhuk*.

RIVERINE MONITORS: about 126:

19 *Yaz*, 10 *Piyavka*, 7 *Vosh*, 90 *Shmel*.

SPT AND MISC: about 26:

8 *Ivan Susanin* armed icebreakers, 18 *Sorum* armed ocean tugs.

FORCES FOR THE PROTECTION OF THE RUSSIAN FEDERATION: 20,000: org incl elm of

Ground Forces (1 mech inf bde, 1 AB regt).

MVD (*Ministerstvo Vnutrennikh Del*): internal security tps: ε180,000; 1 indep special purpose div (ODON – 5 op regt; 8,000), some indep regt; special motorised units (40,000); special purpose militia (OMON) guards and escorts (some 110,000). Eqpt incl 1,200 ACV (incl BMP-1/-2, BTR-80), 20 D-30.

The Middle East and North Africa

Political and Security Developments

In the Middle East, the Arab–Israeli peace process stumbles on; Kuwait was again threatened by Iraqi forces; and Islamic extremists continue their terrorist campaigns in Algeria and Egypt.

Israeli–Syrian Peace Treaty

While Syrian President Hafez Assad appears to be dragging his feet over progress towards a peace treaty with Israel, a major step forward was taken on 27 June 1995 when the Israeli and Syrian Chiefs of Staff held discussions in Washington. They agreed that a security arrangement should include: a demilitarised zone; an early-warning system; an international presence; and a staged Israeli withdrawal – but the detail under these headings has not been finalised. The Syrians proposed a formula for an asymmetric demilitarised zone which would require them to demilitarise 10 miles of territory to Israel's six. This zone would be astride the international border which has yet to be agreed. The Syrians have rejected Israel's proposal to keep its early-warning station on Mount Hermon while allowing Syria to establish a station near Zefat in northern Israel.

Israeli–Jordanian Peace Treaty

King Hussein of Jordan and Israeli Prime Minister Yitzhak Rabin, in the presence of US President Bill Clinton, signed a peace treaty on 26 October 1994. Israel agreed to the international border being the boundary line drawn by the British in 1922, and to withdraw from territory east of the line captured in 1967. In return, Jordan has leased back to Israel areas in the Arava valley farmed by Israelis. Water issues were addressed in the Treaty with Israel agreeing to Jordan taking an additional 40 million cubic metres annually from the Yarmouk River. Jordan will not join an anti-Israeli alliance and neither side will allow its territory to be used for attacks on the other. Both have committed themselves to creating a Conference on Security and Cooperation in the Middle East on the lines of the Organisation for Security and Cooperation in Europe with confidence-building and transparency measures. A number of ambitious joint schemes for energy, tourism, transport, water and industry have been proposed. Israel completed its withdrawal from Jordanian territory on 9 February 1995.

Palestinian Self-Rule

Both Israeli Foreign Minister Shimon Peres and Palestinian Chairman Yasser Arafat are making great efforts to reach agreement over the next stage of Israeli withdrawal from the West Bank and the handover of responsibilities to the Palestinian National Authority. The programme agreed in the Declaration of Principles signed on 13 September 1993 is well behind schedule. Although not all details of the next stage have been agreed, it is clear that Israel intends to withdraw totally from the northern Palestinian towns of Jenin, Nablus, Qalqilya and Tulkarm. There would be partial withdrawal and joint patrols in Ramallah and Bethlehem where Israeli settlers use the roads through these towns. There would be no withdrawal from Hebron where a small enclave in the town and the nearby Kiryat Arba are populated by Israeli extremists and an Israeli Army presence is essential not only to protect them, but also to deter them from attacking the Arab population. It had been confidently planned that an agreement on Israeli Defence Force (IDF) withdrawal would be signed in Washington on 25 July 1995 to include provision for some 700 international monitors to deploy in September and the IDF to withdraw at the beginning of November to be replaced by 1,700 Palestinian police. However agreement had not been reached by the end of July. The elections for the self-rule council were to be held before the end of November. Withdrawal from Ramallah and Bethlehem is scheduled for November, but depends on the completion of bypass roads. Until all Palestinian villages can be bypassed, the IDF will continue to patrol through them. While any terrorism is unacceptable to Israel, the level of violence dropped considerably after Islamic *Jihad* suicide bombers killed 21 Israelis at Beit Lid on 22 January 1995, but increased with another suicide bomb on a bus in Tel Aviv on 24 July. Israel has agreed to transfer all remaining spheres of civil authority but detailed agreements still have to be reached. Electricity and water are two of the most difficult areas to agree on. The Israeli Army has started preparing for redeployment, which involves moving some training units into Israel and using their bases for operational units, and constructing bypass roads to allow unhindered settler movement.

In **Lebanon**, *Hizbollah* has intensified its campaign against the IDF and the South Lebanese Army (SLA) with some success. At least 23 Israeli soldiers were killed in Lebanon during 1994 and during the last three months of the year casualties inflicted on *Hizbollah* were roughly equal to those incurred by the IDF and SLA. This situation is likely to continue until an Israeli–Syrian peace treaty, which should contain provision for Syrian control of *Hizbollah*, is signed.

Iraq

On 7 October 1994, US officials revealed that two Iraqi Republican Guard divisions had moved south, close to the border with Kuwait. The news came, after the move had been monitored for several days, just as Iraqi Prime Minister Tariq Aziz was about to address the United Nations. Kuwaiti forces mobilised and deployed to the border. The US reacted quickly, sending several aircraft squadrons to bases in Saudi Arabia. The first US ground troops, equipped from the stockpile maintained in Kuwait, arrived on 10 October. The UK also sent a marine battalion group with artillery and six additional *Tornado* GR-1 FGA aircraft. The US reinforcement included some 12,000 ground forces with two brigades of the 24th Mechanized Division (the US Marine Expeditionary Force stood by for deployment, but did not in the event do so), the aircraft carrier USS *Washington*, and some 50 extra combat aircraft plus tankers and transports. The UAE also sent naval and ground forces to Kuwait. By 12 October, Iraqi forces were being withdrawn and, although allied deployment continued, the crisis was over. The US tabled a UN Resolution forbidding future Iraqi southern deployments, but backed down from calling for a heavy-weapon exclusion zone in southern Iraq. On 15 October, the UN Security Council adopted Resolution 949 which condemned the Iraqi action, but only warned of serious consequences if it was repeated. Five days later, the US Ambassador to the UN, Madeleine Albright, warned Iraq that units north of the 32nd parallel on 20 September 1994 could no longer be deployed south of that line. The UN Security Council has so far voted against lifting the economic sanctions imposed on Iraq, most recently on 11 July 1995, on the grounds that Iraq has not yet revealed all the details of its biological weapons (BW) programme and that many Kuwaiti citizens and much Kuwaiti military and civil property are still unaccounted for. Iraq has now admitted that it had produced botulism and anthrax BW agents and has handed over to UNSCOM a 530-page document said to detail its BW programme. It has been reported that Russia has already signed contracts to develop the West Qurno and North Rumaila oil fields when sanctions are lifted.

The level of political dissent within Iraq can perhaps be judged by the government's efforts to have sanctions lifted. These include:

- The release of two Americans imprisoned for border crossing.
- The release of information on the BW programme.
- The decree releasing all political prisoners and dropping charges against Iraqis living abroad.
- The diplomatic campaign to re-enter the Arab world.

There have been several reports of unsuccessful mutinies in the Army. The defection of two of Saddam Hussein's sons-in-law on 10 August 1995 was a serious blow to the regime. One, General Hussein Kamel Hassan, who was head of the military industry, may reveal more about Iraq's weapon-of-mass-destruction programme.

Iran remains, to some extent, isolated from the world. President Clinton imposed a total ban on US trade with Iran at the end of April 1995, a move which has been supported only by Israel. The US is concerned that Iran has embarked on a nuclear weapons programme, supports Islamic

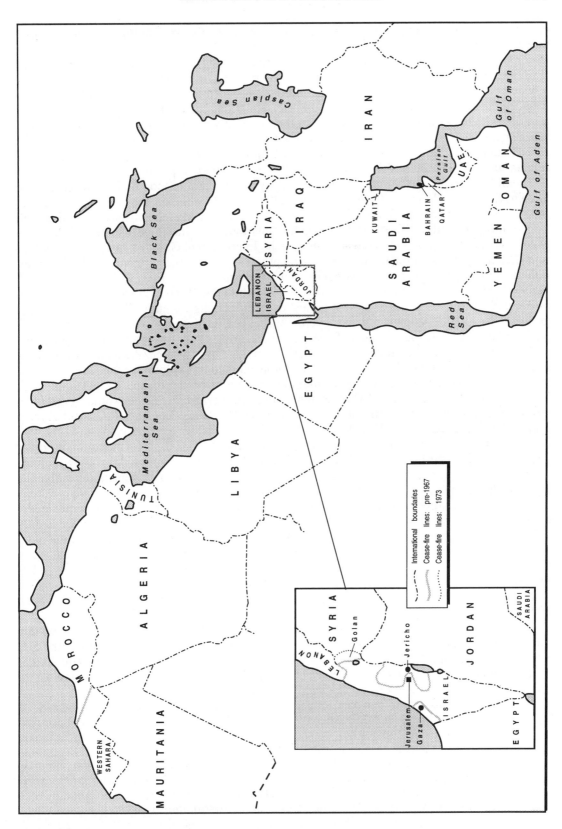

extremism and terrorism in a number of countries, opposes the Middle East process and may threaten international shipping in the Straits of Hormuz. In June, Iran rejected the European Union's offer of better relations in return for the end of the *fatwa* imposed on British author Salman Rushdie. Norway recalled its Ambassador from Tehran on 3 July. There is a growing divergence of views within Iran between the religious authorities and President Rafsanjani and his government, essentially over who has ultimate authority. Relations between Iran and Iraq appear to be improving and delegations have visited each other's capitals. Official talks, if established, would focus on questions over prisoners still unaccounted for from the Iran–Iraq War and the support given to opposition groups (such as the Iranian *Mujahedin-e-Khalq*, based in eastern Iraq, and Iranian support for Iraqi Shi'i). There are also unresolved border questions.

The Gulf States have experienced some instability over the past 12 months. In **Qatar,** the Amir, Sheikh Khalifa bin Hamad al Thani, was peacefully deposed by his son, the Crown Prince, on 26 June 1995 while out of the country. The new ruler, who was quickly recognised by the other Gulf Cooperation Council (GCC) states, is known to want to solve the maritime dispute with Bahrain. Qatar referred its claim to the Huwar islands to the International Court of Justice (ICJ), which ruled that it had jurisdiction, but there can be no progress without the agreement of both parties. Bahrain will only accept Qatar's claim if its own claim against Qatar in the Zubarah area is dealt with by the ICJ at the same time. In December 1994, while Bahrain was hosting an international conference, it was the scene of violent protest as economic discontent was fuelled by Islamist groups and at least 12 people died. The government has been criticised by Amnesty International, but maintains that there have been far fewer deaths and arrests than Amnesty claims. Opposition to the **Saudi** regime is becoming more vocal, but is divided over whether the whole Saud family should be overthrown or whether a split in the family should be exploited.

Some progress has been made by **Yemen** in resolving its border disputes. On 3 June 1995, Yemen and the Oman concluded a border agreement which returns to Yemen some 5,000km^2 of territory ceded to Oman in 1992 by the now-exiled former Vice-President Ali Salim al-Bid. Having achieved this success, Yemeni President Ali Abdullah Salih was able to visit Riyadh on 5 June with some confidence. He agreed to renew the Treaty of Ta'if which defines a part of the common border without amendment in the hope that Saudi Arabia would provide economic aid and allow Yemeni workers to return to Saudi Arabia. However, as yet there has been no movement to resolve the question of the undefined and disputed border east of Najran.

Talks between **Algerian** President Liamine Zeroual and Abassi Madani, the moderate leader of the Islamic Salvation Front (FIS), which had appeared to be going well, broke down in July 1995. The government maintains that the breakdown was caused by the insistence of the more extreme opposition factions that imprisoned FIS leaders must be released before there can be an end to violence. While the failure of the talks sets back any progress towards a settlement, it has to some extent caused a rift between the FIS and the other opposition factions which the government will hope to exploit. The death toll in the three-year civil war is now put at between 30,000 and 40,000, although the government argues for a much lower number.

United Nations efforts to identify and register those eligible in Western Sahara to vote in a referendum continue to be obstructed by the **Moroccan** authorities. In April 1995, the UN Secretary-General announced yet another postponement, this time of six months, with the start of the transitional period considered unachievable until 1 January 1996 at the earliest. The Western Saharans have threatened to resume the war, but have not yet done so.

Egyptian relations with Sudan deteriorated sharply following the attempted assassination of Egypt's President Mubarak in Addis Ababa on 26 June 1995 when Sudan was initially accused of being behind the attack. Tension heightened along the Halaib border area, where Egypt forced the withdrawal of 70 Sudanese police from their posts, and shots were exchanged. Both sides issued warnings to the other and the Sudanese threatened to abrogate the 1959 Nile Water Treaty. Meanwhile an Egyptian group – 'the Islamic Group' – claimed responsibility for the assassination attempt. Terrorist activity by Muslim extremists has continued over the last 12 months with an upsurge in the Minya Province of Upper Egypt in the first months of 1995.

Nuclear and Missile Developments

Nuclear Weapons

At present, of the Middle Eastern states, only Iran is considered to be pursuing a nuclear weapons programme, although no doubt Iraq still has ambitions in this respect. However, little is known beyond a general acknowledgement that Iran wants nuclear weapons and that it is planning a large-scale nuclear energy programme. Contracts have been placed with Russia to provide a 1,000 megawatt (MW) light-water reactor at Bushehr with options for a second 1,000 MW and two 400 MW reactors. Iran has also approached China to construct further nuclear power stations, but this project appears to have been stalled by a number of problems. One view is that Iran, with its known oil and gas reserves, has no need of an expensive nuclear-energy programme, while the Iranians themselves argue that it makes sense to diversify. Iran is known to have three working uranium mines, one of which has been visited by International Atomic Energy Agency (IAEA) officials who reported that they had found nothing inconsistent with a civil nuclear programme. China has delivered an electromagnetic isotope separator, or calutron, which, while it could be used to separate weapons-grade uranium, is, as reported by the IAEA, of a scale that could only produce isotopes for medical purposes. Iranians have received training in nuclear physics at two institutes in Pakistan, and also in the US and Europe.

Iran joined the Nuclear Non-Proliferation Treaty (NPT) and a safeguards agreement with the IAEA came into force in May 1994. Since then, IAEA inspectors have seen no evidence of a weapons programme and congratulate Iran on its cooperation with the Agency which goes beyond the obligations of the NPT.

President Clinton, at the May 1995 summit in Moscow, is reported to have shown Russian President Boris Yeltsin intelligence regarding Iran's nuclear-weapons programme. While this was sufficient to cause Yeltsin to halt plans to sell Iran a centrifuge-based enrichment plant, he would not agree to halt the sale of the nuclear reactor. There are a number of estimates of how long it would take for Iran to acquire deliverable nuclear weapons. While Israel and some in the US claim that Iran is within three to five years of doing so, the general consensus tends more to a seven- to ten-year time-frame.

Ballistic Missiles

The only new deployments of surface-to-surface missiles during the last 12 months are in **Iran** where four more North Korean *Scud*-C launchers and 5 more CSS-8 (M-7) launchers have been acquired. There are unconfirmed reports that *No-Dong* SSM bought from North Korea were delivered, but *The Military Balance* considers this to be unlikely.

Military Developments

In **Algeria**, the 28 Mi-2 helicopters shown last year as belonging to the Gendarmerie are actually part of the Air Force's inventory. **Mauritania** has commissioned a French OPV-54 (*Aboubekr Ben Amer*) patrol craft. The **Tunisian** Navy has acquired three more Chinese *Shanghai*-class (*Gafsah*) inshore patrol craft. The **Egyptian** Army has taken delivery of 150 more M-60 and 50 M-1 *Abrams* tanks, 600 YPR-765 infantry fighting vehicles and 76 122mm SP artillery. The Air Force has acquired 24 AH-64A *Apache* attack helicopters and a further 30 F-16C fighters (produced in Turkey). The Navy has leased two US *Knox*-class frigates.

The **Israeli** Navy has commissioned two more *Eilat*-class and one more *Romat*-class missile craft. The Army now has 9 MLRS in service with the artillery, and six more have been ordered. Israel and the US reached agreement in May 1995 for the continued US funding for the next five years of Israel's *Arrow* anti-tactical ballistic-missile system. An annual provision of $40m has been reported, rather less than the amount sought by the Israelis. A series of test flights are expected to take place shortly. On 5 April 1995, Israel launched the *Ofek*-3 satellite which is confidently reported as having an intelligence collection capability. **Lebanon** has 16 UH-1H utility helicopters not previously listed in *The Military Balance* whose serviceability is doubtful.

The US is planning to provide a further 225 M-113 APCs. The **Syrian** Army has taken delivery of 100 T-72 tanks, and the Air Force has received six *Mashak* basic training aircraft from Pakistan.

The **Iranian** Air Force has ten Swiss PC-6B liaison aircraft not previously listed. The Revolutionary Guard naval forces have taken delivery of five Chinese *Hudong*-class missile craft. The Navy expects to take delivery of its third *Kilo*-class submarine before the end of 1995, and there have been reports of Iranian moves to acquire the use of naval facilities at Port Sudan. The Army has taken delivery of about one-third of the 100 T-72 tanks ordered from Poland. There are 200 more Chinese Type 69 tanks and 200 more BMP 1/2 than listed before. The number of Chinese 107mm Type 63 MRL held is some 500. The first production of the *Zufuqar*-4 tank, an Iranian built T-72, and of an indigenous APC, the *Boraq* are reported. There have been no reports of **Iraqi** armaments acquisitions or of domestic production.

The **UAE** Air Force has acquired seven Spanish CN-23M-100 and four Russian *Ilyushin*-76 transport aircraft. Seven AS-565 anti-submarine warfare helicopters have been ordered from France. The Army has received its first two French *Leclerc* tanks; 45 of the total order of 396 should be delivered before the end of 1995. 70 more BMP-3 infantry fighting vehicles have also been delivered. Army manpower strength has risen by 8,000. The UAE Navy has commissioned a US *Oliver Hazard Perry*-class frigate. In **Qatar**, the Army has acquired 12 AMX-VCI infantry fighting vehicles, 12 AMX-10RC reconnaissance vehicles and eight V-150 APC. The Air Force has taken delivery of two *Mistral* SAM launchers and has ordered 12 *Mirage* 2000-5 fighters for delivery by the end of 1997. The Navy has four fast patrol craft on order from Vospers of the UK for delivery in 1995. The **Kuwaiti** Army's inventory has increased greatly with 60 *TOW* ATGW mounted on HMMVW, 76 BMP-3 and the first eight, of an order of 254, *Desert Warrior* infantry fighting vehicles. An order has been placed for *Starburst* close air-defence systems worth £50m. The **Saudi Arabian** Army now has 315 M-1 *Abrams* tanks, an increase of 285, and 400 M-2 *Bradley* fighting vehicles (200 more than last year). The Navy has commissioned a third UK *Sandown* (*Al Jawf*) coastal minesweeper and ordered two French *La Fayette*-class frigates. Aircraft orders include 20 *Hawk* advanced trainers for delivery in 1996 and 20 PC-9 primary trainers also from the UK. The delivery schedule for 48 *Tornado* IDS ordered in 1993 for delivery in 1996 appears to have slipped by one to two years. A major reorganisation of the **Bahraini** Army is taking place with the formation of an armoured, an infantry and an artillery brigade and an increase of 1,700 in manpower. 26 more M-60 tanks have also been acquired. The Navy has commissioned a US *Oliver Hazard Perry*-class frigate. The **Omani** Air Force has withdrawn its elderly *Hunter* FGA aircraft from service and taken delivery of eight more *Hawk* 203 aircraft. The Army has acquired 18 *Challenger*-2 tanks which will be delivered by the end of 1995, 20 *Piranha* APCs and six G-6 155mm SP guns – a further 19 have still to be delivered. The Navy has ordered three fast patrol craft from France.

Defence Spending

The IISS estimates that regional defence spending dropped from $44.5bn in 1993 to $42.7bn in 1994 in constant 1993 dollars. Budgetary data for 1995 indicate a further decline to $41bn in 1995. The region spends more on defence as a proportion of GDP than any other region, and the per capita spending is also relatively high. GCC countries account for about half of the total.

Saudi Arabia's defence budget in 1995 is $13.2bn. The government has released defence expenditure figures for 1992 ($15.4bn), 1993 ($16.5bn) and 1994 ($14.3bn) which reflect the scale of Saudi weapons acquisitions and orders (over $30bn) in the aftermath of the war with Iraq. Questions have been raised about the government's ability to pay for these arms purchases given the prolonged fiscal and current-account deficits exacerbated by the squeeze on government revenue following the sharp decline in the price of oil in 1993. These factors contributed to contract renegotiations with major suppliers announced in 1994, which involved rescheduling deliveries and payments due in 1994–95, but did not result in any programme cancellations. A marked decline in new Saudi arms purchases in 1994 and 1995 has accompanied these adjustments. However, there seems no reason why the existing substantial procurement programme should not remain effective. In 1995, the government repaid the last tranche of the $4.5bn war loan of 1991, and mid-1995 indications are that there has been a material improvement in both the fiscal and current balance. High procurement spending is also evident from the recent defence budgets of other GCC states. In 1995, **Kuwait's** budget drops from $3.1bn in 1994 to $2.9bn, excluding supplementary expenditure of $232m for the 1994 deployment of coalition forces and $170m for joint exercises. Procurement amounts to $1.4bn. The cost of UNIKOM was about $69m in 1994. UNSCOM's budget for 1995 amounts to $25m, to which the GCC states are contributing $12m. In **Oman**, both the 1993 and 1994 out-turn were higher than budget, with procurement the reason for the overspend. The defence budget for 1995 is $1.7bn, up from the 1994 figure of $1.6bn, but down from out-turn of $1.9bn. Actual **UAE** spending levels are uncertain because no details of the defence budget are published in advance and there are conflicting figures for past expenditure. The International Monetary Fund (IMF) cite a figure of $1.6bn for 1993, whereas estimates attributed to the Central Bank cite $2.1bn for 1993 and a similar level for 1994.

Israel's defence budget for 1995 remains static in real terms at $6.7bn, and continues to be supported by the largest individual allocation of US Foreign Military Assistance (FMA) – $3bn, including $1.8bn for equipment. The cost of UNTSO in 1994 was about $29m. **Syria's** defence spending accounts for one-quarter of public spending, and in 1995 the defence budget obtains a small increase to £S40bn or an estimated $2.6bn. The cost of UNDOF in 1994 was about $30m. In the case of **Iran**, there are discrepancies between the official spending reported to the IMF and independent estimates. This variation has partly to do with the devaluation of the rial, which makes for problems in dollar conversion, and partly to do with unreported extra-budgetary expenditure. According to the IMF, 1993 out-turn was R1.8bn ($1.4bn at the average annualised exchange rate) or 7% of public spending. The defence budget for 1994 was $2.3bn, and remains about the same in 1995. **Iraq's** military spending is certain to be substantial by regional comparison, but serious data limitations allow for order-of-magnitude estimates only. **Egypt's** defence budget for 1993 was $1.6bn, $1.8bn in 1994, and rises to $2bn in 1995. The budget continues to be supported by the second largest individual allocation of US FMA – unchanged in 1995 at $2.1bn including $1.3bn for equipment. The cost of UNIFIL's operation in **Lebanon** during 1994 was some $142m. In the case of **Yemen,** no reliable details are available on the military expenditure incurred as a result of the 1994 civil war. The UN has estimated the costs of war damage at $200m, of which $20m is required for emergency repair work. In **North Africa**, the cost of MINURSO in 1994 was about $41m. **Algeria's** defence budget has increased by a nominal 48%, and by some 12% in dollar terms to $1.3bn.

It is not clear what economic repercussions for the GCC states will accompany any relaxation of UN sanctions on Iraq's oil trade. Oil is the major source of government revenue for the GCC states, and directly or indirectly determines the level of their arms purchases from foreign sources. The larger GCC producers (Saudi Arabia, the UAE and Kuwait) are members of the 12-nation Organisation of Petroleum-Exporting Countries (OPEC) cartel – which seeks to optimise its members' revenue by agreements on production quotas and prices. In 1994, OPEC supplied about 37% (about 24.8m barrels a day) of total global demand (about 67.9mb/d). Saudi Arabia has the largest share of OPEC production quotas (almost one-third or about 8mb/d in 1994). In 1994, UAE oil output was about 2.2mb/d, while that of Kuwait was about 1.9mb/d. Oil production in Oman and Bahrain, which are not OPEC members, and Qatar, which is, amounted to about 1.3mb/ per day in 1994. In 1994, the combined oil output of the six GCC states amounted to about 13.5m/ per day-worth, valued at some $69bn for the year, or about one-fifth of global production. By comparison, Iraq's quota, which was about 3.2mb/d in 1989 (capacity about 3.5mb/d), is currently 600,000b/d and for domestic use only since Iraq rejected the UN offer in 1995 to export oil worth some $2bn (up from the 1991 offer of $1.6bn) over six months to pay for food and medical supplies, but also to pay war reparations and to fund continuing UN operations. It is estimated that, on the lifting of sanctions, output could be raised to 2.6mb/d within a year and thereafter to the level of the pre-Gulf War production capacity. The Iraqi government's ambition is to export 5.5mb/d by 2000 with the help of foreign investment.

There are several possible options open to OPEC for accommodating Iraqi production. First, if global demand for oil is more or less static, the pressure will be on OPEC producers to agree to reduce individual quotas *pro rata*. This is likely to be more acceptable to smaller producers than the larger ones – and to Iran, which has tended to argue in favour of keep supply levels below those of demand in order to maximise prices. However, the largest OPEC producer, Saudi Arabia, has already signalled its intention to maintain current market share within the OPEC cartel when sanctions on Iraq are lifted. Before the war with Iraq, Saudi Arabia's oil production was about 5mb/d. Dislocation of Kuwaiti production and sanctions on Iraq resulted in current levels of about 8mb/d. A second option, again assuming demand is relatively static, is to raise production levels in an attempt to win market share from non-OPEC producers. The danger of this strategy is that it would probably lead to declining oil prices, a price war between OPEC and non-OPEC producers, and conceivably one between OPEC member-states themselves (several of which are already inclined to breach quota agreements). A third option arises if demand for oil increases, since Iraqi output could be permitted to absorb much of the extra demand. Again, Saudi Arabia – with a production capacity of 10mb/d against a quota of 8mb/d – may attempt to gain a share of the extra demand.

For the Gulf States, the likely cost of each of these options will determine their bargaining stance within OPEC. Assuming an eventual Iraqi quota of 3.5mb/d, a *pro rata* cut in GCC quotas at existing OPEC aggregate production levels implies a revenue decline of 11–12% – probably representing the least acceptable outcome for the large GCC producers. Alternatively, given a decision to increase production despite static demand, the consequences for GCC oil revenue are less predictable and would depend on actual pricing levels. Undoubtedly, the most favourable outcome for the GCC states would be an increase in global demand which would absorb the extra supply from Iraq.

ALGERIA

GDP	1993: D 1,093bn ($46.82bn):
	per capita $5,800
	1994ε: D 1,692bn ($48.28bn):
	per capita $6,000

Growth	1993: -2.0%	1994ε: 1.1%
Inflation	1993: 20.5%	1994: 29.0%
Debt 1993:	$26.4bn	1994: $29.5bn
Def exp	1993: D 31.8bn ($1.36bn)	
Def bdgt	1994: D 39.7bn ($1.13bn)	
	1995: D 58.8bn ($1.33bn)	
FMA	1994: $0.06m (IMET)	
	1995: $0.08m (IMET)	
	1996: $0.08m (IMET)	
$1 = D	1993: 23.4	1994: 35.1
	1995: 44.3	
D = dinar		

Population: 28,144,000

	13–17	18–22	23–32
Men	1,796,400	1,551,800	2,416,200
Women	1,674,800	1,458,800	2,264,000

TOTAL ARMED FORCES:
ACTIVE: 121,700 (90,000 conscripts).

Terms of service: Army 18 months (6 months basic, 1 year civil projects).

RESERVES: Army: some 150,000, to age 50.

ARMY: 105,000 (90,000 conscripts).
6 Military Regions. Reorganisation into div structure on hold. Numbers of indep bde, regt unclear.
2 armd div (each 3 tk, 1 mech regt).
2 mech div (each 3 mech, 1 tk regt).
5 mot inf bde (4 inf, 1 tk bn).
1 AB div.
7 indep arty, 5 AD bn.
EQPT:
MBT: some 960: 330 T-54/-55, 330 T-62, 300 T-72.
RECCE: 120 BRDM-2.
AIFV: 915: 690 BMP-1, 225 BMP-2.
APC: 460 BTR-50/-60.
TOWED ARTY: 405: **122mm:** 25 D-74, 100 M-1931/37, 60 M-30 (M-1938), 190 D-30; **130mm:** 10 M-46; **152mm:** 20 ML-20 (M-1937).
SP ARTY: 185: **122mm:** 150 2S1; **152mm:** 35 2S3.
MRL: 126: **122mm:** 48 BM-21; **140mm:** 48 BM-14-16; **240mm:** 30 BM-24.
MOR: 330: **82mm:** 150 M-37; **120mm:** 120 M-1943; **160mm:** 60 M-1943.
RCL: 178: **82mm:** 120 B-10; **107mm:** 58 B-11.

ATK GUNS: 298: **57mm:** 156 ZIS-2; **85mm:** 80 D-44; **100mm:** 12 T-12, 50 SU-100 SP.
AD GUNS: 895: **14.5mm:** 80 ZPU-2/-4; **20mm:** 100; **23mm:** 100 ZU-23 towed, 210 ZSU-23-4 SP; **37mm:** 150 M-1939; **57mm:** 75 S-60; **85mm:** 20 KS-12; **100mm:** 150 KS-19; **130mm:** 10 KS-30.
SAM: SA-7/-8/-9.

NAVY: ε6,700 (incl ε630 Coast Guard).
BASES: Mers el Kebir, Algiers, Annaba, Jijel.
SS: 2 Sov *Kilo* with 533mm TT (one refitting in Russia).
FF: 3 *Mourad Rais* (Sov *Koni*) with 2 x 12 ASW RL.
PATROL AND COASTAL COMBATANTS: 22:
CORVETTES: 3 *Rais Hamidou* (Sov *Nanuchka* II) with 4 x SS-N-2C *Styx* SSM.
MSL CRAFT: 11 *Osa* with 4 x SS-N-2 SSM.
PATROL CRAFT: 8:
COASTAL: 2 *Djebel Chinoise*.
INSHORE: about 6 *El Yadekh* PCI.
MCM: 1 Sov T-43 MSC.
AMPH: 3:
2 *Kalaat beni Hammad* LST: capacity 240 tps, 10 tk, hel deck.
1 *Polnocny* LSM: capacity 180 tps, 6 tk.
SPT AND MISC: 3:
1 *El Idrissi* AGHS, 1 div spt, 1 *Poluchat* torpedo recovery vessel.

COAST GUARD (under naval control): ε630.
Some 7 Ch *Chui-E* PCC, about 6 *El Yadekh* PCI, 16 PCI⟨, 1 spt, plus boats.

AIR FORCE: 10,000; 170 cbt ac, 60 armed hel.
Average annual flying hours: 100+.
FGA: 3 sqn:
1 with 10 Su-24.
2 with 40 MiG-23BN.
FTR: 5 sqn:
1 with 10 MiG-25.
1 with 20 MiG-23B/E.
3 with 70 MiG-21MF/bis.
RECCE: 1 sqn with 3 MiG-25R, 1 sqn with 6 MiG-21.
MR: 1 sqn with 2 *Super King Air* B-200T.
TPT: 2 sqn with 10 C-130H, 6 C-130H-30, 5 Il-76.
VIP: 2 *Falcon* 900, 3 *Gulfstream* III, 2 F-27.
HEL: 6 sqn:
ATTACK: 2 with 30 Mi-24, 1 with 30 Mi-8/-17.
TPT: 1 with 15 Mi-8, 1 with 12 Mi-4, 2 with 28 Mi-2.
TRG: 3* MiG-21U, 5* MiG-23U, 3* MiG-25U, 6 T-34C, 30 L-39, plus 30 ZLIN-142.
AAM: AA-2, AA-6.
AD GUNS: 3 bde+: **85mm, 100mm, 130mm. SAM:** 3 regt: with SA-3, SA-6, SA-8.

FORCES ABROAD:
UN AND PEACEKEEPING:
ANGOLA (UNAVEM III): 10 Obs. **HAITI** (UNMIH): 15 civ pol.

PARAMILITARY:
GENDARMERIE (Ministry of Interior): 24,000; 44 Panhard AML-60/M-3, 200 *Fahd* APC.
NATIONAL SECURITY FORCES (Ministry of Interior): 16,000; small arms.
REPUBLICAN GUARD BDE: 1,200; AML-60, M-3 recce.

OPPOSITION:
GROUPE ISLAMIQUE ARMÉE (GIA).
ARMÉE ISLAMIQUE DU SALUT (AIS).

BAHRAIN

GDP	1993: D 1.72bn ($4.6bn): per capita $8,000		
	1994ε: D1.73bn ($4.6bn): per capita $8,100		
Growth	1993: 4%	1994ε: -1%	
Inflation	1993: 2.4%	1994: 1.0%	
Debt	1993: $2.6bn	1994ε: $2.7bn	
Def exp[ab]	1993: D 94.4m ($251m)		
Def bdt[b]	1994: D 93.3m ($248m)		
	1995ε: D 95.0m ($253m)		
FMA	1994: $0.1m (IMET)		
	1995: $0.1m (IMET)		
	1996: $0.1m (IMET)		
$1 = D	1993–95: 0.38		
D = dinar			

[a] Incl public order and safety exp.
[b] Excl a subsidy from the Gulf Cooperation Council (GCC) of $1.8bn (1984–94) shared between Bahrain and Oman.

Population: 572,000 (Nationals 68%, other Arab 10%, Asian 13%, Iranian 8%, European 1%)

	13–17	18–22	23–32
Men	25,600	20,800	40,800
Women	24,800	20,800	38,400

TOTAL ARMED FORCES:
ACTIVE: 10,700.

ARMY: 8,500.
1 armd bde (-) (2 tk, 1 recce bn) forming.

1 inf bde (2 mech, 1 mot inf bn).
1 arty 'bde' (1 hy, 2 med, 1 lt, 1 MRL bty).
1 AD bn (2 SAM, 1 AD gun bty).
EQPT:
MBT: 106 M-60A3.
RECCE: 22 AML-90, 8 *Saladin*, 8 *Ferret*, 8 *Shorland*.
APC: some 10 AT-105 *Saxon*, 110 Panhard M-3, 115 M-113A2.
TOWED ARTY: 105mm: 8 lt; **155mm:** 28 M-198.
SP ARTY: 203mm: 13 M-110.
MRL: 227mm: 9 MLRS.
MOR: 81mm: 9; **120mm:** 9.
ATGW: 15 BGM-71A *TOW*.
RCL: 106mm: 30 M-40A1; **120mm:** 6 MOBAT.
AD GUNS: 35mm.
SAM: 40+ RBS-70, 18 *Stinger*, 7 *Crotale*, 8 I HAWK (reported).

NAVY: 700.
BASE: Mina Sulman.
FF: 1 *Oliver Hazard Perry*-class FFG.
PATROL AND COASTAL COMBATANTS: 10:
CORVETTES: 2 *Al Manama* (Ge Lürssen 62-m) with 2 x 2 MM-40 *Exocet* SSM, hel deck.
MSL CRAFT: 4 *Ahmad el Fateh* (Ge Lürssen 45-m) with 2 x 2 MM-40 *Exocet*.
PATROL CRAFT: 4:
2 *Al Riffa* (Ge Lürssen 38-m) PFI.
2 PFI⟨.
SPT AND MISC: 4 *Ajeera* LCU-type spt.

AIR FORCE: 1,500; 24 cbt ac, 10 armed hel.
FGA: 1 sqn with 8 F-5E, 4 F-5F.
FTR: 1 sqn with 8 F-16C, 4 F-16D.
TPT: 2 *Gulfstream* (1 -II, 1 -III; VIP), 1 Boeing 727.
HEL: 1 sqn with 12 AB-212 (10 armed), 4 Bo-105, 1 UH-60L (VIP), 1 S-70A (VIP).
MSL:
ASM: AS-12, AGM-65 *Maverick*.
AAM: AIM-9P *Sidewinder*, AIM-7F *Sparrow*.

PARAMILITARY:
COAST GUARD (Ministry of Interior): ε250; 1 PCI, some 20 PCI⟨, 2 spt/landing craft, 1 hovercraft.
POLICE (Ministry of Interior): 9,000; 2 Hughes 500, 2 Bell 412, 1 Bell 205 hel.

EGYPT

| GDP | 1993: £E 145.9bn ($43.29bn): per capita $4,100 |
| | 1994: £E 156.0bn ($46.15bn): per capita $4,500 |

Growth	1993:	3.0%	1994:	3.8%
Inflation	1993:	12.1%	1994:	8.2%
Debt	1993:	$40.6bn	1994:	$40.0bn
Def exp	1993:	£E 8.35bn ($2.48bn)		
Def bdgt	1994:	£E 9.20bn ($2.71bn)		
	1995:	£E 10.04bn ($2.96bn)		
FMA	1994:	$2.1bn (FMF, IMET, Econ aid)		
	1995:	$2.1bn (FMF, IMET, Econ aid)		
	1996:	$2.1bn (FMF, IMET, Econ aid)		
$1 = £E	1993:	3.37	1994:	3.39
	1995:	3.39		

£E = Egyptian pound

Population: 57,741,000

	13–17	18–22	23–32
Men	3,264,000	2,739,600	4,650,200
Women	3,072,200	2,572,000	4,344,200

TOTAL ARMED FORCES:
ACTIVE: 436,000 (some 222,000 conscripts).
Terms of service: 3 years (selective).
RESERVES: 254,000: Army 150,000; Navy 14,000; Air Force 20,000; AD 70,000.

ARMY: 310,000 (perhaps 200,000 conscripts).
4 Military Districts, 2 Army HQ.
4 armd div (each with 2 armd, 1 mech, 1 arty bde).
7 mech inf div (each with 2 mech, 1 armd, 1 arty bde).
1 inf div (2 inf, 1 mech, 1 arty bde).
1 Republican Guard armd bde.
4 indep armd bde.   1 air-mobile bde.
2 indep inf bde.   1 para bde.
4 indep mech bde.   6 cdo gp.
15 indep arty bde.
2 SSM bde (1 with *FROG*-7, 1 with *Scud*-B).
EQPT:[a]
MBT: 3,500: 840 T-54/-55, 260 *Ramses* II (mod T-54/55), 500 T-62, 1,700 M-60 (600 M-60A1, 1,100 M-60A3), ε200 M1A1 *Abrams*.
RECCE: 300 BRDM-2, 112 *Commando Scout*.
AIFV: 1,080: 220 BMP-1, 260 BMR-600P, some 600 YPR-765 (being delivered).
APC: 3,834: 650 *Walid*, 165 *Fahd*/-30, 1,075 BTR-50/OT-62, 1,900 M-113A2, 44 M-577.
TOWED ARTY: 971: **122mm:** 36 M-31/37, 359 M-1938, 156 D-30M; **130mm:** 420 M-46.
SP ARTY: 122mm: 76 SP 122 (delivery reported), **155mm:** 200 M-109A2.
MRL: 122mm: 96 BM-11, 200 BM-21/*as-Saqr*-10/-18/-36.
MOR: 82mm (some 50 SP); **107mm:** some M-30 SP; **120mm:** 1,800 M-43; **160mm:** 60 M-160.
SSM: launchers: 12 *FROG*-7, *Saqr*-80 (trials), 9 *Scud*-B.
ATGW: 1,400 AT-3 *Sagger* (incl BRDM-2); 220

Milan; 200 *Swingfire*; 530 *TOW* (incl I-*TOW*, *TOW*-2A (with 52 on M-901 SP)).

RCL: 107mm: B-11.

AD GUNS: 14.5mm: 475 ZPU-2/-4; **23mm:** 550 ZU-23-2, 117 ZSU-23-4 SP, 45 *Sinai*; **37mm:** 150 M-1939; **57mm:** 300 S-60, 40 ZSU-57-2 SP.

SAM: 2,000 SA-7/*'Ayn as-Saqr*, 20 SA-9, 26 M-54 SP *Chaparral*.

SURV: AN/TPQ-37 (arty/mor), RASIT (veh, arty).

UAV: R4E-50 *Skyeye*.

---

a Most Soviet eqpt now in store, incl MBT and some cbt ac.

NAVY: ε16,000 (incl ε2,000 Coast Guards and ε12,000 conscripts).

BASES: Alexandria (HQ, Mediterranean), Port Said, Mersa Matruh, Safaqa, Port Tewfig; Hurghada (HQ, Red Sea).

SS: 4:

2 Sov *Romeo* with 533mm TT†.

2 Ch Romeo with Sub *Harpoon* and 533mm TT (plus 2 undergoing modernisation).

PRINCIPAL SURFACE COMBATANTS: 7:

DD: 1 *El Fateh* (UK 'Z') (trg) with 4 x 114mm guns, 5 x 533mm TT.

FF: 6:

2 *El Suez* (Sp *Descubierta*) with 2 x 3 ASTT, 1 x 2 ASW RL; plus 2 x 4 *Harpoon* SSM.

2 *Al Zaffir* (Ch *Jianghu*-I) with 2 x ASW RL; plus 2 x CSS-N-2 (HY-2) SSM.

2 *Damyat* (US *Knox*) with 8 *Harpoon*, 127mm gun, 4 x 324mm TT.

PATROL AND COASTAL COMBATANTS: 43:

MSL CRAFT: 25:

6 *Ramadan* with 4 *Otomat* SSM.

5 Sov *Osa*-I with 4 x SS-N-2A *Styx* SSM (plus 1 non-op).

6 *6th October* with 2 *Otomat* SSM.

2 Sov *Komar* with 2 x SSN-2A *Styx* (plus 2 non-op).

6 Ch *Hegu* (*Komar*-type) with 2 HY-2 SSM.

PATROL CRAFT: 18:

8 Ch *Hainan* PFC with 4 x ASW RL.

6 Sov *Shershen* PFI; 2 with 4 x 533mm TT and BM-21 (8-tube) 122mm MRL; 4 with SA-N-5 and 1 BM-24 (12-tube) 240mm MRL.

4 Ch *Shanghai* II PFI.

MCM: 7:

3 *Aswan* (Sov *Yurka*) MSC.

4 *Assiout* (Sov T-43 class) MSC.

AMPH: 3 Sov *Polnocny* LSM, capacity 100 tps, 5 tk, plus 11 LCU (some in reserve).

SPT AND MISC: 20:

7 AOT (small), 5 trg, 6 tugs, 1 diving spt, 1 *Tariq* (ex-UK FF) trg.

NAVAL AVIATION: 14 armed Air Force hel: 5 *Sea King* Mk 47 (ASW, anti-ship); 9 SA-342 (anti-ship).

COASTAL DEFENCE (Army tps, Navy control):

GUNS: 130mm: SM-4-1.

SSM: *Otomat*.

AIR FORCE: 30,000 (10,000 conscripts); 564 cbt ac, 103 armed hel.

FGA: 7 sqn:

2 with 42 *Alpha Jet*.

2 with 44 Ch J-6.

2 with 29 F-4E.

1 with 20 *Mirage* 5E2.

FTR: 21 sqn:

2 with 28 F-16A.

6 with 74 MiG-21.

6 with 113 F-16C.

3 with 53 *Mirage* 5D/E.

3 with 53 Ch J-7.

1 with 18 *Mirage* 2000C.

RECCE: 2 sqn with 6 *Mirage* 5SDR, 14 MiG-21.

EW: ac: 2 C-130H (ELINT), 4 Beech 1900 (ELINT); **hel:** 4 *Commando* 2E (ECM).

AEW: 5 E-2C.

ASW: 9 SA-342L, 5 *Sea King* 47 (with Navy).

MR: 2 Beech 1900C surv ac.

TPT: 19 C-130H, 5 DHC-5D, 1 *Super King Air,* 3 *Gulfstream* III, 1 *Gulfstream* IV, 3 *Falcon* 20.

HEL: 15 sqn:

ATTACK: 4 sqn with 65 SA-342K (44 with *HOT*, 30 with 20mm gun), 24 AH-64A (to be delivered by end 95).

TAC TPT: hy: 14 CH-47C; **med:** 40 Mi-8, 25 *Commando* (5 -1 tpt, 17 -2 tpt, 3 -2B VIP), 2 S-70 (VIP); **lt:** 12 Mi-4, 17 UH-12E (trg), 2 UH-60A, 3 AS-61.

TRG: incl 4 DHC-5, 54 EMB-312, 15* F-16B, 6* F-16D, 36 *Gumhuria*, 16* JJ-6, 40 L-29, 48 L-39, 25* L-59E, MiG-21U, 5* *Mirage* 5SDD, 3* *Mirage* 2000B.

MSL:

ASM: AGM-65 *Maverick*, *Exocet* AM-39, AS-12, AS-30, AS-30L *HOT*.

ARM: *Armat*.

AAM: AA-2 *Atoll*, AIM-7E/F/M *Sparrow*, AIM-9F/L/P *Sidewinder*, R-530, R-550 *Magic*.

RPV: 23 R4E-50 *Skyeye*, 32 Teledyne-Ryan 324 *Scarab*.

AIR DEFENCE COMMAND: 80,000 (50,000 conscripts).

5 div: regional bde.

100 AD arty bn.

40 SA-2, 53 SA-3, 14 SA-6 bn.

12 bty I HAWK.

12 bty *Chaparral*.

14 bty *Crotale*.

EQPT:
AD GUNS: some 2,000: **20mm, 23mm, 37mm, 57mm, 85mm, 100mm.**
SAM: some 738: some 360 SA-2, 210 SA-3, 60 SA-6, 72 I HAWK, 36 *Crotale.*
AD SYSTEMS: some 18 *Amoun* (*Skyguard*/RIM-7F *Sparrow*, some 36 twin 35mm guns, some 36 quad SAM); *Sinai*-23 short-range AD (Dassault 6SD-20S radar, 23mm guns, 'Ayn as-Saqr SAM).

FORCES ABROAD:
Advisers in Oman, Saudi Arabia, Zaire.
UN AND PEACEKEEPING:
ANGOLA (UNAVEM III): 10 Obs plus 10 civ pol. **BOSNIA** (UNPROFOR): 434; 1 inf bn plus 8 Obs, 1 civ pol. **CROATIA** (UNCRO): 8 Obs, 31 civ pol. **GEORGIA** (UNOMIG): 5 Obs. **LIBERIA** (UNOMIL): 3 Obs. **WESTERN SAHARA** (MINURSO): 12 Obs plus 11 civ pol.

PARAMILITARY:
COAST GUARD: ε2,000 (incl in Naval entry).
PATROL, INSHORE: 33:
12 *Timsah* PCI, 10 *Swiftships*, 5 *Nisr*†, 6 *Crestitalia* PFI⟨, plus some 60 boats.
CENTRAL SECURITY FORCES (Ministry of Interior): 100,000; 110 *Hotspur Hussar, Walid* APC.
NATIONAL GUARD: 60,000; 8 bde (each of 3 bn; cadre status).
BORDER GUARD FORCES: 12,000; 19 Border Guard Regt.

FOREIGN FORCES:
PEACEKEEPING (MFO Sinai): some 1,900 from Australia, Canada, Colombia, Fiji, France, Hungary, Italy, New Zealand, Norway, Uruguay, the US.

GAZA AND JERICHO

GDP	1994ε: $2.4bn:	
	per capita $1,700	
Gaza:	$580m:	
	per capita $900	
West Bank:	$1.82bn:	
	per capita $1,800	
Growth	1994ε: 0%	
Inflation	1994ε: 15%	
Debt	1994ε: $0.0	
Sy bdgt	1994ε: $84m	1995ε: $90m

Population:[a] *West Bank and Gaza:* ε1,944,000 (Israeli 7%); *Gaza:* ε795,000 (Israeli ε5,000); *West Bank:* ε1,149,000 (Israeli ε11%); *Jericho only:* ε18,000

Gaza

	13–17	18–22	23–32
Men	44,400	38,200	58,600
Women	43,000	37,200	58,200

West Bank

	13–17	18–22	23–32
Men	66,400	60,400	100,600
Women	62,200	56,000	91,800

[a] ε500,000 Palestinian refugees live in camps in Lebanon. A further ε250,000 have non-permanent status in Jordan.

PARAMILITARY:
SECURITY FORCES: ε16,500: incl Public Security (ε7,000), Civil Police (ε4,000), General Intelligence (3,000), Preventive Security (ε2,500), Presidential Security, Military Intelligence, Coastal Police, Civil Defence, others reported; small arms, 45 APC allowed. Perhaps 12,000 more after next Israeli withdrawal, Israel agrees to 2,000 more.

PALESTINIAN GROUPS:
All significant Palestinian factions are listed irrespective of the countr(ies) where they are based. The faction leader is given after the full title. Str are est of the number of active 'fighters'; these could be doubled perhaps to give an all-told figure. In 1991, the Lebanon Armed Forces (LAF), backed by the Syrians, entered refugee camps in southern Lebanon to disarm many Palestinian groups of their heavier weapons, such as tanks, artillery and armoured personnel carriers. The LAF conducted further disarming operations against Fatah Revolutionary Council (FRC) refugee camps in spring 1994.

PLO (Palestine Liberation Organisation; Leader: Yasser Arafat):
FATAH: Political wing of the PLO.
PNLA (Palestine National Liberation Army): 8,000. Based in Algeria, Egypt, Lebanon, Libya, Jordan, Iraq, Sudan and Yemen. Effectively the mil wing of the PLO. Its units in various Middle East countries are closely monitored by host nations' armed forces.
PLF (Palestine Liberation Front; Leader: Al Abas): ε300–400. Based in Iraq. Tal al Yaqub faction: ε100–150. Based in Syria.
DFLP (Democratic Front for the Liberation of Palestine; Leader: Hawatmah): ε500–600. Based in Syria, Lebanon, elsewhere. Abd Rabbu faction: ε150–20. Based in Jordan.
PFLP (Popular Front for the Liberation of Palestine; Leader: Habash): ε800. Based in Syria, Lebanon, Occupied Territories.
PSF (Popular Struggle Front; Leader: Samir Ghansha): ε600–700. Based in Syria.

ARAB LIBERATION FRONT: ε500. Based in Lebanon and Iraq.

GROUPS OPPOSED TO THE PLO:

FATAH DISSIDENTS (Abu Musa gp): ε1,000. Based in Syria and Lebanon.

FRC (Fatah Revolutionary Council, Abu Nidal Group): ε300. Based in Lebanon, Syria, Iraq, elsewhere.

PFLP (GC) (Popular Front for the Liberation of Palestine (General Command); Leader: Jibril): ε600.

PFLP (SC) (Popular Front for the Liberation of Palestine – Special Command): ε50–100. Based in Lebanon, Iraq, Syria.

SAIQA (Leader: al-Khadi): ε1,000. Based in Syria.

HAMAS: ε300. Based in Occupied Territories.

PIJ (Palestine Islamic Jihad): ε350 all factions. Based in Occupied Territories.

PALESTINE LIBERATION FRONT: Abd al-Fatah Ghanim faction. Based in Syria:

PLA (Palestine Liberation Army): ε4,500. Based in Syria.

IRAN

GDP[a]	1993: r 93,801bn ($57.8bn):
	per capita $4,900
	1994ε: r 104,641bn ($59.8bn):
	per capita $4,800

Growth	1993: 1.8%	1994ε: 1.0%	
Inflation	1993: 22.3%	1994: 31.5%	
Debt	1993: $20.6bn	1994: $20.0bn	
Def exp	1993ε: r 6,159bn ($4.86bn)		
Def bdgt[a]	1994: r 4,020bn ($2.30bn)		
	1995ε: r 4,300bn ($2.46bn)		
$1 = r	1993: 1,268	1994: 1,749	
	1995: 1,750		
r = rial			

[a] 1995 def bdgt includes r 2,180bn ($1.25bn) for procurement.

Population: 64,805,000 (Shi'i 95%, Azeri 25%, Kurdish 9%, Gilaki/Mazandarani 8%, Sunni 4%)

	13–17	18–22	23–32
Men	3,844,400	3,159,000	4,828,600
Women	3,715,000	2,994,800	4,601,400

TOTAL ARMED FORCES:

ACTIVE: 513,000 (perhaps 250,000 plus conscripts).
Terms of service: 24 months.
RESERVES: Army: 350,000, ex-service volunteers.

ARMY: 345,000 (perhaps 250,000 conscripts).
4 Army HQ.
4 armd div.
1 AB bde.
7 inf div.
2 SF div (3 bde)
Some indep armd, inf, cdo bde.
5 arty gps.
EQPT:†
MBT: 1,440, incl: 110 T-54/-55, 220 Ch Type-59, 150 T-62, 200 T-72, 250 *Chieftain* Mk 3/5, 150 M-47/-48, 160 M-60A1, 200 Ch Type-69.
LT TK: 80 *Scorpion*.
RECCE: 35 EE-9 *Cascavel*.
AIFV: 300 BMP-1, 100 BMP-2.
APC: 550: BTR-50/-60, M-113.
TOTAL ARTY: 2,948 (excl mor):
TOWED: 1,995: **105mm:** 130 M-101A1; **122mm:** 550 D-30, 100 Ch Type-54; **130mm:** 1,000 M-46/Type-59; **152mm:** 30 D-20; **155mm:** 15 WAC-21, 70 M-114; 80 GHN-45; **203mm:** 20 M-115.
SP: 289: **122mm:** 60 2S1; **155mm:** 160 M-109; **170mm:** 9 M-1978; **175mm:** 30 M-107; **203mm:** 30 M-110.
MRL: 664: **107mm:** 500 Ch Type-63; **122mm:** 50 *Hadid/Arash/Noor*, 100 BM-21, 5 BM-11; **240mm:** 9 M-1985; **320mm:** *Oghab*; **333mm:** *Shahin* 1/-2; **355mm:** *Nazeat*; *Iran*-130 reported.
MOR: 3,500, incl: **60mm; 81mm; 82mm; 107mm:** 4.2-in M-30; **120mm.**
SSM: ε10 *Scud*-B/-C (210 msl), ε25 CSS-8 (200 msl), local manufacture msl reported under development.
ATGW: *TOW*, AT-3 *Sagger* (some SP).
RL: 73mm: RPG-7.
RCL: 75mm: M-20; **82mm:** B-10; **106mm:** M-40; **107mm:** B-11.
AD GUNS: 1,700: **14.5mm:** ZPU-2/-4; **23mm:** ZU-23 towed, ZSU-23-4 SP; **35mm; 37mm:** M-1939, Ch Type-55; **57mm:** ZSU-57-2 SP.
SAM: SA-7.
AC: incl 50 Cessna (150, 180, 185, 310), 19 F-27, 8 *Falcon* 20.
HEL: 100 AH-1J (attack); 40 CH-47C (hy tpt); 130 Bell 214A, 35 AB-214C; 40 AB-205A; 90 AB-206; 12 AB-212; 30 Bell 204; 5 Hughes 300C; 9 RH-53D; 10 SH-53D, 10 SA-319; 45 UH-1H.

REVOLUTIONARY GUARD CORPS

(*Pasdaran Inqilab*): some 120,000.
GROUND FORCES: some 100,000; grouped into perhaps 13 inf, 2 armd div and many indep bde, incl inf, armd, para, SF, arty (incl SSM), engr, AD and border defence units, serve indep or with Army; limited numbers of tk, APC and arty; controls *Basij* (see Paramilitary) when mob.
NAVAL FORCES: some 20,000; five island bases (Al Farsiyah, Halul (oil platform), Sirri, Abu Musa,

Larak); some 40 Swedish Boghammar Marin boats armed with ATGW, RCL, machine guns. 5 *Hudong* with C-802 SSM. Controls coast-defence elm incl arty and CSSC-3 (HY-2) *Seersucker* SSM bty. Now under joint command with Navy.

MARINES: 3 bde reported.

NAVY: 18,000 (incl 2,000 Naval Air and Marines).

BASES: Bandar Abbas (HQ), Bushehr, Kharg, Bandar-e-Anzelli, Bandar-e-Khomeini, Chah Bahar.

SS: 2 Sov *Kilo* SS with 6 x 533mm TT (possibly wake homing) (unit 2 probably not fully op). (Plus some 2 SS1s.)

PRINCIPAL SURFACE COMBATANTS: 5:

DD: 2 *Babr* (US *Sumner*) with 4 x 2 SM-1 SSM (boxed), 2 x 2 127mm guns; plus 2 x 3 ASTT.

FF: 3 *Alvand* (UK Vosper Mk 5) with 1 x 5 *Sea Killer* SSM, 1 x 3 AS mor, 1 x 114mm gun.

PATROL AND COASTAL COMBATANTS: 38:

CORVETTES: 2 Bayandor (US PF-103).

MSL CRAFT: 10 *Kaman* (Fr *Combattante* II) PFM, some fitted for 4 *Harpoon* SSM.

PATROL, INSHORE: 26:

3 *Kaivan*, 3 *Parvin* PCI, 1 ex-Iraqi *Bogomol* PFI, some 10 other PFI⟨, plus some 9 hovercraft⟨ (not all op).

MCM: 3:

1 *Shahrokh* MSC (in Caspian Sea as trg ship).
1 *Riazi* (US *Cape*) MSI.
1 *Iran Ajr* LST (used for mine-laying.)

AMPH: 8:

4 *Hengam* LST, capacity 225 tps, 9 tk, 1 hel.
2 *Iran Hormuz 24* (S. Korean) LST, capacity 140 tps, 8 tk.
1 *Iran Ajr* LST (plus 1 non-op).
1 *Polnochny* (ex Iraq) LSM.
Plus craft: 3 LCT.

SPT AND MISC: 20:

1 *Kharg* AOE with 2 hel, 2 *Bandar Abbas* AOR with 1 hel, 1 repair, 4 water tankers, 2 *Delvar* and 8 *Hendijan* spt vessels, 1 AT, 1 *Shahrokh* msc trg.

NAVAL AIR: 9 armed hel.

ASW: 1 hel sqn with ε3 SH-3D, 6 AB-212 ASW.
MCM: 1 hel sqn with 2 RH-53D.
TPT: 1 sqn with 4 *Commander*, 4 F-27, 1 *Falcon* 20 ac; AB-205, AB-206 hel.

MARINES: 3 bn.

AIR FORCE: 30,000 (incl 12,000 Air Defence); some 295 cbt ac (probably less than 50% of US ac types serviceable); no armed hel.

FGA: 9 sqn:

4 with some 60 F-4D/E.
4 with some 60 F-5E/F.
1 with 30 Su-24 (including former Iraqi ac).
FTR: 7 sqn:
4 with 60 F-14.
1 with 25 F-7.
2 with 30 MiG-29 (incl former Iraqi ac).
MR: 5 P-3F, 1 RC-130.
RECCE: 1 sqn (det) with some 8 RF-4E.
TKR/TPT: 1 sqn with 4 Boeing 707.
TPT: 5 sqn with 9 Boeing 747F, 11 Boeing 707, 1 Boeing 727, 19 C-130E/H, 3 *Commander* 690, 15 F-27, 5 *Falcon* 20 1 *Jetstar*, 10 PC-6B.
HEL: 2 AB-206A, 39 Bell 214C, 5 CH-47.
TRG: incl 26 Beech F-33A/C, 10 EMB-312, 45 PC-7, 7 T-33, 5* MiG-29B, 5* FT-7, 20* F-5B.
MSL:
ASM: AGM-65A *Maverick*, AS-10, AS-11, AS-14.
AAM: AIM-7 *Sparrow*, AIM-9 *Sidewinder*, AIM-54 *Phoenix*, probably AA-8, AA-10, AA-11 for MiG-29, PL-7.
SAM: 12 bn with 150 I HAWK, 5 sqn with 30 *Rapier*, 15 *Tigercat*, 45 HQ-2J (Ch version of SA-2). SA-5, FM-80 (Ch version of *Crotale*).

FORCES ABROAD:
LEBANON: ε150 Revolutionary Guard.
SUDAN: mil advisers.

PARAMILITARY:
BASIJ ('Popular Mobilisation Army'): ε200,000 peacetime volunteers, mostly youths; str up to 1 million during periods of offensive ops. Small arms only. Not currently embodied for mil ops.
LAW-ENFORCEMENT FORCES: 45,000, incl border-guard elm; **ac:** Cessna 185/310 lt; **hel:** AB-205/-206; patrol boats: about 90 inshore, 40 harbour craft.

OPPOSITION:
KURDISH COMMUNIST PARTY OF IRAN (KOMALA): strength unknown.
KURDISH DEMOCRATIC PARTY OF IRAN (KDP–Iran): ε8,000.
NATIONAL LIBERATION ARMY (NLA): some 15,000 reported, org in bde, armed with captured eqpt. Perhaps 160+ T-54/-55 tanks. BMP-1 AIFV, D-30 122mm arty, BM-21 122mm MRL, Mi-8 hel. Iraq-based.

IRAQ

GDP	1993ε: $18.0bn	
	1994ε: $18.5bn	
Growth	1993ε: 0%	1994ε: 1%
Inflation	1993ε: 170%	1994ε: 250%

Debt[a] 1993: $86bn 1994ε: $90bn
Def exp 1993ε: $2.6bn 1994ε: $2.7bn
$1 = D[b] 1993–1995: 0.31
D = dinar

[a] excl liabilities up to $80bn for Gulf War reparations.
[b] Informal market rates in June 1995: $1 = d1,200–1,800.

Population: 21,038,000 (Shi'i 60-65%, Sunni 32–37%, Kurdish 17%, other Arab 5%)

	13–17	18–22	23–32
Men	1,293,000	1,063,000	1,562,600
Women	1,234,200	1,018,400	1,505,200

TOTAL ARMED FORCES:
ACTIVE: ε382,500.
Terms of service: 18–24 months.
RESERVES: ε650,000.

ARMY: ε350,000 (incl ε100,000 recalled Reserves).
6 corps HQ.
19 armd/mech/inf div.
7 Republican Guard Force div (4 armd/mech, 3 inf).
Presidential Guard/Special Security Force.
10 SF/cdo bde.
EQPT:
MBT: perhaps 2,700, incl 500 T-54/-55/M-77, Ch T-59/-69, 400 T-62, T-72 (total incl *Chieftain* Mk 3/5, M-60 and M-47 which are mostly inoperable).
RECCE: perhaps 1,500, incl BRDM-2, AML-60/-90, EE-9 *Cascavel*, EE-3 *Jararaca*.
AIFV: perhaps 900 BMP-1/-2.
APC: perhaps 2,000, incl BTR-50/-60/-152, OT-62/-64, MTLB, YW-531, M-113A1/A2, Panhard M-3, EE-11 *Urutu*.
TOWED ARTY: perhaps 1,500, incl **105mm:** incl M-56 pack; **122mm:** D-74, D-30, M-1938; **130mm:** incl M-46, Type 59-1; **155mm:** some G-5, GHN-45, M-114.
SP ARTY: 230, incl **122mm:** 2S1; **152mm:** 2S3; **155mm:** M-109A1/A2, AUF-1 (GCT).
MRL: perhaps 250, incl **107mm; 122mm:** BM-21; **127mm:** *ASTROS* II; **132mm:** BM-13/-16, **262mm:** *Ababeel*.
MOR: 81mm; 120mm; 160mm: M-1943; **240mm.**
ATGW: AT-3 *Sagger* (incl BRDM-2), AT-4 *Spigot* reported, SS-11, *Milan*, *HOT* (incl 100 VC-TH).
RCL: 73mm: SPG-9; **82mm:** B-10; **107mm.**
ATK GUNS: 85mm; 100mm towed.
HEL: ε500 (120 armed), incl:
ATTACK: ε120 Bo-105 with AS-11/*HOT*, Mi-24, SA-316 with AS-12, SA-321 (some with *Exocet*), SA-342.
TPT: ε350 **hy:** Mi-6; **med:** AS-61, Bell 214 ST, Mi-4, Mi-8/-17, SA-330; **lt:** AB-212, BK-117 (SAR), Hughes 300C, Hughes 500D, Hughes 530F.

AD GUNS: ε5,500: **23mm:** ZSU-23-4 SP; **37mm:** M-1939 and twin; **57mm:** incl ZSU-57-2 SP; **85mm; 100mm; 130mm.**
SAM: SA-2/-3/-6/-7/-8/-9/-13/-14/-16, *Roland*.
SURV: RASIT (veh, arty), *Cymbeline* (mor).

NAVY: ε2,500.
BASES: Basra (limited facilities), Az Zubayr, Umm Qasr (currently closed).
FF: 1 *Ibn Marjid* (ex-*Khaldoum*) (trg) with 2 x ASTT.
PATROL AND COASTAL COMBATANTS: 7:
MSL CRAFT: 1 Sov *Osa*-I with 4 SS-N-2A *Styx*.
PATROL, INSHORE: 7:
1 Sov *Bogomol* PFI, 5 PFI⟨, 1 PCI⟨ plus boats.
MCM: 4:
2 Sov *Yevgenya*.
2 Yug *Nestin* MSI⟨.
SPT AND MISC: 3:
1 *Damen* AGS.
1 *Aka* (Yug *Spasilac*-class) AR.
1 Yacht with hel deck.
(Plus 1 *Agnadeen* (It *Stromboli*) AOR laid-up in Alexandria. 3 *Al Zahraa* ro-ro AK with hel deck. Capacity 16 tk, 250 tps. Inactive in foreign ports.)

AIR FORCE: 30,000 (incl 15,000 AD personnel).
The serviceability of fixed-wing aircraft is probably good, but serviceability of helicopters is poor.
BBR: ε6, incl: H-6D, Tu-22.
FGA: ε130, incl MiG-23BN, *Mirage* F1EQ5, Su-7, Su-20, Su-25.
FTR: ε180, incl F-7, MiG-21, MiG-23, MiG-25, *Mirage* F-1EQ, MiG-29.
RECCE: incl MiG-25.
AEW: incl Il-76 *Adnan*.
TKR: incl 2 Il-76.
TPT: incl An-2, An-12, An-24, An-26, Il-76.
TRG: incl AS-202, EMB-312, some 50 L-29, some 50 L-39, *Mirage* F-1BQ, 25 PC-7, 30 PC-9.
MSL:
ASM: AM-39, AS-4, AS-5, AS-11, AS-9, AS-12, AS-30L, C-601.
AAM: AA-2/-6/-7/-8/-10, R-530, R-550.

PARAMILITARY:
FRONTIER GUARDS: ε20,000.
SECURITY TROOPS: 4,800.

OPPOSITION:
KURDISH DEMOCRATIC PARTY (KDP): 25,000 (30,000 more in militia); small arms, some Iranian lt arty, MRL, mor, SAM-7.

PATRIOTIC UNION OF KURDISTAN (PUK):
ε12,000 cbt (plus 6,000 spt); some T-54/-55 MBT; 450
mor (60mm, 82mm, 120mm); 106mm RCL; some 200
14.5mm AA guns; SA-7 SAM.
SOCIALIST PARTY OF KURDISTAN: ε500.
**SUPREME ASSEMBLY OF THE ISLAMIC
REVOLUTION** (SAIRI):ε1 'bde'; Iran-based; Iraqi
dissidents, ex-prisoners of war.

FOREIGN FORCES:
UNITED NATIONS (UNIKOM): some 869 tps and
242 mil obs from 32 countries.
MILITARY COORDINATION COMMITTEE
(Kurdish area): 21 US, UK, France, Turkey mil and civ
personnel.

ISRAEL

GDP	1993: NS 184.1bn ($65.04bn):
	per capita $15,000
	1994: NS 214.0bn ($71.07bn):
	per capita $15,400
Growth	1993: 3.0%	1994: 6.8%
Inflation	1993: 10.9%	1994: 14.0%
Debt	1993: $40bn	1994: $42bn
Def exp[a]	1993: NS 17.54bn ($6.2bn)
Def bdgt[a]	1994: NS 20.24bn ($6.7bn)
	1995: NS 20.43bn ($6.9bn)
	1996ε:[a] NS 21.88bn ($7.4bn)
FMA[b]	1994: $3bn (FMF, Econ aid)
	1995: $3bn (FMF, Econ aid)
	1996: $3bn (FMF, Econ aid)
$1 = NS	1993: 2.83	1994: 3.01
	1995: 2.96

NS = new sheqalim

[a] The defence budget excludes several items of military-related
expenditure which are charged to other government accounts,
including defence industry structural funds (est at $800m for
1992–94), civil defence funds ($510m), civilian administration
expenses in the Occupied Territories, and maintenance of
emergency inventories. In addition, the social security account
reimburses reservists for wages lost while on military service.
[b] The 1994 cost of UNDOF was $32m.

Population:[c] 5,628,000 (Jewish 82%, Arab 14%,
Christian 2%, Druze 2%, Circassian ε3,000).

	13–17	18–22	23–32
Men	266,000	262,600	476,800
Women	252,600	256,400	466,800

[c] Incl ε140,000 Jewish settlers in Gaza, the West Bank and East
Jerusalem, and ε13,000 in Golan.

TOTAL ARMED FORCES:
ACTIVE: ε172,000 (ε138,500 conscripts).
Terms of service: officers 48 months, men 36 months,
women 21 months (Jews and Druze only; Christians,
Circassians and Muslims may volunteer). Annual trg as
cbt reservists to age 42 (some specialists to age 54) for
men, 24 (or marriage) for women.
RESERVES: 430,000: Army 365,000; Navy 10,000;
Air Force 55,000. Reserve service can be followed by
voluntary service in Civil Guard or Civil Defence.

STRATEGIC FORCES:
It is widely believed that Israel has a nuclear capability
with up to 100 warheads. Delivery means could include
ac, *Jericho* 1 SSM (range up to 500km), *Jericho* 2
(tested 1987–89, range ε1,500km).

ARMY: 134,000 (114,700 conscripts, male and
female); some 598,000 on mob.
3 territorial, 1 home front comd.
3 corps HQ.
3 armd div (2 armd, 1 arty bde, plus 1 armd, 1
mech inf bde on mob).
2 div HQ (op control of anti-*intifada* units).
3 regional inf div HQ (border def).
4 mech inf bde (incl 1 para trained).
3 arty bn with 203mm M-110 SP.
RESERVES:
9 armd div (2 or 3 armd, 1 affiliated mech inf, 1 arty
bde).
1 air-mobile/mech inf div (3 bde manned by para
trained reservists).
10 regional inf bde (each with own border sector).
4 arty bde.
EQPT:
MBT: 4,095: 1,080 *Centurion*, 325 M-48A5, 400 M-
60, 600 M-60A1, 200 M-60A3, 150 *Magach* 7, 300
Ti-67 (T-54/-55), 110 T-62, 930 *Merkava* I/II/III.
RECCE: about 400, incl RAMTA RBY, BRDM-2, ε8
Fuchs.
APC: 5,900 M-113A1/A2, ε80 *Nagmashot*, some
Achzarit, BTR-50P, 3,500 M-2/-3 half track.
TOWED ARTY: 400: **105mm:** 60 M-101; **122mm:** 100
D-30; **130mm:** 100 M-46; **155mm:** 40 Soltam M-68/
-71, 50 M-839P/-845P, 50 M-114A1.
SP ARTY: 1,150: **105mm:** 34 M-7; **155mm:** 200 L-
33, 120 M-50, 530 M-109A1/A2; **175mm:** 230 M-
107; **203mm:** 36 M-110.
MRL: 100+: **122mm:** 40 BM-21; **160mm:** LAR-160;
227mm: 9 MLRS; **240mm:** 30 BM-24; **290mm:**
MAR-290.
MOR: 2,740: **81mm:** 1,600; **120mm:** 900; **160mm:** 240
(some SP) plus about 5,000 smaller calibre (60mm).
SSM: 20 *Lance* (in store), some *Jericho* 1/2.

ATGW: 200 *TOW* (incl *Ramta* (M-113) SP), 780 *Dragon*, AT-3 *Sagger*, 25 *Mapats*.
RL: 82mm: B-300.
RCL: 84mm: *Carl Gustav*; **106mm:** 250 M-40A1.
AD GUNS: 20mm: 850: incl TCM-20, M-167 *Vulcan*, 35 M-163 *Vulcan*/M-48 *Chaparral* gun/msl systems; **23mm:** 100 ZU-23 and 60 ZSU-23-4 SP; **37mm:** M-39; **40mm:** L-70.
SAM: *Stinger*, 900 *Redeye*, 45 *Chaparral*.
SURV: EL/M-2140 (veh), AN/TPQ-37 (arty), AN/PPS-15 (arty).

NAVY: ε6,000–7,000 (2,000–3,000 conscripts), 10,000–12,000 on mob.
BASES: Haifa, Ashdod, Eilat.
SS: 2 *Gal* (UK Vickers) SSC with Mk 37 HWT, *Harpoon* USGW (plus 1 in maintenance).
PATROL AND COASTAL COMBATANTS: 55:
CORVETTES: 3 *Eilat* (Sa'ar 5) with 8 *Harpoon*, 8 *Gabriel*-II SSM, 2 *Barak* VLS SAM (2 x 32 mls), 6 x 324mm ASTT plus 1 SA-366G hel.
MSL CRAFT: 23 PFM:
2 *Aliya* with 4 *Harpoon*, 4 *Gabriel* SSM, 1 SA-366G *Dauphin* hel (OTHT).
3 *Romat* with 8 *Harpoon*, 8 *Gabriel*.
4 *Hetz* (ex-*Nirit*) with 4 *Harpoon*, 6 *Gabriel* and *Barak* VLS.
8 *Reshef* with 2–4 *Harpoon*, 4–6 *Gabriel*.
6 *Mivtach* with 2–4 *Harpoon*, 3–5 *Gabriel*.
PATROL, INSHORE: about 40 *Super Dvora/Dabur* PFI⟨, some with 2 x 324mm TT.
AMPH: 1 *Bat Sheva* LST type tpt.
Plus craft: 3 *Ashdod* LCT, 1 US type LCM.

NAVAL CDO: 300 mainly underwater trained.

AIR FORCE: 32,000 (21,800 conscripts, mainly in AD), 37,000 on mob; 449 cbt ac (plus perhaps 250 stored), 116 armed hel. Flying hours: regular pilots, 190; Reserve pilots, 75.
FGA/FTR: 16 sqn: active 10 sqn, reserve (4 A-4N, 5 *Kfir*, 1 F4E-2000):
5 with 50 F-4E-2000, 25 F-4E.
3 with 63 F-15 (-A: 36; -B: 2; -C: 18; -D: 7).
7 with 205 F-16 (-A: 67; -B: 8; -C: 76; -D: 54).
1 with 20 *Kfir* C7 (plus 120 C2/C7 in store).
FGA: 4 sqn with 50 A-4N, plus 130 in store.
RECCE: 14* RF-4E, 6* *Kfir* RC-2, 2* F-15D.
AEW: 4 E-2C.
EW: 6 Boeing 707 (ELINT/ECM), 6 RC-12D, 3 IAI-200, 15 Do-28, 6 *King Air* 2000.
MR: 3 IAI-1124 *Seascan*.
TKR: 3 Boeing-707, 5 KC-130H.

TPT: 1 wing: incl 4 Boeing 707, 12 C-47, 24 C-130H, 7 IAI-201.
LIAISON: 2 *Islander*, 20 Cessna U-206, 8 *Queen Air* 80.
TRG: 80 CM-170 *Tzukit*, 10 *Kfir* TC2/7, 30 *Super Cub*, 10* TA-4H, 4* TA-4J, 4 *Queen Air* 80.
HEL:
ATTACK: 39 AH-1F, 35 Hughes 500MD, 42 AH-64A.
SAR: 2 HH-65A.
TPT: 42 CH-53D, 10 UH-60; 54 Bell 212, 39 Bell 206.
UAV: *Scout, Pioneer, Searcher, Firebee, Samson, Delilah*.
MSL:
ASM: AGM-45 *Shrike*, AGM-62A *Walleye*, AGM-65 *Maverick*, AGM-78D *Standard*, *Gabriel* III (mod), *Hellfire*, TOW.
AAM: AIM-7 *Sparrow*, AIM-9 *Sidewinder*, R-530, *Shafrir*, *Python* III, IV.
SAM: 17 bty with MIM-23 I HAWK, 3 bty *Patriot*, 8 bty *Chapparal*.

===

PARAMILITARY:
BORDER POLICE: 6,000; some *Walid* 1, 600 BTR-152 APC.
COAST GUARD: ε50; 1 US PBR, 3 other patrol craft.

JORDAN

GDP	1993: D 3.88bn ($5.6bn): per capita $5,600		
	1994: D 4.27bn ($6.1bn): per capita $6,000		
Growth	1993: 5.8%	1994: 5.7%	
Inflation	1993: 4.7%	1994: 3.6%	
Debt	1993: $6.87bn	1994: $5.64bn	
Def exp	1993: D 304m ($430m)		
	1994: D 303m ($433m)		
Def bdgt	1994: D 288m ($411m)		
	1995: D 308m ($448m)		
FMA	1994: $9.8m (FMF, IMET)		
	1995: $8.3m (FMF, IMET)		
	1996: $31.2m (FMF, IMET)		
$1 = D	1993: 0.69	1994: 0.70	
	1995: 0.69		

D = dinar

Population:[a] 4,407,000 (Palestinian est 50%)

	13–17	18–22	23–32
Men	246,400	232,600	410,000
Women	238,600	225,400	384,400

[a] Population data do not include Palestinian refugees whose number is est to be at least 250,000.

TOTAL ARMED FORCES:
ACTIVE: 98,600.
RESERVES: 35,000 (all services): Army 30,000 (obligation to age 40).

ARMY: 90,000.
2 armd div (each 2 tk, 1 mech inf, 1 arty, 1 AD bde).
2 mech inf div (each 2 mech inf, 1 tk, 1 arty, 1 AD bde).
1 indep Royal Guard bde.
1 SF bde (3 AB bn).
1 fd arty bde (4 bn).
EQPT:
MBT: some 1,141: 270 M-47/-48A5 (in store), 218 M-60A1/A3, 360 *Khalid/Chieftain*, 293 *Tariq* (*Centurion*).
LT TKS: 19 *Scorpion*.
RECCE: 150 *Ferret*.
AIFV: some 35 BMP-2.
APC: 1,100 M-113.
TOWED ARTY: 115: **105mm:** 50 M-102; **155mm:** 30 M-114 towed, 10 M-59/M-1; **203mm:** 25 M-115 towed (in store).
SP ARTY: 370: **105mm:** 30 M-52; **155mm:** 20 M-44, 220 M-109A1/A2; **203mm:** 100 M-110.
MOR: **81mm:** 450 (incl 130 SP); **107mm:** 50 M-30; **120mm:** 300 *Brandt*.
ATGW: 330 *TOW* (incl 70 SP), 310 *Dragon*.
RL: **94mm:** 2,500 LAW-80; **112mm:** 2,300 *APILAS*.
RCL: **106mm:** 330 M-40A1.
AD GUNS: 360: **20mm:** 100 M-163 *Vulcan* SP; **23mm:** 44 ZSU-23-4 SP; **40mm:** 216 M-42 SP.
SAM: SA-7B2, 50 SA-8, 50 SA-13, 300 SA-14, 240 SA-16, 250 *Redeye*.
SURV: AN-TPQ-36/-37 (arty, mor).

NAVY: ε600.
BASE: Aqaba.
PATROL: 5:
3 *Al Hussein* (Vosper 30-m) PFI, 2 Ge *Bremse* PCI⟨ (ex-GDR). Plus 3 Rotork craft (capacity 30 tps) and other armed boats.

AIR FORCE: 8,000 (incl 2,000 AD); 82 cbt ac, 24 armed hel.
FGA: 3 sqn with 50 F-5E/F.
FTR: 2 sqn with 30 *Mirage* F-1 (-CJ: 14; -EJ: 16).
TPT: 1 sqn with 6 C-130 (-B: 2; -H: 4), 2 C-212A.
VIP: 1 sqn with **ac:** 2 *Gulfstream* III, IL-1011; **hel:** 3 S-70, SA-319.
HEL: 4 sqn:
ATTACK: 3 with 24 AH-1S (with *TOW* ASM).
TPT: 1 with 9 AS-332M, 3 Bo-105, 8 Hughes 500D.
TRG: 16 *Bulldog*, 15 C-101, 12 PA-28-161, 6 PA-34-

200, 2* *Mirage* F-1B.
AD: 2 bde: 14 bty with 80 I HAWK.
MSL:
ASM: *TOW*.
AAM: AIM-9 *Sidewinder*, R-530, R-550 *Magic*.

FORCES ABROAD:
UN AND PEACEKEEPING:
ANGOLA (UNAVEM III): 21 Obs, 20 civ pol. **BOSNIA** (UNPROFOR): 100; arty loc unit, 25 Obs. **CROATIA** (UNCRO): 3,283; 3 inf bn, 23 Obs, 59 civ pol. **GEORGIA** (UNOMIG): 9 Obs. **HAITI** (UNMIH): 146 civ pol. **LIBERIA** (UNOMIL): 8 Obs. **FYROM** (UNPREDEP): 1 Obs. **RWANDA** (UNAMIR): 3 civ pol. **TAJIKISTAN** (UNMOT): 5 Obs.

PARAMILITARY:
PUBLIC SECURITY DIRECTORATE
(Ministry of Interior): ε10,000; some *Scorpion* lt tk, 25 EE-11 *Urutu*, 30 *Saracen* APC.
CIVIL MILITIA 'PEOPLE'S ARMY': ε200,000; men 16–65, women 16–45.

KUWAIT

| GDP | 1993: D 6.77bn ($23.06bn): per capita $15,400 |
| | 1994: D 7.57bn ($25.43bn): per capita $16,800 |

Growth	1993: 8.0%	1994: 7.8%
Inflation	1993: 0.7%	1994: 1.6%
Debt	1993: $8.77bn	1994: $9.43bn
Def exp	1993: D 883m ($3.01bn)	
	1994:[a] D 920m ($3.09bn)	
Def bdgt	1995:[a] D 849m ($2.91bn)	
FMA[ab]		
$1 = D	1993: 0.29	1994: 0.30
	1995: 0.29	

D = dinar

[a] Excl costs to Kuwait for 1994 deployment to the Persian Gulf by US and UK forces of ε$300m funded by a 1995 supplementary allocation.
[b] The 1994 cost of UNIKOM was $69m.

Population: 1,505,000 (Nationals 39%, other Arab 35%, South Asian 9%, Iranian 4%).

	13–17	18–22	23–32
Men	102,000	78,400	140,800
Women	75,600	59,800	97,600

TOTAL ARMED FORCES:
ACTIVE: 16,600 (some conscripts; incl 1,600

foreign personnel).

Terms of service: voluntary, conscripts 2 years.

RESERVES: 23,700: obligation to age 40; 1 month annual trg.

ARMY: ε10,000.

2 mech bde (-).   1 reserve bde (-)
2 armd bde (-).   1 arty bde (-).
1 Amiri gd bde.   1 engr bde.
1 cdo bn.

EQPT:

MBT: 150 M-84, 50 M-1A2 (being delivered), 20 *Chieftain.*

AIFV: 46 BMP-2, 76 BMP-3, 8 *Desert Warrior.*

APC: 153 M-113, 6 M-577, 40 *Fahd.*

SP ARTY: 155mm: 22 M-109A2, 18 GCT (in store), 16 F-3.

MOR: 81mm: 6 SP; **107mm:** 6 M-30 SP.

ATGW: *TOW/Imp TOW* (8 M-901 SP, 60 on HMMWV). (Captured eqpt returned by Iraq incl 48 *Chieftain* MBT, 12 120mm mor which may be refurbished and added to the inventory.)

NAVY: ε2,500 (incl Coast Guard).

BASE: Ras al Qalaya.

PATROL AND COASTAL COMBATANTS: 2:

MSL CRAFT: 2:

1 *Istiqlal* (Ge Lürssen FPB-57) PFM with 2 x 2 MM-40 *Exocet* SSM.

1 *Al Sanbouk* (Ge Lürssen TNC-45) with 2 x 2 MM-40 *Exocet.*

AIR FORCE: ε2,500; 76 cbt ac, 16 armed hel.

FTR/FGA: 40 F/A-18 (-C 32, -D 8).

FTR: 8 *Mirage* F1-CK/BK.

COIN/TRG: 1 sqn with 12 *Hawk* 64, 16 Shorts *Tucano.*

TPT: 3 L-100-30, 1 DC-9.

HEL: 3 sqn:

TPT: 4 AS-332 (tpt/SAR/attack), 8 SA-330.

TRG/ATK: 16 SA-342 (with *HOT*).

AIR DEFENCE: 4 *Hawk* Phase III bty with 24 launchers. 6 bty *Amoun* (each bty, 1 *Skyguard* radar, 2 *Aspede* launchers, 2 twin 35mm *Oerliken*), 48 *Starburst.*

PARAMILITARY:

NATIONAL GUARD: 5,000: 3 gd, 1 armd car, 1 SF, 1 mil police bn.

COAST GUARD: 4 *Inttisar* (Aust 31.5m) PFI. Plus some 55 armed boats.

FOREIGN FORCES:

UNITED NATIONS (UNIKOM): some 869 tps and 242 Obs from 32 countries.

US: Army prepositioned eqpt for 1 armd bde (2 tk, 1 mech, 1 arty bn. Air Force: **ac:** 24 A-10; **hel:** 12 UH-60A *Blackhawk.*

LEBANON

GDP	1993ε: LP 10,934bn ($6.28bn):
	per capita $3,700
	1994ε: LP 11,918bn ($7.09bn):
	per capita $3,800

Growth	1993ε: 7.0%	1994ε: 10.5%
Inflation	1993ε: 9.2%	1994ε: 18.5%
Debt	1993: $1.36bn	1994: $1.40bn
Def exp	1993: LP 479bn ($275m)	
Def bdgt	1994ε: LP 520bn ($310m)	
	1995ε: LP 540bn ($343m)	
FMA[a]	1994: $8.3m (IMET, Other)	
	1995: $4.4m (IMET, Other)	
	1996: $4.8m (IMET, Other)	
$1 = LP	1993: 1,741	1994: 1,680
	1995: 1,633	

LP = Lebanese pound

[a] The 1994 cost of UNIFIL was $142m.

Population: 4,005,000 (Christian 30%, Druze 6%, Armenian 4%) excl ε300,000 Syrian nationals and ε500,000 Palestinian refugees.

	13–17	18–22	23–32
Men	197,000	198,200	361,200
Women	201,800	203,600	381,800

TOTAL ARMED FORCES:

ACTIVE: 44,300.

Terms of Service: 1 year.

ARMY: some 43,000.

11 inf bde (-).
1 Presidential Guard bde.
1 cdo/Ranger, 3 SF regt.
2 arty regt.
1 air aslt regt.

EQPT:

MBT: some 100 M-48A1/A5, 200 T-54/-55.

LT TK: 30 AMX-13.

RECCE: 40 *Saladin*, 5 *Ferret*, 70 AML-90, 30 *Staghound.*

APC: 550 M-113, 20 *Saracen*, 60 VAB-VCI, 25 VAB-VTT, 70 AMX-VCI, 15 *Panhard* M3/VTT.

TOWED ARTY: 105mm: 15 M-101A1, 10 M-102; **122mm:** 30 M-1938, 10 D-30; **130mm:** 25 M-46; **155mm:** 60, incl some Model 50, 15 M-114A1, 35 M-198.

MRL: 122mm: 5 BM-11, 25 BM-21.

MOR: **81mm:** 150; **120mm:** 130.
ATGW: *ENTAC, Milan,* 20 BGM-71A *TOW.*
RL: **85mm:** RPG-7; **89mm:** M-65.
RCL: **106mm:** M-40A1.
AD GUNS: **20mm; 23mm:** ZU-23; **40mm:** 10 M-42A1.

NAVY: 500.
BASES: Juniye, Beirut, Tripoli.
PATROL CRAFT, INSHORE: 9 PCI⟨, 5 UK *Attacker*
and 4 UK *Tracker* PCI⟨, plus armed boats.
AMPH: craft only: 2 *Sour* (Fr *Edic*) LCT.

AIR FORCE: some 800; 3† cbt ac; 4† armed hel.
EQPT:
FTR: 3 *Hunter*† (2 F-70, 1 T-66).
HEL:
ATTACK: 4 SA-342 with AS-11/-12 ASM.
TPT: 16 UH-1H, 4† AB-212, 16 AB-205, 6 SA-330;
2 SA-318, 2 SA-319.
TRG: 3 *Bulldog,* 3 CM-170.
TPT: 1 *Dove,* 1 *Turbo-Commander* 690A.

PARAMILITARY:
INTERNAL SECURITY FORCE (Ministry of
Interior): ε13,000 (incl Regional and Beirut Gendarmerie
coy plus Judicial Police); 30 *Chaimite* APC.
CUSTOMS: 5 armed boats.
MILITIAS: most militias, except *Hizbollah* and the
SLA, have been substantially disbanded and hy wpns
handed over to the National Army.
HIZBOLLAH ('Party of God'; Shi'i, fundamentalist,
pro-Iranian): ε3,000 (-) active; total spt unknown.
EQPT: incl APC, arty, MRL, RL, RCL, ATGW (AT-
3 *Sagger*), AA guns.
SOUTH LEBANESE ARMY (SLA): ε2,500 active
(mainly Christian, some Shi'i and Druze, trained, equipped
and supported by Israel, occupies the 'Security Zone'
between Israeli border and area controlled by UNIFIL).
EQPT:
MBT: 30 T-54/-55.
APC: M-113, BTR-50.
TOWED ARTY: **122mm:** D-30; **130mm:** M-46;
155mm: M-1950.
MOR: **160mm:** some.

FOREIGN FORCES:
UNITED NATIONS (UNIFIL): some 4,963; 6 inf bns: 1
each from Fiji, Finland, Ghana, Ireland, Nepal, Nor-
way, plus spt units from France, Italy, Norway, Poland.
IRAN: ε150 Revolutionary Guard.
SYRIA: 30,000.
BEIRUT: 1 corps HQ, 1 SF div HQ, elm 1 armd bde,
elm 5 SF regt.

METN: elm 1 armd bde.
BEKAA: 1 mech div HQ, elm 2 mech inf bde.
TRIPOLI: 2 SF regt.

LIBYA

GDP	1993ε: D 9.8bn ($29.7bn):	
	per capita $6,000	
	1994ε: D 10.1bn ($29.7bn):	
	per capita $5,800	
Growth	1993ε: 1%	1994ε: 1%
Inflation	1993ε: 10%	1994ε: 12%
Debt	1989: $5.4bn	
Def exp[a]	1993ε: $1,091m	
Def bdgt[a]	1994ε: $967m	
	1995ε: $960m	
$1 = D	1993: 0.33	1994: 0.34
	1995: 0.33	
D = dinar		

[a] Revised from previous year entries.

Population: 5,410,000

	13–17	18–22	23–32
Men	312,400	262,200	389,000
Women	300,800	252,200	366,800

TOTAL ARMED FORCES:
ACTIVE: ε80,000.
Terms of service: selective conscription, 1–2 years.
RESERVES: People's Militia, some 40,000.

ARMY: ε50,000 (ε25,000 conscripts).
7 Military Districts.
5 elite bde (regime sy force).

10 tk bn.	22 arty bn.
21 inf bn.	8 AD arty bn.
8 mech inf bn.	15 para/cdo bn.

5 SSM bde.
EQPT:
MBT: 2,210 (incl 1,200 in store): 1,600 T-54/-55, 350
T-62, 260 T-72.
RECCE: 250 BRDM-2, 380 EE-9 *Cascavel.*
AIFV: 1,000 BMP-1.
APC: 750 BTR-50/-60, 100 OT-62/-64, 40 M-113,
100 EE-11 *Urutu.*
TOWED ARTY: some 720: **105mm:** some 60 M-101;
122mm: 270 D-30, 60 D-74; **130mm:** 330 M-46.
SP ARTY: some 450: **122mm:** 130 2S1; **152mm:** 60
2S3, 80 *DANA;* **155mm:** 160 *Palmaria,* 20 M-109.
MRL: some 700: **107mm:** Type 63; **122mm:** 350 BM-
21/RM-70, 300 BM-11.

MOR: 82mm; 120mm: M-43; **160mm:** M-160.
SSM: launchers: 40 *FROG*-7, 80 *Scud*-B.
ATGW: 3,000: *Milan*, AT-3 *Sagger* (incl BRDM SP),
AT-4 *Spigot*.
RCL: 106mm: 220 M-40A1.
AD GUNS: 600: **23mm:** ZU-23, ZSU-23-4 SP; **30mm:**
M-53/59 SP.
SAM: SA-7/-9/-13, 24 quad *Crotale*.
SURV: RASIT (veh, arty).

NAVY: 8,000 (incl Coast Guard).
BASES: Tripoli, Benghazi, Derna, Tobruk, Sidi
Bilal, Al Khums.
SS: 4 *Al Badr* † (Sov *Foxtrot*) with 533mm and
406mm TT.
FF: 2 *Al Hani* (Sov *Koni*) with 4 x ASTT, 2 x ASW
RL; plus 4 SS-N-2C SSM.
(Plus 1 *Dat Assawari* † (UK Vosper Mk 7) with 2 x 3
ASTT; plus 4 *Otomat* SSM, 1 x 114mm gun (non-op).)
PATROL AND COASTAL COMBATANTS: 36:
CORVETTES: 4:
1 *Assad al Bihar*† (It *Assad*) with 4 *Otomat* SSM;
    plus 2 x 3 ASTT (A244S LWT) (plus 3 more non-op).
3 *Ean al Gazala* (Sov *Nanuchka*-II) with 2 x 2 SS-N-
    2C *Styx* SSM.
MSL CRAFT: 24:
9 *Sharaba* (Fr *Combattante* II) with 4 *Otomat* SSM.
12 *Al Katum* (Sov *Osa* II) with 4 SS-N-2C SSM.
3 *Susa* with 8 SS-12M SSM.
PATROL, INSHORE: 8:
4 *Garian*, 3 *Benina*, 1 Sov *Poluchat* (Diving Support).
MCM: 8 *Ras al Gelais* (Sov *Natya* MSO).
(*El Temsah* and about 5 other ro-ro tpt have minelaying capability.)
AMPH: 5:
2 *Ibn Ouf* LST, capacity 240 tps, 11 tk, 1 SA-316B hel.
3 Sov *Polnocny* LSM, capacity 180 tps, 6 tk.
Plus craft: 3 LCT.
SPT AND MISC: 10:
1 *Zeltin* log spt/dock, 1 *Tobruk* trg, 1 salvage, 1
diving spt, 1 *El Temsah* and about 5 other ro-ro tpt.

NAVAL AVIATION: 30 armed hel.
HEL: 2 sqn:
1 with 25 Mi-14 (ASW), 1 with 5 SA-321.

AIR FORCE: 22,000 (incl Air Defence Command);
417 cbt ac, 52 armed hel (many ac in store, number n.k.).
Flying hours: 85.
BBR: 1 sqn with 6 Tu-22.
FGA: 11 sqn with 40 MiG-23BN, 15 MiG-23U, 30
Mirage 5D/DE, 14 *Mirage* 5DD, 14 *Mirage* F-1AD,
6 Su-24, 45 Su-20/-22.
FTR: 9 sqn with 50 MiG-21, 75 MiG-23, 60 MiG-25,

3 -25U, 15 *Mirage* F-1ED, 6 -BD.
COIN: 1 sqn with 30 J-1 *Jastreb*.
RECCE: 2 sqn with 4 *Mirage* 5DR, 7 MiG-25R.
TPT: 9 sqn with 15 An-26, 12 Lockheed (7 C-130H, 2 L-
100-20, 3 L-100-30), 16 G-222, 20 Il-76, 15 L-410.
ATTACK HEL: 40 Mi-25, 12 Mi-35.
TPT HEL: hy: 18 CH-47C; **med:** 34 Mi-8/17; **lt:** 30
Mi-2, 11 SA-316, 5 AB-206.
TRG: ac: 80 *Galeb* G-2; **hel:** 20 Mi-2; **other ac incl** 1
Tu-22, 150 L-39ZO, 20 SF-260WL.
MSL:
ASM: AT-2 *Swatter* ATGW (hel-borne), AS-7, AS-9,
AS-11.
AAM: AA-2 *Atoll*, AA-6 *Acrid*, AA-7 *Apex*, AA-8
Aphid, R-530, R-550 *Magic*.

AIR DEFENCE COMMAND:
'Senezh' AD comd and control system.
4 bde with SA-5A: each 2 bn of 6 launchers, some 4
    AD arty gun bn; radar coy.
5 Regions: 5–6 bde each 18 SA-2; 2–3 bde each 12
    twin SA-3; ε3 bde each 20–24 SA-6/-8.

PARAMILITARY:
CUSTOMS/COAST GUARD (Naval control):
a few patrol craft incl in naval totals, plus armed boats.

MAURITANIA

GDP	1993: OM 152.2bn ($1.26bn):		
	per capita $1,400		
	1994: OM 165.5bn ($1.34bn):		
	per capita $1,500		
Growth	1993: 4.9%	1994ε: 4.2%	
Inflation	1993: 9.3%	1994: 3.7%	
Debt	1993: $2.4bn	1994: $2.5bn	
Def exp	1993ε: OM 4.3bn ($36m)		
Def bdgt	1994ε: OM 4.5bn ($36m)		
	1995ε: OM 4.6bn ($37m)		
$1 = OM	1993: 124	1994: 125	
	1995: 128		
OM = Mauritanian ouguiya			

Population: 2,255,000

	13–17	*18–22*	*23–32*
Men	123,000	108,000	161,600
Women	117,400	102,600	161,000

TOTAL ARMED FORCES:
ACTIVE: ε15,650.
Terms of service: conscription (2 years) authorised.

ARMY: 15,000.
6 Military Regions.

7 mot inf bn.	3 arty bn.
8 inf bn.	4 AD arty bty.
1 para/cdo bn.	1 Presidential sy bn.
2 Camel Corps bn.	1 engr coy.
1 armd recce sqn.	

EQPT:
MBT: 35 T-54/-55.
RECCE: 60 AML (-60: 20; -90: 40), 40 *Saladin*, 5 *Saracen*.
TOWED ARTY: 105mm: 35 M-101A1/HM-2; **122mm:** 20 D-30, 20 D-74.
MOR: 81mm: 70; **120mm:** 30.
ATGW: *Milan*.
RCL: 75mm: M-20; **106mm:** M-40A1.
AD GUNS: 23mm: 20 ZU-23-2; **37mm:** 15 M-1939; **57mm:** S-60; **100mm:** 12 KS-19.
SAM: SA-7.

NAVY: ε500.
BASES: Nouadhibou, Nouakchott.
PATROL CRAFT: 7:
1 *Aboubekr Ben Amer* (Fr OPV 54) OPV.
1 *N'Madi* (UK *Jura*) PCO (fishery protection).
3 *El Vaiz* (Sp *Barcelo*) PFI†.
1 *El Nasr* (Fr *Patra*) PCI.
1 *Z'Bar* (Ge *Neustadt*) PFI.
Plus 4 armed boats.

AIR FORCE: 150; 7 cbt ac, no armed hel.
COIN: 5 BN-2 *Defender*, 2 FTB-337 *Milirole*.
MR: 2 *Cheyenne* II.
TPT: 2 Cessna F-337, 1 DHC-5D, 1 *Gulfstream* II.

PARAMILITARY:
GENDARMERIE (Ministry of Interior): ε3,000; 6 regional coy.
NATIONAL GUARD (Ministry of Interior): 2,000, plus 1,000 auxiliaries.

MOROCCO

GDP	1993: D 253.8bn ($27.29bn): per capita $3,300
	1994ε: D 263.9bn ($28.67bn): per capita $3,500
Growth	1993: -0.3% 1994ε: 3.0%
Inflation	1993: 5.2% 1994: 5.2%
Debt	1993: $21.43bn 1994: $22.23bn
Def exp	1993: D 10.1bn ($1.09bn)
Def bdgt	1994ε: D 11.3bn ($1.23bn)
	1995ε: D 10.1bn ($1.21bn)
FMA[a]	1994: $270m (IMET, Other)
	1995: $0.8m (IMET)
	1996: $0.8m (IMET)
$1 = D	1993: 9.30 1994: 9.20
	1995: 8.38
D = dirham	

[a] The 1994 cost of MINURSO was $41m.

Population: 27,724,000

	13–17	18–22	23–32
Men	1,599,600	1,439,400	2,314,800
Women	1,543,000	1,387,200	2,281,200

TOTAL ARMED FORCES:
ACTIVE: 195,500 (ε100,000 conscripts).
Terms of service: conscription 18 months authorised; most enlisted personnel are volunteers.
RESERVES: Army 150,000: obligation to age 50.

ARMY: 175,000 (ε100,000 conscripts).
2 Comd (Northern Zone, Southern Zone).

3 mech inf bde.	1 lt sy bde.
2 para bde.	8 mech inf regt.

Indep units:

12 arty bn.	3 mot (camel corps) bn.
1 AD gp.	2 cav bn.
10 armd bn.	1 mtn bn.
37 inf bn.	7 engr bn.
4 cdo units.	2 AB bn.

ROYAL GUARD: 1,500; 1 bn, 1 cav sqn.
EQPT:
MBT: 224 M-48A5, 300 M-60 (60-A1, 240-A3).
LT TK: 100 SK-105 *Kuerassier*.
RECCE: 16 EBR-75, 80 AMX-10RC, 190 AML-90, 38 AML-60-7, 20 M-113.
AIFV: 60 *Ratel* (30 -20, 30 -90), 45 VAB-VCI, 10 AMX-10P.
APC: 420 M-113, 320 VAB-VTT, some 45 OT-62/-64 may be op.
TOWED ARTY: 105mm: 35 lt (L-118), 20 M-101, 36 M-1950; **130mm:** 18 M-46; **155mm:** 20 M-114, 35 FH-70.
SP ARTY: 105mm: 5 Mk 61; **155mm:** 98 F-3, 44 M-109, 20 M-44.
MRL: 122mm: 39 BM-21.
MOR: 81mm: 1,100; **120mm:** 600 (incl 20 VAB SP).
ATGW: 440 *Dragon*, 80 *Milan*, 150 *TOW* (incl 42 SP), 50 AT-3 *Sagger*.
RL: 89mm: 150 3.5-in M-20.
RCL: 106mm: 350 M-40A1.
ATK GUNS: 90mm: 28 M-56; **100mm:** 8 SU-100 SP.
AD GUNS: 14.5mm: 200 ZPU-2, 20 ZPU-4; **20mm:** 40 M-167, 60 M-163 *Vulcan* SP; **23mm:** 90 ZU-23-

2; **100mm:** 15 KS-19 towed.
SAM: 37 M-54 SP *Chaparral*, 70 SA-7.
SURV: RASIT (veh, arty).
UAV: R4E-50 *Skyeye*.

NAVY: 7,000 (incl 1,500 Marines).
BASES: Casablanca, Agadir, Al Hoceima, Dakhla, Tangier.
FF: 1 *Lt Col. Errhamani* (Sp *Descubierta*) with 2 x 3 ASTT (Mk 46 LWT), 1 x 2 375mm AS mor (fitted for 4 x MM-38 *Exocet* SSM).
PATROL AND COASTAL COMBATANTS: 29:
CORVETTES: 2 *Assad* with 3 x 2 *Otomat* SSM; plus 2 x 3 ASTT (A244S LWT) (reported purchased, but not yet delivered).
MSL CRAFT: 4 *Cdt El Khattabi* (Sp *Lazaga* 58-m) PFM with 4 x MM-38 *Exocet* SSM.
PATROL CRAFT: 23:
COASTAL: 13:
2 *Okba* (Fr PR-72) PFC.
6 *LV Rabhi* (Sp 58-m B-200D) PCC.
5 *El Hahiq* (Dk *Osprey* 55) PCC (incl 2 with customs).
INSHORE: 10 *El Wacil* (Fr P-32) PFI〈 (incl 4 with customs).
AMPH: 4:
3 *Ben Aicha* (Fr *Champlain BATRAL*) LSM, capacity 140 tps, 7 tk.
1 *Sidi Mohammed Ben Abdallah* (US Newport) LST, capacity 400 troops.
Plus craft: 1 *Edic*-type LCU.
SPT: 4: 2 log spt, 1 tpt, 1 AGOR (US lease).

MARINES: (1,500). 1 naval inf bn.

AIR FORCE: 13,500; 99 cbt ac, 24 armed hel.
Annual flying hours for F-5 and *Mirage*: over 100.
FGA: 2 sqn:
1 with 16 F-5E, 4 F-5F.
1 with 14 *Mirage* F-1EH.
FTR: 1 sqn with 15 *Mirage* F-1CH.
COIN: 2 sqn:
1 with 23 *Alpha Jet*.
1 with 23 CM-170, 4 OV-10.
RECCE: 1 sqn with 2 C-130H (with side-looking radar).
EW: 2 C-130 (ELINT), 1 *Falcon* 20 (ELINT).
TKR: 1 Boeing 707; 2 KC-130H (tpt/tkr).
TPT: 11 C-130H, 7 CN-235, 3 Do-28, 3 *Falcon 20*, 1 *Falcon 50* (VIP), 2 *Gulfstream* II (VIP), 5 *King Air* 100, 3 *King Air* 200.
HEL:
ATTACK: 24 SA-342 (12 with *HOT*, 12 with cannon).
TPT: hy: 7 CH-47; **med:** 27 SA-330, 27 AB-205A; **lt:** 20 AB-206, 3 AB-212, 4 SA-319.
TRG: 10 AS-202, 2 CAP-10, 4 CAP-230, 12 T-34C.
LIAISON: 2 *King Air 200*, 2 UH-60 *Blackhawk*.

AAM: AIM-9B/D/J *Sidewinder*, R-530, R-550 *Magic*.
ASM: AGM-65B *Maverick* (for F-5E), *HOT*.

FORCES ABROAD:
UAE: some 2,000; (incl gendarmerie and police).
UN AND PEACEKEEPING:
ANGOLA (UNAVEM III): 2 Obs.

PARAMILITARY: 42,000.
GENDARMERIE ROYALE: 12,000; 1 bde, 4 mobile gp, 1 para sqn, air sqn, coast guard unit; 18 boats, **ac:** 2 *Rallye*; **hel:** 3 SA-315, 3 SA-316, 2 SA-318, 6 *Gazelle*, 6 SA-330, 2 SA-360.
FORCE AUXILIAIRE: 30,000, incl 5,000 Mobile Intervention Corps.
CUSTOMS/COAST GUARD: 2 PCC, 4 PFI (incl in Navy), plus boats.

OPPOSITION:
POLISARIO: Mil wing of Sahrawi People's Liberation Army: ε3–6,000, org in bn.
EQPT: 100 T-55, T-62 tk; 50+ BMP-1, 20–30 EE-9 *Cascavel* MICV; 25 D-30/M-30 **122mm** how; 15 BM-21 **122mm** MRL; 20 **120mm**, mor; AT-3 *Sagger* ATGW; 50 ZSU-23-2, ZSU-23-4 **23mm** SP AA guns; SA-6/-7/-8/-9 SAM. (Captured Moroccan eqpt incl AML-90, *Eland* armd recce, *Ratel* 20, Panhard APC, Steyr SK-105 *Kuerassier* lt tks.)

FOREIGN FORCES:
UNITED NATIONS (MINURSO): some 48 tps, 238 mil obs and 112 civ pol in Western Sahara from 28 countries.

OMAN

GDP	1993: R 4.4bn ($11.69bn):		
	per capita $10,200		
	1994: R 4.6bn ($11.96bn):		
	per capita $10,000		
Growth	1993: 1.7%	1994: 0.3%	
Inflation	1993: 1.0%	1994: -0.8%	
Debt	1993: $2.66bn	1994: $2.41bn	
Def exp	1993: R 738.2m ($1.92bn)		
	1994: R 732.4m ($1.90bn)		
Def bdgt	1995: R 667.0m ($1.59bn)		
FMA[a]	1994: $0.05m (IMET)		
	1995: $0.10m (IMET)		
	1996: $0.10m (IMET)		
$1 = R	1993–95: 0.39		
R = rial			

a Excl $1.8bn military subsidy from GCC 1984–94, shared with Bahrain, and ε$100m over 1990–99 from US Access Agreement renewed in 1990.

Population: 1,881,000 (expatriates 27%)

	13–17	18–22	23–32
Men	105,600	83,400	127,800
Women	102,600	80,400	114,000

TOTAL ARMED FORCES:
ACTIVE: 43,500 (incl Royal Household tps, and some 3,700 foreign personnel).

ARMY: 25,000 (regt are bn size).
1 div, 2 bde HQ.
2 armd regt (3 tk sqn).
1 armd recce regt (3 armd car sqn).
4 arty (2 fd, 1 med (2 bty), 1 AD (2 bty)) regt.
8 inf regt (incl 3 Baluch).
1 inf recce regt (3 recce coy), 2 indep recce coy.
1 fd engr regt (3 sqn).
1 AB regt.
Musandam Security Force (indep rifle coy).
EQPT:
MBT: 6 M-60A1, 43 M-60A3, 24 *Qayid al-Ardh* (*Chieftain* Mk 7/-15), 18 *Challenger* 2 (delivery complete by end 1995).
LT TK: 37 *Scorpion*.
APC: 6 *Spartan*, 13 *Sultan*, 20 *Piranha* (being delivered).
TOWED ARTY: 96: **105mm:** 42 ROF lt; **122mm:** 30 D-30; **130mm:** 12 M-46, 12 Type 59-1.
SP ARTY: 155mm: 6 G-6 (being delivered).
MOR: 81mm: 54; **107mm:** 20 4.2-in M-30.
ATGW: 18 *TOW*, 32 *Milan* (incl 2 VCAC).
AD GUNS: 23mm: 4 ZU-23-2; **40mm:** 12 *Bofors* L/60.
SAM: *Blowpipe*, 28 *Javelin*, 34 SA-7.

NAVY: 4,200.
BASES: Seeb (HQ), Wudam (main base), Raysut, Ghanam Island, Alwi.
PATROL AND COASTAL COMBATANTS: 12:
MSL CRAFT: 4 *Dhofar*, 1 with 2 x 3 MM-40, 3 with 2 x 4 MM-40 *Exocet* SSM.
PATROL CRAFT: 8:
2 *Al Bushra* (Fr P-400) with 1 x 76m gun, 2 x 406mm TT.
2 *Al Wafi* (Brooke-Marine 37-m) PCI, 4 *Seeb* (Vosper 25-m) PCI⟨.
AMPH: 2:
1 *Nasr el Bahr* LST†, capacity 240 tps, 7 tk, hel deck (in reserve).
1 *Al Munassir* LST, capacity 200 tps, 8 tk, hel deck (non-op, harbour trg).
Plus craft: 3 LCM, 1 LCU.

SPT: 2:
1 *Al Sultana*, 1 *Al Mabrukah* trg with hel deck (also used in offshore patrol role).

AIR FORCE: 4,100; 46 cbt ac, no armed hel.
FGA: 2 sqn with 15 *Jaguar* S(O) Mk 1, 4 T-2.
FGA/RECCE: 12 *Hawk* 203.
COIN/TRG: 1 sqn with 11* BAC-167 Mk 82, 7 BN-2 *Defender,* 4* *Hawk* 103.
TPT: 3 sqn:
1 with 3 BAC-111.
2 with 15 *Skyvan* 3M (7 radar-equipped, for MR), 3 C-130H.
HEL: 2 med tpt sqn with 20 AB-205, 3 AB-206, 3 AB-212, 5 AB-214.
TRG: 4 AS-202-18, 3 MFI-17B *Mushshak*.
AD: 2 sqn with 28 *Rapier* SAM, *Martello* radar.
MSL:
ASM: *Exocet* AM-39.
AAM: AIM-9P *Sidewinder*.

ROYAL HOUSEHOLD: 6,500 (incl HQ staff).
Royal Guard bde: (5,000): 9 VBC-90 lt tk, 14 VAB-VCI APC, 9 VAB-VDAA, *Javelin* SAM.
2 SF regt: (1,000).
Royal Yacht Squadron (based Muscat): (150):
   1 Royal Yacht, 3,800t with hel deck.
   1 *Fulk Al Salamah* tps and veh tpt with up to 2 AS-332C *Puma* hel.
   1 *Zinat Al Bihaar Dhow*.
Royal Flight: (250): **ac:** 2 Boeing-747 SP, 1 DC-8-73CF, 2 *Gulfstream* IV; **hel:** 3 AS-330, 2 AS-332C, 1 AS-332L.

PARAMILITARY:
TRIBAL HOME GUARD (*Firqat*): 4,000.
POLICE COAST GUARD: 400; 15 AT-105 APC, some 18 inshore patrol craft.
POLICE AIR WING: ac: 1 Do-228, 2 CN 235M, 1 BN-2T Islander; **hel:** 3 Bell 205A, 6 Bell 214ST.

QATAR

GDP	1993: R 27.88bn ($7.66bn): per capita $16,000 1994ε: R 28.57bn ($7.85bn): per capita $15,800	
Growth	1993: 0.5%	1994ε: 1.0%
Inflation	1993: 3%	1994: 4%
Debt	1993ε: $1.7bn	1994ε: $1.9bn
Def exp	1993ε: R 1.2bn ($330m)	
Def bdgt	1994ε: R 1.1bn ($302m) 1995ε: R 1.2bn ($326m)	
$1 =R	1993–95: 3.64	
R = rial		

Population: 544,000 (nationals 25%, expatriates 75%, of which Pakistani 18%, Indian 18%, Iranian 10%)

	13–17	18–22	23–32
Men	21,200	17,600	38,800
Women	22,600	17,400	27,400

TOTAL ARMED FORCES:
ACTIVE: ε11,100.

ARMY: 8,500.

1 Royal Guard regt.	1 SF 'bn' (coy).
1 tk bn.	1 fd arty regt.
4 mech inf bn.	

EQPT:
MBT: 24 AMX-30.
RECCE: 6 VBL, 12 AMX-10RC, 8 V-150.
AIFV: 40 AMX-10P.
APC: 160 VAB, 12 AMX-VCI.
TOWED ARTY: 155mm: 12 G5.
SP ARTY: 155mm: 28 AMX Mk F-3.
MRL: 4 ASTROS II.
MOR: 81mm: 24 L16 (some SP); **120mm:** 15.
ATGW: 100 Milan, HOT (incl 24 VAB SP).
RCL: 84mm: Carl Gustav.

NAVY: ε1,800 (incl Marine Police).
BASE: Doha.
PATROL AND COASTAL COMBATANTS: 9:
MSL CRAFT: 3 Damsah (Fr Combattante III) with 2 x 4 MM-40 Exocet SSM.
PATROL, INSHORE: 6 Barzan (UK 33-m) PCI.
Plus some 44 small craft operated by Marine Police.
AMPH: craft only: 1 LCU.
COASTAL DEFENCE: 4 x 3 quad MM-40 Exocet bty.

AIR FORCE: 800; 12 cbt ac, 20 armed hel.
FGA/FTR: 1 sqn with 6 alpha jets and 5 Mirage F-1 EDA, 1 Mirage F1-DDA.
TPT: 1 sqn with 2 Boeing 707, 1 Boeing 727, 1 Falcon 900, 1 Airbus A340.
HEL:
ATTACK: 12 SA-342L (with HOT), 8 Commando Mk 3 (Exocet).
TPT: 4 Commando (3 Mk 2A tpt, 1 Mk 2C VIP).
LIAISON: 2 SA-341G.
MSL:
ASM: Exocet AM-39, HOT.
SAM: 9 Roland 2, Mistral, Stinger, SA-7 Grail.

FOREIGN FORCES:
US: prepositioned eqpt for 1 armd bde (forming).

SAUDI ARABIA

GDP	1993: R 470bn ($124.8bn):
	per capita $10,200
	1994ε: R 480bn ($128.1bn):
	per capita $10,100
Growth	1993: 0.7% 1994ε: 0.6%
Inflation	1993: 1.1% 1994: 0.6%
Debt	1993ε: $15bn 1994ε: $12bn
Def exp	1993: R 61.7bn ($16.5bn)
Def bdgt	1994: R 53.5bn ($14.3bn)
	1995: R 49.5bn ($13.2bn)
$1 = R	1993–95: 3.75
R = rial	

Population: 18,613,000 (nationals 69% (Bedouin up to 10%, Shi'i 6%); expatriates 31%, of which Asians 21%, Arabs 8%, Africans 2% and Europeans (1%).

	13–17	18–22	23–32
Men	1,128,400	907,400	1,396,200
Women	1,009,000	802,400	1,138,600

TOTAL ARMED FORCES:
ACTIVE: 105,500 (plus 57,000 active National Guard).

ARMY: 70,000.
3 armd bde (each 3 tk, 1 mech, 1 fd arty, 1 recce, 1 AD, 1 ATK bn).
5 mech bde (each 3 mech, 1 tk, 1 fd arty, 1 AD, 1 spt bn).
1 AB bde (2 AB bn, 3 SF coy).
1 Royal Guard regt (3 bn).
8 arty bn.
1 army avn comd.
EQPT:
MBT: 315 M-1A2 Abrams, 290 AMX-30 (50% in store), 450 M60A3.
RECCE: 235 AML-60/-90.
AIFV: 570+ AMX-10P, 400 M-2 Bradley.
APC: 1,700 M-113 (incl variants), 150 Panhard M-3.
TOWED ARTY: 105mm: 100 M-101/-102 (in store); **155mm:** 40 FH-70 (in store), 90 M-198, M-114; **203mm:** 8 M-115 (in store).
SP ARTY: 155mm: 110 M-109A1B/A2, 90 GCT.
MRL: 60 ASTROS II.
MOR: 400, incl: **107mm:** 4.2-in M-30; **120mm:** 175 Brandt.
SSM: some 10 Ch CSS-2 (40 msl).
ATGW: TOW-2 (incl 200 VCC-1 SP), M-47 Dragon, HOT (incl 90 AMX-10P SP).
RCL: 84mm: 300 Carl Gustav; **90mm:** M-67; **106mm:** M-40A1.
HEL: 12 AH-64, 12 S-70A-1, 10 UH-60 (tpt, 4 medevac), 6 SA-365N (medevac), 15 Bell 406CS.
SAM: Crotale, Stinger, 500 Redeye.
SURV: AN/TPQ-36/-37 (arty, mor).

NAVY: ε13,500 (incl 3,000 Marines).
BASES: Riyadh (HQ Naval Forces); Western Fleet: Jiddah (HQ), Yanbu; Eastern Fleet: Al-Jubayl (HQ), Ad-Dammam, Ras al Mishab, Ras al Ghar.
FF: 8:
4 *Madina* (Fr F.2000) with 4 x 533mm, 2 x 406mm ASTT, 1 x AS-365N hel (AS 15 ASM); plus 8 *Otomat-2* SSM, 1 x 100mm gun.
4 *Badr* (US Tacoma) (ASUW) with 2 x 4 *Harpoon* SSM, 2 x 3 ASTT (Mk 46 LWT).
PATROL AND COASTAL COMBATANTS: 29:
MSL CRAFT: 9 *Al Siddiq* (US 58-m) PFM with 2 x 2 *Harpoon*.
TORPEDO CRAFT: 3 *Dammam* (Ge *Jaguar*) with 4 x 533mm TT (trg, incl 1 in reserve).
PATROL CRAFT: 17 US Halter Marine PCI⟨ (some with Coast Guard).
MCM: 7:
3 *Al Jawf* (UK *Sandown* MCC).
4 *Addriyah* (US MSC-322) MCC.
AMPH: craft only: 4 LCU, 4 LCM.
SPT AND MISC: 7:
2 *Boraida* (mod Fr *Durance*) AO with 1 or 2 hel, 3 ocean tugs, 1 salvage tug, 1 Royal Yacht with hel deck.

NAVAL AVIATION: 23 armed hel.
HEL: 21 AS-365N (4 SAR, 17 with AS-15TT ASM), 12 AS 332B/F (6 tpt, 6 with AM-39 *Exocet*).

MARINES: (3,000).
1 inf regt (2 bn), with 140 BMR-600P.

AIR FORCE: 18,000; 295 cbt ac, no armed hel.
FGA: 5 sqn:
3 with 56 F-5E, 14 F-5F, 2 with 42 *Tornado* IDS.
FTR: 6 sqn:
4 with 78 F-15C, 20 F-15D.
2 with 24 *Tornado* ADV.
RECCE: 1 sqn with 10* RF-5E (6 *Tornado* in FGA sqn).
AEW: 1 sqn with 5 E-3A.
TKR: 8 KE-3A (tkr/tpt), 8 KC-130H.
OCU: 2 sqn with 14* F-5B, 7* F-5F.
TPT: 3 sqn with 41 C-130 (7 -E, 34 -H), 8 L-100-30HS (hospital ac).
HEL: 2 sqn with 22 AB-205, 25 AB-206B, 27 AB-212.
TRG: 36 BAC-167 Mk-80/80A, 30* *Hawk* Mk 65, 30 PC-9, 1 *Jetstream* 31.
ROYAL FLT: ac: 1 Boeing-747SP, 1 Boeing-737-200, 4 BAe 125-800, 2 C-140, 4 CN-235, 2 *Gulfstream* III, 2 *Learjet* 35, 6 VC-130H, 1 Cessna 310; **hel:** 3 AS-61, AB-212, 1 -S70.
MSL:
ASM: AGM-65 *Maverick*, AS-15, AS-30, *Sea Eagle*, *Shrike* AGM-45.
ARM: ALARM.

AAM: AIM-9J/L/P *Sidewinder*, AIM-7F *Sparrow*, *Skyflash*.

AIR DEFENCE FORCES: 4,000.
33 SAM bty:
  16 with 128 I HAWK.
  17 with 68 *Shahine* fire units and AMX-30SA 30mm SP AA guns.
73 *Shahine/Crotale* fire units as static defence.
EQPT:
AD GUNS: 20mm: 92 M-163 *Vulcan*; **30mm:** 50 AMX-30SA; **35mm:** 128; **40mm:** 150 L/70 (in store).
SAM: 141 *Shahine*, 128 MIM-23BI HAWK, 40 *Crotale*.

NATIONAL GUARD: 77,000 (57,000 active, 20,000 tribal levies).
2 mech inf bde, each 4 all arms bn.
6 inf bde.
1 ceremonial cav sqn.
EQPT:
LAV: 262 LAV-25.
APC: 1,100 V-150 *Commando* (50% in store), 65 *Piranha*.
TOWED ARTY: 105mm: 40 M-102; **155mm:** 30 M-198.
RCL: 106mm: M-40A1.
ATGW: *TOW*.

PARAMILITARY:
FRONTIER FORCE: 10,500.
COAST GUARD: 4,500; 4 *Al Jouf* PFI, about 30 PCI⟨, about 20 hovercraft, 1 trg, 1 Royal Yacht (5,000t) with 1 Bell 206B hel, about 350 armed boats.
GENERAL CIVIL DEFENCE ADMINISTRATION UNITS: 10 KV-107 hel.
SPECIAL SECURITY FORCE: 500; UR-416 APC.

FOREIGN FORCES:
PENINSULAR SHIELD FORCE: ε7,000; 1 inf bde (elm from all GCC states).
FRANCE: 130; 6 *Mirage* 2000C, 1 C 135FR, 1 N-262.
US: Air Force units on rotational det, numbers vary (incl: F-15, F-16, F-117, C-130, KC-135, U-2 E-3), 1 *Patriot* bn.
UK: 6 *Tornado* GR-1A, 2 VC-10 (tkr).

SYRIA

GDP	1993:ª £S 398.5bn ($26.75bn): per capita $6,000	
	1993:ª £S 429.0bn ($28.09bn): per capita $6,200	
Growth	1993: 3.9%	1994ε: 3.0%

Inflation	1993: 11.8%	1994ε: 13.0%
Debt	1993: $19.8bn	1994ε: $20.0bn
Def exp	1993:[a] £S 35.52bn ($2.38bn)	
Def bdgt	1994:[a] £S 37.60bn ($2.46bn)	
	1995:[a] £S 39.98bn ($2.62bn)	
$1 = £S	1993–95:	11.3
£S = Syrian pound		

[a] Dollar conversions not based on official exchange rates cited here.

Population: 14,284,000

	13–17	18–22	23–32
Men	869,600	702,400	1,075,000
Women	837,800	677,600	1,025,400

TOTAL ARMED FORCES:
ACTIVE: ε423,000.
Terms of service: conscription, 30 months.
RESERVES (to age 45): 650,000. Army 550,000 active; Navy 8,000; Air Force 92,000.

ARMY: 315,000 (250,000 conscripts).
3 corps HQ.
6 armd div (each 3 armd, 1 mech bde, 1 arty regt).
3 mech div (-) (each 2 armd, 2 mech bde, 1 arty regt).
1 Republican Guard div (3 armd, 1 mech bde, 1 arty regt).
1 SF div (3 SF regt).
3 indep inf bde.
1 Border Guard bde.
2 indep arty bde.
2 indep ATK bde.
8 indep SF regt.
1 indep tk regt.
3 SSM bde (each of 3 bn):
  1 with *FROG*; 1 with *Scud*; 1 with SS-21.
1 coastal def SSM bde with SS-C-1B *Sepal* and SS-C-3 *Styx*.
RESERVES: 1 armd div HQ (cadre), 30 inf, arty regt.
EQPT:
MBT: 4,600: 2,100 T-54/-55, 1,000 T-62M/K, 1,500 T-72/-72M. (Total incl some 1,200 in static positions and in store.)
RECCE: 1,000 BRDM-2.
AIFV: 2,250 BMP-1, 60 BMP-2.
APC: 1,500 BTR-40/-50/-60/-152.
TOWED ARTY: some 1,630, incl: **122mm:** 100 M-1931/-37 (in store), 150 M-1938, 500 D-30; **130mm:** 800 M-46; **152mm:** 20 D-20, 50 M-1937; **180mm:** 10 S23.
SP ARTY: **122mm:** 400 2S1; **152mm:** 50 2S3.
MRL: **107mm:** 200 Type-63; **122mm:** 280 BM-21.
MOR: **82mm:** 200; **120mm:** 350 M-1943; **160mm:** 100 M-160; **240mm:** ε8 M-240.
SSM: launchers: 18 *FROG*-7, some 18 SS-21, 25

Scud-B/-C; SS-C-1B *Sepal*, SS-C-3 coastal.
ATGW: 3,000 AT-3 *Sagger* (incl 2,500 SP), 150 AT-4 *Spigot*, 40 AT-5 *Spandrel* and 200 *Milan*.
AD GUNS: 2,060: **23mm:** 650 ZU-23-2 towed, 400 ZSU-23-4 SP; **37mm:** 300 M-1939; **57mm:** 675 S-60, 10 ZSU-57-2 SP; **100mm:** 25 KS-19.
SAM: 4,000 SA-7, 20 SA-9; 35 SA-13.

NAVY: ε8,000.
BASES: Latakia, Tartus, Minet el-Baida.
SS: 1 Sov *Romeo* † with 533mm TT (plus 2 more non-op).
FF: 2 Sov *Petya*-II with 4 x ASW RL, 5 x 533mm TT.
PATROL AND COASTAL COMBATANTS: 29:
MSL CRAFT: 18:
14 Sov *Osa*-I and II PFM with 4 SS-N-2 *Styx* SSM.
4 Sov *Komar*⟨ † with 2 SS-N-2 *Styx* SSM.
PATROL CRAFT: 11:
8 Sov *Zhuk* PFI⟨ .
1 Sov *Natya* (ex-MSO).
About 2 *Hamelin* PFI⟨ (ex-PLF).
MCM: 7:
1 Sov T-43, 1 *Sonya* MSC.
5 *Yevgenya* MSI.
AMPH: 3 *Polnocny* LSM, capacity 100 tps, 5 tk.
SPT AND MISC: 3: 1 spt, 1 trg, 1 div spt.

NAVAL AVIATION: 29 armed hel.
ASW: 20 Mi-14, 5 Ka-25, 4 Ka-28 (Air Force manpower).

AIR FORCE: 40,000; 579 cbt ac; 100 armed hel (some may be in store).
FGA: 9 sqn:
5 with 90 Su-22.
2 with 44 MiG-23 BN.
2 with 20 Su-24.
FTR: 18 sqn:
8 with 160 MiG-21.
5 with 90 MiG-23.
2 with 30 MiG-25.
3 with 20 MiG-29.
RECCE: 6 MiG-25R, 8 MiG-21H/J.
EW: 10 Mi-8 *Hip* J/K hel.
TPT: ac: 4 An-24, civil-registered ac incl: 5 An-26, 2 *Falcon* 20, 4 Il-76, 7 Yak-40, 1 *Falcon* 900, 6 Tu-134; **hel:** 18 Mi-2, 100 Mi-8/-17.
ATTACK HEL: 50 Mi-25, 50 SA-342L.
TRG: incl 10 L-29, 80* L-39, 20 MBB-223, 20* MiG-21U, 6* MiG-23UM, 5* MiG-25U, 6 *Mashshak*.
MSL:
ASM: AT-2 *Swatter*, AS-7 *Kerry*, AS-12, *HOT*.
AAM: AA-2 *Atoll*, AA-6 *Acrid*, AA-7 *Apex*, AA-8 *Aphid*, AA-10 *Alamo*.

AIR DEFENCE COMMAND: ε60,000.
25 AD bde (some 130 SAM bty):
Some 450 SA-2/-3, 200 SA-6 and AD arty.
2 SAM regt (each 2 bn of 2 bty) with some 48 SA-5,
60 SA-8.

FORCES ABROAD:
LEBANON: 30,000; 1 corps HQ, 1 mech div HQ, 1
SF div HQ, elm 2 armd, 2 mech bde, 7 SF, 2 arty regt.

PARAMILITARY:
GENDARMERIE (Ministry of Interior): 8,000.
BA'TH PARTY: Workers' Militia (People's Army).

FOREIGN FORCES:
UNITED NATIONS (UNDOF): 1,036; contingents
from Austria (468), Canada (214) and Poland (354).
RUSSIA: ε500 advisers, mainly AD.

TUNISIA

GDP	1993: D 14.69bn ($14.63bn):		
	per capita $5,200		
	1994: D 16.13bn ($15.95bn):		
	per capita $5,400		
Growth	1993: 2.6%	1994: 4.4%	
Inflation	1993: 4.3%	1994: 4.8%	
Debt	1993: $8.7bn	1994: $8.0bn	
Def exp[a]	1993: D 232m ($231m)		
Def bdgt	1994: D 228m ($225m)		
	1995: D 242m ($262m)		
FMA	1994: $0.5m (IMET)		
	1995: $0.8m (IMET)		
	1996: $0.8m (IMET)		
$1 = D	1993: 1.00	1994: 1.01	
	1995: 0.92		
D = dinar			

[a] Previous year entries included police and interior sy exp.

Population: 9,031,000

	13–17	18–22	23–32
Men	499,000	450,400	786,400
Women	477,800	434,600	763,400

TOTAL ARMED FORCES:
ACTIVE: 35,500 (26,400 conscripts).
Terms of service: 12 months selective.

ARMY: 27,000 (25,000 conscripts).

3 mech bde (each with 1 armd, 2 mech inf, 1 arty, 1
AD regt).
1 Sahara bde.
1 SF bde.
1 engr regt.
EQPT:
MBT: 84: 54 M-60A3, 30 M-60A1.
LT TK: 55 SK-105 *Kuerassier.*
RECCE: 24 *Saladin*, 35 AML-90.
APC: 268: 140 M-113A1/-A2, 18 EE-11 *Urutu*, 110
Fiat F-6614.
TOWED ARTY: 117: **105mm:** 48 M-101A1/A2; **155mm:**
12 M-114A1, 57 M-198.
MOR: 81mm: 95; **107mm:** 40 4.2-in.
ATGW: 65 *TOW* (incl some SP), 500 *Milan.*
RL: 89mm: 300 LRAC-89, 300 3.5-in M-20.
RCL: 57mm: 140 M-18; **106mm:** 70 M-40A1.
AD GUNS: 20mm: 100 M-55; **37mm:** 15 Type-55/-65.
SAM: 48 RBS-70, 25 M-48 *Chaparral.*
SURV: RASIT (veh, arty).

NAVY: ε5,000 (ε700 conscripts).
BASES: Bizerte, Sfax, Kelibia.
PATROL AND COASTAL COMBATANTS: 23:
MSL CRAFT: 6:
3 *La Galite* (Fr *Combattante* III) PFM with 8 MM-40
Exocet SSM.
3 *Bizerte* (Fr P-48) with 8 x SS-12 SSM.
PATROL, INSHORE: 17:
5 *Gafsah* (Ch *Shanghai*) PFI, 2 *Tazarka* (UK Vosper
31-m) PCI, some 10 PCI⟨.
SPT AND MISC: 1 *Salambo* (US *Conrad*) survey/trg.

AIR FORCE: 3,500 (700 conscripts); 32 cbt ac,
7 armed hel.
FGA: 15 F-5E/F.
COIN: 1 sqn with 3 MB-326K, 2 MB-326L.
TPT: 2 C-130B, 2 C-130H, 1 *Falcon* 20.
LIAISON: 2 S-208M.
TRG: 18 SF-260 (6-C, *12-W), 5 MB-326B.
ARMED HEL: 5 SA-341 (attack) 2 HH-3 (ASW).
TPT HEL: 1 wing with 15 AB-205, 6 AS-350B, 1 AS-
365, 6 SA-313, 3 SA-316, 2 UH-1H, 2 UH-1N.
AAM: AIM-9J *Sidewinder.*

FORCES ABROAD:
UN AND PEACEKEEPING:
CROATIA (UNCRO): 12 civ pol. **RWANDA**
(UNAMIR): 834 plus 10 Obs. **WESTERN SAHARA**
(MINURSO): 9 Obs.

PARAMILITARY:
NATIONAL POLICE: 13,000.
NATIONAL GUARD: 10,000; incl Coastal Patrol

with 4 (ex-GDR) *Kondor*-I-class PCC, 5 (ex-GDR) *Bremse*-class PCI⟨, plus some 10 other PCI⟨.

UNITED ARAB EMIRATES (UAE)

GDP	1993:	Dh 131.6bn ($35.85bn):	
		per capita $19,900	
	1994ε:	Dh 134.8bn ($36.72bn):	
		per capita $20,400	
Growth	1993:	0.5%	1994: 2.9%
Inflation	1993:	4.2%	1994: 5.1%
Debt	1993:	$10.64bn	1994: $10.49bn
Def exp	1993:	Dh 7.8bn ($2.11bn)	
Def bdgt	1994ε:	Dh 7.0bn ($1.91bn)	
	1995ε:	Dh 6.9bn ($1.88bn)	
$1 = Dh	1993–95:	3.67	
Dh = dirham			

Population: 1,830,000 (nationals 24%, expatriates 76%, of which Indian 30%, Pakistani 16%, other Asian 12%, other Arab 12%, European 1%)

	13–17	*18–22*	*23–32*
Men	82,600	72,000	140,400
Women	79,200	63,400	79,400

TOTAL ARMED FORCES:

The Union Defence Force and the armed forces of the UAE (Abu Dhabi, Dubai, Ras Al Khaimah and Sharjah) were formally merged in 1976 and centred on Abu Dhabi. Dubai still maintains its independence, and other emirates a smaller degree of independence.

ACTIVE: 70,000 (perhaps 30% expatriates).

ARMY: 65,000 (incl Dubai: 15,000) (being reorganised). MoD (Dubai); GHQ (Abu Dhabi).
INTEGRATED:
1 Royal Guard 'bde'.
1 armd bde.
1 mech inf bde.
2 inf bde.
1 arty bde.
NOT INTEGRATED:
2 inf bde (Dubai).
EQPT:
MBT: 133: 95 AMX-30, 36 OF-40 Mk 2 (*Lion*), 2 *Leclerc*.
LT TK: 76 *Scorpion*.
RECCE: 90 AML-90, 50 *Saladin* (in store), 20 *Ferret* (in store).
AIFV: 18 AMX-10P, 330 BMP-3.
APC: 80 VCR (incl variants), 240 Panhard M-3, 60 EE-11 *Urutu*.
TOWED ARTY: 105mm: 62 ROF lt; **130mm:** 20 Ch Type-59-1.

SP ARTY: 155mm: 18 Mk F-3, 72 G-6.
MRL: 122mm: 48 *FIROS*-25.
MOR: 81mm: 80; **120mm:** 21 *Brandt*.
SSM: 6 *Scud*-B (Dubai only).
ATGW: 230 *Milan*, *Vigilant*, 25 *TOW*, *HOT* (20 SP).
RCL: 84mm: *Carl Gustav*; **106mm:** 30.
AD GUNS: 20mm: 42 M-3VDA SP; **30mm:** 20 GCF-BM2.
SAM: 20+ *Blowpipe*, *Mistral*.

NAVY: ε1,500.
BASES: Abu Dhabi (main base): Dalma, Mina Zayed, Ajman; Dubai: Mina Rashid, Mina Jabal, Al Fujairah; Ras al Khaimah: Mina Sakr; Sharjah: Mina Khalid, Khor Fakkan.
FF: 1 *Oliver Hazard Perry*-class FFG scheduled for lease from US in 1995.
PATROL AND COASTAL COMBATANTS: 19:
CORVETTES: 2 *Muray Jip* (Ge Lürssen 62-m) with 2 x 2 MM-40 *Exocet* SSM, plus 1 SA-316 hel.
MSL CRAFT: 8:
6 *Ban Yas* (Ge Lürssen TNC-45) with 2 x 2 MM-40 *Exocet* SSM.
2 *Mubarraz* (Ge Lürssen 45-m) with 2 x 2 MM-40 *Exocet* SSM, plus 1 x 6 *Sadral* SAM.
PATROL, INSHORE: 9:
6 *Ardhana* (UK Vosper 33-m) PFI, 3 *Kawkab* PCI⟨.
AMPH: craft only: 3 *Al Feyi* LCT, 1 LCM.
SPT AND MISC: 3:
1 div spt, 1 log spt, 1 tug.

AIR FORCE (incl Police Air Wing): 3,500; 97 cbt ac, 42 armed hel. Flying hours: 110.
FGA: 3 sqn:
1 with 9 *Mirage* 2000E.
1 with 18 *Hawk* 102.
1 with 14 *Hawk* Mk 63A (FGA/trg).
FTR: 1 sqn with 22 *Mirage* 2000 EAD.
COIN: 1 sqn with 6 MB-326 (4 -KD, 2 -LD), 5 MB-339A.
OCU: *7 *Hawk* Mk 61, *2 MB-339A, *6 *Mirage* 2000 DAD.
RECCE: 8 *Mirage* 2000 RAD.
TPT: incl 1 BN-2, 4 C-130H, 2 L-100-30, 4 C-212, 7 CN-235M-100, 4 Il-76 (on lease).
HEL:
ATTACK: 5 AS-332F (anti-ship, 3 with *Exocet* AM-39), 10 SA-342K (with *HOT*), 7 SA-316/-319 (with AS-11/-12), 20 AH-64A.
TPT: 2 AS-332 (VIP), 1 AS-350, 26 Bell (-205: 8; -206A: 9; -206L: 5; -214: 4), 10 SA-330.
SAR: 3 Bo-105.
TRG: 30 PC-7, 5 SF-260 (-TP: 4; -W: 1).
MSL:
ASM: *HOT*, AS-11/-12, *Exocet* AM-39, *Hellfire*,

Hydra-70.
AAM: R-550 *Magic*, AIM 9L.
AIR DEFENCE:
1 AD bde (3 bn).
5 bty I HAWK.
12 *Rapier*, 9 *Crotale*, 13 RBS-70, 100 *Mistral* SAM.

PARAMILITARY:
COAST GUARD (Ministry of Interior): some 40 PCI⟨, plus boats.

FOREIGN FORCES:
MOROCCO: some 2,000; army, gendarmerie and police.

REPUBLIC OF YEMEN

The Republic of Yemen was formed in May 1990 by the Yemen Arab Republic (north) and the People's Democratic Republic of Yemen (south). Civil war broke out between the forces of the two former states in May 1994 and ended in victory for the north in July.

GDP[a]   1993ε: R n.k.($7.7bn):
           per capita $1,300
           1994ε: R n.k. ($7.9bn):
           per capita $1,300

Growth	1993ε: 2.5%	1994ε: 1.0%
Inflation	1993ε: 55%	1994ε: 60%
Debt	1993: $5.9bn	1994: $7.1bn
Def exp	1993ε: R19.2bn ($355m)	
Def bdgt	1994ε: R n.k. ($318m)	
	1995ε: R n.k. ($345m)	
$1 = R	1993: 54	1994: 85
	1995: 140	

R = rial

[a] Prior to the unification of the Yemen Arab Republic and the People's Democratic Republic of Yemen in 1990, the GDP of the north comprised about 80% of the combined GDP.

Population: 14,244,000 (North 79%, South 21%)

	13–17	18–22	23–32
Men	800,400	707,800	1,120,400
Women	773,200	660,400	1,012,400

TOTAL ARMED FORCES:
ACTIVE: 39,500 (perhaps 25,000 conscripts).
Terms of service: conscription, 3 years.
RESERVES: Army: perhaps 40,000.

ARMY: 37,000 (perhaps 25,000 conscripts).

7 armd bde.	1 SF bde.
18 inf bde.	4 arty bde.
5 mech bde.	1 SSM bde.
2 AB/cdo bde.	1 central guard force.
3 AD arty bn.	2 AD bn (1 with SA-2 SAM).

EQPT:
MBT: 250 T-34, 675 T-54/-55, 150 T-62, 50 M-60A1.
RECCE: 60 AML-245, 125 AML-90, 125 BRDM-2.
AIFV: 270 BMP-1/-2.
APC: 60 M-113, 500 BTR-40/-60/-152.
TOWED ARTY: 76mm: 200 M-194; **105mm:** 35 M-101; **122mm:** 30 M-1931/37, 40 M-1938, 125 D-30; **130mm:** 70 M-46; **152mm:** D-20; **155mm:** 12 M-114.
ASLT GUNS: 100mm: 30 SU-100.
COASTAL ARTY: 130mm: 36 SM-4-1.
MRL: 122mm: 185 BM-21; **140mm:** BM-14.
MOR: 81mm; 82mm; 120mm: 50 M-43; **160mm.**
SSM: *Frog-*7, 12 SS-21 *Scud-*B.
ATGW: 12 *TOW*, 24 *Dragon,* AT-3 *Sagger.*
RL: 66mm: M72 *LAW.*
RCL: 75mm: M-20; **82mm:** B-10; **107mm:** B-11.
ATK GUNS: 85mm: D-44; **100mm.**
AD GUNS: 20mm: 52 M-167, 20 M-163 *Vulcan* SP; **23mm:** 30 ZU-23, ZSU-23-4; **37mm:** 150 M-1939; **57mm:** 120 S-60; **85mm:** KS-12.
SAM: SA-7/-9.

NAVY: 1,500.
BASES: Aden, Hodeida.
FACILITIES: Al Mukalla, Perim Island, Socotra.
PATROL AND COASTAL COMBATANTS: 10:
3 *Sana'a* (US *Broadsword* 32-m) PFI.
5 Sov *Zhuk*⟨, 2 Sov *Osa*-II with 4 x SSN-2B *Styx* SSM.
MCM: 3 Sov *Yevgenya* MSI.
AMPH: 2 Sov *Ondatra* LCU, 2 Sov *Polocny* LSM, capacity 100tps, 5 tk.

AIR FORCE: 1,000; 69 cbt ac (plus some 40 in store), 8 attack hel.
FGA: 11 F-5E, 16 Su-20/-22.
FTR: 25 MiG-21, 5 MiG-29.
TPT: 1 An-12, 6 An-24, 4 An-26, 2 C-130H, 2 *Skyvan* 3M, 4 IL-14.
HEL: 1 AB-212, 3 AB-214, 14 Mi-8, 1 AB-47, 2 Ka-26, 8 Mi-24 (attack).
TRG: 2 F-5B*, 2 MiG-15*, 4 MiG-21U*, 4 Su-22U*.
AIR DEFENCE: some SA-2, -3, -5, -6.
AAM: AA-2 *Atoll*, AIM-9 *Sidewinder.*

PARAMILITARY:
MINISTRY OF NATIONAL SECURITY FORCE: 10,000.
TRIBAL LEVIES: at least 20,000.

Central and Southern Asia

Central Asia

The separate civil wars in Afghanistan and on the Afghan–Tajikistan border continued unabated. In **Afghanistan,** the appearance in January 1995 of a new major faction, *Taleban* – formed primarily by religious students and organised in southern Afghanistan – both complicated and increased the intensity of the civil war. Initially, *Taleban* was extremely successful. By March 1995 the group appeared to control the southern half of the country, threatening Kabul. In the capital, *Taleban* soon found itself fighting elements of the forces of General Ahmad Shah Masud and of Gulbuddin Hekmatyar, halting their further advance. *Taleban* appears to have Pakistan's backing, but hopes that the group would rise above Afghanistan's acknowledged factionalism have not been realised. Throughout the last 12 months there have been numerous reports of defections and groups changing sides. *Taleban* has not yet joined or allied itself to either of the main factions, but the war is expected to continue between the Northern Farsi (Uzbek, Turkmen and Tajik) groups, and *Taleban* and the southern Pashtun groups.

On 16 December 1994, the UN Security Council adopted Resolution 968 which established an observer mission (UNMOT) for six months to monitor the cease-fire agreed to by the government of **Tajikistan** and the Islamic opposition. The cease-fire has not been respected and fighting flared up again in April 1995 when rebels based in Afghanistan made a series of raids along the Tajik border. This prompted a strong response from Russian forces, including reported air attacks on targets in Afghanistan. Peace talks took place at Almaty in June, but no agreement was reached on how to integrate the opposition into the Tajik government.

In February 1995, **Kazakhstan** and Russia signed a number of cooperative agreements and issued a joint declaration that they 'would begin to form unified armed forces'. This does not mean a single armed force, but a close alliance whose forces would be unified when necessary to face a common threat. The five former Soviet Central Asian states signed two Commonwealth of Independent States (CIS) agreements: the Memorandum on Maintaining Peace and Stability in March; and the Agreement on Creating a Joint Air Defence System in May. Also in May, Kazakhstan, Kyrgyzstan and Tajikistan signed an agreement protecting CIS external borders.

Southern Asia

In **India** it has been a relatively quiet year, although there is still no solution to the violence in Kashmir. The worst incidence of violence occurred in May 1995 when, during a fight between the Indian Army and Muslim militants, a holy shrine and several hundred homes were destroyed in the Muslim town of Charar-e-Sharief, some 20 miles south-west of Srinagar. Both sides blame the other for the shrine's destruction. After visiting Kashmir, Bhuvanesh Chaturvedi, Minister of State in the Prime Minister's office, said on 3 July that the government was ready to hold unconditional talks with 'anyone' to end the violence there.

In January, **Myanmar's** Army launched a major campaign against the Karen rebels, one of the few groups still able to oppose the government. The Karen main stronghold of Manerplaw was taken at the end of the month and another, Kawmoora, some three weeks later. The Karen movement decided to stop attempting to control territory and to revert to guerrilla warfare instead. Although a substantial number of arms were handed into the government, the fight continues with some Karens escaping over the border to Thailand.

In **Pakistan**, there has been a major outbreak of communal violence in Karachi caused by the Mohajiv Qaumi Movement formed by Urdu-speaking Muslims who migrated to Pakistan after partition in 1947. So far, around 1,000 people have died and the city is virtually ungovernable.

In **Sri Lanka**, the ruling United National Party was defeated in elections in August 1994 and was replaced by a coalition government led by Chandrika Kumaratunga's People's Alliance. The new government quickly eased the economic blockade on the region controlled by the Liberation

Tigers of Tamil Eelam (LTTE), lifted the state of emergency and invited the Tamil Tigers to peace talks. But armed clashes continued until midnight on 7 January 1995 when a cease-fire agreed by the Sri Lanka government and the LTTE, and monitored by Canadian, Dutch and Norwegian officials, came into force. Later that month the LTTE dropped its demand for independence and was willing to accept autonomy with Sri Lanka. The cease-fire ended when two naval patrol boats were sunk by mines in Trincomalee harbour on 19 April. The following day the Tamil Tigers attacked two army posts and the police rounded up some 1,000 Tamils across the country. In June it was revealed that India was providing naval ships and maritime aircraft to prevent supplies from reaching the LTTE across the Palk Strait. The worst incident in the renewed fighting occurred on 28 June when up to 1,000 LTTE raided the island of Mandaitivu, killing over 100 government soldiers.

Nuclear Developments

Kazakhstan has made good progress towards achieving non-nuclear status. Russia's Strategic Rocket Forces announced that the transfer of nuclear warheads from Kazakhstan was completed on 24 April 1995. In the December 1994 START Memorandum of Understanding, Kazakhstan declared it had 69 deployed ICBM and had destroyed no launcher silos. There were still 31 ICBM at Derzhavinsk and 38 at Zhangiz-Tobe. On 1 June 1995 there were only 48 ICBM left in Kazakhstan. Also in June, the **Indian** Foreign Minister ruled out halting fissile-material production until there is a satisfactory global convention to ban its use for weapons. **Pakistan** continues to reject US proposals to put its enrichment facilities under International Atomic Energy Agency (IAEA) safeguards (in return for F-16 aircraft) as there is no guarantee of a similar monitoring measure in India. Pakistan has, however, halted production of uranium-235, but is continuing with the construction of a so-called 'research reactor' at Khushab which, it is suspected, could produce plutonium.

Missile Proliferation

It is still unclear whether **Pakistan** has received either complete missiles, missile components or technology from China for the M-11 missile system, although US intelligence officials believe that up to 30 missiles have been delivered to Lahore. Both China and Pakistan deny this. China also refutes claims that the M-11 is covered by Missile Technology Control Regime (MTCR) parameters (missiles which can carry a 500kg payload over 300km). They claim its range is 185 miles (296km) and its payload 1,000lbs (453kg), but have accepted the US concept of 'inherent capability'. There have been no reports in the last 12 months of tests of **Indian** ballistic missiles, although development is thought to be continuing. It is now accepted that a regiment of short-range (150km) *Privthi* SSM has been formed, but may not yet be operational. Although under international pressure to end missile production, the Indian government declared on 9 May 1995 that there was no question of halting the programme.

Conventional Military Developments

Kazakhstan no longer has a regiment of 48 Mi-24 attack helicopters, which are presumed to have returned to Russia. 20 Su-27 fighter aircraft are due to be delivered in 1995. **Turkmenistan** has disposed of some 500 of the over 1,000 aircraft held in store. In **Uzbekistan**, the Army has formed a Corps HQ and a special forces brigade. The cadre airborne division has been redesignated a brigade, the motor rifle division has converted to three independent brigades, and the artillery has been expanded by two regiments. Tank strength has risen by 50 and fresh information has allowed a more detailed inventory to be compiled. The Air Force has formed a reconnaissance unit with 10 Su-24 aircraft and has 10 more An-2 transport planes.

The **Bangladeshi** Navy has commissioned four *Shapla* (ex-UK *River*-class) and one Chinese inshore (probably a *Wosoa*-class) mine-sweepers. The Air Force has retired its elderly 12 Su-7 aircraft.

The **Indian** Army's order of battle has been reassessed. It is now considered to comprise three armoured divisions (one more than in 1994), no mechanised division, 17 infantry divisions (five less) and ten mountain divisions (no change). Four Reorganised Army Plains Infantry Divisions

(RAPID) have been formed which have both mechanised and infantry brigades. A missile regiment armed with *Privthi* SSM has been formed, but it is not known how many launchers it is equipped with nor when it will be fully operational. Army manpower strength is now considered to be under one million. The number of tanks in service is much reduced, mainly because several hundred have been withdrawn for upgrading, probably at the expense of producing the Indian-designed *Arjun*. The Army was incorrectly shown as having 50 SA-11 SAM last year. The Navy has commissioned two more V*ibhuti*-class corvettes and acquired ten more Do-228 maritime reconnaissance aircraft. The Navy has ambitious plans for the future, including the indigenous production of nuclear submarines and an aircraft carrier. The submarine programme is still in the research and development phase, and the boat is not planned to be operational until 2003–5. The aircraft carrier will also take some years to produce, and until then the two current carriers will need extensive refits. As yet, no decision has been reached over whether to buy the Russian carrier *Gorshkhov* or not. The Indian Defence Minister has said that negotiations have been under way to buy six Russian frigates. The Air Force has formed an additional MiG-27 FGA squadron and acquired 28 more aircraft. Ten MiG-29 aircraft (including two trainers) have been ordered and may be the first of a larger purchase. Refurbishment of the MiG-21 force is considered essential, but as yet it has not been decided whether the contract should be awarded to Russia or Israel.

During the last 12 months, **Myanmar** has taken delivery of 150 Chinese Type-85 APCs. There have been unconfirmed reports of Chinese plans to construct a naval base at Hainggyi Island at the mouth of the River Bassein south-west of the capital, and a SIGINT station on Great Coco Island north of the Andamans. China is already involved in port improvements at Akyab, Kyaukpyu and Mergui. It is conjectured that in return for Chinese naval rights in the Bay of Bengal, Myanmar will receive a further package of arms, estimated to be worth $400m. Orders reportedly include some 30 older aircraft (F-7, A-5), two Y-8 transport aircraft, six *Hainan*-class coastal patrol boats plus 20 helicopters, 60 armoured fighting vehicles and 50 artillery pieces (all unspecified).

The **Pakistani** Army has acquired 100 more Chinese Type-85 tanks, and the Navy has commissioned two more *Tariq* (UK *Amazon*)-class frigates. Three French *Agosta* 90B submarines are on order, the first to be built in France, the other two in Pakistan, and six more Type-21 (*Amazon*-class) frigates have been ordered from the UK.

The **Sri Lankan** Army has acquired 15 BMP armoured fighting vehicles for training purposes, the first of a much larger order – now postponed or cancelled – to be delivered. The Navy has lost three patrol boats. In September 1994, the *Sagarawardene* was sunk by a Tamil Tiger suicide squad, and in April 1995 two more were sunk by mines in Trincomalee harbour. The Tamil Tigers have also shot down two Air Force transport planes, probably BAe 748 (*Andover*) aircraft.

Defence Spending

Expenditure by India and Pakistan in recent years accounts for about three-quarters of all spending by the countries in this section, excluding the costs of the civil war in Afghanistan which are not known. In 1995, India and Pakistan both increased their defence budgets by 6–7% in real terms, and there are more substantial increases in the case of Sri Lanka and Myanmar.

India's defence budget for 1995 is R255bn ($8.1bn), a real increase of some 6% over the enlarged 1994 out-turn of R235bn ($7.5bn). In recent years the Army has received about half of the total defence budget (see Table 1). In 1995 its allocation is R124bn ($4bn). The Air Force takes about 16% of the budget and in 1995 receives R41bn ($1.3bn). Funding for the Navy is the lowest priority (about 12%), and in 1995 it receives R15bn ($480m). This excludes certain items in its budget, including procurement for which details are not yet available. Other funding is for central Ministry of Defence (MoD) organisation, the Defence Ordnance Factories and pensions.

The Indian method of classifying defence expenditure follows the UK practice of including operational spending under manpower and procurement costs, and consequently does not make use of an Operations and Maintenance (O&M) heading. This funding may also be found under 'Other', shown in Table 2. Funds for procurement, R&D and construction are classified as capital outlay.

Table 1:   Indian Defence Expenditure by Service Organisation ($ million)

	1993	%	1994	%
Army	3,512	49.8	3,665	50.0
Navy	883	12.5	861	11.7
Air Force	1,148	16.3	1,178	16.1
Subtotal	5,544	78.6	5,704	77.8
MoD	640	9.1	713	9.7
Pensions	830	11.8	877	12.0
Defence Ordnance Factories	37	0.5	37	0.5
Total	7,051	100	7,331	100

The largest part of the procurement budget is spent on aircraft and aero-engines ($740m in 1993 and $820m in 1994). Capital spending on the naval fleet was $340m in 1993 and $330m in 1994. MoD policy on weapons procurement generally reflects a continuing struggle between ends and means, exacerbated by supply problems and deteriorating terms of trade with Russia and other former Soviet states as they have increasingly demanded hard currency (in place of rupees). Some policy shift is now becoming apparent towards long-term commitment to indigenous R&D and production supported by foreign joint ventures rather than licensed production. Any move away from licensed production is likely to require a sustained effort over the long term. Although Indian experience with indigenous production has been mixed to date (generally programmes have run up against technological and financial barriers and time-scales have consequently been compromised) it has laid the foundation for an extensive defence industrial base.

Table 2:   Indian Armed Services Expenditure by Function ($ million)

	Army		Navy		Air Force		Total	
	1993	1994	1993	1994	1993	1994	1993	1994
Personnel	1,356	1,445	160	164	265	279	1,782	1,888
Procurement	1,278	1,312	426	441	779	791	2,232	2,275
R&D			226	234	25	27	251	261
Construction	201	223	44	43	64	67	310	334
Other	251	250	225	236	37	39	339	353
Total	3,313	3,465	855	884	1,170	1,202	4,913	5,110

Cost escalation in indigenous programmes has squeezed resources for buying new equipment from foreign sources. According to the US Arms Control and Disarmament Agency (ACDA), imports of defence equipment have declined sharply from their peak in 1988, when they amounted to $4.3bn (at constant 1993 prices) to $2bn in 1990, $615 in 1992 and a provisional $10m in 1993. Accumulating debt has been one factor in curtailing procurement from abroad. According to a Ministry of Finance report, imported defence equipment accounted for about 9% of India's external debt in 1993 – of which about 90% was owed to Russia in unrequited rupee credits, but with a sizeable dollar-denominated component of almost $1bn. Delays in development are another factor which has held up several new production programmes. This has resulted in priority being switched to spares provisioning and limited modernisation programmes in order to keep existing equipment in service. While a less costly option than purchasing new weapons systems from abroad, this policy is still relatively expensive in hard-currency terms, with over 80% of the $300–500m annual budget reportedly sourced from abroad, and the MoD reportedly seeking to reduce its dependence on Russia as its major supplier (some 75–80% of Indian defence equipment is of Soviet origin and most was produced under licence in India).

In 1995, **Pakistan's** defence budget amounts to R115bn ($3.7bn) – a real increase of some 7% over 1994. No other statistical details are released by the government. As a proportion of gross domestic product (GDP), defence expenditure is about three times that of India. According to ACDA, arms imports in 1993 amounted to $430m. **Sri Lanka's** military expenditure is increasing sharply as a result of the counter-insurgency operations against the Tamil Tigers. In mid-1995, the government announced supplementary funding of R4.5bn ($90m) – almost one-fifth of the 1994 budget – to cover additional costs of this campaign. **Myanmar** added K2.8bn (about $108m at market exchange rates) of supplementary funds for the 1994 military budget, while the defence budget for 1995 (K15.5bn or nearly $600m) has increased by 40% over 1994.

Budgetary information from **Kazakhstan, Kyrgyzstan, Tajikistan, Turkmenistan** and **Uzbekistan** has improved since 1994 with the publication by the International Monetary Fund (IMF) of external audits of government expenditure, including defence. However, lack of transparency in military accounting, high inflation, and uncertainty over the purchasing power of domestic currencies still create difficulties in estimating real expenditures. According to NATO, these states appear to have adopted differing policies towards accepting financial responsibility for the residual Russian armed forces on their territory. In general, defence expenditure has been concentrated on manpower and O&M functions rather than on R&D and procurement. In Tajikistan, the projected cost for 1995 of UNMOT – the first UN operation in the Central Asian republics of the former Soviet Union – is $7m.

AFGHANISTAN

GDP	1989ε: Afs 152.0bn ($3.0bn):	
	per capita $700	
Inflation	1991ε: 56.7%	1992: n.k.
Debt	1992: $2.3bn	1993ε: $2.5bn
Def exp	1990ε: Afs 22bn ($430m)	
FMA	1990ε: $3.5–4.5bn	
$1 = Afs[a]	1993–95: 50.6	
Afs = afghani		

[a] In July 1995 the market rate was $1 = Afs 4,448

Population:[b] ε16,060,000 (Pashtun 38%, Tajik 25%, Hazara 19%, Uzbek 6%, Aimaq 4%, Baluchi 0.5%)

	13–17	18–22	23–32
Men	1,208,800	1,098,400	1,813,600
Women	1,154,200	1,041,000	1,713,400

[b] Includes ε3,751,000 refugees in Pakistan and 1,278,000 (400,000 to return in 1995) in Iran. More than half reportedly returned during 1993.

It is becoming increasingly difficult to differentiate between the sides, movements and groups in the Afghan civil war, and to distinguish which represents the official government, as the number of reports of defections and re-defections is growing.

EQPT: It is not possible to show how ground forces' equipment has been divided among the different factions. The list below represents weapons known to be in the country in April 1992.

MBT: 700 T-54/-55, 170 T-62.
LT TK: 60 PT-76.
RECCE: 250 BRDM-1/-2.
AIFV: 550 BMP-1/-2.
APC: 1,100 BTR-40/-60/-70/-80/-152.
TOWED ARTY: 1,000+: **76mm:** M-1938, M-1942; **85mm:** D-48; **100mm:** M-1944; **122mm:** M-30, D-30; **130mm:** M-46; **152mm:** D-1, D-20, M-1937 (ML-20).
MRL: 185: **122mm:** BM-21; **140mm:** BM-14; **220mm:** 9P140 *Uragan*.
MOR: 1,000+ incl **82mm:** M-37; **107mm; 120mm:** 100 M-43.
SSM: 30: *Scud, FROG*-7 launchers.
ATGW: AT-1 *Snapper*, AT-3 *Sagger*.
RCL: **73mm:** SPG-9; **82mm:** B-10.
AD GUNS: 600+ incl **14.5mm; 23mm:** ZU-23, 20 ZSU-23-4 SP; **37mm:** M-1939; **57mm:** S-60; **85mm:** KS-12; **100mm:** KS-19.
SAM: SA-7/-13.

AIR FORCE:
Air Force org and loyalty following the fall of the government is uncertain. The majority is controlled either by the Defence Ministry or by General Rashid Dostum. The inventory shows ac in service in April 1992. Since then an unknown number of fixed-wing ac and hel have either been shot down or destroyed on the ground. The serviceability of the remainder is doubtful, but reports are still received of air attacks.
FGA: 30 MiG-23, 80 Su-7/-17/-22.
FTR: 80 MiG-21F.
ARMED HEL: 25 Mi-8, 35 Mi-17, 20 Mi-25.
TPT: ac: 2 Il-18D; 50 An-2, An-12, An-26, An-32; **hel:** 12 Mi-4.
TRG: 25 L-39*, 18 MiG-21*.

AIR DEFENCE:
SAM: 115 SA-2, 110 SA-3, 37mm, 85mm and 100mm guns.

MUJAHEDDIN GROUPS:
Afghan insurgency was a broad national movement, united only against the Najibullah government.

GROUPS ORIGINALLY BASED IN PESHAWAR:
TRADITIONALIST MODERATE:
NATIONAL LIBERATION FRONT[a] (*Jabha't-Nija't-Milli'*): ε15,000. Leader: Sibghatullah Modjaddi. Area: enclaves in Kandahar, Zabol provinces, eastern Konar. Ethnic group: Pashtun.

NATIONAL ISLAMIC FRONT (*Mahaz-Millin Isla'mi*): ε15,000. Leader: Sayyed Amhad Gailani. Area: eastern Paktia (Vardak/Lowgar border). Ethnic group: Pashtun.

ISLAMIC REVOLUTIONARY MOVEMENT (*Haraka't-Inqila'b-Isla'mi*): ε25,000. Leader: Mohammed Nabi Mohammed. Area: Farah, Zabol, Paktika, southern Ghazni, eastern Lowgar, western Paktia, northern Nimruz, northern Helmand, northern Kandahar. Ethnic group: Pashtun. Has backed *Taleban*.

ISLAMIC FUNDAMENTALIST:
ISLAMIC PARTY (*Hizbi-Isla'mi-Kha'lis*): ε40,000. Leader: Yu'nis Kha'lis. Area: central Paktia, Nangarhar, south-east Kabul. Ethnic group: Pashtun.

ISLAMIC PARTY (*Hizbi-Isla'mi-Gulbuddin*)[a]: ε50,000. Leader: Gulbuddin Hekmatyar. Area: northern and southern Kabul, Parvan, eastern Laghman, northern Nangarhar, south-eastern Konar; large enclave at Badghis/Ghowr/Jowzjan junction, western Baghlan; enclaves in Farah, Nimruz, Kandahar, Oruzgan and Zabol. Ethnic groups: Pashtun/Turkoman/Tajik.

ISLAMIC UNION (*Ittiha'd-Isla'mi Barai Azadi*): ε18,000. Leader: Abdul Rasul Sayyaf. Area: east of Kabul. Ethnic group: Pashtun.

ISLAMIC SOCIETY (*Jamia't Isla'mi*): ε60,000. Leader: Burhanuddin Rabbani. Area: eastern and northern Farah, Herat, Ghowr, Badghis, Faryab, northern Jowzjan, northern Balkh, northern Kondoz, Takhar, Baghlan, Kapisa, northern Laghman, Badakhshan. Ethnic groups: Turkoman/Uzbek/Tajik.

TALEBAN: ε25,000. Leaders: Maulewi Mohamed Omar, Maulewi Mohamed Rabbi. Area: southern Afghanistan. Ethnic group: Pashtun. Formed originally from religious students in Madrassahs (both Pashtun and non-Pashtun).

GROUPS ORIGINALLY BASED IN IRAN:
Shi'i groups have now formed an umbrella party, the ***Hezbi-Wahdat*** (Unity Party).[a] It includes:

Sazman-e-Nasr: some 50,000. Area: Bamian, northern Oruzgan, eastern Ghowr, southern Balkh, southern Samangan, south-western Baghlan, south-eastern Parvan, northern Vardak. Ethnic group: Hazara.

Harakat-e-Islami: 20,000. Area: west of Kabul; enclaves in Kandahar, Ghazni, Vardak, Samangan, Balkh. Ethnic groups: Pashtun/Tajik/Uzbek.

Pasdaran-e-Jehad: 8,000.

Hizbollah: 4,000.

Nehzat: 4,000.

Shura-Itifaq-Islami: some 30,000+. Area: Vardak, eastern Bamian. Ethnic group: Hazara.

NATIONAL ISLAMIC MOVEMENT (NIM):[a]
Formed in March 1992 by Uzbek militia commander General Dostum, mainly from troops of former Northern Comd of the Afghan Army. Predominantly Uzbek, Tajik, Turkomen, Ismaeli and Hazara Shi'i. Strε65,000 (120–150,000 in crisis). 2 Corps HQ, 5–7 inf div, some indep bde. Now supports Gulbuddin Hekmatyar.

[a] Now form the Supreme Coordination Council.

BANGLADESH

GDP	1993: Tk 947.9bn ($23.96bn): per capita $1,250		
	1994: Tk 1,035.5bn ($25.75bn): per capita $1,300		
Growth	1993: 4.3%		1994: 4.6%
Inflation	1993: 0%		1994: 3.6%
Debt	1993: $13.9bn		1994: $15.4bn
Def exp	1993: Tk 18.24bn ($461m)		
Def bdgt	1994: Tk 18.76bn ($467m)		
	1995: Tk 19.35bn ($483m)		
FMA	1994: $0.2m (IMET)		
	1995: $0.2m (IMET)		
	1996: $0.3m (IMET)		
$1 = Tk	1993: 39.6		1994: 40.2
	1995: 40.1		

Tk = taka

Population: 121,110,000 (Hindu 16%)

	13–17	18–22	23–32
Men	7,692,000	6,694,200	10,224,600
Women	7,231,000	6,335,000	9,684,000

TOTAL ARMED FORCES:
ACTIVE: ε115,500.

ARMY: 101,000.
7 inf div HQ.
16 inf bde (some 26 bn).
1 armd bde (2 armd regt).
2 armd regt.
2 arty bde (4 arty regt).
1 engr bde.
1 AD bde.
EQPT:†
MBT: some 80 Ch Type-59/-69, 60 T-54/-55.

LT TK: some 40 Ch Type-62.
APC: 58 BTR-70 (UNPROFOR).
TOWED ARTY: 105mm: 30 Model 56 pack, 50 M-101;
122mm: 20 Ch Type-54; **130mm:** 40+ Ch Type-59.
MRL: 122mm: reported.
MOR: 81mm; 82mm: Ch Type-53; **120mm:** 50 Ch Type-53.
RCL: 106mm: 30 M-40A1.
ATK GUNS: 57mm: 18 6-pdr; **76mm:** 50 Ch Type-54.
AD GUNS: 37mm: 16 Ch Type-55; **57mm:** Ch Type-59.

NAVY:† ε8,000.
BASES: Chittagong (HQ), Dhaka, Khulna, Kaptai.
FF: 4:
1 *Osman* (Ch *Jianghu I*) with 2 x 5 ASW mor, plus 2 x 2 CSS-N-2 *Hai Ying*-2 (HY-2) SSM, 2 x 2 100mm guns (second unit fitting out).
1 *Umar Farooq* (UK *Salisbury*) with 1 x 3 *Squid* ASW mor, 1 x 2 114mm guns.
2 *Abu Bakr* (UK *Leopard*) with 2 x 2 114mm guns.
PATROL AND COASTAL COMBATANTS: 40:
MSL CRAFT: 8:
4 *Durdarsha* (Ch *Huangfeng*) with 4 x HY-2 SSM.
4 *Durbar* (Ch *Hegu*) PFM⟨ with 2 x HY-2 SSM.
TORPEDO CRAFT: some 8 Ch *Huchuan* PFT⟨ with 2 x 533mm TT.
PATROL, OFFSHORE: 1 *Shaeed Ruhul Amin* (UK *Island*) PCO (training role).
PATROL, COASTAL: 5:
2 *Durjoy* (Ch *Hainan*) with 4 x 5 ASW RL.
2 *Meghna* fishery protection.
1 *Shahjalal*.
PATROL, INSHORE: 13:
8 *Shahead Daulat* (Ch *Shanghai II*) PFI.
2 *Karnaphuli*, 2 *Padma*, 1 *Bishkali* PCI.
RIVERINE: 5 *Pabna*⟨.
MCM: 5:
4 *Shapla* (UK *River*) MSI, 1 OH (Ch) MSI.
AMPH: 1 *Shahamanat* LCU; plus craft: 4 LCM, 3 LCVP.
SPT AND MISC: 3:
1 coastal tkr, 1 repair, 1 ocean tug.

AIR FORCE:† 6,500; 57 cbt ac, no armed hel.
FGA: 3 sqn with 17 J-6/JJ-6 (F-6/FT-6), 13 Q-5 (A-5 *Fantan*).
FTR: 2 sqn with 17 J-7 (F-7M), 4 MiG-21MF, 2 MiG-21U.
TPT: 1 sqn with 1 An-24, 4 An-26, 2 An-32, 1 DHC-3.
HEL: 3 sqn with 2 Bell 206L, 10 Bell 212, 7 Mi-8, 4 Mi-17, 3 UH-1N.
TRG: 20 Ch CJ-6, 8 CM-170, 4* JJ-7 (FT-7), 4 MiG-15UTI.

FORCES ABROAD:
UN AND PEACEKEEPING:
ANGOLA (UNAVEM III): 10 Obs plus 11 civ pol.

BOSNIA (UNPROFOR): 1,263 incl 18 Obs. **CROATIA** (UNPROFOR I): 23 Obs, 33 civ pol. **GEORGIA** (UNOMIG): 11 Obs. **HAITI** (UNMIH): 1,067 plus 84 civ pol. **IRAQ/KUWAIT** (UNIKOM): 775; incl 9 Obs. **LIBERIA** (UNOMIL): 13, incl 6 Obs. **FYROM** (UNPREDEP): 2 civ pol. **RWANDA** (UNAMIR): 37, incl 36 Obs. **TAJIKISTAN** (UNMOT): 7 Obs. **WESTERN SAHARA** (MINURSO): 7 Obs.

PARAMILITARY:
BANGLADESH RIFLES: 30,000 (border guard); 37 bn.
ARMED POLICE: 5,000.
ANSARS (Security Guards): 20,000.

OPPOSITION:
SHANTI BAHINI (Peace Force): ε5,000. Chakma tribe, Chittagong Hills.

INDIA

GDP	1993: Rs 7,863.6bn ($257.9bn):			
	per capita $1,200			
	1994: Rs 8,478.0bn ($270.2bn):			
	per capita $1,300			
Growth	1993: 3.5%		1994: 4.8%	
Inflation	1993: 6.4%		1994: 10.2%	
Debt	1993: $91.8bn		1994: $90.5bn	
Def exp	1993: Rs 217.8bn ($7.14bn)			
	1994ε: Rs 233.0bn ($7.43bn)			
Def bdgt	1994: Rs 230.0bn ($7.33bn)			
	1995: Rs 255.0bn ($8.12bn)			
FMA[a]	1994: $0.2m (IMET)			
	1995: $0.2m (IMET)			
	1996: $0.4m (IMET)			
$1 = Rs	1993: 30.5		1994: 31.4	
	1995: 31.4			

Rs = rupee

[a] The cost of UNMOGIP in 1994 was $7m.

Population: 934,228,000 (Muslim 11%, Sikh 2%)

	13–17	18–22	23–32
Men	49,677,800	45,932,000	79,803,800
Women	46,133,000	42,203,800	72,685,800

TOTAL ARMED FORCES:
ACTIVE: 1,145,000 (incl 200 women).
RESERVES: Army 300,000 (first-line reserves within 5 years of full-time service; a further 650,000 have commitment until the age of 50); Territorial Army (volunteers) 160,000; Air Force 140,000; Navy 55,000.

ARMY: 980,000.

HQ: 5 Regional Comd (= Fd Army), 12 Corps.
3 armd div (each 2/3 armed, 1 SP arty (2 SP fd, 1
    med regt) bde).
4 'RAPID' div (each 2 inf, 1 mech bde).
17 inf div (each 2–5 inf, 1 arty bde; some have armed regt).
10 mtn div (each 3–4 bde, 1 or more arty regt).
14 indep bde: 5 armd, 7 inf, 1 mtn, 1 AB/cdo; 3 indep
    arty bde.
1 SSM regt (*Privthi*).
16 AD bde (ε10 cadre).
3 engr bde.
These formations comprise:
59 tk regt (bn).
355 inf bn (incl 25 mech, 9 AB/cdo).
290 arty regt (bn) reported: incl 1 hy, 2 MRL, 50 med
    (11 SP), 69 fd (3 SP), 39 mtn, 29 AD arty regt;
    perhaps 10 SAM gp (3–5 bty each).
14 hel sqn: 6 ATK, 8 air obs.

EQPT:
MBT: 2,400: some 500 T-55, 1,100 T-72/-M1, 800
Vijayanta, some in store.
RECCE: BRDM-2.
AIFV: 900 BMP-1/-2 (*Sarath*).
APC: 157 OT-62/-64.
TOWED ARTY: 4,075 incl: **75mm:** 900 75/24 mtn,
215 Yug M-48; **105mm:** some 1,200 IFG Mk I/II, 50
M-56; **122mm:** some 550 D-30; **130mm:** 750 M-46;
155mm: 410 FH-77B.
SP ARTY: 105mm: 80 *Abbot*; **130mm:** 100 mod M-46.
MRL: 122mm: 80 BM-21, LRAR.
MOR: 81mm: L16A1, E1; **120mm:** 1,000 incl M-43,
500 *Brandt* AM-50, E1; **160mm:** 200 M-160.
SSM: *Prithvi* (3–5 launchers).
ATGW: *Milan*, AT-3 *Sagger*, AT-4 *Spigot*, AT-5 *Spandrel*.
RCL: 57mm: M-18; **84mm:** *Carl Gustav*; **106mm:**
1,000+ M-40A1.
AD GUNS: 2,468: **20mm:** *Oerlikon* (reported); **23mm:**
140 ZU 23-2, 75 ZSU-23-4 SP; **30mm:** 8 2S6 SP
(reported); **40mm:** 500 L40/60, 1,000 L40/70.
SAM: 100 SA-6, 620 SA-7, 48 SA-8A/-B, 200 SA-9,
45 SA-13, 500 SA-16.
SURV: MUFAR, *Green Archer* (mor).
HEL: 199 *Chetak*, *Cheetah*.
LC: 2 LCVP.

RESERVES: Territorial Army: 25 inf bn, plus 31
'departmental' units.

DEPLOYMENT:
North: 2 Corps with 7 inf, 2 mtn div.
West: 3 Corps with 1 armd, 5 inf div, 1 mtn, 3 RAPID.
Central: 1 Corps with 1 armd, 1 inf, 1 mtn div, 1 RAPID.
East: 3 Corps with 1 inf, 7 mtn div.
South: 2 Corps with 1 armd, 3 inf div.

NAVY: 55,000 (incl 5,000 Naval Aviation and

ε1,000 Marines).
PRINCIPAL COMD: Western, Eastern, Southern.
SUB-COMD: Submarine, Naval Air.
BASES: Bombay (HQ Western Comd), Goa (HQ
Naval Air), Karwar (under construction), Cochin (HQ
Southern Comd), Visakhapatnam (HQ Eastern and
Submarines), Calcutta, Madras, Port Blair (Andaman
Is), Arakonam (Naval Air).
FLEETS: Western (base Bombay); Eastern (base
Visakhapatnam). (Only 50% of warships est combat-
capable.)
SS: 15:
8 *Sindhughosh* (Sov *Kilo*) with 533mm TT.
4 *Shishumar* (Ge T-209/1500) with 533mm TT.
3 *Kursura* (Sov *Foxtrot*) with 533mm TT trg (plus
    3 op reserve).
PRINCIPAL SURFACE COMBATANTS: 25:
CARRIERS: 2:
1 *Viraat* (UK *Hermes*) (29,000t) CVV.
1 *Vikrant* (UK *Glory*) (19,800t) CVV.
Air group typically: **ac:** 12 (*Viraat*) and 6 (*Vikrant*)
Sea Harrier ftr/attack; **hel:** 7 (*Viraat*) and 9 (*Vikrant*)
Sea King ASW/ASUW (*Sea Eagle* ASM).
DDG: 5 *Rajput* (Sov *Kashin*) with 2 x 2 SA-N-1 *Goa*
SAM; plus 4 SS-N-2C *Styx* SSM, 5 x 533mm TT, 2
x ASW RL, 1 Ka-25 or 27 hel (ASW).
FF: 18:
3 *Godavari* FFH with 1 x *Sea King* hel, 2 x 3 324mm
    ASTT; plus 4 x SS-N-2C *Styx* SSM and 1 x 2 SA-
    N-4 SAM.
6 *Nilgiri* (UK *Leander*) with 2 x 3 ASTT, 4 with 1
    x 3 *Limbo* ASW mor, 1 *Chetak* hel, 2 with 1 *Sea
    King*, 1 x 2 ASW RL; plus 2 x 114mm guns (all).
4 *Kamorta* (Sov *Petya*) with 4 ASW RL, 3 x 533mm TT.
5 *Khukri* (ASUW) with 2 or 4 SS-N-2C (*Styx*), hel deck.
Additional in store: some 2 ex-UK FF and 4 *Kamorta* FF.
PATROL AND COASTAL COMBATANTS: 41:
CORVETTES: 17:
3 *Vijay Durg* (Sov *Nanuchka* II) with 4 x SS-N-2B
    Styx SSM.
5 *Veer* (Sov *Tarantul*) with 4 x *Styx* SSM.
5 *Vibhuti* (similar to *Tarantul*) with 4 x *Styx* SSM.
4 *Abhay* (Sov *Pauk*-II) (ASW) with 4 x ASTT, 2 x
    ASW mor.
MSL CRAFT: 6 *Vidyut*† (Sov *Osa* II) with 4 x *Styx*.
PATROL, OFFSHORE: 7 *Sukanya* PCO.
PATROL, INSHORE: 11 SDB Mk 2/3.
MINE WARFARE: 20:
MINELAYERS: none, but *Kamorta* FF and *Pondicherry*
MSO have minelaying capability.
MCM: 20:
12 *Pondicherry* (Sov *Natya*) MSO.
2 *Bulsar* (UK *Ham*) MSI.
6 *Mahé* (Sov *Yevgenya*) MSI⟨.
AMPH: 9:
1 *Magar* LST, capacity 200 tps, 12 tk, 1 hel.

8 *Ghorpad* (Sov *Polnocny* C) LSM, capacity 140 tps, 6 tk (includes 2 in reserve).
Plus craft: 7 *Vasco da Gama* LCU.
SPT AND MISC: 23:
2 *Deepak* AO, 5 small AO, 1 *Amba* (Sov *Ugra*) sub spt, 1 div spt, 2 ocean tugs, 6 *Sandhayak* and 4 *Makar* AGHS, 1 *Tir* trg, 1 *Sagardhwani* AGOR.

NAVAL AVIATION: (5,000); 68 cbt ac, 75 armed hel. Flying hours: some 180.
ATTACK: 2 sqn with 20 *Sea Harrier* FRS Mk-51, 2 T-60 trg.
ASW: 6 hel sqn with 26 *Chetak*, 7 Ka-25, 10 Ka-28, 32 *Sea King* Mk 42A/B.
MR: 3 sqn with 5 Il-38, 8 Tu-142M *Bear* F, 20 Do-228, 13 BN-2 *Defender*.
COMMS: 1 sqn with **ac:** 5 BN-2 *Islander*, 26 Do-228; **hel:** 3 *Chetak*.
SAR: 1 hel sqn with 6 *Sea King* Mk 42C.
TRG: 2 sqn with **ac:** 6 HJT-16, 8 HPT-32; **hel:** 2 *Chetak*, 4 Hughes 300.
MSL:
AAM: R-550 *Magic* I and II.
ASM: *Sea Eagle, Sea Skua*.

MARINES: (ε1,000).
1 regt (2nd forming).

AIR FORCE: 110,000; 844 cbt ac, 32 armed hel.
5 Air Comd. Flying hours: 240.
FGA: 22 sqn:
3 with 54 MiG-23 BN/UM.
4 with 97 *Jaguar* S(I).
6 with 148 Mig-27.
9 with 144 MiG-21 MF/PFMA.
FTR: 20 sqn:
4 with 74 MiG-21 FL/U.
9 with 170 MiG-21 bis/U.
2 with 26 MiG-23 MF/UM.
3 with 67 MiG-29
2 with 35 *Mirage* 2000H/TH.
ECM: 5 *Canberra* B(I) 58.
ELINT: 2 Boeing 707.
AWAC: 2 HS-748 (test).
MARITIME ATTACK: 8 *Jaguar* S(I) with *Sea Eagle*.
ATTACK HEL: 2 sqn with 32 Mi-25/35.
RECCE: 2 sqn:
1 with 8 *Canberra* (6 PR-57, 2 PR-67).
1 with 6 MiG-25R, 2 MiG-25U.
MR/SURVEY: 2 *Gulfstream* IV SRA, 2 *Learjet* 29.
TPT:
AC: 12 sqn:
6 with 105 An-32 *Sutlej*.
2 with 30 Do-228.
2 with 29 BAe-748.
2 with 19 Il-76 *Gajraj*.

HEL: 11 sqn with 74 Mi-8, 50 Mi-17, 10 Mi-26 (hy tpt).
VIP: 1 HQ sqn with 2 Boeing 737-200, 7 BAe-748, 6 Mi-8.
TRG: ac: 28 BAe-748 (trg/tpt), 7 *Canberra* (2 T54, 5 TT18), 120 *Kiran* I, 56 *Kiran* II, 88 HPT-32, *Hunter* (20 F-56, 18 T-66), 14* *Jaguar* B(1), 7 MiG-29UB, 44 TS-11 *Iskara*; **hel:** 20 *Chetak*, 2 Mi-24, 2 Mi-35.
MSL:
ASM: AS-7 *Kerry*, AS-11B (ATGW), AS-12, AS-30, *Sea Eagle*.
AAM: AA-2 *Atoll*, AA-7 *Apex*, AA-8 *Aphid*, AA-10 *Alamo*, AA-11 *Archer*, R-550 *Magic*, *Super* 530D.
SAM: 30 sqn: 280 *Divina* V75SM/VK (SA-2), *Pechora* (SA-3), SA-3, SA-5.

FORCES ABROAD:
UN AND PEACEKEEPING:
ANGOLA (UNAVEM III): 236 incl 22 Obs plus 20 civ pol. **HAITI** (UNMIH): 123. **IRAQ/KUWAIT** (UNIKOM): 6 Obs. **LIBERIA** (UNOMIL): 4 Obs. **RWANDA** (UNAMIR): 954 incl 20 Obs.

PARAMILITARY:
NATIONAL SECURITY GUARDS (Cabinet Secretariat): 7,500: anti-terrorism contingency deployment force. Comprises elements of the Armed Forces, CRPF and Border Security Force.
CENTRAL RESERVE POLICE FORCE (CRPF) (Ministry of Home Affairs): 120,000; 70 bn incl 10 rapid action, internal security duties, only lightly armed, deployable throughout the country.
STATE ARMED POLICE: 400,000. For duty in parent state only, incl 24 bn India Reserve Police (commando trained).
BORDER SECURITY FORCE (BSF) (Ministry of Home Affairs): 185,000; some 149 bn, small arms, some lt arty, tpt/liaison air spt.
ASSAM RIFLES (Ministry of Home Affairs): 52,000; 31 bn, security within north-eastern states, mainly Army-officered, better trained than BSF.
INDO-TIBETAN BORDER POLICE (Ministry of Home Affairs): 35,000; 28 bn, Tibetan border security.
SPECIAL FRONTIER FORCE (Cabinet Secretariat): 10,000; mainly ethnic Tibetans.
NATIONAL RIFLES (*Rashtriya Rifles*) (Ministry of Defence): 30,000; 30 bn (6 more to form).
CENTRAL INDUSTRIAL SECURITY FORCE (Ministry of Home Affairs):[a] 90,000.
DEFENCE SECURITY CORPS:[a] 31,000; provides security at Defence Ministry Sites.
RAILWAY PROTECTION FORCES: 70,000.
HOME GUARD (R): 472,000; men on lists, no trg.
COAST GUARD: ε5,000.
PATROL CRAFT: 51:

1 *Samar* OPV, 9 *Vikram* PCO, 11 *Tara Bai* PCC, 5
Rajhans PFI, 7 *Jija Bai* PCI, 18⟨.
AVN: 3 sqn with **ac:** 20 Do-228, 2 Fokker F-27; **hel:**
13 *Chetak.*

a Lightly armed security guards only.

KAZAKHSTAN

GDP	1993ε:t 31.6bn ($18.2bn)	
	per capita $4,300	
	1994ε:t 446.4bn ($14.0bn)	
	per capita $3,300	
Growth	1993ε:-12%	1994ε:-25%
Inflation	1993ε:1,570%	1994ε:1,681%
Debt	1993: $1.6bn	1994: $2.5bn
Def exp	1993ε:t 744m ($429m)	
Def bdgt	1994ε:t 15.6bn ($414m)	
	1995ε:t 19.29bn ($297m)	
FMA*a*	1994: $0.1m (IMET)	
	1995: $0.1m (IMET)	
	1996: $0.4m (IMET)	
$1 = t	1993: 5.5	1994: 37.6
	1995: 65.0	

t = tenge*b*

a Excl US Cooperative Threat Reduction funds for nuclear
dismantlement and demilitarisation.
b The tenge was introduced in November 1993 to replace the old
Russian rouble.

Population: 16,763,000 (Kazakh 42%, Russian 37%,
Ukrainian 5%, German 5%, Uzbek 2%, Tatar 2%)

	13–17	*18–22*	*23–32*
Men	831,000	744,800	1,252,400
Women	814,600	732,600	1,212,600

TOTAL ARMED FORCES:
ACTIVE: ε40,000.

STRATEGIC NUCLEAR FORCES
(Russian-controlled forces on Kazakhstan territory):
ICBM: 48 SS-18 *Satan* (RS-20), at 2 sites (all nuclear
warheads returned to Russia).

ARMY: ε25,000.
1 Corps HQ.
1 TD.
1 arty bde.
2 MRD (1 trg).
1 arty regt.
1 indep MRR.
1 MRL bde.
1 air aslt bde.

EQPT:
MBT: 624 T-62, T-72 (plus some 470 in store).
RECCE: 140 BRDM.
ACV: 1,200 incl BMP-1/-2, BRM AIFV, BTR-70/-
80, MT-LB APC (plus some 1,000 in store).
TOTAL ARTY: ε1,850:
TOWED ARTY: 1,000: **100mm:** M-1944 (BS-3);
122mm: D-30, M-30; **130mm:** M-46; **152mm:** D-1,
D-20, M-1937, 2A65, 2A36.
SP ARTY: 200: **122mm:** 2S1; **152mm:** 2S3.
MRL: 350: **122mm:** BM-21; **220mm:** 9P140 *Uragan.*
MOR: 300: **120mm:** 2B11, M-120.
ATK GUNS: 100mm: 125 T-12.
(In 1991 the former Soviet Union transferred some
2,680 T-64/-72), 2,428 ACV and 6,900 arty pieces to
open storage bases in Kazakhstan. This eqpt is under
Kazakh control, but has deteriorated considerably.)

NAVY: none. Has announced intention to form a
maritime force. Caspian Sea Flotilla (see Russia) is
operating as a joint Russian, Kazakhstan and
Turkmenistan flotilla under Russian comd based at Astrakhan.

AIR FORCE: ε15,000; 1 Air Force div, 133 cbt ac
(plus some 40 instore). Flying hours: 25.
FTR: 1 regt with 12 MiG-29, 9 MiG-29UB, 12 MiG-
23, 4 MiG-23UB.
FGA: 2 regt: 1 with 34 MiG-27, 9 MiG-23UB; 1 with
26 Su-24.
RECCE: 1 regt with 12 Su-24*, 13 MiG-25 RB*, 2
MiG-25 RU*.
HEL: 1 regt (tpt), 44 Mi-8.
STORAGE: some 40 MiG-27/MiG-23/MiG-23UB.
AD: 1 PVO regt, 32 cbt ac.
FTR: 1 regt with 32 MiG-31.
SAM: 100 SA-2, SA-3, SA-5.

FORCES ABROAD:
TAJIKISTAN: ε500: 1 border gd bn.

PARAMILITARY:
REPUBLICAN GUARD: 2,500.
INTERNAL SECURITY TROOPS (Ministry of
Interior): ε20,000.
BORDER GUARDS (National Security Committee):
ε12,000.

KYRGYZSTAN

GDP	1993ε:s 10.2bn ($3.37bn)
	per capita $2,600
	1994ε:s 11.4bn ($3.40bn)
	per capita $2,600

Growth	1993ε: -13%	1994ε: -0.2%
Inflation	1993ε 1,209%	1994ε: 283%
Debt	1993: $308m	1994: $489m
Def exp	1993ε: s 321m ($51m)	
	1994ε: s 529m ($49m)	
Def bdgt	1995: s 149m ($13m)	
FMA	1994: $0.05m (IMET)	
	1995: $0.05m (IMET)	
	1996: $0.30m (IMET)	
$1 = s	1993ε: 6.3	1994ε: 10.8
	1995ε: 11.2	

s = som[a]

[a] The som was introduced in May 1993 replacing the old Russian rouble at a conversion rate of 1 som = 200 roubles. Since then the som has floated against the rouble.

Population: 4,636,000 (Russian 21%, Uzbek 13%, other 14%)

	13–17	18–22	23–32
Men	248,400	209,600	329,000
Women	244,800	206,200	323,600

TOTAL ARMED FORCES:
ACTIVE: ε7,000.
Terms of service: 12–18 months.

ARMY: ε7,000.
1 MRD (3 MR, 1 tk, 1 arty, 1 AA regt).
1 indep MR bde (mtn).
EQPT:
MBT: 204 T-72.
RECCE: 42 BRDM-2.
AIFV: 349 BMP-1, 28 BRM.
APC: 96 BTR-70.
TOTAL ARTY: 216:
TOWED ARTY: 100mm: 18 M-1944 (BS-3); **122mm:** 27 D-30, 110 M-30; **152mm:** 16 D-1.
COMBINED GUN/MOR: 120mm: 12 2S9.
MOR: 120mm: 6 2S12, 27 M-120.
ATGW: 30 AT-3 *Sagger*.
AD GUNS: 57mm: 24 S-60.

AIR FORCE:
Ac and hel assets inherited from the Soviet Air Force trg school. Kyrgyzstan hoped to maintain pilot trg for foreign students, but without success.
AC: 96 L-39.
HEL: 40 Mi-24, 25 Mi-8/17/25/35. About 100 decommissioned MiG21/MiG-21UB.
AD:
SAM: 20 SA-2, SA-3.

MYANMAR (BURMA)

GDP[a]	1993: K 339.1bn ($13.0bn):	
	per capita $810	
	1994: K 359.0bn ($13.8bn)	
	per capita $860	
Growth	1993: 6.0%	1994: 6.4%
Inflation	1993: 31.8%	1994: 35%
Debt	1993: $5.48bn	1994: $5.24bn
Def exp[a]	1993: K 10.5bn ($403m)	
Def bdgt[a]	1994: K 11.1bn ($425m)	
	1995: K 15.5n ($594m)	
$1 = K	1993: 6.16	1994: 5.97
	1995: 5.45	

K = kyat

[a] PPP est.

Population: 46,759,000 (Shan 9%, Karen 7%, Rakhine 4%, Chinese 3+%, other (Chin, Kachin, Mon, Palaung, Wa, Pao, Lahu, Kayan) 5%)

	13–17	18–22	23–32
Men	2,442,800	2,325,600	3,856,000
Women	2,390,000	2,258,000	3,930,000

TOTAL ARMED FORCES:
ACTIVE: 286,000.

ARMY: 265,000.
10 lt inf div (each 3 tac op comd (TOC)).
10 Regional Comd (8 with 3 TOC, 2 with 4 TOC).
32 TOC with 145 garrison inf bn.
Summary of cbt units:
245 inf bn.
7 arty bn.
3 armd bn.
1 AA arty bn.
EQPT:†
MBT: 26 *Comet*, 36 Ch T-69II.
LT TK: 60 Type-63.
RECCE: 45 *Ferret*, 40 *Humber*, 30 *Mazda* (local manufacture).
APC: 20 *Hino* (local manufacture), 150 Type-85 (reported).
TOWED ARTY: 76mm: 100 M-1948; **88mm:** 50 25-pdr; **105mm:** 96 M-101; **140mm:** 5.5-in.
MRL: 107mm: 30 Type-63.
MOR: 81mm; 82mm: Type-53; **120mm:** Type-53, 80 Soltam.
RCL: 84mm: 500 *Carl Gustav*; **106mm:** M40A1.
ATK GUNS: 60: **57mm:** 6-pdr; **76.2mm:** 17-pdr.
AD GUNS: 37mm: 24 Type-74; **40mm:** 10 M-1; **57mm:** 12 Type-80.
SAM: HN-5A (reported).

NAVY:† 12,000–15,000 (incl 800 Naval Infantry).
BASES: Bassein, Mergui, Moulmein, Seikyi, Rangoon (Monkey Point), Sittwe.
PATROL AND COASTAL COMBATANTS: 56:
CORVETTES: 2:
1 *Yan Taing Aung* (US PCE-827)†.
1 *Yan Gyi Aung* (US *Admirable* MSF)†.
PATROL, COASTAL: 10 *Yan Sit Aung* (Ch *Hainan*).
PATROL, INSHORE: 15: 12 US PGM-401/412, 3 Yug PB-90 PFI⟨.
RIVERINE: 29: 2 *Nawarat,* 2 imp Yug Y-301 and 10 Yug Y-301, about 15⟨, plus some 25 boats.
AMPH: 5 LCU, plus craft: 10 LCM.
SPT: 4: 1 coastal tpt, 2 AGHS, 1 PC/div spt.

NAVAL INFANTRY: (800): 1 bn.

AIR FORCE: 9,000; 91 cbt ac, 10 armed hel.
FTR: 3 sqn with 30 F-7, 6 FT-7.
FGA: 2 sqn with 24 A-5M.
COIN: 2 sqn with 15 PC-7, 4 PC-9, 12 *Super Galeb* G4.
TPT: 1 F-27, 4 FH-227, 5 PC-6A/-B, 2 Y-8D.
LIAISON: 6 Cessna 180, 1 Cessna 550.
HEL: 4 sqn with 12 Bell 205, 6 Bell 206, 9 SA-316, 10 Mi-2 (armed), 12 PZL W-3 *Sokol.*

PARAMILITARY:
PEOPLE'S POLICE FORCE: 50,000.
PEOPLE'S MILITIA: 35,000.
PEOPLE'S PEARL AND FISHERY MINISTRY: ε250; 11 patrol boats (3 *Indaw* (Dk *Osprey)* PCC, 3 US *Swift* PGM PCI, 5 Aust *Carpentaria* PCI⟨).

OPPOSITION AND FORMER OPPOSITION:
GROUPS WITH CEASE-FIRE AGREEMENTS:
KACHIN INDEPENDENCE ARMY (KIA): some 8,000; northern Myanmar, incl Kuman range, the Triangle. Reached cease-fire agreement with government in October 1993.
DEMOCRATIC KAREN BUDDHIST ORGANISATION (DKBO): ε100–500 armed.
NEW DEMOCRATIC ARMY (NDA): ε500; along Chinese border in Kachin state; was Communist Party of Burma (CPB).
MYANMAR NATIONAL DEMOCRATIC ALLIANCE ARMY (MNDAA): 2,000; north-east Shan state.
PALAUNG STATE LIBERATION ARMY (PSLA): ε700; hill tribesmen north of Hsipaw.
UNITED WA STATE ARMY (UWSA): ε12,000, Wa hills between Salween river and Chinese border; was part of CPB.

SHAN STATE ARMY (SSA): ε3,000; Shan state.
NATIONAL DEMOCRATIC ALLIANCE ARMY (NDAA): ε1,000; eastern corner of Shan state on China–Laos border; was part of CPB.
MON NATIONAL LIBERATION ARMY (MNLA): ε1,000; on Thai border in Mon state.
GROUPS STILL IN OPPOSITION:
MONG TAI ARMY (MTA) (formerly Shan United Army): 10,000+; along Thai border and between Lashio and Chinese border.
KAREN NATIONAL LIBERATION ARMY (KNLA): ε4,000; based in Thai border area.
KARENNI ARMY (KA): ›1,000; Kayah state, Thai border.
ALL BURMA STUDENTS DEMOCRATIC FRONT: ε2,000.

NEPAL

GDP	1993: NR 170.0bn ($3.5bn):	
	per capita $1,100	
	1994: NR 197.0bn ($4.0bn):	
	per capita $1,200	
Growth	1993: 3.1%	1994: 7.6%
Inflation	1993: 7.5%	1994ε: 7.2%
Debt	1993: $2.07bn	1994: $2.17bn
Def exp	1993: NR 2.0bn	($41.0m)
Def bdgt	1994: NR 2.1bn	($42.5m)
	1995: NR 2.2bn	($42.9m)
FMA	1994: $0.1m (IMET)	
	1995: $0.1m (IMET)	
	1996: $0.1m (IMET)	
$1 = NR	1993: 48.6	1994: 49.4
	1995: 50.4	

NR = Nepalese rupee

Population: 21,406,000

	13–17	18–22	23–32
Men	1,246,000	1,017,000	1,574,000
Women	1,167,000	943,600	1,455,800

TOTAL ARMED FORCES:
ACTIVE: 35,000 (to be 40,000).

ARMY: 34,800.
1 Royal Guard bde: incl 1 cav sqn, 1 garrison bn.
5 inf bde (14 inf bn).
1 spt bde: incl AB bn, arty regt, engr bn, armd recce sqn.
EQPT:
RECCE: 25 *Ferret.*
TOWED ARTY: 75mm: 6 pack; **94mm:** 5 3.7-in mtn; **105mm:** 14 pack.
MOR: 81mm; 120mm: 70 M-43.
AD GUNS: 14.5mm: 30 Ch; **40mm:** 2 L/60.

AIR FORCE: 200; no cbt ac, nor armed hel.
TPT: ac: 1 BAe-748, 2 *Skyvan*, 1 *Twin Otter*; 2 Y-11;
hel: 2 AS-332 (Royal Flight), 1 Bell 206L, 3 SA-316B *Chetak*, 2 SA-330.

FORCES ABROAD:
UN AND PEACEKEEPING:
CROATIA (UNPROFOR 1): 896; 1 inf bn, plus 3 Obs, 43 civ pol. **HAITI** (UNMIH): 414 plus 53 civ pol. **LEBANON** (UNIFIL): 666; 1 inf bn.

PARAMILITARY:
POLICE FORCE: 28,000.

PAKISTAN

GDP	1993: Rs 1,342bn ($47.7bn):		
	per capita $2,100		
	1994: Rs 1,565bn ($51.2bn):		
	per capita $2,200		
Growth	1993: 1.9%		1994: 4.0%
Inflation	1993: 4.2%		1994: 12.5%
Debt	1993: $26.1bn		1994: $27.4bn
Def exp	1993: Rs 93.8bn ($3.3bn)		
Def bdgt	1994: Rs 101.9bn ($3.4bn)		
	1995: Rs 115.3bn ($3.7bn)		
FMA[a]	1994: $2.5m (Narcs)		
	1995: $2.5m (Narcs)		
	1996: $2.5m (Narcs)		
$1 = Rs	1993: 28.1		1994: 30.6
	1995: 30.9		

Rs = rupee

[a] The cost of UNMOGIP in 1994 was $7m.

Population: 129,704,000 (less than 3% Hindu)			
	13–17	*18–22*	*23–32*
Men	7,581,600	6,581,200	10,622,600
Women	6,905,600	5,849,600	9,482,800

TOTAL ARMED FORCES:
ACTIVE: 587,000.
RESERVES: 513,000; Armyε500,000: obligation to age 45 (men) or 50 (officers); active liability for 8 years after service; Navy 5,000; Air Force 8,000.

ARMY: 520,000.
9 Corps HQ.
2 armd div.
9 corps arty bde.
19 inf div.
7 engr bde.
1 area comd (div).
3 armd recce regt.
7 indep armd bde.
1 SF gp (3bn).
9 indep inf bde.
1 AD comd (3 AD gp: 8 bde).
Avn: 17 sqn: 7 ac, 8 hel, 1 VIP, 1 obs flt.
EQPT:
MBT: 2,050+: 120 M-47, 280 M-48A5, 50 T-54/-55, 1,200 Ch Type-59, 200 Ch Type-69, 200+ Ch Type-85.
APC: 850 M-113, 169 BTR-70 (UNPROFOR).
TOWED ARTY: 1,566: **85mm:** 200 Ch Type-56; **105mm:** 300 M-101, 50 M-56 pack; **122mm:** 200 Ch Type-60, 400 Ch Type-54; **130mm:** 200 Ch Type-59-1; **155mm:** 30 M-59, 60 M-114, 100 M-198; **203mm:** 26 M-115.
SP ARTY: 240: **105mm:** 50 M-7; **155mm:** 150 M-109A2; **203mm:** 40 M-110A2.
MRL: 122mm: 45 *Azar* (Ch Type-83).
MOR: 81mm: 500; **120mm:** 225 AM-50, M-61.
SSM: 18 *Hatf*-1, *Hatf*-2 (under development).
ATGW: 800: *Cobra, TOW* (incl 24 on M-901 SP), *Green Arrow* (Ch *Red Arrow*).
RL: 89mm: M-20 3.5-in.
RCL: 75mm: Type-52; **106mm:** M-40A1.
AD GUNS: 2,000+ incl **14.5mm; 35mm:** 200 GDF-002; **37mm:** Ch Type-55/-65; **40mm:** M1, 100 L/60; **57mm:** Ch Type-59.
SAM: 350 *Stinger, Redeye,* RBS-70, 500 *Anza* Mk-1/-2.
SURV: RASIT (veh, arty), AN/TPQ-36 (arty, mor).
AC:
SURVEY: 1 *Commander* 840.
LIAISON: 1 Cessna 421, 2 *Commander* 690, 80 *Mashshaq,* 1 F-27.
OBS: 40 O-1E, 50 *Mashshaq.*
HEL:
ATTACK: 20 AH-1F (*TOW*).
TPT: 12 Bell 47G, 7 Bell 205, 10 Bell 206B, 16 Mi-8, 6 IAR/SA-315B, 23 IAR/SA-316, 35 SA-330, 5 UH-1H.

NAVY: 22,000 (incl Naval Air, ε1,200 Marines and ε2,000 Maritime Security Agency (see Paramilitary)).
BASE: Karachi (Fleet HQ).
SS: 9:
2 *Hashmat* (Fr *Agosta*) with 533mm TT (F-17 HWT), *Harpoon* USGW.
4 *Hangor* (Fr *Daphné*) with 533mm TT (L-5 HWT), *Harpoon* USGW.
3 SX-756 SSI SF *Midget* submarines.
PRINCIPAL SURFACE COMBATANTS: 11:
DD: 3 *Alamgir* (US *Gearing*) (ASW) with 1 x 8 ASROC; plus 2 x 3 ASTT, 2 x 2 127mm guns, 3 x 2 *Harpoon* SSM and hel deck (1 trg).
FF: 8:
6 *Tariq* (UK *Amazon*) with 2 x 3 324mm ASTT; 1 x

114mm gun (2 *Lynx* hel delivered).
2 *Shamsher* (UK *Leander*) with SA-319B hel, 1 x 3
　ASW mor, plus 2 x 114mm guns.
PATROL AND COASTAL COMBATANTS: 13:
MSL CRAFT: 8:
4 Ch *Huangfeng* with 4 x *Hai Ying 2* SSM.
4 Ch *Hegu⟨* with 2 x *Hai Ying 2*.
PATROL, COASTAL: 1 *Larkana* PCO.
PATROL, INSHORE: 4:
3 *Quetta* (Ch *Shanghai*) PFI.
1 *Rajshahi* PCI.
MCM: 3: 1 *Munsif* (Fr *Eridan*) MHC, 2 *Mahmood*
(US-MSC 268) MSC.
SPT AND MISC: 3: 1 *Nasr* (Ch *Fuqing*) AO, 1 *Dacca*
AO, 1 AGOR.

NAVAL AIR: 4 cbt ac, 13 armed hel.
ASW/MR: 1 sqn with 4 *Atlantic* plus 3 in store
(operated by Air Force).
ASW/SAR: 2 hel sqn with 4 SA-319B (ASW), 6 *Sea
King* Mk 45 (ASW), 3 *Lynx* HAS Mk-3 (ASW).
COMMS: 3 Fokker F-27 ac (Air Force).
ASM: *Exocet* AM-39.

MARINES: (ε1,200); 1 cdo/SF gp.

AIR FORCE: 45,000; 430 cbt ac, no armed hel.
Flying hours: some 210.
FGA: 7 sqn:
1 with 18 *Mirage* (15 IIIEP (some with AM-39
　ASM), 3 IIIDP (trg)).
3 (1 OCU) with 56 *Mirage 5* (54 -5PA/PA2,
　2-5DPA/DPA2).
3 with 49 Q-5 (A-5 *Fantan*).
FTR: 10 sqn:
4 with 100 J-6/JJ-6, (F-6/FT-6).
3 (1 OCU) with 34 F-16A/B.
2 (1 OCU) with 79 J-7 (F-7P).
1 with 30 *Mirage* 1110.
RECCE: 1 sqn with 12 *Mirage* IIIRP*.
ASW/MR: 1 sqn with 4 *Atlantic*.*
SAR: 1 hel sqn with 6 SA-319.
TPT: ac: 12 C-130 (5 -B, 7 -E), 1 L-100, 3 Boeing
707, 3 *Falcon 20*, 2 F-27-200 (1 with Navy), 2 Beech
(1 *Travel Air*, 1 *Baron*); **hel:** 1 sqn with 12 SA-316,
4 SA-321, 12 SA-315B *Lama*.
TRG: 12 CJ-6A (PT-6A), 30 JJ-5 (FT-5), *45 MFI-
17B *Mashshaq*, 6 MiG-15UTI, 10 T-33A, 44 T-37B/
C, 6 K-8.
AD: 7 SAM bty: 6 each with 24 *Crotale*, 1 with 6
CSA-1 (SA-2).
MSL:
ASM: AM-39 *Exocet*.
AAM: AIM-7*Sparrow*, AIM-9*Sidewinder*, R-530, R-
550 *Magic*.

FORCES ABROAD:
UN AND PEACEKEEPING:
ANGOLA (UNAVEM III): 5 Obs. **BOSNIA** (UNPRO-
FOR): 2,994 incl 16 Obs. **CROATIA** (UNCRO): 19
Obs plus 16 civ pol. **GEORGIA** (UNOMIG): 8 Obs.
HAITI(UNMIH): 870 plus 51 civ pol.**IRAQ/KUWAIT**
(UNIKOM): 7 Obs. **LIBERIA** (UNOMIL): 8 Obs.
FYROM (UNPREDEP): 1 Obs plus 2 civ pol.
WESTERN SAHARA (MINURSO): 5 Obs.

PARAMILITARY:
NATIONAL GUARD: 185,000; incl Janbaz Force;
Mujahid Force; National Cadet Corps; Women Guards.
FRONTIER CORPS (Ministry of Interior): 35,000;
45 UR-416 APC.
PAKISTAN RANGERS (Ministry of Interior):
ε35,000; 11 regt (40 bn), 1 indep armd cor sqn.
MARITIME SECURITY AGENCY: (ε2,000);
1 *Alamgir* (US *Gearing* DD) (no *ASROC* ar TT), 4
Barakat PCC, 2 (Ch *Shanghai*) PFI.
COAST GUARD: some 23 PFI, plus boats.

SRI LANKA

GDP	1993: Rs 496.5bn ($10.27bn):
	per capita $3,100
	1994: Rs 537.4bn ($10.88bn):
	per capita $3,200

Growth	1993: 5.7%	1994: 5.9%
Inflation	1993: 11.7%	1994: 8.5%
Debt	1993: $6.78bn	1994: $7.20bn
Def exp	1993: Rs 24.05bn ($498m)	
	1994ε:Rs 25.52bn ($516m)	
Def bdgt	1995ε:Rs 30.12bn ($605m)	
FMA	1994: $0.1m (IMET)	
	1995: $0.1m (IMET)	
	1996: $0.2m (IMET)	
$1 = Rs	1993: 48.3	1994: 49.4
	1995: 49.7	

Rs = rupee

Population: 18,079,000 (Tamil 18%, Moor 7%)

	13–17	18–22	23–32
Men	929,600	840,600	1,530,800
Women	891,600	813,400	1,516,400

TOTAL ARMED FORCES:
ACTIVE: some 125,300 (incl recalled reservists).
RESERVES: Army 1,100; Navy 1,100; Air Force
2,000. Obligation: 7 years post-regular service.

ARMY: 105,000 (incl 42,000 recalled reservists).
3 div, 4 task force HQ.
1 mech inf bde.
1 air mobile bde.
23 inf bde.
1 indep SF bde (1 cdo, 1 SF regt).
1 armd regt.
3 armd recce regt (bn).
4 fd arty (1 reserve), 4 fd engr regt (1 reserve).
EQPT:
MBT: 25 T-55.
RECCE: 26 *Saladin*, 15 *Ferret*, 12 Daimler *Dingo*.
AIFV: 15 BMP (trg).
APC: 35 Ch Type-85, 10 BTR-152, 31 *Buffel*, 30
Unicorn, 8 Shorland, 9 *Hotspur*, 30 *Saracen*.
TOWED ARTY: 76mm: 14 Yug M-48; **85mm:** 12 Ch
Type-56; **88mm:** 12 25-pdr; **130mm:** 12 Ch Type-59-1.
MRL: 107mm: 1.
MOR: 81mm: 276; **82mm:** 19; **107mm:** 12; **120mm:**
36 M-43.
RCL: 105mm: 15 M-65; **106mm:** 34 M-40.
AD GUNS: 40mm: 7 L-40; **94mm:** 3 3.7-in.

NAVY: 10,300 (incl 1,100 recalled reservists).
BASES: Colombo (HQ), Trincomalee (main base),
Karainagar, Tangalle, Kalpitiya, Galle, Welisara.
PATROL AND COASTAL COMBATANTS: 40:
PATROL, COASTAL: 1 *Jayesagara* PCC.
PATROL, INSHORE: 39:
4 *Sooraya*, 2 *Rana* (Ch MOD *Shanghai* II) PFI.
11 Is *Dvora* PFI⟨.
3 S. Korean *Killer* PFI⟨.
19 PCI⟨, plus some 30 boats.
AMPH: craft only: 3 LCM (1 non-op), 2 fast personnel carrier.
SPT AND MISC: 2 *Abheetha* spt/cmd.

AIR FORCE: 10,000; 27 cbt ac, 26 armed hel.
Flying hours: 420.
FGA: 4 F-7M.
COIN: 8 SF-260TP, 3 FMA IA58A *Pucar*⟨.
ATTACK HEL: 12 Bell 212, 4 Bell 412.
MR: 1 sqn with **ac:** 6 Cessna 337; **hel:** 2 SA-365.
TPT: 1 sqn with 3 BAe 748, 1 Cessna 421C, 1 *Super
King Air*, 3 Ch Y-8, 9 Y-12, 3 AN-2.
HEL: 9 Bell 206, 6 Mi-17.
TRG: incl 3 Cessna 150, 4 DHC-1, 2* FT-5, 1* FT-7,
8* SF-260 MB.

RESERVES: Air Force Regt, 3 sqn; Airfield
Construction Regt, 1 sqn.

PARAMILITARY:
POLICE FORCE (Ministry of Defence): 80,000
incl reserves and 1,000 women. Total incl Special Task

Force: 3,000-man anti-guerrilla unit.
NATIONAL GUARD: ε15,000.
HOME GUARD: 15,200.

OPPOSITION:
**LIBERATION TIGERS OF TAMIL EELAM
(LTTE):** Leader: Velupillai Prabhakaran; ε4,000
active, plus 3,000 spt and log.

TAJIKISTAN

GDP[a]	1993ε: r 631.7bn ($2.5bn)	
	per capita $1,700	
	1994ε: r n.k. ($2.2bn)	
	per capita $1,400	
Growth	1993ε: -28%	1994ε: -15%
Inflation	1993ε: 2,195%	1994ε: 1,500%
Debt	1993: $41.5m	1994: $45.1m
Def exp[a]	1993ε: r 31.6bn ($126m)	
Def bdgt[a]	1994ε: r 34.7bn ($68m)	
	1995: r 73.8bn ($67m)	
$1 = Tr[b]	1995ε: 51	
r = rouble		
Tr = Tajik rouble		

[a] PPP est.
[b] The Tajik rouble was introduced in May 1995 replacing the old
Russian rouble and valued initially at 1 Tr = 100 roubles.

Population: 6,002,000 (Uzbek 25%, Russian 4%, Tatar 2%)

	13–17	18–22	23–32
Men	339,800	272,000	421,000
Women	331,000	264,000	419,000

TOTAL ARMED FORCES
ACTIVE: some 2–3,000.
Tajikistan has not yet formed any mil units. A number
of potential officers are being trained at the Higher
Army Officers and Engineers College, Dushanbe. It is
planned to form an Air Force sqn and to acquire Su-25
from Belarus. 5 Mi-24 and 10 Mi-8 have been procured.

PARAMILITARY:
BORDER GUARDS (Ministry of Interior): ε15,000.

OPPOSITION:
ISLAMIC MOVEMENT OF TAJIKISTAN.

FOREIGN FORCES:
RUSSIA:
ARMY: 12,000+. 1 MRD.

EQPT:
MBT: 180 T-72.
AIFV: 340 BMP-1, BTR-60/-70/-80.
TOTAL ARTY: 180:
TOWED: 122mm: D-30, M-1938.
SP: 122mm: 2S1; **152mm:** 2S3.
MRL: 122mm: 18 BM-21.
MOR: 120mm: 36 PM-38.
AD:
SAM: 15: SA-2/-3; 20 SA-8.
KAZAKHSTAN: ε500: 1 border gd bn.

TURKMENISTAN

GDP	1993ε: r 5,584bn ($6.0bn)	
	per capita $4,400	
	1994ε: m n.k. ($5.8bn)	
	per capita $4,300	
Growth	1993ε: -8.0%	1994ε: -5.0%
Inflation	1993ε: 3,102%	1994ε: 2,001%
Debt	1993: $9.7m	1994ε: $890.0m
Def exp[a]	1993ε: r 69bn ($74m)	
Def bdgt	1994ε: m 1,380m ($65m)	
	1995ε: m 4,588m ($61m)	
FMA	1994: $0.05m (IMET)	
	1995: $0.05m (IMET)	
	1996: $0.20m (IMET)	
$1 = m	1994ε: 75	1995ε: 230
r = rouble		
m = manat[b]		

[a] PPP est.
[b] The manat was introduced in November 1993 replacing the Russian rouble.

Population: 4,124,000 (Russian 10%, Uzbek 9%, Kazakh 2%)

	13–17	18–22	23–32
Men	224,800	191,200	315,600
Women	221,000	189,400	310,200

FORCES UNDER JOINT CONTROL:
TURKMENISTAN/RUSSIA:
ARMY: 11,000.
3 MRD (1 trg).
1 arty bde.
1 MRL regt.
1 atk regt.
1 engr bde.
1 indep hel sqn.
EQPT:
MBT: 530 T-72.
RECCE: 14 BRDM-2.
AIFV: 250 BMP-1, 288, BMP-2, 51 BRM.
APC: 344 BTR, 199 BTR-70.

TOWED ARTY: 122mm: 197 D-30; **152mm:** 76 D-1, 72 2A65.
SP ARTY: 152mm: 16 2S3.
COMBINED GUN/MOR: 120mm: 12 2S9.
MRL: 122mm: 60 BM-21; **220mm:** 54 9P140.
MOR: 82mm: 31; **120mm:** 42 PM-38.
ATGW: AT-2 *Swatter*, AT-3 *Sagger*, AT-4 *Spigot*, AT-5 *Spandrel*.
ATK GUNS: 85mm: 6 D-44; **100mm:** 48 MT-12.
AD GUNS: 23mm: 28 ZSU-23-4 SP; **57mm:** 22 S-60.

NAVY: none. Has announced intention to form a Navy/ Coast Guard. Caspian Sea Flotilla (see Russia) is operating as a joint Russian, Kazakhstan and Turkmenistan flotilla under Russian comd based at Astrakhan.

AIR FORCE: 171 cbt ac (plus 218 in store).
FGA/FTR: 1 composite regt with 22 MiG-29, 2 MiG-29U, 65 Su-17.
FTR: 2 regt with 48 MiG-23, 10 MiG-23U 24 MiG-25.
TRG: 1 unit with 3 Su-7B, 3 MiG-21, 2 L-39, 8 Yak-28, 3 An-12.
TPT/GENERAL PURPOSE: 1 composite sqn with 1 An-24, 10 Mi-24, 10 Mi-8.
SAM: 50: SA-2/-3/-5.
IN STORE: 172 MiG-23, 46 Su-25.

UZBEKISTAN

GDP[a]	1993ε: r 4,428.1bn ($13.8bn)	
	per capita $2,600	
	1994ε: s n.k. ($13.8bn)	
	per capita $2,600	
Growth	1993ε: -2.4%	1994: -2.6%
Inflation	1993ε: 885%	1994: 423%
Debt	1993: $238.0m	1994ε: $554.0m
Def exp[a]	1993ε: r 110bn ($344m)	
Def bdgt[a]	1994ε: s n.k. ($325m)	
	1995: s 8.69bn ($315m)	
FMA	1995: $0.05m (IMET)	
	1996: $0.30m (IMET)	
$1 = s	1994ε: 25	1995ε: 28
r = rouble		
s = sum [b]		

[a] PPP est.
[b] The Uzbek sum was introduced in July 1994 replacing the sum coupon and Russian rouble.

Population: 23,028,000 (Russian 8%, Tajik 5%, Kazakh 4%, Tatar 2%, Karakalpak 2%)

	13–17	18–22	23–32
Men	1,274,200	1,060,000	1,701,600
Women	1,255,000	1,047,200	1,715,400

TOTAL ARMED FORCES: 25,000 (incl

MOD staff and centrally controlled units).
Terms of service: conscription, 18 months.

ARMY: some 20,400.
1 Corps HQ.
3 MR bde.
1 AB bde
1 SF bde.
1 tk regt.
1 arty bde.
2 arty regt.
EQPT:
MBT: 179 T-62.
RECCE: 21 BRDM-2.
AIFV: 97 BMP-2, 110 BMD-1.
APC: 11 BTR-70, 95 BTR-80, 70 BTR-D.
TOTAL ARTY: 325:
TOWED ARTY: 122mm: 54 D-30, 36 D-1; **152mm:** 54 D-20, 36 2A36.
SP ARTY: 122mm: 18 2S1; **152mm:** 16 2S3.
COMBINED GUN/MOR: 120mm: 54 2S9.
MRL: 122mm: 21 BM-21.
MOR: 120mm: 18 PM-38, 18 2S12.

ATK GUNS: 100mm: 15 MT-12.
(In 1991 the former Soviet Union transferred some 2,000 tanks (T-64), 1,200 ACV and 750 arty pieces to open storage bases in Uzbekistan. This eqpt is under Uzbek control, but has deteriorated considerably.)

AIR FORCE: some 4,000; 126 cbt ac, 43 attack hel.
FGA: 30 Su-17, 22 Su-24.
FTR: 32 MiG-29, 32 Su-27.
RECCE: 10* Su-24.
TPT: 30 An-2, plus 20 light tpt ac.
HEL:
ATTACK: 43 Mi-24.
ASLT: 43 Mi-8T.
TPT: 23 Mi-6, 1 Mi-26.
RECCE: 6 Mi-24K, 2 Mi-24 R.
SAM: 45 SA-2/-3/-5.

PARAMILITARY: 16,000:
INTERNAL SECURITY TROOPS (Ministry of Interior): 15,300.
NATIONAL GUARD (Ministry of Defence): 700; 1 bde.

East Asia and Australasia

The two most serious developments in the region are North Korea's nuclear programme and the rising tension in the South China Sea.

Regional Cooperation

In January 1995, **Cambodia** obtained observer status and candidate membership of the Association of South-East Nations (ASEAN) when it agreed to adhere to its Treaty of Amity and Cooperation. In July, **Vietnam** became a full member of ASEAN, following a decision first taken in July 1994.

The South China Sea

The long-simmering dispute among the South-east Asian states and China for the territory and resources of the South China Sea took a turn for the worse when, for the first time, Chinese forces came into direct conflict with an ASEAN state. In January 1995, Chinese troops, said by Beijing to be fishermen, removed Filipino fishermen from Mischief Reef which lies within the Exclusive Economic Zone (EEZ) of the Philippines. In April, the Philippine Navy destroyed a number of Chinese markers on several other reefs, all closer to the Philippines than Mischief Reef, and arrested over 50 Chinese fishermen. In May, another confrontation between the Navy and Chinese fishing boats took place at Mischief Reef when the latter attempted to block a naval ship carrying a group of international journalists. Two Chinese frigates were also in the area at the time. The Philippines reinforced its forces by sending five F-5 aircraft to its airstrip on Thitu island. Various other claimants to the Spratly Islands, including Vietnam and Taiwan, were also engaged in incidents in the region. On 25 March, Taiwanese artillery fired on a Vietnamese supply ship close to Ban Than island where Taiwan had earlier begun construction work to which Vietnam had protested, asking the Taiwanese to leave. Indonesia, which had previously believed that China's claim in the Spratly Island area did not include their lucrative gas field near Natuna island, became concerned when China declined to confirm that it had no claim to Indonesian resources. While these infrequent clashes are worrying, the ability of regional claimants to sustain military operations in the Spratlys is extremely limited. Particularly lacking is in-flight refuelling capability, possessed only by China, naval afloat support, although this can be considered a luxury, and amphibious warfare shipping.

Sino-American Relations

Relations between China and the United States have also worsened. Trade disputes over intellectual property rights have been settled temporarily, but Beijing has been unable to ensure that all its citizens comply fully with the agreed terms. China was also unsuccessful in persuading the US to grant it favourable terms for membership of the World Trade Organisation. Human-rights issues also featured with China's arrest of Harry Wu, a former Chinese dissident with US citizenship. Various other issues continued to aggravate Sino-American relations, including China's continuing nuclear-weapon testing programme, uncertainty over its missile exports to Pakistan and Chinese nuclear assistance to Iran. China's most vituperative response to US policy came after the US Administration reversed in May 1995 its previous assurance that a visa would not be granted to the President of Taiwan for a private visit to the United States.

The Koreas

In February 1995, North Korea demanded the withdrawal of the Polish delegation to the Neutral Nations Supervisory Commission. The UN Forces Command protested, claiming that this was a violation of the 1953 Armistice Agreement. The other (originally communist) Czech delegation which operated in North Korea had been expelled in 1993. More recently, North Korean troops have openly violated the Demilitarised Zone (DMZ). North Korea withdrew from the Military

Armistice Commission (MAC) in April 1994 and persuaded the Chinese to withdraw in September. In June 1995, the North Korean government informed the UN Command that it would soon declare the Armistice Agreement null and void. These developments are striking when viewed in the context of a seemingly more accommodating approach by North Korea on the nuclear issue.

Internal Conflicts

Clashes between **Philippine** security forces and the insurgent Moro Islamic Liberation Front (MILF) continued throughout the second half of 1994 in the southern island of Mindanao. The worst incident occurred in April 1995 when the MILF launched a major attack on the town of Ipil, burning it down and killing over 40 people. In February 1995, MILF leaders claimed that they had some 120,000 active supporters organised in six divisions but admitted that, as yet, only half were armed. This may be an exaggerated claim, but MILF strength is certainly more than Vice-Chief of Staff General Alfredo Filler's claim of only 6,000. A Regional Army Commander covering three of Mindanao's 17 provinces reported 5,000 MILF in his region alone. In **Cambodia**, the Khmer Rouge continues to control some areas and to attack road and rail links.

On 5 June, a UN-sponsored meeting of **East Timorese** activists agreed on a common declaration calling for respect of human rights, and to hold further meetings. This was the result of an earlier meeting between Portugal, Indonesia and the UN in January 1995 when Indonesia announced that it would withdraw two of its seven battalions stationed in East Timor. In May 1995, **Papua New Guinea** announced an amnesty for all concerned in the civil war in Bougainville.

Nuclear Developments

China has carried out three further nuclear tests since its test on 10 June 1994. The first of these took place on 7 October 1994 and had an estimated yield of 40–150 kilotons. The second occurred on 15 May 1995, only 48 hours after the Nuclear Non-Proliferation Treaty (NPT) had been extended indefinitely. Its yield has also been estimated as being between 40 and 150 kilotons and the explosion measured 5.8 on the Richter Scale. The third took place on 17 August, measured 5.6 on the Richter Scale and is estimated as having a yield of between 20 and 80 kilotons. Chinese officials have said that more tests are planned before the Comprehensive Test Ban Treaty (CTBT) comes into force. While the continuation of Chinese testing was widely regretted, only Japan has taken action, cutting grant aid to China.

France has decided to resume nuclear testing at the Muroroa site. Australia and New Zealand have protested, freezing military cooperation and trade with France and Australia has withdrawn its Ambassador in Paris. French commandos boarded a Greenpeace ship on 9 July 1995 which had violated the 12-mile exclusion zone in the Pacific, ensuring maximum publicity for those opposed to testing.

Chemical Weapon Terrorism

The first recorded major attempt to use Chemical Weapons (CW) for terrorism was in Japan on 20 March 1995. A weak version of the nerve gas Sarin was released at five locations on the Tokyo underground railway system. Some 4,695 people were treated immediately after the event and four weeks later the death toll had reached 12. A sect known as *Aum Shinrikyo* is considered responsible for the attack and its leaders have been arrested. *Aum Shinrikyo* was also suspected of two earlier, similar, but less serious, incidents of gas attacks in 1994. Since the March attack, two devices containing chemicals which, when combined, form cyanide gas were discovered at railway stations in Japan on 4 and 5 July. There have been no 'copy-cat' incidents elsewhere in the world.

Missile Developments

It was reported in June 1995 that **China** had test-fired a new missile, said to be the DF-31, reportedly propelled by solid fuel and fired from a mobile launcher. Its range has been estimated

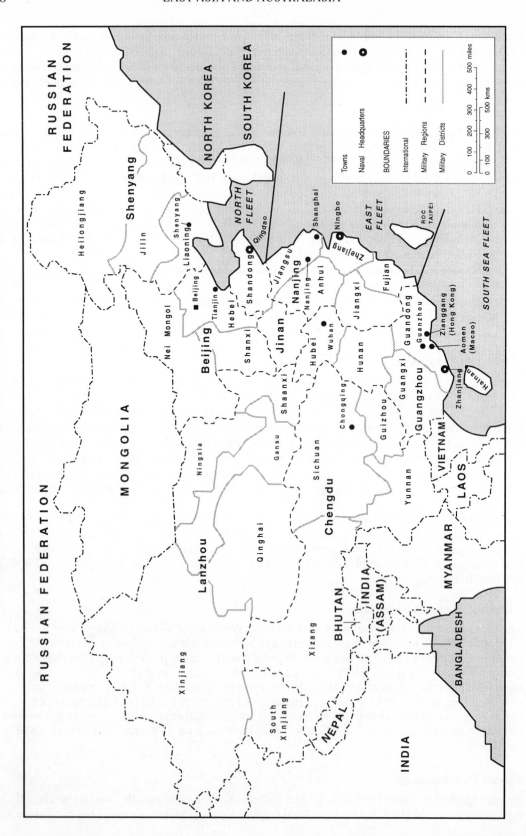

CHINESE MILITARY REGIONS AND DISTRICTS

as up to 8,000 km, bringing the US west coast and all of Europe within its scope. The CSS-5 (or DF-21) 1,800km-range ballistic missile is coming into service, and up to ten are already believed to have been operationally deployed. There are more CSS-4 (DF-5) ICBM deployed than the four listed for some years in *The Military Balance*. Some sources suggest as many as ten, but *The Military Balance* considers seven the correct number. In July 1995, China held a naval exercise north of Taiwan which included firing ballistic missiles on two days. Taiwan has taken this as a political display of Chinese strength.

On 20 February 1995, **North Korea** also tested a new ballistic missile. Whether this was a *No-Dong* or a *Taepo-Dong* is not clear, but according to South Korean sources, the tested missile could have a range of 1,500km, which suggests the latter. Although there has been one report that North Korea has deployed six operational *No-Dong* mobile launchers, *The Military Balance* has not listed these as a confirmed deployment.

Military Developments

Although **Australian** active Army strength has been reduced by some 4,000, it has acquired 12 more *Rapier* SAM launchers and four CH-47D *Chinook* transport helicopters. Australia is to build 30 1,200-ton corvettes of which 18 are destined for Malaysia.

Fresh information has allowed a reassessment of the **Chinese** Army (PLA) order of battle. The Navy has commissioned one more *Ming*-class and its first *Kilo*-class submarine; a second *Kilo* is due to be delivered by the end of 1995. Just how many *Kilos* have been ordered is uncertain. There will be no less than four, but the total could be much higher. The fourth *Jiangwei*-class frigate, three more *Houxin*-class missile craft and two more *Yukan*-class and the first of a new class, the *Yuting*, tank landing ships have been commissioned. Two *Jiangnan*-class frigates have been retired. China has bought 15 *Ilyushin* 76M transport aircraft from Uzbekistan, and China and Pakistan are jointly developing the FC-1 combat aircraft which is planned to have a capability similar to the US F-16. There is growing evidence that the Chinese Navy is now its paramount service.

The **Japanese** Self Defense Force (SDF) has acquired ten MLRS and introduced 120mm mortars and the Type-10 SAM. The Maritime SDF has commissioned its sixth *Harushio*-class submarine and its second *Kongo*-class destroyer. Four 8,900-ton amphibious ships with a lift capacity of 1,000 troops and tanks, and a helicopter and hovercraft capability, are to be built and are intended to support peacekeeping operations. The first is due to be delivered in 1998. For the second year running, orders for new aircraft and helicopters are large. The total for both 1994 and 1995 is: Army 63; Air Force 43; Navy 23. This includes four Boeing 767-200 AWACS aircraft for delivery in 1998 and 1999. The FS-X indigenous fighter programme continues with the first model due to fly in 1995. The original planned buy of 130 aircraft may be scaled down because of escalating cost.

The strength of the **North Korean** Air Force has been reassessed. It is now thought to have over 200 fewer aircraft than listed last year, but 30 more Mi-24 attack helicopters. The **South Korean** Army has acquired 200 more KIFV (indigenous infantry fighting vehicles), 16 more *Kooryong* 130mm, 36 tube MRL and ten more AH-1 *Cobra* attack helicopters. The Navy has commissioned its third *Chang Bogo*-class (German T-209/1200) submarine and one more *Po Hang*-class frigate, and has eight more P-3C ASW aircraft. The Air Force has taken delivery of the first 12 of an order for 120 F-16 aircraft.

The **Republic of China, Taipei**, Army has reduced its manpower strength by some 49,000 over the last 12 months. 20 M-60 tanks, 24 AH-1 *Cobra* attack helicopters and 12 OH-58D *Kiowa* armed scout helicopters have been acquired. The Navy has commissioned two more *Cheng Kung*-class frigates and leased three *Knox*-class frigates from the US. The first *Jin Chiang*-class missile craft, armed with four *Hsiung Feng* 1 SSM, has also been commissioned. It is planned to order ten more of this class. Four US *Aggressive*-class off-shore minesweepers have been acquired. The Air Force has retired 40 F-104 fighters and has added 38 more *Ching-Kuo* FGA/fighter aircraft to its inventory; the first of this indigenously produced aircraft came into service in 1994. A squadron of four E-2C *Hawkeye* AEW aircraft is now operational and four E-2D have been ordered.

The **Thai** Navy has commissioned one *Naresuan*-class frigate, the first of two being built in China, and has leased one US *Knox*-class frigate. The Navy has two more P-3A *Orion* maritime aircraft, and is taking delivery of 14 A-7E *Corsair* maritime attack aircraft during July 1995. The Air Force has retired its 15 A-37B COIN aircraft. It is reported that **Cambodia** is to take delivery of 40 Czech T-55 tanks in the near future. **Vietnam** has acquired six Russian Su-27 air-defence fighters. **Fiji** has taken delivery of two more Pacific Forum (*Kulu*-class) patrol craft built in Australia.

The **Malaysian** Army has taken delivery of 69 more KIFV. The original buy of KIFV has been deployed with the Malaysian battalion in Bosnia. The Navy has acquired a third US LST 511 and has leased from the US a *Newport*-class tank landing ship, thereby doubling its amphibious capability. The first of two UK-built frigates was launched in December 1994. The Air Force has taken delivery of 12 more *Hawk* 208 FGA aircraft. The last of 18 MiG-29 aircraft was delivered in July 1995 and six CN 235 transport aircraft were ordered from Indonesia. In **Singapore**, the first of six *Fearless*-class patrol ships has been launched; a second batch of six may be armed with SSM. The second Swedish-designed (*Landsort*), Singaporean-built, *Bedok*-class mine-hunter has been commissioned. There are suggestions that Singapore is to buy a number (four and six have been mentioned) of redundant Type 206 submarines from Germany. Delivery is unlikely before 1997–98, and then only if agreement can be reached on performance guarantees and a support package including training. The **Brunei** Army has recruited an extra 500 men. **Indonesia** has acquired 26 British *Scorpion* light tanks plus eight APC variants. 24 *Hawk* 100/200 are on order for delivery in 1996–97 and 20 MD3-160 trainers have been ordered from Malaysia.

Defence Spending

The *Military Balance 1993–1994* included a loose wall-map with statistics showing the marked rise in defence capability of several countries in the region since the 1985 benchmark. This trend is set to continue in 1995. The IISS estimates that regional defence spending increased by about 9% in real terms between 1992 and 1994. For 1995, defence budgets denominated in national currency show a 6% nominal rise before discounting for inflation. By comparison, the same budgets show a 10% rise when measured in US dollars – the variation being a consequence of currency appreciation (particularly that of the Japanese yen) against the US dollar.

The most dramatic case concerns **Japan** itself. Although the 1995 defence budget denominated in yen increases by less than 1% over 1994, its dollar rises by over one-fifth at the April 1995 exchange rate (from $46bn to $56bn). By comparison, the 1995 defence spending of France and the UK is $37bn and $34bn respectively. With the possible exception of Russia, Japan now spends appreciably more on defence than any other country apart from the US. This first became apparent in 1993 when Japan exceeded the defence expenditures of Germany, France and the UK, and since then the spending gap measured in US dollars has quickly widened.

The weakness of the US dollar has been accompanied by a strengthening of several other currencies (notably in **New Zealand**, **South Korea**, **Malaysia** and **Singapore**). One of the consequences of such currency appreciation is that the external purchasing power of defence budgets increases. It would be incorrect, however, to see in these increasing levels of defence expenditure an arms race threatening regional stability. In several cases, strong and sustained economic performance has allowed for increased investment in non-offensive defence and security. **China** is the possible exception, as a separate commentary suggests. The economic growth trend in the immediate future is likely to be similar to recent years, and the Organisation for Economic Cooperation and Development (OECD) projects strong regional economic performance over 1995–96, with only some moderation of recent very high rates.

China and the five countries with the most dynamic economies (**South Korea, Malaysia, Singapore, Taiwan** and **Thailand**) have projected real growth rates of 6–10%, well above the global trend for both industrialised and developing countries. The underlying upward regional trend in defence spending is most marked for this grouping. In 1995, **South Korea's** defence budget increased from $13.3bn to $14.4bn. **Malaysia's** budget for 1995 is $2.4bn; final out-turn figures for 1994 have not yet been released, but it is reported that the 1994 manpower budget was cut by 6% to accommodate a 27% increase in the procurement budget for arms purchases. **Singapore**, which increases its budget by over 20% from $3.1bn to $4.0bn, has the largest per capita increase. **Thailand's** spending is to rise from $3.6bn to $4.0bn. Excluding the special appropriations for F-16 and Mirage 2000 acquisition, **Taiwan's** budget declines from $9.9bn in 1994 to $9.6bn in 1995 before returning to the $9.9bn level in 1996.

Indonesia's budget increases from $2.3bn to $2.6bn with procurement rising from $530m to $600m. The **Philippines** defence budget for 1995 is $1bn, and is to be supplemented by funds from the 15-year Armed Forces' Modernisation Plan. The first tranche of $1.9bn over the next five years was approved in 1995.

Despite the **Japanese** government's claim that defence spending amounts to no more than 1% of gross domestic product (GDP), some independent analysts believe that the defence budget excludes items which would be classified as military expenditure under NATO definitions – and whose inclusion would raise defence spending to around 1.5% of GDP. Categories of expenditure which may qualify as military include pensions for the Japanese Imperial Army, dual-use Research and Development in aerospace and other advanced technology sectors, and the Maritime Safety Agency.

AUSTRALIA

GDP	1993: $A 415.7bn ($396.2bn):
	per capita $17,600
	1994: $A 442.6bn ($415.7bn):
	per capita $18,400

Growth	1993: 4.0%	1994: 4.9%
Inflation	1993: 1.8%	1994: 1.9%
Publ Debt	1993: 30.7%	1994: 35.0%
Def exp	1993: $A 10.95bn ($7.45bn)	
	1994: $A 10.22bn ($7.47bn)	
Def bdgt	1994: $A 9.67bn ($7.08bn)	
	1995: $A 9.99bn ($7.35bn)	
$1 = $A	1993: 1.47	1994: 1.37
	1995: 1.36	

$A = Australian dollar

Population: 18,240,000 (Aborigines ⟨1%⟩)

	13–17	18–22	23–32
Men	664,200	695,800	1,530,000
Women	624,400	663,600	1,474,000

TOTAL ARMED FORCES:
ACTIVE: 56,100 (incl ε7,200 women).
RESERVES: 38,250 (incl Standby Reserve).
READY RESERVE: 2,750: Army 2,450; Navy 100; Air Force 200.
GENERAL RESERVE: 25,400: Army 22,850; Navy 1,300; Air Force 1,250.
STANDBY RESERVE: 10,100: Army 3,600; Navy 3,550; Air Force 2,950.

ARMY: 23,700 (incl ε2,600 women).
1 Land HQ, 1 northern comd.
1 inf div, 2 bde HQ.
1 armd regt HQ (1 active, 2 reserve sqn).
1 recce regt (2 sqn).
1 APC sqn.
4 inf bn (incl 1 AB, 1 mech, 1 more forming).
2 arty regt (1 fd, 1 med (each 2 bty)).
1 AD regt (2 bty), 1 indep AD bty.
2 cbt engr regt.
1 SF regt (3 sqn).
2 avn regt.
RESERVES:
READY RESERVE: 2,450: 1 bde HQ, 2 recce sqn, 1 armd sqn, 3 inf bn, 1 fd arty regt, 1 engr regt.
GENERAL RESERVE: 22,850: 1 div HQ, 7 bde HQ, 1 armd sqn, 1 APC regt, 2 APC sqn, 2 recce regt, 1 recce sqn, 1 APC/recce regt, 14 inf bn, 1 cdo (2 coy), 4 arty regt (3 fd, 1 med), 4 indep arty bty, 4 engr (1 fd, 1 spt, 2 construction) regt, 4 indep fd engr sqn, 3 regional surv units.
EQPT:
MBT: 90 *Leopard* 1A3 (excl variants).
AIFV: 47 M-113 with **76mm** gun.
APC: 724 M-113 (incl variants, 119 in store), 15 LAV.
TOWED ARTY: 105mm: 246 M2A2/L5, 104 *Hamel*; **155mm:** 33 M-198.
MOR: 81mm: 302.
ATGW: 10 *Milan*.
RCL: 84mm: 608 *Carl Gustav*; **106mm:** 67 M-40A1.
SAM: 31 *Rapier*, 19 RBS-70.
AC: 22 GAF N-22/-24 *Missionmaster*.
HEL: 38 S-70 A-9 (Army/Air Force crews), 45 OH-58 *Kalkadoon*, 25 UH-1H (armed), 18 AS-35OB, 4 CH-47D.
MARINE: 15 LCM, 53 LARC-5 amph craft.

SURV: RASIT (veh, arty); AN-TPQ-36 (arty, mor).

NAVY: 15,000 (incl 900 Fleet Air Arm, 1,950 women).
Maritime Comd, Support Comd, 6 Naval Area comd.
BASES: Sydney, NSW (Maritime Comd HQ). Base
for: 1 SS (on occasion), 3 DDG, 5 FF, 1 patrol, 1
LST, 1 AOR, 2 LCT.
Cockburn Sound, WA. Base for: 4 SS, 3 FF, 3
patrol, 1 survey, 1 AOR.
Cairns, Qld. Base for: 5 patrol, 1 survey, 2 LCT.
Darwin, NT. Base for: 6 patrol, 1 LCT.
SS: 4 *Oxley* (mod UK *Oberon*) (incl 1 in refit) with Mk
48 HWT and *Harpoon* SSM (plus 1 alongside trg).
PRINCIPAL SURFACE COMBATANTS: 11 (incl 2
at 14 days' notice for ops):
DD: 3 *Perth* (US *Adams*) DDG with 1 SM-1 MR
SAM/*Harpoon* SSM launcher; plus 2 x 3 ASTT (Mk
46 LWT), 2 x 127mm guns.
FF: 8:
6 *Adelaide* (US *Perry*), with S-70B-2 *Sea Hawk*, 2 x 3
ASTT; plus 1 x SM-1 MR SAM/*Harpoon* SSM launcher.
2 *Swan* with 2 x 3 ASTT; plus 2 x 114mm guns.
PATROL AND COASTAL COMBATANTS: 16:
PATROL, INSHORE: 16:
15 *Fremantle* PFI.
1 *Banks* PCC (reserve trg).
MCM: 6:
2 *Rushcutter* MHI.
2 *Bandicoot* and 2 *Brolga* auxiliary MSI.
AMPH: 1 *Tobruk* LST, capacity 22 tk, 378 tps, hel
deck. Plus craft: 3 *Balikpapan* LCT, capacity 3 tk
(plus 3 in store).
(Plus 2 ex-US *Newport*-class LST under conversion,
no beach landing capability and equipping for 6
Army *Blackhawk* hel.)
SPT AND MISC: 9:
1 *Success* (mod Fr *Durance*), 1 *Westralia* AO, 1
Protector sub trials and safety, 2 AGHS, 4 small AGHS.
FLEET AIR ARM: (900); no cbt ac, 23 armed hel.
ASW: 1 hel sqn with 7 *Sea King* Mk 50/50A, 1 hel sqn
with 16 S-70B-2.
UTILITY/SAR: 1 sqn with 6 AS-350B, 3 Bell 206B
and 2 BAe-748 (EW trg).
SURVEY: 1 F-27.

AIR FORCE: 17,425 (incl 2,700 women); 125
cbt ac incl MR, no armed hel. Flying hours: F-111,
200; F/A-18, 175.
FGA/RECCE: 2 sqn with 17 F-111C, 15 F-111G, 4
RF-111C.
FTR/FGA: 3 sqn with 52 F-18 (-A: 50; -B: 2).
OCU: 1 with 18* F-18B.
TAC TRG: 1 sqn with 16 MB-326H, 2 PC-9A.
MR: 2 sqn with 19 P-3C.
FAC: 1 fleet with 4 PC-9.

TKR: 4 Boeing 707-32OC.
TPT: 7 sqn:
2 with 24 C-130 (-E: 12; -H: 12).
1 with 5 Boeing 707 (4 fitted for air-to-air refuelling).
2 with 14 DHC-4 (*Caribou*).
1 VIP with 5 *Falcon*-900.
1 with 10 HS-748 (8 for navigation trg, 2 for VIP tpt).
TRG: 56 PC-9, 12 MB-326.
SPT: 4 *Dakota*, 2 *Nomad*.
AD: *Jindalee* OTH radar: 1 experimental, 3 planned.
3 control and reporting units (1 mobile).
MSL:
ASM: AGM-84A.
AAM: AIM-7 *Sparrow*, AIM-9M *Sidewinder*.

FORCES ABROAD:
Advisers in Fiji, Indonesia, Solomon Islands, Thailand,
Vanuatu, Tonga, W. Samoa, Kiribati.
MALAYSIA: Army: 1 inf coy (on 3-month rotational
tours); Air Force: det with 2 P-3C ac.
PAPUA NEW GUINEA: 100; trg unit, 2 engr unit, 75
advisers.
UN AND PEACEKEEPING:
CYPRUS (UNFICYP): 20 civ pol. **EGYPT** (MFO): 26
Obs. **MIDDLE EAST** (UNTSO): 13 Obs. **RWANDA**
(UNAMIR): 301.

PARAMILITARY:
AUSTRALIAN CUSTOMS SERVICE: ac: 3
Seascan, 3 *Nomad*, 11 *Strike Aerocommander 500*;
hel: 4 AS-350; about 6 boats.

FOREIGN FORCES:
US: 370. Air Force: 270; Navy: 100; joint facilities at
NW Cape, Pine Gap and Nurrungar.
NEW ZEALAND: Air Force: 90; 6 A-4K/TA-4K
(providing trg for Australian Navy).
SINGAPORE: (160) Flying Training School with
27 S-211 **ac**.

BRUNEI

GDP	1993: $B 8.1bn ($5.0bn)		
	per capita $6,600		
	1994ε: $B 8.2bn ($5.3bn):		
	per capita $6,700		
Growth	1993ε: 4%		1994ε: 4%
Inflation	1993ε: 2.0%		1994ε: 2.5%
Debt	1993ε: $0.0		1994ε: $0.0
Def exp	1993ε: $B 348m ($212m)		
	1994: $B 371m ($239m)		
Def bdgt[a]	1995ε: $B 70m ($48m)		
$1 = $B	1993: 1.64		1994: 1.55
	1995: 1.45		

$B = Brunei dollar

[a] Excl procurement budget.

Population: 295,000 (Malay 64%, expatriates ε29%, Chinese 20%, non-Muslim indigenes and other 16%)

	13–17	18–22	23–32
Men	13,600	12,600	27,800
Women	14,000	12,800	22,200

TOTAL ARMED FORCES (all services

form part of the Army; Malays only eligible for service):
ACTIVE: 4,900 (incl 250 women).
RESERVES: Army 700.

ARMY: 3,900.
3 inf bn.
1 armd recce sqn.
1 SAM bty: 2 tps with *Rapier*.
1 SF sqn.
1 engr sqn.
EQPT:
LT TK: 16 *Scorpion*.
APC: 22 VAB.
MOR: 81mm: 24.
SAM: 12 *Rapier* (with *Blindfire*).

RESERVES: 1 bn (forming).

NAVY: 700.
BASE: Muara.
PATROL AND COASTAL COMBATANTS: 6†:
MSL CRAFT: 3 *Waspada* PFM with 2 x MM-38 *Exocet* SSM.
PATROL, INSHORE: 3 *Perwira* PFI⟨.
RIVERINE: 3 *Rotork* Marine FPB plus boats.
AMPH: craft only: 2 LCM⟨.

AIR FORCE: 300; 2 cbt ac, 6 armed hel.
COIN: 1 sqn with 6 Bo-105 armed hel (81mm rkts).
HEL: 1 sqn with 10 Bell 212, 1 Bell 214 (SAR).
MARITIME: 3 CN-235, 1 S-70 *Blackhawk*.
SULTAN'S FLT: 1 A-320 *Airbus*, 1 B747-400, 1 B727-200, 2 *Gulfstream* IV hel, 1 S-76, 1 S-70A.
VIP TPT: 2 S-70 hel, 2 Bell 214ST.
TRG: ac: *2 SF-260W (COIN, trg); **hel:** 2 Bell 206B.

PARAMILITARY:
GURKHA RESERVE UNIT: 2,300+; 2 bn.
ROYAL BRUNEI POLICE: 1,750; 7 PCI⟨.

FOREIGN FORCES:
UK: some 900 (Army): 1 Gurkha inf bn, 1 hel flt.
SINGAPORE: ε500: trg school incl hel det (5 UH-1).

CAMBODIA

GDP	1993: r 5,414bn ($2.4bn):		
	per capita $520		
	1994ε: r 7,020bn ($2.6bn):		
	per capita $590		
Growth	1993: 5.7%		1994: 7.5%
Inflation	1993: 41%		1994: 9%
Debt	1993: $383m		1994: $124m
Def exp	1993ε: r 181bn ($64m)		
Def bdgt	1994: r 164bn ($61m)		
	1995: r 220bn ($84m)		
FMA[a]	1994: $0.1m (IMET)		
	$2.3m (Australia)		
	1995: $0.2m (IMET)		
	$3.8m (Australia)		
	1996: $3.3m (FMF, IMET)		
$1 = r	1993: 2,816		1994: 2,700
	1995: 2,609		

r = riel

[a] The reported costs of UNAMIC and UNTAC are $1.58bn for November 1991–December 1993, and $8.6m for 1994.

Population: 9,756,000 (Vietnamese 5%, Chinese 1%)

	13–17	18–22	23–32
Men	499,400	433,000	851,800
Women	490,800	424,800	873,000

TOTAL ARMED FORCES:
ACTIVE: some 88,500 (incl Provincial Forces).
Terms of service: conscription, 5 years; ages 18 to 35. Militia serve 3 to 6 months with Regulars.

ARMY: some 36,000.
6 Military Regions.
7 inf div.[a]
3 indep inf bde.
9 indep inf regt.
3 armd regt.
Some indep recce, arty, AD bn.
EQPT:
MBT: 250 T-54/-55, Ch Type-59.
LT TK: 10 PT-76.
APC: 210 BTR-60/-152, M-113, 40 OT-64 (SKOT).
TOWED ARTY: some 400: **76mm:** M-1942; **122mm:** M-1938, D-30; **130mm:** Type 59.
MRL: 107mm: Type-63; **122mm:** 8 BM-21; **132mm:** BM-13-16; **140mm:** 20 BM-14-16.

MOR: **82mm:** M-37; **120mm:** M-43; **160mm:** M-160.
RL: *Armbrust.*
RCL: **82mm:** B-10; **107mm:** B-11.
AD GUNS: **14.5mm:** ZPU 1/-2/-4; **37mm:** M-1939;
57mm: S-60.
SAM: SA-7.

ª Inf div strength est 5,000.

NAVY: ε2,000.
PATROL AND COASTAL COMBATANTS: 12:
2 Sov *Turya* PFI (no TT).
2 Sov *Stenka* PFI (no TT), about 2 Sov Zhuk PCI⟨
and about 4 Sov Shmel PCI⟨, 2 PCF and PCI⟨
plus boats.
AMPH: craft only: 3 Sov LCVP.

AIR FORCE: 500; 25 cbt ac†; no armed hel.
FTR: 19 MiG-21.
TPT: 3 An-24, 1 An-26, Tu-134.
HEL: 9 Mi-8/-17.
TRG: 6* L-39, 5 Tecnam P-92.

PROVINCIAL FORCES: some 50,000. Reports
of at least 1 inf regt per province, with varying number of
inf bn with lt wpn.

PARAMILITARY:
MILITIA: org at village level for local defence: ε10–20
per village. Not all armed.

OPPOSITION:
KHMER ROUGE (National Army of Democratic
Kampuchea): some 9,000 org in 25 'bde', plus 2
indep regt.

CHINA

GDPª		
	1993: Y 3,151.4bn ($473bn):	
	per capita $2,200	
	1994: Y 4,380.0bn ($509bn):	
	per capita $2,400	
Growth	1993: 13.0%	1994: 11.8%
Inflation	1993: 13.0%	1994: 21.8%
Debt	1993: $83.5bn	1994: $92.8bn
Def expᵇ	1993: $27.4bn	1994: $28.5bn
Def bdgtᶜ	1993: Y 43.2bn ($6.49bn)	
	1994: Y 55.1bn ($6.74bn)	
	1995: Y 63.1bn ($7.48bn)	
$1 = Y	1993: 5.76	1994: 8.62
	1995: 8.43	
Y = yuan		

ª Calculations of GDP using PPP give a larger GDP. An IMF
study est GDP at $1,413bn in 1991; other est for 1991 incl
$1,931bn (World Bank) and $3,439bn (Penn World Table).
ᵇ PPP est.
ᶜ Def bdgt shows official figures converted at market exchange rates.

Population: 1,201,248,000 (Tibetan and other non-
Han 9%)

	13–17	18–22	23–32
Men	48,432,000	57,360,200	122,784,800
Women	45,199,200	53,777,600	114,525,800

TOTAL ARMED FORCES:
ACTIVE: some 2,930,000 (perhaps 1,275,000
conscripts, some 136,000 women), being reduced.
Terms of service: selective conscription; Army, Marines
3 years; Navy, Air Force 4 years.
RESERVES: 1,200,000+ militia reserves being
formed on a province-wide basis.

STRATEGIC MISSILE FORCES:
OFFENSIVE: 90,000.
MSL: org in 6 bases (army level) with bde/regt incl 1
msl testing and trg regt; org varies by msl type.
ICBM: some 17:
7 CSS-4 (DF-5); mod tested with MIRV.
10+ CSS-3 (DF-4).
IRBM: some 70+.
60+ CSS-2 (DF-3), some updated.
ε10 CSS-5 (DF-21).
SLBM: 1*Xia* SSBN with 12 CSS-N-3 (J-1).
DEFENSIVE:
Tracking stations: Xinjiang (covers Central Asia)
and Shanxi (northern border).
Phased-array radar complex: ballistic-missile
early-warning.

ARMY: 2,200,000 (incl Strategic Rocket Units,
perhaps 1,075,000 conscripts) (reductions continue).
7 Mil Regions, 28 Mil Districts, 3 Garrison Comd.
24 Integrated Group Armies (GA, equivalent to
Western corps), org varies, normally with 3 inf
div, 1 tk, 1 arty, 1 AAA bde or 3 inf, 1 tk div, 1
arty, 1 AAA bde, cbt readiness category varies.
Summary of Cbt units:
Group Army: 73 inf div (incl 2 mech inf).
9 div (main force div with rapid-reaction role).
11 tk div, 13 tk bde.
5 arty div, 20 arty bde.
Independent: 5 inf div, 1 tk, 2 inf bde.
1 arty div, 3 arty bde.
4 AAA bde.
Local Forces (Garrison, Border, Coastal): 12 inf div, 4

inf bde, 87 inf regt.

Avn: 7 hel regt.

AB (manned by Air Force): 1 corps of 3 div. Spt tps, incl 50 engr, 50 sigs regt.

EQPT:

MBT: some 7,500–8,000: incl 700 T-34/85, some T-54, 6,000 Type-59, 200 Type-69I/-II (mod Type-59), some Type-79, Type-80, Type-85 IIM.

LT TK: 1,200 Type-63 amph, 800 Type-62.

AIFV/APC: 4,500 incl Type-63, YW-531C, Type-85, some Type-77 (BTR-50), Type-90, WZ-523, WZ-551.

TOWED ARTY: 14,500: **100mm:** Type-59 (fd/ATK); **122mm:** 6,000 Type-54, Type-60, Type-83, D-30; **130mm:** 1,000 Types-59/-59-1; **152mm:** Type-54, 1,400 Type-66, Type-83; **155mm:** ε30 WAC-21.

SP ARTY: 122mm: Type-54-1 (Type-531 chassis), Type-85; **152mm:** Type-83.

MRL: 3,800: **107mm:** Types-63 towed /-81 SP (being replaced by 122mm); **122mm:** Type-81, Type-83; **130mm:** Type-63, Type-70 SP, Type-82, Type-85; **140mm:** BM-14-16; **273mm:** Type-83; **284mm:** Type-74 minelayer; **320mm:** WS-1; **425mm:** Type-762 mine clearance.

MOR: 82mm: Type-53 (incl SP); **120mm:** Type-55 (incl SP); **160mm:** Type-56.

SSM: M-9 (CSS-6/DF-15) (range 600km), M-11 (CSS-7/DF-11) (range 120–150km).

ATGW: HJ-73 (*Sagger*-type), HJ-8 (*TOW*/Milan-type).

RCL: 75mm: Type-52, Type-56; **82mm:** Type-65.

RL: 90mm: Type-51.

ATK GUNS: 57mm: Type-55; **76mm:** Type-54; **100mm:** Type-73, Type-86.

AD GUNS: 15,000: incl **23mm:** (ZSU-23 type); **37mm:** Types-55/-65/-74, -63 twin SP; **57mm:** Types-59, -80 SP; **85mm:** Type-56; **100mm:** Type-59.

SAM: HN-5, HN-5A/-C (SA-7 type); HQ-61 twin SP.

SURV: Cheetah (arty), Type-378 (veh), RASIT (veh, arty).

HEL: 28 Mi-17, 20 S-70C-2, 25 Mi-8, 30 Z-9, 8 SA-342 (with *HOT*), 24 S-70.

UAV: *Chang Hong* 1, ASN-104/105.

RESERVES (undergoing major reorganisation on a provincial basis): perhaps 900,000; ε80 inf div.

DEPLOYMENT: (Group Army units only).

North-East: Shenyang MR (Heilongjiang, Jilin, Liaoning MD): 5 GA, 3 tk, 15 inf, 1 arty div.

North: Beijing MR (Beijing, Tianjin Garrison, Nei Monggol, Hebei, Shanxi MD): 6 GA, 2 tk, 20 inf, 2 arty, 2 AD div.

West: Lanzhou MR (incl Ningxia, Shaanxi, Gansu, Qinghai, Xinjiang, South Xingiang MD): 2 GA, 1 tk, 12 inf div.

South-West: Chengdu MR (incl Sichuan, Guizhou, Yunnan, Xizang MD): 2 GA, 7 inf, 1 arty div.

South: Guangzhou MR (Hubei, Hunan, Guangdong, Guangxi, Hainan): 2 GA, 6 inf, 3 AB (Air Force) div.

Centre: Jinan MR (Shandong, Henan MD): 4 GA, 2 tk, 13 inf, 1 arty div.

East: Nanjing MR (Shanghai Garrison, Jiangsu, Zhejiang, Fujian, Jiangxi, Anhui MD): 3 GA, 2 tk, 11 inf, 1 arty, 1 AD div.

NAVY: ε260,000 (incl 25,000 Coastal Regional Defence Forces, 25,000 Naval Air Force, some 5,000 Marines and some 40,000 conscripts).

SUBMARINES: 52:

STRATEGIC: 1 SSBN.

TAC: 50:

SSN: 5 *Han* with 533mm TT, 2 with 12 x C801 SSM.

SSG: 1 mod *Romeo* (Type ES5G), with 6 C-801 (YJ-6, *Exocet* derivative) SSM; plus 533mm TT.

SS: 44:

1 *Kilo*-class (Type EKM 877) with 533mm.

10 imp *Ming* (Type ES5E) with 533mm TT.

About 33 *Romeo* (Type ES3B)† with 533mm TT (probably some 50 additional *Romeo*-class non-op.)

OTHER ROLES: 1 *Golf* (SLBM trials).

PRINCIPAL SURFACE COMBATANTS: 50:

DDG: 18

1 *Luhu* with 4 x 2 C-801 SSM, 1 x 2 100mm gun, 2 Z-9A (Fr *Dauphin*) hel, plus 2 x 3 ASTT, 1 x 8 *Crotale* SAM.

2 mod *Luda*, 1 with 2 x 3 CSS-N-2 *Hai Ying-2* (HY-2 *Styx* derivative) and 1 with 4 x 2 C-801 SSM, 1 x 2 130mm guns, 2 Z-9A (Fr *Dauphin*) hel (OTHT), 2 x 3 ASTT, 1 x 8 *Crotale* SAM.

15 *Luda* (Type-051) (ASUW) with 2 x 3 HY-2 SSM, 2 x 2 130mm guns; plus 2 x 12 ASW RL.

FFG: 32:

4 *Jiangwei* with 2 x 3 C-801 SSM, 2 x 5 ASW RL, 1 x 2 100mm gun, 1 Z-9A (Fr *Dauphin*) hel.

About 26 *Jianghu*; 3 variants:

About 21 Type I, with 4 x 5 ASW RL, plus 2 x 2 HY-2 SSM, 2 x 100mm guns.

About 2 Type II, with 2 x 5 ASW RL, plus 2 x 2 HY-2, 2 x 2 100mm guns.

About 3 Type III, with 8 x C-801 SSM, 2 x 2 100mm guns; plus 4 x 5 ASW RL.

2 *Chengdu* with 1 x 2 HY-2 SSM, 3 x 100mm guns.

PATROL AND COASTAL COMBATANTS: about 870:

MSL CRAFT: 220:

1 *Huang* with 6 x C-801 SSM.

9 *Houxin* with 4 x C-801 SSM.

Some 120 *Huangfeng/Hola* (Sov *Osa-I*-type) with 6 or 8 x C-801 SSM; some with 4 x HY-2.

About 90 *Hegu/Hema*⟨ (Komar-Type) with 2 x HY-2 or 4 x C-801 SSM.

TORPEDO CRAFT: about 160:

100 *Huchuan*, some 60 P-6, all ⟨ with 2 x 533mm TT.

PATROL: about 495:

COASTAL: about 100:

4 *Haijui* with 3 x 5 ASW RL.

About 96 *Hainan* with 4 x ASW RL.
INSHORE: about 350:
300 *Shanghai*, 5 *Huludao* PFI, about 45 *Shantou*⟨.
RIVERINE: about 45⟨.
(Note: some minor combatants have reportedly been assigned to paramilitary forces (People's Armed Police, border guards, the militia) to the Customs Service, or into store. Totals, therefore, may be high.)
MINE WARFARE: about 121:
ML: 1 *Beleijan* reported. In addition, *Luda, Anshan, Jiangnan, Chengdu*-class DD/FF, *Hainan, Shanghai* PC and T-43 MSO have minelaying capability.
MCM: about 120:
35 Sov T-43 MSO.
1 *Wosao* MSC.
About 80 *Lienyun* aux MSC.
3 *Wochang* and 1 *Shanghai* II MSI; plus about 60 drone MSI⟨.
AMPH: 54:
5 *Yukan* LST, capacity about 200 tps, 10 tk.
13 *Shan* (US LST-1) LST, capacity about 150 tps, 16 tk.
1 *Yuting* LST.
30 *Yuliang*, 1 *Yuling*, 4 *Yudeng* LSM, capacity about 100 tps, 3 tk.
Plus about 400 craft: 320 LCU, 40 LCP, 10 LCT.
SPT AND MISC: about 164: 2 *Fuqing* AO, 33 AOT, 14 AF, 10 submarine spt, 1 sub rescue, 2 repair, 9 *Qiong Sha* tps tpt, 30 tpt, 33 survey/research/experimental, 4 icebreakers, 25 ocean tugs, 1 trg.
COASTAL REGIONAL DEFENCE FORCES:
(25,000).
ε35 indep arty and SSM regt deployed in 25 coastal defence regions to protect naval bases, offshore islands and other vulnerable points.
GUNS: 85mm, 100mm, 130mm.
SSM: CSS-C-2 (*Hai Ying 2* variant, *Silkworm*), some with *Hai Ying* 4/C-201.

MARINES (Naval Infantry): (some 5,000).
1 bde; special recce units.
RESERVES: on mob to total 8 div (24 inf, 8 tk, 8 arty regt), 2 indep tk regt. (3 Army div also have amph role.)
EQPT:
MBT: T-59.
LT TK: T-60/-63, PT-76.
APC: Type-531, LVT; some Type-77.
ARTY: how: **122mm:** Type-54 (incl -54-1 SP).
MRL: 107mm: Type-63.

NAVAL AIR FORCE: (25,000); 855 shore-based cbt ac, 68 armed hel. 3 bbr, 6 ftr div:
BBR: some 25 H-6, some H-6D reported with two C-601 anti-ship ALCM.
About 130 H-5 torpedo-carrying lt bbr.
FGA: some 100 Q-5.
FTR: some 600, incl J-5/-6/-7/-8.

RECCE: H-5.
MR/ASW: 15 ex-Sov Be-6 *Madge*, 5 PS-5 (SH-5).
HEL: ASW: 15 SA-321, 40 Z-5, 3 Z-8, 10 Z-9.
MISC: some 60 lt tpt ac incl Y-8; JJ-5/-6 trg ac.
ALCM: FL-1/C-601.
Naval fighters are integrated into the national AD system.

DEPLOYMENT AND BASES:
NORTH SEA FLEET: coastal defence from Korean border (Yalu River) to south of Lianyungang (approx 35°10'N); equates to Shenyang, Beijing and Jinan Military Regions, and to seaward.
BASES: Qingdao (HQ), Dalian (Luda), Huludao, Weihai, Chengshan.
9 coastal defence districts.
FORCES: 2 submarine, 3 escort, 1 mine warfare, 1 amph sqn; plus Bohai Gulf trg flotillas. About 300 patrol and coastal combatants.
EAST SEA FLEET: coastal defence from south of Lianyungang to Dongshan (approx 35°10'N to 23°30'N); equates to Nanjing Military Region, and to seaward.
BASES: Shanghai (HQ), Wusong, Dinghai, Hangzhou.
7 coastal defence districts.
FORCES: 2 submarine, 2 escort, 1 mine warfare, 1 amph sqn. About 250 patrol and coastal combatants.
Marines: 1 cadre div.
Coastal Regional Defence Forces: Nanjing Coastal District.
SOUTH SEA FLEET: coastal defence from Dongshan (approx 23°30'N) to Vietnamese border; equates to Guangzhou Military Region, and to seaward (including Paracel and Spratly Islands).
BASES: Zhanjiang (HQ), Shantou, Guangzhou, Haikou, Yulin, Beihai, Huangpu; plus outposts on Paracel and Spratly Islands.
9 coastal defence districts.
FORCES: 2 submarine, 2 escort, 1 mine warfare, 1 amph sqn. About 300 patrol and coastal combatants.
Marines: 1 bde.

AIR FORCE: 470,000 (incl strategic forces, 220,000 AD personnel and 160,000 conscripts); some 4,970 cbt ac, few armed hel.
7 Military Air Regions, HQ Beijing.
Combat elm org in armies of varying numbers of air div (each with 3 regt of 3 sqn of 3 flt of 4–5 ac, 1 maint unit, some tpt and trg ac); tpt ac in regt only.
MED BBR: 120 H-6 (some may be nuclear-capable). Some carry C-601 ASM.
LT BBR: some 300+ H-5 (some with C-801 ASM).
FGA: 400+ Q-5.
FTR: ε4,000, some 60 regt with about 400 J-5, 3,000 J-6/B/D/E, 500 J-7, 100 J-8, 22 Su-27, 4 Su-27B.
RECCE: ε40 HZ-5, 150 JZ-5, 100 JZ-6 ac.

TPT: some 600, incl 18 BAe *Trident* 1E/2E, 30 Il-14, 10 Il-18, 10 Il-76, 50 Li-2, 300 Y-5, 25 Y-7, 25 Y-8 (some tkr), 15 Y-11, 2 Y-12.
HEL: some 190: incl 6 AS-332, 4 Bell 214, 30 Mi-8, 100 Z-5, 100 Z-6, 15 Z-8, 50 Z-9.
TRG: incl CJ-5/-6, HJ-5, J-2, JJ-2, JJ-4/-5/-6.
MSL:
AAM: PL-2/-2A, PL-5B *Atoll*-type, PL-7, PL-8.
ASM: C-601 subsonic ALCM (anti-ship, perhaps HY-2 SSM derivative); C-801 surface skimmer.
AD ARTY: 16 div: 16,000 **35mm**, **57mm**, **85mm** and **100mm** guns; 28 indep AD regts (100 SAM units with HQ-2/-2B, -2J (CSA-1), -61 SAM, SA-10).

FORCES ABROAD:
UN AND PEACEKEEPING:
MIDDLE EAST (UNTSO): 4 Obs. **LIBERIA** (UNOMIL): 5 Obs. **IRAQ/KUWAIT** (UNIKOM): 15 Obs. **WESTERN SAHARA** (MINURSO): 20 Obs.

PARAMILITARY:
PEOPLE'S ARMED POLICE (Ministry of Defence): 600,000: 60 div, duties incl border and internal security (returned to PLA control June 1993).

FIJI

GDP	1993: $F 2.54bn ($1.65bn): per capita $4,800		
	1994: $F 2.66bn ($1.82bn): per capita $5,000		
Growth	1993: 1.8%	1994: 3.2%	
Inflation	1993: 5.2%	1994: 1.2%	
Debt	1993: $294m	1994: $310m	
Def exp	1993: $F 49.4m ($32m)		
	1994: $F 40.8m ($28m)		
Def bdgt	1995ε: $F 41.0m ($30m)		
$1 = $F	1993: 1.54	1994: 1.46	
	1995: 1.38		

$F = Fiji dollar

Population: 775,000 (Fijian 49%, Indian 46%)

	13–17	*18–22*	*23–32*
Men	46,600	39,000	60,400
Women	44,600	37,000	59,600

TOTAL ARMED FORCES:
ACTIVE: 3,900 (incl recalled reserves).
RESERVES: some 5,000 (to age 45).

ARMY: ε3,600 (incl Reserves).

7 inf bn (incl 4 cadre).
1 engr bn.
EQPT:
MOR: 81mm: 12.

NAVY: 300.
BASE: Suva.
PATROL AND COASTAL COMBATANTS: 9:
3 *Kulu* (*Pacific Forum*) PCI.
4 *Vai* (Is *Dabur*) PCI⟨.
2 *Levuka* PCI⟨.
SPT AND MISC: 2:
1 *Kiro* (US *Redwing*-class) trg.
1 *Cagidonu* presidential yacht (trg).

AIR WING:
1 AS-350 F-2, 1 SA-365N.

FORCES ABROAD:
UN AND PEACEKEEPING:
ANGOLA (UNAVEM III): 8 Obs. **EGYPT** (MFO): 340; 1 inf bn(-). **IRAQ/KUWAIT** (UNIKOM): 7 Obs. **LEBANON** (UNIFIL): 50; 1 inf bn. **RWANDA** (UNAMIR): 1 Obs.

INDONESIA

GDP	1993: Rp 302,018bn ($144.7bn): per capita $3,200		
	1994: Rp 354,824bn ($154.8bn): per capita $3,500		
Growth	1993: 6.5%	1994: 7.0%	
Inflation	1993: 9.7%	1994: 8.5%	
Debt	1993: $87.9bn	1994: $90.5bn	
Def exp[a]	1993: Rp 4,239.1bn ($2.03bn)		
Def bdgt	1994: Rp 5,008.1bn ($2.32bn)		
	1995: Rp 5,704.2bn ($2.57bn)		
FMA	1996: $0.6m (IMET)		
$1 = Rp	1993: 2,087	1994: 2,161	
	1995: 2,222		

Rp = rupiah

[a] Excl defence industrial funding.

Population: 192,543,000 (Javanese 45%, Sundanese 14%, Madurese 8%, Malay 8%, Chinese and other 26%)

	13–17	*18–22*	*23–32*
Men	11,130,200	9,925,200	15,501,400
Women	10,645,000	9,642,800	16,767,200

TOTAL ARMED FORCES:
ACTIVE: 274,500.

Terms of service: 2 years selective conscription authorised.

RESERVES: 400,000: Army: cadre units; numbers, strengths unknown, obligation to age 45 for officers.

ARMY: 214,000.

Strategic Reserve (KOSTRAD): (20,000):
- 2 inf div HQ.
- 3 inf bde (9 bn).
- 3 AB bde (9 bn).
- 2 fd arty regt (6 bn).
- 1 AD arty regt (2 bn).
- 2 engr bn.

10 Military Area Comd (KODAM): (190,500) (Provincial (KOREM) and District (KODIM)comd):
- 1 inf bde (3 bn).
- 59 inf bn (incl 4 AB).
- 8 cav bn.
- 11 fd arty, 10 AD bn.
- 8 engr bn.
- 1 composite avn sqn, 1 hel sqn.

SF (KOPASSUS): (3,500):
- 2 SF gp (each 2 bn).

EQPT:
LT TK: some 275 AMX-13, 30 PT-76, 26 *Scorpion* (being delivered).
RECCE: 69 *Saladin* (16 being upgraded), 55 *Ferret* (13 being upgraded).
APC: 200 AMX-VCI, 55 *Saracen* (14 being upgraded), 200 V-150 *Commando*, 22 *Commando Ranger*, 80 BTR-40, 14 BTR-50, 8 *Stormer* (incl 2 comd being delivered).
TOWED ARTY: 76mm: M48; **105mm:** 170 M-101, 10 M-56.
MOR: 81mm: 800; **120mm:** 75 Brandt.
RCL: 90mm: 90 M-67; **106mm:** 45 M-40A1.
RL: 89mm: 700 LRAC.
AD GUNS: 20mm: 125; **40mm:** 90 L/70; **57mm:** 200 S-60.
SAM: 51 *Rapier*, 42 RBS-70.
AC: 1 BN-2 *Islander*, 2 C-47, 4 NC-212, 2 Cessna 310, 2 *Commander* 680, 18 *Gelatik* (trg).
HEL: 9 Bell 205, 14 Bo-105, 3 NB-412, 10 Hughes 300C (trg).

NAVY: ε40,500 (incl ε1,000 Naval Air and 12,000 Marines).

PRINCIPAL COMD:
WESTERN FLEET (HQ Tanjung Priok (Jakarta)).
BASES: Jakarta, Belawan (Sumatra); Minor Facilities: Tanjung Pinang (Riau Is.), Sabang.
EASTERN FLEET (HQ Surabaya):
BASES: Surabaya, Ujung Pandang, Jayapura (Irian Jaya); Minor Facilities: Manado (Celebes), Ambon (Moluccas).

MILITARY SEALIFT COMD (KOLINLAMIL): controls some amph and tpt ships used for inter-island comms and log spt for Navy and Army (assets incl in Navy and Army listings).
SS: 2 *Cakra* (Ge T-209/1300) with 533mm TT (Ge HWT) (1 in long-term refit).
FF: 13:
6 *Ahmad Yani* (Nl *Van Speijk*) with 1 *Wasp* hel (ASW) (Mk 44 LWT), 2 x 3 ASTT; plus 2 x 4 *Harpoon* SSM.
3 *Fatahillah* with 2 x 3 ASTT (not *Nala*), 1 x 2 ASW mor, 1 *Wasp* hel (*Nala* only); plus 2 x 2 MM-38 *Exocet*, 1 x 120mm gun.
3 *M. K. Tiyahahu* (UK *Tribal*) with 1 *Wasp* hel, 1 x 3 *Limbo* ASW mor; plus 2 x 114mm guns.
1 *Hajar Dewantara* (Yug) (trg) with 2 x 533mm TT, 1 ASW mor; plus 2 x 2 MM-38 *Exocet*.
(Plus 4 *Samadikun* (US *Claud Jones*) with 2 x 3 ASTT (in reserve).)
PATROL AND COASTAL COMBATANTS: 44:
CORVETTES: 4 *Kapitan Patimura* (GDR Parchim) (plus 13 non-op and poss not delivered).
MSL CRAFT: 4 *Mandau* PFM with 4 x MM-38 *Exocet* SSM (possibly non-op).
TORPEDO CRAFT: 2 *Singa* (Ge Lürssen 57-m (NAV I)) with 2 x 533mm TT and 1 x 57mm gun.
PATROL CRAFT: 34:
COASTAL: 7:
2 *Pandrong* (Ge Lürssen 57-m (NAV II)) PFC, with 1 x 57mm gun.
2 *Barakuda* (Sov *Kronshtadt*)†.
3 *Kakap* (Ge Lürssen 57-m (NAV III)) PFC, with 40mm gun and hel deck.
INSHORE: 27:
8 *Sibarau* (Aust *Attack*) PCI, 1 *Bima Samudera* PHM, 18⟨.
MCM: 6:
2 *Pulau Rengat* (mod Nl *Tripartite*) MCC (mainly used for coastal patrol).
2 *Pulau Rani* (Sov *T-43*) MCC (mainly used for coastal patrol).
2 *Palau Rote* (Ge *Kondor* II) MSC (plus 7 non op; poss not all delivered yet).
AMPH: 14:
6 *Teluk Semangka* LST, capacity about 200 tps, 17 tk, 4 with 3 hel (2 fitted as comd ships and 1 as hospital ship).
1 *Teluk Amboina* LST, capacity about 200 tps, 16 tk.
7 *Teluk Langsa* (US LST-512) and 2 *Teluk Banten* (mod US LST-512) LST, capacity: 200 tps, 16 tks).
(3 *Teluk Gilimanuk* (Ge *Frosch I/II*) LST (plus 11 non-op, poss not all delivered) assigned to Military Sealift Comd.)
Plus about 80 craft, incl 4 LCU, some 45 LCM.
SPT AND MISC: 17:
1 *Sorong* AO, 1 *Arun* AO (UK *Rover*), 2 Sov *Khobi*

AOT, 1 cmd/spt/replenish, 1 repair, 4 tpt (Military Sea Lift Comd), 1 ocean tug, 6 survey/research.

NAVAL AIR: (ε1,000); 24 cbt ac, 14 armed hel.
ASW: 6 *Wasp* HAS-1 hel, 4 AS-332L.
MR: 9 N-22 *Searchmaster* B, 6 *Searchmaster* L, 6 CN-235-100 IPTN/CASA.
TPT: 4 *Commander*, 4 NC-212;
TRG: 2 *Bonanza* F33, 6 PA-38.
HEL: 4 NAS-332F, *4 NBo-105, 4 Bell-412.

MARINES: (12,000).
2 inf bde (6 bn).
1 SF bn(-).
1 cbt spt regt (arty, AD).
EQPT:
LT TK: 100 PT-76†.
RECCE: 14 BRDM.
AIFV: 10 AMX-10 PAC-90.
APC: 24 AMX-10P, 60 BTR-50P.
TOWED ARTY: 105mm: some LG-1 Mk II; **122mm:** 28 M-38.
MRL: 140mm: 15 BM-14.
AD GUNS: 40mm, 57mm.

AIR FORCE: 20,000; 73 cbt ac, no armed hel.
2 Air Operations Areas.
FGA: 4 sqn:
2 with 24 A-4 (22 -E, 2 TA-4H).
1 with 11 F-16 (7 -A, 4 -B).
1 with 14 I HAWK Mk 53 (FGA/trg).
FTR: 1 sqn with 12 F-5 (8 -E, 4 -F).
COIN: 1 sqn with 12 OV-10F.
MR: 1 sqn with 3 Boeing 737-200.
TKR: 2 KC-130B.
TPT: 19 C-130 (-B: 9; -H: 3; -H-30: 7), 1 L100-30. 1 Boeing 707, 5 Cessna 401, 2 Cessna 402, 7 F-27-400M, 1 F-28-1000, 10 NC-212, 1 *Skyvan* (survey), 6 CN-235M.
HEL: 3 sqn:
1 with 12 S-58T.
2 with 2 Bell 204B, 10 Hughes 500, 12 NSA-330.
TRG: 4 sqn with 40 AS-202, 2 Cessna 172, 22 T-34C, 6 T-41D.

AIRFIELD DEFENCE: 4 bn *Rapier*.

FORCES ABROAD:
UN AND PEACEKEEPING:
BOSNIA(UNPROFOR): 8 Obs. **CROATIA**(UNCRO): 252 incl 16 Obs plus 13 civ pol. **GEORGIA**(UNOMIG): 6 Obs. **IRAQ/KUWAIT** (UNIKOM): 6 Obs. **FYROM** (UNPREDEP): 1 Obs plus 2 civ pol.

PARAMILITARY:
POLICE (POLRI): some 174,000: incl 6,000 Police 'Mobile bde' (BRIMOB) org in coy, incl Police COIN unit (GEGANA); **ac:** 3 *Commander*, 1 Beech 18, 7 lt; **hel:** 10 Bo-105, 3 Bell 206.
MARINES: about 10 PCC, 9 PCI and 6 PCI⟨ (all armed).
KAMRA (People's Security): 1.5m: some 300,000 undergo 3 weeks' basic trg each year. Part-time police auxiliary.
WANRA (People's Resistance): part-time local military auxiliary force under Regional Military Comd (KOREM).
CUSTOMS: about 72 PFI⟨, armed.
SEA COMMUNICATIONS AGENCY (responsible to Department of Transport): 5 *Kujang* PCI, 4 *Golok* PCI (SAR), plus boats.

OPPOSITION:
FRETILIN (Revolutionary Front for an Independent East Timor): FALINTIL mil wing with some 170 incl spt; small arms.
FREE PAPUA MOVEMENT (OPM): perhaps 200–300 (100 armed).
FREE ACEH MOVEMENT (Gerakan Aceh Merdeka): 50 armed reported.

JAPAN

GDP	1993: ¥ 468,769bn ($4,216bn): per capita $20,700		
	1994: ¥ 469,300bn ($4,592bn): per capita $20,900		
Growth	1993: -0.2%	1994: 0.6%	
Inflation	1993: 1.2%	1994: 0.7%	
Publ Debt	1993: 75.1%	1994: 81.7%	
Def bdgt^a	1994: ¥ 4,683.5bn ($45.8bn)		
	1995: ¥ 4,723.6bn ($53.8bn)		
Request	1996: ¥ 4,860.6bn ($55.4bn)		
$1 = ¥	1993: 111	1994: 102	
	1995: 88		

¥ = yen

[a] See regional commentary.

Population: 125,213,000

	13–17	18–22	23–32
Men	4,139,000	4,813,200	9,078,200
Women	3,933,400	4,577,200	8,701,800

TOTAL ARMED FORCES:
ACTIVE: 239,500 (incl 160 Central Staffs (reducing), 9,500 women).

RESERVES: 47,900: Army 46,000; Navy 1,100;
Air Force 800.

ARMY (Ground Self-Defense Force): 151,200.
5 Army HQ (Regional Comds).
1 armd div.
12 inf div (6 at 7,000, 6 at 9,000 each).
2 composite bde.
1 AB bde.
1 arty bde; 2 arty gp.
2 AD bde; 4 AD gp.
4 trg bde (incl 1 spt); 2 trg regt.
5 engr bde.
1 hel bde.
5 ATK hel sqn.
EQPT:
MBT: some 1,160: some 190 Type-61 (retiring),
some 870 Type-74, some 100 Type-90.
RECCE: some 80 Type-87.
AIFV: some 40 Type-89.
APC: some 380 Type-60, some 310 Type-73, some
200 Type-82.
TOWED ARTY: some 500: **105mm:** some 110 M-101;
155mm: some 380 FH-70; **203mm:** some 10 M-115.
SP ARTY: 310: **105mm:** 20 Type-74; **155mm:** 200
Type-75; **203mm:** some 90 M-110A2.
MRL: 130mm: some 70 Type-75 SP; **227mm:** some
10 MLRS
MOR: some 1,360, incl **81mm:** 770 (some SP);
107mm: some 490 (some SP); **120mm:** some 100.
SSM: some 50 Type-88 coastal.
ATGW: some 220 Type-64, some 220 Type-79, some
180 Type-87.
RL: 89mm: some 2,970.
RCL: some 3,170: **84mm:** some 2,720 Carl Gustav;
106mm: some 450 (incl Type 60 SP).
AD GUNS: 90: **35mm:** some 50 twin, some 40 Type-87 SP.
SAM: 330 Stinger, some 60 Type 81, some 50 Type
91, some 10 Type 93, some 200 I HAWK.
AC: some 20 LR-1.
ATTACK HEL: some 80 AH-1S.
TPT HEL: 3 AS-332L (VIP), some 30 CH-47J, some
10 KV-107, some 180 OH-6D/J, some 130 UH-1H/J,
some TH-55 (trg).
SURV: Type-92 (mor), J/MPQ-P7 (arty).

NAVY (Maritime Self-Defense Force): 43,700 (incl
ε12,000 MSDF Air Arm and 3,000 women).
BASES: Yokosuka, Kure, Sasebo, Maizuru, Ominato.
Fleet: Surface units org into 4 escort flotillas of 8 DD/FF
each; 1 based at Yokosuka, 1 at Kare, 1 at Sasebo, 1 at
Maizuru. SS org into 2 flotillas based at Kure and Yokosuka.
Remainder assigned to 10 regional/district units.
SS: 18:
6 Harushio with 533mm TT (Jap Type-89 HWT)

with Harpoon USGW.
10 Yuushio with 533mm TT (Jap Type-89 HWT), 7
with Harpoon USGW.
2 Uzushio (trg).
PRINCIPAL SURFACE COMBATANTS: 63:
DDG: 8:
2 Kongo with 2 x VLS for Standard SAM and ASROC
SUGW (29 cells forward, 61 cells aft); plus 2 x 4
Harpoon SSM, 2 x 3 ASTT and hel deck.
2 Hatakaze with 1 x SM-1-MR Mk 13 SAM; plus
2 x 4 Harpoon SSM, 1 x 8 ASROC SUGW (Mk
46 LWT) 2 x 3 ASTT, 2 x 127mm guns.
3 Tachikaze with 1 x SM-1-MR; plus 1 x 8 ASROC,
2 x 3 ASTT, 2 x 127mm guns.
1 Amatsukaze with 1 x SM-1-MR; plus 1 x 8
ASROC, 2 x 3 ASTT, 2 x 76mm guns.
FRIGATES: 55 (incl 1 trg):
FFH: 24:
2 Shirane with 3 x SH-60J ASW hel, 1 x 8
ASROC, 2 x 3 ASTT; plus 2 x 127mm guns.
2 Haruna with 3 x SH-60J hel, 1 x 8 ASROC, 2 x
3 ASTT; plus 2 x 127mm guns.
8 Asagiri with 1 SH-60J hel, 1 x 8 ASROC, 2 x 3
ASTT; plus 2 x 4 Harpoon SSM.
12 Hatsuyuki with 1 SH-60J, 1 x 8 ASROC, 2 x 3
ASTT; plus 2 x 4 Harpoon SSM.
FF: 31:
6 Abukuma with 1 x 8 ASROC, 2 x 3 ASTT; plus 2
x 4 Harpoon SSM.
4 Takatsuki with 1 x 8 ASROC, 2 x 3 ASTT, 1 x 4
ASW RL; plus 2 x 127mm gun.
3 Yamagumo with 1 x 8 ASROC, 2 x 3 ASTT, 1 x
4 ASW RL.
3 Minegumo with 1 x 8 ASROC, 2 x 3 ASTT, 1 x
4 ASW RL (2 trg, 1 trg support).
2 Yubari with 2 x 3 ASTT, 1 x 4 ASW RL; plus 2
x 4 Harpoon SSM.
1 Ishikari with 2 x 3 ASTT, 1 x 4 ASW RL; plus 2
x 4 Harpoon SSM.
11 Chikugo with 1 x 8 ASROC, 2 x 3 ASTT.
1 Katori (trg) with 2 x 3 ASTT, 1 x ASW RL.
PATROL AND COASTAL COMBATANTS: 6:
MSL CRAFT: 3 Ichi-Go Type PHM with 4 SSM-1B.
PATROL: 3 Jukyu-Go PCI⟨.
MINE WARFARE: 39:
MINELAYERS: 1 Souya plus hel deck, 2 x 3 ASTT,
also MCM spt/comd.
MCM: 38:
1 Hayase MCM cmd with hel deck, 2 x 3 ASTT,
plus minelaying capacity.
22 Hatsushima MCC.
7 Uwajima MCC.
3 Yaeyama MSO.
4 Nana-go MSI⟨.
1 Fukue coastal MCM spt.
AMPH: 6:

3 *Miura* LST, capacity 200 tps, 10 tk.
3 *Atsumi* LST, capacity 130 tps, 5 tk.
Plus craft: 2 *Yura* and 2 *Ichi-Go* LCM.
SPT AND MISC: 19:
3 *Towada* AOE, 1 *Sagami* AOE (all with hel deck),
2 sub depot/rescue, 2 *Yamagumo* trg, 2 trg spt, 8
survey/experimental, 1 icebreaker.

MSDF AIR ARM: (ε12,000); 110 cbt ac, 99 armed
hel. Average annual flying hours for P-3 aircrew: 500.
7 Air Groups.
MR: 10 sqn (1 trg) with 100 P-3C.
ASW: 6 hel sqn (1 trg) with 60 HSS-2B, 39 SH-60J.
MCM: 1hel sqn with 9 MH-53E.
EW: 1 sqn with 2 EP-3C.
TPT: 1 sqn with 4 YS-11M.
TEST: 1 sqn with **ac**: 3 P-3C; **hel**: 2 HSS-2B, 2 SH-60J.
SAR: 2 sqn with 9 US-1A, 11 UH-605.
3 rescue sqn with 10 S-61 hel, 10 UH-60J.
TRG: 5 sqn with **ac**: 10 KM-2, 10* P-3C, 30 T-5, 30 TC-
90/UC-90, 10 YS-11T/M; **hel**: 10 HSS-2B, 10 OH-6D/J.

AIR FORCE (Air Self-Defense Force): 44,600; 450
cbt ac, no armed hel, 7 cbt air wings. Flying hours: 150.
FGA: 3 sqn with 50 F-I.
FTR: 10 sqn:
7 with 180 F-15J/DJ.
3 with 110 F-4EJ.
RECCE: 1 sqn with 20* RF-4E/EJ.
AEW: 1 sqn with 10 E-2C.
EW: 1 fleet with 1 EC-1, 4 YS-11 E.
AGGRESSOR TRG: 1 sqn with a few F-15DJ.
TPT: 8 sqn:
3 with 20 C-1, 13 C-130H, 10 YS-11.
1 with 2 747-400 (VIP).
4 heavy-lift hel sqn with 10 CH-47J.
SAR: 1 wing (10 det) with **ac**: 25 MU-2; **hel**: 20 KV-
107, 10 CH-47J, 9 UH-60J.
CAL: 1 sqn with 1 YS-11, 2 U-125-800.
TRG: 5 wings: 11 sqn: 40* T-1A/B, 50* T-2, 40 T-3,
50 T-4, 10 T-400.
LIAISON: U-65, 40 T-33, 70 T-4.
TEST: 1 wing with F-15J, T-4.

AIR DEFENCE: ac control and warning: 4 wings; 28
radar sites.
6 SAM gp (23 sqn) with 115 *Patriot*. Air Base Defence
Gp with 20mm *Vulcan* AA guns, Type 81, Type 91,
Stinger SAM.
MSL:
ASM: ASM-1.
AAM: AAM-3, AIM-7 *Sparrow*, AIM-9 *Sidewinder*.

PARAMILITARY:
MARITIME SAFETY AGENCY (Coast Guard)

(Ministry of Transport, no cbt role): 12,000.
PATROL VESSELS: some 328:
OFFSHORE (over 1,000 tons): 42, incl 1 *Shikishima*
with 2 *Super Puma* hel, 2 *Mizuho* with 2 Bell 212, 8
Soya with 1 Bell 212 hel, 2 *Izu,* 28 *Shiretoko* and 1
Kojima (trg).
COASTAL (under 1,000 tons): 36.
INSHORE: about 250 patrol craft most⟨.
MISC: about 90 service, 80 tender/trg vessels.
AC: 5 NAMC YS-11A, 2 Short *Skyvan*, 16 *King Air*,
1 Cessna U-206G.
HEL: 32 Bell 212, 4 Bell 206, 2 Hughes 369.

FOREIGN FORCES:
US: 45,500: Army (2,000): 1 Corps HQ; Navy (7,300)
bases at Yokosuka (HQ 7th Fleet) and Sasebo; Marines
(21,000): 1 MEF in Okinawa; Air Force (15,200): 1 Air
Force HQ: 102 cbt ac, 2 ftr wings (5 sqn) with 54 F-15C/
D, 48 F-16, 2 C-21A, 3 UH-1N (hel), 1 sqn with 2 E-3
AWACS, 1 airlift wg with 16 C-130E/H, 1 sqn with 15
KC-135 tkr, 1 SAR sqn with 8 HH-60, 1 SF gp with 5
HC-130N/P and 4 MC-130.

KOREA: DEMOCRATIC PEOPLE'S REPUBLIC OF (NORTH)

GNP[a]	1993ε: won 44.4bn ($20.8bn):	
	per capita $1,000	
	1994ε: won 44.9bn ($20.9bn)	
	per capita $ 950	
Growth	1993ε: -4.3%	1994ε: 1.8%
Inflation	1993ε: 5%	1994ε: 5%
Debt	1993ε:$8.4bn	1994ε: $8.8bn
Def exp	1993ε: won 11.3bn ($5.3bn)	
	1994ε:won 11.9bn ($5.6bn)	
Def bdgt	1994: won 4.8bn ($2.2bn)	
	1995ε: won 4.9bn ($2.2bn)	
$1 = won	1993: 2.13	1994: 2.14
	1995: 2.20	

[a] GNP shows an increase over GDP because of remitted
earnings of N. Korean expatriates in Japan.

Population: 23,927,000

	13–17	18–22	23–32
Men	956,400	1,165,600	2,535,200
Women	962,400	1,176,600	2,567,600

TOTAL ARMED FORCES:
ACTIVE: ε1,128,000.
Terms of service: Army 5–8 years; Navy 5–10 years;

Air Force 3–4 years, followed by compulsory part-time service to age 40. Thereafter service in the Worker/Peasant Red Guard to age 60.

RESERVES: 4,700,000 of which Army 750,000, Navy 40,000 are assigned to units (see Paramilitary).

ARMY: 1,000,000.

16 Corps (1 armd, 4 mech, 8 inf, 2 arty, 1 capital defence).
26 inf/mot inf div.
14 armd bde.
23 mot/mech inf bde.
5 indep inf bde.
Special Purpose Forces Comd (88,000): 10 *Sniper* bde (incl 2 amph, 2 AB), 14 lt inf bde (incl 3 AB) 17 recce, 1 AB bn.
'Bureau of Reconnaissance SF' (8 bn).
Army tps: 6 hy arty bde (incl MRL), 1 *Scud* SSM bde, 1 *Frog* SSM regt.
Corps tps: 14 arty bde incl 122mm, 152mm SP, MRL.
RESERVES: 23 inf div, 6 inf bde.
EQPT:
MBT: some 3,400: T-34, 1,600 T-54/-55, 1,800 T-62, Type-59.
LT TK: 540 PT-76, M-1985.
APC: 2,200 BTR-40/-50/-60/-152, Ch Type-531, N. Korean Type M-1973.
TOWED ARTY: 3,000: **122mm:** M-1931/-37, D-74, D-30; **130mm:** M-46; **152mm:** M-1937, M-1938, M-1943.
SP ARTY: 4,500: **122mm:** M-1977, M-1981, M-1985; **130mm:** M-1975, M-1991; **152mm:** M-1974, M-1977; **170mm:** M-1978, M-1989.
MRL: 2,200: **107mm:** Type-63; **122mm:** BM-21, BM-11, M-1977/-1985/-1992/-1993; **240mm:** M-1985/-1989/-1991.
MOR: 7,200: **82mm:** M-37; **120mm:** M-43; **160mm:** M-43.
SSM: 54 *FROG*-3/-5/-7; some 30 *Scud*-C.
ATGW: 8,500: AT-1 *Snapper*, AT-3 *Sagger*, AT-4 *Spigot*, AT-5 *Spandrel*.
RCL: **82mm:** 1,700 B-10.
AD GUNS: 4,800 plus 3,000 in static positions: **14.5mm:** ZPU-1/-2/-4 SP, M-1983 SP; **23mm:** ZU-23, ZSU-23-4 SP; **37mm:** M-1939; **57mm:** S-60; **85mm:** KS-12; **100mm:** KS-19.
SAM: 10,000+ SA-7/-16.

NAVY: ε46,000.

BASES: East Coast: Toejo (HQ), Changjon, Munchon, Songjon-pardo, Mugye-po, Mayang-do, Chaho Nodongjagu, Puam-Dong, Najin.
West Coast: Nampo (HQ), Pipa Got, Sagon-ni, Chodo-ri, Koampo, Tas-ri.
2 Fleet HQ.

SS: 25:
21 Ch Type-031/Sov *Romeo* with 533mm TT.
4 Sov *Whiskey*† with 533mm and 406mm TT.
(Plus some 50 midget and 11 coastal submarines mainly used for SF ops, but some with 2 x TT.)
FF: 3:
1 *Soho* with 4 x ASW RL, plus 4 x SS-N-2 *Styx* SSM, 1 x 100mm gun and hel deck.
2 *Najin* with 2 x 5 ASW RL, plus 2 SS-N-2 *Styx* SSM, 2 x 100mm guns.
PATROL AND COASTAL COMBATANTS: about 413:
CORVETTES: 4 *Sariwon* with 1 x 100mm gun.
MSL CRAFT: 42: 10 *Soju*, 12 Sov *Osa*, 4 Ch *Huangfeng* PFM with 4 x SS-N-2 *Styx*, 6 *Sohung*, 10 Sov *Komar* PFM with 2 x SS-N-2.
TORPEDO CRAFT: 198:
3 Sov *Shershen* with 4 x 533mm TT.
Some 155 with 2 x 533mm TT.
40 *Sin Huag* PHT.
PATROL CRAFT: 169:
COASTAL: 18 PFC:
6 *Hainan* with 4 x ASW RL, 12 *Taechong* with 2 x ASW RL.
INSHORE: some 151:
16 SO-1, 12 *Shanghai* II, 3 *Chodo*, some 120⟨.
MCM: about 25 MSI⟨.
AMPH: craft only: 15 LCM, 15 LCU, about 100 *Nampo* LCVP , plus about 130 hovercraft.
SPT AND MISC: 7: 2 ocean tugs, 1 AS, 1 ocean and 3 inshore survey.

COAST DEFENCE:

2 SSM regt: *Silkworm* in 6 sites.
GUNS: **122mm:** M-1931/-37; **130mm:** SM-4-1; **152mm:** M-1937.

AIR FORCE: 82,000; 509 cbt ac, 80 armed hel.

Flying hours: some 30.
BBR: 3 lt regt with 80 H-5 (Il-28).
FGA/FTR: 16 regt:
4 with 110 J-5 (MiG-17).
3 with 130 J-6 (MiG-19).
4 with 130 J-7 (MiG-21).
1 with 46 MiG-23.
2 with 40 MiG-29.
1 with 18 Su-7.
1 with 35 Su-25.
ATTACK HEL: 80 Mi-24.
TPT: ac: 282 An-2/Y-5, 6 An-24, 2 Il-18, 4 Il-62M, 2 Tu-134, 4 Tu-154; **hel:** 80 Hughes 500D, 140 Mi-2, 15 Mi-8/-17, 48 Z-5.
TRG: incl 10 CJ-5, 7 CJ-6, 6 MiG-21, 170 Yak-18.
AAM: AA-2 *Atoll*, AA-7 *Apex*.
SAM: 240 SA-2, 36 SA-3, 24 SA-5.

FORCES ABROAD: advisers in some 12 African countries.

PARAMILITARY:

SECURITY TROOPS (Ministry of Public Security): 115,000, incl border guards.
WORKER/PEASANT RED GUARD: some 3.8m. Org on a provincial/town/village basis. Comd structure is bde – bn – coy – pl. Small arms with some mor and AD guns (but many units unarmed).

KOREA: REPUBLIC OF (SOUTH)

GDP	1993: won 267,146bn ($332.8bn):
	per capita $10,000
	1994: won 305,008bn ($379.6bn):
	per capita $11,000

Growth	1993: 5.5%	1994: 8.6%
Inflation	1993: 4.8%	1994: 6.2%
Debt	1993: $47.2bn	1994: $34.3bn
Def exp	1993: won 9,627bn ($11.99bn)	
	1994: won 10,857bn ($13.51bn)	
Def bdgt	1994: won 10,683bn ($13.30bn)	
	1995: won 11,023bn ($14.36bn)	
$1 = won	1993: 803	1994: 804
	1995: 768	

Population: 44,825,000

	13–17	18–22	23–32
Men	1,986,400	2,197,200	4,394,600
Women	1,845,000	2,051,600	4,103,400

TOTAL ARMED FORCES:
ACTIVE: 633,000.

Terms of service: conscription: Army 26 months; Navy and Air Force 30 months; then First Combat Forces (Mobilisation Reserve Forces) or Regional Combat Forces (Homeland Defence Forces) to age 33.
RESERVES: 4,500,000; being reorganised.

ARMY: 520,000 (140,000 conscripts).
HQ: 3 Army, 11 Corps.
3 mech inf div (each 3 bde: 3 mech inf, 3 tk, 1 recce, 1 engr bn; 1 fd arty bde).
19 inf div (each 3 inf regt, 1 recce, 1 tk, 1 engr bn; 1 arty regt (4 bn)).
2 indep inf bde.
7 SF bde.
3 counter-infiltration bde.
3 SSM bn with NHK-I/-II (*Honest John*).
3 AD arty bde.
3 I HAWK bn (24 sites), 2 *Nike Hercules* bn (10 sites).
1 avn comd.
RESERVES: 1 Army HQ, 23 inf div.
EQPT:
MBT: 2,050: 800 Type 88, 400 M-47, 850 M-48.
APC: some 2,460, incl 1,700 KIFV, 420 M-113, 140 M-577, 200 Fiat 6614/KM-900/-901.
TOWED ARTY: some 3,500: **105mm:** 1,700 M-101, KH-178; **155mm:** M-53, M-114, KH-179; **203mm:** M-115.
SP ARTY: 1,000: **155mm:** M-109A2; **175mm:** M-107; **203mm:** M-110.
MRL: 130mm: 156 *Kooryong* (36-tube).
MOR: 6,000: **81mm:** KM-29; **107mm:** M-30.
SSM: 12 NHK-I/-II.
ATGW: *TOW*-2A, *Panzerfaust.*
RCL: 57mm, 75mm, 90mm: M67; **106mm:** M40A2.
ATK GUNS: 76mm: 8 M-18; **90mm:** 50 M-36 SP.
AD GUNS: 600: **20mm:** incl KIFV (AD variant), 60 M-167 *Vulcan;* **30mm:** 20 BI HO SP; **35mm:** 20 GDF-003; **40mm:** 80 L60/70, M-1.
SAM: 350 *Javelin,* 60 *Redeye,* 130 *Stinger,* 170 *Mistral,* 110 I HAWK, 200 *Nike Hercules.*
AC: 5 O-1A.
HEL:
ATTACK: 75 AH-1F/-J, 68 Hughes 500 MD.
TPT: 15 CH-47D.
UTILITY: 170 Hughes 500, 130 UH-1H, 80 UH-60P.
SURV: RASIT (veh, arty), AN/TPQ-36 (arty, mor).

NAVY: 60,000 (incl 25,000 Marines and ε19,000 conscripts).
BASES: Chinhae (HQ), Cheju, Inchon, Mokpo, Mukho, Pukpyong, Pohang, Pusan.
3 Fleet Commands.
SS: 3 *Chang Bogo* (Ge T-209/1200) with 8 x 533 TT. Plus 3 KSS-1 *Dolgorae* SSI (175t) with 2 x 406mm TT.
PRINCIPAL SURFACE COMBATANTS: 40:
DD: 7 *Chung Buk* (US *Gearing*) with 2 or 3 x 2 127mm guns; plus 2 x 3 ASTT; 5 with 2 x 4 *Harpoon* SSM, 2 with 1 x 8 *ASROC,* 1 *Alouette* III hel (OTHT).
FF: 33:
9 *Ulsan* with 2 x 3 ASTT (Mk 46 LWT); plus 2 x 4 *Harpoon* SSM.
24 *Po Hang* with 2 x 3 ASTT; some with 2 x 1 MM-38 *Exocet.*
PATROL AND COASTAL COMBATANTS: 122:
CORVETTES: 4 *Dong Hae* (ASW) with 2 x 3 ASTT.
MSL CRAFT: 11:
8 *Pae Ku*-52, 3 with 4 *Standard* (boxed) SSM, 5 with 2 x 2 *Harpoon* SSM.
1 *Pae Ku*-51 (US *Asheville*), with 2 x *Standard* SSM.

2 *Kilurki*-71 (*Wildcat*) with 2 x MM-38 *Exocet* SSM.
PATROL, INSHORE: 107:
92 *Kilurki*-11 ('*Sea Dolphin*') 37-m PFI.
15 *Chebi*-51 ('*Sea Hawk*') 26-m PFI⟨ (some with 2 x MM-38 *Exocet* SSM).
MCM: 14:
6 *Kan Keong* (mod It *Lerici*) MHC.
8 *Kum San* (US MSC-268/289) MSC.
AMPH: 15:
8 *Un Bong* (US LST-511) LST, capacity 200 tps, 16 tk.
7 *Ko Mun* (US LSM-1) LSM, capacity 50 tps, 4 tk.
Plus about 36 craft; 6 LCT, 10 LCM, about 20 LCVP.
SPT AND MISC: 12:
2 AOE, 2 spt tankers, 2 ocean tugs, 2 salv/div spt, about 4 survey (civil-manned, Ministry of Transport-funded).

NAVAL AIR: 23 cbt ac; 47 armed hel.
ASW: 3 sqn:
2 **ac**: 1 with 15 S-2E, 1 with 8 P-3C.
1 **hel** with 25 Hughes 500MD.
1 fleet with 10 SA-316 hel, 12 *Lynx* (ASW).

MARINES: (25,000).
2 div, 1 bde.
spt units.
EQPT:
MBT: 60 M-47.
APC: 60 LVTP-7.
TOWED ARTY: 105mm, 155mm.
SSM: *Harpoon* (truck-mounted).

AIR FORCE: 53,000; 461 cbt ac, no armed hel.
8 cbt, 2 tpt wings.
FGA: 8 sqn:
2 with 60 F-16.
6 with 195 F-5A/E.
FTR: 4 sqn with 130 F-4D/E.
COIN: 1 sqn with 23 A-37B.
FAC: 10 O-2A.
RECCE: 1 sqn with 18 RF-4C, 10 RF-5A.
SAR: 1 hel sqn, 15 UH-60.
TPT: ac: 2 BAe 748 (VIP), 1 Boeing 737-300 (VIP), 1 C-118, 10 C-130H, 12 CN-235Ml; **hel:** 6 UH-1H/N, 6 CH-47, 3 Bell-412, 3 AS-332, 3 VH-60.
TRG: 25* F-5B, 50 T-37, 25 T-41B, 18 *Hawk* Mk-67.
MSL:
ASM: AGM-65A *Maverick*, AGM-88 HARM.
AAM: AIM-7 *Sparrow*, AIM-9 *Sidewinder*, AIM-120 AMRAAM.
SAM: *Nike-Hercules* I HAWK, *Javelin*, *Mistral*.

FORCES ABROAD:
UN AND PEACEKEEPING:
GEORGIA (UNOMIG) 6 Obs: **INDIA/PAKISTAN**

(UNMOGIP): 5 Obs. **WESTERN SAHARA** (MINURSO): 42 incl 2 Obs.

PARAMILITARY:
CIVILIAN DEFENCE CORPS (to age 50): 3,500,000.
COAST GUARD: ε4,500.
PATROL CRAFT: 74:
OFFSHORE: 10:
3 *Mazinger* (HDP-1000) (1 CG flagship).
1 *Han Kang* (HDC-1150).
6 *Sea Dragon/Whale* (HDP-600).
COASTAL: 26:
22 *Sea Wolf/Shark*.
2 *Bukhansan*, 2 *Hyundai*-type.
INSHORE: 38:
18 *Seagull*; about 20⟨, plus numerous boats.
SPT AND MISC: 2 salvage.
HEL: 9 Hughes 500.

FOREIGN FORCES:
US: 36,400. Army (27,500): 1 Army HQ, 1 inf div; Air Force (8,950): 1 Air Force HQ: 2 ftr wings: 90 cbt ac, 72 F-16, 6 A-10, 12 0A-10, 1 spec ops sqn with 5 MH -53J, recce det with 3 U-2, 2 C-12.

LAOS

GDP	1993: kip 951bn ($1.33bn):	
	per capita $2,000	
	1994: kip 1,037bn ($1.44bn):	
	per capita $2,200	
Growth	1993: 6.1%	1994: 8.4%
Inflation	1993: 6.3%	1994: 6.7%
Debt	1993: $2.0bn	1994: $2.0bn
Def exp[a]	1993: kip 75.5bn ($105m)	
Def bdgt[a]	1994: kip 81.9bn ($114m)	
	1995ε: kip 87.6bn ($121m)	
FMA	1994: $2.0m (Narcs)	
	1995: $2.2m (Narcs)	
	1996: $2.0m (Narcs)	
$1 = kip	1993: 717	1994: 720
	1995: 725	

[a] Incl Public Security budget.

Population: 4,774,000 (Phoutheung 15%, Thai 20% Hmong 10%)

	13–17	18–22	23–32
Men	252,200	212,600	336,200
Women	248,800	210,800	335,800

TOTAL ARMED FORCES:
ACTIVE: 37,000.

Terms of service: conscription, 18 months minimum.

ARMY: 33,000.
4 Military Regions.
5 inf div.
7 indep inf regt.
5 arty, 9 AD arty bn.
3 engr (2 construction) regt.
65 indep inf coy.
1 lt ac liaison flt.
EQPT:
MBT: 30 T-54/-55, T-34/85.
LT TK: 25 PT-76.
APC: 70 BTR-40/-60/-152.
TOWED ARTY: 75mm: M-116 pack; **105mm:** 25 M-101; **122mm:** 40 M-1938 and D-30; **130mm:** 10 M-46; **155mm:** M-114.
MOR: 81mm; 82mm; 107mm: M-2A1, M-1938; **120mm:** M-43.
RCL: 57mm: M-18/A1; **75mm:** M-20; **106mm:** M-40; **107mm:** B-11.
AD GUNS: 14.5mm: ZPU-1/-4; **23mm:** ZU-23, ZSU-23-4 SP; **37mm:** M-1939; **57mm:** S-60.
SAM: SA-3, SA-7.

NAVY (Army Marine Section): ε500.
PATROL CRAFT, river: some 12 PCI⟨, 4 LCM, plus about 40 boats.

AIR FORCE: 3,500; 31 cbt ac; no armed hel.
FGA: 1 regt with some 29 MiG-21.
TPT: 1 sqn with 5 An-24, 2 An-26, 2 Yak-40.
HEL: 1 sqn with 2 Mi-6, 10 Mi-8.
TRG: *2 MiG-21U.
AAM: AA-2 *Atoll.*

PARAMILITARY:
MILITIA SELF-DEFENCE FORCES:
100,000+: village 'homeguard' org for local defence.

OPPOSITION:
Numerous factions/groups. Total armed strength:ε2,000. Largest group, United Lao National Liberation Front (ULNLF).

MALAYSIA

GDP	1993: r 165.9bn ($64.4bn):		
	per capita $8,400		
	1994: r 183.2bn ($69.9bn):		
	per capita $9,000		

Growth	1993: 8.3%	1994: 8.5%	
Inflation	1993: 3.6%	1994: 3.7%	
Debt	1993: $23.3bn	1994: $25.0bn	
Def exp	1993ε: r 6.8bn ($2.64bn)		
Def bdgt	1994: r 5.37bn ($2.05bn)		
	1995: r 5.98bn ($2.41bn)		
FMA:	1994: $0.3m (IMET)		
	1995: $0.5m (IMET)		
	1996: $0.6m (IMET)		
$1 = r	1993: 2.57	1994: 2.62	
	1995: 2.48		

r = ringgit

Population: 19,876,000 (Chinese 32%, Indian 9%; in Sabah and Sarawak non-Muslim Bumiputras form the majority of the population; 1 million+ Indonesian illegal immigrants)

	13–17	18–22	23–32
Men	1,040,000	918,200	1,646,600
Women	990,400	883,400	1,618,800

TOTAL ARMED FORCES:
ACTIVE: 114,500.
RESERVES: 58,300: Army 55,000; Navy 2,700; Air Force 600.

ARMY: 90,000 (reducing to 85,000).
2 Military Regions.
1 corps, 5 div HQ.
10 inf bde, consisting of 35 inf bn (1 APC, 2 AB), 4 armd, 5 fd arty, 1 AD arty, 5 engr regt.
1 Rapid Deployment Force (incl 1 AB bde).
1 SF regt (3 bn).
Army Avn: 1 hel sqn.
RESERVES: 1 bde HQ; 12 inf regt; 4 highway sy bn.
EQPT:
LT TK: 26 *Scorpion* (90mm).
RECCE: 162 SIBMAS, 140 AML-60/-90, 92 *Ferret* (60 mod).
AIFV: 111 KIFV (incl variants).
APC: 184 V-100/-150 *Commando*, 25 *Stormer*, 459 *Condor*, 37 M-3 *Panhard.*
TOWED ARTY: 105mm: 75 Model 56 pack, 40 M-102A1 († in store); **155mm:** 15 FH-70.
MOR: 81mm: 300.
ATGW: SS-11.
RL: 89mm: M-20.
RCL: 84mm: *Carl Gustav*; **106mm:** 150 M-40.
AD GUNS: 35mm: 16 Oerlikon; **40mm:** 36 L40/70.
SAM: 48 *Javelin, Starburst*, 12 *Rapier.*
HEL: 10 SA-316 (Air Force).
ASLT CRAFT: 165 Damen.

NAVY: 12,000 (incl 160 Naval Air).

2 Regional Comd: plus Fleet.
Area 1: Malayan Peninsula (west of 109°E).
Area 2: Borneo Area (east of 109°E).
BASES: Area 1: Lumut (Fleet HQ), Tanjong Gelang (Area HQ), Kuantan, Woodlands (Singapore), trg base.
Area 2: Labuan (Area HQ), Sungei Antu (Sarawak), Sandakan (Sabah).
FF: 4:
2 *Kasturi* (FS-1500) with 2 x 2 ASW mor, deck for *Wasp* hel; plus 2 x 2 MM-38 *Exocet* SSM, 1 x 100mm gun.
1 *Hang Tuah* (UK *Mermaid*) with 1 x 3 *Limbo* ASW mor, hel deck for *Wasp*; plus 1 x 2 102mm gun (trg).
1 *Rahmat* with 1 x 3 ASW mor, 1 x 114mm gun hel deck.
PATROL AND COASTAL COMBATANTS: 37:
MSL CRAFT: 8:
4 *Handalan* (Sw *Spica*) with 4 MM-38 *Exocet* SSM.
4 *Perdana* (Fr *Combattante* II) with 2 *Exocet* SSM.
PATROL: 29:
OFFSHORE: 2 *Musytari* with 1 x 100mm gun, hel deck.
INSHORE: 27:
6 *Jerong* PFI, 3 *Kedah*, 4 *Sabah*, 14 *Kris* PCI.
MCM: 5:
4 *Mahamiru* (mod It *Lerici*) MCO.
1 diving tender (inshore).
AMPH: 4:
3 *Sri Banggi* (US LST-511) LST, capacity 200 tps, 16 tk (but usually employed as tenders to patrol craft).
1 *Sri Inderapura* (US LST-1192) LST, capacity 400 troops, 10 tk.
Plus 33 craft: 5 LCM, 13 LCU, 15 LCP.
SPT AND MISC: 3:
2 log/fuel spt, 1 survey.

NAVAL AIR: (160); no cbt ac, 12 armed hel.
HEL: 12 *Wasp* HAS-1.

AIR FORCE: 12,500; 120 cbt ac, no armed hel; 4 Comd. Flying hours: 200.
FGA: 2 sqn:
1 with 35 A-4 (30 A-4PTM, 5 TA-4).
1 with 10 HAWK 108, 18 HAWK 208.
FTR: 2 sqn:
1 with 11 F-5E.
1 with 16 MiG-29, 2 MiG-29U.
RECCE: 1 recce/OCU sqn with 2* RF-5E, 3* F-5F.
MR: 1 sqn with 3 C-130HMP, 4 B200T.
TPT:
AC: 4 sqn:
1 with 6 C-130H.
2 with 14 DHC-4.
1 with 2 BAe-125 (VIP), 2 *Falcon*-900 (VIP), 11 Cessna 402B.

HEL: 4 sqn with 33 S-61A, 20 SA-316A/B (liaison).
TRG: ac: 11* MB-339, 39 PC-7 (12* wpn trg); **hel**: 8 SA-316, 6 Bell 47G, 4 S-61.
AAM: AIM-9 *Sidewinder*.

AIRFIELD DEFENCE: 1 sqn.

FORCES ABROAD:
UN AND PEACEKEEPING:
ANGOLA (UNAVEM III): 20 Obs, 20 civ pol. **BOSNIA** (UNPROFOR): 1,547; 1 armd inf bn gp, plus 14 Obs. **CROATIA** (UNCRO): 12 Obs plus 24 civ pol. **IRAQ/ KUWAIT** (UNIKOM): 7 Obs. **LIBERIA** (UNOMIL): 8 Obs. **FYROM** (UNPREDEP): 1 Obs. **WESTERN SAHARA** (MINURSO): 14 Obs, 15 civ pol.

PARAMILITARY:
POLICE FIELD FORCE: 18,000; 4 bde HQ: 21 bn (incl 2 Aboriginal, 1 cdo), 4 indep coy; *Shorland* armd cars, 140 AT-105 *Saxon*, SB-301 APC.
MARINE POLICE: about 2,100; 48 inshore patrol craft:
15 *Lang Hitam* (38-m) PFI.
6 *Sangitan* (29-m) PFI.
27 PCI⟨, plus boats.
POLICE AIR WING: ac: 4 Cessna 206, 7 PC-6; **hel**: 1 Bell 206L3, 2 AS-355F2.
AREA SECURITY UNITS (auxiliary Police Field Force): 3,500 in 89 units.
BORDER SCOUTS (in Sabah, Sarawak): 1,200.
PEOPLE'S VOLUNTEER CORPS (RELA): 168,000.
CUSTOMS SERVICE: 56 patrol craft: 6 *Perak* (Vosper 32-m) armd PFI, about 50 craft⟨.

FOREIGN FORCES:
AUSTRALIA: Army: 1 inf coy; Air Force: det with 2 P-3C ac.

MONGOLIA

GDP	1993:	t 183.3bn ($700m)	
	1994:	t 256.0bn ($735m)	
Growth	1992:	1.2%	1994: 2.5%
Inflation	1993:	268%	1994: 88%
Debt	1993:	$382m	1994: $478m
Def exp	1993:	t 3,119m ($8m)	
	1994:	t 7,100m ($17m)	
Def bdgt	1995:	t 9,300m ($22m)	
FMA	1994:	$0.1m (IMET)	
	1995:	$0.1m (IMET)	
	1996:	$0.1m (IMET)	

$1 = t   1993: 312   1994: 413
1995: 431
t = tugrik
Population: 2,497,000 (Kazakh 4%, Russian 2%, Chinese 2%)

	13–17	*18–22*	*23–32*
Men	140,800	125,000	200,200
Women	134,800	120,200	194,400

TOTAL ARMED FORCES:
ACTIVE: 21,100 (perhaps 12,350 conscripts).
Terms of service: conscription: males 18–28 years, 1 year.
RESERVES: Army 140,000.

ARMY: 20,000 (perhaps 12,000 conscripts).
4 MRD (3 under-strength, 1 cadre).
1 arty bde.
1 AD bde.
2 indep inf bn.
1 AB bn.
EQPT:
MBT: 650 T-54/-55/-62.
RECCE: 135 BRDM-2.
AIFV: 420 BMP-1.
APC: 300 BTR-40/-60/-152.
TOWED ARTY: 300: **122mm:** M-1938/D-30;
130mm: M-46; **152mm:** M-1937.
MRL: **122mm:** 135+ BM-21.
MOR: 140: **82mm, 120mm, 160mm**.
ATK GUNS: **100mm:** T-12.
AD GUNS: 100: **14.5mm:** ZPU-4; **37mm:** M-1939;
57mm: S-60.
SAM: 300 SA-7.

AIR FORCE: 1,100 (350 conscripts); 15 cbt ac;
12 armed hel. Flying hours: 22.
FTR: 1 sqn with 12 MiG-21.
ATTACK HEL: 12 Mi-24.
TPT: at least 2 sqn with 15 An-2, 16 An-24, 3 An-26, 3 Boeing 727, 5 Y-12.
HEL: 1 sqn with 10 Mi-4, 4 Mi-8.
TRG: 2 MiG-15U, 3* MiG-21U, 3 PZL-104, 6 Yak-11, Yak-18.

PARAMILITARY:
MILITIA (Ministry of Public Security):
10,000: internal security troops, frontier guards; BTR-60/-152 APC.

FOREIGN FORCES:
RUSSIA: ε500 (SIGINT station).

NEW ZEALAND

GDP	1993: $NZ 80.86bn ($43.73bn):
	per capita $15,200
	1994: $NZ 84.09bn ($49.94bn):
	per capita $15,500
Growth	1993: 4.8% 1994: 3.0%
Inflation	1993: 1.4% 1994: 1.7%
Publ debt	1993: 50.1% 1994: 42.0%
Def exp	1993: $NZ 1.20bn ($651m)
Def bdgt	1994: $NZ 915m ($544m)
	1995: $NZ 898m ($599m)
$1 = $NZ	1993: 1.85 1994: 1.68
	1995: 1.50

$NZ = New Zealand dollar

Population: 3,531,000 (Maori 9%)

	13–17	*18–22*	*23–32*
Men	128,600	141,000	296,200
Women	121,800	133,800	282,600

TOTAL ARMED FORCES:
ACTIVE: 10,050 (incl 1,450 women).
RESERVES: 6,650. *Regular* 1,300: Army 500, Navy 800, Air Force 10. *Territorial* 5,350: Army 4,600, Navy 400, Air Force 350.

ARMY: 4,500 (incl 500 women).
2 Land Force Gp HQ.
1 APC/Recce regt (-).
2 inf bn.
1 arty regt (2 fd bty).
1 engr regt (-).
2 SF sqn (incl 1 reserve).
RESERVES: Territorial Army: 6 inf bn, 4 fd arty bty, 2 armd sqn (incl 1 lt recce).
EQPT:
LT TK: 26 *Scorpion* (18 in store).
APC: 78 M-113 (incl variants).
TOWED ARTY: **105mm:** 19 M-101A1 (13 in store), 24 *Hamel*.
MOR: **81mm:** 86.
RL: **94mm:** *LAW*
RCL: **84mm:** 65 *Carl Gustav*.
SURV: *Cymbeline* (mor).

NAVY: 2,200 (incl 250 women).
BASE: Auckland (Fleet HQ).
FF: 4 *Waikato* (UK *Leander*) with 1 *Wasp* hel, 2 x 3 ASTT and 3 with 2 x 114mm guns (1 in long refit).
PATROL AND COASTAL COMBATANTS: 4 *Moa* PCI (reserve trg).
SPT AND MISC: 5:

1 *Endeavour* AO, 1 *Monowai* AGHS, 1 *Tui* AGOR, 1 diving spt, 1 *Charles Upham* military sealift.

NAVAL AIR: no cbt ac, 5 armed hel.
HEL: 5 *Wasp* (see Air Force).

AIR FORCE: 3,350 (incl 700 women); 37 cbt ac, no armed hel. Flying hours for A-4: 180.
AIR COMD:
FGA: 2 sqn with 15 A-4K, 5 TA-4K.
MR: 1 sqn with 6 P-3K *Orion*.
LIGHT ATTACK/TRG: 1 sqn for *ab initio* and ftr lead-in trg with 17 MB-339C.
ASW: 5 *Wasp* HAS-1 (Navy-assigned).
TPT: 3 sqn:
AC: 2 sqn:
1 with 5 C-130H, 2 Boeing 727.
1 with 9 *Andover*.
HEL: 1 sqn with 13 UH-1H, 5 Bell 47G (trg).
TRG: 1 sqn with 18 CT-4 ac.
MSL:
ASM: AGM-65B/G *Maverick*.
AAM: AIM-9L *Sidewinder*.

FORCES ABROAD:
AUSTRALIA: 90: 6 A-4*K*/TA-4K, 14 navigation trg.
SINGAPORE: 20: spt unit.
UN AND PEACEKEEPING:
ANGOLA (UNAVEM III): 5 Obs. **BOSNIA** (UNPRO-FOR): 258 incl 4 Obs; 1 inf coy + spt elms. **CROATIA** (UNCRO): 5 Obs. **EGYPT** (MFO): 25. **MIDDLE EAST** (UNTSO): 7 Obs.

PAPUA NEW GUINEA

GDP	1993: K 4.98bn ($5.09bn):		
	per capita $2,200		
	1994: K 5.07bn ($5.1bn):		
	per capita $2,200		
Growth	1993: 16.5%	1994: 0.8%	
Inflation	1993: 5.0%	1994: 1.5%	
Debt	1993: $3.17bn	1994: $2.57bn	
Def exp	1993: K 85.0m ($83.0m)		
Def bdgt	1994: K 54.3m ($54.6m)		
	1995: K 60.0m ($47.4m)		
FMA	1994: $0.05m (IMET)		
	$20m (Australia)		
	1995: $0.1m (IMET)		
	$20m (Australia)		
	1996: $0.2m (IMET)		
$1 = K	1993: 0.98	1994: 1.00	
	1995: 1.19		
K = kina			

Population: 4,345,000

	13–17	18–22	23–32
Men	249,000	227,600	375,600
Women	233,400	210,200	333,000

TOTAL ARMED FORCES:
ACTIVE: about 3,800.

ARMY: 3,200.
2 inf bn.
1 engr bn.

NAVY: 500.
BASES: Port Moresby (HQ and lc sqn), Lombrum (Manus Island) (patrol boat sqn). Forward bases at Kieta and Alotau.
PATROL AND COASTAL COMBATANTS: 4 *Tarangau* (Aust *Pacific Forum* 32-m) PCI.
AMPH: craft only: 2 *Salamaua* (Aust *Balikpapan*) LCT plus 6 other landing craft (4 civilian-manned and operated by Department of Defence).

AIR FORCE: 100; 2 cbt ac, no armed hel.
MR: 2 N-22B *Searchmaster* B.
TPT: 2 N-22B *Missionmaster*, 2 CN-235, 3 IAI-201 *Arava*.
HEL: †4 UH-1H.

OPPOSITION:
BOUGAINVILLE REVOLUTIONARY ARMY: 2,000+.

FOREIGN FORCES:
AUSTRALIA: 100; trg unit, 2 engr unit, 75 advisers.

PHILIPPINES

GDP	1993: P 1,475bn ($54.39bn):		
	per capita $2,600		
	1994: P 1,688bn ($63.88bn):		
	per capita $2,600		
Growth	1993: 2.1%	1994: 4.3%	
Inflation	1993: 7.6%	1994: 9.1%	
Debt	1993: $35.94bn	1994: $36.5bn	
Def exp	1993: P 20.3bn ($749m)		
Def bdgt[a]	1994: P 23.2bn ($878m)		
	1995: P 26.1bn ($1,004m)		
FMA	1994: $10.9m (Econ Aid, IMET)		
	1995: $1.2m (IMET)		
	1996: $1.4m (IMET)		
$1 = P	1993: 27.1	1994: 26.4	
	1995: 26.0		

P = peso

a A 5-year supplementary procurement budget of $1.9bn for 1996–2000 was approved in 1995.

Population: 69,209,000 (Muslim 4%, Chinese 2%)

	13–17	18–22	23–32
Men:	3,839,800	3,406,200	5,677,600
Women:	3,704,400	3,279,000	5,529,600

TOTAL ARMED FORCES:
ACTIVE: ε106,500.
RESERVES: 131,000: Army 100,000 (some 75,000 more have commitments); Navy 15,000; Air Force 16,000 (to age 49).

ARMY: 68,000.
5 Area Unified Comd (joint service).
8 inf div (each with 3 inf bde).
1 lt armd bde ('regt').
1 scout ranger regt.
3 engr bde; 1 construction bn.
8 arty bn.
1 SF regt.
1 Presidential Security Group.
EQPT:
LT TK: 41 *Scorpion*.
AIFV: 85 YPR-765 PRI.
APC: 100 M-113, 20 *Chaimite*, 165 V-150, some 45 *Simba*.
TOWED ARTY: 105mm: 230 M-101, M-102, M-26 and M-56; **155mm:** 12 M-114 and M-68.
MOR: 81mm: M-29; **107mm:** 40 M-30.
RCL: 75mm: M-20; **90mm:** M-67; **106mm:** M-40 A1.

NAVY:† ε23,000 (incl 8,500 Marines).
6 Naval Districts.
BASES: Sangley Point/Cavite, Zamboanga, Cebu.
FF: 1 *Datu Siratuna* (US *Cannon*) with ASW mor, 76mm gun.
PATROL AND COASTAL COMBATANTS: 47:
PATROL, OFFSHORE: 9:
1 *Rizal* (US *Auk*) with hel deck.
7 *Miguel Malvar* (US PCE-827).
1 *Magat Salamat* (US-MSF).
PATROL, INSHORE: 38:
2 *Aguinaldo*, 3 *Kagitingan*, 12 *Sea Hawk* PCI‹ and about 21 other PCI‹.
AMPH: 8:
2 US *F. S. Beeson*-class LST, capacity 32 tk plus 150 tps, hel deck.
Some 6 *Agusan del Sur* (US LST-1/511/542) LST, capacity either 16tk or 10tk plus 200 tps.
Plus about 39 craft: 30 LCM, 3 LCU, some 6 LCVP.

SPT AND MISC: 11:
2 AOT (small), 1 repair ship, 3 survey/research, 3 spt, 2 water tkr.

NAVAL AVIATION: 8 cbt ac, no armed hel.
MR/SAR: ac: 8 BN-2A *Defender*, 1 *Islander*; **hel:** 11 Bo-105 (SAR).

MARINES: (8,500).
4 bde (10 bn).
EQPT:
APC: 30 LVTP-5, 55 LVTP-7.
TOWED ARTY: 105mm: 150 M-101.
MOR: 4.2-in (**107mm**): M-30.

AIR FORCE: 15,500; 43 cbt ac, some 104 armed hel.
FTR: 1 sqn with 7 F-5 (5 -A, 2 -B).
COIN: 4 sqn.
AC: 1 with 23 OV-10 *Broncos*.
HEL: 3 with 62 Bell UH-1H/M, 16 AUH-76 (S-76 gunship conversion), 26 Hughes 500/520MD.
MR: 2 F-27M.
RECCE: 6 RT-33A.
SAR: ac: 4 HU-16; **hel:** 10 Bo-105C.
PRESIDENTIAL AC WG: ac: 1 F-27, 1 F-28; **hel:** 2 Bell 212, 2 S-70A, 2 SA-330.
TPT: 3 sqn:
1 with 2 C-130B, 3 C-130H, 3 L-100-20, 5 C-47, 7 F-27.
2 with 22 BN-2 *Islander*, 14 N-22B *Nomad Missionmaster*.
HEL: 2 sqn with 55 Bell 205, 17 UH-1H.
LIAISON: 10 Cessna (7-180, 2-210, 1-310), 5 DHC-2, 12 U-17A/B.
TRG: 4 sqn:
1 with 6 T-33A.
1 with 10 T-41D.
1 with 16 SF-260TP.
1 with 13* S-211.
AAM: AIM-9B *Sidewinder*.

FORCES ABROAD:
UN AND PEACEKEEPING:
HAITI (UNMIH): 50 civ pol.

PARAMILITARY:
PHILIPPINE NATIONAL POLICE (Department of Interior and Local Government): 40,500; 62,000 active auxiliary; 12 Regional, 73 Provincial Comd.
COAST GUARD: 2,000 (no longer part of Navy).
EQPT:
1 *Kalinga* PCO, 4 *Basilan* (US PGM-39/42 PCI, 2 *Tirad Pass* PCI (SAR), 4 ex-US Army spt ships, plus

some 50 patrol boats, 2 lt ac.

CITIZEN ARMED FORCE GEOGRAPHICAL UNITS (CAFGU): Militia: 60,000, 56 bn. Part-time units which can be called up for extended periods.

OPPOSITION:

NEW PEOPLE'S ARMY (NPA; communist):ε8,000.
BANGSA MORO ARMY (armed wing of Moro National Liberation Front (MNLF); Muslim): ε3,300.
MORO ISLAMIC LIBERATION FRONT (breakaway from MNLF; Muslim): ε6–10,000.
MORO ISLAMIC REFORMIST GROUP (breakaway from MNLF; Muslim): 900.

REPUBLIC OF CHINA (TAIPEI)

GNP	1993: $NT 5,935bn ($226bn): per capita $10,500 1994: $NT 6,298bn ($240bn): per capita $11,100		
Growth	1993: 6.3%	1994:	6.1%
Inflation	1993: 2.9%	1994:	4.1%
Debt	1990: $18.6bn	1994:[a]	$0.0
Def exp	1993[b]: $NT 317.9bn ($11.94bn) 1994[b]: $NT 298.3bn ($11.27bn)		
Def bdgt	1995: $NT 251.2bn ($9.55bn) 1996: $NT 261.2bn ($9.93bn)		
$1 = $NT	1993: 26.6 1995: 26.3	1994:	26.2

$NT = New Taipei dollar

[a] Taipei is a net creditor state.
[b] Incl special appropriations for F-16 and Mirage 2000 acquisition: 1993 $NT 46.9bn; 1994 $NT 39.9bn.

Population: 21,178,000 (mainland Chinese 14%)

	13–17	18–22	23–32
Men	1,015,200	931,800	1,874,400
Women	959,800	876,600	1,779,400

TOTAL ARMED FORCES:
ACTIVE: 376,000.
Terms of service: 2 years.
RESERVES: 1,657,500: Army 1,500,000 with some obligation to age 30; Navy 32,500; Marines 35,000; Air Force 90,000.

ARMY: ε240,000 (incl mil police).
3 Army, 1 AB Special Ops HQ.
10 inf div.
2 mech inf div.
2 AB bde.
6 indep armd bde.
1 tk gp.
2 AD SAM gp with 5 SAM bn: 2 with *Nike Hercules*, 3 with I HAWK.
2 avn gp, 6 avn sqn.
RESERVES: 7 lt inf div.
EQPT:
MBT: 100 M-48A5, 450+ M-48H, ε20 M-60A3.
LT TK: 230 M-24 (**90mm** gun), 675 M-41/Type 64.
AIFV: 225 M-113 with **20/30mm** cannon.
APC: 650 M-113, 300 V-150 *Commando*.
TOWED ARTY: 105mm: 650 M-101 (T-64); **155mm:** M-44, 90 M-59, 250 M-114 (T-65); **203mm:** 70 M-115.
SP ARTY: 105mm: 100 M-108; **155mm:** 45 T-69, 110 M-109A2; **203mm:** 60 M-110.
MRL: 117mm: KF VI; **126mm:** KF III/IV towed and SP.
MOR: 81mm: M-29 (some SP); **107mm**.
ATGW: 1,000; *TOW* (some SP).
RCL: 90mm: M-67; **106mm:** 500 M-40A1/Type 51.
AD GUNS: 40mm: 400 (incl M-42 SP, Bofors).
SAM: 40 *Nike Hercules*, 100 HAWK, *Tien Kung* (*Sky Bow*)-1/-2, some *Chaparral*.
AC: 20 O-1
HEL: 112 UH-1H, 42 AH-1W, 26 OH-58D, 12 KH-4, 7 CH-47, Hughes 500.
UAV: *Mastiff* III.

DEPLOYMENT:
QUEMOY: 55,000.
MATSU: 18,000.

NAVY: 68,000 (incl 30,000 Marines).
3 Naval Districts.
BASES: Tsoying (HQ), Makung (Pescadores), Keelung.
SS: 4:
2 *Hai Lung* (Nl mod *Zwaardvis*) with 533mm TT.
2 *Hai Shih* (US *Guppy* II) with 533mm TT (trg only).
PRINCIPAL SURFACE COMBATANTS: 38:
DESTROYERS: 22:
DDG: 7 *Chien Yang* (US *Gearing*) (*Wu Chin* III conversion) with 10 x SM-1 MR SAM (boxed), plus 1 x 8 *ASROC*, 2 x 3 ASTT, plus 1 *Hughes* MD-500 hel.
DD: 15:
7 *Fu Yang* (US *Gearing*) (ASW); 5 with 1 *Hughes* MD-500 hel, 1 with 1 x 8 *ASROC*, all with 2 x 3 ASTT; plus 1 or 2 x 2 127mm guns, 3 or 5 *Hsiung Feng-I (HF-1)* (Is *Gabriel*) SSM.
4 *Po Yang* (US *Sumner*)† with 1 or 2 x 2 127mm guns; plus 2 x 3 ASTT; 5 or 6 *HF-1* SSM, 2 with 1 *Hughes* MD-500 hel.
4 *Kun Yang* (US *Fletcher*) with 2 or 3 x 127mm guns; 1 x 76mm gun; plus 2 x 3 ASTT with 5 *HF-1* SSM†.

FRIGATES: 16:
FFG: 4 *Cheng Kung* with 1 x SM-1 MR SAM, 2 S-70C
hel, 2 x 3 ASTT plus 2 x 4 *HF-II,* 1 or 2 S-70C hel.
FF: 12:
5 *Tien Shan* (US *Lawrence/Crosley*), some with up to 6
40mm guns (fishing protection and transport 160 tps).
1 *Tai Yuan* (US *Rudderow*) with 2 x 3 ASTT; plus
2 x 127mm guns.
6 *Chin Yang* (US *Knox*) with 1 x 8 ASROC, 1 x
SH-2F hel, 4 x ASTT; plus *Harpoon* (from *ASROC*
launchers), 1 x 127mm gun.
PATROL AND COASTAL COMBATANTS: 98:
MSL CRAFT: 53:
2 *Lung Chiang* PFM with 2 x *HF-1* SSM.
1 *Jinn Chiang* PFM with 4 x *HF-1* SSM.
50 *Hai Ou* (mod Is *Dvora*)⟨ with 2 x *HF-1* SSM.
PATROL, INSHORE: 45 (operated by marine police):
22 Vosper-type 32-m PFI, 7 PCI and about 16 PCI⟨.
MINE WARFARE: 16:
MINELAYERS: nil, but *Tai Yuan* has capability.
MCM: 16:
8 *Yung Chou* (US *Adjutant*) MSC.
4 (ex-US) *Aggressive* ocean-going minesweepers.
4 MSC converted from oil rig spt ships.
AMPH: 21:
1 *Kao Hsiung* (US LST 511) amph comd.
14 *Chung Hai* (US LST 511) LST, capacity 16 tk,
200 tps.
4 *Mei Lo* (US LSM-1) LSM, capacity about 4 tk.
1 *Cheng Hai* (US *Cabildo*) LSD, capacity 3 LCU
or 18 LCM.
1 *Chung Cheng* (US Ashland) LSD, capacity 3
LCU or 18 LCM.
Plus about 400 craft: 22 LCU, some 260 LCM, 120
LCVP.
SPT AND MISC: 19:
3 spt tankers, 2 repair/salvage, 1 *Wu Yi* combat spt
with hel deck, 2 *Yuen Feng* and 2 *Wu Kang* attack tpt
with hel deck, 2 tpt, 7 ocean tugs.

COASTAL DEFENCE: 1 SSM coastal def bn
with *Hsiung Feng* (*Gabriel* type).

NAVAL AIR: 32 cbt ac; 22 armed hel.
MR: 1 sqn with 32 S-2 (-E: 25; -G: 7) (Air Force-
operated).
HEL: 12 Hughes 500MD, 9 S-70C ASW *Defender*, 10
S-70C(M)-1.

MARINES: (30,000).
2 div, spt elm.
EQPT:
AAV: LVTP-4/-5.
TOWED ARTY: 105mm, 155mm.
RCL: 106mm.

AIR FORCE: 68,000; 430 cbt ac, no armed hel.
Flying hours: 180.
FGA/FTR: 15 sqn:
10 with 275 F-5 (-B: 7; -E: 215; -F: 53).
3 with 50 F-104 (models incl D/DJ, G, J and TF).
2 with 40 *Chung-Kuo* (plus 10 Test).
RECCE: 1 sqn with 6 RF-104G.
AEW: 4 E-2T.
SAR: 1 sqn with 14 S-70.
TPT: 8 sqn:
AC: 2 with 8 C-47, 1 C-118B, 1 DC-6B.
3 with 30 C-119G.
1 with 13 C-130H (1 EW).
1 VIP with 4 -727-100, 12 Beech 1900.
HEL: 5 CH-34, 1 S-62A (VIP), 14 S-70.
TRG: ac: incl 59* AT-3A/B, 60 T-38A, 42 T-34C.
MSL:
ASM: AGM-65A *Maverick.*
AAM: AIM-4D *Falcon*, AIM-9J/P *Sidewinder, Shafrir,
Sky Sword* II.

PARAMILITARY:
SECURITY GROUPS: 25,000:
National Police Administration (Ministry of Interior);
Bureau of Investigation (Ministry of Justice); Military
Police (Ministry of Defence).
MARITIME POLICE: ε1,000 with about 38 armed
patrol boats. Also man many of the patrol craft listed
under Navy.
CUSTOMS SERVICE (Ministry of Finance): 650;
5 PCO, 2 PCC, 1 PCI, 5 PCI⟨; most armed.

FOREIGN FORCES:
SINGAPORE: 4 trg camps.

SINGAPORE

GDP	1993:	S89.0bn ($55.1bn):	
	per capita $18,700		
	1994:	S97.9bn ($60.7bn):	
	per capita $19,700		
Growth	1993:	9.9%	1994: 10.1%
Inflation	1993:	2.4%	1994: 3.6%
Debt	1990:	$4.2bn	1993:[a] $0.0
Def exp	1993:	S3,946m ($2.44bn)	
	1994:	S4,679m ($2.91bn)	
Def bdgt	1995:	S5,627m ($4.02bn)	
FMA	1994:	$0.01m (IMET)	
	1995:	$0.02m (IMET)	
	1996:	$0.02m (IMET)	
$1 = S	1993:	1.62	1994: 1.53
	1995:	1.40	

S = Singapore dollar

a Singapore is a net creditor state.

Population: 2,943,000 (Chinese 76%, Malay 15%, Indian 6%)

	13–17	18–22	23–32
Men	104,600	111,200	262,200
Women	97,600	105,400	255,800

TOTAL ARMED FORCES:
ACTIVE: ε53,900 (33,800 conscripts).
Terms of service: conscription 24–30 months.
RESERVES: ε221,000: Army 210,000: annual trg to age 40 for men, 50 for officers; Navy ε3,600; Air Force ε7,500.

ARMY: 45,000 (30,000 conscripts).
3 combined arms div each with 2 inf bde (each 3 inf bn), 1 mech bde, 1 recce, 2 arty, 1 AD, 1 engr bn (mixed active/reserve units).
1 Rapid Deployment (op reserve) div with 3 inf bde (incl 1 air mob, 1 amph, mixed active/reserve units).
1 mech bde.
1 cdo bn.
1 arty, 1 SP mor bn.
1 engr bn.
RESERVES:
1 op reserve div, 1 inf bde HQ; 3 inf bn.
People's Defence Force: some 30,000; org in 2 comd, 7 bde gp, ε21 bn.
EQPT:
MBT: some 60 *Centurion* (reported).
LT TK: ε350 AMX-13SM1.
RECCE: 22 AMX-10 PAC 90.
AIFV: 25 AMX-10P.
APC: 750 M-113, 30 V-100, 250 V-150/-200 *Commando*.
TOWED ARTY: 105mm: 36 LG1; **155mm:** 38 Soltam M-71S, 16 M-114A1 (may be in store), M-68 (may be in store), 52 FH88, some FH2000 reported.
MOR: 81mm (some SP); **120mm:** 50 (some SP in M-113); **160mm:** 12 Tampella.
ATGW: 30 *Milan*.
RL: *Armbrust*; **89mm:** 3.5-in M-20.
RCL: 84mm: *Carl Gustav*; **106mm:** 90 M-40A1 (in store).
AD GUNS: 20mm: 30 GAI-CO1 (some SP).
SAM: RBS-70 (some SP in V-200), some *Mistral*.
SURV: AN/TPQ-36/-37 (arty, mor).

NAVY: ε2,900 (800 conscripts); 3 Comd: Fleet (1st and 3rd Flotillas), Coastal Comd and Naval Logistic Comd.
BASES: Pulau Brani, Tuas (Jurong).

PATROL AND COASTAL COMBATANTS: 26:
CORVETTES: 6 *Victory* (Ge Lürssen 62-m) with 8 x *Harpoon* SSM, 2 x 3 ASTT.
MSL CRAFT: 6 *Sea Wolf* (Ge Lürssen 45-m) PFM with 2 x 2 *Harpoon*, 2 x *Gabriel* SSM.
PATROL, INSHORE: 14:
6 *Independence/Sovereignty* (33-m).
8 *Swift⟨*, plus boats.
MCM: 2 *Bedok* (SW *Landsort*) MHC. (*Jupiter* diving spt has mine-hunting capability.)
AMPH: 5:
1 *Perseverance* (UK *Sir Lancelot*) LSL with 2 *Simbad* (navalised *Mistral*) SAM capacity: 340 tps, 16 tk, hel deck.
4 *Endurance* (US LST-511) LST, capacity 200 tps, 16 tk, hel deck.
Plus craft: 10 LCM, 1 hovercraft and boats.
SPT AND MISC: 2:
1 *Jupiter* diving spt and salvage, 1 trg.

AIR FORCE: 6,000 (3,000 conscripts); 155 cbt ac, 20 armed hel.
FGA: 4 sqn:
3 with 62 A-4S/SI, 13 TA-4S/SI.
1 with 7 F-16 (3 -A, 4 -B) (with a further 11 F-16A/B in US).
FTR: 2 sqn with 29 F-5E, 9 F-5F.
RECCE: 1 sqn with 6* RF-5E.
AEW: 1 sqn with 4 E-2C.
ARMED HEL: 2 sqn with 20 AS 550A2/C2.
TPT: 5 sqn:
AC: 2 sqn:
1 with 4 C-130B (tkr/tpt), 6 C-130H/H-30.
1 with 6 *Skyvan* 3M (tpt/SAR), 4 *Fokker* 50.
HEL: 2 sqn:
1 with 4 Bell 205A, 16 UH1H.
1 with 20 AS-332M (incl 3 SAR), 6 AS-532UL (*Cougar*).
TRG: 3 sqn:
2 with 27* SIAI S-211.
1 with 22 SF-260 (12 -MS, 10 -WS).
UAV: *Scout*.
AIRFIELD DEFENCE: 4 field defence sqn with 10 *Rapier*, 12 I HAWK and **35mm** *Oerlikon* (towed) guns.
MSL:
AAM: AIM-9 J/P *Sidewinder*.
ASM: AGM-65B *Maverick*.

FORCES ABROAD:
AUSTRALIA: (160); flying trg school with 27 S-211 ac.
BRUNEI: (500); trg school, incl hel det (with 5 UH-1).
TAIWAN: 4 trg camps (incl MBT, inf and arty).
THAILAND: 2 trg camps (1 arty, 1 mor).
US: 100; 11 F-16A/B leased from USAF at Luke AFB.

UN AND PEACEKEEPING:
IRAQ/KUWAIT (UNIKOM): 6 Obs.

PARAMILITARY:
POLICE COASTGUARD: 11,600; incl some 750 Gurkhas, 4 Swift PCI⟨, some 4 PCI and about 80 boats.
CIVIL DEFENCE FORCE: ε100,000 (incl regulars, conscripts, ε34,000 former Army reservists); 1 construction bde (2,500 conscripts).

FOREIGN FORCES:
NEW ZEALAND: 20: spt unit.
US: 140: Navy (100); Air Force (40).

THAILAND

GDP	1993: b 3,088bn ($122.0bn):	
	per capita $6,200	
	1994: b 3,350bn ($132.4bn):	
	per capita $6,600	
Growth	1993: 7.8%	1994: 8.5%
Inflation	1993: 3.5%	1994: 5.4%
Debt[a]	1993: $45.8bn	1994: $55.0bn
Def exp	1993: b 78.94bn ($3.12bn)	
Def bdgt	1994: b 90.94bn ($3.62bn)	
	1995ε: b 97.24bn ($4.00bn)	
FMA	1994: $3.9m (IMET, Narcs)	
	1995: $2.3m (IMET, Narcs)	
	1996: $3.1m (IMET, Narcs)	
$1 = b	1993: 25.3	1994: 25.2
	1995: 24.6	
b = baht		

[a] Some reports cite a higher 1994 figure of $68bn.

Population: 60,460,000 (Chinese 14%, Muslims 4%)

	13–17	18–22	23–32
Men	3,204,200	3,145,600	5,845,600
Women	3,101,000	3,047,200	5,692,200

TOTAL ARMED FORCES:
ACTIVE: 259,000.
Terms of service: conscription, 2 years.
RESERVES: 200,000.

ARMY: 150,000 (80,000 conscripts).
4 Regional Army HQ, 2 Corps HQ.
1 armd div.
1 cav (lt armd) div (2 cav, 1 arty regt).
2 mech inf div.
7 inf div (incl Royal Guard, 5 with 1 tk bn) (1 to be mech, 1 to be lt).
2 SF div.
1 arty div, 1 AD arty div (6 AD arty bn).
19 engr bn.
1 indep cav regt.
8 indep inf bn.
4 recce coy.
Armd air cav regt with 3 air-mobile coy.
Some hel flt.
RESERVES: 3 inf div HQ.
EQPT:
MBT: 50+ Ch Type-69 (in store), 150 M-48A5, 53 M-60A1.
LT TK: 154 *Scorpion*, 250 M-41, 106 *Stingray*.
RECCE: 32 *Shorland* Mk 3.
APC: 340 M-113, 150 V-150 *Commando*, 450 Ch Type-85 (YW-531H).
TOWED ARTY: 105mm: 200 M-101/-101 mod, 12 M-102, 32 M-618A2 (local manufacture); **130mm:** 15 Ch Type-59; **155mm:** 56 M-114, 62 M-198, 32 M-71.
MOR: 81mm, 107mm.
ATGW: *TOW*, 300 *Dragon*.
RL: M-72 *LAW*.
RCL: 75mm: M-20; **106mm:** 150 M-40.
AD GUNS: 20mm: 24 M-163 *Vulcan*, 24 M-167 *Vulcan*; **37mm:** 122 Type-74; **40mm:** 80 M-1/M-42 SP, 28 L/70; **57mm:** 24.
SAM: *Redeye*, some *Aspide*.
AC:
TPT: 1 Beech 99, 4 C-47, 10 Cessna 208, 1 Short 330, 1 *Beech King Air*.
LIAISON: 62 O-1A, 17 -E, 5 T-41A, 13 U-17A.
TRG: 16 T-41D.
HEL:
ATTACK: 4 AH-1F.
TPT: 10 Bell 206, 9 Bell 212, 6 Bell 214, 70 UH-1H.
TRG: 36 Hughes 300C, 3 OH-13, 7 TH-55.
SURV: RASIT (veh, arty), AN-TPQ-36 (arty, mor).

NAVY: 66,000 (incl 1,150 Naval Air, 20,000 Marines, Coastal Defence and Coast Guards, and 15,000 conscripts).
3 Fleets: **1st:** East Thai Gulf; **2nd:** West Thai Gulf; **3rd:** Andaman Sea.
2 Naval Air Wings.
BASES: Bangkok, Sattahip (Fleet HQ), Songkhla, Phang Nga, Nakhon Phanom (HQ Mekong River Operating Unit), Trat.
FRIGATES: 10:
FFG: 6:
1 *Naresuan* with 2 x 4 *Harpoon* SSM, 8 cell *Sea Sparrow* SAM, 1 x 127mm gun, 6 x 324mm TT, 1 x SH-2F hel.
2 *Chao Phraya* (Ch *Jianghu*-III) with 8 x C-801 SSM, 2 x 2 100mm guns; plus 2 x 5 ASW RL.
2 *Kraburil* (Ch *Jianghu*-IV type) with 8 x C-801

SSM, 1 x 2 100mm guns; plus 2 x 5 ASW RL and *Bell* 212 hel.

1 *Phutthayotfa Chulalok* (US *Knox*) with 8 x *Harpoon* SSM, 8 x Asroc ASTT, 1 x 127mm gun.

FF: 4:

1 *Makut Rajakumarn* with 2 x 3 ASTT (*Sting Ray* LWT); plus 2 x 114mm guns.

2 *Tapi* (US PF-103) with 2 x 3 ASTT (Mk 46LWT).

1 *Tachin* (US *Tacoma*) with 2 x 3 ASTT (trg).

PATROL AND COASTAL COMBATANTS: 62:

CORVETTES: 5:

2 *Rattanakosin* with 2 x 3 ASTT (*Sting Ray* LWT); plus 2 x 4 *Harpoon* SSM.

3 *Khamronsin* with 2 x 3 ASTT; plus 1 x 76mm gun.

MSL CRAFT: 6:

3 *Ratcharit* (It Breda 50-m) with 4 x MM-38 *Exocet* SSM.

3 *Prabparapak* (Ge Lürssen 45-m) with 5 *Gabriel* SSM.

PATROL: 51:

COASTAL: 11:

3 *Chon Buri* PFC, 6 *Sattahip*, 2 *Sarasin* (US PC-461) PCC.

INSHORE: 40: 7 T-11 (US PGM-71), about 33 PCI⟨.

MCM: 6:

2 *Bang Rachan* (Ge Lürssen T-48) MCC.

3 *Ladya* (US '*Bluebird*' MSC) MSC.

1 *Thalang* MCM spt with minesweeping capability. (Plus some 5 MSB.)

AMPH: 9:

2 *Sichang* (Fr PS-700) LST, capacity 14 tk, 300 tps with hel deck (trg).

5 *Angthong* (US LST-511) LST, capacity 16 tk, 200 tps.

2 *Kut* (US LSM-1) LSM, capacity about 4 tk.

Plus about 51 craft: 9 LCU, about 24 LCM, 1 LCG, 2 LSIL, 3 hovercraft, 12 LCVP.

SPT AND MISC: 11:

1 *Chula* AO, 4 small tankers, 3 survey, 3 trg (incl 1 *Pin Klao* (US *Cannon*) (plus 2 *Tachin* FF and 2 *Sichang* LST listed above).

NAVAL AIR: (1,150); 49 cbt ac; 8 armed hel.

MR/ASW: 2 P-3T *Orion*, 1 UP-3T, 3 Do-228, 5 F-27 MPA, 5 N-24A *Searchmaster* L, 5 S-2F (plus 2 P-3A in store).

ASW HEL: 8 Bell 212 ASW.

MR/SAR: 1 sqn with 2 CL-215.

MR/ATTACK: 10 Cessna T-337 *Skymasters*, 14 A-7E, 4 TA-7C (delivery starts Jul 95).

SAR: 1 hel sqn with 8 Bell 212, 2 Bell 214, 4 UH-1H.

ASM: AGM-84 *Harpoon* (for F-27MPA).

MARINES: (20,000).

1 div HQ, 6 inf regt, 1 arty regt (3 fd, 1 AA bn); 1 amph aslt bn; recce bn.

EQPT:

APC: 33 LVTP-7.

TOWED ARTY: 155mm: 18 GC-45.

ATGW: *TOW*, *Dragon*.

AIR FORCE: 43,000; 197 cbt ac, no armed hel.

FGA: 2 sqn:

1 with 8 F-5A, 4 -B.

1 with 14 F-16A, 4 -B.

FTR: 2 sqn with 37 F-5E, 6 -F.

COIN: 7 sqn:

1 with 7 AC-47.

3 with 24 AU-23A.

2 with 30 OV-10C.

1 with 20* N-22B *Missionmaster* (tpt/COIN).

ELINT: 1 sqn with 3 IAI-201.

RECCE: 4* RF-5A, 3*RT-33A.

SURVEY: 2 *Learjet* 35A, 3 *Merlin* IVA, 3 GAF N-22B Nomads.

TPT: 3 sqn:

1 with 6 C-130H, 6 C-130H-30, 3 DC-8-62F.

1 with 3 C-123-K, 4 BAe-748.

1 with 10 C-47.

VIP: Royal flight: **ac**: 1 Airbus A-310-324, 1 Boeing 737-200, 1 *King Air* 200, 2 Bae-748, 3 *Merlin* IV; **hel**: 2 Bell 412.

TRG: 24 CT-4, 30 *Fantrainer*-400, 16 *Fantrainer*-600, 16 SF-260, 10 T-33A, 20 PC-9, 6 -C, 11 T-41, 36* L-39ZA/MP.

LIAISON: 3 *Commander*, 2 *King Air* E90, 30 O-1 *Bird Dog*, 2 *Queen Air*.

HEL: 2 sqn:

1 with 18 S-58T.

1 with 21 UH-1H.

AAM: AIM-9B/J *Sidewinder*, *Python* 3.

AD: *Blowpipe* and *Aspide* SAM. 1 AA arty bty: 4 *Skyguard*, 1 *Flycatcher* radars, each with 4 fire units of 2 x 30mm Mauser guns.

FORCES ABROAD:

UN AND PEACEKEEPING:

IRAQ/KUWAIT (UNIKOM): 6 Obs.

PARAMILITARY:

THAHAN PHRAN ('Hunter Soldiers'): 18,500; volunteer irregular force; 27 regt of some 200 coy.

NATIONAL SECURITY VOLUNTEER CORPS: 50,000.

MARINE POLICE: 2,500; 3 PCO, 3 PCC, 8 PFI, some 110 PCI⟨.

POLICE AVN: 500; **ac**: 1 *Airtourer*, 3 AU-23, 1 C-47, 2 Cessna 310, 1 CT-4, 3 DHC-4, 1 Do-28, 4 PC-6, 1 Short 330; **hel**: 27 Bell 205A, 14 Bell 206, 3 Bell 212, 6

UH-12, 5 KH-4, 1 S-62.
BORDER PATROL POLICE: 40,000.
PROVINCIAL POLICE: ε50,000, incl Special
Action Force (ε500).

VIETNAM

GDP	1993ε: $17.6bn:	
	per capita $800	
	1994ε: $19.1bn:	
	per capita $850	
Growth	1993: 8.1%	1994: 8.7%
Inflation	1993: 8.5%	1994: 9.9%
Debt	1993: $24.2bn	1994: $24.7bn
Def exp	1993ε: d 7,812bn ($720m)	
Def bdgt	1994ε: d 15,000bn ($860m)	
	1995ε: d 16,000bn ($890m)	
$1 = d	1993ε: 10,850	1994ε: 17,500
	1995ε: 18,000	

d = dong

Population: 74,109,000 (Chinese 3%, Montagnard
1–5%)

	13–17	18–22	23–32
Men	4,090,400	3,699,000	6,419,400
Women	3,944,400	3,596,600	6,386,200

TOTAL ARMED FORCES:
ACTIVE: ε572,000 (referred to as 'Main Force').
Terms of service: 2 years, specialists 3 years, some
ethnic minorities 2 years.
RESERVES: 'Strategic Rear Force', some 3–4m
manpower potential (see also Paramilitary).

ARMY: 500,000.
8 Military Regions, 2 special areas.
14 Corps HQ.
50 inf div.[a]
3 mech div.
10 armd bde.
15 indep inf regt.
SF incl AB bde, demolition engr regt.
Some 10 fd arty bde.
8 engr div.
10–16 economic construction div; 20 indep engr bde.
EQPT:
MBT: 1,300: 1,000 T-34/-54/-55, 200 T-62, Ch Type-
59, M-48A3.
LT TK: 600 PT-76, Ch Type-62/63.
RECCE: 100 BRDM-1/-2.
AIFV: 300 BMP.
APC: 1,100 BTR-40/-50/-60/-152, YW-531, M-113.
TOWED ARTY: 2,300: **76mm; 85mm; 100mm:** M-

1944, T-12; **105mm:** M-101/-102; **122mm:** Type-
54, Type-60, M-1938, D-30, D-74; **130mm:** M-46;
152mm: D-20; **155mm:** M-114.
SP ARTY: 152mm: 30 2S3; **175mm:** M-107.
COMBINED GUN/MOR: 120mm: 2S9 reported.
ASLT GUNS: 100mm: SU-100; **122mm:** ISU-122.
MRL: 107mm: 360 Type 63; **122mm:** 350 BM-21;
140mm: BM-14-16.
MOR: 82mm, 120mm: M-43; **160mm:** M-43.
ATGW: AT-3 *Sagger*.
RCL: 75mm: Ch Type-56; **82mm:** Ch Type-65, B-10;
87mm: Ch Type-51.
AD GUNS: 12,000: **14.5mm; 23mm:** incl ZSU-23-4
SP; **30mm; 37mm; 57mm; 85mm; 100mm**.
SAM: SA-7/-16.

[a] Inf div strengths vary from 5,000 to 12,500.

NAVY: ε42,000 (incl 30,000 Naval Infantry).
Four Naval Regions.
BASES: Hanoi (HQ), Cam Ranh Bay, Da Nang,
Haiphong, Ha Tou, Ho Chi Minh City, Can Tho, plus
several smaller bases.
FF: 7:
1 *Phan Ngu Lao* (US *Barnegat*) (ASUW), with 2 x
  SS-N-2 *Styx* SSM, 1 x 127mm gun.
5 Sov *Petya-II* with 4 x ASW RL, 3 x 533mm TT.
1 *Dai Ky* (US *Savage*) with 2 x 3 ASTT (trg).
PATROL AND COASTAL COMBATANTS: 57:
MSL CRAFT: 10:
8 Sov *Osa-II* with 4 x SS-N-2 SSM.
2 Sov *Tarantul* with 4 x SS-N-2D *Styx* SSM.
TORPEDO CRAFT: 19:
3 Sov *Turya* PHT with 4 x 533mm TT.
16 Sov *Shershen* PFT with 4 x 533mm TT.
PATROL, INSHORE: 28:
8 Sov SO-1, 3 US PGM-59/71, 11 *Zhuk*⟨, 4⟨, 2 Sov
Turya (no TT).
MCM: 11:
2 *Yurka* MSC, 4 *Sonya* MSC, 2 Ch *Lienyun* MSC, 1
Vanya MSI, 2 *Yevgenya* MSI, plus 5 K-8 boats.
AMPH: 7:
3 US LST-510-511 LST, capacity 200 tps, 16 tk.
3 Sov *Polnocny* LSM, capacity 180 tps, 6 tk.
1 US LSM-1 LSM, capacity about 50 tps, 4 tk.
Plus about 30 craft: 12 LCM, 18 LCU.
SPT AND MISC: 30+, incl:
1 survey, 4 small tankers, about 12 small tpt, 2 ex-
Sov Floating Docks and 3 div spt.

NAVAL INFANTRY: (30,000) (amph, cdo).

AIR FORCE: 15,000; 190 cbt ac, 33 armed hel
(plus many in store). 4 Air Div.
FGA: 1 regt with 65 Su-22, Su-27.

FTR: 5 regt with 125 MiG-21bis/PF.
ATTACK HEL: 25 Mi-24.
MR: 4 Be-12.
ASW HEL: 8 Ka-25.
SURVEY: 2 An-30.
TPT: 3 regt: incl 12 An-2, 4 An-24, 30 An-26, 8 Tu-134, 14 Yak-40.
HEL: some 70, incl Mi-4, Mi-6, Mi-8.
TRG: 3 regt with 52 ac, incl L-39, MiG-21U, Yak-18
AAM: AA-2 *Atoll*.

AIR DEFENCE FORCE: 15,000.
14 AD div:
SAM: some 66 sites with SA-2/-3/-6.

4 AD arty bde: **37mm, 57mm, 85mm, 100mm, 130mm;** plus People's Regional Force: ε1,000 units.
6 radar bde: 100 sites.

PARAMILITARY:
LOCAL FORCES: some 4–5m, incl People's Self-Defence Force (urban units), People's Militia (rural units); these comprise: static and mobile cbt units, log spt and village protection pl; some arty, mor and AD guns; acts as reserve.
BORDER DEFENCE CORPS: ε50,000.

FOREIGN FORCES:
RUSSIA: 500: naval base; ELINT station.

Caribbean and Latin America

Nuclear and Non-proliferation Developments

Argentina joined the Nuclear Non-Proliferation Treaty (NPT) on 10 February 1995 and Chile on 25 May 1995; Cuba is the only country in the region not to have joined. On 25 March 1995, Cuba signed the Treaty of Tlatelolco, which prohibits nuclear weapons in Latin America and the Caribbean, but it has not deposited its instrument of ratification. Guyana remains the only country in the region not to have signed this Treaty.

CARIBBEAN

Political Developments

The situation in **Haiti** has dominated events in the Caribbean over the last 12 months. In September 1994, US President Bill Clinton despatched a mission – former President Jimmy Carter, General Colin Powell, Senator Sam Nunn – to Haiti to negotiate the departure of General Raoul Cédras and other leaders of the military junta. Although the mission was ultimately successful, the 82nd Airborne Division was already airborne and a multinational force, predominantly from the US and under US command, had deployed before agreement was reached. The force's main task was to establish a secure and stable environment and to disarm the Haitian population. Seven Caribbean Community and Common Market (CARICOM) nations formed a multinational unit which, joined by three more states, has remained with the UN Mission in Haiti (UNMIH). UNMIH has an American commander. President Jean-Bertrand Aristide returned to Haiti on 15 October 1994, and the US handed over responsibility to UNMIH on 31 March 1995. Elections took place on 25 June with a second round in some constituencies to take place on 13 August.

Military Developments

The Haitian Armed Forces (FADH) and Civil Police have been disbanded and their weapons collected by the multinational force. As a short-term measure, an Interim Public Security Force (IPSF) has been formed but will be progressively demobilised as the new National Police Force is recruited and trained. The IPSF, although working alongside UN Civilian Police, is seen by many as the last remnant of the old regime as most of its 3,000 recruits are former FADH members. UNMIH is mandated to transfer responsibility to the Haitian authorities by the end of February 1996.

CENTRAL AMERICA

Political Developments

The mandate of the UN Mission in **El Salvador** (ONUSAL) was extended for a further six months in October 1994 to 30 April 1995, when the mission ended. In **Nicaragua**, General Humberto Ortega finally retired from the Army on 21 February 1995. **Guatemala** and **Mexico** are taking steps to improve their military and political cooperation in the battle against their separate guerrilla movements, both of which operate in their common border area. Mexico believes it can learn from Guatemala's counter-insurgency experience, while Guatemala expects that the Guatemalan National Revolutionary Unity (URNG) will no longer be free to operate in Mexico City.

In Mexico, the government has had to deal with a massive economic crisis and continued problems in the Chiapas province. The financial crisis of late 1994 was caused by sharply deteriorating balance-of-payments and fiscal deficits, probably as a result of rising internal security costs and regional subsidies to alleviate poverty which threatened the government's ability to meet its external debt repayments. An unprecedented rescue package was provided by the International Monetary Fund (IMF), the World Bank and the US government which could amount to some $50bn in loans and credit guarantees. A cease-fire arranged with the *Ejército Zapatista de Liberación Nacional* (EZLN) has been successfully maintained despite lack of progress in peace talks, and a large-scale military operation took place peacefully in February 1995 to demonstrate that the Army could exercise full control in the area. A round of peace talks began in April on how the Army would deploy and how the EZLN would be responsible for law and order.

Military Developments

There has been a major reorganisation of the **Mexican** Marines. The previous organisation based on security and police companies has been altered to one with a security battalion subordinate to each of the 17 naval zones. The Marine paratroop brigade, which had no combat or service support elements, has been retitled a regiment and has two battalions but no amphibious capability. The **Honduran** Army is now 2,000 stronger with a total manpower of 16,000. The reorganisation of the **Nicaraguan** Army into centrally controlled forces and territorial units is nearly complete. The five regional commands control a total of ten infantry and one tank battalion. The main elements are a special forces brigade with three battalions (previously there was only one SF battalion) and a light mechanised brigade with one tank, one mechanised infantry and one armoured transport battalion and two artillery units (one with D-20, one with BM-21). There is no longer a separate artillery brigade and manpower has been reduced by 3,500. There are now an additional 40 BTR-60 APCs and the total of 64 is split between the mechanised and the armoured transport battalion.

LATIN AMERICA

Political Developments

In January 1995, after a series of border incidents, fighting broke out between **Peru** and **Ecuador** in the Cenepa River valley. This has its origins in the 1941 war which resulted in Ecuador handing over territory to Peru and has led to disputes ever since. Following the violence, both sides reinforced the border region and mobilised reserves. President Alberto Fujimori of Peru, who rejected Organisation of American States (OAS) and UN mediation, and President Durán Ballén of Ecuador agreed to mediation by the four guarantors (US, Argentina, Brazil and Chile) of the 1942 Rio Protocol Treaty (which followed the 1941 war), who agreed to send 50 military officers to form the Ecuador–Peru Military Observers Mission (MOMEP). Cease-fires were agreed to on 1 and 14 February, but have been continually violated. MOMEP's mandate to supervise the cease-fire and monitor the withdrawal of both sides was to last for 90 days (until 10 June) and it completed its deployment on 13 March. By the end of the 90-day period the separation and demobilisation of troops in the border region had been achieved. In **Peru**, the *Sendero Luminoso* (Shining Path) guerrillas are still active despite government claims that they are on the brink of defeat.

A major development in the war against drugs in **Colombia** was the arrest on 11 June 1995 of the leader of the Cali cartel, Gilbert Orejuda, and the surrender a week later of Cali's military leader, Henry Loaiza. Government security forces are making determined efforts to destroy the poppy and coca crops mainly by aerial spraying. The guerrilla war waged by the Revolutionary Armed Forces of Colombia (FARC) continues, but in June 1995 the smaller opposition groups, the National Liberation Army (ELN) and the People's Liberation Army (EPL), responded positively to President Ernesto Samper's offer of talks. A relatively new development has been the increasing number of attacks by the ELN and other guerrilla forces on **Venezuelan** military posts. Venezuela increased its border surveillance activities in November 1994 and further reinforced the frontier region with 5,000 more troops in March 1995 following the most serious incident when eight Venezuelan Marines were killed. Venezuela has stressed that its action is not hostile to Colombia, but any 'hot pursuit' operations might result in clashes between the two armies.

Military Developments

Conscription ended in **Argentina** on 1 January 1995. The number of armoured vehicles in the Army has increased: there are now 200 TAM tanks (30 more than previously); 216 TAM infantry fighting vehicles (50 more); and 111 MOWAG *Grenadier* APCs (30 more). The **Brazilian** Navy has commissioned a second *Tupi*-class (German T-209/1400) submarine and a UK *Broadsword*-class frigate (three more have been purchased from the UK). One US *Gearing*-class (*Marcilio Dias*) destroyer has been retired. The Navy has ordered nine *Lynx* naval helicopters and upgrades for the five already in service. It is also obtaining eight ex-US SH-3 naval helicopters under the Excess Defence Articles (EDA) programme, which will be delivered in December 1995. A contract for the modernisation of the six *Niteroi*-class of frigates was announced in early 1995. The third Type 209 submarine out of five planned (the second from indigenous production under licence) is undergoing sea trials in 1995 prior to entry into service in 1996. Development work on a nuclear submarine programme continues, reportedly at a lower priority than before. The Brazilian Army has an additional $800 million to spend on procurement between 1994 and 1997 – an indication of the government's growing reliance on the Army for internal security. So far the Army has ordered 61 German *Leopard* 1 tanks, some 50 L-118 105mm light guns for $60m and heavy mortars from the UK (these may be for Marine use), and *Eryx* anti-tank missiles from France. An agreement to purchase *Mistral* SAMs from France has also been finalised. The Air Force is expected to award a contract for ALX advanced trainer/light-attack aircraft prototypes as the precursor to an order for as many as 100 aircraft. Manpower has been reduced in each of the three services and overall by some 40,000. In **Chile** the Army has increased the number of its Cardoen/MOWAG *Piranha* APCs by 100. The Navy has retired one *Almirante Riveros*-class destroyer; a fourth *Micalvi*-class and four more Israeli *Dabur*-class (*Grumete Diaz*) PCC have been brought into service. The Air Force has retired its very old *Hunter* FGA aircraft and is taking delivery of 20 *Mirage* 5 (15 BA and 5 -BD) aircraft from Belgium. The Air Force remains the only one in South America allowed to operate US F-16 aircraft. However, US Department of Defense ambitions to sell early-model F-16 aircraft and other advanced weaponry may induce a change in US regional sales policy and encourage other states to modernise their inventories. The Air Force has also acquired one converted Boeing 707 from Israel which will have an airborne early-warning role. The **Colombian** Navy has retired its US *Courtney*-class (*Boyaca*) frigate. The **Peruvian** Air Force has acquired eight more attack helicopters (Mi-24/-25). The **Uruguayan** Army has acquired 60 Polish OT-64 SKOT APCs and 44 120mm mortars. New information has allowed a reassessment of the Uruguayan Air Force. It has 36 combat-capable aircraft (not 24 as shown in previous years): seven T-33A are in squadron service; 12 T-34A/B trainers are considered combat-capable; while six AT-6 trainers have been disposed of.

Defence Spending

Under the impetus of democratisation and economic liberalisation, there have been some great changes in the pattern and structure of military expenditure in the region over the last decade. First, military spending is now more a function of economic strength than of military rule and civil war. Second, priority has shifted from procurement to manpower and operations. The IISS estimates that regional military expenditure in 1994 was $18.4bn and about 1.7% of regional gross domestic product (GDP). By comparison, aggregate expenditure in 1985 was slightly higher at $18.5bn (at constant 1993 prices), but represented nearly twice the proportion of GDP (3.1%). It is worth noting that the precipitous reduction in Cuban military expenditure accounts for much of the regional fall. Excluding Cuba, the aggregate spending level in 1994 is actually at similar levels to the years of peak expenditure in the early and mid-1980s. The resilience of military spending is due in part to improved economic performance resulting in higher fiscal revenues, but is also evidence that the new set of national-security challenges confronting the region are no less demanding in terms of military effort than of old.

Recent conflicts in the region have confirmed the high cost of modern warfare and military intervention. According to official reports, the undeclared month-long border war in early 1995 between Ecuador and Peru cost Ecuador $250m and Peru in the region of $100–350m. In Mexico, the Chiapas campaign has added at least $300m to annual military expenditure, and these extra costs are set to persist in 1995. Military intervention through UN-sponsored operations is hardly less expensive. The Haiti operation is said to have cost the US over $1bn since October 1994. This is a voluntary contribution, since these costs are not reimbursed by the UN. The projected cost of UNMIH for 1995 ($258m) is less great, but still sizeable by comparison with Haiti's own military expenditure in recent years. In El Salvador, the UN Security Council extended the ONUSAL mandate in November 1994 for a final period to 30 April 1995. The operation cost some $29m in 1994.

Because of the residual influence of military hierarchies in the affairs of civil government, the evidence on military expenditure should be treated with caution. In particular, assessment of the real cost of the military effort is often difficult because of under-reporting. Similarly, several governments tend, first, to classify paramilitary spending, military pensions and defence industrial subsidies outside the defence budget without giving specific details under other budget headings and, second, to withhold details of extra-budgetary accounts related, for example, to industrial and commercial revenues for the military. If these revenues and expenditures were added to the official figures, a rather different picture of regional spending would probably emerge. Two examples illustrate the point. This year, *The Military Balance* has obtained information on Chile's military pensions and extra-budgetary military funding from industrial sources. When these are added to the final expenditure figure, it increases by over two-thirds. In the case of Ecuador, the official defence budget is said to be augmented by oil revenues and profits from commercial enterprises run by the military as well as by contingency funds allocated from the executive budget. These extra funds increase the defence budget by one-third. Unfortunately there is little systematic information of this kind, and for want of hard evidence it can only be observed that some military expenditures may be significantly higher than official figures indicate. Latin American inhibitions over transparency have resulted in only six countries in 1993 responding to the annual UN questionnaire on military expenditure.

Functional Categories as % of Military Expenditure in 1993, Selected Countries

	Argentina	Brazil	Chile	Mexico	Peru
Personnel	76.7	72.7	59.1	55.8	19.1
O&M	16.0	19.1	36.5	29.6	73.0
Procurement	5.5	6.5	4.5	7.5	7.2
R&D	0.9	1.9	–	–	–
Construction	0.9	–	–	7.1	0.7

For those countries which report military expenditure to the UN, some evidence of the composition of the official defence spending is available. The table shows spending in the constituent functions as a proportion of total expenditure for five countries in 1993. Despite the statistical anomalies created by non-standardised classification of expenditure, the data provide a clear indication of the priority attached to personnel and O&M expenditure, and the very small proportions taken by procurement and R&D. Official 1994 data for Brazil show that this trend continues. Personnel accounts for 72%, O&M 13%, and Procurement and R&D just 14%. It should be added that these figures are difficult to reconcile with evidence on indigenous weapons procurement and R&D (as opposed to imported arms and technology transfers) in the countries concerned, and most probably exclude defence industrial subsidies and extra-budgetary funding.

In general the decline in procurement concerned foreign supply until the trend began to reverse in 1994. Up to 1993, regional arms imports and exports declined sharply from typical 1980 levels. According to the US Arms Control and Disarmament Agency (ACDA), the mid-1980s were the peak years for arms imports. In 1985, for example, arms worth some $5.7bn (at constant 1993 prices) were imported into the region; by 1990 this figure had declined to $2.6bn; and in 1993 arms imports were valued at $380m. A large part of the decline can be attributed to the loss of Soviet influence and the curtailment of Soviet arms transfers. Since the latter often involved grant, soft-loan or barter arrangements rather than hard currency, it is also probable that the 1980s statistics overstate the prices actually paid by recipients. In two known cases – those of Peru and Nicaragua – Russia is still seeking to recoup debt allegedly owed to the former Soviet Union. Official arms exports (mostly involving Brazil, Argentina and Chile) have also declined sharply since the 1980s. In the peak year of 1988, arms exports were worth $1.2bn; by 1993 the value had declined to $60m.

Beginning in 1994, there has been an observable increase in arms purchases from both outside and within the region. The momentum is being maintained in 1995. The increased activity is primarily due to three factors. First, the Ecuador–Peru conflict, during which several Latin American countries supplied arms mainly to Ecuador. Second, the re-emergence of Russia in the Latin American arms market. Recent transactions have included 56 SA-18 SAM launchers for Brazil, and supplies of weaponry and spare parts to Peru have resumed. Third, a modernisation programme is under way in Brazil.

US aid to the region has fallen dramatically as a result of changing foreign-policy priorities in the aftermath of the Cold War, particularly in respect of military equipment transfers. The aggregate level of US assistance of all kinds has declined from $1,366m in 1992 (or 14% of all US bilateral aid) to $858m in 1995 (7%) and a request for $813m (8%) in 1996. Security and military assistance has dropped from $775m in 1990 (of which $545m was security-related economic aid and $218m equipment-related) to $268m in 1992 (of which $110m was equipment-related and $84m for narcotics-related law enforcement) to $90m in 1995 (of which $53m is for anti-drugs operations and $16m for equipment). In 1996 the budget request for regional military assistance has grown to $170m, due almost entirely to a large increase for narcotics-related law-enforcement funding ($150m).

This year the dollar GDP figures for several countries in the Latin American region have been revised according to the estimates of the Inter-American Development Bank, and in some cases the dollar conversion rates are different from the average exchange-rate values shown under the country entry. Consequently, dollar GDP figures may vary from those cited in *The Military Balance* in previous years. Defence budgets and expenditures have been converted at the dollar exchange rate used for GDP and may also differ from figures in previous years.

ANTIGUA AND BARBUDA

GDP	1993: EC $1.05bn ($390m):	
	per capita $4,700	
	1994ε:EC $1.12bn ($410m):	
	per capita $4,900	
Growth	1993: 3.4%	1994ε: 3.5%
Inflation	1992: 4.5%	1993: 7.0%
Ext Debt	1992: $328m	1993: $309m
Def bdgt	1993ε: EC $8.5m ($3.2m)	
	1994ε: EC $8.8m ($3.3m)	
	1995ε: EC $9.0m ($3.3m)	
$1 = EC $	1993: 2.70	1994: 2.70
	1995: 2.70	

EC $ = East Caribbean dollar

Population: 68,000

	13–17	18–22	23–32
Men	5,000	4,000	4,000
Women	5,000	4,000	6,000

TOTAL ARMED FORCES: (all services form combined Antigua and Barbuda Defence Force).
ACTIVE: 150.
RESERVES: 75.

ARMY: 125.

NAVY: 25.
BASES: St Johns.
PATROL CRAFT: 1 *Swift* PCI with 1 x 12.7mm, 2 x 7.62mm gun (plus 2 *Boston* Whalers, 1 boat).

FORCES ABROAD:
UN AND PEACEKEEPING:
HAITI (UNMIH):15.

ARGENTINA

GDP	1993: P 255.3bn ($181.9bn):	
	per capita $6,000	
	1994: P 281.3bn ($200.3bn):	
	per capita $6,300	
Growth	1993: 6.0%	1994: 4.7%
Inflation	1993: 10.6%	1994: 3.9%
Debt	1993: $74.5bn	1994: $82.3bn
Def exp	1993: P 4.25bn ($3.03bn)	
	1994: P 4.78bn ($3.09bn)	

Def bdgt	1995: P 4.86bn ($3.14bn)	
FMA	1994: $0.1m (IMET)	
	1995: $0.1m (IMET)	
	1996: $0.3m (IMET)	
$1 = P[a]	1993: 1.00	1994: 1.00
	1995: 1.00	

P = Argentinean peso

[a] The peso Argentino, equal to 10,000 australes, was introduced on 1 January 1992. The official rate shown above is pegged to the US$.

Population: 34,254,000

	13–17	*18–22*	*23–32*
Men	1,633,000	1,491,000	2,480,000
Women	1,579,000	1,447,000	2,422,000

TOTAL ARMED FORCES:
ACTIVE: 67,300 (18,100 conscripts).
Terms of service: Conscription ended 1 April 1995.
RESERVES: 377,000: Army 250,000 (National Guard 200,000; Territorial Guard 50,000); Navy 77,000; Air Force 50,000.

ARMY: 40,400 (13,400 conscripts).
3 Corps:
1 with 1 armd, 1 mech bde, 1 trg bde.
1 with 1 inf, 1 mtn bde.
1 with 1 armd, 2 mech, 1 mtn bde.
Corps tps: 1 lt armd cav regt (recce), 1 arty, 1 AD arty, 1 engr bn in each Corps.

STRATEGIC RESERVE:
1 AB bde.
1 mech bde (4 mech, 1 armd cav, 2 SP arty bn).
Army tps:
1 mot inf bn (Army HQ Escort Regt).
1 mot cav regt (Presidential Escort).
1 SF coy, 3 avn bn.
1 AD arty bn, 2 engr bn.

EQPT:
MBT: 96 M-4 *Sherman* (in store), ε200 TAM.
LT TK: 58 AMX-13, 106 SK-105 *Kuerassier*.
RECCE: 48 AML-90.
AIFV: 30 AMX-VCI, 216 TAM VCTP.
APC: 129 M-3 half-track, 262 M-113, 80 MOWAG *Grenadier* (mod *Roland*).
TOWED ARTY: 105mm: 88 M-56; **155mm:** 119 CITEFA Models 77/-81.
SP ARTY: 155mm: 24 Mk F3.
MRL: 105mm: 30 SLAM *Pampero*; **127mm:** 20 SLAM SAPBA-1.
MOR: 81mm: 1,000; **120mm:** 330 *Brandt* (50 SP in VCTM AIFV).
ATGW: 600 SS-11/-12, *Cobra (Mamba)*, 2,100

Mathogo.
RCL: 75mm: 75 M-20; **90mm:** 100 M-67; **105mm:** 930 M-1968.
AD GUNS: 20mm: 30; **30mm:** 30; **35mm:** 100 GDF-001; **40mm:** 95 L/60/-70 (in store); **90mm:** 20.
SAM: *Tigercat*, *Blowpipe*, 6 *Roland*.
SURV: RASIT (veh, arty), *Green Archer* (mor).
AC: 1 C212-200, 5 Cessna 207, 5 *Commander* 690, 2 DHC-6, 3 G-222, 1 *Merlin* IIIA, 4 *Merlin* IV, 3 *Queen Air*, 1 *Sabreliner*, 5 T-41, 23 OV-1D.
HEL: 6 A-109, 3 AS-332B, 5 Bell 205, 4 FH-1100, 4 SA-315B, 2 SA-330, 9 UH-1H, 8 UH-12.

NAVY: 18,000 (incl 3,000 Naval Aviation, 4,000 Marines and 3,500 conscripts).
3 Naval Areas: *Centre*: from River Plate to 42° 45' S; *South:* from 42° 45' S to Cape Horn; and *Antarctica.*
BASES: Buenos Aires, Ezeiza (Naval Air), La Plata, Rio Santiago (submarine base), Puerto Belgrano (HQ Centre), Punta Indio (Naval Air), Mar del Plata (submarine base), Ushuaia (HQ South).
SS: 3:
2 *Santa Cruz* (Ge TR-1700) with 533mm TT (SST-4 HWT).
Plus 1 *Salta* (Ge T-209/1200) with 533mm TT (SST-4 HWT) (plus 1 in major refit/modernisation).
PRINCIPAL SURFACE COMBATANTS: 13:
DD: 6:
2 *Hercules* (UK Type 42) with 1 x 2 *Sea Dart* SAM; plus 1 SA-319 hel (ASW), 2 x 3 ASTT, 4 x MM-38 *Exocet* SSM, 1 x 114mm gun.
4 *Almirante Brown* (Ge *MEKO-360*) ASW with 2 x SA-316 hel, 2 x 3 ASTT; plus 8 x MM-40 *Exocet* SSM, 1 x 127mm gun.
FF: 7:
4 *Espora* (Ge *MEKO-140*) with 2 x 3 ASTT, hel deck; plus 8 x MM-40 *Exocet*.
3 *Drummond* (Fr A-69) with 2 x 3 ASTT; plus 4 x MM-38 *Exocet*, 1 x 100mm gun.
ADDITIONAL AWAITING REFIT: 1 *Veinticinco de Mayo* (UK *Colossus*) CV.
PATROL AND COASTAL COMBATANTS: 14:
TORPEDO CRAFT: 2 *Intrepida* (Ge Lürssen 45-m) PFT with 2 x 533mm TT (SST-4 HWT).
PATROL CRAFT: 12:
OFFSHORE: 8:
1 *Teniente Olivieri* (ex-US oilfield tug).
3 *Irigoyen* (US *Cherokee* AT).
2 *King* (trg) with 3 x 105mm guns.
2 *Sorbral* (US *Sotoyomo* AT).
INSHORE: 4 *Baradero* PCI(.
MCM: 6:
4 *Neuquen* (UK '*Ton*') MSC.
2 *Chaco* (UK '*Ton*') MHC.
AMPH: 1 *Cabo San Antonio* LST (hel deck), capacity

600 tps, 18 tk.
Plus 20 craft: 4 LCM, 16 LCVP.
SPT AND MISC: 9:
1 AGOR, 3 tpt, 1 ocean tug, 1 icebreaker, 2 trg, 1 research.

NAVAL AVIATION: (3,000); 45 cbt ac, 13 armed hel.
ATTACK: 1 sqn with 12 *Super Etendard*.
MR/ASW: 1 sqn with 3 L-188, 9 S-2E/T.
EW: 2 L-188E.
HEL: 2 sqn:
1 ASW/tpt with 7 ASH-3H (ASW) and 4 AS-61D (tpt).
1 spt with 6 SA-316/-319 (with SS-11).
TPT: 1 sqn with 1 BAe-125, 3 F-28-3000, 3 L-188, 4 *Queen Air* 80, 9 *Super King Air*, 4 US-2A.
SURVEY: 3 PC-6B (Antarctic flt).
TRG: 2 sqn with 7* EMB-326, 9* MB-326, 5* MB-339A, 10 T-34C.
MSL:
ASM: AGM-12 *Bullpup*, AM-39 *Exocet*, AS-12, *Martín Pescador*.
AAM: AIM-9 *Sidewinder*, R-550 *Magic*.

MARINES: (4,000).
Fleet Forces: 2, each with 2 bn, 1 amph recce coy, 1 fd arty bn, 1 ATK, 1 engr coy.
Amph spt force: 1 marine inf bn.
1 AD arty regt (bn).
2 SF bn.
EQPT:
RECCE: 12 ERC-90 *Lynx*.
AAV: 21 LVTP-7.
APC: 6 MOWAG *Grenadier*, 35 Panhard VCR.
TOWED ARTY: 105mm: 15 M-101/M-56; **155mm:** 6 M-114.
MOR: 81mm: 70.
ATGW: 50 *Bantam*, *Cobra (Mamba)*.
RL: 89mm: 60 3.5-in M-20.
RCL: 105mm: 30 1974 FMK1.
AD GUNS: 30mm: 10 HS-816; **35mm:** GDF-001.
SAM: *Blowpipe, Tigercat*.

AIR FORCE: 8,900 (1,200 conscripts); 237 cbt ac, 11 armed hel, 9 air bde, 10 AD arty bty, 1 SF (AB) coy.
AIR OPS COMD (9 bde):
FGA/FTR: 3 sqn:
2 (1 OCU) with 20 *Mirage* IIIC (-CJ: 17; -BE: 1; -BJ: 2), 15 *Mirage* IIIEA.
1 with 7 *Mirage* 5P, 22 *Dagger Nesher* (-A: 19; -B: 3).
FGA: 4 sqn with 16 A-4B/C, 32 A-4M, 4 OA-4M.
COIN: 3 sqn:
2 with 45 IA-58A, 30 MS-760.
1 armed hel with 11 Hughes MD500, 3 UH-1H.
MR: 1 Boeing 707.
SURVEY: 3 *Learjet* 35A, 4 1A-50.
TKR: 2 Boeing 707, 2 KC-130H.

SAR: 4 SA-315 hel.
TPT: 5 sqn with: **ac:** 5 Boeing 707, 2 C-130E, 3 C-130B, 5 -H, 1 L-100-30, 6 DHC-6, 10 F-27, 4 F-28, 15 IA-50, 2 *Merlin* IVA, 1 S-70A (VIP). Antarctic spt unit with 1 DHC-6; **hel:** 5 Bell 212, 2 CH-47C, 1 S-61R (*Sea King*).
CAL: 1 sqn with 2 Boeing 707, 3 IA-50, 2 *Learjet* 35, 1 PA-31.
LIAISON: 1 sqn with 20 Cessna 182, 1 Cessna 320, 7 *Commander*, 1 *Sabreliner*.
AIR TRG COMD: ac: 28 EMB-312, 16* IA-63, 30* MS-760, 29 T-34B; **hel:** 3 Hughes 500D.
MSL:
ASM: ASM-2 *Martín Pescador*.
AAM: AIM-9B *Sidewinder*, R-530, R-550, *Shafrir*.

FORCES ABROAD:
UN AND PEACEKEEPING:
ANGOLA (UNAVM II): 2 Obs, 1 civ pol. **CROATIA** (UNCRO): 859; 1 inf bn. **CYPRUS** (UNFICYP): 392; 1 inf bn. **HAITI** (UNMIH): 15 plus 100 civ pol. **IRAQ/ KUWAIT** (UNIKOM): 50 engr plus 7 Obs. **MIDDLE EAST** (UNTSO): 6 Obs. **RWANDA** (UNAMIR): 10 Obs. **WESTERN SAHARA** (MINURSO): 7 Obs.

PARAMILITARY:
GENDARMERIE (Ministry of Defence): 18,000; 5 Regional Comd.
EQPT: *Shorland* recce, 40 UR-416; **81mm** mor; **ac:** 3 Piper, 5 PC-6; **hel:** 5 SA-315.
PREFECTURA NAVAL (Coast Guard): 13,240; 7 comd.
EQPT: 6 PCO: 5 *Mantilla*, 1 *Delfin*; 4 PCI, 19 PCI‹; **ac:** 5 C-212; 4 Short *Skyvan*; **hel:** 3 SA-330, 6 MD-500, 2 Bell-47.

BAHAMAS

GDP	1993: $B3.30bn ($3.30bn):	
	per capita $11,100	
	1994: $B3.43bn ($3.43bn):	
	per capita $11,200	
Growth	1993: 0.8%	1994: 1.5%
Inflation	1993: 2.8%	1994: 1.5%
Debt	1993: $455m	1994: $470m
Def exp	1993: $B18m ($18m)	
	1994: $B18m ($18m)	
Def bdgt	1995ε: $B20m ($20m)	
FMA	1994: $0.7m (Narcs, IMET)	
	1995: $0.7m (Narcs)	
	1996: $0.8m (Narcs, IMET)	
$1 = $B	1993–95: 1.00	
$B = Bahamian dollar		

Population: 275,000

	13–17	*18–22*	*23–32*
Men	15,000	16,200	28,400
Women	13,600	15,200	27,000

TOTAL SECURITY FORCES:
ACTIVE: 2,000: Police (1,200); Defence Force (850).

NAVY (ROYAL BAHAMIAN DEFENCE FORCE): 800 (incl 60 women).
BASE: Coral Harbour, New Providence Island.
PATROL AND COASTAL COMBATANTS: 15:
INSHORE: 3 *Yellow Elder* PFI, 1 *Marlin*, 6 *Fenrick Sturrup* (ex-USCG *Cape Higgon* Cl) PCI, 5 PCI⟨, plus some ex-fishing vessels and boats.
MISC: 2: 1 converted LCM (ex-USN), 1 small auxiliary.
AC: 1 Cessna 404, 1 Cessna 421.

FORCES ABROAD:
UN AND PEACEKEEPING:
HAITI (UNMIH): 36.

BARBADOS

GDP	1993: B$3.28bn ($1.73bn):		
	per capita $5,300		
	1994: B$3.41bn ($1.84bn):		
	per capita $5,500		
Growth	1993: 0.8%	1994: 4.0%	
Inflation	1993: 1.2%	1994: 0.1%	
Debt	1993: $568m	1994: $620m	
Def exp	1993ε:B$25m ($13m)		
	1994: B$26m ($14m)		
	1995ε:B$26 m ($14m)		
$1 = B$	1993–95: 2.01		

B$ = Barbados dollar

Population: 261,000

	13–17	*18–22*	*23–32*
Men	11,000	12,200	25,000
Women	11,000	11,600	23,000

TOTAL ARMED FORCES:
ACTIVE: 610.
RESERVES: 430

ARMY: 500.

NAVY: 110.

BASES: St Ann's Fort Garrison (HQ). Bridgetown.
PATROL AND COASTAL COMBATANTS: 5:
1 *Kebir* PCO with 2 x 12.7mm gun.
3 *Guardian II* PCI⟨.
1 *Enterprise* PCO⟨ with 1 x12.7mm gun.

FORCES ABROAD:
UN AND PEACEKEEPING:
HAITI (UNMIH): 24 plus 10 civ pol.

BELIZE

GDP	1993: $BZ1,048m ($550m):		
	per capita $2,400		
	1994: $BZ1,150m ($570m):		
	per capita $2,400		
Growth	1993: 3.5%	1994: 2.2%	
Inflation	1993: 1.5%	1994: 2.3%	
Debt	1993: $18m	1994: $21m	
Def bdgt	1993ε:$BZ20m ($10m)		
	1994ε:$BZ22m ($11m)		
	1995ε:$BZ28m ($14m)		
FMA[a]	1994: $0.20m (FMF, IMET)		
	1995: $0.04m (IMET)		
	1996: $0.30m (IMET)		
$1 = $BZ	1993–95: 2.00		

$BZ = Belize dollar

[a] UK defence expenditure in Belize was $55m in 1992–93, $51m in 1993–94 and $23m in 1994–95.

Population: 215,000

	13–17	*18–22*	*23–32*
Men	12,800	10,800	16,200
Women	12,800	10,800	16,200

TOTAL ARMED FORCES:
ACTIVE: 1,050.
RESERVES: 700.

ARMY: 1,000.
1 inf bn (3 inf, 1 spt, 1 trg, 3 Reserve coy).
EQPT:
MOR: 81mm: 6.
RCL: 84mm: 8 *Carl Gustav*.

MARITIME WING: 50.
PATROL CRAFT: 1 PCI⟨, plus some 8 armed boats and 3 ramped lighters.

AIR WING: 15: 2 cbt ac, no armed hel.
MR/TPT: 2 BN-2B *Defender*.

FORCES ABROAD:
UN AND PEACEKEEPING:
HAITI (UNMIH): 3.

BOLIVIA

GDP	1993: B 36.48bn ($8.55bn):	
	per capita $2,500	
	1994: B 42.38bn ($9.17bn):	
	per capita $2,600	
Growth	1993: 4.0%	1994: 4.2%
Inflation	1993: 8.5%	1994: 8.3%
Debt	1993: $4.2bn	1994: $4.3bn
Def exp	1993: B 538m ($126m)	
Def bdgt	1994ε: B 602m ($130m)	
	1995ε: B 642m ($136m)	
FMA	1994: $19.5m (FMF, Narcs, IMET)	
	1995: $16.2m (Narcs)	
	1996: $60.5m (Narcs, IMET)	
$1 = B	1993: 4.27	1994: 4.62
	1995: 4.71	

B = Boliviano

Population: 8,075,000

	13–17	18–22	23–32
Men	460,200	398,400	599,600
Women	457,800	402,600	621,800

TOTAL ARMED FORCES:
ACTIVE: 33,500 (some 20,000 conscripts).
Terms of service: 12 months, selective.

ARMY: 25,000 (some 18,000 conscripts).
HQ: 6 Military Regions.
Army HQ direct control:
  2 armd bn.
  1 mech cav regt.
  1 Presidential Guard inf regt.
10 'div'; org, composition varies; comprise:
  8 cav gp (5 horsed, 2 mot, 1 aslt); 1 mot inf 'regt'
  with 2 bn; 22 inf bn (incl 5 inf aslt bn); 1 armd bn;
  1 arty 'regt' (bn); 5 arty gp (coy); 1 AB 'regt' (bn);
  6 engr bn.
EQPT:
LT TK: 36 SK-105 *Kuerassier*.
RECCE: 24 EE-9 *Cascavel*.
APC: 108: 50 M-113, 10 V-100 *Commando*,
24 MOWAG *Roland*, 24 EE-11 *Urutu*.
TOWED ARTY: 75mm: 70 incl M-116 pack,ε10 Bofors
M-1935; **105mm:** 30 incl M-101, FH-18;
122mm: 36 Ch Type -54.
MOR: 81mm: 50; **107mm:** M-30.

AC: 2 C-212, 1 *King Air* B90, 1 *Super King Air* 200 (VIP).

NAVY: 4,500 (incl Naval Aviation and 2,000 Marines).
6 Naval Districts covering Lake Titicaca and the
rivers; each 1 Flotilla.
BASES: Riberalta (HQ), Tiquina (HQ), Puerto
Busch, Puerto Guayaramerín (HQ), Puerto Villaroel,
Trinidad (HQ), Puerto Suárez (HQ), Cobija (HQ).
RIVER PATROL CRAFT: some 9⟨; plus some 15 US
Boston whalers.
SPT: some 20 riverine craft/boats.

NAVAL AVIATION:
AC: 1 Cessna U206G, 1 Cessna 402C.

MARINES: (2,000): 6 bn (1 in each District).

AIR FORCE: 4,000 (perhaps 2,000 conscripts);
48 cbt ac, 10 armed hel.
FTR: 1 sqn with 6 AT-33N, 4 F-86F (ftr/trg).
COIN: 15 PC-7.
SPECIAL OPS: 1 sqn with 10 Hughes 500M hel.
SAR: 1 hel sqn with 4 HB-315B, 2 SA-315B, 1 UH-1.
SURVEY: 1 sqn with 5 Cessna 206, 1 Cessna 210, 1
Cessna 402, 3 *Learjet* 25/35.
TPT: 3 sqn:
1 VIP tpt with 1 L-188, 1 *Sabreliner*, 2 *Super King Air*.
2 tpt with 10 C-130A/B/H, 4 F-27-400, 1 IAI-201, 2
  King Air, 2 C-47, 1 Convair 580.
LIAISON: ac: 9 Cessna 152, 2 Cessna 185, 13 Cessna 206,
1 Cessna 208, 2 Cessna 402; 2 Beech Bonanza, 2 Beech
Barons, PA-31, 4 PA-34; **hel:** 2 Bell 212, 22 UH-1H.
TRG: 1 Cessna 152, 2 Cessna 172, 11* PC-7, 4 SF-
260CB, 15 T-23, 12* T-33A, 1 Lancair 320.
AD: 1 air-base defence regt (Oerlikon twin **20mm,**
18 Ch type-65 **37mm,** some truck-mounted guns).

PARAMILITARY:
NATIONAL POLICE: some 30,000; 9 bde, 2
rapid action regt, 27 frontier units.
NARCOTICS POLICE: some 600.

BRAZIL

GDP	1993: R 14.1bn ($381.3bn):	
	per capita $5,600	
	1994: R n.k. ($415.0bn):	
	per capita $6,000	
Growth	1993: 4.1%	1994: 5.7%
Inflation	1993: 2,148%	1994: 2,669%
Debt	1993: $132.7bn	1994: $134.9bn
Def exp	1993: R 188m ($6.27bn)	

Def bdgt

	1994:	R 4,108m ($6.42bn)
	1994:	R 5,723m ($6.73bn)
	1995:	R 11,564m ($7.23bn)
FMA	1994:	$0.5m (Narcs, IMET)
	1995:	$0.7m (Narcs, IMET)
	1996:	$1.2m (Narcs, IMET)
$1 = R	1993: 0.03	1994 0.64
	1995: 0.91	

R = real[a]

[a] The cruzeiro real, equal to 1,000 cruzeiros, was introduced in August 1993. This was followed by the introduction of the real, equal to 2,750 cruzeiros reals, in July 1994. The nominal values denominated in reals for GDP, defence budget and defence expenditure are not comparable since they are based on official figures that use a different indexation value.

Population: 161,374,000

	13–17	18–22	23–32
Men	8,418,000	7,658,000	13,771,800
Women	8,377,000	7,670,200	13,825,000

TOTAL ARMED FORCES:
ACTIVE: 295,000 (132,000 conscripts).
Terms of service: 12 months (can be extended by 6 months).
RESERVES: trained first-line: 1,115,000; 400,000 subject to immediate recall. Second-line: 225,000.

ARMY: 195,000 (incl 125,000 conscripts).
HQ: 7 Mil Comd, 11 Mil Regions.
8 div (3 with Region HQ).
1 armd cav bde (2 mech, 1 armd, 1 arty bn).
3 armd inf bde (each 2 inf, 1 armd, 1 arty bn).
4 mech cav bde (each 3 inf, 1 arty bn).
13 motor inf bde (26 bn).
1 mtn bde.
4 'jungle' bde.
1 frontier bde (6 bn).
1 AB bde (3 AB, 1 SF bn).
2 coast and AD arty bde.
3 cav guard regt.
28 arty gp (4 SP, 6 med, 18 fd).
2 engr gp each 4 bn; 10 bn (incl 2 railway) (to be increased to 34 bn).
Avn: hel bde forming, to comprise 52 hel per bn.
EQPT:
LT TK: 546: some 250 M-3, 296 M-41B/C.
RECCE: 409 EE-9 *Cascavel*, 30 M-8.
APC: 823: 219 EE-11 *Urutu*, 20 M-59, 584 M-113.
TOWED ARTY: 377: **105mm:** 264 M-101/-102, 21 Model 56 pack; **155mm:** 92 M-114.
SP ARTY: 105mm: 72 M-7/-108.
COASTAL ARTY: some 240 incl **57mm, 75mm, 120mm, 150mm, 152mm, 305mm**.

MRL: 108mm: SS-06; 4 *ASTROS* II.
MOR: 81mm; 107mm: 209 M-30; **120mm:** 77.
ATGW: 300 *Cobra*.
RCL: 57mm: 240 M-18A1; **75mm:** 20 M-20; **105mm; 106mm:** M-40A1.
AD GUNS: 200 incl **20mm; 35mm:** GDF-001; **40mm:** L-60/-70 (some with BOFI).
SAM: 2 *Roland* II.
HEL: 36 SA-365, 18 AS-550 *Fennec*, 16 AS-350 (armed).

NAVY: 50,000 (incl 1,200 Naval Aviation, 15,000 Marines and 2,000 conscripts).
5 Oceanic Naval Districts plus 1 Riverine; 1 Comd.
BASES: Ocean: Rio de Janeiro (HQ I Naval District), Salvador (HQ II District), Natal (HQ III District), Belém (HQ IV District), Rio Grande do Sul (HQ V District). River: Ladario (HQ VI District), Manaus.
SS: 5:
2 *Tupi* (Ge T-209/1400) with 533mm TT (UK *Tigerfish* HWT).
3 *Humaitá* (UK *Oberon*) with 533mm TT (*Tigerfish* HWT).
PRINCIPAL SURFACE COMBATANTS: 21:
CARRIER: 1 *Minas Gerais* (UK *Colossus*) CV (ASW), capacity 20 ac: typically **ac** 6 S-2E ASW, **hel** 4–6 ASH-3H, 3 AS-332 and 2 AS-355.
DD: 5:
1 *Marcilio Dias* (US *Gearing*) ASW with 1 *Wasp* hel (Mk 46 LWT), 1 x 8 *ASROC*, 2 x 3 ASTT; plus 2 x 2 127mm guns.
4 *Sergipe* (US *Sumner*) ASW, 4 with 1 *Wasp* hel, all with 2 x 3 ASTT; plus 3 x 2 127mm guns.
FF: 15:
1 *Greenhaigh* (ex-UK *Broadsword*) with 4 x MM-38 *Exocet* SSM, *Seawolf* MOD 4 SAM.
4 *Para* (US *Garcia*) with 1 x 8 *ASROC*, 2 x 3 ASTT, 1 x *Lynx* hel; plus 2 x 127mm guns.
4 *Constitucao* ASW with 1 *Lynx* hel, 2 x 3 ASTT, *Ikara* SUGW, 1 x 2 ASW mor; plus 2 x MM-40 *Exocet* SSM, 1 x 114mm gun.
2 *Niteroi*; weapons as ASW, except 4 x MM-40 *Exocet*, 2 x 114mm guns, no *Ikara*.
4 *Inhauma*, with 1 *Lynx* hel, 2 x 3 ASTT, plus 4 x MM-40 *Exocet*, 1 x 114mm gun.
PATROL AND COASTAL COMBATANTS: 29:
9 *Imperial Marinheiro* PCO.
1 *Grajaü* PCC.
6 *Piratini* (US PGM) PCI.
3 *Aspirante Nascimento* PCI (trg).
4 *Tracker* PCI〈.
PATROL, RIVERINE: 6:
3 *Roraima* and 2 *Pedro Teixeira*, 1 *Parnaiba*.
MCM: 6:
6 *Aratü* (Ge *Schütze*) MSI.
AMPH: 4:

2 *Ceara* (US *Thomaston*) LSD capacity 350 tps, 38 tk.
1 *Duque de Caxais* (US *de Soto County* LST), capacity 600 tps, 18 tk.
1 *Mattoso Maia* (US *Newport* LST) capacity 400 tps, 500 tons veh, 3 LCVP, 1 LCPL.
Plus some 49 craft: 3 LCU, 11 LCM, 35 LCVP.
SPT AND MISC: 26:
1 *Marajo* AO, 1 *Almirante G. Motta* AO, 1 repair ship, 1 submarine rescue, 4 tpt, 9 survey/oceanography, 1 *Brasil* trg, 5 ocean tugs, 3 buoy tenders (UK River).

NAVAL AVIATION: (1,200); 33 armed hel.
ASW: 1 hel sqn with 7 SH-3A.
ATTACK: 1 with 5 *Lynx* HAS-21.
UTL: 2 sqn with 5 AS-332, 12 AS-350 (armed), 9 AS-355 (armed).
TRG: 1 hel sqn with 13 TH-57.
ASM: AS-11, AS-12, *Sea Skua*.

MARINES: (15,000).
Fleet Force:
1 amph div (1 comd, 3 inf bn, 1 arty gp).
Reinforcement Comd:
5 bn incl 1 engr, 1 SF.
Internal Security Force:
8+ regional gp.
EQPT:
RECCE: 6 EE-9 Mk IV *Cascavel*.
AAV: 12 LVTP-7A1.
APC: 30 M-113, 5 EE-11 *Urutu*.
TOWED ARTY: 105mm: 15 M-101, 10 L118; **155mm:** 6 M-114.
MOR: 81mm: incl 2 SP.
RL: 89mm: 3.5-in M-20.
RCL: 106mm: 8 M-40A1.
AD GUNS: 40mm: 6 L/70 with BOFI.

AIR FORCE: 50,000 (5,000 conscripts); 273 cbt ac, 29 armed hel.
AD COMD: 1 gp.
FTR: 2 sqn with 16 F-103E/D (*Mirage* IIIE/DBR).
TAC COMD: 10 gp.
FGA: 3 sqn with 56 F-5E/-B/-F, 28 AMX.
COIN: 2 sqn with 58 AT-26 (EMB-326).
RECCE: 2 sqn with 4 RC-95, 10 RT-26, 12 *Learjet* 35 Recce/VIP, 3 RC-130E.
LIAISON/OBS: 7 sqn: 1 with **ac:** 8 T-27; 5 with **ac:** 31 U-7; **hel:** 29 UH-1H (armed).
MARITIME COMD: 4 gp.
ASW (afloat): 1 sqn with S-2: 13; -A: 7; - E: 6.
MR/SAR: 3 sqn with 11 EMB-110B, 20 EMB-111.
TPT COMD: 6 gp (6 sqn), plus 7 regional indep sqns:
1 with 9 C-130H, 2 KC-130H.
1 with 4 KC-137 (tpt/tkr).
1 with 12 C-91.
1 with 23 C-95A/B/C.

1 with 17 C-115.
1 (VIP) with **ac:** 1 VC-91, 12 VC/VU-93, 2 VC-96, 5 VC-97, 5 VU-9, 2 Boeing 737-200; **hel:** 3 VH-4.
7 (regional) with 7 C-115, 86 C-95A/B/C, 6 EC-9 (VU-9).
HEL: 6 AS-332 (armed), 8 AS-355, 4 Bell 206, 27 HB-350B.
LIAISON: 50 C-42, 3 Cessna 208, 30 U-42.
TRG COMD: ac: 38* AT-26, 97 EMB-110, 25 T-23, 98 T-25, 63* T-27 (*Tucano*), 14* AMX-T; **hel:** 4 OH-6A, 25 OH-13.
CAL: 1 unit with 2 C-95, 1 EC-93, 4 EC-95, 1 U-93.
AAM: AIM-9B *Sidewinder*, R-530, *Magic* 2.

FORCES ABROAD:
UN AND PEACEKEEPING:
ANGOLA (UNAVEM III): 30, incl 11 Obs plus 17 civ pol. **BOSNIA** (UNPROFOR): 14 Obs plus 1 civ pol. **CROATIA** (UNCRO): 19 Obs, 4 civ pol. **FYROM** (UNPREDEP): 1 Obs.

PARAMILITARY:
PUBLIC SECURITY FORCES (R): some 385,600 in state mil pol org (State Militias) under Army control and considered an Army Reserve.

CHILE

GDP	1993: pCh 18,454bn ($51.64bn): per capita $8,700	
	1994: pCh 21,918bn ($55.31bn): per capita $9,200	
Growth	1993: 6.3%	1994: 4.2%
Inflation	1993: 12.1%	1994: 11.4%
Debt	1993: $20.6bn	1994: $20.9bn
Def exp[a]	1993ε: pCh 628bn ($1.76bn)	
	1994ε: pCh 776bn ($1.96bn)	
Def bdgt	1994: pCh 450bn ($1.14bn)	
	1995: pCh 472bn ($1.17bn)	
FMA	1994: $0.1m (IMET)	
	1995: $0.1m (IMET)	
	1996: $0.3m (IMET)	
$1 = pCh	1993: 431	1994: 404
	1995: 404	

pCh = Chilean peso

[a] Incl Codelco (state company) copper fund est to be 10% of earnings ($200m in 1993 and $216m in 1994) and extra-budgetary pension costs est to be $560m in 1993 and $629m in 1994.

Population: 14,241,000

	13–17	*18–22*	*23–32*
Men	640,400	615,000	1,232,400
Women	617,000	595,800	1,207,400

TOTAL ARMED FORCES:
ACTIVE: ε99,000 (31,000 conscripts).
Terms of service: Army 1 year; Navy and Air Force 2 years.
RESERVES: Army 50,000.

ARMY: 54,000 (27,000 conscripts).
7 Mil Regions, 2 Corps HQ.
7 div:
  1 with 3 mot inf, 1 armd cav, 1 arty, 1 engr regt.
  1 with 3 mot inf, 4 mtn, 1 armd cav, 1 arty, 1 engr regt.
  1 with 3 mot inf, 2 mtn, 2 armd cav, 1 arty, 1 engr regt.
  1 with 1 mot inf, 2 mtn, 3 armd cav, 1 arty, 1 engr regt.
  1 with 2 mot inf, 2 armd cav, 1 arty, 1 engr regt.
  1 with 1 mot inf, 1 armd cav, 1 arty, 1 engr regt.
  1 with 1 mot inf, 1 mtn inf, 2 arty, 1 engr regt.
  1 bde with 1 armd cav, 1 mtn regt.
  1 bde with 1 mot inf, 1 cdo regt.
Army tps: 1 avn, 1 engr, 1 AB regt (1 AB, 1 SF bn).
EQPT:
MBT: 100 M-4A3, 19 AMX-30.
LT TK: 81: 21 M-24, 60 M-41.
RECCE: 50 EE-9 *Cascavel*.
AIFV: 20 MOWAG *Piranha* with **90mm** gun.
APC: 100 M-113, 180 Cardoen/MOWAG *Piranha*, 30 EE-11 *Urutu*.
TOWED ARTY: 114: **105mm**: 66 M-101, 36 Model 56; **155mm**: 12 M-71.
SP ARTY: 155mm: 12 Mk F3.
MOR: 81mm: 300 M-29; **107mm:** 15; **120mm:** 125 FAMAE (incl 50 SP).
ATGW: *Milan/Mamba, Mapats*.
RL: 89mm: 3.5-in M-20.
RCL: 150 incl: **57mm:** M-18; **106mm:** M-40A1.
AD GUNS: 20mm: 60 incl some SP (Cardoen/MOWAG).
SAM: 50 *Blowpipe, Javelin*.
AC:
TPT: 6 C-212, 1 *Citation* (VIP), 3 CN-235, 4 DHC-6, 3 PA-31, 8 PA-28 Piper *Dakota*.
TRG: 16 Cessna R-172.
HEL: 2 AB-206, 3 AS-332, 15 Enstrom 280 FX, 5 Hughes 530F (armed trg), 10 SA-315, 9 SA-330.

NAVY: 31,000 (incl 500 Naval Aviation, 5,000 Marines, 1,500 Coast Guard and 3,000 conscripts).
DEPLOYMENT AND BASES:
3 main comd: Fleet (includes DD and FF), Submarine Flotilla, Transport. Remaining forces allocated to 4 Naval Zones:
1st Naval Zone (26°S – 36°S approx): Valparaiso (HQ), Vina Del Mar.
2nd Naval Zone (36°S – 43°S approx): Talcahuano (HQ), Puerto Montt.
3rd Naval Zone (43°S to Cape Horn): Punta Arenas (HQ), Puerto Williams.
4th Naval Zone (north of 26°S approx): Iquique (HQ).
SS: 4:
2 *O'Brien* (UK *Oberon*) with 8 x 533mm TT (Ge HWT).
2 *Thompson* (Ge T-209/1300) with 8 x 533mm TT (HWT).
PRINCIPAL SURFACE COMBATANTS: 9:
DD: 5:
2 *Prat* (UK *Norfolk*) DDG with 1 x 2 *Seaslug-2* SAM, 4 x MM-38 *Exocet* SSM, 1 x 2 114mm guns, 1 AB-206B hel plus 2 x 3 ASTT (Mk 44).
2 *Blanco Encalada* (UK *Norfolk*) DDH with 4 x MM-38, 1 x 2 114 mm guns, 2 AS-332F hel; plus 2 x 3 ASTT (Mk 44) (*Barak* SAM in unit 1).
1 *Almirante Riveros* (ASUW) with 4 x MM-38 *Exocet* SSM, 4 x 102mm guns; plus 2 x 3 ASTT (Mk 44 LWT), 2 x 3 ASW mor (1 prob non-op).
FF: 4 *Condell* (mod UK *Leander*) 3 with 2 x 3 ASTT (Mk 44), 1 hel; plus 2 x 2 MM-40 (2 with 4 x MM-38) *Exocet*, 1 x 2 114mm guns.
PATROL AND COASTAL COMBATANTS: 25:
MSL CRAFT: 4:
2 *Casma* (Is *Reshef*) PFM with 4 *Gabriel* SSM.
2 *Iquique* (Is *Sa'ar*) PFM with 6 *Gabriel* SSM.
TORPEDO CRAFT: 4 *Guacolda* (Ge Lürssen 36-m) with 4 x 533mm TT.
PATROL: 17:
1 PCO (ex-US tug).
4 *Micalvi* PCC.
1 *Papudo* PCC (ex-US PC-1638).
1 *Viel* (ex-US) icebreaker.
10 *Grumete Diaz* (Is *Dabur*) PCI⟨.
AMPH: 3 *Maipo* (Fr *BATRAL*) LSM, capacity 140 tps, 7 tk.
Plus craft: 2 *Elicura* LCT.
SPT AND MISC: 11:
1 *Almirante Jorge Montt* (UK 'Tide') AO, 1 *Araucano* AO, 1 tpt, 1 survey, 1 *Uribe* trg, 1 Antarctic patrol, 5 tugs/spt.
NAVAL AVIATION: (500); 16 cbt ac, 18 armed hel. 4 sqn.
MR: 1 sqn with 6 EMB-111N, 2 *Falcon* 200, 8 P-3 *Orion*.
ASW HEL: 8 AS-332, 7 Bo-105, 3 AB-206AS.
LIAISON: 1 sqn with 3 C-212A, 3 EMB-110CN, 2 IAI-1124.
HEL: 1 sqn with 3 AB-206-B, 3 SH-57.
TRG: 1 sqn with 10 PC-7.

MARINES: (ε5,000).
4 gp: each 1 inf bn (+), 1 cdo coy, 1 fd arty, 1 AD arty bty.
1 amph bn.
EQPT:
LT TK: 30 *Scorpion* (being delivered)
AAV: 30 LVTP-5 (in store).
APC: 40 MOWAG *Roland*.
TOWED ARTY: 105mm: 16 M-101; **155mm:** 36 M-114.
COASTAL GUNS: 155mm: 16 GPFM-3.

MOR: **60mm**: 50; **81mm**: 50.
RCL: **106mm**: ε30 M-40A1.
SAM: *Blowpipe*.

COAST GUARD: (1,500).
PATROL CRAFT: 17:
2 PCC (Buoy Tenders), 1 *Castor* PCI, 2 *Alacalufe*
PCI, 12 PCI⟨, plus about 12 boats.

AIR FORCE: 14,000 (1,000 conscripts); 110 cbt
ac, no armed hel. 5 Air Bde: 5 wings.
FGA: 2 sqn:
1 with 15 *Mirage* 5BA (MRIS), 6 *Mirage* BD (MRIS).
1 with 16 F-5 (13 -E, 3 -F).
COIN: 2 sqn with 30 A-37B, 24 A-36.
FTR/RECCE: 1 sqn with 15 *Mirage* 50 (-FCH: 8; -CH:
6; -DCH: 1); 4 *Mirage* 5-BR.
RECCE: 2 photo units with 1 *Canberra* PR-9, 1 *King
Air* A-100, 2 *Learjet* 35A.
AEW: 1 IAI-707 *Phalcon*.
TPT: 1 sqn with: **ac:** 4 Boeing 707(2 tkr), 2 C-130H,
4 C-130B, 4 C-212, 9 Beech 99 (ELINT, tpt, trg), 14
DHC-6 (5 -100, 9 -300); **hel:** 5 SA-315B.
LIAISON HEL: 6 Bo-105CB, 4 UH-1H.
TRG: 1 wing, 3 flying schools: **ac:** 16 PA-28, 50 T-
35A/B, 20 T-36, 20 T-37B/C, 8 T-41D, 6 *Extra* 300;
hel: 10 UH-1H.
MSL:
ASM: AS-11/-12.
AAM: AIM-9B *Sidewinder, Shafrir, Python* III.
AD: 1 regt (5 gp) with: **20mm**: S-639/-665, GAI-CO1
twin; **35mm**: 36, K-63 twin; *Blowpipe*, 12 *Cactus*
(*Crotale*), MATRA *Mistral*.

FORCES ABROAD:
UN AND PEACEKEEPING:
INDIA/PAKISTAN (UNMOGIP): 3 Obs. **MIDDLE
EAST** (UNTSO): 3 Obs.

PARAMILITARY:
CARABINEROS (Ministry of Interior): 31,000; 8
zones, 38 districts.
EQPT:
APC: 20 MOWAG *Roland*.
MOR: 60mm, 81mm.
AC: 22 Cessna (-150: 6; -182: 10; -206: 6), 1 *Metro*.
HEL: 2 Bell 206, 12 Bo-105.

OPPOSITION:
**FRENTE PATRIOTICO MANUEL RODRIGUEZ/
DISSIDENT (FPMR/D):** ε800; leftist.
**MOVEMENT OF THE REVOLUTIONARY LEFT
(MIR):** some 500.

COLOMBIA

GDP	1993: pC 41,932bn ($49.6bn):
	per capita $6,200
	1994: pC 44,278bn ($52.4bn):
	per capita $6,600
Growth	1993: 5.3%	1994: 5.7%
Inflation	1993: 22.6%	1994: 22.8%
Debt	1993: $17.2bn	1994: $19.1bn
Def exp	1993ε: pC 1,039bn ($1.23bn)
	1994ε: pC 1,022bn ($1.21bn)
Def bdgt	1994: pC 715bn ($846m)
	1995: pC 799bn ($923m)
FMA	1994: $28.6m (FMF, Narcs, IMET)
	1995: $29.6m (Narcs)
	1996: $35.9m (Narcs, IMET)
$1 = pC	1993: 863	1994: 845
	1994: 866

pC = Colombian peso

Population: 35,101,000

	13–17	18–22	23–32
Men	1,907,600	1,708,800	3,252,200
Women	1,824,600	1,652,400	3,226,800

TOTAL ARMED FORCES:
ACTIVE: 146,400 (some 67,300 conscripts).
Terms of service: 1–2 years, varies (all services).
RESERVES: 60,700, incl 2,000 first-line: Army
54,700; Navy 4,800; Air Force 1,200.

ARMY: 121,000 (63,800 conscripts).
4 div HQ.
16 inf bde (Regional) each with 3 inf, 1 arty, 1 engr
bn, 1 mech gp (1 more bde forming).
Army Tps:
2 COIN bde (each with 1 cdo unit, 4 COIN bn) (3rd
bde forming).
1 Presidential Guard bn.
1 AD arty bn.
EQPT:
LT TK: 12 M-3A1 (in store).
RECCE: 12 M-8, 120 EE-9 *Cascavel*.
APC: 80 M-113, 76 EE-11 *Urutu*.
TOWED ARTY: 105mm: 130 M-101.
MOR: 81mm: 125 M-1; **120mm**: 120 Brandt.
ATGW: *TOW*.
RCL: 106mm: M-40A1.
AD GUNS: 40mm: 30 Bofors.

NAVY (incl Coast Guard): 18,100 (incl 8,800 Marines and 100 Naval Aviation).

BASES: Ocean: Cartagena (main), Buenaventura, Málaga (Pacific).
River: Puerto Leguízamo, Barrancabermeja, Puerto Carreño, Leticia, Puerto Orocue, Puerto Inirida.
SS: 2 *Pijao* (Ge T-209/1200) with 8 x 533mm TT (Ge HWT). (Plus 2 *Intrepido* (It SX-506) SSI (SF delivery).)
FF: 4 *Almirante Padilla* with 1 x Bo-105 hel (ASW), 2 x 3 ASTT; plus 8 x MM-40 *Exocet* SSM.
PATROL AND COASTAL COMBATANTS: 40:
PATROL: 40:
OFFSHORE: 3 *Pedro de Heredia* (ex-US tugs). 1 *Cormoran* PCO.
INSHORE: 11: 6 *Quito Sueno* (US *Asheville*) PFI, 2 *Castillo Y Rada* (Swiftships 32-m) PCI, 3 *José Palas* PCI⟨.
RIVERINE: 25: 3 *Arauca*, 16 *Juan Lucioá*, 6 *Capitan* tugs.
AMPH: 8 *Morrosquillo* (ex-US) LCUS.
SPT AND MISC: 4:
1 tpt, 2 research, 1 trg.

MARINES: (8,800); 2 bde (each of 2 bn), 1 amph aslt, 1 river ops (15 amph patrol units), 1 SF, 1 sy bn. No hy eqpt (to get EE-9 *Cascavel* recce, EE-11 *Urutu* APC).

NAVAL AVIATION: (100).
AC: 2 *Commander*, 2 PA-28, 2 PA-31.
HEL: 4 Bo-105.

AIR FORCE: 7,300 (some 3,500 conscripts); 74 cbt ac, 75 armed hel.
AIR COMBAT COMD:
FGA: 2 sqn:
1 with 13 *Mirage* 5.
1 with 13 *Kfir* (11 -C2, 2 -TC2).
TAC AIR SPT COMD:
COIN: ac: 1 AC-47, 2 AC-47T, 3 IA-58A, 23 A-37B, 6 AT-27, 13 OV-10; **hel:** 5 Bell 212, 12 Bell 205, 2 Bell 412, 26 UH-1H, 2 UH-1B, 12 UH-60, 11 MD-500ME, 2 MD-500D, 3 MD-530F.
MIL AIR TPT COMD: 1 Boeing 707, 7 C-130B, 2 C-130H, 1 C-117, 2 C-47, 2 CASA 212, 2 *Bandeirante*, 1 F-28.
AIR TRG COMD: ac: 14 T-27 (*Tucano*), 6 T-34M, 13 T-37, 8 T-41; **hel:** 2 UH-1B, 4 UH-1H.
AAM: AIM-9 *Sidewinder*, R-530.

FORCES ABROAD:
UN AND PEACEKEEPING:
EGYPT (MFO): 358.

PARAMILITARY:
NATIONAL POLICE FORCE: 87,000; **ac:** 2 C-47, 2 DHC-6, 9 Cessna (-152: 2; -206G: 6; -208: 1), 1 Beech C-99, 5 *Turbo Thrush*; **hel:** 12 Bell (-206L: 7; -212: 5), 21 UH-1H, 3 Hughes 500D.

COAST GUARD: integral part of Navy.

OPPOSITION:
COORDINADORA   NACIONAL GUERRILLERA   SIMON   BOLIVAR (CNGSB): loose coalition of guerrilla gp incl: Revolutionary Armed Forces of Colombia (FARC): ε5,700 active; National Liberation Army (ELN): ε2,500, pro-Cuban; People's Liberation Army (EPL): ε500.

COSTA RICA

GDP	1993: C 1,069bn ($7.12bn):		
	per capita $6,100		
	1994: C 1,309bn ($7.64bn):		
	per capita $6,500		
Growth	1993: 6.3%	1994: 4.5%	
Inflation	1993: 9.8%	1994: 13.5%	
Debt	1993: $3.9bn	1994: $3.8bn	
Sy bdgt[a]	1994: C 6.33bn ($37m)		
	1995: C 7.77bn ($47m)		
FMA	1994: $0.10m (IMET)		
	1995: $0.05m (IMET)		
	1996: $0.20m (IMET)		
$1 = C	1993: 142	1994: 157	
	1995: 165		

C = colon

[a] No armed forces. Budgetary data are for border and maritime policing and internal security.

Population: 3,405,000

	13–17	18–22	23–32
Men	177,200	155,000	292,800
Women	169,800	148,600	283,000

TOTAL SECURITY FORCES:
ACTIVE: 7,500 (Paramilitary).

CIVIL GUARD: 4,300 (incl ε400 Marines).
2 Border Sy Comd (North, South).
5 border gd bn(-).
2 COIN bn.
7 Civil Guard Comd (bn).

MARINES: (ε400).
PATROL CRAFT, INSHORE: 7:
1 *Isla del Coco* (US *Swift* 32-m) PFI, 1 *Astronauta Franklin Chang* (US *Cape Higgon*) PCI, 5 PCI⟨; plus about 10 boats.
AC: 4 Cessna 206, 1 *Commander* 680, 3 O-2 (surv), 2 PA-23, 3 PA-28, 1 PA-31, 1 PA-34.
HEL: 2 *Hughes* 500E, 1 *Hiller* FH-1100.

RURAL GUARD (Ministry of Government and Police): 3,200; small arms only.

CUBA

GDP	1993ε: $11.37bn:	
	per capita $1,800	
	1994ε: $11.45bn:	
	per capita $1,800	
Growth	1993ε: -16.0%	1994: 0.7%
Inflation	1992ε: 35%	1993ε: 47%
Debt[a]	1993ε: $5.0bn	1994ε: $5.0bn
Def exp	1993ε: $426m	
	1994ε: $350m	
Def bdgt	1995ε: $274m	
$1 = pC[b]	1993–95: 1.0	
pC = Cuban peso		

[a] Excl debt to Russia of convertible roubles 21bn.
[b] Official exchange rates. Informal market rates were about pC 50 to $1 in 1995.

Population: 10,992,000

	13–17	18–22	23–32
Men	386,400	489,400	1,134,600
Women	362,400	460,000	1,079,600

TOTAL ARMED FORCES:
ACTIVE: 105,000 (incl Ready Reserves; 74,500 conscripts).
Terms of service: 2 years.
RESERVES: Army: 135,000 Ready Reserves (serve 45 days per year) to fill out Active and Reserve units; see also Paramilitary.

ARMY: ε85,000 (incl Ready Reservists and conscripts).
HQ: 3 Regional Comd: 3 Army.
4–5 armd bde.
9 mech inf bde (3 mech inf, 1 armd, 1 arty, 1 AD arty regt).
1 AB bde.
14 reserve bde.
1 frontier bde.
AD: AD arty regt and SAM bde.
EQPT: (some 75% in store).
MBT: 1,575: 75 T-34, 1,100 T-54/-55, 400 T-62.
LT TK: 50 PT-76.
RECCE: 100 BRDM-1/-2.
AIFV: 400 BMP-1.
APC: 800 BTR-40/-50/-60/-152.
TOWED ARTY: 620: **76mm**: M-1942; **122mm**: M-1931/37, D-74; **130mm**: M-46; **152mm**: M-1937, D-20, D-1.
SP ARTY: 40: **122mm**: 2S1; **152mm**: 2S3.

MRL: 300: **122mm**: BM-21; **140mm**: BM-14.
MOR: 1,000: **82mm**: M-41/-43; **120mm**: M-38/-43.
STATIC DEF ARTY: some 15 JS-2 (**122mm**) hy tk, T-34 (**85mm**), SU-100 (**100mm**) SP guns.
ATGW: AT-1 *Snapper*, AT-3 *Sagger*.
ATK GUNS: 200: **85mm**: D-44; **100mm**: SU-100 SP.
AD GUNS: 500 incl **23mm**: ZU-23, ZSU-23-4 SP; **30mm**: M-53 (twin)/BTR-60P SP; **37mm**: M-1939; **57mm**: S-60 towed, ZSU-57-2 SP; **85mm**: KS-12; **100mm**: KS-19.
SAM: ε1,600: SA-6/-7/-8/-9/-13/-14.

NAVY: ε5,000 (ε3,000 conscripts).
2 Naval Districts: Western: HQ Cabanas; Eastern: HQ Holquin. 4 Operational Flotillas.
BASES: Cienfuegos, Cabanas, Havana, Mariel, Punta Movida, Nicaro.
SS: 2 Sov *Foxtrot*† with 533mm and 406mm TT.
PRINCIPAL SURFACE COMBATANTS:
FF: 3 Sov *Koni* with 2 x ASW RL.
PATROL AND COASTAL COMBATANTS: 24:
MSL CRAFT: 17 Sov *Osa*-I/-II with 4 x SS-N-2 *Styx* SSM.
TORPEDO CRAFT: some of *Turya* listed below have 4 x 533mm TT.
PATROL: 7:
COASTAL: 1 Sov *Pauk* II PFC with 2 x ASW RL, 4 x ASTT.
INSHORE: some 6 Sov *Turya* PHT.
MCM: 15:
3 Sov *Sonya* MSC.
12 Sov *Yevgenya* MSI.
AMPH: 2 Sov *Polnocny* LSM, capacity 180 tps, 6 tk.
SPT AND MISC: 2:
1 AGI, 1 survey.

NAVAL INFANTRY: (550+).
2 amph aslt bn.
COASTAL DEF:
ARTY: 122mm: M-1931/37; **130mm**: M-46; **152mm**: M-1937.
SSM: 2 SS-C-3 systems.

AIR FORCE: ε15,000 (incl AD and conscripts); 130† cbt ac, 40 armed hel.
Annual flying hours: less than 50.
FGA: 2 sqn with 10 MiG-23BN.
FTR: 4 sqn:
2 with 30 MiG-21F.
1 with 50 MiG-21bis.
1 with 20 MiG-23MF, 6 MiG-29.
(Probably only some 3 MiG-29, 10 MiG-23, 11 MiG-21bis in operation.)
ATTACK HEL: 40 Mi-8/-17 (plus 40 in store).
ASW: 5 Mi-14 hel.
TPT: 4 sqn: 8 An-2, 1 An-24, 15 An-26, 2 An-32, 4

Yak-40, 2 Il-76 (Air Force ac in civilian markings).
HEL: 60 Mi-8/-17.
TRG: 25 L-39, 8* MiG-21U, 4* MiG-23U, 2* MiG-29UB, 20 Z-326.
MSL:
ASM: AS-7.
AAM: AA-2, AA-7, AA-8, AA-10, AA-11.
SAM: 200+ SAM launchers: SA-2, SA-3.
Civil Airline: 10 Il-62, 7 Tu-154, 12 Yak-42 used as troop tpt.

FORCES ABROAD:
UN AND PEACEKEEPING:
GEORGIA (UNOMIG): 4 Obs.

PARAMILITARY:
YOUTH LABOUR ARMY: 70,000.
CIVIL DEFENCE FORCE: 50,000.
TERRITORIAL MILITIA (R): 1,300,000.
STATE SECURITY (Ministry of Interior): 15,000.
BORDER GUARDS (Ministry of Interior): 4,000; about 22 Sov *Zhuk* and 3 Sov *Stenka* PFI⟨, plus boats.

FOREIGN FORCES:
US: 2,550: Navy: 1,900; Marine: 650.
RUSSIA: 810: 800 SIGINT; ε10 mil advisers.

DOMINICAN REPUBLIC

GDP	1993: pRD 120.6bn ($9.1bn): per capita $3,400 1994: pRD 136.1bn ($9.8bn): per capita $3,600	
Growth	1993: 3.0%	1994: 4.3%
Inflation	1993: 5.3%	1994: 8.3%
Debt	1993: $4.6bn	1994: $4.1bn
Def exp	1993: pRD 1,432m ($108m)	
Def bdgt	1994ε: pRD 1,007m ($73m)	
	1995ε: pRD 1,048m ($78m)	
FMA	1994: $0.6m (FMF, IMET)	
	1995: $0.2m (IMET)	
	1996: $0.5m (IMET)	
$1 = pRD	1993: 12.7	1994: 13.2
	1995: 13.3	

pRD = peso República Dominicana

Population: 7,701,000

	13–17	18–22	23–32
Men	422,600	385,000	686,800
Women	412,200	376,200	672,400

TOTAL ARMED FORCES:
ACTIVE: 24,500.

ARMY: 15,000.
3 Def Zones.
4 inf bde (with 10 inf, 1 armd, 1 arty).
1 armd, 1 Presidential Guard, 1 SF, 1 arty, 1 engr bn.
EQPT:
LT TK: 12 AMX-13 (**75mm**), 12 M-41A1 (**76mm**).
RECCE: 8 V-150 *Commando*.
APC: 20 M-2/M-3 half-track.
TOWED ARTY: 105mm: 22 M-101.
MOR: 81mm: M-1; **120mm:** 24 ECIA.

NAVY: 4,000 (incl marine security unit and 1 SEAL unit).
BASES: Santo Domingo (HQ), Las Calderas.
PATROL AND COASTAL COMBATANTS: 17:
PATROL, OFFSHORE: 9:
1 *Mella* (Cdn *River*) (comd/trg).
3 *Cambiaso* (US *Cohoes*).
3 armed ocean tugs (USCG *Argo*-class).
2 *Prestol* (US *Admirable*).
PATROL, INSHORE: 8:
1 *Betelgeuse* (US PGM-71), 1 *Capitan Alsina* (trg), some 6 PCI⟨.
AMPH: craft only: 1 LCU.
SPT AND MISC: 4:
1 AOT (small harbour), 3 ocean tugs.

AIR FORCE: 5,500; 10 cbt ac, no armed hel.
Annual flying hours: probably less than 60.
COIN: 1 sqn with 8 A-37B.
TPT: 1 sqn with 3 C-47, 1 *Commander* 680, 1 MU-2.
LIAISON: 1 Cessna 210, 2 PA-31, 3 *Queen Air* 80, 1 *King Air*.
HEL: 8 Bell 205, 1 OH-6A, 2 SA-318C, 1 SA-365 (VIP).
TRG: 2* AT-6, 6 T-34B, 3 T-41D.
AB: 1 SF (AB) bn.
AD: 1 bn with 4 **20mm** guns.

PARAMILITARY:
NATIONAL POLICE: 15,000.

ECUADOR

GDP	1993: ES 27,451bn ($17.62bn): per capita $4,500 1994: ES 36,368bn ($18.88bn): per capita $4,800	
Growth	1993: 2.0%	1994: 4.0%
Inflation	1993: 45.0%	1994: 27.3%

Debt	1993: $14.1bn	1994: $13.2bn
Def exp	1993ε: ES 956bn ($614m)	
Def bdgt	1994ε: ES 1,028bn ($534m)	
	1995ε: ES 1,260bn ($550m)	
FMA	1994: $1.0m (FMF, Narcs, IMET)	
	1995: $0.8m (Narcs, IMET)	
	1996: $1.3m (Narcs, IMET)	
$1 = ES	1993: 1,919	1994: 2,197
	1995: 2,287	

ES = Ecuadorean sucre

Population: 11,721,000

	13–17	18–22	23–32
Men	622,800	600,400	997,000
Women	644,600	585,800	979,200

TOTAL ARMED FORCES:
ACTIVE: 57,100.
Terms of service: conscription 1 year, selective.
RESERVES: 100,000; ages 18–55.

ARMY: 50,000.
4 Defence Zones.
1 div with 2 inf bde (each 3 inf, 1 armd, 1 arty bn).
1 armd bde (3 armd, 1 mech inf, 1 SP arty bn).
2 inf bde (5 inf, 3 mech inf, 2 arty bn).
3 jungle bde (2 with 3, 1 with 4 jungle bn).
Army tps:
1 SF (AB) bde (4 bn).
1 AD arty gp.
1 avn gp (4 bn).
3 engr bn.
EQPT:
LT TK: 45 M-3, 108 AMX-13.
RECCE: 27 AML-60/-90, 22 EE-9 *Cascavel,* 10 EE-3 *Jararaca.*
APC: 20 M-113, 60 AMX-VCI, 20 EE-11 *Urutu.*
TOWED ARTY: 105mm: 50 M2A2, 30 M-101, 24 Model 56; **155mm:** 12 M-198, 12 M-114.
SP ARTY: 155mm: 10 Mk F3.
MOR: 300: **81mm:** M-29; **107mm:** 4.2-in M-30; **160mm:** 12 Soltam.
RCL: 90mm: 380 M-67; **106mm:** 24 M-40A1.
AD GUNS: 20mm: 20 M-1935; **35mm:** 30 GDF-002 twin; **40mm:** 30 L/70.
SAM: 75 *Blowpipe.*
AC:
SURVEY: 1 Cessna 206, 1 *Learjet* 24D.
TPT: 1 CN-235, 1 DHC-5, 3 IAI-201, 1 *King Air* 200, 2 PC-6.
LIAISON/TRG/OBS: 1 Cessna 172, 1 -182.
HEL:
SURVEY: 3 SA-315B.
TPT/LIAISON: 10 AS-332, 4 AS-350B, 1 Bell 214B, 3 SA-315B, 3 SA-330, 30 SA-342.

NAVY: 4,100 (incl 250 Naval Aviation and 1,500 Marines).
BASES: Guayaquil (main base), Jaramijo, Galápagos Islands.
SS: 2 *Shyri* (Ge T-209/1300) with 533mm TT (Ge SUT HWT).
FF: 2 *Presidente Eloy Alfaro* (ex-UK *Leander Batch II*) with 1 206B hel; plus 4 x MM-38 *Exocet* SSM.
PATROL AND COASTAL COMBATANTS: 12:
CORVETTES: 6 *Esmeraldas* with 2 x 3 ASTT, hel deck; plus 2 x 3 MM-40 *Exocet* SSM.
MSL CRAFT: 6:
3 *Quito* (Ge Lürssen 45-m) with 4 x MM-38 *Exocet.*
3 *Manta* (Ge Lürssen 36-m) with 4 x *Gabriel* II SSM.
AMPH: 1 *Hualcopo* (US LST-511) LST, capacity 200 tps, 16 tk.
SPT AND MISC: 8:
1 survey, 1 ex-GDR depot ship, 1 AOT (small), 1 *Calicuchima* (ex-UK *Throsk*) armament carrier, 1 water carrier, 2 armed ocean tugs, 1 trg.

NAVAL AVIATION: (250):
LIAISON: 1 *Citation* I, 1 *Super King Air*, 1 CN-235, 3 Cessna 337.
TRG: 3 T-34C.
HEL: 4 Bell 206.

MARINES: (1,500); 3 bn: 2 on garrison duties, 1 cdo (no hy weapons/veh).

AIR FORCE: 3,000; 72 cbt ac, no armed hel.
OP COMD: 2 wings, 5 sqn:
FGA: 2 sqn:
1 with 8 *Jaguar* S (6 -S(E), 2 -B(E)).
1 with 8 *Kfir* C-2, 1 TC-2.
FTR: 1 sqn with 13 *Mirage* F-1JE, 1 F-1JB.
COIN: 1 sqn with 8 A-37B.
COIN/TRG: 1 sqn with 2 *Strikemaster* Mk 89, 7 *Strikemaster* Mk 89A.
MILITARY AIR TPT GP:
2 civil/military airlines:
TAME: 6 Boeing 727, 2 BAe-748, 2 C-130H, 3 DHC-6, 1 F-28, 1 L-100-30.
ECUATORIANA: 3 Boeing 707-320, 1 DC-10-30, 2 Airbus A-310.
LIAISON: 1 *King Air* E90, 1 *Sabreliner.*
LIAISON/SAR: hel fleet: 2 AS-332, 1 Bell 212, 6 Bell-206B, 5 SA-316B, 1 SA-330, 2 UH-1B, 24 UH-1H.
TRG: incl 22* AT-33, 20 Cessna 150, 5 Cessna 172, 17 T-34C, 2 T-41.
AAM: R-550 *Magic, Super* 530, *Shafrir.*
AB: 1 AB sqn.

PARAMILITARY:
COAST GUARD: 270.
PATROL, INSHORE: 6 PCI:
2 *25 De Julio* PCI.
2 *5 De Agosto* PCI.
2 *10 De Agosto* PCI⟨, plus some 20 boats.

EL SALVADOR

GDP	1993: C 60.52bn ($6.99bn):
	per capita $2,400
	1994: C 71.02bn ($7.33bn):
	per capita $2,600

Growth	1993: 7.4%	1994: 6.0%
Inflation	1993: 18.6%	1994: 10.5%
Debt	1993: $2.0bn	1994: $2.2bn
Def exp	1993ε: C 1.05bn ($121m)	
	1994ε: C 1.37bn ($141m)	
Def bdgt	1994: C 866.5m ($89.4m)	
	1995: C 961.4m ($109.0m)	
FMA[a]	1994: $0.4m (IMET)	
	1995: $17.3m (IMET, Econ Aid)	
	1996: $0.5m (IMET)	
$1 = C	1993: 8.67	1994: 8.75
	1995: 8.82	

C = colon

[a] The cost of ONUSAL in 1994 was $29.2m.

Population: 5,669,000

	13–17	18–22	23–32
Men	365,000	321,600	416,600
Women	351,600	318,200	454,000

TOTAL ARMED FORCES:
ACTIVE: 30,500.
Terms of service: selective conscription, 2 years.
RESERVES: ex-soldiers registered.

ARMY: 28,000 (some conscripts).
3 Mil Zones.
6 inf bde (10 inf bn).
1 special sy bde (2 MP, 2 border gd bn).
8 inf det (bn).
1 engr comd (1 engr bn).
1 arty bde (3 fd, 1 AD bn).
1 mech cav regt (2 bn).
2 indep bn (1 Presidential Guard, 1 sy).
1 special ops gp (1 para, 1 naval inf, 1 SF coy).
EQPT:
RECCE: 10 AML-90.
APC: 45 M-37B1 (mod), 14 M-113, 9 UR-416.
TOWED ARTY: 105mm: 36 M-101/102, 14 M-56 (in store).

MOR: 81mm: incl 300 M-29; **120mm:** 60 UB-M52, M-74 (all in store).
RL: 94mm: LAW; **82mm:** B-300.
RCL: 90mm: 400 M-67; **106mm:** 20+ M-40A1.
AD GUNS: 20mm: 24 Yug M-55, 4 SP.
SAM: some captured SA-7 may be in service.

NAVY: 500 (incl some 150 Naval Infantry and spt forces).
BASES: La Unión, La Libertad, Acajutla, El Triunfo.
PATROL AND COASTAL COMBATANTS: 5:
PATROL, INSHORE: 3 Camcraft 30-m, 2 PCI⟨, plus boats.
AMPH: craft only: 2 LCM.

NAVAL INFANTRY (Marines): (some 150).
1 Marine coy (150).

AIR FORCE: 2,000 (incl AD and ε500 conscripts); 21 cbt ac, 18 armed hel.
Annual flying hours for A-37 pilots: less than 50.
COIN: 3 sqn:
1 with 10 A-37B, 2 AC-47, 9 O-2A.
1 with 10 Hughes (armed: 3 MD 500D, 7 -E), 15 UH-1M armed hel.
1 with 24 UH-1H tpt hel (incl 4 SAR).
TPT: 1 sqn with 4 C-47, 2 C-47 Turbo-67, 1 *Commander*, 1 DC-6B, 1 *Merlin* IIIB, 9 *Rallye*.
LIAISON: 6 Cessna 180, 1 Cessna 182, 1 Cessna 185.
TRG: 6 CM-170, 3 T-41C/D.

FORCES ABROAD:
UN AND PEACEKEEPING:
WESTERN SAHARA (MINURSO): 2 Obs.

PARAMILITARY:
NATIONAL CIVILIAN POLICE (Ministry of Interior): some 8,000: small arms; **ac:** 1 Cessna; **hel:** 1 UH-1H.

GUATEMALA

GDP	1993: q 63.73bn ($11.28bn):
	per capita $3,700
	1994: q 67.45bn ($11.73bn):
	per capita $3,800

Growth	1993: 3.9%	1994: 4.0%
Inflation	1993: 11.9%	1994: 11.6%
Debt	1993: $3.0bn	1994: $3.1bn
Def exp	1994ε: q 694m ($123m)	
	1995ε: q 765m ($133m)	
Def bdgt	1994: q 634m ($110m)	

FMA 1995: q 678m ($120m)
1994: $2.0m (Narcs, IMET)
1995: $2.7m (Narcs)
1996: $2.8m (Narcs, IMET)
$1 = q 1993: 5.64 1994: 5.75
1995: 5.69
q = quetzal

Population: 10,602,000

	13–17	18–22	23–32
Men	636,200	531,600	783,000
Women	619,200	520,200	776,000

TOTAL ARMED FORCES (National
Armed Forces are combined; the Army provides log
spt for Navy and Air Force):
ACTIVE: 44,200 (30,000 conscripts).
Terms of service: conscription; selective, 30 months.
RESERVES: Army ε35,000 (trained), Navy
(some), Air Force 200.

ARMY: 42,000 (30,000 conscripts).
19 Mil Zones (39 inf, 1 trg bn, 6 armd sqn).
2 strategic bde (6 inf, 1 lt armd bn, 1 recce sqn, 2
arty bty).
1 SF gp (3 coy incl 1 trg).
2 AB bn.
1 inf bn gp (3 inf coy, 1 recce sqn, 1 AA bty).
1 MP bn.
1 Presidential Guard bn.
1 engr bn.
EQPT:
LT TK: 10 M-41A3.
RECCE: 8 M-8, 10 RBY-1.
APC: 9 M-113, 7 V-100 *Commando*, 30 *Armadillo*.
TOWED ARTY: 75mm: 8 M-116; **105mm:** 12 M-101,
8 M-102, 56 M-56.
MOR: 81mm: 55 M-1; **107mm:** 12 M-30; **120mm:** 18 ECIA.
RL: 89mm: 3.5-in M-20.
RCL: 57mm: M-20; **105mm:** 64 Arg M-1974 FMK-
1; **106mm:** 20 M-40A1.
AD GUNS: 20mm: 16 M-55.

RESERVES: ε19 inf bn.

NAVY: ε1,500 (incl some 650 Marines).
BASES: Santo Tomás de Castilla (Atlantic), Puerto
Quetzal (Pacific).
PATROL CRAFT, INSHORE: 9:
1 *Kukulkan* (US *'Broadsword'* 32-m) PFI, 8 PCI⟨,
plus boats.

MARINES: (some 650); 2 under-str bn.

AIR FORCE: 700; 14† cbt ac, 7 armed hel.
Serviceability of ac is less than 50%.
COIN: 1 sqn with 2 Cessna A-37B, 8 PC-7, 4 IAI-201.
ARMED HEL: 6 Bell 212, 1 Bell 412.
TPT: 1 sqn with 1 C-47, 3 T-67 (mod C-47 *Turbo*), 2
F-27, 1 *Super King Air* (VIP), 1 DC-6B.
LIAISON: 1 sqn with 3 Cessna 206, 1 Cessna 310.
HEL: 1 sqn with 9 Bell 206, 5 UH-1D/-H, 3 S-76.
TRG: 6 T-41.
TAC SECURITY GP: 3 COIN coy, 1 armd sqn,
1 AD bty (army units for air-base sy).

FORCES ABROAD:
UN AND PEACEKEEPING:
LIBERIA (UNOMIL): 124.

PARAMILITARY:
NATIONAL POLICE: 9,800: 21 departments, 1 SF
bn, 1 integrated task force (incl mil and treasury police).
TREASURY POLICE: 2,500.
TERRITORIAL MILITIA (R) (CVDC): ε300,000.

OPPOSITION:
**UNIDAD REVOLUCIONARIA NACIONAL
GUATEMALTECA** (URNG): some 800–1,100;
coalition of 3 main groups: Ejército Guerrillero de
los Pobres (EGP): 300–400; Fuerzas Armadas
Rebeldes (FAR): ε300–400; Organización del Pueblo
en Armas (ORPA): 200–300.

GUYANA

GDP	1993: $G 56.65bn ($450m):	
	per capita $2,500	
	1994: $G 67.23bn ($480m):	
	per capita $2,800	
Growth	1993: 12.9%	1994: 8.5%
Inflation	1993: 10.0%	1994: 16.1%
Debt	1993: $1.9bn	1994: $2.0bn
Def exp	1993: $G 773m ($6m)	
Def bdgt	1994: $G 923m ($7m)	
	1995: $G 1,005m ($7m)	
FMA	1994: $0.2m (FMF, IMET)	
	1995: $0.1m (FMF, IMET)	
	1996: $0.2m (IMET)	
$ 1 = $G	1993: 127	1994: 138
	1995: 143	

$G = Guyanese dollar

Population: 824,000

	13–17	18–22	23–32
Men	41,600	41,800	80,400
Women	39,600	39,800	79,200

TOTAL ARMED FORCES (Combined
Guyana Defence Force):
ACTIVE: some 1,600.
RESERVES: some 1,500 People's Militia (see Paramilitary).

ARMY: 1,400 (incl 500 Reserves).
1 inf bn, 1 SF, 1 spt wpn, 1 engr coy.
EQPT:
RECCE: 3 *Shorland*.
TOWED ARTY: 130mm: 6 M-46.
MOR: 81mm: 12 L16A1; **82mm:** 18 M-43; **120mm:** 18 M-43.

NAVY: Authorised: 30 plus 300 reserves. Actual: 17 plus 170 reserves.
BASES: Georgetown, New Amsterdam.
2 boats.

AIR FORCE: 100; no cbt ac, no armed hel.
TPT: ac: 1 BN-2A; **hel:** 1 Bell 206, 1 Bel 202.

FORCES ABROAD:
UN AND PEACEKEEPING:
HAITI (UNMIH): 51.

PARAMILITARY:
GUYANA PEOPLE'S MILITIA (GPM): some 1,500.

HAITI

GDP	1993: G 15.72bn ($1.69bn)	
	per capita $1,000	
	1994: G 21.01bn ($1.56bn):	
	per capita $925	
Growth	1993: -4.2%	1994: -10.6%
Inflation	1993: 18.9%	1994: 36.1%
Debt	1994: $773m	1994: $870m
Def exp	1993ε: G 422m ($33m)	
	1994ε: G 453m ($35m)	
Sy bdgt	1995ε: G 893m ($47m)	
FMA[a]	1996: $7.4m (FMF, IMET)	
$1 = G	1993: 12.8	1994: 13.0
	1995: 19.0	

G = gourde

[a] The cost of UNMIH in 1994 was $5.3m and was borne by the participating member-states, of which the US incurred expenditure of $1bn from Oct 1994 to March 1995.

Population: 7,090,000

	13–17	18–22	23–32
Men	389,800	348,800	558,200
Women	383,200	345,000	564,000

TOTAL ARMED FORCES:
In 1994 the military government of Haiti was replaced by a civilian administration. The armed forces and police have been disbanded and an Interim Public Security Force (IPSF) of 3,000 formed. A National Police Force of some 4,000 personnel is being formed. Equipment details shown represent the situation prior to the change of administration.

The United Nations Mission in Haiti (UNMIH) has deployed 6,106 troops and 874 civ pol to ensure maintenance of a secure and stable environment leading to free and fair elections, and to supervise the professionalisation of the armed forces and creation of a separate national police force.
EQPT:
APC: 5 M-2, 6 V-150 *Commando*.
TOWED ARTY: 75mm: 5 M-116; **105mm:** 4 M-101.
MOR: 60mm: 36 M-2; **81mm:** M-1.
ATK GUNS: 37mm: 10 M-3A1; **57mm:** 10 M-1.
RCL: 57mm: M-18; **106mm:** M-40A1.
AD GUNS: 20mm: 6 TCM-20, 4 other; **40mm:** 6 M-1.

NAVY: (Coast Guard).
BASE: Port au Prince.
PATROL CRAFT: boats only.

AIR FORCE: 5 cbt ac, no armed hel.
COIN: 5 Cessna 0-2/337.
TPT: 1 *Baron*, 1 DHC-6.
TRG: 3 Cessna 150, 3 Cessna 172, 5 SF-260TP, 1 *Twin Bonanza*.

HONDURAS

GDP	1993: L 22.44bn ($3.40bn):	
	per capita $2,000	
	1994: L 27.36bn ($3.35bn):	
	per capita $2,100	
Growth	1993: 6.1%	1994: -1.4%
Inflation	1993: 10.8%	1994: 21.7%
Debt	1993: $3.9bn	1994: $4.2bn
Def exp	1993: L 329m ($50m)	
Def bdgt	1994: L 355m ($44m)	
	1995ε: L 445m ($49m)	

FMA 1994: $0.5m (IMET)
1995: $0.3m (IMET)
1996: $0.4m (IMET)
$1 = L 1993: 7.26 1994: 9.40
1995: 9.04
L = lempira

Population: 5,924,000

	13–17	18–22	23–32
Men	348,200	305,800	465,800
Women	338,000	297,400	459,200

TOTAL ARMED FORCES:
ACTIVE: 18,800 (13,200 conscripts).
Terms of service: conscription, 24 months (to end 1995).
RESERVES: 60,000 ex-servicemen registered.

ARMY: 16,000 (12,000 conscripts).
10 Mil Zones.
2 inf bde (each with 3 inf, 1 arty bn).
1 inf bde with 1 inf, 1 arty, 1 engr bn.
1 special tac gp with 1 inf, 1 ranger bn, 2 trg units.
1 territorial force (2 inf, 1 SF, 1 AB bn).
1 armd cav regt (2 bn).
1 arty, 1 engr bn.
RESERVES:
3 inf bde.
EQPT:
LT TK: 12 *Scorpion*.
RECCE: 3 *Scimitar*, 1 *Sultan*, 72 *Saladin*, 12 RBY Mk 1.
TOWED ARTY: 105mm: 24 M-102; **155mm:** 4 M-198.
MOR: 400: **60mm**; **81mm**; **120mm:** 60 Brandt; **160mm:** 30 *Soltam*.
RL: 84mm: 120 *Carl Gustav*.
RCL: 106mm: 80 M-40A1.

NAVY: 1,000 (incl 400 Marines and 500 conscripts).
BASES: Puerto Cortés, Puerto Castilla (Atlantic), Amapala (Pacific).
PATROL CRAFT, INSHORE: 11:
3 *Guaymuras* (US Swiftships 31-m) PFI, 2 *Copan* (US Lantana 32-m) PFI⟨, 6 PCI⟨, plus boats.
AMPH: craft only; 1 *Punta Caxinas* LCT; plus some 3 ex-US LCM.

MARINES: (400); 1 bn.

AIR FORCE: some 1,800 (700 conscripts); 40 cbt† ac plus 8 in store, no armed hel.
FGA: 2 sqn:
1 with 13 A-37B.
1 with 10 F-5E, 2 -F.

FTR: 8 *Super Mystère* B2 (in store).
TPT: 9 C-47, 2 C-130A, 1 L-188, 2 IAI-201, 2 IAI-1123.
LIAISON: 1 sqn with 1 *Baron*, 3 Cessna 172, 2 Cessna 180, 2 Cessna 185, 4 *Commander*, 1 PA-31, 1 PA-34.
HEL: 9 Bell 412, 4 Hughes 500, 5 TH-55, 8 UH-1B, 7 UH-1H, 1 S-76.
TRG: 4* C-101BB, 6 U-17A, 11* EMB-312, 5 T-41A.

FORCES ABROAD:
UN AND PEACEKEEPING:
HAITI (UNMIH): 120. **WESTERN SAHARA** (MINURSO): 14 Obs.

PARAMILITARY:
PUBLIC SECURITY FORCES (Ministry of Public Security and Defence): 5,500; 11 regional comd.

FOREIGN FORCES:
US: 350: Army: (200); Air: (150).

JAMAICA

GDP	1993: $J 95.8bn ($3.0bn):	
	per capita $4,000	
	1994: $J 101.3bn ($3.1bn):	
	per capita $4,000	
Growth	1993: 1.2%	1994: 0.8%
Inflation	1993: 22.1%	1994: 35.1%
Debt	1993: $4.3bn	1994: $4.3bn
Def exp	1994: $J 673m ($21m)	
Def bdgt	1994: $J 908m ($27m)	
	1995ε: $J 937m ($29m)	
FMA:	1994: $1.1m (FMF, Narcs, IMET)	
	1995: $0.8m (Narcs, IMET)	
	1996: $1.5m (Narcs, IMET)	
$1 = $J	1993: 25.0	1994: 33.1
	1995: 33.1	

$J = Jamaican dollar

Population: 2,454,000

	13–17	18–22	23–32
Men	126,600	127,000	227,200
Women	123,200	123,200	234,200

TOTAL ARMED FORCES (all services
form combined Jamaican Defence Force):
ACTIVE: some 3,320.
RESERVES: some 870: Army 800; Coast Guard 50; Air Wing 20.

ARMY: 3,000.
2 inf bn, 1 spt bn.
EQPT:
APC: 14 V-150 *Commando.*
MOR: 81mm: 12 L16A1.

RESERVES: 800: 1 inf bn.

COAST GUARD: ε150.
BASE: Port Royal.
PATROL CRAFT, INSHORE: 5:
1 *Fort Charles* PFI (US 34-m), 1 *Paul Bogle* (US-31m), 3 PFI⟨, plus boats.

AIR WING: 170; no cbt ac, no armed hel.
AC: 2 BN-2A, 1 Cessna 210, 1 *King Air.*
HEL: 4 Bell 206, 3 Bell 212, 4 UH-1H.

FORCES ABROAD:
UN AND PEACEKEEPING:
HAITI (UNMIH): 10.

MEXICO

GDP	1993: Np 1,128bn ($235bn): per capita $7,900			
	1994: Np 1,225bn ($243bn): per capita $8,100			
Growth	1993: 0.8%		1994: 3.5%	
Inflation	1993: 9.7%		1994: 7.0%	
Debt	1993: $118.0bn		1993: $124.2bn	
Def exp	1994: Np 7.77bn ($1.62bn)			
Def bdgt	1994ε: Np 8.78bn ($1.74bn)			
	1995ε: Np 13.76bn ($2.05bn)			
FMA	1994: $ 0.2m (IMET)			
	1995: $0.2m (IMET)			
	1996: $1.0m (IMET)			
$1[a] = Np	1993: 3.12		1994: 3.38	
	1995: 6.70			

Np = new peso

[a] The new peso, equal to 1,000 pesos, was introduced on 1 January 1993.

Population: 90,464,000 (Chiapas administrative region 4%)

	13–17	18–22	23–32
Men	4,979,000	4,846,000	7,971,600
Women	4,852,600	4,766,200	8,016,800

TOTAL ARMED FORCES:
ACTIVE: 175,000 (60,000 conscripts).

Terms of service: 1 year conscription (4 hours per week) by lottery.

RESERVES: 300,000.

ARMY: 130,000 (incl ε60,000 conscripts).
36 Zonal Garrisons: incl 1 armd, 19 mot cav, 1 mech inf, 7 arty regt, plus 3 arty, 80 inf bn.
1 armd bde (3 armd, 1 mech inf regt).
1 Presidential Guard bde (4 inf, 1 arty bn).
1 mot inf bde (3 mot inf regt).
2 inf bde (each 3 inf bn, 1 arty bn).
1 AB bde (3 bn).
AD, engr and spt units.
EQPT:
RECCE: 50 M-8, 120 ERC-90F *Lynx,* 40 VBL, 70 DN-3/-5 *Caballo,* 30 MOWAG, 40 Mex-1.
APC: 40 HWK-11, 30 M-3 halftrack, 40 VCR/TT.
TOWED ARTY: 75mm: 18 M-116 pack; **105mm:** 16 M-2A1/M-3, 60 M-101, 24 M-56.
SP ARTY: 75mm: 5 M-8.
MOR: 81mm: 1,500; **120mm:** 20 *Brandt.*
ATGW: *Milan* (incl 8 VBL).
RL: 82mm: B-300.
ATK GUNS: 37mm: 30 M-3.
AD GUNS: 12.7mm: 40 M-55.
SAM: RBS-70

NAVY: 37,000 (incl 1,100 Naval Aviation and 8,600 Marines).
6 Navy regions covering 2 areas:
Gulf: 6 Naval Zones.
Pacific: 11 Naval Zones.
BASES: Gulf: Vera Cruz (HQ), Tampico, Chetumal, Ciudad del Carmen, Yukalpetén, Lerna, Frontera, Coatzacoalcos, Isla Mujéres.
Pacific: Acapulco (HQ), Ensenada, La Paz, San Blas, Guaymas, Mazatlán, Manzanillo, Salina Cruz, Puerto Madero, Lázaro Cárdenas, Puerto Vallarta.
PRINCIPAL AND SURFACE COMBATANTS: 5:
DD: 3:
2 *Ilhuicamina* (ex-*Quetzalcoatl*) (US *Gearing*) ASW with 1 x 8 *ASROC,* 2 x 3 ASTT; plus 2 x 2 127mm guns and 1 Bo-105 hel.
1 *Cuitlahuac* (US *Fletcher*) with 5 x 533mm TT, 5 x 127mm guns.
FF: 2 *H. Galeana* (US *Bronstein*) with 1 x 8 ASROC, 2 x 3 ASTT, 1 x 2 76mm guns.
PATROL AND COASTAL COMBATANTS: 105:
PATROL, OFFSHORE: 41:
4 *S. J. Holzinger* (ex-*Uxmal*) (imp *Uribe*) with Bo-105 hel.
6 *Cadete Virgilio Uribe* (Sp '*Halcon*') with Bo-105 hel.
1 *Comodoro Manuel Azueta* (US *Edsall*) (trg).
1 *Zacatecas* (US *Lawrence/Crosley*) with 1 x 127mm gun.
16 *Leandro Valle* (US *Auk* MSF).

1 *Guanajuato* with 2 x 102mm gun.
12 D-01 (US *Admirable* MSF), 3 with hel deck.
PATROL, INSHORE: 44:
4 *Halter* XFPB (US).
4 *Isla Coronada* PFI.
31 *Quintana Roo* (UK *Azteca*) PCI.
3 *Cabo* (US *Cape Higgon*) PCI.
2 *Punta* (US *Point*) PCI.
PATROL, RIVER: 20⟨.
AMPH:
2 *Panuco* (US-511) LST.
SPT AND MISC: 22:
3 AOT, 1 PCI spt, 4 log spt, 6 ocean tugs, 5 survey,
1 *Durango* tpt, plus 2 other tpt.

NAVAL AVIATION: (1,100); 9 cbt ac, no armed hel.
MR: 1 sqn with 9 C-212-200M.
MR HEL: 12 Bo-105 (8 afloat).
TPT: 1 C-212, 2 Cessna 180, 3 Cessna 310, 1 DHC-5, 1 FH-227, 1 *King Air* 90, 1 *Learjet* 24.
HEL: 3 Bell 47, 4 SA-319, 2 UH-1H, 4 MD-500 (trg), 8 Mi-8/17, 4 AS-335.
TRG: 8 Cessna 152, 2 Cessna 337, 2 Cessna 402, 10 F-33C *Bonanza*.

MARINES: (8,600).
1 AB regt (2 bn).
1 sy, 1 Presidential Guard bn.
17 bn (1 per Naval Zone).
EQPT:
AAV: 25 VAP-3550.
TOWED ARTY: 105mm: 8 M-56.
MRL: 51mm: *Firos*-6.
MOR: 100 incl **60mm, 81mm.**
RCL: 106mm: M-40A1.
AD GUNS: 20mm, 40mm.

AIR FORCE: 8,000 (incl 1,500 AB bde); 101 cbt ac, 25 armed hel.
FTR: 1 sqn with 9 F-5E, 2 -F.
COIN: 5 sqn:
3 with 40 PC-7.
1 with 15 AT-33.
1 hel with 5 Bell 205, 5 Bell 206, 15 Bell 212.
RECCE: 2 photo sqn with 10 *Commander* 500S.
SAR: 1 sqn with 5 IAI-201.
TPT: 5 sqn with 2 BN-2, 12 C-47, 1 C-54, 10 C-118, 9 C-130A, 5 *Commander* 500, 1 -680, 5 DC-6 *Skytrain*, 2 F-27.
HEL: 4 Bell 205, 12 Bell 206, 15 Bell 212, 3 SA-330, 2 UH-60.
PRESIDENTIAL TPT: ac: 7 Boeing 727, 1 Boeing 737, 1 Boeing 757, 1 L-188, 3 FH-227, 2 *Merlin*, 4 *Sabreliners*; **hel:** 1 AS-332, 2 SA-330, 2 UH-60.
LIAISON/UTL: 2 *King Air*, 1 *Musketeer*, 40 *Beech Bonanza* F-33A, 10 *Beech, Musketeer.*

TRG: ac: 20 CAP-10, 20 PC-7, 5 T-39 *Sabreliner*, 35* AT-33; **hel:** 10 MD 530F (SAR/paramilitary/trg).

PARAMILITARY:
RURAL DEFENCE MILITIA (R): 14,000.

NICARAGUA

GDP	1993: Co 11.02bn ($1.89bn):	
	per capita $2,700	
	1994: Co 12.22bn ($1.98bn):	
	per capita $2,700	
Growth	1993: -0.4%	1994: 3.2%
Inflation	1993: 20.4%	1994: 7.8%
Debt	1993: $10.4bn	1994: $10.7bn
Def exp	1993ε: Co 224m ($38m)	
Def bdgt	1994: Co 242m ($39m)	
	1995: Co 260m ($37m)	
FMA	1995: $0.1m (IMET)	
	1996: $0.2m (IMET)	
$1 = Co	1993: 5.62	1994: 6.72
	1995: 7.11	
Co = Cordoba oro		

Population: 4,212,000

	13–17	*18–22*	*23–32*
Men	276,200	208,600	269,000
Women	249,400	210,600	330,600

TOTAL ARMED FORCES:
ACTIVE: 12,000.
Terms of service: voluntary, 18–36 months.
RESERVES: ε12,000.

ARMY: 10,000.
Reorganisation in progress.
5 Regional Comd (10 inf, 1 tk bn).
2 mil det (2 inf bn).
1 lt mech bde (1 mech inf, 1 tk, 1 armd tpt bn, 1 fd arty gp (2 bn).
1 comd regt (1 inf, 1 sy bn)
1 SF bde (3 SF bn).
1 engr bn.
EQPT:
MBT: some 130 T-55 (66 in store).
LT TK: 22 PT-76.
RECCE: 79 BRDM-2.
APC: 102 BTR-152, 64 BTR-60.
TOWED ARTY: 122mm: 36 D-30, 332 *Grad* 1P (single-tube rocket launcher); **152mm:** 60 D-20.
MRL: 107mm: 33 Type-63; **122mm:** 18 BM-21.
MOR: 82mm: 579; **120mm:** 24 M-43; **160mm:** 4 M-160.

ATGW: AT-3 *Sagger* (12 on BRDM-2).
RCL: 82mm: B-10.
ATK GUNS: 57mm: 354 ZIS-2; **76mm:** 83 Z1S-3;
100mm: M-1944.
SAM: 400+ SA-7/-14/-16.

NAVY: ε800.
BASES: Corinto, Puerto Cabezzas, El Bluff.
PATROL AND COASTAL COMBATANTS: 12:
PATROL, INSHORE: 12†:
2 Sov *Zhuk* PFI⟨, 4 N. Korea *Sin Hung* PFI⟨,
6 PCI⟨.
MCM: 2 Sov *Yevgenya* MHI.

AIR FORCE: 1,200; no cbt ac, 15 armed hel.
TPT: 6 An-2, 4 An-26.
HEL: 15 Mi-17 (tpt armed).
UTL/TRG: ac: 1 Cessna 172, 1 Cessna 185, 1 Cessna
404, 2 *Piper* PA-18, 2 *Piper* PA-28; **hel:** 4 Mi-2.
ASM: AT-2 *Swatter* ATGW.
AD GUNS: 1 air def gp, 18 ZU-23, 18 C3-*Morigla* M1.

OPPOSITION:
FRENTE NORTE: ε1,200 (former Contra rebels),
perhaps 500 armed.

PANAMA

GDP	1993:	B6.56bn ($6.56bn):	
	per capita $5,800		
	1994:	B6.99bn ($6.99bn):	
	per capita $6,100		
Growth	1993: 5.4%	1994: 4.7%	
Inflation	1993: 0.5%	1994: 1.3%	
Debt	1993: $6.8bn	1994: $6.9bn	
Def exp	1993: B79m ($79m)		
Sy bdgt	1994: B86m ($86m)		
	1995: B91m ($91m)		

$1 = B 1993–95: 1.0
B = balboa

Population: 2,660,000

	13–17	*18–22*	*23–32*
Men	138,000	134,800	236,600
Women	132,000	129,400	234,000

TOTAL PUBLIC FORCES:
ACTIVE: 11,800.

NATIONAL POLICE FORCE: 11,000.
Presidential Guard bn (-).

1 MP bn plus 8 coys.
18 Police coy.
No hy mil eqpt, small arms only.

NATIONAL MARITIME SERVICE: ε400.
BASES: Amador (HQ), Balboa, Colón.
PATROL CRAFT, INSHORE: 7:
2 *Panquiaco* (UK Vosper 31.5-m), 1 *Tres de Noviembre*
(ex-USCG *Cape Higgon*), 3 ex-US MSB 5-class, 1⟨
(plus about 4 other ex-US patrol/spt craft⟨.
AMPH: craft only: 6 LCM.

NATIONAL AIR SERVICE: 400.
TPT: 1 CN-235-2A, 1 BN-2B, 1 PA-34, 3 CASA-
212M *Aviocar*.
TRG: 6 T-35D.
HEL: 2 Bell 205, 3 Bell 212, 1 UH-H, 1-N.

FOREIGN FORCES:
US: 9,120. Army: 6,300; 1 inf bde (1 inf bn), 1 avn bde.
Navy: 700. Marines: 120. Air Force: 2,000; 1 air div.

PARAGUAY

GDP	1993:	Pg 11,992bn ($5.72bn):	
	per capita $3,800		
	1994:	Pg 13,600bn ($6.07bn):	
	per capita $3,900		
Growth	1993: 4.1%	1994: 3.5%	
Inflation	1993: 18.2%	1994: 18.7%	
Debt	1993: $1.6bn	1994: $1.6bn	
Def exp[a]	1993: Pg 154bn ($74m)		
	1994: Pg 186bn ($83m)		
Def bdgt	1995: Pg 239bn ($107m)		
FMA	1994: $0.1m (IMET)		
	1995: $0.1m (IMET)		
	1996: $0.2m (IMET)		
$1 = Pg	1993: 1,744	1994: 1,912	
	1995: 1,972		

Pg = Paraguayan guarani

[a] Does not include extra-budgetary funds from military enterprises.

Population: 4,940,000

	13–17	*18–22*	*23–32*
Men	267,200	233,200	398,400
Women	257,400	224,800	384,600

TOTAL ARMED FORCES:
ACTIVE: 20,300 (12,900 conscripts).
Terms of service: 12 months; Navy 2 years.

RESERVES: some 164,500.

ARMY: 15,000 (10,400 conscripts).
3 corps HQ.
9 div HQ (6 inf, 3 cav).
7 inf regt (bn).
4 cav regt (horse).
1 armd cav regt.
2 mech cav regt.
20 frontier det.
6 arty gp (bn).
1 AD arty bn.
4 engr bn.
EQPT:
MBT: 5 M-4A3.
RECCE: 8 M-8, 5 M-3, 30 EE-9 *Cascavel*.
APC: 10 EE-11 *Urutu*.
TOWED ARTY: 75mm: 20 Model 1927/1934; **105mm:**
15 M-101; **152mm:** 6 Mk V 6-in (anti-ship).
MOR: 81mm: 80.
RCL: 75mm: M-20.
AD GUNS: 20mm: 20 Bofors; **40mm:** 10 M-1A1.

NAVY: 3,600 (incl 900 Marines, 800 Naval Aviation,
Harbour and River Guard, and ε1,900 conscripts).
BASES: Asunción (Puerto Sajonia), Bahía Negra,
Ciudad Del Este.
PATROL AND COASTAL COMBATANTS: 7:
COASTAL: 7:
2 *Paraguay* with 4 x 120mm guns.
3 *Nanawa* PCO with 4 x 40mm and 2 x 12.7mm guns.
1 *Itapu* PCR with 1 x 40mm, 6 x 12.7mm guns, 2 x
81mm mor.
1 *Capitan Cabral* PCR with 1 x 40mm, 2 x 20mm, 2
x 12.7mm guns.
SPT AND MISC: 6:
1 tpt, 1 *Boqueron* spt (ex-US LSM with hel
deck), 1 trg/tpt, 1 survey⟨, 2 LCT.

MARINES: (900) (incl 200 conscripts).
2 bn.

NAVAL AVIATION: (800); 2 cbt ac, no armed hel.
COIN: 2 AT-6G.
LIAISON: 2 Cessna 150, 2 Cessna 206, 1 Cessna 210.
HEL: 2 HB-350, 1 OH-13.

AIR FORCE: 1,700 (600 conscripts); 17 cbt ac,
no armed hel.
COMPOSITE SQN:
COIN: 5 AT-6, 7 EMB-326.
LIAISON: 1 Cessna 185, 4 Cessna 206, 2 Cessna 402,
2 T-41.

HEL: 3 HB-350, 1 UH-1B, 4 UH-12, 4 Bell 47G.
TPT: 1 sqn with 5 C-47, 4 C-212, 3 DC-6B, 1 DHC-
6 (VIP), 1 C-131D.
TRG: 5* EMB-312, 6 T-6, 10 T-23, 5 T-25, 10 T-35,
1 T-41.

PARAMILITARY:
SPECIAL POLICE SERVICE: 8,000.

PERU

GDP	1993: NS 81.64bn ($37.07bn):		
	per capita $3,400		
	1994: NS 91.91bn ($41.78bn):		
	per capita $3,800		
Growth	1993: 6.4%	1994: 12.7%	
Inflation	1993: 48.6%	1994: 23.7%	
Debt	1993: $20.3bn	1994: $21.0bn	
Def exp[a]	1993: NS 1,531m ($696m)		
Def bdgt	1994ε: NS 1,646m ($750m)		
	1995ε: NS 1,715m ($784m)		
FMA	1994: $8.4m (Narcs)		
	1995: $12.3m (Narcs)		
	1996: $42.5m (Narcs, IMET)		
$1 = NS	1993: 1.99	1994: 2.20	
	1995: 2.25		

NS = new sol

[a] Does not include some extra-budgetary funds.

Population: 23,681,000

	13–17	18–22	23–32
Men	1,303,800	1,209,600	2,030,000
Women	1,292,600	1,201,400	2,023,600

TOTAL ARMED FORCES:
ACTIVE: 115,000 (65,500 conscripts).
Terms of service: 2 years, selective.
RESERVES: 188,000 (Army only).

ARMY: 75,000 (50,000 conscripts).
6 Mil Regions.
Army tps:
1 AB div (3 cdo, 1 para bn, 1 arty gp).
1 Presidential Escort regt.
1 AD arty gp.
Regional tps:
3 armd div (each 2 tk, 1 armd inf bn, 1 arty gp, 1 engr bn).
1 armd gp (3 indep armd cav, 1 fd arty, 1 AD arty, 1
engr bn).
1 cav div (3 mech regt, 1 arty gp).
7 inf div (each 3 inf bn, 1 arty gp).

1 jungle div.
2 med arty gp; 2 fd arty gp.
1 indep inf bn.
1 indep engr bn.
3 hel sqn.
EQPT:
MBT: 300 T-54/-55 (ε50 serviceable).
LT TK: 110 AMX-13 (ε30 serviceable).
RECCE: 60 M-8/-20, 10 M-3A1, 50 M-9A1, 15 Fiat 6616, 30 BRDM-2.
APC: 130 M-113, 12 BTR-60, 130 UR-416, 4 *Repontec*.
TOWED ARTY: 105mm: 20 Model 56 pack, 130 M-101; **122mm:** 30 D-30; **130mm:** 30 M-46.
SP ARTY: 155mm: 12 M-109A2, 12 Mk F3.
MRL: 122mm: 14 BM-21.
MOR: 81mm: incl some SP; **107mm:** incl some SP; **120mm:** 300 Brandt, ECIA.
RCL: 106mm: M40A1.
AD GUNS: 23mm: 80 ZSU-23-2, 35 ZSU-23-4 SP; **40mm:** 45 M-1, 80 L60/70.
SAM: SA-7, 120 SA-14/-16.
AC: 1 Cessna 182, 2 -U206, 1 -337, 1 *Queen Air* 65, 3 U-10, 3 U-17.
HEL: 2 Bell 47G, 2 Mi-6, 26 Mi-8, 14 Mi-17, 6 SA-315, 5 SA-316, 3 SA-318, 2 *Agusta* A-109.

NAVY: 25,000 (incl some 700 Naval Aviation, 3,000 Marines and 13,500 conscripts).
3 Naval Force Areas: Pacific, Lake Titicaca, Amazon River.
BASES: Ocean: Callao, San Lorenzo Island, Paita, Talara. **Lake:** Puno. **River:** Iquitos, Puerto Maldonado.
SS: 6 *Casma* (Ge T-209/1200) with 533mm TT (It A184 HWT).
(Plus 1 *Pedrera* (US *Guppy* I) with 533mm TT (Mk 37 HWT) alongside trg only.)
PRINCIPAL SURFACE COMBATANTS: 11:
CC: 2:
1 *Almirante Grau* (Nl *De Ruyter*) with 4 x 2 152mm guns, 8 *Otomat* SSM.
1 *Aguirre* (Nl *De 7 Provincien*) with 3 x SH-3D *Sea King* hel (ASW/ASUW) (Mk 46 LWT/AM-39 *Exocet*), 2 x 2 152mm guns.
DD: 5:
1 *Palacios* (UK *Daring*) with 4 x 2 MM-38 *Exocet*, 3 x 2 114mm guns, hel deck.
4 *Bolognesi* (Nl *Friesland*) with 4 x 120mm guns, 2 x 4 ASW RL.
FF: 4 *Carvajal* (mod It *Lupo*) with 1 AB-212 hel (ASW/OTHT), 2 x 3 ASTT; plus 8 *Otomat* Mk 2 SSM, 1 x 127mm gun.
PATROL AND COASTAL COMBATANTS: 7:
MSL CRAFT: 6 *Velarde* PFM (Fr PR-72 64-m) with 4 x MM-38 *Exocet*.
PATROL: 1 *Unanue* (ex-US *Sotoyomo*) PCC (Antarctic ops).

MCM: 2 *Dokkum* (NL *Abcoude*).
AMPH: 3 *Paita* (US *Terrebonne Parish*) LST, capacity 395 tps, 16 tk.
SPT AND MISC: 8:
3 AO, 1 AOT, 1 tpt, 2 survey, 1 ocean tug (SAR).
RIVER AND LAKE FLOTILLAS: 9:
some 4 gunboats, 5 patrol⟨.

NAVAL AVIATION: (some 700); 7 cbt ac, 14 armed hel.
ASW/MR: 4 sqn with: **ac:** 7* S-2, 6 *Super King Air* B 200T; 3 EMB-111A; **hel:** 6 AB-212 ASW, 8 SH-3D (ASW).
TPT: 2 C-47.
LIAISON: 4 Bell 206B, 6 UH-1D hel, 2 SA-319, 3 Mi-8.
TRG: 1 Cessna 150, 5 T-34C.
ASM: *Exocet* AM-39 (on SH-3 hel).

MARINES: (3,000).
1 Marine bde (5 bn, 1 recce, 1 cdo coy).
EQPT:
RECCE: V-100.
APC: 15 V-200 *Chaimite*, 20 BMR-600.
MOR: 81mm; 120mm e18 .
RCL: 84mm: *Carl Gustav*; **106mm:** M-40A1.
AD GUNS: twin 20mm SP.

COASTAL DEFENCE: 3 bty with 18 155mm how.

AIR FORCE: 15,000 (2,000 conscripts); 90 cbt ac, 23 armed hel.
BBR: 1 gp (2 sqn) with 15 *Canberra* (4 -B(1) 12, 8 -B1(68), 1 T-4, 2 -T54).
FGA: 2 gp: 6 sqn:
3 with 28 Su-22 (incl 4* Su-22U).
3 with 23 Cessna A-37B.
FTR: 3 sqn:
1 with 10 *Mirage* 2000P, 2 -DP.
2 with 10 *Mirage* 5P, 2 -DP.
ATTACK HEL: 1 sqn with 23 Mi-24/-25.
RECCE: 1 photo-survey unit with 2 *Learjet* 25B, 2 -36A.
TKR: 1 Boeing KC 707-323C.
TPT: 3 gp (7 sqn):
AC: 14 An-32, 3 AN-72, 4 C-130A, 6 -D, 5 L-100-20, 2 DC-8-62F, 12 DHC-5, 8 DHC-6, 1 FH-227, 9 PC-6, 6 Y-12.
PRESIDENTIAL FLT: 1 F-28, 1 *Falcon* 20F.
HEL: 3 sqn with 8 Bell 206, 15 Bell 212, 5 Bell 214, 1 Bell 412, 10 Bo-105C, 5 Mi-6, 3 Mi-8, 35 Mi-17, 5 SA-316.
LIAISON: ac: 2 Beech 99, 3 Cessna 185, 1 Cessna 320, 15 *Queen Air* 80, 3 *King Air* 90, 1 PA-31T; **hel:** 8 UH-1D.
TRG: ac: 2 Cessna 150, 25 EMB-312, 13 MB-339A, 20 T-37B/C, 15 T-41A/-D; **hel:** 12 Bell 47G.
MSL:
ASM: AS-30.
AAM: AA-2 *Atoll*, R-550 *Magic*.
AD: 3 SA-2, 6 SA-3 bn with 18 SA-2, 24 SA-3 launchers.

PARAMILITARY:

NATIONAL POLICE: 60,000 (amalgamation of Guardia Civil, Republican Guard and Policia Investigacionara Peruana); MOWAG *Roland* APC.
COAST GUARD: 600; 5 *Rio Nepena* PCC, 3 PCI, 8 riverine PCI⟨.
RONDAS CAMPESINAS (peasant self-defence force): perhaps 2,000 *rondas* 'groups', up to pl strength, some with small arms. Deployed mainly in emergency zone.

OPPOSITION:

SENDERO LUMINOSO (Shining Path): ε3,000; Maoist.
MOVIMIENTO REVOLUCIONARIO TUPAC AMARU (MRTA): ε500; mainly urban gp.

SURINAME

GDP	1993: gld 23.18bn ($490bn):		
	per capita $3,500		
	1994: gld n.k. ($490bn):		
	per capita $3,300		
Growth	1993: -4.8%	1994: -2.2%	
Inflation	1993: 143.5%	1994: 368.6%	
Debt	1992: $206m	1993: $208m	
Def exp	1993: gld 520m ($71m)		
Def bdgt	1994ε: gld 2,046m ($11m)		
	1995ε: gld 7,200m ($12m)		
FMA	1995: $0.05m (IMET)		
	1996: $0.05m (IMET)		
$1 = gld	1993: 47	1994: 186	
	1995: 671		

gld = guilder

Population: 410,000

	13–17	*18–22*	*23–32*
Men	19,600	19,200	38,400
Women	19,600	18,600	39,600

TOTAL ARMED FORCES (all services form part of the Army):
ACTIVE: ε1,800.

ARMY: 1,400.
1 inf bn (4 inf coy).
1 mech cav sqn.
1 MP 'bde' (bn).
EQPT:
RECCE: 6 EE-9 *Cascavel.*
APC: 9 YP-408, 15 EE-11 *Urutu.*
MOR: 81mm: 6.

RCL: 106mm: M-40A1.

NAVY: 240.
BASE: Paramaribo.
PATROL CRAFT, INSHORE: 5:
3 S-401 (Nl 32-m), 2⟨, plus boats.

AIR FORCE: ε150; 5 cbt ac, no armed hel.
COIN: 4 BN-2 *Defender*, 1 PC-7.
LIAISON: 1 Cessna U206.
HEL: 2 SA-319, 1 AB-205.

FORCES ABROAD:
UN AND PEACEKEEPING:
HAITI (UNMIH): 31 plus 15 civ pol.

TRINIDAD AND TOBAGO

GDP	1993: $TT 24.28bn ($5.58bn):		
	per capita $8,700		
	1994: $TT 31.55bn ($5.84bn):		
	per capita $9,000		
Growth	1993: -1.3%	1994: 4.7%	
Inflation	1993: 10.8%	1994: 9.5%	
Debt	1993: $2.2bn	1994: $2.1bn	
Def exp	1993ε: $TT 343m ($79m)		
Def bdgt	1994ε: $TT 450m ($83m)		
	1995ε: $TT 485m ($82m)		
FMA	1994: $0.10m (FMF, IMET)		
	1995: $0.05m (IMET)		
	1996: $0.05m (IMET)		
$1 = $TT	1993: 5.35	1994: 5.92	
	1995: 5.92		

$TT = Trinidad and Tobago dollar

Population: 1,305,000

	13–17	*18–22*	*23–32*
Men	66,800	57,800	105,400
Women	65,800	58,000	110,200

TOTAL ARMED FORCES (all services are part of the Army):
ACTIVE: 2,100.

ARMY: 1,400.
2 inf bn.
1 spt bn.
EQPT:
MOR: 60mm: ε40; **81mm:** 6 L16A1.
RL: 82mm: 13 B-300.
RCL: 84mm: *Carl Gustav.*

COAST GUARD: 700 (incl 50 Air Wing).
BASE: Staubles Bay (HQ), Hart's Cut, Point Fortin, Tobago.
PATROL CRAFT, INSHORE: 9 (some non-op):
2 *Barracuda* PFI (Sw *Karlskrona* 40-m).
7 PCI⟨, plus boats and 3 ex-marine police spt vessels.

AIR WING: 1 Cessna 310, 1 Cessna 402, 1 Cessna 172.

FORCES ABROAD:
UN PEACEKEEPING:
HAITI (UNMIH): 55.

PARAMILITARY:
POLICE: 4,800.

URUGUAY

GDP	1993:	pU 51.90bn ($11.57bn):
		per capita $7,700
	1994:	pU 61.06bn ($12.09bn):
		per capita $8,100
Growth	1993: 1.5%	1994: 4.5%
Inflation	1993: 54.1%	1994: 44.8%
Debt	1993: $7.3bn	1994: $7.3bn
Def exp	1993: pU 1,147m ($256m)	
Def bdgt	1994: pU 1,499m ($297m)	
	1995ε: pU 1,745m ($302m)	
FMA	1994: $0.2m (IMET)	
	1995: $0.1m (IMET)	
	1996: $0.3m (IMET)	
$1 = pU[a]	1993: 3.95	1994: 5.05
	1995: 5.77	
pU = Uruguyan peso		

[a] The Uruguayan peso, equal to 1,000 new Uruguayan pesos, was introduced in March 1993.

Population: 3,179,000

	13–17	18–22	23–32
Men	137,400	135,000	228,200
Women	132,000	129,400	228,200

TOTAL ARMED FORCES:
ACTIVE: 25,600.

ARMY: 17,600.
4 Mil Regions/div HQ.
5 inf bde (4 of 3 inf bn, 1 of 1 mech, 1 mot, 1 para bn).
3 cav bde (10 cav bn (4 horsed, 3 mech, 2 mot, 1 armd)).

1 arty bde (2 arty, 1 AD arty bn).
1 engr bde (3 bn).
3 arty, 4 cbt engr bn.
EQPT:
LT TK: 17 M-24, 29 M-3A1, 22 M-41A1.
RECCE: 16 EE-3 *Jararaca*, 10 EE-9 *Cascavel*.
APC: 15 M-113, 50 *Condor*, 60 OT-64 SKOT.
TOWED ARTY: 75mm: 12 Bofors M-1902; **105mm:** 48 M-101A/M-102; **155mm:** 5 M-114A1.
MOR: 81mm: 97; **107mm:** 8 M-30; **120mm:** 44.
ATGW: 5 *Milan*.
RCL: 57mm: 30 M-18; **106mm:** 30 M-40A1.
AD GUNS: 20mm: 6 M-167 *Vulcan*; **40mm:** 8 L/60.

NAVY: 5,000 (incl 280 Naval Aviation, 400 Naval Infantry, 1,600 Prefectura Naval (Coast Guard)).
BASES: Montevideo (HQ), La Paloma, Fray Bentos.
FF: 3: *General Artigas* (Fr *Cdt Rivière*) with 2 x 3 ASTT, 1 x 2 ASW mor, 2 x 100mm guns.
PATROL AND COASTAL COMBATANTS: 10:
PATROL, INSHORE: 10:
2 *Colonia* PCI (US *Cape*).
3 *15 de Noviembre* PFI (Fr *Vigilante* 42-m).
1 *Salto* PCI, 1 *Paysandu* PCI⟨, and 3 other⟨.
MCM: 4 *Temerario* MSC (Ge *Kondor* II).
AMPH: craft only: 2 LCM, 2 LCVP.
SPT AND MISC: 5:
1 *Presidente Rivera* AOT, 1 *Vanguardia* Salvage, 1 *Campbell* (US *Auk* MSF) PCO (Antarctic patrol/research), 1 spt (ex-GDR *Elbe*-Class), 1 trg.

NAVAL AVIATION: (280); 6 cbt ac, no armed hel.
ASW: 1 flt with 3 S-2A, 3 -G.
MR: 1 *Super King Air* 200T.
TRG/LIAISON: 1 *Super Cub*, 2 T-28, 2 T-34B, 2 T-34C, 1 PA-34-200T, 1 C-182 *Skylane*.
HEL: 2 Wessex 60, 1 Bell 47G, 1 Bell 222, 2 SH-34J.

NAVAL INFANTRY: (430); 1 bn.

AIR FORCE: 3,000; 36 cbt ac, no armed hel.
Flying hours: 120.
COIN: 2 sqn:
1 with 12 A-37B, 7 T-33A.
1 with 5 IA-58B.
SURVEY: 1 EMB-110B1.
SAR: 1 sqn with: 2 Bell 212, 3 UH-1H hel.
TPT: 3 sqn with 3 C-212 (tpt/SAR), 3 EMB-110C, 1 F-27, 3 C-130B.
LIAISON: 3 Cessna 182, 2 *Queen Air* 80, 5 U-17.
TRG: *12 T-34A/B, 5 T-41D, 5 PC-7U.

FORCES ABROAD:
UN AND PEACEKEEPING:

ANGOLA (UNAVEM III): 839 incl 10 Obs plus 9 civ pol. **EGYPT** (MFO): 64. **GEORGIA** (UNOMIG): 4 Obs. **INDIA/PAKISTAN** (UNMOGIP): 3 Obs. **IRAQ/ KUWAIT** (UNIKOM): 6 Obs. **LIBERIA** (UNOMIL): 3 Obs. **RWANDA** (UNAMIR): 26 Obs. **TAJIKISTAN** (UNMOT): 5 Obs. **WESTERN SAHARA** (MINURSO): 15 Obs plus 10 civ pol.

PARAMILITARY:
GUARDIA DE GRANADEROS: 450.
GUARDIA DE CORACEROS: 470.
COAST GUARD: the Prefectura Naval (PNN) is part of the Navy.

VENEZUELA

GDP	1993:	Bs 5.45bn ($60.0bn):	
		per capita $9,100	
	1994:	Bs 8.31bn ($58.0bn):	
		per capita $8,800	
Growth	1993:	-0.4%	1994: -3.3%
Inflation	1993:	38.1%	1994: 60.8%
Debt	1993:	$37.5bn	1994: $37.8bn
Def exp	1993:	Bs 93.5bn ($1,029m)	
	1994ε:	Bs 136.0bn ($950m)	
Def bdgt	1994:	Bs 111bn ($775m)	
	1995:	Bs 151bn ($890m)	
FMA	1994:	$0.6m (Narcs, IMET)	
	1995:	$0.8m (Narcs, IMET)	
	1996:	$0.8m (Narcs, IMET)	
$1 = Bs	1993:	91	1994: 149
	1995:	170	
Bs = bolivar			

Population: 21,883,000

	13–17	18–22	23–32
Men	1,183,200	1,069,800	1,854,800
Women	1,140,000	1,034,600	1,806,200

TOTAL ARMED FORCES:
ACTIVE: 79,000 (incl National Guard and ε31,000 conscripts).
Terms of service: 30 months selective, varies by region for all services.
RESERVES: Army: ε8,000.

ARMY: 34,000 (incl 27,000 conscripts).
6 inf div.
1 armd bde.
1 cav bde.
7 inf bde (18 inf, 1 mech inf, 4 fd arty bn).
1 AB bde.
1 Ranger bde (6 Ranger bn).
1 avn regt.
RESERVES: ε6 inf, 1 armd, 1 arty bn.
EQPT:
MBT: 70 AMX-30.
LT TK: 75 M-18, 36 AMX-13, ε50 *Scorpion* 90.
RECCE: 10 AML-60/-90, 30 M-8.
APC: 25 AMX-VCI, 100 V-100, 30 V-150, 100 *Dragoon* (some with 90mm gun), 35 EE-11 *Urutu*.
TOWED ARTY: 105mm: 40 Model 56, 40 M-101; **155mm:** 12 M-114.
SP ARTY: 155mm: 5 M-109, 10 Mk F3.
MRL: 160mm: 20 LAR SP.
MOR: 81mm: 165; **120mm:** 65 Brandt.
ATGW: AT-4, AS-11, 24 *Mapats*.
RCL: 84mm: *Carl Gustav*; **106mm:** 175 M-40A1.
SURV: RASIT (veh, arty).
AC: 3 IAI-202, 2 Cessna 182, 2 Cessna 206, 2 Cessna 207.
ATTACK HEL: 5 A-109 (ATK).
TPT HEL: 4 AS-61A, 3 Bell 205, 6 UH-1H.
LIAISON: 2 Bell 206.

NAVY: 15,000 (incl 1,000 Naval Aviation, 5,000 Marines, 1,000 Coast Guard and ε4,000 conscripts).
5 Comds: Fleet, Marines, Naval Avn, Coast Guard, Fluvial (River Forces).
5 Fleet sqn: submarine, frigate, patrol, amph, service.
BASES: Caracas (HQ), Puerto Cabello (submarine, frigate, amph and service sqn), Punto Fijo (patrol sqn). Minor bases: Puerto de Hierro, Puerto La Cruz, El Amparo (HQ Arauca River), Maracaibo, La Guaira, Ciudad Bolivar (HQ Fluvial Forces).
SS: 2 *Sabalo* (Ge T-209/1300) with 533mm TT (SST-4 HWT) (1 refitting in Germany).
FF: 6 *Mariscal Sucre* (It *Lupo*) with 1 AB-212 hel (ASW/OTHT), 2 x 3 ASTT (A-244S LWT); plus 8 *Teseo* SSM, 1 x 127mm gun, 1 x 8 *Aspide* SAM.
PATROL AND COASTAL COMBATANTS: 6:
MSL CRAFT: 6:
3 *Constitución* PFM (UK Vosper 37-m), with 2 x *Teseo*.
3 *Constitución* PFI with 4 x *Harpoon* SSM.
AMPH: 4 *Capana* LST, capacity 200 tps, 12 tk.
Plus craft: 2 LCU (river comd), 12 LCVP.
SPT AND MISC: 3:
1 log spt, 1 trg, 1 *Punta Brava* AGHS.

NAVAL AVIATION: (1,000); 4 cbt ac, 8 armed hel.
ASW: 1 hel sqn (afloat) with 8 AB-212.
MR: 1 sqn with 4 C-212.
TPT: 2 C-212, 1 DHC-7, 1 *Rockwell Commander* 680.
LIAISON: 1 Cessna 310, 1 Cessna 402, 1 *King Air* 90.
HEL: 2 Bell 47J.

MARINES: (5,000).
4 inf bn.

1 arty bn (3 fd, 1 AD bty).
1 amph veh bn.
1 river patrol, 1 engr, 2 para/cdo unit.
EQPT:
AAV: 11 LVTP-7 (to be mod to -7A1).
APC: 25 EE-11 *Urutu*, 10 *Fuchs/Transportpanzer* 1.
TOWED ARTY: 105mm: 18 Model 56.
AD GUNS: 40mm: 6 M-42 twin SP.

COAST GUARD: (1,000).
BASE: La Guaira; operates under Naval Command and Control, but organisationally separate.
PATROL, OFFSHORE: 3:
2 *Almirante Clemente* (It FF type).
1 *Miguel Rodriguez* (ex-US ocean tug).
PATROL, INSHORE: 6:
2 *Petrel* (USCG *Point*-class) PCI⟨, 4 riverine PCI⟨, plus boats.

AIR FORCE: 7,000 (some conscripts); 119 cbt
ac, 27 armed hel.
FTR/FGA: 3 air gp:
1 with 15 CF-5A/B, 15 T-2D; 1 with 2 *Mirage* IIIEV, 5 *Mirage* 50EV; 1 with 18 F-16A, 6 -B.
COIN: 1 air gp with 10 EMB-312, 24 OV-10E, 17 T-2D *Buckeye*.
ARMED HEL: 1 air gp with 10 SA-316, 12 UH-1D, 5 UH-1H.
TPT: ac: 7 C-123, 6 C-130H, 8 G-222, 2 HS-748, 2 B-707 (tkr); **hel:** 3 Bell 214, 4 Bell 412, 5 AS-332B, 2 UH-1N.
PRESIDENTIAL FLT: 1 Boeing 737, 3 *Falcon* 20, 1 *Gulfstream* II, 1 *Gulfstream* III, 1 *Learjet* 24D.
LIAISON: 9 Cessna 182, 1 *Citation* I, 1 *Citation* II, 2 *Queen Air* 65, 5 *Queen Air* 80, 5 *Super King Air* 200, 9 SA-316B *Alouette III*.
TRG: 1 air gp: 12 EMB-312, *7 F-5 (1 CF-5D, 6 NF-5B), 20 T-34.
AAM: R-530 *Magic*, AIM-9L *Sidewinder*, AIM-9P *Sidewinder*.
AD GUNS: 20mm: some Panhard M-3 SP; **35mm**; **40mm:** 114: Bofors L/70 towed, Breda towed.
SAM: 10 *Roland*.

NATIONAL GUARD (Fuerzas Armadas de Cooperación): 23,000 (internal sy, customs).
8 regional comd.
EQPT: 20 UR-416 AIFV, 24 Fiat-6614 APC, 100 60mm mor, 50 81mm mor.
AC: 1 *Baron*, 1 BN-2A, 2 Cessna 185, 5 -U206, 4 IAI-201, 1 *King Air* 90, 1 *King Air* 200C, 2 *Queen Air* 80.
HEL: 4 A-109, 20 Bell 206.
PATROL CRAFT, INSHORE: 22; some 60 boats.

FORCES ABROAD:
UN AND PEACEKEEPING:
IRAQ/KUWAIT (UNIKOM): 2 Obs. **WESTERN SAHARA** (MINURSO): 1 Obs.

Sub-Saharan Africa

On 2 June 1995, the Organisation of African Unity (OAU) – which includes, in addition to the states listed in this section of *The Military Balance*, Sao Tome and Principe, Swaziland, the Comoros, and the North African states of Algeria, Egypt, Libya, Mauritania and Tunisia, but not Morocco – adopted a draft Nuclear-Weapons-Free Zone treaty. Drafting of the treaty began in 1993 after the end of apartheid in South Africa. It is being submitted to the UN General Assembly and, once approved, will be opened for signature. The draft includes a protocol (considered stronger than the similar commitment in the Nuclear Non-Proliferation Treaty (NPT)) under which nuclear-armed states would pledge not to use nuclear weapons against African states. The status of Diego Garcia, where US nuclear weapons are suspected of being stored, is a potential problem.

Only two African countries, Djibouti and the Comoros, have not signed the NPT. Angola, Botswana, Mozambique, Sao Tome and Principe, Somalia and Sudan are non-signatories of the Chemical Weapons Convention (CWC), but only Lesotho, Mauritius and the Seychelles have ratified it.

In general, there have been very few changes in either the order of battle or the manpower strengths or weapons holdings of African states in the last 12 months. However, the instances listed are significant when the overall armed strength of the country concerned is taken into account.

Political and Strategic Developments

Horn of Africa

In **Djibouti** the government and the Front for the Restoration of Unity and Democracy (FRUD) signed an agreement on 26 December 1994 which provided for an immediate cease-fire, a revision of the Constitution and the integration of FRUD militia into the national army. In December 1994, the **Ethiopian** Constituent Assembly adopted a new Constitution establishing a federal government and dividing the country into nine states with considerable autonomy and the right to secede. The United Nations peacekeeping force (UNOSOM) completed its withdrawal from **Somalia** on 1 March 1995, its mission unaccomplished. Also in March, two Mogadishu-based leaders, Mohammed Farah Aideed and Ali Mahdi Mohammed, reached agreement over joint control of the port and airport (although Aideed had effective control) and an attempt was made to form a Benadir regional authority. In the north, Somaliland still maintains its independence, although it has been the scene of some inter-factional fighting and has not yet received international recognition. The civil war in **Sudan** has been interrupted by a two-month cease-fire agreed to after a peace initiative by former US President Jimmy Carter. The cease-fire was declared by the government on 27 March 1995 and accepted by the Sudanese People's Liberation Army (SPLA) on 30 March and by the Southern Sudan Independence Movement on 3 April. A two-month extension was accepted by the SPLA on 4 June 1995 after it complained of government violations. Khartoum's links with Iran appeared to be confirmed by an agreement signed on 13 April 1995 which is believed to have included provisions for Iran to use naval facilities at Port Sudan, an increase in other areas of military cooperation such as intelligence and training, and the supply of arms by Iran.

Central Africa

A Forum for the Promotion of Peace in Central Africa met in December 1994 in Brazzaville, organised jointly by the United Nations Educational, Scientific and Cultural Organisation (UNESCO) and the Congo. An action plan was reportedly adopted for humanitarian intervention and to establish a cooperative and security mechanism. A committee to take charge of the reorganisation of security forces in **Congo** has been established.

In **Chad,** the government reached agreement with the Chadian National Front (FNT) on 12 October 1994 for a cease-fire and the integration of FNT members into the national army. In **Rwanda**, the French *Operation Turquoise* force completed its withdrawal on 30 September 1994, but it was some time later before the UN force (UNAMIR) completed its deployment. UNAMIR now numbers just over 6,000, provided by 27 countries, including 3,662 troops and police from 12 African states. This is the largest UN force after those in Bosnia, Croatia and Haiti. The UN has voted to cut the size of UNAMIR by about two-thirds by November 1995.

West Africa

In December 1994, the warring parties in **Liberia** agreed to a cease-fire starting at midnight on 28 December. There have, however, been numerous major violations of the cease-fire. The UN Secretary-General has warned that the UN peacekeeping mission (UNOMIL) may be withdrawn if no agreement can be reached over the proposed joint council of state. Tanzania has withdrawn its troops from the West African peacekeeping force (ECOMOG) and Uganda has also decided to withdraw. In **Niger**, the government and Tuareg rebel Organisation of the Armed Resistance (ORA) have signed an agreement providing for a cease-fire, a general amnesty, disarmament and weapons collection, and the integration of ORA members into government service. In **Mali** despite earlier peace talks, the government attacked a Tuareg base in November 1994 and the rebels responded with an attack on Timbuktu in January 1995. However, in June 1995 the Tuareg rebel group, the Arab Islamic Front (FIAA), unilaterally declared an end to hostilities and peace talks are expected shortly. The rebel Revolutionary United Front (RUF) in **Sierra Leone** released the last of a number of European hostages on 20 April 1995. The government is unclear whether to negotiate with the rebels, or to intensify the war effort in which it is supported by troops from Guinea and Nigeria and, reportedly, a mercenary group of Gurkhas. In **Nigeria**, General Sani Abacha, who took control of the country in November 1993, has continued to lead an increasingly repressive regime. Mashood K. O. Abiola, the winner of the presidential election in June 1993, remains in prison following his arrest in June 1994 and there seems to be little prospect of either his release or his trial. In February 1994, the Abacha regime, suspecting that the Army was planning a coup, made many arrests. Those arrested included General Olusegun Obasananjo, a former president, and his deputy, retired Major General Shehu Yar Adua. It is rumoured that Obasananjo has been secretly tried and given a long prison sentence. Abacha has said that he will announce his programme to return the country to an elected civilian government on 1 October 1995.

Southern Africa

A peace agreement was signed in November 1994 by **Angolan** President José dos Santos and rebel UNITA leader Jonas Savimbi. After assurances from the Angolan Foreign Minister that 'this time peace has come to stay' in February 1995, the UN Security Council adopted Resolution 976 providing for a 7,000-strong force and observers to assist in the disengagement of forces, set up a verification regime and a communications network, and start mine clearance. By the end of May, some 2,000 troops had deployed, including logistic and communications units as well as one infantry battalion. Nearly 350 military observers have been deployed to 50 sites in all six regions of Angola. The United Nations peacekeeping force (ONUMOZ) withdrew from **Mozambique** in January 1995. It had been planned to incorporate some 30,000 men from both the national army and Renamo into the new Mozambique Democratic Armed Forces (FADM), but by February only 12,000 had agreed to join and President Joaquim Alberto Chissano announced that conscription would be necessary. In **South Africa**, the armed forces have concentrated on integrating men from Umkhontowe Sizwe (MK) (the military wing of the African National Congress), the Azanian People's Liberation Army, the Zulu Inkatha movement and the armed forces of the Homelands into the South African National Defence Force (SANDF), leaving its reorganisation, including the numerous reserves, until integration is complete. Some 35,000 men have registered for service and, by May 1995, 15,000 of these applications had been processed with 11,000 accepted.

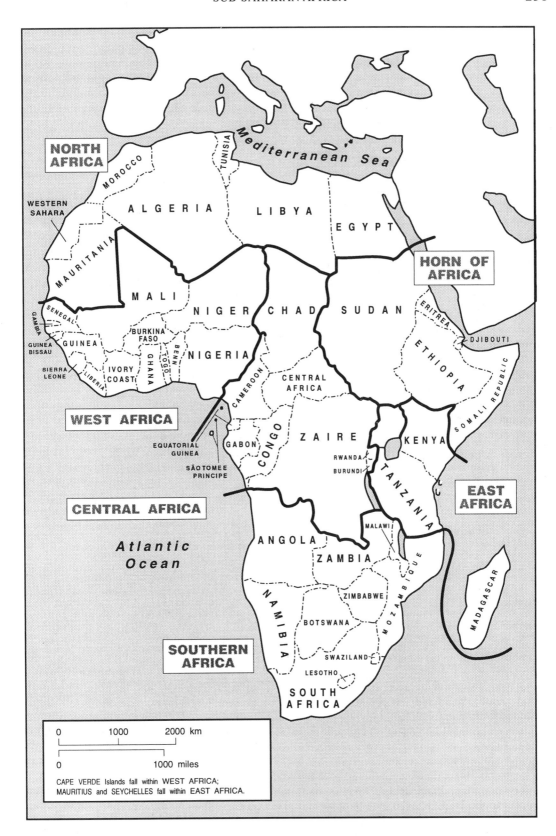

NORTH
AFRICA

WESTERN
SAHARA

Mediterranean Sea

MOROCCO

TUNISIA

ALGERIA   LIBYA

EGYPT

HORN OF
AFRICA

MAURITANIA

MALI

NIGER   CHAD   SUDAN

ERITREA

DJIBOUTI

SENEGAL

GAMBIA

GUINEA
BISSAU   GUINEA

BURKINA
FASO

BENN

ETHIOPIA

SIERRA
LEONE   LIBERIA

IVORY
COAST

GHANA

TOGO

NIGERIA

CAMEROON

CENTRAL
AFRICA

SOMALI REPUBLIC

WEST AFRICA

EQUATORIAL
GUINEA

SÃO TOME E
PRINCIPE

GABON

CONGO

ZAIRE

KENYA

RWANDA

BURUNDI

TANZANIA

EAST
AFRICA

CENTRAL AFRICA

Atlantic
Ocean

MALAWI

ANGOLA

ZAMBIA

MOZAMBIQUE

MADAGASCAR

NAMIBIA

ZIMBABWE

BOTSWANA

SOUTHERN
AFRICA

SWAZILAND

LESOTHO

SOUTH
AFRICA

0   1000   2000 km

0   1000 miles

CAPE VERDE Islands fall within WEST AFRICA;
MAURITIUS and SEYCHELLES fall within EAST AFRICA.

Military Developments

The number of MiG-23 aircraft in the **Ethiopian** Air Force is six (not 18 as listed in *The Military Balance 1994–1995*). The **Kenyan** Army has acquired 20 more AML-60/-90 armoured reconnaissance vehicles. The **Mauritius** Navy will be taking delivery of a Chilean-built 1,650 ton offshore patrol vessel probably in March 1996. The **Tanzanian** armed forces have been reduced by 15,000 to some 35,000 in the last 12 months and are planned to reduce further to 25,000 in 1996. The three divisional headquarters and three infantry brigades have been disbanded. **Equatorial Guinea** has taken delivery of two SA-316 helicopters.

The **Congolese** Air Force has acquired two Mi-8 helicopters. The Air Force inventory for **Guinea** has been reassessed. The **Guinea-Bissau** Navy has commissioned one inshore patrol craft acquired from India. In **Mali**, the Air Force has acquired three AS-350 helicopters. A Presidential Guard Brigade has been formed in **Nigeria**. The Army has 32 more Vickers Mark 3 tanks and six more 122mm APR-21 MRL. **Sierra Leone** has increased the manpower of its army by 7,000, virtually doubling its size; three new infantry battalions have been formed. The Army now has one Mi-24 attack helicopter. 36 *Scorpion* armoured vehicles including variants are being delivered to the **Botswana** Army and the Air Force has acquired two BN-2 *Defender* COIN aircraft. The **Malawi** Army has 2,000 fewer men than it had last year. **Namibia** has formed an Air Wing which is equipped with five Cessna 337/02-A aircraft, two SA-315 and two SA-319 helicopters. There are now no conscripts in the **South African** National Defence Force which is 131,000 strong and which will continue to grow before it is reduced to around 91,000 in about three years' time. A decision to purchase four corvettes to give the Navy some reach has been postponed. Two more battalions, one of commandos, have been formed in **Zimbabwe**. The Army now has a total of 60 122mm RM-70 MRL, and has acquired 20 *Eland* 60 armoured reconnaissance vehicles.

Defence Spending

The IISS estimates that regional military expenditure declined in real terms from some $8.6bn, 3% of gross domestic product (GDP), in 1993 to about $8bn, or 2.6% of GDP, in 1994 (all at 1993 prices). The 1994 level is about one-fifth down by comparison with 1985 ($10bn and 3.6% of GDP). Unlike in the Asia-Pacific region and Latin America, there has been little real GDP growth over the same period (just 2.5% in 1986–94, according to the International Monetary Fund (IMF)) to stimulate investment in defence and security, and GDP per capita has actually declined by 0.5%.

Three factors have determined the scale of military spending and its relative decline in recent years. First, the large cost of civil war arising from high levels of military consumption with concomitant economic and humanitarian costs. But spending has declined in recent years because the incidence of civil war is less prevalent than before, although it remains a significant cost for several countries. Second, while national-security costs in the region have declined, the UN and its member-states have taken on a large financial burden as a result of regional peacekeeping. In Mozambique, the cost of ONUMOZ in 1994 – its final year – amounted to about $295m. Other costs for UN peacekeeping in 1994 were about $198m for UNAMIR (inclusive of costs related to UNOMUR), some $862m for UNOSOM II, about $36m for UNOMIL (excluding estimated ECOMOG costs of $15m which, for a 5,000-strong military force, compares favourably with the UN's $36m for 70 Observers), and about $26m for UNAVEM II. UNAVEM III seems likely to be another costly UN effort in the region. All told, the cost in 1994 of UN peacekeeping operations and ECOMOG (about $1.4bn) added up to nearly one-fifth of regional military expenditure. The latter has thus declined because there are fewer civil wars and because the UN is increasing its financial contribution to regional security. A third reason concerns those countries that have managed to disengage from civil war. The legacy of repressive regimes has often meant unproductive and largely unaccountable military expenditure.

The impact of changing policy priorities – particularly in respect of economic development – has led several countries to seek to reduce unproductive military spending – a frequent target for the IMF's Structural Adjustment Programmes. These aim to reduce central government intervention in the economy through a policy of liberalisation intended to promote the private sector, improve economic competitiveness, particularly in the field of foreign trade, and thus create a more robust regime in the balance of payments through which to reduce the burden of external debt. Some countries, notably Kenya and Ghana, have adjusted strongly and are better placed to increase investment in national security. Others are adjusting more slowly, including several of the Francophone countries where government spending remains under tight constraints following the 1994 devaluation of the Communauté française Africaine (CFA) franc.

From an accounting perspective, the lack of transparency in regional military expenditure remains a problem. Few countries (in 1993 only Madagascar and Burkina Faso) report military expenditure to the UN and only a slightly larger number (among them Ghana, Kenya and Mauritius) allow the IMF to publish reasonably timely external audits. No recipient countries reported to the UN Conventional Arms Register in 1993, although counterpart supplier data showed that Angola, Nigeria and Malawi had taken delivery of weapons systems in the qualifying categories. About half the states in the region publish a defence budget for the coming or current financial year, but in some cases provide information on recurrent expenditure only (manpower and operations) and give no details of investment (equipment and construction). If the lack of transparency is one reason to treat official figures on military spending with caution, another is that military expenditure by opposition groups is not subject to systematic reporting for those countries engaged in – or liable to engage in – civil war. In some cases – for example, Angola and Somalia – the sums involved are likely to be considerable.

As a result of the incidence of civil war and weak government controls, systematic data on the market for small arms, ammunition and explosives – the staple *materiel* of regional civil war – are virtually non-existent. As there are only a small number of transactions in advanced weaponry and technology, these are generally conspicuous. The real problem lies in identifying the vast traffic in light weaponry and associated equipment. According to the US Arms Control and Disarmament Agency (ACDA), arms sales to the region have declined sharply since 1987. In that peak year recorded transfers amounted to some $6.1bn (at constant 1993 prices), reducing to $1.7bn in 1990. In contrast, recorded transfers (excluding South Africa) to the region were valued at $605m in 1991 and $240m in 1993. It must be emphasised that these figures are unlikely to capture much, if any, of the covert arms trade to the recent regional flashpoints, such as Angola, Somalia, Burundi, Rwanda, Sierra Leone, Liberia and Sudan.

South Africa accounts for nearly half of military spending in Sub-Saharan Africa. The new government has made more information available than its predecessor. In 1994 the defence budget amounted to R12.1bn ($3.1bn) and was supplemented by R1.5bn ($419m) for the amalgamation of the 'homeland' defence forces, R223m ($63m) for the integration of African National Congress (ANC) personnel, and R385m ($108m) for the operations of the National Peacekeeping Force – giving a total defence budget of R14.2bn ($4bn). Out-turn was some R700m ($197m) less because of a government spending freeze. Equipment spending for 1994 amounted to R2.2bn ($619m) – 20% of the unsupplemented budget – and R&D R329bn ($93m or 3%). The relatively low cost of indigenous procurement of advanced weaponry is illustrated by figures released for the Cheetah-C multi-role fighter modernisation programme, which is priced at R6.5bn ($1.8bn) for 38 aircraft, and the Rooivalk attack helicopter programme – R1.2bn ($338m) for development. The attempt to sell the latter to the UK proved unsuccessful. Imported defence equipment was valued at R833m ($235m) and exports at R519m ($146m). The defence budget for 1995 is R9.8bn ($2.7bn) and the military are requesting release of a further R700m held over from 1994 to bring the defence allocation up to R10.5bn ($3m).

ANGOLA

GDP	1993ε: K n.k. ($5.68bn):
	per capita $950
	1994ε: K n.k. ($5.93bn):
	per capita $1,000

Growth	1993ε: -22.3%	1994ε: 4.5%
Inflation	1993ε: 1,379%	1994ε: 673%
Debt	1993: $9.7bn	1994: $10.9bn
Def exp	1993ε: K n.k. ($780m)	
	1994ε: K n.k. ($515m)	

FMA*a*

$1 = K	1993ε: 6,500	1994ε: 610,000
	1995ε: 2,216	

K = kwanza

a The cost of UNAVEM II was about $26m in 1994.

Population: 10,636,000

	13–17	18–22	23–32
Men	584,600	492,600	741,600
Women	586,200	497,000	758,000

TOTAL ARMED FORCES:
ACTIVE: ε82,000.

ARMY: 75,000.
25 regts (armd, inf, engr, comd – str vary).
EQPT:†
MBT: 100 T-34†, 100 T-54/-55, some T-62, T-72 reported.
LT TK: some 10 PT-76.
AIFV: 50+ BMP-1, some BMP-2 reported.
RECCE: some 40+ BRDM-2.
APC: 100 BTR-60/-152.
TOWED ARTY: 300: incl **76mm:** M-1942 (ZIS-3); **85mm:** D-44; **122mm:** D-30; **130mm:** M-46.
ASLT GUNS: 100mm: SU-100.
MRL: 122mm: 50 BM-21; **240mm:** some BM-24.
MOR: 82mm: 250; **120mm:** 40+ M-43.
ATGW: AT-3 *Sagger*.
RCL: 500: **82mm:** B-10; **107mm:** B-11.
AD GUNS: 200+: **14.5mm:** ZPU-4; **23mm:** ZU-23-2, 20 ZSU-23-4 SP; **37mm:** M-1939; **57mm:** S-60 towed, 40 ZSU-57-2 SP.
SAM: SA-7/-14.

NAVY: ε1,500–2,000.
BASES: Luanda (HQ), Lobito, Namibe.
PATROL AND COASTAL COMBATANTS: 10:
MSL CRAFT: 6 Sov *Osa*-II† with 4 x SS-N-2 *Styx* SSM.
TORPEDO CRAFT: 4 *Shershen*† with 4 x 533mm HWT.
PATROL, INSHORE 7:

2 Sov *Poluchat*†, 1 Sov *Zhuk*⟨†.
4 *Mandume* type 31.6m PCI.
MCM: 2 Sov *Yevgenya* MHI.
AMPH: 2 Sov *Polnocny* LSM, capacity 100 tps, 6 tk.
Plus craft: 1 LCT, about 5 LCM.

COASTAL DEFENCE: SS-C-1 *Sepal* at Luanda.

AIR FORCE/AIR DEFENCE: 5,500†;
109 cbt ac, 40 armed hel.
FGA: 19 MiG-23, 18 Su-22, 10 Su-25.
FTR: 15 MiG-21 MF/bis.
COIN/RECCE: 18 PC-7, 18 PC-9.
MR: 2 EMB-111, 1 F-27MPA.
ATTACK HEL: 28 Mi-25/35, 6 SA-365M (guns), 6 SA-342 (*HOT*).
TPT: 2 sqn with 8 An-26, 6 BN-2, 9 C-212, 4 PC-6B, 2 L-100-20, 2 Boeing-707, 1 *Gulfstream* III.
HEL: 2 sqn with 30 IAR-316, 16 SA-316, 16 Mi-8, 6 Mi-17, 5 SA-341, 4 SA-365.
LIAISON: 5 An-2, 5 Do-27.
TRG: 3 Cessna 172, 3 MiG-15UTI, 6* MiG-21U, 5* Su-22, 6 Yak-11.
AD: 5 SAM bn†. 10 bty with 40 SA-2, 12 SA-3, 25 SA-6, 15 SA-8, 20 SA-9, 10 SA-13.
MSL:
ASM: *HOT*.
AAM: AA-2 *Atoll*.

PARAMILITARY:
INTERNAL SECURITY POLICE: 40,000.

OPPOSITION:
UNITA (Union for the Total Independence of Angola): ε55,000.
EQPT: captured T-34/-85, 70 T-55 MBT reported, misc APC (not in service); BM-21 122mm MRL; 75mm, 76mm, 122mm, 130mm fd guns; 81mm, 82mm, 120mm mor; 85mm RPG-7 RL; 75mm RCL; 12.7mm hy machine guns; 14.5mm, 20mm, ZU-23-2 23mm AA guns; *Stinger*, SAM-7.
FLEC (Front for the Liberation of the Cabinda Enclave): claims 5,000, actual str ε600; small arms only.

FOREIGN FORCES:
UNITED NATIONS (UNAVEM III): 1,969 tps, 341 mil obs and 212 civ pol from 33 countries.

BENIN

GDP	1993: fr 569.2bn ($1.6bn):
	per capita $1,700

1994ε: fr 733.0bn ($1.7bn):
per capita $1,700

Growth	1993: 3.6%	1994: 2.2%
Inflation	1993: 3.5%	1994: 26.0%
Debt	1993: $1.49bn	1994: $1.56bn
Def exp	1993: fr 9.1bn ($26.0m)	
Def bdgt	1994ε: fr 10.9bn ($26.1m)	
	1995ε: fr 12.1bn ($25.0m)	
FMA	1994: $0.1m (IMET) $1.5m (France)	
	1995: $0.1m (IMET)	
	1996: $0.2m (IMET)	
$1 = fr	1993: 283	1994: 555
	1995: 484	

fr = CFA franc

Population: 5,470,000

	13–17	18–22	23–32
Men	316,400	249,600	365,600
Women	329,800	267,400	399,800

TOTAL ARMED FORCES:
ACTIVE: 4,800.
Terms of service: conscription (selective), 18 months.

ARMY 4,500.
3 inf, 1 AB/cdo, 1 engr bn, 1 armd sqn, 1 arty bty.
EQPT:
LT TK: 20 PT-76 (op status uncertain).
RECCE: 9 M-8, 14 BRDM-2, 10 VBL.
TOWED ARTY: 105mm: 4 M-101.
MOR: 81mm.
RL: 89mm: LRAC.

NAVY:† ε150.
BASE: Cotonou.
PATROL COMBATANTS: 1 *Patriote* PFI (Fr 38-m)⟨.
In store: 4 Sov *Zhuk*⟨ PFI†.

AIR FORCE:† 150; no cbt ac.
AC: 2 An-26, 2 C-47, 1 *Commander* 500B, 2 Do-128, 1 Boeing 707-320 (VIP), 1 F-2 (VIP), 1 DHC-6.
HEL: 2 AS-350B, 1 SE-3130.

FORCES ABROAD:
UN AND PEACEKEEPING:
HAITI (UNMIH): 35 civ pol.

PARAMILITARY:
GENDARMERIE: 2,500; 4 mobile coy.

BOTSWANA

GDP	1993: P 8.43bn ($2.8bn):	
	per capita $5,000	
	1994: P 9.11bn ($2.9bn):	
	per capita $4,800	
Growth	1993: -0.7%	1994: 20.0%
Inflation	1993: 14.3%	1994: 10.6%
Debt	1993: $674m	1994: $735m
Def exp	1993: P 415m ($129m)	
	1994: P 615m ($196m)	
Def bdgt	1994: P 455m ($145m)	
	1995ε: P 625m ($200m)	
FMA	1994: $0.4m (IMET)	
	1995: $0.5m (IMET)	
	1996: $0.5m (IMET)	
$1 = P	1993: 2.42	1994: 2.68
	1995: 2.72	

P = pula

Population: 1,483,000

	13–17	18–22	23–32
Men	88,800	75,200	109,400
Women	90,200	75,600	116,600

TOTAL ARMED FORCES:
ACTIVE: 7,500.

ARMY: 7,000 (to be 10,000).
2 bde: 4 inf bn, 2 fd arty, 2 AD arty, 1 engr regt, 1 cdo unit.
EQPT:
LT TK: 36 *Scorpion* (incl variants, being delivered).
RECCE: 12 V-150 *Commando* (some with **90mm** gun), RAM-V.
APC: 30 BTR-60 (15 serviceable).
TOWED ARTY: 105mm: 12 lt, 4 Model 56 pack.
MOR: 81mm: 10; **120mm:** 6 M-43.
ATGW: 6 *TOW* (some SP on V-150).
RCL: 84mm: 30 *Carl Gustav.*
AD GUNS: 20mm: 7 M-167.
SAM: 12 SA-7, 10 SA-16, 5 *Javelin.*

AIR FORCE: 500; 21 cbt ac, no armed hel.
COIN: 1 sqn with 7 BAC-167 Mk 90, 7 BN-2 *Defender.*
TPT: 1 sqn with 2 CN-235, 2 *Skyvan* 3M, 1 BAe 125-800 (VIP), 1 *Gulfstream* IV.
TRG/COIN: 2 sqn with 2 Cessna 152, 7* PC-7.
HEL: 1 sqn with 2 AS-350L, 5 Bell 412 (VIP).

PARAMILITARY:
POLICE MOBILE UNIT: 1,000 (org interritorial coy).

BURKINA FASO

GDP	1993: fr 844bn ($2.51bn):
	per capita $850
	1994: fr 1,003bn ($2.66bn):
	per capita $850

Growth	1993: 0.4%	1994:	3.3%
Inflation	1993: 0.5%	1994:	31.2%
Debt	1993: $1.14bn	1994:	$1.30bn
Def exp[a]	1993: fr 17.4bn ($61m)		
Def bdgt	1994ε: fr 23.8bn ($43m)		
	1995ε: fr 33.7bn ($61m)		
FMA	1994: $0.7m (France)		
$1 = fr	1993: 283	1994:	555
	1995: 484		

fr = CFA franc

[a] Reported to UN.

Population: 10,439,000

	13–17	18–22	23–32
Men	592,000	480,200	753,600
Women	574,600	479,600	766,400

TOTAL ARMED FORCES:
ACTIVE: 10,000 (incl Gendarmerie).

ARMY: 5,600.
6 Military Regions.
5 inf 'regt': HQ, 3 'bn' (each 1 coy of 5 pl).
1 AB 'regt': HQ, 1 'bn', 2 coy.
1 tk 'bn': 2 pl.
1 arty 'bn': 2 tp.
1 engr 'bn'.
EQPT:
RECCE: 83: 15 AML-60/-90, 24 EE-9 *Cascavel*, 10 M-8, 4 M-20, 30 *Ferret*.
APC: 13 M-3.
TOWED ARTY: 122mm: 6; **105mm:** 8 M-101.
MRL: 107mm: Ch Type-63.
MOR: 81mm: Brandt.
RL: 89mm: LRAC, M-20.
RCL: 75mm: Ch Type-52.
AD GUNS: 14.5mm: 30 ZPU.
SAM: SA-7.

AIR FORCE: 200; 10 cbt ac, no armed hel.
COIN: 4 SF-260W, 6 SF-260WP.
TPT: 2 C-47, 1 *Beech Super King*, 1 *Commander* 500B. 2 HS-748, 2 N-262, 1 Boeing 727 (VIP).
LIAISON: 2 Cessna 150/172, 1 SA-316B, 1 AS-350, 3 Mi-8/17.

PARAMILITARY:
GENDARMERIE: 4,200.
SECURITY COMPANY (CRG): 250.
PEOPLE'S MILITIA (R): 45,000 trained.

BURUNDI

GDP	1993: fr 250.7bn ($1.03bn):
	per capita $600
	1994: fr 269.6bn ($1.07bn):
	per capita $530

Growth	1993: -15.5%	1994:	-8.9%
Inflation	1993: 9.7%	1994:	14.9%
Debt	1993: $1.06bn	1994:	$1.13bn
Def exp	1993ε: fr 6.41bn ($26m)		
Def bdgt	1994ε: fr 8.09bn ($32m)		
	1995ε: fr 8.49bn ($34m)		
FMA:	1994: $0.1m (IMET) $1.1m (France)		
	1995: $0.1m (IMET)		
	1996: $0.1m (IMET)		
$1 = fr	1993: 243	1994:	253
	1995: 235		

fr = Burundi franc

Population: 6,301,000 (Hutu 85%, Tutsi 14%)

	13–17	18–22	23–32
Men	366,000	299,600	487,200
Women	335,000	275,600	453,000

TOTAL ARMED FORCES:
ACTIVE: ε14,600 (incl: Gendarmerie).

ARMY: ε12,500.
5 inf bn.
2 lt armd bn.
EQPT:
RECCE: 18 AML (6-60, 12-90) 7 *Shorland*.
APC: 29: 9 *Panhard* M-3, 20 BTR-40 and *Walid*.
MOR: 82mm: 18 M-43.
RL: 83mm: *Blindicide*.
RCL: 75mm: 15 Ch Type-52.
AD GUNS: 14.5mm: 15 ZPU-4.

AIR FORCE: 100; 5 cbt ac, no armed hel.
COIN: 5 SF-260W.
HEL: 3 SA-316B, 4 SA-342L.
LIAISON: 2 Reims-Cessna 150, 1 Do-27Q.
TRG: 7 SF-260 (-C: 3; -TP: 4).

PARAMILITARY:
GENDARMERIE: ε2,000 (incl ε50 Marine Police):

Base: Bujumbura.
PATROL BOATS: 4 *Huchuan* (Ch026) PHT.

CAMEROON

GDP	1993: fr 3,773bn ($8.24bn):	
	per capita $2,200	
	1994: fr 4,545bn ($8.19bn):	
	per capita $2,200	
Growth	1993: -5.9%	1994: -0.7%
Inflation	1993: 12.8%	1994: 18.8%
Debt	1993: $6.6bn	1994: $7.1bn
Def exp	1993ε: fr 40.7bn ($144m)	
Def bdgt	1994ε: fr 57.0bn ($103m)	
	1995ε: fr 51.0bn ($105m)	
FMA	1994: $0.1m (IMET) $0.5m (France)	
	1996: $0.1m (IMET)	
$1 = fr	1993: 283	1994: 555
	1995: 485	

fr = CFA franc

Population: 13,368,000

	13–17	18–22	23–32
Men	760,600	635,000	941,000
Women	759,000	638,000	958,600

TOTAL ARMED FORCES:
ACTIVE: 23,600 (incl Gendarmerie).

ARMY: 13,000.
8 Military Regions each 1 inf bn under comd.
Presidential Guard: 1 guard, 1 armd recce bn, 3 inf coy.
1 AB/cdo bn.   1 arty bn (5 bty).
5 inf bn (1 trg).   1 AA bn (6 bty).
1 engr bn.
EQPT:
RECCE: 8 M-8, *Ferret*, 8 V-150 *Commando* (**20mm** gun), 5 VBL.
AIFV: 14 V-150 *Commando* (**90mm** gun).
APC: 21 V-150 *Commando*, 12 M-3 half-track.
TOWED ARTY: 34: **75mm:** 6 M-116 pack; **105mm:** 16 M-101; **130mm:** 12 Type-59.
MOR: **81mm** (some SP); **120mm:** 16 *Brandt*.
ATGW: *Milan*.
RL: **89mm:** LRAC.
RCL: **57mm:** 13 Ch Type-52; **106mm:** 40 M-40A2.
AD GUNS: **14.5mm:** 18 Ch Type-58; **35mm:** 18 GDF-002; **37mm:** 18 Ch Type-63.

NAVY: ε1,300.
BASES: Douala (HQ), Limbe, Kribi.
PATROL AND COASTAL COMBATANTS: 2:

MSL CRAFT: 1 *Bakassi* (Fr P.48) PFM with 2 x 4 MM-40 *Exocet* SSM.
PATROL, INSHORE: 1 *L'Audacieux* (Fr P.48) PFI.
RIVERINE: boats only, some 30 US *Swift*-38 (not all op), 6 SM 30/36 types.
AMPH: craft only: 2 LCM.

AIR FORCE: 300; 14 cbt ac, 4 armed hel.
1 composite sqn. 1 Presidential Flt.
FGA/COIN: 4† *Alpha Jet*, 10 CM-170.
MR: 2 Do-128D-6.
ATTACK HEL: 4 SA-342L (with *HOT*).
TPT: ac: 3 C-130H/-H-30, 1 DHC-4, 4 DHC-5D, 1 IAI-201, 2 PA-23, 1 *Gulfstream* III, 1 Do-128, 1 Boeing 707; **hel:** 3 Bell 206, 3 SE-3130, 1 SA-318, 3 SA-319, 1 AS-332, 1 SA-365.

PARAMILITARY:
GENDARMERIE: 9,000; 10 regional groups.
PATROL BOATS: about 10 US *Swift*-38 (incl in Navy entry).

CAPE VERDE

GDP	1993: CV E 30.3bn ($380m):	
	per capita $1,800	
	1994: CV E 32.1bn ($392m):	
	per capita $1,800	
Growth	1993: 3.9%	1994: 3.2%
Inflation	1993: 10.6%	1994: 5.6%
Debt	1993: $158m	1994: $178m
Def exp	1993: CV E 252m ($3.1m)	
Def bdgt	1994: CV E 288m ($3.5m)	
	1995: CV E 301m ($3.8m)	
FMA	1993: $0.2m (IMET)	
	1995: $0.1m (IMET)	
	1996: $0.1m (IMET)	
$1 = CV E	1993: 80.4	1994: 81.9
	1995: 80.4	

CV E = Cape Verde escudo

Population: 417,000

	13–17	18–22	23–32
Men	24,600	20,000	35,800
Women	25,200	21,600	39,800

TOTAL ARMED FORCES:
ACTIVE: ε1,100.
Terms of service: conscription (selective).

ARMY: 1,000.
2 bn.

EQPT:
RECCE: 10 BRDM-2.
TOWED ARTY: 75mm: 12; **76mm:** 12.
MOR: 82mm: 12; **120mm:** 6 M-1943.
RL: 89mm: 3.5-in.
AD GUNS: 14.5mm: 18 ZPU-1; **23mm:** 12 ZU-23.
SAM: 50 SA-7.

COAST GUARD: nucleus of ε50 with 1 *Zhuk* PCI⟨, 1 *Espadarte* PCI⟨.

AIR FORCE: under 100; no cbt ac.
MR: 1 Do-228.

CENTRAL AFRICAN REPUBLIC

GDP	1993: fr 368.4bn ($1.14bn):		
	per capita $1,100		
	1994: fr 497.3bn ($1.21bn):		
	per capita $1,100		
Growth	1993: -3.0%	1994: 2.5%	
Inflation	1993: -2.1%	1994: 35.0%	
Debt	1993: $904m	1994: $973m	
Def exp	1993ε: fr 8.7bn ($27m)		
Def bdgt	1994ε: fr 10.0bn ($24m)		
	1995ε: fr 10.3bn ($21m)		
FMA	1994: $0.2m (IMET) $2.5m (France)		
	1995: $0.2m (IMET)		
	1996: $0.1m (IMET)		
$1 = fr	1993: 283	1994: 555	
	1995: 485		
fr = CFA franc			

Population: 3,403,000

	13–17	18–22	23–32
Men	175,800	167,200	252,600
Women	180,800	167,200	248,000

TOTAL ARMED FORCES:
ACTIVE: 4,950 (incl Gendarmerie).
Terms of service: conscription (selective), 2 years; reserve obligation thereafter, term n.k.

ARMY: 2,500.
1 Republican Guard regt (2 bn).
1 territorial defence regt (bn).
1 combined arms regt (1 mech, 1 inf bn).
1 spt/HQ regt.
1 Presidential Guard bn.
EQPT:†
MBT: 4 T-55.

RECCE: 10 *Ferret*.
APC: 4 BTR-152, some 10 VAB, 25+ ACMAT.
MOR: 81mm; 120mm: 12 M-1943.
RL: 89mm: LRAC.
RCL: 106mm: 14 M-40.
RIVER PATROL CRAFT: 9⟨.

AIR FORCE: 150; no cbt ac, no armed hel.
TPT: 1 Cessna 337, 1 *Mystère Falcon* 20, 1 *Caravelle*.
LIAISON: 8 AL-60, 6 MH-1521.
HEL: 1 AS-350, 1 SE-3130.

PARAMILITARY:
GENDARMERIE: 2,300;
3 Regional legions, 8 'bde'.

FOREIGN FORCES:
FRANCE: 1,300; 1 inf bn gp, 1 armd cav sqn, 1 arty bty; 5 *Jaguar*, 2 C-160, 4 SA-330.

CHAD

GDP	1993: fr 339bn ($1.09bn):		
	per capita $750		
	1994ε: fr 510bn ($1.18bn):		
	per capita $770		
Growth	1993: -3.7%	1994: 4.7%	
Inflation	1993: 2.1%	1994: 43.3%	
Debt	1993: $757m	1994: $843m	
Def exp	1993: fr 9.9bn ($32m)		
Def bdgt	1994ε: fr 13.4bn ($31m)		
	1995ε: fr 12.7bn ($26m)		
FMA	1994: $0.2m (IMET) $10m (France)		
	1995: $0.2m (IMET)		
	1996: $0.1m (IMET)		
$1 = fr	1993: 283	1994: 555	
	1995: 485		
fr = CFA franc			

Population: 6,448,000

	13–17	18–22	23–32
Men:	333,000	282,200	454,600
Women:	332,800	284,400	463,800

TOTAL ARMED FORCES:
ACTIVE: ε30,350 (incl Republican Guard).
Terms of service: conscription authorised.

ARMY: ε25,000 (being re-organised).
7 Military Regions.

EQPT:
MBT: 60 T-55.
AFV: some 63: 4 Panhard ERC-90, some 50 AML-60/
-90, 9 V-150 with **90mm**, some EE-9 *Cascavel*.
TOWED ARTY: 105mm: 5 M-2.
MOR: 81mm; 120mm: AM-50.
ATGW: *Milan.*
RL: 89mm: LRAC.
RCL: 106mm: M-40A1; **112mm:** *APILAS.*
AD GUNS: 20mm, 30mm.

AIR FORCE: 350; 4 cbt ac, no armed hel.
COIN: 2 PC-7, 2 SF-260W.
TPT: ac: 3 C-47, 1 C-130A, 2 -B, 1 -H, 1 C-212, 2 DC-
4, **hel:** 2 SA-316.
LIAISON: 2 PC-6B, 5 Reims-Cessna FTB 337.

FORCES ABROAD:
UN AND PEACEKEEPING:
RWANDA (UNAMIR): 2 plus 5 civ pol.

PARAMILITARY:
REPUBLICAN GUARD: 5,000.
GENDARMERIE: 4,500.

OPPOSITION:
WESTERN ARMED FORCES: str n.k.
**MOVEMENT FOR DEVELOPMENT AND
DEMOCRACY:** str n.k.

FOREIGN FORCES:
FRANCE: 800; 2 inf coy, AD arty units; 2 C-160 ac.

CONGO

GDP	1993: fr 676bn ($2.86bn):	
	per capita $2,800	
	1994: fr 926bn ($2.87bn):	
	per capita $2,800	
Growth	1993: -1.5%	1994: -2.4%
Inflation	1993: 1.6%	1994: 40.3%
Debt	1993: $5.01bn	1994: $5.29bn
Def exp	1993ε: fr 13.9bn ($59m)	
	1994ε: fr 15.6bn ($48m)	
Def bdgt	1995ε: fr 24.5bn ($50m)	
FMA	1993: $21m (France)	
	1994: $0.1m (IMET) $1.8m (France)	
	1995: $0.2m (IMET) $2.1m (France)	
	1996: $0.2m (IMET)	
$1 = fr	1993: 283	1994: 555
	1995: 485	
fr = CFA franc		

Population: 2,673,000

	13–17	18–22	23–32
Men:	148,400	127,000	200,600
Women:	140,600	121,200	192,800

TOTAL ARMED FORCES:
ACTIVE: 10,000.

ARMY: 8,000.
2 armd bn.
2 inf bn gp (each with lt tk tp, 76mm gun bty).
1 inf bn.
1 arty gp (how, MRL).
1 engr bn.
1 AB/cdo bn.
EQPT:†
MBT: 25 T-54/-55, 15 Ch Type-59 (some T-34 in
store).
LT TK: 10 Ch Type-62, 3 PT-76.
RECCE: 25 BRDM-1/-2.
APC: M-3, 50 BTR (30 -60, 20 -152).
TOWED ARTY: 76mm: M-1942; **100mm:** 10 M-1944;
122mm: 10 D-30; **130mm:** 5 M-46; **152mm:** some D-20.
MRL: 122mm: 8 BM-21; **140mm:** BM-14-16.
MOR: 82mm; 120mm: 10 M-43.
RCL: 57mm: M-18.
ATK GUNS: 57mm: 5 M-1943.
AD GUNS: 14.5mm: ZPU-2/-4; **23mm:** ZSU-23-4
SP; **37mm:** 28 M-1939; **57mm:** S-60; **100mm:** KS-19.

NAVY:† ε800.
BASE: Pointe Noire.
PATROL AND COASTAL COMBATANTS: 6:
PATROL, INSHORE: 6:
3 *Marien N'gouabi* PFI (Sp *Barcelo* 33-m)†.
3 Sov *Zhuk* PFI⟨.
RIVERINE: boats only.

AIR FORCE:† 1,200; 22 cbt ac, no armed hel.
FGA: 10 MiG-17, 12 MiG-21.
TPT: 5 An-24, 1 An-26, 1 Boeing 727, 1 N-2501.
TRG: 4 L-39, 1 MiG-15UTI.
HEL: 2 SA-316, 2 SA-318, 1 SA-365, 2 Mi-8.

FORCES ABROAD:
UN AND PEACEKEEPING:
ANGOLA (UNAVEM III): 8 Obs. **RWANDA**
(UNAMIR): 8 Obs.

PARAMILITARY: 5,000:
GENDARMERIE: (2,000); 20 coy.

PEOPLE'S MILITIA: (3,000): being absorbed into national army.
PRESIDENTIAL GUARD: (forming).

CÔTE D'IVOIRE

GDP	1993: fr 3,200bn ($8.84bn):			
	per capita $1,600			
	1994: fr 4,419bn ($9.19bn):			
	per capita $1,600			
Growth	1993: -1.0%		1994: 2.0%	
Inflation	1993: 2.9%		1994: 35.4%	
Debt	1993: $19.2bn		1994: $20.2bn	
Def exp	1993ε: fr 35.6bn ($98m)			
Def bdgt	1994ε: fr 33.8bn ($61m)			
	1995ε: fr 36.5bn ($75m)			
FMA	1994: $0.2m (IMET) $2.2m (France)			
	1995: $0.2m (IMET)			
	1996: $0.2m (IMET)			
$1 = fr	1993: 283		1994: 555	
	1995: 485			
fr = CFA franc				

Population: 14,342,000

	13–17	18–22	23–32
Men	816,800	647,800	973,400
Women	819,200	650,600	959,200

TOTAL ARMED FORCES:
ACTIVE: ε13,900 (incl Presidential Guard, Gendarmerie).
Terms of service: conscription (selective), 6 months.
RESERVES: 12,000.

ARMY: 6,800.
4 Military Regions.
1 armd, 3 inf bn, 1 arty gp.
1 AB, 1 AA, 1 engr coy.
EQPT:
LT TK: 5 AMX-13.
RECCE: 7 ERC-90 *Sagaie*, 16 AML-60/-90.
APC: 16 M-3, 13 VAB.
TOWED ARTY: 105mm: 4 M-1950.
MOR: 81mm; 120mm: 16 AM-50.
RL: 89mm: LRAC.
RCL: 106mm: M-40A1.
AD GUNS: 20mm: 16, incl 6 M-3 VDA SP; 40mm: 5 L/60.

NAVY: ε900.
BASE: Locodjo (Abidjan).

PATROL AND COASTAL COMBATANTS: 4:
MSL CRAFT: 2 *L' Ardent* (Fr *Auroux* 40-m) with 4 x SS-12 SSM.
PATROL: 2 *Le Vigilant* (Fr SFCN 47-m) PCI.
AMPH: 1 *L'Eléphant* (Fr *Batral*) LSM, capacity 140 tps, 7 tk, hel deck, plus some 8 craft.

AIR FORCE: 700; 4 cbt ac, no armed hel.
FGA: 1 sqn with 4 *Alpha Jet*.
TPT: 1 hel sqn with 1 SA-318, 1 SA-319, 1 SA-330, 4 SA-365C.
PRESIDENTIAL FLT: ac: 1 F-28, 1 *Gulfstream* IV, 3 Fokker 100; **hel:** 1 SA-330.
TRG: 3 Beech F-33C, 2 Reims Cessna 150H.
LIAISON: 1 Cessna 421, 1 *Super King Air* 200.

PARAMILITARY: 7,800:
PRESIDENTIAL GUARD: 1,100.
GENDARMERIE: 4,400; VAB APC, 4 patrol boats.
MILITIA: 1,500.
MILITARY FIRE SERVICE: 800.

FOREIGN FORCES:
FRANCE: 700; 1 marine inf bn; 1 AS-355 hel.

DJIBOUTI

GDP	1993: frD 73.3bn ($413m):		
	per capita $1,100		
	1994: frD 72.9bn ($410m):		
	per capita $1,000		
Growth	1993: -0.5%	1994: -3.2%	
Inflation	1993: 5.3%	1994: 9.2%	
Debt	1993: $225m	1994: $259m	
Def exp	1993: frD 4.98bn ($28m)		
	1994: frD 4.50bn ($25m)		
Def bdgt	1995ε: frD 4.30bn ($24m)		
FMA	1994: $0.2m (IMET) $1.1m (France)		
	1995: $0.1m (IMET)		
	1996: $0.2m (IMET)		
$1 = frD	1993–95: 178		
frD = Djibouti franc			

Population: 633,000

	13–17	18–22	23–32
Men	34,400	29,000	46,400
Women	33,600	30,200	50,200

TOTAL ARMED FORCES:
ACTIVE: ε9,600 (incl Gendarmerie).

ARMY: ε8,000.

3 Comd (North, Central, South).

1 inf bn, incl mor, ATK pl.	1 arty bty.
1 armd sqn.	1 border cdo bn.
1 AB coy.	1 spt bn.

EQPT:

RECCE: 15 M-11 VBL, 4 AML-60†.

APC: 12 BTR-60 (op status uncertain).

TOWED ARTY: 122mm: 6 D-30.

MOR: 81mm: 25; **120mm:** 20 *Brandt*.

RL: 73mm; 89mm: LRAC.

RCL: 106mm: 16 M-40A1.

AD GUNS: 20mm: 5 M-693 SP; **23mm:** 5 ZU-23; **40mm:** 5 L/70.

NAVY: ε200.

BASE: Djibouti.

PATROL CRAFT, INSHORE: 8:

5 *Sawari* PCI⟨.

2 *Moussa Ali* PCI⟨.

1 *Zena* PCI⟨†; plus boats.

AIR FORCE: 200; no cbt ac or armed hel.

TPT: 2 C-212, 2 N-2501F, 2 Cessna U206G, 1 Socata 235GT.

HEL: 3 AS-355, 1 AS-350.

(Defected from Ethiopia: Mi-8, Mi-24 hel.)

PARAMILITARY:

GENDARMERIE (Ministry of Defence): 1,200; 1 bn, 1 patrol boat.

NATIONAL SECURITY FORCE (Ministry of Interior): ε3,000.

OPPOSITION:

FRONT FOR THE RESTORATION OF UNITY AND DEMOCRACY: ε2,500 (peace agreement signed in 1994; to be absorbed into national army).

FOREIGN FORCES:

FRANCE: 3,900; incl 1 marine inf, 1 Foreign Legion regt, 1 sqn: **ac:** 10 *Mirage* F-1C, 1 C-160; **hel:** 3 SA-319.

EQUATORIAL GUINEA

GDP	1993: fr 53.1bn ($148m):	
	per capita $850	
	1994: fr 78.2bn ($167m):	
	per capita $900	
Growth	1993: 7.1%	1993: 8.9%

Inflation	1993: 4.0%	1994: 35.2%	
Debt	1993: $268m	1994: $284m	
Def exp	1993ε: fr 920m ($2.6m)		
Def bdgt	1994ε: fr 1,130m ($2.4m)		
	1995ε: fr 1,190m ($2.5m)		
FMA	1994: $0.2m (France)		
$1 = fr	1993: 283	1994: 555	
	1995: 485		
fr = CFA franc			

Population: 467,000

	13–17	18–22	23–32
Men:	23,000	20,400	34,000
Women:	23,600	20,800	34,000

TOTAL ARMED FORCES:

ACTIVE: 1,320.

ARMY: 1,100.

3 inf bn.

EQPT:

RECCE: 6 BRDM-2.

APC: 10 BTR-152.

NAVY†: 120.

BASES: Malabo (Santa Isabel), Bata.

PATROL COMBATANTS: 4:

2 *Vambola* (Ge *Kondor*) MSO (prob unarmed).

2 *Zhuk* PCI⟨.

AIR FORCE: 100; no cbt ac or armed hel.

TPT: ac: 1 Yak-40, 3 C-212, 1 Cessna-337; **hel:** 2 SA-316.

PARAMILITARY:

GUARDIA CIVIL: 2 coy.

COAST GUARD: 1 PCI⟨.

FOREIGN FORCES:

MOROCCO: 360; 1 bn.

ERITREA

GDP	1993ε: EB 2,915m ($583m)		
	per capita $400		
	1994ε: EB 3,879m ($652m)		
	per capita $400		
Growth	1993: -2.0%	1994: 9.0%	
Inflation	1993: n.k.	1994: n.k.	
Debt	1993: n.k.	1994: n.k.	

Def exp	1993ε: EB 180m ($36m)
Def bdgt	1994ε: EB 234m ($39m)
	1995ε: EB 232m ($40m)
FMA	1994: $0.1m (IMET)
	1995: $0.2m (IMET)
	1996: $0.3m (IMET)
$ = EB	1993: 5.0 1994: 6.0
	1995: 5.8

EB = Ethiopian birr

Population: ε3,574,000 (Tigray/Christian 50%, Tigre, Kunama, Afar mainly Muslim 44%)

	13–17	18–22	23–32
Men	209,800	175,800	267,800
Women	208,400	174,800	265,400

Eritrea declared itself independent from Ethiopia on 27 April 1993. Demob of some Eritrean forces began in late 1993. Est strength of these forces is currently about 55,000 to be reduced to 35,000. A conscription period of 18 months is authorised to incl 6 months mil trg. No info on div of mil assets between Ethiopia and Eritrea is available. Eritrea holds some air and naval assets, but holdings of army assets are unknown. Close cooperation with Ethiopia is likely to continue to the possible extent of sharing mil assets. Numbers given should be treated with caution.

NAVY: str n.k.
BASES: Massawa, Assab, Dahlak.
FF: 1 *Zerai Deres* (Sov *Petya*-II) with 2 x ASW RL, 10 x 406mm TT†.
PATROL AND COASTAL COMBATANTS: 13:
MSL CRAFT: 1 Sov *Osa* with 2 x SS-N-2 *Styx* SSM†.
TORPEDO CRAFT: 1 *Mol* PFT† with 4 x 533mm TT.
PATROL, INSHORE: 5 PFI: 2 US *Swiftships* 32-m, 2 Sov *Zhuk*⟨, 1 *Super Dvora* PCF⟨.
MCM: 2:
1 *Natya* MSO, 1 *Sonya* MSC.
AMPH: 2 Sov *Polnocny* LSM, capacity 100 tps, 6 tk. Plus craft: 3 LCT (1 Fr EDIC and 2 *Chamo* (Ministry of Transport)), 4 LCM.
SPT AND MISC: 1 AOT.

ETHIOPIA

GDP	1993: EB 26.1bn ($3.50bn):
	per capita $410
	1994: EB 27.4bn ($4.09bn):
	per capita $420
Growth	1993: 13.7% 1994: 1.6%
Inflation	1993: 3.5% 1994: 6.3%
Debt	1993: $4.73bn 1994: $4.98bn

Def exp	1993ε: EB 755m ($119m)
	1994: EB 700m ($109m)
Def bdgt	1995ε: EB 115m ($19m)
FMA	1994: $0.3m (FMF,IMET)
	1995: $0.3m (IMET)
	1996: $0.3m (IMET)
$1 = EB	1993: 5.0 1994: 6.0
	1995: 5.8

EB = birr

Population: 57,091,000 (Oromo 40%, Amhara, Tigray 32%)

	13–17	18–22	23–32
Men	3,165,200	2,633,400	3,979,400
Women	3,007,000	2,504,600	3,824,600

Following the declaration of independence by Eritrea in April 1993, est strength of Ethiopian armed forces is some 120,000. Most are former members of the Tigray People's Liberation Front (TPLF) with maybe 10–15,000 from the Oromo Liberation Front. No info on div of mil assets between Ethiopia and Eritrea is available, although close cooperation is likely between the two countries. All ground and air force assets are listed under Ethiopia and naval assets under Eritrea. Reports indicate that large quantities of eqpt are in preservation. Est numbers in service must be treated with caution.

ARMY:†
MBT: ε350 T-54/-55, T-62.
RECCE/AIFV/APC: ε200, incl BRDM, BMP, BTR-60/-152.
TOWED ARTY: 76mm: ZIS-3; **85mm:** D-44; **122mm:** D-30/M-30; **130mm:** M-46.
MRL: BM-21.
MOR: 81mm: M-1/M-29; **82mm:** M-1937; **120mm:** M-1938.
ATGW: AT-3 *Sagger*.
RCL: 82mm: B-10; **107mm:** B-11.
AD GUNS: 23mm: ZU-23, ZSU-23-4 SP; **37mm:** M-1939; **57mm:** S-60.
SAM: 20 SA-2, 30 SA-3, 300 SA-7, SA-9.

AIR FORCE:† 22 cbt ac, 18 armed hel.
Most of the Air Force is grounded. Air Force activity is believed to be limited to reorganisation, some ground-crew training and maintenance. Priority has been given to helicopter and transport aircraft operations. Types and numbers of remaining ac are assessed as follows:
FGA: 16 MiG-21MF, 6 MiG-23BN.
TPT: 2 C-130B, 4 An-12, 2 DH-6, 1 Yak-40 (VIP), 2 Y-12.
TRG: 14 L-39.
ATTACK HEL: 18 Mi-24.
TPT HEL: 21 Mi-8, 2 UH-1, 2 Mi-14.

GABON

GDP	1993: fr 1,762bn ($5.28bn):	
	per capita $5,000	
	1994ε: fr 2,296bn ($5.39bn):	
	per capita $5,000	
Growth	1993: 2.6%	1994: -0.8%
Inflation	1993: 1.2%	1994: 31.7%
Debt	1993: $3.82bn	1994: $4.15bn
Def exp	1993ε: fr 43.1bn ($129m)	
Def bdgt	1994ε: fr 51.7bn ($93m)	
	1995ε: fr 47.5bn ($98m)	
FMA	1993: $0.1m (IMET) $13.3m (France)	
	1994: $12.1m (France)	
$1 = fr	1993: 283	1994: 555
	1995: 485	

fr = CFA franc

Population: 1,306,000

	13–17	18–22	23–32
Men	60,400	52,400	89,000
Women	61,200	54,400	91,400

TOTAL ARMED FORCES:
ACTIVE: ε4,700.

ARMY: 3,200.
Presidential Guard bn gp (1 recce/armd, 3 inf coy, arty, AA bty) (under direct Presidential control).
8 inf, 1 AB/cdo, 1 engr coy.
EQPT:
RECCE: 14 EE-9 *Cascavel*, 24 AML, 6 ERC-90 *Sagaie*, 12 EE-3 *Jararaca*, 14 VBL.
AIFV: 12 EE-11 *Urutu* with **20mm** gun.
APC: 9 V-150 *Commando*, Panhard M-3, 12 VXB-170.
TOWED ARTY: 105mm: 4 M-101.
MRL: 140mm: 8 *Teruel*.
MORS: 81mm: 35; **120mm:** 4 Brandt.
ATGW: 4 *Milan*.
RL: 89mm: LRAC.
RCL: 106mm: M40A1.
AD GUNS: 20mm: 4 ERC-20 SP; **23mm:** 24 ZU-23-2; **37mm:** 10 M-1939; **40mm:** 3 L/70.

NAVY: ε500.
BASE: Port Gentil (HQ).
PATROL AND COASTAL COMBATANTS: 3:
MSL CRAFT: 1 *General Nazaire Boulingu* PFM (Fr 42-m) with 4 SS-12 SSM.
PATROL, COASTAL: 2 *General Ba'Oumar* (Fr P.400 55-m).
AMPH: 1 *President Omar Bongo* (Fr *Batral*) LSM,

capacity 140 tps, 7 tk.
Plus craft: 1 LCM.

AIR FORCE: 1,000; 16 cbt ac, 5 armed hel.
FGA: 9 *Mirage* 5 (2 -G, 4 -GII, 3 -DG).
MR: 1 EMB-111.
TPT: 1 C-130H, 2 L-100-30, 2 EMB-110, 2 YS-11A.
HEL:
ATTACK: 5 SA-342.
TPT: 3 SA-330C/-H.
LIAISON: 3 SA-316/-319.
PRESIDENTIAL GUARD:
COIN: 4 CM-170, 3 T-34.
TPT: ac: 1 ATR-42F, 1 EMB-110, 1 *Falcon* 900; **hel:** 1 AS-332.

PARAMILITARY:
COAST GUARD: ε2,800; boats only.
GENDARMERIE: 2,000; 3 'bdes', 11 coy, 2 armd sqn, air unit with 1 AS-355, 2 AS-350.

FOREIGN FORCES:
FRANCE: 600; 1 marine inf bn; **ac:** 1 C-160, 1 *Atlantic*; **hel:** 1 AS-355.

THE GAMBIA

GDP	1993: D 3,230m ($364m):	
	per capita $800	
	1994: D 3,610m ($377m):	
	per capita $800	
Growth	1993: 4.5%	1994: 0.7%
Inflation	1993: 6.5%	1994: 1.7%
Debt	1993: $386m	1994: $415m
Def exp	1993ε: D 118.1m ($13m)	
Def bdgt	1994: D 132.2m ($14m)	
	1995: D 139.0m ($15m)	
FMA	1993: $0.1m (IMET)	
	1994: $0.1m (IMET)	
	1995: $0.1m (IMET)	
$1 = D	1993: 9.13	1994: 9.58
	1995: 9.51	

D = dalasi

Population: 1,071,000

	13–17	18–22	23–32
Men	56,600	47,000	73,000
Women	55,800	46,200	74,600

TOTAL ARMED FORCES:
ACTIVE: 800.

GAMBIAN NATIONAL ARMY (GNA): 800.
Presidential Guard (reported).
2 inf bn, engr sqn.
MARINE UNIT: about 70.
BASE: Banjul.
PATROL, INSHORE: 4:
2 *Gonjur* (Ch *Shanghai-II*) PFI, 2 PFI‹, boats.

GHANA

GDP	1993: C 3,932bn ($7.28bn):		
	per capita $1,900		
	1994ε: C 5,306bn ($7.53bn):		
	per capita $2,000		
Growth	1993: 5.0%	1994: 3.8%	
Inflation	1993: 25.0%	1994: 34.2%	
Debt	1993: $4.59bn	1994: $4.82bn	
Def exp	1994: C 39.5bn ($76m)		
Def bdgt	1993: C 47.5bn ($82m)		
	1995ε: C 55.8bn ($53m)		
FMA	1994: $0.5m (FMF, IMET)		
	1995: $0.2m (IMET)		
	1996: $0.3m (IMET)		
$1 = C	1993: 649	1994: 957	
	1995: 1,047		
C = cedi			

Population: 17,236,000

	13–17	*18–22*	*23–32*
Men	1,004,200	827,000	1,234,000
Women	998,000	825,000	1,247,000

TOTAL ARMED FORCES:
ACTIVE: 7,000.

ARMY: 5,000.
2 Comd HQ.
2 bde (6 inf bn (incl 1 trg, 1 UNIFIL, 1 ECOMOG), spt unit).
1 recce regt (2 sqn).
1 arty 'regt' (mor bn).
1 AB force (incl 1 para coy).
1 fd engr regt (bn).
EQPT:
RECCE: 3 EE-9 *Cascavel*.
AIFV: 50 MOWAG *Piranha*.
MOR: 81mm: 50; **120mm:** 28 Tampella.
RCL: 84mm: 50 *Carl Gustav*.
AD GUNS: 14.5mm: 4 ZPU-2, ZPU-4; **23mm:** 4 ZU-23-2.
SAM: SA-7.

NAVY: 1,000; Western and Eastern Comd.

BASES: Sekondi (HQ, West); Tema (HQ, East).
PATROL AND COASTAL COMBATANTS: 4:
PATROL, COASTAL: 2 *Achimota* (Ge Lürssen 57-m) PFC.
PATROL, INSHORE: 2 *Dzata* (Ge Lürssen 45-m) PCI.

AIR FORCE: 1,000; 18 cbt ac, no armed hel.
COIN: 1 sqn with 4 MB-326K†, 2 MB-339.
TPT: 5 Fokker (4 F-27, 1 F-28 (VIP)); 1 C-212, 6 *Skyvan*.
HEL: 2 Bell 212 (VIP), 2 Mi-2, 4 SA-319.
TRG: 1 sqn with 12* L-29, 6 MB 326F.

FORCES ABROAD:
LIBERIA: about 900 forming part of ECOMOG.
UN AND PEACEKEEPING:
BOSNIA (UNPROFOR): 13 Obs. **CROATIA** (UNCRO): 17 Obs. **LEBANON** (UNIFIL): 784; 1 inf bn. **RWANDA** (UNAMIR): 871 incl 35 Obs plus 10 civ pol. **WESTERN SAHARA** (MINURSO): 14 incl Obs plus 8 civ pol.

PARAMILITARY:
PEOPLE'S MILITIA: 5,000: part-time force with police duties.
PRESIDENTIAL GUARD: 1 inf bn.

GUINEA

GDP	1993: G fr 3,027bn ($3.4bn):		
	per capita $750		
	1994ε: G fr 3,445bn ($3.6bn):		
	per capita $800		
Growth	1993: 4.5%	1994: 4.7%	
Inflation	1993: 17.0%	1994: 4.0%	
Debt	1993: $2.9bn	1994: $3.1bn	
Def exp	1993ε: G fr 38bn ($43m)		
Def bdgt	1994ε: G fr 41bn ($43m)		
	1995ε: G fr 42bn ($43m)		
FMA	1994: $0.1m (IMET) $1m (France)		
	1995: $0.2m (IMET)		
	1996: $0.2m (IMET)		
$1 = G fr	1993: 956	1994: 967	
	1995: 986		
G fr = Guinean franc			

Population: 6,618,000

	13–17	*18–22*	*23–32*
Men	370,800	306,600	462,900
Women	377,200	311,400	472,200

TOTAL ARMED FORCES:
ACTIVE: 9,700 (perhaps 7,500 conscripts).

Terms of service: conscription, 2 years.

ARMY: 8,500.

1 armd bn.	1 arty bn.
1 cdo bn.	1 engr bn.
5 inf bn.	1 AD bn.
1 SF bn.	

EQPT:†
MBT: 30 T-34, 8 T-54.
LT TK: 20 PT-76.
RECCE: 25 BRDM-1/-2, 2 AML-90.
APC: 40 BTR (16 -40, 10 -50, 8 -60, 6 -152).
TOWED ARTY: 76mm: 8 M-1942; **85mm:** 6 D-44; **122mm:** 12 M-1931/37.
MOR: 82mm: M-43; **120mm:** 20 M-1938/43.
RCL: 82mm: B-10.
ATK GUNS: 57mm: M-1943.
AD GUNS: 30mm: twin M-53; **37mm:** 8 M-1939; **57mm:** 12 S-60, Ch Type-59; **100mm:** 4 KS-19.
SAM: SA-7.

NAVY: 400.

BASES: Conakry, Kakanda.
PATROL AND COASTAL COMBATANTS: 9:
PATROL: 9:
Some 3 Sov *Bogomol* PFI.
2 Sov *Zhuk*, 1 US Swiftships-77, 3 other PCI, all‹.

AIR FORCE:† 800; 8 cbt ac, no armed hel.

FGA: 4 MiG-17F, 4 MiG-21.
TPT: 4 An-14, 1 An-24.
TRG: 2 MiG-15UTI.
HEL: 1 IAR-330, 1 Mi-8, 1 SA-316B, 1 SA-330, 1 SA-342K.

FORCES ABROAD:

SIERRA LEONE: 300 reported.
UN AND PEACEKEEPING:
LIBERIA: some 1,000, forming part of ECOMOG.
RWANDA: (UNAMIR): 17 Obs. **WESTERN SAHARA** (MINURSO): 1 Obs.

PARAMILITARY: 9,600:

PEOPLE'S MILITIA: (7,000).
GENDARMERIE: (1,000).
REPUBLICAN GUARD: (1,600).

GUINEA-BISSAU

GDP	1993:	pG 2,366bn ($235m):
		per capita $760
	1994ε:	pG 3,197bn ($248m):
		per capita $760
Growth	1993: 3.7%	1994: 2.9%
Inflation	1993: 48.1%	1994: 23.0%
Debt	1993: $691m	1994: $822m
Def exp	1993ε: pG 86.7bn ($8.6m)	
Def bdgt	1994ε: pG 106.2bn ($8.2m)	
	1995ε: pG 130.3bn ($8.0m)	
FMA	1994: $0.1m (IMET) $0.1m (France)	
	1995: $0.1m (IMET)	
	1996: $0.1m (IMET)	
$1 = pG	1993: 10,082	1994: 12,892
	1995: 16,584	

pG = Guinean peso

Population: 1,084,000

	13–17	18–22	23–32
Men	61,600	54,600	81,000
Women	57,800	50,200	79,200

TOTAL ARMED FORCES (all services, incl Gendarmerie, are part of the armed forces):

ACTIVE: ε9,200.

Terms of service: conscription (selective).

ARMY: 6,800.

1 armd 'bn' (sqn).
5 inf, 1 arty bn, 1 recce, 1 engr coy.
EQPT:
MBT: 10 T-34.
LT TK: 20 PT-76.
RECCE: 10 BRDM-2.
APC: 35 BTR-40/-60/-152, 20 Ch Type-56.
TOWED ARTY: 85mm: 8 D-44; **122mm:** 18 M-1938/D-30.
MOR: 82mm: M-43; **120mm:** 8 M-1943.
RL: 89mm: M-20.
RCL: 75mm: Ch Type-52; **82mm:** B-10.
AD GUNS: 23mm: 18 ZU-23; **37mm:** 6 M-1939; **57mm:** 10 S-60.
SAM: SA-7.

NAVY: ε350.

BASE: Bissau.
PATROL AND COASTAL COMBATANTS: 8:
PATROL, INSHORE: 8:
2 *Alfeitc* PCC‹, 1 ex-Ge *Kondor*-I PCI†, 2 Sov *Bogomol*, 1 Indian SDB Mk III PCI, some 2 PCI†‹ (incl 1 customs service).
AMPH: 1 LCM.

AIR FORCE: 100; 3 cbt ac, no armed hel.

FTR: 3 MiG-17.
HEL: 1 SA-318, 2 SA-319.

FORCES ABROAD:
UN AND PEACEKEEPING:
ANGOLA (UNAVEM III): 20 Obs plus 6 civ pol.
HAITI: (UNMIH): 20 Obs. **LIBERIA** (UNOMIL):
3 Obs. **RWANDA:** (UNAMIR): 2 Obs plus 5 civ pol.

PARAMILITARY:
GENDARMERIE: 2,000.

KENYA

GDP	1993: sh 323bn ($8.15bn):		
	per capita $1,500		
	1994: sh 477bn ($8.51bn):		
	per capita $1,500		
Growth	1993: 0.2%	1994: 3.0%	
Inflation	1993: 45.8%	1994: 28.8%	
Debt	1993: $6.99bn	1994: $7.37bn	
Def exp	1993ε: sh 7,094m ($179m)		
Def bdgt	1994ε: sh 7,050m ($126m)		
	1995ε: sh 6,200m ($140m)		
FMA	1994: $0.3m (IMET)		
	1995: $0.3m (IMET)		
	1996: $0.4m (IMET)		
$1 = sh	1993: 58.0	1994: 56.1	
	1995: 44.0		

sh = Kenyan shilling

Population: 27,751,000

	13–17	18–22	23–32
Men	1,764,200	1,436,000	2,024,000
Women	1,761,200	1,440,000	2,039,200

TOTAL ARMED FORCES:
ACTIVE: 24,200.

ARMY: 20,500.
1 armd bde (3 armd bn).
2 inf bde (1 with 2, 1 with 3 inf bn); 1 indep inf bn.
1 arty bde (2 bn).   1 AD arty bn.
1 engr bde.   2 engr bn.
1 AB bn.   1 indep air cav bn.
EQPT:
MBT: 76 Vickers Mk 3.
RECCE: 72 AML-60/-90, 12 *Ferret*, 8 *Shorland*.
APC: 52 UR-416, 10 Panhard M-3 (in store).
TOWED ARTY: 105mm: 40 lt, 8 pack.
MOR: 81mm: 50; **120mm:** 12 Brandt.
ATGW: 40 *Milan*, 14 *Swingfire*.
RCL: 84mm: 80 *Carl Gustav*.
AD GUNS: 20mm: 50 TCM-20, 11 *Oerlikon*; **40mm:**
13 L/70.

NAVY: 1,200.
BASE: Mombasa.
PATROL AND COASTAL COMBATANTS: 6:
MSL CRAFT: 6:
2 *Nyayo* (UK Vosper 57-m) PFM, with 4 *Ottomat* SSM.
1 *Mamba*, 3 *Madaraka* (UK Brooke Marine 37-m/
32-m) PFM with 4 x *Gabriel* II SSM.
SPT AND MISC: 1 tug.
2 *Galana* LCM (civilian use).

AIR FORCE: 2,500; 28 cbt ac, 34 armed hel.
FGA: 10 F-5 (-E: 8; -F: 2).
COIN: 6 *Hawk* Mk 52, 12 *Tucano*.
TPT: 7 DHC-5D, 6 Do-28D-2, 1 PA-31, 3 DHC-8.
TRG: 7 *Bulldog* 103/127.
ATTACK HEL: 11 Hughes 500MD (with TOW), 8
Hughes 500ME, 15 Hughes 500M.
TPT HEL: 9 IAR-330, 3 SA-330, 1 SA-342.
TRG: 2 Hughes 500D.
MSL:
ASM: AGM-65 *Maverick*, *TOW*.
AAM: AIM-9 *Sidewinder*.

FORCES ABROAD:
UN AND PEACEKEEPING:
ANGOLA (UNAVEM III): 10 Obs. **BOSNIA** (UN-
PROFOR): 21 Obs. **CROATIA** (UNCRO): 973; 1
inf bn plus 24 Obs, 34 civ pol. **IRAQ/KUWAIT**
(UNIKOM): 6 Obs. **LIBERIA** (UNOMIL): 9 incl 8
Obs. **FYROM** (UNPREDEP): 1 Obs. **WESTERN
SAHARA** (MINURSO): 10 Obs.

PARAMILITARY:
POLICE GENERAL SERVICE UNIT: 5,000.
POLICE AIR WING: ac: 7 Cessna lt; **hel:** 3 Bell
(1 206L, 2 47G).
CUSTOMS/POLICE NAVAL SQN: about 5
PCI⟨ (2 Lake Victoria), some 12 boats.

LESOTHO

GDP	1993: M 2,587m ($510m):	
	per capita $2,100	
	1994: M 3,012m ($560m):	
	per capita $2,200	
Growth	1993: 4.9%	1994: 7.5%
Inflation	1993: 13.1%	1994: 8.3%
Debt	1993: $512m	1994: $612m
Def exp[a]	1993ε: M 96.1m ($19m)	
Def bdgt[a]	1994: M 90.3m ($18m)	
	1995: M 102.5m ($28m)	

FMA   1994: $0.1m (IMET)
                1995: $0.1m (IMET)
                1996: $0.1m (IMET)
$1 = M   1993: 3.26   1994: 3.55
                1995: 3.60

M = maloti

a Excl capital expenditure.

Population: 1,985,000

	13–17	*18–22*	*23–32*
Men	114,000	94,600	144,400
Women	113,000	94,200	146,800

TOTAL ARMED FORCES:
ACTIVE: 2,000.

ARMY: 2,000.
7 inf coy.
1 spt coy (incl recce/AB, 81mm mor).
1 air sqn.
EQPT:
RECCE: 10 Is RAMTA, 8 *Shorland,* AML-90.
TOWED ARTY: 105mm: 2.
MOR: 81mm: some.
RCL: 106mm: M-40.
AC: 2 C-212 *Aviocar* 300, 1 Cessna 182Q.
HEL: 2 Bo-105 CBS, 1 Bell 47G, 2 Bell 412 SP.

LIBERIA

GDP   1993: $L n.k. ($1.34bn):
                per capita $1,000
                1994: $L n.k. ($1.38bn):
                per capita $1,000
Growth   1993: -0.4%   1994: -0.4%
Inflation   1993: 6.8%   1994: 6.4%
Debt   1993: $1.93bn   1994: $1.94bn
Def exp   1993ε:$L n.k. ($35m)
                1994: $L n.k. ($37m)
FMA*a*
$1 = $L*b*   1993–1995: 1.0
$L= Liberian dollar

a The cost of UNOMIL in 1993 was about $65m and in 1994
about $36m. Voluntary contributions by non-participating
countries in support of ECOMOG were $18m between Sept
1993 and Nov 1994. Estimated cost for participating
ECOMOG states in 1994 was $16m (incl Nigeria $11m and
Ghana $3m) paid as voluntary contributions.
b Official exchange rate is based on a par relationship with
the US dollar. Unofficial rate: 1995ε: $1 = $L40–50.

Population: 2,379,000

	13–17	*18–22*	*23–32*
Men	144,000	113,400	154,200
Women	139,400	107,200	144,600

As a result of civil war, the Armed Forces of Liberia
(AFL), with a cbt strength of ε2–3,000, are now confined
to the capital, Monrovia. Eqpt held by the AFL has been
destroyed or is unserviceable. The area west of Monrovia,
up to the Sierra Leone border, is controlled by the
United Liberation Movement for Democracy in Liberia
(ULIMO), which has split into two factions with a
combined cbt strength of ε7,000 (ε4,000 plus ε3,000).
Both are opposed by the National Patriotic Forces of
Liberia (NPFL), which has also split into two factions
and controls most of the country with a combined cbt
strength of ε12,000 (ε8,000 plus ε3–4,000). The Liberian Peace Council (LPC) based in eastern Liberia has
a cbt strength of ε2,000. A four-nation peacekeeping
force (ECOMOG) provided by the Economic Community of West African States (ECOWAS) is deployed
within the country and is composed of forces from
Ghana (900), Guinea (1,000), Nigeria (ε6,000) and
Sierra Leone (700).
The United Nations Observer Mission in Liberia
(UNOMIL) has deployed some 70 military obs and spt
tps to supervise the disarming of the various factions.

MADAGASCAR

GDP   1993: fr 6,451bn ($3.37bn):
                per capita $810
                1994: fr 9,069bn ($3.48bn):
                per capita $800
Growth   1993: 2.1%   1994ε: 1.3%
Inflation   1993: 10.0%   1994: 39.0%
Debt   1993: $4.59bn   1994: $4.79bn
Def exp*a*   1993: fr 424.2bn ($222m)
Def bdgt*b*   1994: fr 73.9bn ($38m)
                1995: fr 90.1bn ($29m)
FMA   1993: $0.3m (IMET)
                1994: $1.3m (France)
                1996: $0.1m (IMET)
$1 = fr   1993: 1,914   1994: 3,067
                1995: 4,135
fr = Malagasy franc

a As reported to the UN.
b Excl capital expenditure.

Population: 13,485,000

	13–17	*18–22*	*23–32*
Men	764,800	632,200	973,200
Women	746,400	621,600	969,400

TOTAL ARMED FORCES:
ACTIVE: 21,000.
Terms of service: conscription (incl for civil purposes), 18 months.

ARMY: some 20,000.
2 bn gp.
1 engr regt.
EQPT:
LT TK: 12 PT-76.
RECCE: 8 M-8, ε20 M-3A1, 10 *Ferret*, ε35 BRDM-2.
APC: ε30 M-3A1 half-track.
TOWED ARTY: 76mm: 12 ZIS-3; **105mm:** some M-101; **122mm:** 12 D-30.
MOR: 82mm: M-37; **120mm:** 8 M-43.
RL: 89mm: LRAC.
RCL: 106mm: M-40A1.
AD GUNS: 14.5mm: 50 ZPU-4; **37mm:** 20 Type 55.

NAVY:† 500 (incl some 100 Marines).
BASES: Diégo-Suarez, Tamatave, Fort Dauphin, Tuléar, Majunga.
PATROL CRAFT: 1 *Malaika* (Fr PR48-m) PCI†.
AMPH: 1 *Toky* (Fr *BATRAM*) LSM, with 8 x SS-12 SSM, capacity 30 tps, 4 tk†.
Plus craft: 1 LCT (Fr EDIC), 1 LCA, 3 LCVP.
SPT AND MISC: 1 tpt/trg.

AIR FORCE: 500; 12 cbt ac, no armed hel.
FGA: 1 sqn with 4 MiG-17F, 8 MiG-21FL.
TPT: 4 An-26, 1 BN-2, 2 C-212, 2 Yak-40 (VIP).
HEL: 1 sqn with 6 Mi-8.
LIAISON: 1 Cessna 310, 2 Cessna 337, 1 PA-23.
TRG: 4 Cessna 172.

PARAMILITARY:
GENDARMERIE: 7,500, incl maritime police with some 5 PCI⟨.

MALAWI

GDP	1993: K 8,862m ($1.82bn): per capita $750 1994: K 10,166m ($1.78bn): per capita $710	
Growth	1993: 11.1%	1994: -4.6%
Inflation	1993: 19.6%	1994: 24.6%
Debt	1993: $1.82bn	1994: $1.93bn
Def exp	1993ε: K 103m ($21m)	
Def bdgt	1994ε: K 115m ($20m) 1995ε: K 180m ($20m)	
FMA	1994: $0.1m (IMET)	

	1995: $0.1m (IMET) 1996: $0.3m (IMET)	
$1 = K	1993: 4.40 1995: 15.27	1994: 8.74

K = kwacha

Population: 9,727,000

	13–17	18–22	23–32
Men:	542,600	447,600	675,000
Women:	537,600	457,000	719,800

TOTAL ARMED FORCES (all services form part of the Army):
ACTIVE: 8,000.
RESERVES: Army: 10,000 (militia).

ARMY: 7,800.
3 inf bn; 1 spt bn (incl 1 recce sqn).
EQPT:
RECCE: 20 *Fox*, 10 *Ferret*, 13 *Eland*.
TOWED ARTY: 105mm: 9 lt.
MOR: 81mm: 8 L16.
RL: 89mm: M-20.
RCL: 57mm: M-18.
AD GUNS: 14.5mm: 50 ZPU-4.
SAM: 15 *Blowpipe*.

MARINES: 200.
BASE: Monkey Bay (Lake Nyasa).
PATROL CRAFT: 1 PCI⟨, 2 LCVP, some boats.

AIR WING: 200; no cbt ac, 1 armed hel.
TPT AC: 1 sqn with 2 Do-228, 2 C-47, 1 HS-125-800 (VIP), 1 *King Air* C90.
ATTACK HEL: 1 AS-350.
TPT HEL: 3 SA-319, 3 SA-330, 1 SA-365.

FORCES ABROAD:
UN AND PEACEKEEPING:
RWANDA (UNAMIR): 197 incl 14 Obs.

PARAMILITARY:
MOBILE POLICE FORCE (MPF): 1,500; 8 Shorland armd car; **ac:** 3 BN-2T *Defender* (border patrol), 1 *Skyvan* 3M, 4 Cessna; **hel:** 2 AS-365.

MALI

GDP	1993: fr 798bn ($2.1bn): per capita $650

1994ε: fr 957bn ($2.2bn):
per capita $700

Growth	1993: -0.8%	1994: 2.4%	
Inflation	1993: -0.3%	1994: 25.8%	
Debt	1993: $2.65bn	1994: $2.82bn	
Def exp	1993ε: fr 16.3bn ($42m)		
Def bdgt	1994ε: fr 19.4bn ($45m)		
	1995ε: fr 23.0bn ($47m)		
FMA	1994: $0.1m (IMET) $2.0m (France)		
	1995: $0.2m (IMET)		
	1996: $0.2m (IMET)		
$1 = fr	1993: 283	1994: 555	
	1995: 485		

fr = CFA franc

Population: 9,833,000 (Tuareg 6–10%)

	13–17	18–22	23–32
Men	537,800	444,600	672,400
Women	559,000	464,000	712,600

TOTAL ARMED FORCES (all services

form part of the Army):
ACTIVE: 7,350.
Terms of service: conscription (incl for civil purposes),
2 years (selective).

ARMY: 6,900.
2 tk, 4 inf, 1 AB, 2 arty, 1 engr, 1 SF bn, 2 AD, 1 SAM bty.
EQPT:†
MBT: 21 T-34, T-54/-55 reported.
LT TK: 18 Type 62.
RECCE: 20 BRDM-2.
APC: 30 BTR-40, 10 BTR-60, 10 BTR-152.
TOWED ARTY: 85mm: 6 D-44; **100mm:** 6 M-1944;
122mm: 8 D-30; **130mm:** M-46 reported.
MRL: 122mm: 2 BM-21.
MOR: 82mm: M-43; **120mm:** 30 M-43.
AD GUNS: 37mm: 6 M-1939; **57mm:** 6 S-60.
SAM: 12 SA-3.

NAVY:† about 50.
BASES: Bamako, Mopti, Segou, Timbuktu.
RIVER PATROL CRAFT: 3⟨.

AIR FORCE: 400; 16† cbt ac, no armed hel.
FGA: 5 MiG-17F.
FTR: 11 MiG-21.
TPT: 2 An-2, 2 An-24, 2 An-26.
TRG: 6 L-29, 1 MiG-15UTI, 4 Yak-11, 2 Yak-18, 1
SN-601 (VIP).
HEL: 2 Mi-4, 1 Mi-8, 3 AS-350.

FORCES ABROAD:
UN AND PEACEKEEPING:
ANGOLA (UNAVEM III): 10 Obs plus 9 civ pol.
HAITI (UNMIH): 25 civ pol. **RWANDA** (UNAMIR):
228 incl 30 Obs plus 10 civ pol.

PARAMILITARY:
GENDARMERIE: 1,800; 8 coy.
REPUBLICAN GUARD: 2,000.
MILITIA: 3,000.
NATIONAL POLICE: 1,000.

OPPOSITION:
**MOVEMENT FOR A UNITED FRONT OF
AZAOUAD** (MFUA): ε1,000 armed.

MAURITIUS

GDP	1993: R 54.93bn ($2.38bn):		
	per capita $12,000		
	1994: R 60.61bn ($2.57bn):		
	per capita $12,400		
Growth	1993: 5.4%	1994: 5.1%	
Inflation	1993: 10.5%	1994: 7.4%	
Debt	1993: $999m	1994: $1,049m	
Def exp	1993: R 180.1m ($10.2m)		
	1994: R 202.6m ($11.3m)		
Def bdgt	1995ε: R 224.5m ($13.2m)		
FMA	1993: $0.07m (IMET)		
$1 = R	1993: 17.7	1994: 18.0	
	1995: 17.0		

R = rupee

Population: 1,133,000

	13–17	18–22	23–32
Men	55,400	51,600	103,600
Women	54,400	51,200	103,600

PARAMILITARY:
SPECIAL MOBILE FORCE: 1,300.
6 rifle, 2 mobile, 1 engr coy, spt tp.
EQPT:
APC: 10 VAB.
MOR: 81mm: 2.
RL: 89mm: 4 LRAC.
COAST GUARD: ε500.
PATROL CRAFT: 4:
1 *Amar* PCI, 1 SDB-3 PFI, 2 Sov *Zhuk* PCI⟨, plus boats.
MR: 2 Do-228-101, 1 BN-2T *Defender*, 3 SA-316B.
POLICE AIR WING: 2 *Alouette* III.

MOZAMBIQUE

GDP	1993: M 5,463m ($1.41bn):
	per capita $700
	1994: M 8,877m ($1.47bn):
	per capita $730

Growth	1993: 8.0%	1994: 4.3%
Inflation	1993: 76.2%	1994: 46.2%
Debt	1993: $5.26bn	1994: $5.59bn
Def exp[a]	1993: M 456bn ($118m)	
	1994: M 631bn ($104m)	
Def bdgt	1995: M 626bn ($89m)	
FMA[b]	1994: $0.2m (IMET)	
	1995: $0.1m (IMET)	
	1996: $0.1m (IMET) $2m (France)	
$1 = M	1993: 3,874	1994: 6,039
	1995: 7,010	

M = metical

[a] Incl costs of demob programme and new org est at $31m in 1993 and $19m in 1994.
[b] The cost of ONUMOZ was about $327m in 1993 and about $295m in 1994.

Population: 17,732,000

	13–17	18–22	23–32
Men	986,400	810,600	1,277,800
Women	1,002,000	826,600	1,317,400

TOTAL ARMED FORCES:

Under the terms of the 1992 peace accord, government and Renamo forces are to merge forming a new National Army some 30,000 strong. The unified force has a current str of ε12,000 from which 6 inf bn have formed. Weaponry is mainly of Soviet manufacture and of poor serviceability.

ARMY: to be 30,000.
EQPT:† (all est at 10% or less serviceability).
MBT: some 80 T-54/-55 (300+ T-34, T-54/-55 non-op).
RECCE: 30 BRDM-1/-2.
AIFV: 40 BMP-1.
APC: 150+ BTR-60, 100 BTR-152.
TOWED ARTY: 100+: **76mm:** M-1942; **85mm:** 150+: D-44, D-48, Type-56; **100mm:** 24 M-1944; **105mm:** M-101; **122mm:** M-1938, D-30; **130mm:** 24 M-46; **152mm:** 20 D-1.
MRL: **122mm:** 30 BM-21.
MOR: **82mm:** M-43; **120mm:** M-43.
RCL: **75mm;** **82mm:** B-10; **107mm:** B-11.
AD GUNS: 400: **20mm:** M-55; **23mm:** 90 ZU-23-2; **37mm:** 100 M-1939; **57mm:** 90: S-60 towed, ZSU-57-2 SP.
SAM: SA-7.

NAVY†: ε750.
BASES: Maputo (HQ), Beira, Nacala, Pemba, Inhambane, Quelimane (ocean); Metangula (Lake Nyasa) where 3 PCI⟨ (non-op) are based.
PATROL AND COASTAL COMBATANTS: 10 (none believed to be op).
PATROL, INSHORE: some 10 (non-op).
3 *Zhuk* PFI⟨, some 7 PCI⟨ (non-op).
MCM: 2 Sov *Yevgenya* MSI (non-op).
AMPH: craft only: 2 LCU (non-op).

AIR FORCE: 4,000 (incl AD units); 43 cbt ac†, 4 armed hel†.
FGA: 5 sqn with 43 MiG-21.
TPT: 1 sqn with 5 An-26, 2 C-212.
HEL:
ATTACK: 4 Mi-24.
TPT: 5 Mi-8.
TRG: 4 PA-32, 1 Cessna 182, 7 ZLIN-326.
AD SAM:† SA-2, 10 SA-3.

NAMIBIA

GDP	1993: $N 8.19bn ($2.17bn):
	per capita $2,600
	1994: $N 9.18bn ($2.35bn):
	per capita $2,700

Growth	1993: 0.4%	1994: 5.8%
Inflation	1993: 8.6%	1994: 10.8%
Debt	1993: $59m	1994: $62m
Def exp	1993: $N 187m ($50m)	
Def bdgt	1994: $N 198m ($51m)	
	1995: $N 234m ($60m)	
FMA	1994: $0.2m (IMET)	
	1995: $0.2m (IMET)	
	1996: $0.3m (IMET)	
$1 = $N	1993: 3.27	1994: 3.55
	1995: 3.60	

$N= Namibian dollar

Population: 1,647,000

	13–17	18–22	23–32
Men	94,200	78,600	119,200
Women	92,800	77,600	118,800

TOTAL ARMED FORCES:
ACTIVE: 8,100.

ARMY: 8,000.
1 Presidential Guard bn.
4 mot inf bn.

1 cbt spt bde with 1 arty, 1 AD, 1 ATK regt.

EQPT:
RECCE: BRDM-2.
APC: some *Casspir, Wolf,* BTR-152.
MRL: 122mm: 5 BM-21.
MORS: 81mm; 82mm.
RCL: 82mm: B-10.
ATK GUNS: 57mm; 76mm;:M-1942 (ZIS-3).
AD GUNS: 14.5mm: 50 ZPU-4; **23mm:** 15 ZU-23.
SAM: SA-7.
AC: 6 Cessna O-2A.
HEL: 2 SA-315 *Cheetah,* 2 SA-319 *Chetak.*
AIR WING: ac: 5 Cessna 337/02-A; **hel:** 2 SA-315 (*Cheetah*), 2 SA-319 (*Chetak*).

COAST GUARD: ε100.
BASE: Walvis Bay.
PATROL: 3 PCO plus boats.

NIGER

GDP	1993: fr 630bn ($2.23bn):
	per capita $1,000
	1994ε: fr 897bn ($2.30bn):
	per capita $1,000
Growth	1993: 1.4% 1994: 3.9%
Inflation	1993: -1.2% 1994: 36.7%
Debt	1993: $1.70bn 1994: $1.80bn
Def exp	1993: fr 6.2bn ($21m)
Def bdgt	1994: fr 7.9bn ($20m)
	1995: fr 8.9bn ($22m)
FMA	1994: $0.2m (IMET) $1.8m (France)
	1995: $0.2m (IMET)
	1996: $0.3m (IMET)
$1 = fr	1993: 283 1994: 555
	1995: 485
fr = CFA franc	

Population: 9,037,000

	13–17	18–22	23–32
Men:	498,000	400,200	604,800
Women:	502,200	408,800	624,600

TOTAL ARMED FORCES:
ACTIVE: 5,300.
Terms of service: selective conscription (2 years).

ARMY: 5,200.
3 Military Districts.
4 armd recce sqn.
7 inf, 2 AB, 1 engr coy.

EQPT:
RECCE: 90 AML-90, 35 AML-60/20, 7 VBL.
APC: 22 M-3.
MOR: 81mm: 19 Brandt; **82mm:** 17; **120mm:** 4 Brandt.
RL: 89mm: 36 LRAC.
RCL: 75mm: 6 M-20; **106mm:** 8 M-40.
ATK GUNS: 85mm; 90mm.
AD GUNS: 20mm: 39 incl 10 M-3 VDA SP.

AIR FORCE: 100; no cbt ac or armed hel.
TPT: 2 C-130H, 1 Do-228, 1 Boeing 737-200 (VIP).
LIAISON: 2 Cessna 337D, 1 Do-28D.

PARAMILITARY:
GENDARMERIE: 1,400.
REPUBLICAN GUARD: 2,500.
NATIONAL POLICE: 1,500.

NIGERIA

GDP	1993: N 821.9bn ($37.25bn):
	per capita $1,400
	1994: N 830.1bn ($37.74bn):
	per capita $1,400
Growth	1993: 2.6% 1994: 1.3%
Inflation	1993: 57.2% 1994: 64.3%
Debt	1993: $32.53bn 1994: $33.44bn
Def exp[a]	1993ε: N 25,520m ($1.16bn)
	1994ε: N 25,739m ($1.17bn)
Def bdgt[a]	1995ε: N 7,023m ($319m)
FMA	1993: $0.2m (IMET)
$1 = N	1993: 22.1 1994: 22.0
	1995: 22.0
N = naira	

[a] IMF external audits of Nigerian central gov exp have not been published since 1987. Def exp est cited here include extra-budgetary mil and paramil funding.

Population:[b] 111,273,000 (*North:* Hausa and Fulani; *South-west:* Yoruba; *South-east:* Ibos. These 4 tribes make up ε65% of population.)

	13–17	18–22	23–32
Men	6,614,800	5,482,400	8,114,800
Women	6,650,400	5,636,200	8,446,400

[b] The 1991 census indicated a population of 90,500,000 (a large discrepancy against UN estimates).

TOTAL ARMED FORCES:
ACTIVE: 77,100.
RESERVES: planned; none organised.

ARMY: 62,000.

1 armd div (2 armd bde).

1 composite div (1 mot inf, 1 amph bde, 1 AB bn).

2 mech div (each 1 mech, 1 mot inf bde).

1 Presidential Guards bde (2 bn).

1 AD bde.

div tps: each div 1 arty, 1 engr bde, 1 recce bn.

EQPT:

MBT: 210: 60 T-55†, 150 Vickers Mk 3.

LT TK: 100 *Scorpion*.

RECCE: 20 *Saladin*, ε120 AML-60, 60 AML-90, 55 *Fox*, 75 EE-9 *Cascavel*.

APC: 10 *Saracen*, 300 *Steyr* 4K-7FA, 70 MOWAG *Piranha*.

TOWED ARTY: 105mm: 200 M-56; **122mm:** 200 D-30/-74; **130mm:** 7 M-46; **152mm:** 4; **155mm:** 24 FH-77B (in store).

SP ARTY: 155mm: 27 *Palmaria*.

MRL: 122mm: 11 APR-21.

MOR: 81mm: 200; **82mm:** 100; **120mm:** 30+.

RCL: 84mm: *Carl Gustav*; **106mm:** M-40A1.

AD GUNS: 20mm: some 60; **23mm:** ZU-23, 30 ZSU-23-4 SP; **40mm:** L/60.

SAM: 48 *Blowpipe*, 16 *Roland*.

SURV: *Rasit* (veh, arty).

NAVY: 5,600 (incl Coast Guard).

BASES: Apapa (Lagos; HQ Western Comd), Calabar (HQ Eastern Comd), Warri, Port Harcourt, Ibaka (Akwa Ibom state).

FF: 1 *Aradu* (Ge *Meko*-360) with 1 *Lynx* hel, 2 x 3 ASTT; plus 8 x *Otomat* SSM, 1 x 127mm gun.

PATROL AND COASTAL COMBATANTS: 53:

CORVETTES: 2† *Erinomi* (UK Vosper Mk 9) with 1 x 3 *Seacat*, 1 x 76mm gun, 1 x 2 ASW mor†.

(Plus 1 *Otobo* (UK Vosper Mk 3) in Italy since 1988, refitting to PCO.)

MSL CRAFT: 6:

3 *Ekpe* (Ge Lürssen 57-m) PFM with 4 x *Otomat* SSM.

3 *Siri* (Fr *Combattante*) PFM with 2 x 2 MM-38 *Exocet* SSM.

PATROL, INSHORE: 45:

4 *Makurdi* (UK Brooke Marine 33-m), some 41 PCI‹.

MCM: 2 *Ohue* (mod It *Lerici*) MCC.

AMPH: 2 *Ambe* (Ge) LST (1 non-op), capacity 220 tps 5 tk.

TRG: 1 *Obuma* (ex-NI frigate), believed converted to trg role.

SPT AND MISC: 6

1 *Lana* AGHS, 4 tugs, 1 nav trg.

NAVAL AVIATION:

HEL: †2 *Lynx* Mk 89 MR/SAR.

AIR FORCE: 9,500; 92 cbt ac†, 15 armed hel†.

FGA/FTR: 3 sqn:

1 with 20 *Alpha Jet* (FGA/trg).

1 with †6 MiG-21MF, †4 MiG-21U, †12 MiG-21B/FR.

1 with †15 *Jaguar* (12 -SN, 3 -BN).

COIN/TRG: 23 L-39MS, 12 MB-339AN.

ARMED HEL: †15 Bo-105D.

TPT: 2 sqn with 5 C-130H, 3 -H-30, 18 Do-128-6, 3 Do-228 (VIP), 5 G-222.

PRESIDENTIAL FLT: 1 Boeing 727, 1 *Falcon*, 2 *Gulfstream*, 1 BAe 125-700, 1 BAe 125-1000.

HEL: 4 AS-332, 2 SA-330.

TRG: ac:† 25 *Bulldog*; **hel:** 14 Hughes 300.

MSL:

AAM: AA-2 *Atoll*.

FORCES ABROAD:

UN AND PEACEKEEPING:

ANGOLA (UNAVEM III): 21 Obs plus 16 civ pol. **BOSNIA** (UNPROFOR): 13 Obs. **CROATIA** (UNCRO): 16 Obs, 66 civ pol. **IRAQ/KUWAIT** (UNIKOM): 7 Obs. **LIBERIA** (ECOMOG): some 6,000; 2 inf bde. **FYROM** (UNPREDEP): 1 Obs plus 2 civ pol. **RWANDA** (UNAMIR): 356 incl 17 Obs plus 10 civ pol. **SIERRA LEONE:** 1,000; 1 inf bn+. **WESTERN SAHARA** (MINURSO): 4 Obs plus 15 civ pol.

PARAMILITARY:

COAST GUARD: incl in Navy entry.

PORT SECURITY POLICE: ε2,000; about 60 boats and some 5 hovercraft.

SECURITY AND CIVIL DEFENCE CORPS (Ministry of Internal Affairs): Police: UR-416, 70 AT-105 *Saxon*† APC; **ac:** 1 Cessna 500, 3 Piper (2 *Navajo*, 1 *Chieftain*); **hel:** 4 Bell (2 -212, 2 -222).

RWANDA

GDP	1993: fr 225.2bn ($1.6bn):	
	per capita $700	
	1994ε: fr n.k. ($1.5bn):	
	per capita $600	
Growth	1993: -6.9%	1994: -10.0%
Inflation	1993: 9.6%	1994: 12.3%
Debt	1993: $910m	1994: $942m
Def exp	1992ε: fr 13.7bn ($107m)	
	1993ε: fr 15.9bn ($113m)	
Def bdgt	1994ε: fr 16.5bn ($116m)	
FMA[a]	1993: $0.2m (IMET)	
	1994: $0.1m (IMET) $2.2m (France)	
	1995: $0.2m (IMET)	
$1 = fr	1992: 133	1993: 144
	1994: 148	

fr = Rwandan franc

[a] The costs of UNAMIR (including those related to UNOMUR) were $98m in 1993 and $198m in 1994.

Population: 7,794,000 (Hutu 90%, Tutsi 9%)

	13–17	18–22	23–32
Men	470,200	378,000	552,400
Women	486,200	392,800	577,200

TOTAL ARMED FORCES (all services form part of the Army):

ACTIVE: 40,000 reported.

No reliable information has been received since the civil war ended in 1994. Data in respect of current org and eqpt are not available.

ARMY:
EQPT:
RECCE: 12 AML-60, 16 VBL.
APC: 16 M-3.
TOWED ARTY: 105mm; 122mm: 6 D-30.
MOR: 81mm: 8; **82mm; 120mm.**
RL: 83mm: *Blindicide.*
ATK GUNS: 57mm: 6.
AC: 2 C-47, 1 Do-27Q-4.
HEL: 2 SE-316.

AIR FORCE: 200; 2 cbt ac, no armed hel.
COIN: 2 R-235 *Guerrier.*
TPT: 2 BN-2, 1 N-2501.
LIAISON: 5 SA-316, 6 SA-342L hel.

OPPOSITION:
Former govt tps based in Burundi, Tanzania (10,000) and Zaire (10,000).

FOREIGN FORCES (1 June 1995):
UNITED NATIONS (UNAMIR): some 5,636 tps, 315 mil obs and 68 civ pol from 27 countries.

SENEGAL

GDP	1993: fr 1,518bn ($3.99bn):
	per capita $1,900
	1994: fr 1,540bn ($4.17bn):
	per capita $1,900

Growth	1993: -2.6%	1994: 1.8%
Inflation	1993: -0.6%	1994: 32.3%
Debt	1993: $3.67bn	1994: $3.89bn
Def exp	1993: fr 35.8bn ($94m)	

Def bdgt	1994ε: fr 33.5bn ($91m)	
	1995ε: fr 37.0bn ($76m)	
FMA	1994: $0.5m (IMET) $4.0m (France)	
	1995: $0.6m (IMET)	
	1996: $0.6m (IMET)	
$1 = fr	1993: 283	1994: 555
	1995: 485	

fr = CFA franc

Population: 8,468,000

	13–17	18–22	23–32
Men	500,400	409,800	598,400
Women	494,000	410,400	606,000

TOTAL ARMED FORCES:
ACTIVE: 13,350.
Terms of service: conscription, 2 years selective.
RESERVES: exists, but no details known.

ARMY: 12,000 (mostly conscripts).
4 Military Zone HQ.

1 armd bn.	1 engr bn.
6 inf bn.	1 Presidential Guard (horsed)
1 arty bn.	3 construction coy.
1 cdo bn.	1 AB bn.
1 engr bn.	

EQPT:
RECCE: 10 M-8, 4 M-20, 30 AML-60, 27 AML-90.
APC: some 16 Panhard M-3, 12 M-3 half-track.
TOWED ARTY: 18: **75mm:** 6 M-116 pack; **105mm:** 6 M-101/HM-2; **155mm:** ε6 Fr Model-50.
MOR: 81mm: 8 Brandt; **120mm:** 8 Brandt.
ATGW: 4 *Milan.*
RL: 89mm: 31 LRAC.
AD GUNS: 20mm: 21 M-693; **40mm:** 12 L/60.

NAVY: 700.
BASES: Dakar, Casamance.
PATROL AND COASTAL COMBATANTS: 10:
PATROL, COASTAL: 2:
1 *Fouta* (Dk *Osprey*) PCC.
1 *Njambuur* (Fr SFCN 59-m) PFC.
PATROL, INSHORE: 8:
3 *Saint Louis* (Fr 48-m) PCI.
3 *Senegal* II PFI⟨.
2 *Challenge* (UK *Tracker*) PCI⟨.
AMPH: craft only: 1 LCT.

AIR FORCE: 650; 8 cbt ac, no armed hel.
COIN: 1 sqn with 4 CM-170, 4 R-235 *Guerrier.*
MR/SAR: 1 EMB-111.
TPT: 1 sqn with 6 F-27-400M, 2 MH-1521, 1 Boeing 727-200 (VIP).

HEL: 2 SA-318C, 2 SA-330, 1 SA-341H.
TRG: 2 *Rallye* 160, 2 R-235A.

FORCES ABROAD:
UN AND PEACEKEEPING:
ANGOLA (UNAVEM III): 10 Obs. **IRAQ/KUWAIT** (UNIKOM): 6 Obs. **FYROM** (UNPREDEP): 2 civ pol. **RWANDA** (UNAMIR): 238 plus 2 Obs.

PARAMILITARY:
GENDARMERIE: 4,000; 12 VXB-170 APC.
CUSTOMS: 2 PCI⟨, boats.

OPPOSITION:
CASAMANCE MOVEMENT OF DEMOCRATIC FORCES: str n.k.

FOREIGN FORCES:
FRANCE: 1,500; 1 marine inf bn, MR *Atlantic*; **ac:** 1 C-160; **hel:** 1 SA-319.

SEYCHELLES

GDP	1993: SR 2,316m ($338m): per capita $3,900		
	1994ε: SR 2,433m ($356m): per capita $4,000		
Growth	1993: 4.0%	1994: 2.7%	
Inflation	1993: 1.3%	1994: 1.9%	
Debt	1993: $163m	1994: $185m	
Def exp	1993: SR 63.0m ($9.0m)		
Def bdgt	1994: SR 63.4m ($9.3m)		
	1995ε: SR 65.4m ($9.6m)		
FMA	1993: $0.1m (IMET)		
	1996: $0.1m (IMET)		
$1 = SR	1993: 5.18	1994: 5.06	
	1995: 4.59		

SR = Seychelles rupee

Population: 71,000

	13–17	18–22	23–32
Men	4,000	4,000	8,000
Women	4,000	4,000	7,400

TOTAL ARMED FORCES (all services form part of the Army):
ACTIVE: 300.

ARMY: 300.
1 inf bn (3 coy).

2 arty tps.
EQPT:†
RECCE: 6 BRDM-2.
TOWED ARTY: 122mm: 3 D-30.
MOR: 82mm: 6 M-43.
RL: RPG-7.
AD GUNS: 57mm: S-60.
SAM: 10 SA-7.

PARAMILITARY:
NATIONAL GUARD: 1,000.
COAST GUARD: ε500 incl 100 Air Wing and ε80 Marines.
BASE: Port Victoria.
PATROL AND COASTAL COMBATANTS: 4:
PATROL, INSHORE: 4:
1 *Andromache* (It Pichiotti 42-m) PFI.
1 *Zoroaster* (Sov *Turya*, no foils or TT) PCI.
2 *Zhuk* PFI⟨ (1 non op).
AMPH: craft only: 1 LCT.
AIR WING: 100; 1 cbt ac, no armed hel.
MR: 1 BN-2 *Defender*.
TPT: 1 Cessna Citation.
HEL: 1† *Chetak*.
TRG: 1 Cessna 152.

SIERRA LEONE

GDP	1993: Le 396.1bn ($698m): per capita $700		
	1994: Le 474.8bn ($809m): per capita $750		
Growth	1993: 1.7%	1994: 3.6%	
Inflation	1993: 22.2%	1994: 24.2%	
Debt	1993: $1.39bn	1994: $1.51bn	
Def exp	1993ε: Le 10.8bn ($19m)		
	1994ε: Le 21.0bn ($36m)		
Def bdgt[a]	1994e: Le 14.0bn ($24m)		
	1995ε: Le 17bn ($27m)		
FMA	1994: $0.3m (IMET)		
	1995: $0.1m (IMET)		
	1996: $0.1m (IMET)		
$1 = Le	1993: 568	1994: 587	
	1995: 638		

Le = leone

[a] 1995 def bdgt is for July–Dec 1995.

Population: 4,707,000

	13–17	18–22	23–32
Men	249,200	212,400	328,600
Women	247,200	212,200	332,800

TOTAL ARMED FORCES:
ACTIVE: ε6,200.

ARMY: 6,000.
4 inf bn.
2 arty bty.
1 engr sqn.
EQPT:
MOR: 81mm: 3; **82mm:** 2; **120mm:** 2.
RCL: 84mm: *Carl Gustav.*
AD GUNS: 12.7mm: 4; **14.5mm:** 3.
SAM: SA-7.
HEL: 1 Mi-24.

NAVY: ε200.
BASE: Freetown.
PATROL AND COASTAL COMBATANTS: 3:
2 Ch *Shanghai-II* PFI, 1 Swiftship 32-m PFI. Plus
some 3 modern boats.

FORCES ABROAD:
LIBERIA (ECOMOG): 700.

PARAMILITARY:
STATE SECURITY DIVISION: 2,000: incl 1 SF bn.

OPPOSITION:
REVOLUTIONARY UNITED FRONT: ε1,000
with perhaps 300 active.

FOREIGN FORCES:
GUINEA: 300.
NIGERIA: 1,000; 1 inf bn+.

SOMALI REPUBLIC

GDP	1993ε: ($810m):	
	per capita $800	
	1994ε: ($864m):	
	per capita $830	
Growth	1993: -0.6%	1994: 3.7%
Inflation	1992: 10.5%	1993: 24.6%
Debt	1993: $2.50bn	1994: $2.54bn
FMA[a]		
$1 = S sh	1992–95: 2,620	
S sh = Somali shillings		

[a] The costs of UNOSOM I and II for May 1992–February 1994
inclusive are $959m. The cost of UNOSOM II in 1994 was
about $862m, excl voluntary contributions from participating
UN member-states. The cost of US forces supporting UNOSOM
II in 1993–94 and funded by voluntary contributions by the US
is est at $1.3bn.

Population: 8,994,000

	13–17	18–22	23–32
Men	507,600	407,800	608,400
Women	504,400	403,600	616,000

Following the 1991 revolution, no national armed forces
have yet been formed. The Somali National Movement
has declared northern Somalia as the independent
Republic of Somaliland, while in the south, insurgent
groups compete for local supremacy. Heavy military
equipment is in a poor state of repair or inoperable.

CLAN/MOVEMENT GROUPINGS:
'SOMALILAND' (northern Somalia):
UNITED SOMALIA FRONT: sub-clan Issa.
SOMALIA DEMOCRATIC FRONT: sub-clan
Gadabursi.
SOMALIA NATIONAL MOVEMENT: clan Isaq,
5–6,000, 3 factions (Tur, Dhegaweyne, Kahin).
UNITED SOMALI PARTY: sub-clan Dolbuhunta,
leader Abdi Hasai.
SOMALIA:
**SOMALIA SALVATION DEMOCRATIC
FRONT:** sub-clan Majerteen, 3,000, leaders 'Colonel'
Yusuf, Abshir Musa (loose alliance).
UNITED SOMALI CONGRESS: (Somali National
Army) clan Hawije; Aideed Faction: leader Osman
Hassan Ali al'Atto/Mohammed Farah Aideed, 10,000,
Habar Gadir sub-clan.
Ali Mahdi Faction: leader Mohammed Ali Mahdi,
10,000(-), Marehan sub-clan.
SOMALI NATIONAL FRONT: sub-clan Marehan,
2–3,000, leaders Mohamed Said Hersi Morgan, Hashi
Ganni, Warsame Hashi.
SOMALI DEMOCRATIC MOVEMENT: clan
Dighil and Rahenwein.
SOMALI PATRIOTIC MOVEMENT: sub-clan
Ogaden, 203,000, leaders Ahmed Omar Jeso, Aden Nar
Gabiyu.

SOUTH AFRICA

GDP	1993: R 383.1bn ($117.5bn):	
	per capita $5,900	
	1994: R 432.8bn ($121.9bn):	
	per capita $5,900	
Growth	1993: 1.2%	1994: 2.5%
Inflation	1993: 9.8%	1994: 9.0%
Debt	1993: $16.4bn	1994: $17.5bn

Def exp	1993: R 12.8bn ($3.91bn)	
Def bdgt	1994:[a] R 12.1bn ($3.41bn)	
	1995: R 10.2bn ($2.87bn)	
FMA	1994: $0.1m (IMET)	
	1995: $0.3m (IMET)	
	1996: $0.5m (IMET)	
$1 = R	1993: 3.26	1994: 3.55
	1995: 3.56	
R = rand		

[a] Excl funds for SANDF reorganisation of R2.09bn ($590m) in 1994 and εR3.29bn ($924m) in 1995.

Population: 42,505,000

	13–17	18–22	23–32
Men:	2,309,000	2,069,000	3,312,000
Women:	2,278,800	2,052,800	3,295,600

TOTAL ARMED FORCES:
ACTIVE: ε136,900 (incl 5,400 Medical Services, 4,200 women).

Terms of service: conscription ended when the new Constitution became effective in 1994. Voluntary service of 2–6 years is followed by part-time service in Citizen Force (CF), duty not to exceed 60 days trg in any 2-year period.

An est 35,000 personnel from other forces, incl MK and the Homelands, are being absorbed into the new South African National Defence Force (SANDF). Of this total some 11,000 are now SANDF members. The total force strength will be reduced over a 3-year period once the integration process is complete.

RESERVES:
Citizen Force: 475,000. Active Citizen Force Reserve, 275,000; Commandos, ε140,000.

ARMY: ε118,000 (ε11,000 White; ε103,000 Black and Coloured; ε4,000 women).
FULL TIME FORCE (FT):
9 Province (forming), 10 regional comd (regional comd consist of HQ and a number of unit HQ, but no tps which are provided when necessary by FT and CF units).
1 AB bde.
1 special ops/AB bde (3 bn incl 1 CF).
1 indep mech bde (forms from trg units).
9 inf bn.
Trg/Holding Units (incl armd, inf, arty, engr). Cbt role is to provide sub-units either for regional comd for internal sy tasks or for mech bde for ops.
JOINT FORCES: Rapid Deployment Force HQ
(elms earmarked by all 3 services incl 1 mech/mot inf bde of 1 mech bn gp, 1 AB bn, 1 armd recce coy, allocated according to op requirement).

RESERVES:
CITIZEN FORCE (CF):
3 div (each 2 armd recce, 2 tk, 2 mech inf, 2 mot inf, 2 arty, 1 MRL, 2 AD, 1 engr bn).
(Corps and 2 div HQ have skeleton FT staff.)
COMMANDOS:
some 250 inf coy home defence units.
EQPT:
MBT: some 250 *Olifant* 1A/-B.
RECCE: 1,600 *Eland*-60/-90, 100 *Rooikat*-76.
AIFV: 1,500 *Ratel*-20/-60/-90.
APC: 1,500 *Buffel*, *Casspir*, 160+ *Mamba*.
TOWED ARTY: 350, **88mm:** incl 25-pdr, 30 G-1 (in store); **140mm:** 5.5-in , 75 G-2; **155mm:** ε75 G-5, some G-4.
SP ARTY: 155mm: ε20 G-6.
MRL: 127mm: 120 *Bateleur* (40 tube), 60 *Valkiri* 22 SP (24 tube); some *Valkiri* 5 towed.
MOR: 81mm: 4,000 (incl some SP); **120mm:** +120.
ATGW: ZT-3 *Swift* (some SP), *Milan*.
RL: 92mm: FT-5.
RCL: 106mm: M-40A1.
AD GUNS: 600: **20mm:** GAI, *Ystervark* SP; **23mm:** 36 *Zumlac* (ZU-23-2) SP; **35mm:** 150 GDF-002 twin.
SAM: SA-7/-14.
SURV: *Green Archer* (mor), *Cymbeline* (mor).
UAV: RPV-2 *Seeker*, *Scout*.

NAVY: ε4,500 (ε300 women).
Naval HQ: Pretoria.
Three flotillas: submarine; strike; mine warfare.
BASES: Simon's Town, Durban (Salisbury Island).
SS: 3 *Maria van Riebeek* (Mod Fr *Daphné*) with 550mm TT.
PATROL AND COASTAL COMBATANTS: 12:
MSL CRAFT: 9 *Minister* (Is *Reshef*) with 6–8 *Skerpioen* (Is *Gabriel*) SSM (incl 3 non-op), class being modernised.
PATROL, INSHORE: 3 PFI⟨.
MCM: 8:
4 *Kimberley* (UK *Ton*) MSC.
4 *River* (Ge *Navors*) MHC.
SPT AND MISC: 8:
1 *Drakensberg* AO with 2 hel and extempore amph capability (perhaps 60 tps and 2 small landing craft), 1 *Outeniqua* AO with similar capability as *Drakensberg*, 1 AGHS, 1 diving spt, 1 Antarctic tpt with 2 hel (operated by Department of Economic Affairs), 3 tugs.

AIR FORCE: ε9,000 (ε400 women); 243 cbt ac
(plus 11 in store), 14+ armed hel.
1 Territorial Area Comd, AD, tac spt, log, trg comd.
FGA: 3 sqn:
1 with 75 *Impala* II.

1 with 29 *Mirage* F-1AZ.
1 with 11 *Cheetah* E.
FTR: 11 *Mirage* F-1 CZ (in store).
TKR/EW: 1 sqn with 4 Boeing 707-320 (EW/tkr).
MR: 1 sqn with 8 C-47TP, 5 C-212.
TPT: 3 sqn:
1 with 7 C-130B.
1 (VIP) with 3 HS-125 -400B (civil registration), 2 *Super King Air* 200, 2 *Citation*, 2 *Falcon* 50, 1 *Falcon* 900, 200 Cessna *Caravan*.
1 with 19 C-47 (being modified to C-4 TP).
LIAISON/FAC: 24 Cessna 185.
HEL: 4 sqn with 63 SA-316/-319 (some armed), 63 SA-330C/H/L, 10 BK-117.
TRG COMD (incl OCU): 6 schools: **ac:** 12 C-4TP, *14 *Cheetah* D, 55 T-6G *Harvard* IIA/III, *114 *Impala* I, 60 PC-7 (being delivered); **hel:** 37 SA-316/SA-330.
MSL:
ASM: AS-11/-20/-30.
AAM: R-530, R-550 *Magic*, AIM-9 *Sidewinder*, V-3C *Darter*, V-3A/B *Kukri*.
GROUND DEFENCE: 1 regt (South African Air Force Regt) *Rhino* APC.
RADAR: 2 Air Control Sectors, 3 fixed and some mobile radars.
SAM: 2 wings (2 sqn each), some *Bofors* 40mm L/70, 20 *Cactus* (*Crotale*), SA-8/-9/-13.

MEDICAL SERVICE: 5,400 (1,500 women).
A separate service within the SANDF.

PARAMILITARY:
SOUTH AFRICAN POLICE SERVICE: 140,000; Police Reserves: 37,000. Air Wing: **ac:** 1 *King Air*, 1 Cessna 402, 1 Beech 400, 8 PC-6; **hel:** 2 BK-117, 16 Bo-105 CBS, 2 *Hughes* 500.

SUDAN

GDP	1993ε: £S 1,210.8bn ($7.87bn):
	per capita $1,100
	1994ε: £S 2,400.0bn ($8.64bn):
	per capita $1,100
Growth	1993: 3.0% 1994: 7.6%
Inflation	1993: 118.7% 1994: 80.0%
Debt	1993: $16.56bn 1994: $16.85bn
Def exp	1993ε: £S 46.9bn ($304m)
	1994ε: £S 85.0bn ($306m)
Def bdgt[a]	1994ε: £S 72.8bn ($262m)
	1995: £S 42.0bn ($134m)
$1 = £S	1993: 154 1994: 278
	1995: 313

£S = Sudanese pound

[a] 1995 def bdgt is for July–Dec only.

Population: 28,776,000

	13–17	18–22	23–32
Men	1,683,000	1,400,000	2,111,000
Women	1,606,400	1,335,600	2,034,400

TOTAL ARMED FORCES:
ACTIVE: 118,500.
Terms of service: conscription (males 18–30), 3 years.

ARMY: 115,000 (ε30,000 conscripts).

1 armd div.	1 recce bde.
6 inf div (regional comd).	10 arty bde.
1 AB div (incl 1 SF bde).	3 arty regt.
1 mech inf bde.	1 engr div.
24 inf bde.	12 AD arty

EQPT:
MBT: 250 T-54/-55, 20 M-60A3, 50 Ch Type-59.
LT TK: 70 Ch Type-62.
RECCE: 6 AML-90, 90 *Saladin*, 80 *Ferret*, 60 BRDM-1/-2.
APC: 426: 90 BTR-50/-152, 80 OT-62/-64, 36 M-113, 100 V-100/-150, 120 *Walid*.
TOWED ARTY: 489: **105mm:** 18 M-101 pack, 24 Model 56 pack; **122mm:** 35 D-74, 24 M-1938, 270 Type-54/D-30; **130mm:** 100 M-46/Ch Type 59-1; **155mm:** 18 M-114A1.
SP ARTY: 155mm: 6 AMX Mk F-3.
MRL: 107mm: 600 Type-63; **122mm:** 30 BM-21.
MOR: 81mm: 138; **120mm:** 12 M-43, 24 AM-49.
ATGW: 4 *Swingfire*.
RCL: 106mm: 72 M-40A1.
ATK GUNS: 76mm: 18 M-1942; **100mm:** 40 M-1944.
AD GUNS: 20mm: M-167 towed, M-163 SP; **23mm:** ZU-23-2; **37mm:** 120 M-1939/Type-63, 200 Type-55; **40mm:** 60 L/60; **57mm:** 160 Type-59; **85mm:** 37 M-1939/1944; **100mm:** KS-19 towed.
SAM: SA-7, *Redeye*.
SURV: RASIT (veh, arty).

NAVY: ε1,500.
BASES: Port Sudan (HQ), Flamingo Bay (Red Sea), Khartoum (Nile).
PATROL CRAFT: 3 *Kadir* PCI‹; plus 4 riverine PCI‹ and about 10 armed boats.
AMPH: craft only: some 7 *Sobat* (Yug DTK-221) LCT (used for transporting stores).

AIR FORCE: 3,000 (incl Air Defence); 50† cbt ac, 2 armed hel.
FGA: 9 F-5 (-E: 7; -F: 2), 9 Ch J-5 (MiG-17), 9 Ch J-6 (MiG-19).

FTR: 4 MiG-21, 3 MiG-23, 4 Ch J-6 (MiG-19).
MR: 2 C-212.
TPT: 5 An-24, 5 C-130H, 4 C-212, 3 DHC-5D, 6 EMB-110P, 1 F-27, 2 *Falcon* 20/50.
HEL: 1 sqn with 11 AB-412, 8 IAR/SA-330, 4 Mi-4, 8 Mi-8, 2 Mi-24 (armed).
TRG: incl 4 MiG-15UTI*, 4 MiG-21U*, 2 JJ-5*, 2 JJ-6*.
AD: 5 bty SA-2 SAM (18 launchers).
AAM: AA-2 *Atoll*.

PARAMILITARY:
POPULAR DEFENCE FORCE: ε5–10,000 active (to be 15,000), 60,000 reserve; mil wing of National Islamic Front.

OPPOSITION:
SUDANESE PEOPLE'S LIBERATION
ARMY (SPLA): ε60–100,000: four factions, each org in bn; mainly small arms plus 60mm mor, 14.5mm AA, SA-7 SAM; arty reported; operating mainly in southern Sudan.

FOREIGN FORCES:
IRAN: some mil advisers.

TANZANIA

GDP	1993: sh 845.5bn ($2.84bn):		
	per capita $500		
	1994: sh 916.6bn ($3.00bn):		
	per capita $500		
Growth	1993: 2.1%	1994: 3.6%	
Inflation	1993: 23.4%	1994: 28.1%	
Debt	1993: $7.52bn	1994: $7.80bn	
Def exp	1993: sh 36.5bn ($90m)		
	1994: sh 32.4bn ($106m)		
Def bdgt	1994: sh 25.0bn ($82m)		
	1995ε: sh 35.0bn ($114m)		
FMA	1994: $0.1m (IMET)		
	1995: $0.1m (IMET)		
	1996: $0.2m (IMET)		
$1 = sh	1993: 405	1994: 510	
	1995: 546		
sh = Tanzanian shilling			

Population: 28,463,000

	13–17	18–22	23–32
Men	1,597,400	1,295,400	1,949,400
Women	1,684,400	1,351,000	2,124,800

TOTAL ARMED FORCES:
ACTIVE: ε34,600 (reducing to 25,000 by 1996).

Terms of service: incl civil duties, 2 years.
RESERVES: Citizens' Militia: 80,000.

ARMY: 30,000+.

5 inf bde.	1 tk bde.
2 arty bn.	2 AD arty bn.
2 mor bn.	2 ATK bn.
1 engr regt (bn).	

EQPT:†
MBT: 30 Ch Type-59 (15 op), 35 T-54 (all non-op).
LT TK: 30 Ch Type-62, 40 *Scorpion*.
RECCE: 40 BRDM-2.
APC: 66 BTR-40/-152, 30 Ch Type-56.
TOWED ARTY: 76mm: 45 ZIS-3; **85mm:** 80 Ch Type-56; **122mm:** 20 D-30, 100 M-30; **130mm:** 40 M-46.
MRL: 122mm: 58 BM-21.
MOR: 82mm: 350 M-43; **120mm:** 135 M-43.
RCL: 75mm: 540 Ch Type-52.

NAVY:† ε1,000.
BASES: Dar es Salaam, Zanzibar, Mwanza (Lake Victoria – 4 boats).
PATROL AND COASTAL COMBATANTS: 22:
TORPEDO CRAFT: 4 Ch *Huchuan* PHT⟨ with 2 x 533mm TT.
PATROL, INSHORE: 18:
8 Ch *Shanghai* II PFI, some 10 PCI⟨ (4 in Zanzibar), plus boats.

AIR FORCE: 3,600 (incl ε2,600 AD tps); 24 cbt ac†, no armed hel.
FTR: 3 sqn with 3 Ch J-5 (MiG-17), 10 J-6 (MiG-19), 11 J-7 (MiG-21).
TPT: 1 sqn with 4 DHC-5D, 1 Ch Y-5, 2 CH Y-12, 3 HS-748, 2 F-28, 1 HS-125-700.
HEL: 4 AB-205.
LIAISON: ac: 5 Cessna 310, 2 Cessna 404, 1 Cessna 206; **hel:** 6 Bell 206B.
TRG: 2 MiG-15UTI, 5 PA-28.
AD GUNS: 14.5mm: 40 ZPU-2/-4; **23mm:** 40 ZU-23; **37mm:** 120 Ch Type-55.
SAM: 20 SA-3, 20 SA-6, 120 SA-7.

PARAMILITARY:
POLICE FIELD FORCE: 1,400 in 18 sub-units incl Police Marine Unit.
POLICE AIR WING: ac: 1 Cessna U-206; **hel:** 2 AB-206A, 2 -B, 2 Bell 206L, 2 Bell 47G.
POLICE MARINE UNIT: (100); boats only.
CITIZENS' MILITIA: 80,000.

TOGO

GDP	1993: fr 424bn ($950m):	
	per capita $1,300	
	1994: fr 517bn ($1.13bn):	
	per capita $1,500	
Growth	1993: -3.5%	1994: 16.1%
Inflation	1993: -1.0%	1994: 25.0%
Debt	1993: $1.29bn	1994: $1.30bn
Def exp	1993ε: fr 13.7bn ($31m)	
Def bdgt	1994ε: fr 13.9bn ($30m)	
	1995ε: fr 14.1bn ($29m)	
$1 = fr	1993: 283	1994: 555
	1995: 485	

fr = CFA franc

Population: 4,164,400

	13–17	18–22	23–32
Men:	235,600	188,800	281,800
Women:	245,400	203,400	310,600

TOTAL ARMED FORCES:
ACTIVE: some 6,950.
Terms of service: conscription, 2 years (selective).

ARMY: 6,500.
2 inf regt: 1 with 1 mech bn, 1 mot bn; 1 with 2 armd
   sqn, 3 inf coy; spt units (trg).
1 Presidential Guard regt: 2 bn (1 cdo), 2 coy.
1 para cdo regt: 3 coy.
1 spt regt: 1 fd arty bty; 2 AD arty bty; 1 log/tpt/engr bn.
EQPT:
MBT: 2 T-54/-55.
LT TK: 9 *Scorpion.*
RECCE: 6 M-8, 3 M-20, 10 AML (3 -60, 7 -90), 36
EE-9 *Cascavel*, 2 VBL.
APC: 4 M-3A1 half-track, 30 UR-416.
TOWED ARTY: 105mm: 4 HM-2.
MORS: 82mm: 20 M-43.
RCL: 57mm: 5 ZIS-2; **75mm:** 12 Ch Type-52/-56;
82mm: 10 Ch Type-65.
AD GUNS: 14.5mm: 38 ZPU-4; **37mm:** 5 M-39.

NAVY: ε200 (incl Marine Infantry unit).
BASE: Lomé.
PATROL AND COASTAL COMBATANTS: 2:
PATROL, INSHORE: 2 *Kara* (Fr *Esterel*) PFI⟨.

AIR FORCE: †250; 16 cbt ac, no armed hel.
COIN/TRG: 5 *Alpha Jet*, 4 CM-170, 4 EMB-326G, 3
TB-30.

TPT: 2 *Baron*, 2 DHC-5D, 1 Do-27, 1 F-28-1000
(VIP), 1 Boeing 707 (VIP), 2 Reims-Cessna 337.
HEL: 1 AS-332, 2 SA-315, 1 SA-319, 1 SA-330.

FORCES ABROAD:
UN AND PEACEKEEPING:
HAITI (UNMIH): 20 civ pol. **WESTERN SAHARA**
(MINURSO): 9 civ pol.

PARAMILITARY:
GENDARMERIE (Ministry of Interior): 750; 1
trg school, 2 regional sections, 1 mobile sqn.

UGANDA

GDP	1993: U sh 4,105bn ($3.44bn):	
	per capita $1,300	
	1994: U sh 4,310bn ($3.68bn):	
	per capita $1,400	
Growth	1993: 6.5%	1994: 5.0%
Inflation	1993: 6.2%	1994: 11.6%
Debt	1993: $3.06bn	1994: $3.28bn
Def exp	1993: U sh 65bn ($54m)	
Def bdgt	1994ε: U sh 62bn ($53m)	
	1995ε: U sh 87bn ($94m)	
FMA[a]	1994: $0.1m (IMET)	
	1995: $0.2m (IMET)	
	1996: $0.2m (IMET)	
$1 = U sh	1993: 1,195	1994: 979
	1995: 926	

U sh = Ugandan shilling

[a] Excl demob costs. Since 1992 ε$45m has been committed by
the World Bank.

Population: 19,156,000

	13–17	18–22	23–32
Men	1,122,000	916,400	1,322,200
Women	1,106,400	951,000	1,501,800

TOTAL ARMED FORCES:
ACTIVE: ε50,000 (incl ε400 Marines, 800 Air Wing).

NATIONAL RESISTANCE ARMY (NRA):
4 'div' (closer to weak bde).
EQPT:†
MBT: 20 T-54/-55.
LT TK: 20 PT-76.
APC: 20 BTR-60, 4 OT-64 SKOT.
TOWED ARTY: 76mm: 60 M-1942; **122mm:** 20 M-1938.
MRL: 122mm: BM-21; **240mm:** BM-24.

MOR: 81mm: L 16; **82mm:** M-43; **120mm:** Soltam.
ATGW: 40 AT-3 *Sagger*.
AD GUNS: 14.5mm: ZPU-1/-2/-4; **23mm:** 20 ZU-23;
37mm: 20 M-1939.
SAM: 10 SA-7.
AVN: 4 cbt ac†, 5 armed hel.
FGA: 4 MiG-17F.†
TRG: 3 L-39, 5 SF-260.
ATTACK HEL: 5 AB-412.
TPT HEL: 3 Bell 206, 2 Bell 412, 1 Bell 212.
TPT/LIAISON HEL: 2 AS-202 *Bravo*, 1-L100, 1
Gulfstream II.

PARAMILITARY:
BORDER DEFENCE UNIT: ε600: small arms.
POLICE AIR WING: ac: 1 DHC-2, 1 DHC-4, 1
DHC-6; **hel:** 2 Bell 206, 4 Bell 212.
MARINES: (ε400).
8 riverine patrol craft⟨, plus boats.

OPPOSITION:
LORDS RESISTANCE ARMY: ε1,000 (ε400
in Uganda, remainder in Sudan).

ZAIRE

GDP	1993: NZ n.k. ($6.47bn):		
	per capita $500		
	1994: NZ n.k. ($6.16bn):		
	per capita $450		
Growth	1993: -8.2%	1994: -7.4%	
Inflation	1993: 1,890%	1994: 23,769%	
Debt	1993: $11.28bn	1994: $11.79bn	
Def exp	1993: NZ 1,258m ($417m)		
Def bdgt	1994ε: NZ 140bn ($117m)		
	1995ε: NZ 595bn ($112m)		
$1 = NZ[a]	1993: 2.51	1994: 1,194	
	1995: 5,330		

NZ = new zaire

[a] Estimates of the value of the zaire are unreliable due to its rapid
devaluation since 1990. The new zaire, equal to 3m old zaires,
was introduced in October 1993.

Population: 43,436,000

	13–17	18–22	23–32
Men:	2,493,400	2,009,000	2,993,800
Women:	2,478,200	2,009,000	3,020,200

TOTAL ARMED FORCES:
ACTIVE: 49,100 (incl Gendarmerie).

ARMY: 25,000.
8 Military Regions.
1 inf div (3 inf bde).
1 Presidential Guard div.
1 para bde (3 para, 1 spt bn) (2nd forming).
1 SF (cdo/COIN) bde.
1 indep armd bde.
2 indep inf bde (each 3 inf bn, 1 spt bn).
EQPT:
MBT: 20 Ch Type-59, some 40 Ch Type-62.
RECCE:† 60 AML (30 -60, 30 -90).
APC: 12 M-113, 12 YW-531, 60 *Panhard* M-3.
TOWED ARTY: 75mm: 30 M-116 pack; **85mm:** 20
Type 56; **122mm:** 20 M-1938/D-30, 15 Type 60;
130mm: 8 Type 59.
MRL: 107mm: 20 Type 63; **122mm:** 10 BM-21.
MOR: 81mm; 107mm: M-30; **120mm:** 50 *Brandt*.
RCL: 57mm: M-18; **75mm:** M-20; **106mm:** M-40A1.
AD GUNS: 14.5mm: ZPU-4; **37mm:** 40 M-1939/
Type 63; **40mm:** L/60.
SAM: SA-7.

NAVY:† ε1,300 (incl 600 Marines).
BASES: Banana (coast), Boma, Matadi, Kinshasa
(all river), Kalémié (Lake Tanganyika – 4 boats).
PATROL AND COASTAL COMBATANTS: 4:
PATROL, INSHORE: 2 Ch *Shanghai* II PFI, about 2
Swiftships⟨, plus about 6 armed boats.

MARINES: (600).

AIR FORCE: 1,800; 22 cbt ac, no armed hel.
FGA/FTR: 1 sqn with 7 *Mirage* 5M, 1 -5DM.
COIN: 1 sqn with 8 MB-326 GB, 6 -K.
TPT: 1 wg with 1 Boeing 707-382, 1 BN-2, 8 C-47, 5
C-130H, 3 DHC-5.
HEL: 1 sqn with 1 AS-332, 4 SA-319, 4 SA-330.
LIAISON: 6 Cessna 310R, 2 Mu-2J (VIP).
TRG: ac: 12 Cessna 150, 3 Cessna 310, 9 SF-260C;
hel: 6 Bell 47.

PARAMILITARY:
GENDARMERIE: 21,000 (to be 27,000); 40 bn.
CIVIL GUARD: 10,000; some *Fahd* APC.

ZAMBIA

GDP	1993: K 1,440.7bn ($3.80bn):	
	per capita $600	
	1994: K 1,804.0bn ($3.61bn):	
	per capita $550	
Growth	1993: 1.0%	1994: -7.4%

Inflation   1993: 189.0%   1994: 35.2%
Debt   1993: $6.79bn   1994: $6.99bn
Def exp   1993: K 25.30bn ($58m)
Def bdgt   1994: K 30.98bn ($38m)
             1995: K 37.39bn ($45m)
FMA   1994: $0.1m (IMET)
             1995: $0.1m (IMET)
             1996: $0.2m (IMET)
$1 = K   1993: 435   1994ε: 825
             1995: 825

K = kwacha

Population: 9,072,200

	13–17	18–22	23–32
Men	534,000	436,000	644,000
Women	527,200	443,600	687,000

TOTAL ARMED FORCES:
ACTIVE: 21,600.

ARMY: 20,000 (incl 3,000 reserves).
3 bde HQ.
1 arty regt.
9 inf bn (3 reserve).
1 engr bn.
1 armd regt (incl 1 armd recce bn).
EQPT:
MBT: 10 T-54/-55, 20 Ch Type-59.
LT TK: 30 PT-76.
RECCE: 88 BRDM-1/-2.
APC: 13 BTR-60.
TOWED ARTY: 76mm: 35 M-1942; **105mm:** 18 Model 56 pack; **122mm:** 25 D-30; **130mm:** 18 M-46.
MRL: 122mm: 50 BM-21.
MOR: 81mm: 55; **82mm:** 24; **120mm:** 14.
ATGW: AT-3 *Sagger*.
RCL: 57mm: 12 M-18; **75mm:** M-20; **84mm:** *Carl Gustav*.
AD GUNS: 20mm: 50 M-55 triple; **37mm:** 40 M-1939; **57mm:** 55 S-60; **85mm:** 16 KS-12.
SAM: SA-7.

AiR FORCE: 1,600; 59† cbt ac, some armed hel.
FGA: 1 sqn with 12 Ch J-6 (MiG-19)†.
FTR: 1 sqn with 12 MiG-21 MF†.
COIN/TRG: 12 *Galeb* G-2, 15 MB-326GB, 8 SF-260MZ.
TPT: 1 sqn with 4 An-26, 4 C-47, 3 DHC-4, 4 DHC-5D.
VIP: 1 fleet with 1 HS-748, 3 Yak-40.
LIAISON: 7 Do-28, 2 Y-12.
TRG: 2-F5T, 2 MiG-21U†.
HEL: 1 sqn with 4 AB-205A, 5 AB-212, 12 Mi-8.
LIAISON HEL: 12 AB-47G.

MSL:
ASM: AT-3 *Sagger*.
SAM: 1 bn; 3 bty: SA-3 *Goa*.

FORCES ABROAD:
UN AND PEACEKEEPING:
ANGOLA (UNAVEM III): 10 Obs plus 10 civ pol.
RWANDA (UNAMIR): 850 incl 20 Obs plus 10 civ pol.

PARAMILITARY:
POLICE MOBILE UNIT (PMU): 700; 1 bn of 4 coy.
POLICE PARAMILITARY UNIT (PPMU): 700; 1 bn of 3 coy.

ZIMBABWE

GDP   1993: $Z 35.1bn ($5.4bn):
            per capita $1,900
            1994: $Z 44.0bn ($5.5bn):
            per capita $2,000
Growth   1993: -2.6%   1994: 5.2%
Inflation   1993: 27.6%   1994: 22.2%
Debt   1993: $4.17bn   1994: $4.37bn
Def exp[a] 1993: $Z 1,326m ($204m)
            1994: $Z 1,532m ($193m)
Def bdgt   1995: $Z 2,013m ($238m)
FMA   1994: $0.2m (IMET)
            1995: $0.3m (IMET)
            1996: $0.3m (IMET)
$1 = $Z   1993: 6.50   1994: 8.15
            1995: 8.46

$Z = Zimbabwe dollar

[a] Excl supplementary allocations approved in late FY1994.

Population: 11,105,000

	13–17	18–22	23–32
Men	668,400	550,600	876,400
Women	666,200	551,600	881,200

TOTAL ARMED FORCES:
ACTIVE: 45,000.

ARMY: 41,000.
7 bde HQ (incl 1 Presidential Guard).
1 armd car, 1 tk sqn.
26 inf bn (incl 3 guard, 1 mech, 2 cdo, 2 para).
1 fd arty regt.
1 AD regt.
1 engr regt.
EQPT:

MBT: 40 incl Ch T-59, Ch T-69.
RECCE: 80 EE-9 *Cascavel* (**90mm** gun), 20 *Eland* 60/-90.
APC: 30 YW-531, UR-416, 75 *Crocodile*.
TOWED ARTY: 20: **122mm:** Ch Type-60, Ch Type-54.
MRL: **107mm:** 16 Ch Type-63; **122mm:** 60 RM-70.
MOR: **81mm/82mm** 140; **120mm:** 6 M-43.
RCL: **107mm:** 16 B-12.
AD GUNS: 110 incl **14.5mm:** ZPU-1/-2/-4; **23mm:** ZU-23; **37mm:** M-1939.
SAM: 30 SA-7.

AIR FORCE: 4,000; 52 cbt ac, no armed hel.
Annual flying hours: 100.
FGA/COIN: 2 sqn:
1 with 12 *Hunters* (10 FGA-90: 1 -F80: 1 T-81).
1 with 6 *Hawk* Mk 60 and 5 *Hawk* Mk 60A.
FTR: 1 sqn with 14 Ch J-7 (MiG-21).

COIN/RECCE: 1 sqn with 15 Reims-Cessna 337 *Lynx*.
TRG/RECCE/LIAISON: 1 sqn with 13 SF-260C/W *Genet*, 5 SF-260TP.
TPT: 1 sqn with 6 BN-2, 11 C-212-200 (1 VIP), 10 C-47.
HEL: 1 sqn with 2 AB-205, 7 SA-316, 10 AB-412, 1 AS-332 (VIP).

FORCES ABROAD:
UN AND PEACEKEEPING:
ANGOLA (UNAVEM II): 24 incl 3 Obs plus 17 civ pol. **RWANDA** (UNAMIR): 24 Obs.

PARAMILITARY:
ZIMBABWE REPUBLIC POLICE FORCE:
19,500 (incl Air Wing).
POLICE SUPPORT UNIT: 2,300.
PEOPLE'S MILITIA: 1,000.

2

_____

TABLES AND ANALYSES

International Comparisons of Defence Expenditure and Military Manpower in 1985, 1993 and 1994[a]

Country	$m (1993 constant prices)			$ per capita (1993 constant prices)			% of GDP			Numbers in armed forces (000)		Estimated reservists (000)	Para-military (000)
	1985	1993	1994	1985	1993	1994	1985	1993	1994	1985	1994	1994	1994
NATO													
Belgium	5,409	3,805	3,843	549	379	382	3.0	1.8	1.7	91.6	63.0	228.8	n.a.
Denmark	2,747	2,701	2,667	537	523	513	2.2	2.0	1.9	29.6	27.0	70.0	n.a.
France	42,918	42,898	42,724	778	750	739	4.0	3.4	3.3	464.3	409.6	339.4	91.8
Germany	46,330	36,654	34,848	610	460	428	3.2	2.1	2.0	478.0	367.3	442.7	24.7
Greece	3,060	4,074	4,224	308	402	406	7.0	5.6	5.7	201.5	159.3	406.0	30.5
Italy	22,576	24,400	20,632	395	398	357	2.3	2.1	2.1	385.1	322.3	584.0	256.3
Luxembourg	84	117	120	229	307	301	0.9	1.1	1.2	0.7	0.8	n.a.	0.6
Netherlands	7,814	7,070	6,901	540	464	450	3.1	2.5	2.1	105.5	70.9	130.6	3.6
Norway	2,719	3,320	3,333	655	778	771	3.1	3.1	3.1	37.0	33.5	282.0	0.7
Portugal	1,610	2,360	2,221	157	225	225	3.1	2.6	2.6	73.0	50.7	210.0	49.8
Spain	9,900	7,870	7,416	256	199	187	2.4	1.7	1.6	320.0	206.5	498.0	72.6
Turkey	3,016	7,073	5,242	60	119	86	4.5	4.0	3.2	630.0	503.8	952.3	71.1
United Kingdom	41,891	35,100	33,861	741	606	583	5.2	3.7	3.4	327.1	254.3	376.2	n.a.
Total NATO Europe:	190,074	177,442	168,031	415	401	388	3.1	2.5	2.4	3,143.4	2,469.0	4,520.0	601.8
Canada	10,284	10,267	9,242	405	375	329	2.2	1.9	1.7	83.0	78.1	37.2	6.0
US	339,229	297,300	278,730	1,418	1,156	1,074	6.5	4.7	4.3	2,151.6	1,650.5	2,048.0	106.1
Total NATO:	539,587	485,008	456,002	477	446	427	3.3	2.6	2.5	5,378.0	4,197.6	6,605.2	713.9
Russia	n.a.	107,900	106,927	n.a.	729	718	n.a.	9.3	9.6	n.a.	1,714.0	2,400.0	280.0
USSR	317,000	n.a.	n.a.	1,144	n.a.	n.a.	16.1	n.a.	n.a.	5,300.0	n.a.	n.a.	n.a.
Other Europe													
Albania	248	37	41	84	11	12	5.3	3.4	2.7	40.4	73.0	155.0	13.5
Armenia	n.a.	62	69	n.a.	18	18	n.a.	2.8	3.1	n.a.	32.7	300.0	1.0
Austria	1,696	1,797	1,818	225	231	228	1.2	1.0	0.9	54.7	51.3	119.0	n.a.
Azerbaijan	n.a.	305	245	n.a.	41	33	n.a.	8.0	8.7	n.a.	56.0	560.0	40.0
Belarus	n.a.	661	479	n.a.	63	46	n.a.	2.4	2.2	n.a.	92.5	289.5	8.0
Bosnia	n.a.	875	878	n.a.	206	204	n.a.	58.3	69.2	n.a.	110.0	100.0	n.a.
Bulgaria	7,632	317	274	852	36	33	14.1	2.9	2.5	148.5	101.9	303.0	34.0
Croatia	n.a.	975	1,089	n.a.	205	229	n.a.	9.2	10.2	n.a.	105.0	190.0	45.0
Cyprus	114	492	359	172	684	495	3.6	7.8	5.4	10.0	10.0	88.0	4.0

Czech Republic	n.a.	801	908	n.a.	78	88	n.a.	2.6	2.6	n.a.	92.9	240.0	11.4
Czechoslovakia	6,372	n.a.	n.a.	411	49	51	4.7	n.a.	n.a.	203.3	n.a.	n.a.	3.0
Estonia	n.a.	77	80	n.a.	339	377	n.a.	3.9	3.8	n.a.	2.5	6.0	4.4
Finland	1,974	1,707	1,919	402	14	15	2.8	2.0	2.0	36.50	31.2	700.0	7.5
FYROM	n.a.	30	32	n.a.	25	23	n.a.	1.9	2.2	n.a.	10.4	100.0	5.0
Georgia	n.a.	137	133	n.a.	70	63	n.a.	2.3	2.4	n.a.	10.2	250.0	2.3
Hungary	4,970	723	645	467	163	172	7.2	2.0	1.6	106.00	74.5	195.0	n.a.
Ireland	420	572	607	118	36	40	1.8	1.2	1.2	13.70	13.0	16.2	4.3
Latvia	n.a.	95	105	n.a.	35	37	n.a.	3.5	3.8	n.a.	2.6	18.0	4.0
Lithuania	n.a.	130	137	n.a.	65	73	n.a.	3.8	3.9	n.a.	8.9	12.0	n.a.
Malta	21	24	27	59	7	8	1.4	0.9	1.0	0.8	1.9	n.a.	3.4
Moldova	n.a.	32	38	n.a.	57	57	n.a.	2.7	3.8	n.a.	11.1	100.0	23.4
Poland	7,567	2,200	2,197	203	24	57	8.1	2.6	2.5	319.0	283.6	465.5	72.1
Romania	1,833	554	743	81	49	33	4.5	2.2	2.9	189.5	230.5	427.0	4.0
Slovakia	n.a.	266	301	n.a.	104	56	4.7	2.4	2.5	n.a.	47.0	122.0	9.5
Slovenia	n.a.	205	283	160	606	142	3.8	1.6	2.1	n.a.	8.1	70.0	35.6
Sweden	4,194	5,259	4,818	502	572	549	3.3	2.8	2.5	65.7	64.0	729.0	n.a.
Switzerland	2,536	3,893	4,082	393	16	579	2.1	1.7	1.6	20.0	29.8	625.0	66.0
Ukraine	n.a.	824	868	n.a.	266	17	n.a.	1.5	2.1	n.a.	517.0	1,000.0	n.a.
FY/Serbia/Montenegro	4,390	2,800	2,927	190	275	275	3.8	22.8	23.1	241.0	126.5	400.0	n.a.
Total Other Europe:	43,968	25,850	26,104	270	145	141	4.5	5.7	6.1	1,449.1	2,198.1	7,580.2	401.4
Middle East													
Algeria	1,252	1,360	1,249	57	50	44	1.7	2.9	2.7	170.0	121.7	150.0	41.2
Bahrain	198	251	246	476	475	439	3.5	5.5	5.5	2.8	8.1	n.a.	9.3
Egypt	3,394	2,477	2,641	70	45	47	7.2	5.7	5.9	445.0	440.0	254.0	374.0
Iran	18,689	1,977	2,237	419	34	37	36.0	3.4	3.8	305.0	513.0	350.0	45.0
Iraq	16,909	2,600	2,628	1,064	141	132	25.9	14.4	14.6	520.0	382.0	650.0	24.8
Israel	6,638	6,197	6,543	1,568	1,211	1,230	21.2	9.5	9.5	142.0	172.0	430.0	6.1
Jordan	791	439	422	226	97	96	15.9	7.8	7.1	70.3	98.6	35.0	10.0
Kuwait	2,360	3,110	3,009	1,380	2,032	2,019	9.1	13.1	12.2	12.0	16.6	23.7	5.0
Lebanon	263	275	301	99	71	75	9.0	4.4	4.4	17.4	44.3	n.a.	13.0
Libya	1,774	967	1,062	471	190	210	6.2	3.3	3.7	73.0	70.0	40.0	n.a.
Mauritania	68	36	35	40	17	16	6.5	2.8	2.7	8.5	15.7	n.a.	5.0
Morocco	842	1,086	1,197	38	40	44	5.4	4.0	4.3	149.0	195.5	150.0	42.0
Oman	2,834	1,920	1,854	1,771	951	991	20.8	16.7	15.9	2.5	42.9	n.a.	4.0
Qatar	394	330	294	1,251	685	559	6.0	4.3	3.8	6.0	10.1	n.a.	n.a.
Saudi Arabia	23,603	16,473	13,917	2,045	1,339	1,109	19.6	13.2	11.2	62.5	158.0	n.a.	15.5
Syria	4,577	2,383	2,358	436	172	168	16.4	8.9	8.6	402.5	408.0	400.0	8.0
Tunisia	548	231	219	77	27	25	5.0	1.6	1.4	35.1	35.5	n.a.	23.0
UAE	2,685	2,110	2,055	1,954	1,241	1,149	7.6	5.9	5.7	43.0	61.5	n.a.	n.a.
Yemen	643	356	401	64	27	29	8.9	4.6	5.2	64.1	66.0	85.0	75.0
Total Middle East:	88,462	44,478	42,670	711	465	443	12.2	6.9	6.7	2,530.7	2,859.5	2,567.7	700.9

| Country | Defence Expenditure | | | | | | | | | Numbers in armed forces (000) | | Estimated reservists (000) | Para-military (000) |
| | $m (1993 constant prices) | | | $ per capita (1993 constant prices) | | | % of GDP | | | | | | |
	1985	1993	1994	1985	1993	1994	1985	1993	1994	1985	1994	1994	1994
Central Asia													
Afghanistan	377	n.a.	n.a.	21	n.a.	n.a.	8.7	n.a.	n.a.	47.0	n.a.	n.a.	n.a.
Bangladesh	329	461	463	3	3	4	1.4	1.9	1.8	91.3	115.5	n.a.	55.0
India	8,230	7,142	7,321	11	8	8	3.0	2.8	2.8	1,260.0	1,265.0	1,305.0	906.7
Kazakhstan	n.a.	429	404	n.a.	43	25	n.a.	2.4	3.5	n.a.	40.0	n.a.	34.50
Kyrgyzstan	n.a.	51	48	n.a.	11	11	n.a.	1.5	1.4	n.a.	12.0	n.a.	n.a.
Myanmar (Burma)	640	403	415	17	31	9	7.0	3.1	3.1	186.0	286.0	n.a.	85.3
Nepal	47	41	41	3	2	2	1.5	1.2	1.1	25.0	35.0	n.a.	28.0
Pakistan	2,728	3,337	3,426	28	27	27	6.9	7.0	6.9	482.8	587.0	313.0	277.0
Sri Lanka	300	498	504	19	28	28	3.8	4.8	4.7	21.6	126.0	10.7	70.2
Tajikistan	n.a.	126	66	n.a.	22	11	n.a.	5.0	4.0	n.a.	3.0	n.a.	6.0
Turkmenistan	n.a.	74	63	n.a.	19	16	n.a.	1.2	1.1	n.a.	28.0	n.a.	n.a.
Uzbekistan	n.a.	344	317	n.a.	16	14	n.a.	2.5	2.4	n.a.	45.0	n.a.	8.0
Total Central Asia:	12,650	12,905	13,080	15	14	13	4.6	2.8	2.7	2,113.7	2,542.5	1,628.7	1,470.7
East Asia and Australasia													
Australia	7,155	7,448	7,275	454	417	401	3.4	2.6	2.3	70.4	61.6	29.4	n.a.
Brunei	269	212	233	1,203	756	806	6.0	4.3	4.5	4.1	4.4	0.7	4.1
Cambodia	n.a.	64	59	n.a.	7	6	n.a.	3.3	2.3	35.0	88.5	n.a.	220.0
China	26,083	27,390	27,680	25	23	23	7.9	5.4	5.6	3,900.0	2,930.0	1,200.0	1,200.0
Fiji	18	32	27	26	42	35	1.2	1.9	1.5	2.7	3.9	5.0	n.a.
Indonesia	3,076	2,031	2,256	19	11	11	2.8	1.4	1.4	278.1	276.0	400.0	174.0
Japan	28,240	41,732	44,600	234	334	356	1.0	1.0	1.0	243.0	237.7	47.9	12.0
Korea, North	5,461	5,305	5,412	268	233	234	23.0	25.5	26.6	838.0	1,128.0	540.0	115.0
Korea, South	8,268	11,994	13,153	201	273	294	5.1	3.6	3.6	598.0	633.0	4,500.0	4.5
Laos	72	105	111	20	23	23	7.8	7.9	7.9	53.7	37.0	n.a.	n.a.
Malaysia	2,318	2,642	2,652	149	137	135	5.6	4.1	3.9	110.0	114.5	58.3	25.8
Mongolia	45	10	17	23	4	8	9.0	1.7	2.8	33.0	21.3	140.0	10.0
New Zealand	849	651	529	261	187	151	2.9	1.5	1.1	12.4	10.0	7.9	n.a.
Papua New Guinea	47	87	53	13	21	12	1.5	1.7	1.1	3.2	3.8	n.a.	n.a.
Philippines	623	749	855	11	11	13	1.4	1.4	1.4	114.8	106.5	131.0	40.5
Singapore	1,561	2,442	2,982	610	780	1,043	6.7	4.4	4.8	55.0	54.0	262.0	11.6
Taiwan	8,461	11,939	11,065	436	572	524	7.0	5.5	5.0	444.0	425.0	1,657.5	26.7
Thailand	2,462	3,118	3,313	48	54	56	5.0	2.6	2.6	235.3	256.0	200.0	161.5
Vietnam	3,154	720	837	51	10	12	19.4	4.1	5.7	1,027.0	572.0	3,000.0	50.0
Total East Asia and Australasia:	98,163	118,672	123,108	231	205	218	6.9	4.4	4.5	8,057.7	6,963.2	12,179.2	2,055.7

Caribbean													
Antigua and Barbuda	n.k.	3	3	n.k.	51	49	n.k.	0.8	0.8	n.k.	0.1	0.1	n.a.
Barbados	16	13	13	64	51	51	1.0	0.8	0.8	1.0	0.6	0.4	n.a.
Bahamas	48	18	17	194	68	63	1.4	0.6	0.5	0.5	2.6	n.a.	n.a.
Cuba	2,098	426	292	208	39	27	9.6	3.7	2.7	161.5	106.0	135.0	19.0
Dominican Republic	67	108	112	10	15	15	1.1	1.0	1.1	22.2	24.5	n.a.	15.0
Haiti	41	33	34	7	5	5	1.5	2.0	2.2	6.9	7.3	n.a.	n.a.
Jamaica	26	21	27	11	9	11	0.9	0.7	0.9	2.1	3.3	0.9	0.2
Trinidad and Tobago	96	79	81	81	62	63	1.4	1.4	1.4	2.1	2.6	n.a.	4.8
Central America													
Belize	5	10	11	32	49	51	1.8	1.9	1.9	0.6	1.0	0.7	n.a.
Costa Rica	38	34	36	15	11	11	0.7	0.4	0.5	n.a.	n.a.	n.a.	7.5
El Salvador	331	121	152	69	22	27	4.4	1.7	1.9	41.7	30.7	n.a.	5.9
Guatemala	259	123	129	33	12	13	1.8	1.1	1.1	31.7	44.2	35.0	12.5
Honduras	95	50	42	22	9	7	2.1	1.5	1.3	16.6	16.8	60.0	5.5
Mexico	1,631	1,617	1,694	21	18	18	0.7	0.7	0.7	129.1	175.0	300.0	14.0
Nicaragua	837	38	38	256	9	9	14.2	2.0	2.0	62.9	15.2	150.0	n.a.
Panama	118	83	85	58	33	33	2.0	1.2	1.2	12.0	0.7	n.a.	11.0
Latin America													
Argentina	4,758	3,026	3,262	156	91	97	3.8	1.7	1.7	108.0	69.8	377.0	31.2
Bolivia	167	126	127	26	16	16	2.0	1.5	1.4	27.6	33.5	n.a.	30.6
Brazil	3,088	6,270	6,551	23	39	40	0.8	1.6	1.6	276.0	336.8	1,115.0	385.6
Chile	1,632	1,764	1,906	135	128	137	7.8	3.4	3.5	101.0	93.0	50.0	31.0
Colombia	557	1,232	1,178	20	36	34	1.6	2.5	2.3	66.2	146.4	60.7	79.0
Ecuador	373	498	589	40	45	53	1.8	2.8	3.2	42.5	57.5	100.0	0.4
Guyana	26	6	6	75	8	8	9.7	1.4	1.4	6.6	1.7	n.a.	1.5
Paraguay	79	74	81	21	16	17	1.3	1.4	1.4	14.4	16.5	45.0	8.0
Peru	842	770	730	45	33	31	4.5	2.1	1.8	128.0	115.0	188.0	62.6
Suriname	11	11	13	15	23	27	2.4	2.3	2.8	2.0	1.8	n.a.	n.a.
Uruguay	223	256	289	56	81	91	2.5	2.2	2.5	31.9	25.6	n.a.	1.2
Venezuela	1,083	1,029	925	63	49	43	1.3	1.7	1.6	49.0	79.0	8.0	23.0
Total Caribbean, Central and Latin America:	18,546	17,839	18,423	65	37	37	3.1	1.7	1.7	1,344.1	1,407.2	2,625.8	749.5

Country	Defence Expenditure									Numbers in armed forces (000)		Estimated reservists (000)	Para-military (000)
	$m (1993 constant prices)			$ per capita (1993 constant prices)			% of GDP						
	1985	1993	1994	1985	1993	1994	1985	1993	1994	1985	1994	1994	1994
Sub-Saharan Africa													
Horn of Africa													
Djibouti	42	28	25	124	50	42	7.9	6.8	6.2	3.0	8.4	n.a.	4.2
Eritrea	n.a.	38	38	n.a.	12	13	n.a.	6.2	6.0	n.a.	70.0	n.a.	n.a.
Ethiopia	587	119	106	14	2	2	17.9	2.9	2.6	217.0	120.0	n.a.	n.a.
Somali Republic	60	n.k.	n.k.	11	n.k.	n.k.	6.2	n.k.	n.k.	62.7	n.a.	n.a.	n.a.
Sudan	494	305	298	37	11	11	3.2	3.9	3.5	56.6	118.5	n.a.	15.0
Central Africa													
Burundi	46	26	31	10	4	5	3.0	2.6	3.0	5.2	10.5	n.a.	2.0
Cameroon	209	89	115	21	7	9	1.4	1.1	1.4	7.3	14.6	n.a.	9.0
Cape Verde	5	3	3	15	8	8	0.9	0.8	0.9	7.7	1.1	n.a.	0.5
Central African Republic	23	27	24	9	8	7	1.4	2.4	2.0	2.3	2.7	n.a.	2.3
Chad	49	32	30	10	5	5	2.9	2.9	2.6	12.2	25.4	n.a.	9.5
Congo	74	59	47	39	23	18	1.9	2.1	1.7	8.7	10.0	n.a.	6.7
Equatorial Guinea	4	3	2	11	6	5	2.0	1.7	1.4	2.2	1.3	n.a.	0.3
Gabon	104	129	118	104	105	93	1.8	2.4	2.3	2.4	3.2	n.a.	4.8
Rwanda	43	113	113	7	14	15	1.9	7.1	7.7	5.2	5.0	n.a.	1.2
Zaire	106	417	114	3	10	3	0.9	6.5	1.9	48.0	28.1	n.a.	31.0
East Africa													
Kenya	336	179	180	17	7	6	3.1	2.2	2.2	13.7	24.2	n.a.	5.0
Madagascar	71	222	28	7	17	2	2.0	6.6	0.8	21.1	21.0	n.a.	7.5
Mauritius	3	10	11	24	8	10	1.7	0.4	0.4	1.0	1.3	n.a.	n.a.
Seychelles	11	9	10	162	132	142	2.1	2.7	2.9	1.2	0.8	n.a.	1.0
Tanzania	184	90	103	8	3	4	4.4	3.2	3.5	40.4	49.6	85.0	1.4
Uganda	70	54	87	5	3	5	1.8	1.6	2.4	20.0	50.0	n.a.	0.5
West Africa													
Benin	28	26	25	7	5	5	1.1	1.6	1.5	4.5	4.8	n.a.	2.5
Burkina Faso	45	61	42	6	6	4	1.1	2.4	1.6	4.0	5.8	n.a.	4.5
Côte d'Ivoire	100	98	68	10	7	5	0.8	1.1	0.8	13.2	8.4	12.0	7.8
Gambia	3	13	13	4	14	13	1.5	3.7	3.7	0.5	0.8	n.a.	n.a.
Ghana	83	76	80	7	5	5	1.0	1.0	0.9	15.1	6.9	n.a.	5.8
Guinea	68	43	42	11	7	7	1.8	1.3	1.2	9.9	9.7	n.a.	9.6
Guinea-Bissau	14	9	8	16	8	8	5.7	3.7	3.3	8.6	7.3	n.a.	2.0
Liberia	37	35	34	17	12	14	2.4	2.6	2.5	6.8	5.0	n.a.	n.a.

Mali	39	42	64	5	5	7	1.4	2.0	3.0	4.9	7.4	n.a.	7.8
Niger	16	21	20	2	2	2	0.5	0.9	0.9	2.2	5.3	n.a.	5.4
Nigeria	1,644	1,157	1,139	5	13	10	1.0	3.1	3.1	94.0	76.5	n.a.	12.0
Senegal	83	94	88	13	12	11	1.1	2.4	2.2	10.1	13.4	n.a.	4.0
Sierra Leone	7	19	35	2	4	8	1.0	2.7	4.4	3.1	6.2	n.a.	0.8
Togo	25	31	30	8	8	7	1.3	3.2	2.7	3.6	7.0	n.a.	0.8

South Africa

Angola	850	780	501	172	71	46	22.5	13.7	8.7	49.5	82.0	n.a.	40.0
Botswana	49	136	131	45	100	93	1.1	4.9	4.6	4.0	7.5	n.a.	1.0
Lesotho	60	19	18	39	10	9	4.6	3.7	3.2	2.0	2.0	n.a.	n.a.
Malawi	28	21	20	4	2	2	1.0	1.2	1.1	5.3	10.4	10.0	1.5
Mozambique	314	118	102	23	7	6	22.5	8.3	7.1	15.8	2.0	n.a.	n.a.
Namibia	n.a.	50	49	n.a.	25	31	n.a.	2.3	2.2	n.a.	8.1	n.a.	n.a.
South Africa	3,774	3,911	3,893	113	101	94	2.7	3.3	3.3	106.4	78.5	360.0	110.0
Zambia	53	58	37	8	6	4	1.1	1.5	1.0	16.2	24.0	n.a.	1.4
Zimbabwe	223	204	191	27	19	17	3.1	3.8	3.5	41.0	46.9	n.a.	22.8

Total Sub-Saharan Africa:	10,062	8,971	8,111	28	21	19	3.5	3.3	2.8	958.5	991.6	467.0	341.6

Summary Totals

NATO	539,587	485,008	456,002	477	446	427	3.3	2.6	2.5	5,378.0	4,197.6	6,605.2	713.9
Russia	n.a.	107,900	106,927	n.a.	729	718	n.a.	9.3	9.6	n.a.	1,714.0	2,400.0	280.0
USSR	317,000	n.a.	n.a.	1,144	n.a.	n.a.	16.1	n.a.	n.a.	5,300.0	n.a.	n.a.	n.a.
Europe	43,968	25,850	26,104	270	145	141	4.5	5.7	6.1	1,449.1	2,198.1	7,580.2	401.4
Middle East	88,462	44,478	42,670	711	465	443	12.2	6.9	6.7	2,530.7	2,859.5	2,567.7	700.9
Central Asia	12,650	12,905	13,080	15	14	13	4.6	2.8	2.7	2,113.7	2,542.5	1,628.7	1,470.7
East Asia and Australasia	98,163	118,672	123,108	231	205	218	6.9	4.4	4.5	8,057.7	6,963.2	12,179.2	2,055.7
Caribbean, Central and Latin America	18,546	17,839	18,423	65	37	37	3.1	1.7	1.7	1,344.1	1,407.2	2,625.8	749.5
Sub-Saharan Africa	10,062	8,971	8,111	28	21	19	3.5	3.3	2.8	958.5	991.6	467.0	341.6

Global Totals:	1,128,437	821,622	794,425	232	148	141	4.8	2.8	2.6	27,131.8	22,873.7	36,053.8	6,713.7

Notes:

[a] See *The Military Balance 1994–1995*, pp. 278–281 for an explanation of the IISS methodology for defence expenditure calculations.

China's Military Expenditure

(The general problems of estimating and interpreting defence-economics data are discussed in *The Military Balance 1994–1995*, pp. 278–81.)

Introduction

Few analysts outside the People's Republic of China (PRC) consider the official Chinese defence budget to be a true measure of China's military spending. The uncertainty arises because the Chinese government does not disclose how its defence budget is constituted beyond aggregate figures for recurrent and capital spending – which gives little away. Consistent with this lack of transparency, China does not report its military expenditures to the UN in the standardised format. Such secretive behaviour prompted US Defense Secretary William Perry in 1994 to urge the Chinese to improve the transparency of their military accounting. The absence of reliable information has resulted in widely disparate estimates of China's military spending ranging from $20–140 billion.

The IISS estimates that Chinese military expenditure was over $28bn in 1994 – nearly four times the official figure. The following analysis examines the evidence supporting this conclusion: the enormity of China's Armed Forces and paramilitary and their increasing modernisation since 1989; the strength of the economy and its implications in terms of both the domestic purchasing power of the defence budget and the availability of extra hard currency for foreign equipment and technology; and the falsification in military accounting whereby military-related expenditure is listed under non-defence headings in the central-government budget, and extra-budgetary revenue raised for military application by the regions and the People's Liberation Army (PLA) is not registered at all.

A credibility problem arises primarily because of evidence of a shift in China's intentions and, more obviously, its growing military capability. Although the military doctrine of active defence provides little distinct indication of expansionist intentions, the shift beginning in 1979 from the Maoist concept of a 'people's war' to that of 'local war' confirms some new thinking. The former envisaged the final defeat of the enemy on Chinese soil after a global nuclear war, and in principle involved the tactical yielding of Chinese territory to draw the enemy into defeat. In contrast, the 'local war' doctrine abandons the concept of global war and instead envisages 'localised' conflict through which political objectives can be achieved without nuclear escalation. It might apply, for example, in the case of a conflict with Taiwan or Vietnam over the Spratly Islands. As a consequence of the new doctrine, rapid-reaction forces were formed and equipment modernisation became a top priority.

If the growth in China's military capability were not so demonstrable, the significance of the change in military doctrine could be exaggerated. That growing capability is also a function of an increasingly powerful nuclear capability that aims for global reach, and a massive conventional force, approximately twice the size of any other nation's force. The sheer size of the armed forces (over 4 million including the paramilitary People's Armed Police (PAP)) renders official military accounting implausible. A simple calculation shows that per capita spending amounts to less than $2,000, compared to over $40,000 for Russia and about $160,000 for the US. The PLA ground forces alone number over 2 million and are structured into three distinct parts. About 500,000 troops are selected for the best-equipped and trained units, which include at least six rapid-deployment formations – the so-called 'fist' units. The second tier comprises supporting combat, training and logistic units, while the balance comprises the service organisations engaged in agriculture, construction and, increasingly, commercial activities. According to some estimates, the PLA owns, administers and sometimes mans some 25,000 enterprises, distinct from the defence industries that produce PLA weaponry and technical equipment under the management of state ministries and are manned by a civilian work-force of 3–3.5 million.

Increased momentum in the modernisation of weapon systems and military equipment also warrants scepticism about the official defence budget. As far back as 1979, the Deng Xiaoping regime identified defence as the fourth pillar of the 'Four Modernisations' programme, and this policy was reaffirmed in 1985. But China's defence spending remained static during most of the 1980s, and it was not until the 1989 Tiananmen Square crisis that the modernisation effort gained momentum. Shortly after, the 1990–91 Gulf War provided further impetus, for the Chinese, like others, could not afford to ignore the startling evidence about the nature of modern warfare. That a renewed modernisation effort is under way is evident both from the purely indigenous R&D and procurement programmes and the increasing numbers of programmes involving international industrial cooperation (facilitated by the relaxation of post-Tiananmen sanctions). A range of substantial industrial cooperation programmes, with Russian and Israeli suppliers, for example, are currently in progress. In the nuclear field, China continues to be the only nuclear state in addition to France still testing nuclear devices and rejecting a ban on the production of fissile material.

New development programmes – the more visible elements of the modernisation process – are said to include: a new generation of strategic weapons for launch from mobile ground (DF31, DF-41) and submarine (JL-2) platforms; a new class of SSBN (Type 094); the indigenous fighter J-10 (reportedly based on the defunct Israeli *Lavi*) and the FC-1 fighter joint venture with Pakistan and Russia; the *Luhu*-class destroyer of which series production started in 1994; and the Type-90 main battle tank. To claim, as the Chinese do, that the sizeable increases in the defence budget do no more than compensate for inflation is hardly credible, for modernisation programme funding remains unexplained. It is plausible that technological modernisation is being partly funded by defence budget increases and masked by non-defence funds.

A second method for estimating the value of Chinese military expenditure is to measure the real purchasing power of the defence budget. The official exchange rate fails to capture the real purchasing power of the yuan in a largely autarkic defence economy and, coastal regions apart, in a national economy little influenced by world prices for capital, labour, goods and services. The intrinsic strength of the Chinese economy is better reflected in purchasing-power-parity (PPP) estimates of gross domestic product (GDP). The International Monetary Fund (IMF) GDP estimates for 1991 (which cite various analysts) ranged from $1.3–3.4bn, or 3–9 times the figure of $379bn calculated using the official exchange rate. Using the IMF's own PPP estimate, annual defence expenditure was between $23bn and $32bn from 1990–1995, while the World Bank estimates expenditure at $37–52bn (Table 1). Despite the substantial differences, these estimates yield a more credible value for the Chinese defence budget than an official exchange-rate conversion predicts. They also show the real increase in the defence budget over the period and bolster the argument that the increase is the result of modernisation costs rather than inflation.

Table 1:   Purchasing-power-parity Estimates of the Official Chinese Defence Budget

Year	(yuan bn)	($bn)	% Military/ expenditure/ GDP	($bn) IMF PPP	($bn) World Bank PPP
(official exchange rate)				(constant 1993$)	
1990	29.0	6.1	1.6	27.2	44.0
1991	33.3	6.2	1.6	28.9	46.8
1992	37.8	6.8	1.6	32.7	53.1
1993	43.2	7.4	1.4	34.5	56.2
1994	55.1	6.3	1.5	36.3	59.7
1995	63.1	7.5	1.4	38.7	62.8

A third reason to doubt official defence budget figures is the concealment of military expenditure. Evidence of hidden military expenditure in other central, regional and local government budgets, and the extra-budgetary funds generated from the PLA's industrial and commercial activities, support this proposition. These are the *prima-facie* grounds for the charge that China is not revealing the extent of its military spending.

Budgetary falsification takes two forms: military expenditure not included in the central government's defence budget; and operation of the 'three-thirds' principle, whereby responsibility for raising revenue is shared by the three entities of central government, regional and local government, and PLA units and enterprises. The central government budget provides the primary indication of military funding outside the defence budget. The government includes the defence budget under the heading, 'Building up National Strength', which may be one way of acknowledging that the defence budget does not cover all military spending.

Table 2: The 1995 Chinese Defence Budget and Expenditures for Building Up National Strength

Budget Heading (current market exchange rates)	yuan (bn)	$ (bn)
Central Regular Budget:	76.7	9.1
Administrative Expenses	1.3	0.2
National Defence	62.8	7.4
Central Construction Budget	73.2	8.7
National Defence	0.29	0.034
Total Expenditures for Building Up National Strength:	149.9	17.8
Administrative Expenses	49.9	5.9
National Defence	63.1	7.5

The 1995 Budget for Building up National Strength totals yuan 149.9bn, $17.8bn at the official exchange rates (Table 2). The total budget figure is divided according to two overlapping budgetary classifications: activity or departmental function; and regular or construction expenditure. In 1995, the total budget for Building up National Strength includes yuan 63.1bn for 'National Defence' and yuan 49.9bn for 'Administrative Expenses'. The central budget is subdivided into the 'regular' and 'construction' budget. Thus, the defence budget appears as an aggregate under the National Defence heading (but is not attributed to any single ministry or organisation), and then disaggregated as a line item in the central regular budget and the central construction budget. The central regular budget covers the range of operating expenditure whilst the central construction budget accounts for government procurement and capital investment programmes in industry and the infrastructure.

Two important conclusions can be drawn from the structure of the central government budget. First, there is a real possibility that some, if not most, of the Budget for Building Up National Strength is devoted to military spending. The Chinese appear to have copied this practice from the Soviet Union which used to conceal military-related expenditure as 'Appropriations for Financing the Development of the National Economy'. Second, the very small defence allocation contained in the central construction budget (yuan 290m or $34m) is implausible, and signifies that a large part of the procurement budget may be hidden under the heading, Building Up National Strength.

Regarding the distribution of defence funds, analysts have concluded that the defence budget may cover primarily operational expenses across the range of the PLA's activities and interests. This included a share of manpower costs and procurement of quartermaster stores, equipment and ordnance from the PLA-administered factories, but it excludes procurement of weapons systems and supporting equipment. It may also include a share of the funding for the PLA's Commission on Science, Technology and Industry for National Defence (COSTIND). The PLA's civilian manpower costs may be accounted as Administrative Expenses under the Building Up National Strength heading. Consequently, it also seems plausible that a large part, if not all, of indigenous procurement – research and development (R&D), weapons and associated programmes, and infrastructure – is funded from the capital construction budget for Building up National Strength, with more funds going to COSTIND via this route. Since analysts have reported that the individual defence industries receive direct funding from the State Council, the construction budget may also fund military-related activities of the State Commission for Science and Technology (CAST), and of the main civilian ministries responsible for the defence industry.

It is not clear how the Chinese military account for arms purchases from foreign suppliers. Analysts tend to see these as another major expenditure item that lies outside the defence budget. Although the Chinese seek to trade on barter terms whenever possible, they have been forced to spend hard currency on foreign weaponry and technology (typically from Russia and Israel in recent years). These outlays appear greater than the proceeds from Chinese arms-sales exports (especially in the light of their decline since the end of the Iran–Iraq War), though some analysts argue that they are funded by accumulated proceeds of past sales. Even if this applied in the past, it is probable that arms purchases now require financing through an extra-budgetary account.

Funding for paramilitary organisations, like the PAP, is another military expenditure that does not appear in the defence budget. The budgets of the PAP and other paramilitary forces, such as the Customs Service and the maritime sections of the Public Security Ministry and Border Security Force, are probably listed in the regular budget of Building up National Strength and attributed to the Ministries of Public Security and State Security. The regions also play a role in funding the PLA and the paramilitary; central government allocations for the military subsume some military funds transferred to and administered by the regions. But it also appears that the regions are partly responsible for funding the PAP, as well as regional PLA regular units, reserves and part-time standing militias.

The second form of budgetary falsification is achieved through the three-thirds principle whereby the PLA has official sanction to raise revenue. Since 1979, central government revenue as a proportion of GDP has dropped from 31.6% to an estimated 16.2% in 1994, while defence as a proportion of central government spending declined from 17% to 9%. In the meantime, real GDP has grown threefold, so that government revenue has actually increased by half. The high rate of GDP growth has also provided greater commercial opportunities to the PLA. The value of the PLA's own subsistence and revenue-earning activity is difficult to calculate and subject to considerable speculation. Although some argue that it corrupts rather than contributes to the Chinese military effort (and, in any case, should be excluded from calculations of real military expenditure), the evidence suggests that the PLA is formally responsible for raising revenue to cover a part of its operating expenditure, and that consequently, these funds should be included in the calculation of military expenditure.

PLA revenues are derived from two types of activity. First, PLA units together with the reserves and militia engage in farming and food production. The scale of these activities are such that the PLA claimed a production surplus valued at yuan 700m in 1993 which could be sold commercially after military needs had been met. Second, the PLA runs factories and service organisations to meet its own supply requirements for construction and military equipment (excluding weapons systems produced by the civilian-administered defence industries). These activities are also claimed to generate profits for the PLA. Various sources confirm both the proliferation of PLA commercial enterprises and the extent of their diversification into non-military interests. The sum total of value-added activity performed by the PLA in pursuit of its military needs and commercial interests is difficult to quantify. Some analysts claim that the PLA's annual turnover for military and commercial activity is as large as the total National Defence budget, while one press report claims that PLA revenue was in the order of yuan 30bn ($3.6bn) in 1992. In evaluating the military implications of PLA enterprises (and, hence, whether they should be considered in calculations of military expenditure), a distinction should be made between those that promote military needs and those that do not, and between profit-making activities and those effectively subsidised by the defence budget.

A 1994 study of the Chinese defence budget by the Stockholm International Peace Research Institute (SIPRI) attempts to disaggregate the components of Chinese military revenue and expenditure (Table 3). SIPRI estimates the Chinese military revenue base for 1993 (as distinct from the defence budget) at \$45bn and net military spending at \$36bn, providing evidence of disaggregated expenditures included in and excluded from the official budget.

Table 3:   SIPRI Estimates of Chinese Military Revenue in 1993

1993	$bn
Central government	
Official military budget	7.3
PAP budget	3.0
State direct allocations to military industries	14.3
State direct military R&D allocations	5.0
Subtotal	**(29.6)**
Local/regional government	
Local contributions for regional forces	2.5
Pensions and demobilisation contributions	2.0
Militia levies	1.5
Subtotal	**(6.0)**
Military industries and enterprises	
International arms sales revenue	1.5
Military enterprise commercial revenue	5.0
Regional unit agricultural/associated production	2.5
Subtotal	**(9.0)**
Total	**44.6**

US Arms Control and Disarmament Agency (ACDA) estimates show an even higher level of dollar expenditure for 1993 (\$56bn) than SIPRI. ACDA's estimate for the defence share of gross national product (GNP) in 1993 (2.7%) is nearly double Chinese government estimates (about 1.5%). The variance between SIPRI and ACDA figures may be attributable to differing assumptions about purchasing-power parity, as the SIPRI analysis does not use the PPP estimates. ACDA comments on the exceptional difficulties of estimating yuan costs and converting them to dollars, and cautions that comparative studies of Chinese military spending are subject to a wide margin of error.

The IISS estimate of Chinese military expenditure in 1994 (\$28.5bn) is nearly four times the Chinese defence budget converted at the official rate (Table 4). The IISS estimation method incorporates the three approaches already described: estimating relative (international) cost inputs to the budget (mainly manpower and equipment); estimating the domestic purchasing power of the defence budget; and estimating other military funding contained in central government non-defence accounts and PLA extra-budgetary accounts. The IISS method combines a 'top-down' and 'bottom-up' costing method. The latter involves the calculation of the costs of Chinese military inputs (salaries, operations, R&D, procurement, infrastructure, pensions, etc.), which are derived from equivalent NATO costs and take differences in quality into consideration. These are then converted at IISS-calculated PPP rates. The top-down method supplements the official defence budget with conservative estimates of other funding, including the budget for Building Up National Strength and the PLA's own revenue, and then applies the same PPP conversion rates. The two independently calculated estimates are then reconciled into a final estimate. It should be noted that these estimates are sensitive to the choice of PPP measure, and that there is no consensus among economists on a single PPP yuan/\$ rate. Consequently, using the estimates of either the IMF or World Bank will alter the IISS estimates by a factor of up to 2 – making them compatible with those of SIPRI and ACDA. The IISS has selected a lower PPP measure because estimates derived from costing defence inputs, particularly those applicable to R&D and procurement, are difficult to reconcile with spending levels calculated with higher PPP estimates. In addition, the IISS estimate takes into account that some 5–10% of Chinese military expenditure requires hard-currency funding, to which market exchange rates, and not the higher PPP values, are applicable.

Table 4:   IISS Estimate of China's Military Expenditure in 1994 ($bn)

	$bn	% of defence budget
Manpower	6.3	22
Procurement, of which	6.8	24
Domestic	(5.3)	
External	(1.5)	
R&D	3.0	11
Operations	11.4	40
Infrastructure/other	1.0	4
Total	**28.5**	**100**

Although the Chinese government still maintains that all Chinese military expenditure is accounted in the defence budget and that its level is stable, if not actually in decline, there is a consensus among independent analysts outside China on two counts: Chinese military expenditure is much higher than revealed by the Chinese defence budget; and its military expenditure has increased sharply in real terms since 1989, allowing for inflation. The increase is largely attributable to greater spending on salaries, operations and equipment modernisation. Moreover, the rate of Chinese economic growth continues at such high levels that it would be imprudent to assume that a plateau in military spending has been reached.

Developments in the Field of Weapons of Mass Destruction

The first six months of 1995 were successful in the field of nuclear arms control. The US–Russian Strategic Arms Reductions Talks (START) Treaty came into force, the Nuclear Non-Proliferation Treaty (NPT) was extended indefinitely and the negotiations on a Comprehensive Test Ban Treaty (CTBT) made progress. However, China has continued to test nuclear weapons and France announced a plan to resume testing from September 1995. These and other developments in the control or proliferation of nuclear, chemical and biological weapons and of ballistic missiles are reviewed in this section. Changes in national nuclear and missile forces are reflected in the relevant national entry and are highlighted in the text preceding the relevant regional section.

START I

On 16 November 1994, the Ukrainian Verkhovna Rada (parliament) adopted the law on Ukraine's accession to the NPT. It added a number of reservations mainly concerning compensation for the cost of dismantling weapons and the provision of assurances by the nuclear-weapon states. However, these did not affect Ukraine's unconditional accession to the NPT as a non-nuclear state. The final hurdle was cleared at Budapest on 5 December, where the Conference, now Organisation, on Security and Cooperation in Europe (OSCE) summit was being held, when US President Bill Clinton, Russian President Boris Yeltsin and UK Prime Minister John Major signed an assurance document and President Leonid Kuchma of Ukraine signed the instruments of NPT ratification. With this the START I Treaty came into effect, allowing verification of weapons elimination to be implemented and clearing the way for the ratification of START II, signed by Russia and the US in January 1993. START I requires each side to reduce their strategic forces to no more than 1,600 delivery vehicles armed with no more than 6,000 warheads. Information was released by all states on their holdings of deployed strategic nuclear weapons as at 5 December 1994.

Holdings of Deployed Strategic Nuclear Weapons as at 5 December 1994

	ICBM	SLBM	Bombers	Countable Warheads
US	959	528	351	9,824
Russia	773	728	95	6,914
Kazakhstan	69	–	–	690
Belarus	36	–	–	36
Ukraine	176	–	46	1,592

These figures are somewhat misleading as they refer to all weapons countable under START rules, whether operational or not. For example, 156 of the US bombers were located at the Davis Monthan elimination site and many of the ICBM have had their warheads and other components removed. Counting rules have been interpreted differently. The high number of US ICBM is accounted for by the US-held interpretation that a silo launcher must be considered to contain an ICBM, whether or not a missile is actually deployed at that site, until the silo is destroyed. START I rules that data regarding deployed nuclear forces may not be released to the public for three months after notification. Memorandum of Understanding data is to be fully updated every six months, with the next data as of 5 June 1995 but not releasable until 5 September 1995, too late for inclusion in this edition of *The Military Balance*. *The Military Balance* has received some information on current deployment and operational status which is shown in the relevant country entry, but this must not be confused with Treaty-countable weapons.

START II

The START II Treaty signed by US President George Bush and President Yeltsin on 3 January 1993 has not yet been ratified. The Treaty has been presented to the Russian Duma for ratification and the US Senate began formal hearings on ratification on 31 January 1995. START II requires the US and Russia to have reduced their strategic warheads to between 3,000 and 3,500 by 2003. The Treaty bans ICBM with multiple independently targetable re-entry vehicles (MIRV) and limits SLBM to 1,750 for each side. Counting rules for air-delivered warheads have been altered; bombers will be attributed as having the number of warheads they are equipped to carry.

Nuclear Non-Proliferation Treaty

The NPT was extended indefinitely at the 25-year Extension Conference by consensus on 11 May 1995. Indefinite extension had been opposed by a number of states, mainly Arab, led by Egypt because Israel would not join the Treaty. Israel's position on the NPT is that it will not join until it has achieved peace treaties with all the Arab states; then it will support the establishment of a weapons of mass destruction (WMD) free zone in the Middle East. While the NPT was extended without condition, a number of principles and objectives were adopted. However, these are not legally binding documents. Their main purpose is to allow pressure to be brought to bear on the nuclear-armed states in respect of their commitment to nuclear disarmament. The documents are:

- 'Strengthening the Review Process for the Treaty'.
- 'Principles and Objectives for Nuclear Non-Proliferation and Disarmament'. This stressed the importance of achieving a CTBT no later than 1996 (and pending its entry into force advocated that the nuclear-armed states should exercise utmost restraint); a ban on the production of fissile material for nuclear weapons or other explosive use; the determined pursuit of nuclear disarmament.
- The third document was a resolution, proposed by Russia, the US and the UK, which called for the early accession of all states to the NPT and for Middle Eastern states to establish a Middle East zone free of nuclear, chemical and biological weapons and their delivery systems.

Since June 1994, the following states, most importantly Ukraine (allowing the START I Treaty to enter into force), have acceded to the NPT: Algeria, Argentina, Bosnia-Herzegovina, Chile, Eritrea, the Former Yugoslav Republic of Macedonia (FYROM), Kyrgyzstan, the Marshall Islands, Micronesia, Moldova, Monaco, Palau, Tajikistan and Turkmenistan. Only 13 countries have not joined the NPT: the undeclared nuclear-weapon states of India, Israel and Pakistan, and Andorra, Angola, Brazil, Comoros, Cuba, Djibouti, Oman, Serbia/Montenegro, the UAE and Vanuatu.

Nuclear Test Moratorium

Until the NPT was extended indefinitely, only China of the five recognised nuclear-weapon states had no nuclear-testing moratorium. President Mikhail Gorbachev ended Soviet nuclear tests for one year from 5 October 1991. After this was extended to July 1993, the Russian Foreign Minister said that 'Russia would not be the first to end the moratorium, but to expect any nuclear power to refrain from testing if others resumed would be unreasonable'. France announced a moratorium in April 1992 to last until the end of the year. Former President François Mitterrand then made clear that there would be no more French tests during his presidency, which ended in May 1995. President Clinton extended the Bush administration's US moratorium, instigated in October 1992, for a further year to September 1995. The US moratorium precludes UK testing.

The Chinese have continued testing and have carried out three tests since June 1994. The first, in October 1994, had an estimated yield of 60 kilotonnes. The second, China's 42nd test, came on 15 May 1995, only days after the successful end to the NPT Review Conference. Initial assessments put the yield of the explosion between 40 and 150 kilotonnes. The third took place on 17 August, measured 5.6 on the Richter Scale and is estimated to have had a yield of between 20 and 80 kilotons. Since then an official Chinese spokesman has said that a schedule of further tests is planned, but that China would stop as soon as any test ban treaty came into force. Immediately after the French presidential election in May 1995, the new President, Jacques Chirac, announced that France intended to carry out a series of eight tests at the Mururoa Pacific test site between September 1995 and May 1996. The reasons given for the tests were to collect data to allow France to switch to simulated testing in future and to validate the warhead for the new M-5 SLBM. US Secretary of Defense William Perry also advocated the resumption of US tests, but this was opposed by the US Department of Energy (which is responsible for manufacturing US nuclear weapons) and the Arms Control and Disarmament Agency (ACDA). The US administration has now made it clear that testing will not be resumed. However, if the US had not extended its moratorium there would have been some opportunity until 30 September 1996 when the Energy and Water Development Appropriations Act of 1992 stipulates that no further US tests are to take place unless another state conducts a test after this date. The Act allows a total of five safety-related and one reliability-related test per year. One of the safety-related tests can be carried out by the UK.

Comprehensive Test Ban Treaty

The Nuclear Test Ban (NTB) Committee of the Conference for Disarmament closed its first session for 1994 on 7 April 1995. The second session opened on 1 June and closed on 6 July after progress was made on several contentious issues. The UK and France have withdrawn their proposal to authorise exceptions for safety tests. The US has dropped its demand that the CTBT should only be in force for ten years. China is still pressing for the Treaty to ban a nuclear weapons test which releases nuclear energy; such wording would allow peaceful use of nuclear explosions, but ban what are called hydronuclear tests. Hydronuclear experiments (HNE) are a research technique in which explosions release nuclear energy and small amounts of fission products. The US has opted for a comprehensive ban, but using explosions with the yield of 4lbs as the equivalent of zero. However, the Pentagon is keen to hold tests with a force equivalent to 500 tons of explosive and, having lost the chance to perform these tests before the CTBT comes into force, may argue for the Treaty to allow all such tests. The UK is reported to have conducted safety tests below the 4lbs level, but would prefer a higher limit (100lbs). Russia wants at least 10 tons while France, claiming that it does not have the ability to acquire the information needed at such low thresholds, argues for 200–300 tons. The non-nuclear states of the NTB Committee were originally ready to accept very low-yield hydronuclear tests in order to obtain a timely treaty. This view has now changed, partly as a result of a better understanding of what hydronuclear tests can achieve, partly for fear that the nuclear states are looking for a much higher test threshold, and because of their condemnation of the Chinese nuclear test and French test plans so soon after the NPT extension. They are now pushing for a fully comprehensive ban with no loopholes.

Issues still to be settled include the role of the International Data Centre. Should it purely assemble data, or should it also be responsible for interpretation, which the US believes should be a national responsibility? Agreement has not yet been reached on rules for triggering on-site inspections, nor on whether the International Atomic Energy Agency (IAEA) or another new organisation should be the implementing authority. There are also unresolved issues concerning verification (both the permanent seismic monitoring network, and action to be taken after a suspicious event), on the conditions for bringing the treaty into force, and for allowing states to withdraw.

Fissionable Material Production Ban

In January 1994, the UN Conference for Disarmament (CD) appointed Ambassador Gerald Shannon of Canada as special coordinator for a fissile material cut-off. The CD voted unanimously on 23 March 1995 to establish a committee to negotiate an international and verifiable treaty banning the production of fissile material (plutonium and highly enriched uranium (HEU)) for nuclear weapons. But the establishment of the Committee has been held up as some nations would prefer to establish a Committee on Nuclear Disarmament instead, a proposal strongly resisted by the nuclear-weapon states. The US stopped producing fissile materials for weapons in 1992 and in 1994 signed an agreement with Russia committing them to halting plutonium production and closing plutonium production reactors. Verifying a treaty would probably be the responsibility of the IAEA. A criticism of the proposed treaty is that it makes no provision for the control or destruction of weapons-grade material stockpiles. Progress is already being made in this respect, with the US and Russia agreeing to allow inspection of each other's storage sites for dismantled weapons material, the US agreement to purchase 500 tons of Russian HEU once it had been converted to low-enriched uranium (LEU), and President Clinton's announcement that the US would withdraw 200 tons of plutonium and HEU from the weapons stockpile. The plan for the US to purchase Russian HEU has run into difficulties and so far only one token consignment of the equivalent of under one ton has reached the US. The Russian Atomic Energy Minister, Viktor Mikhailov, has even threatened to cancel the agreement unless the US position changes. However, the main problems, which appear to be over-pricing and the lack of agreement between the US Enrichment Corporation, which would be marketing Russian LEU once it reaches the US, and the Russian Ministry of Atomic Energy, were resolved at the time of US Vice-President Al Gore's meeting with Russian Prime Minister Viktor Chernomyrdin in Moscow in June 1995.

Nuclear-Weapon-Free Zones

On 15 September 1994, the Arab League Council reaffirmed its previous resolution (of 27 March 1994) and called upon its member-states and the General Secretariat to pursue contacts at all levels to make the Middle East a region free of all weapons of mass destruction. The call for a Middle East zone free of WMD was reinforced by the resolution proposed by Russia, the US and the UK and adopted at the NPT review conference. The UN General Assembly voted for a resolution sponsored by Pakistan and Bangladesh to reaffirm its support for the concept of a nuclear-weapon-free zone in South Asia. Only Bhutan, India and Mauritius voted against the resolution and there were ten abstentions. On 25 March 1995, Cuba, in the presence of the Foreign Minister of Mexico, the depository government, signed the Treaty for the Prohibition of Nuclear Weapons in Latin America and the Caribbean (the Treaty of Tlatelolco), but as yet has not deposited its instrument of ratification. Cuba was the last regional state to sign the Treaty.

On 2 June 1995, the Organisation of African Unity (OAU) unanimously adopted the draft of a treaty establishing a nuclear-weapons-free zone in Africa. The draft was submitted to the United Nations on 26 June where it is expected to be approved by the General Assembly.

North Korea

The US and North Korea held negotiations in Geneva between 23 September and 21 October 1994 and signed an Agreed Framework. The key points were that North Korea would:

- not reprocess nor separate plutonium;
- not restart its 5MW reactor;
- freeze construction of two other reactors;
- close and seal its radiochemistry laboratory (considered to be a separation plant) and subject it to IAEA inspections.

The spent fuel rods unloaded from the 5MW reactor in June 1994 were to remain stored in the cooling pond until arrangements for its disposal outside North Korea had been arranged. In return, the US committed itself to:

- organise an international consortium to finance and supply light-water reactors with an approximate generating capacity of 2,000MW by 2003;
- conclude a bilateral agreement for cooperation in the field of peaceful uses of nuclear energy;
- provide alternative energy in the form of 500,000 tons of heavy oil annually.

Both sides agreed to work for a nuclear-weapon-free Korean peninsula and to strengthen the international nuclear non-proliferation regime. When a significant portion of the light-water reactor is completed, but before nuclear components are delivered, North Korea will come into full compliance with IAEA safeguards and allow inspections at facilities not covered by the agreed freeze. North Korea sent an official letter on 2 November 1994 notifying the US that specific action to freeze its nuclear activities had begun.

The Agreed Framework soon ran into trouble when North Korea refused to accept light-water reactors designed, built and installed by South Korea. The US was equally adamant, as South Korea was mainly financing the project, that South Korean reactors must be accepted. Three weeks of meetings were held in Kuala Lumpur in May and June 1995 and on 13 June a joint statement was released by US Deputy Assistant Secretary, Thomas Hubbard, and North Korean Vice-President, Kim Gye Gwan, agreeing that the Korean Peninsula Energy Development Organisation (KEDO) would finance and choose the reactor. Hubbard told the press that North Korea understood that a South Korean reactor would be chosen and that the prime contractor would also be South Korean.

Chemical Weapons

By 1 June 1995, only 29 of the 159 signatory states had ratified the Chemical Weapons Convention (CWC) leaving 32 states still to sign. The earliest the CWC could have come into force was two years after it was opened for signature on 13 January 1993. It now needs a further 36 ratifications before coming into force. The Australia Group, an informal forum of states which abide by an agreed set of export controls, now has 28 members and the Czech Republic, Poland and Slovakia attended their first meeting in Paris on 29 November 1994. Little progress has been made either by Russia or the US in the destruction of their large CW stocks. Destruction of US CW agents continued at the Johnston Atoll facility, but the second facility to be developed at Tooele, Utah, has been found to have numerous flaws. There is growing opposition to CW incineration from local populations close to destruction plants. The first major terrorist use of CW took place in Tokyo on 20 March 1995 when a weak version of the nerve gas sarin was released at five separate points on the underground railway system. A religious cult, *Aum Shinrikyo*, is held responsible for the attacks and raids on their premises discovered sufficient chemicals to produce 5.6 tons of sarin. There were four gas attacks again on railway targets in Japan on 4 July 1995, two of which released cyanide gas. There have been no reports of copy-cat incidents elsewhere.

Biological Weapons

In September 1994, a special conference of the Biological Weapons Convention (BWC) states was held to consider the final report of the VEREX group (an *ad hoc* group of governmental verification experts). There was little agreement at this conference other than to establish another *ad hoc* group to consider 'appropriate measures, including possible verification measures' and to incorporate these into a legally binding protocol. BW verification is far more problematic than that for CW. Sufficient BW agent for use by saboteurs can be produced in research laboratories (which are not prohibited by CWC); BW agents must be produced before protective vaccines can be made; all equipment and materials needed for BW production are 'dual use' in that they are equally necessary for other legitimate purposes. Two sessions will be held by the new *ad hoc* group in July and in November–December 1995.

Missiles

An analysis of the current deployment of ballistic missiles across the world is set out at pp. 281–84. The composition of the Missile Technology Control Regime (MTCR), a group of nations which voluntarily impose mutually agreed export controls on missile technology and equipment, has not altered in the last 12 months. There are 25 members, and six others have agreed to adhere to the regime's criteria. The US is now satisfied that Russia is meeting its commitments and so supports its immediate membership of the MTCR. Ukraine and China are also committed to the MTCR criteria, but in May 1995 China suspended talks with the US on missile and nuclear issues in protest against the granting of a US visa to the Taiwanese President.

Missile Proliferation

Proliferation, that is to say the spread of nuclear, chemical and biological weapons and the missiles capable of delivering them, is one of the world's greatest concerns. This analysis examines the current deployment of ballistic missiles across the world and looks at the potential of those known to be under development. It also comments on the efficacy of the regimes and measures that have been used to attempt to curb missile proliferation.

Missiles are not the only way that weapons of mass destruction (WMD) can be delivered. Both the US and Russia maintain a force of strategic bombers and many NATO and Russian aircraft can be nuclear-capable. Israel, while having its own *Jericho* missiles, has often expressed the opinion that more damage can be assured by aircraft attack than by missiles (an F-15E has an 11,000kg weapons load compared to the 1,000 kg of a *Scud* SSM). At the height of the Cold War, nuclear warheads could be delivered by a wide variety of weapon systems: artillery; free-flight rockets; naval missiles and torpedoes; aircraft bombs; depth-charges; anti-aircraft missiles; and atomic demolition mines. Iraq was found to have a stockpile of chemical weapon-filled *Scud* missiles, aircraft bombs, artillery shells and multi-barrelled launcher rockets. Recently, chemical weapon (CW) agent was released on the Tokyo underground railway network.

Despite the plethora of delivery means, the ballistic missile, mainly on account of its range, speed and cost relative to that of a manned aircraft, is a favoured delivery means for proliferating states and is likely to remain so until a proven anti-ballistic missile defence system has been deployed.

Table 1: **Operational Ballistic Missiles and Free-Flight Rockets (excluding Chinese, Russian and US ICBM and all SLBM)**

Range km	Missile Designation	Payload kgs	Country of Origin	In Service with
40	*Oghab*	300	Iran	Iran
70	*FROG*-7	250	USSR	Afghanistan, Bosnian Serbs, Egypt, Libya, N. Korea, Syria, Yemen
80	*Hatf* 1	500	Pakistan	Pakistan
120	SS-21	500	USSR	Syria, Yemen
130	*Lance*	200	US	Israel
130	*Ching Feng*	400	ROC Taipei	ROC Taipei
135	ATACMS	450	US	US
150	CSS-8/M-7	190	China	China, Iran
150	*Privthi*	1,000	India	India (Army)
250	*Privthi*	500	India	India (Air Force)
280	CSS-7/M-11	800	China	China (possibly supplied to Pakistan)
300	*Scud-B*	1,000	USSR	Afghanistan, Egypt, Iran, Libya, N. Korea, UAE, Yemen,
480	*Hades*	400	France	France (in store)
500	*Scud-C*	700	North Korea	Iran, N. Korea, Syria
500	SS-23	450	USSR	–
600	CSS-6/M-9	500	China	China (Syria suspected)
650	*Jericho* 1	500	Israel	Israel
1,500	*Jericho* 2	500	Israel	Israel
2,700	CSS-2	2,500	China	China, Saudi Arabia
3,500	SSBS S-3D	1,700	France	France

Note: FROG-7 and *Scud*-B also in service with Belarus, Bulgaria*, Czech Republic*, Poland, Romania, Russia, Slovakia and Ukraine*. Those marked * also have SS-23.

Although there are a number of arms-control treaties and regimes aimed at eliminating and restricting ballistic missiles, each is limited in the effect it has on the overall problem of missile proliferation. The Strategic Arms Reduction Talks (START) Treaties at present only limit the ballistic missiles of Russia and the US and cover intercontinental ballistic missiles (ICBM) (with a range of over 5,500km) and submarine-launched ballistic missiles (SLBM) (with a range of over 600km). In May 1995, the Chinese tested a mobile missile which is reported to have a range of 8,000km. The Intermediate Nuclear Forces (INF) Treaty – which banned land-based ballistic and cruise missiles, regardless of warhead role, with ranges between 500 and 5,500km – again applied only to the US (and US dual-key missiles manned by the German Air Force) and the successor states to the Soviet Union. Shortly after the Treaty came into force it was discovered that SS-23 mobile missiles, which, if Soviet-held, would be covered by the Treaty, had been transferred earlier to several of the then Warsaw Pact countries and so were not covered by the INF. As Table 1 shows, a number of states now possess INF category missiles and the number is likely to grow. The terms of Iraq's cease-fire agreement bans Iraq from holding missiles with a range of over 150km, a requirement endorsed by UN Security Council Resolution 687 of April 1991. Perhaps surprisingly, the Syrian–Israeli 1973 armistice, while limiting men, tanks and artillery deployed 20km on either side of the cease-fire line and banning surface-to-air missiles in the zone, did not include any limitations on surface-to-surface missiles (SSM), despite Syria's use of these in the 1973 war.

The main tool to stem proliferation is supplier constraints; in the missile field this is the task of the Missile Technology Control Regime (MTCR). The MTCR is a group of 25 nations which have been invited to work together on a set of agreed self-imposed export controls. A number of other countries (Brazil, China, Israel, Romania, Russia, Slovakia, South Africa, Ukraine) which have not yet been invited to join the MTCR have committed themselves to complying with MTCR guidelines. The US has negotiated a bilateral Memorandum of Understanding with Russia (September 1993) and with Ukraine (April 1994) which formalise their commitment to the MTCR. The US also held negotiations with China which would have led to the lifting of the sanctions imposed by the US on China following China's supply of missile components to Pakistan. China withdrew from these talks as a protest at the granting of a US visa to the President of the Republic of China (Taipei).

The aim of the MTCR is to control the transfer of delivery vehicles (other than manned aircraft) capable of delivering nuclear, CW or biological weapon (BW) warheads. The guidelines cover both complete missile systems and relevant components and technology. The parameters for control are missiles capable of carrying a payload of at least 500kg to a range of 300km or more. The MTCR does not therefore ban the transfer of the Russian *Scud*-B nor, as the Chinese claim, of their M-11 SSM.

The only alternative to control is, of course, active defence measures. The US is developing a series of theatre missile defence programmes (see p. 16) and is looking to its allies to become collaborative parties.

In earlier days countries obtained their missiles from the two superpowers, although the US only provided these to NATO allies and Israel. On the other hand, the Soviet Union provided a number of Middle Eastern countries (in addition to the Warsaw Pact) with *Frog*, SS-21 and *Scud* SSM. The longest-range missiles transferred were the US *Pershing* 1A (720km) (but kept under dual-key control) and the Soviet SS-23 (500km). Neither France nor Israel, which both developed their own missiles (S-3D and *Jericho*), have transferred these to other countries. India and Pakistan are developing indigenous missile systems, primarily to deter each other, but in India's case also to counter the Chinese missile threat. Missile development and production has been abandoned by a number of countries, notably Argentina, Brazil and South Africa. There are now only two known missile-exporting countries, China and North Korea. However, China has pledged to follow the MTCR guidelines.

It is somewhat bizarre that the end of the Cold War has heightened perceptions of the missile threat, but if the threat from the former Soviet Union has receded, that from other, perhaps less deterrable, areas could result in a direct missile threat to North America and Europe. At present no missiles owned by states other than the US, Russia or China (and French and British submarine-launched missiles) can reach European or North American targets. However, that situation could change in coming years. Currently, missile proliferation directly threatens three areas: the Middle East; the Indian subcontinent; and North Korea's neighbours.

The Middle East has long faced the threat of missile attack. SSM were used in both the Iran–Iraq War and the 1991 Gulf War, and against Israel in 1973. In the first, Iraq launched 331 *Scud* and modified *Scud* SSM at Iranian cities, while Iran responded by launching 86 similar missiles plus 253 of the much shorter range (40km) *Oghab* SSM. During *Operation Desert Storm*, Iraq fired 93 missiles at targets in Saudi Arabia and Israel. Neither country responded in kind, although they could have done so: Israel with its *Jericho* series, and Saudi Arabia with its Chinese CSS-2 acquired in 1988. Iraq's *Scuds* were provided by Russia. A total of 819 missiles were delivered, of which over 300 were modified to the *al Hussein* variant with a 600km range compared to the basic *Scud*-B's 280km range, and ten were modified to the *al Abbas* (or *al-Hijara*) variant with a range of 900km. All 819 missiles have been accounted for to the UN Special Committee (UNSCOM), and all are considered to have been destroyed. Iran's SSM were originally Soviet *Scud* B provided by Syria and Libya, but the majority were North Korean versions, most probably financed by Iran and known as *Scud*-Mod B and *Scud*-C, the latter having a 600km range. Iran can now manufacture its own *Scud*-C. Since 1992 there have been persistent rumours that Iran is attempting to buy Chinese M-9 missiles and funding the North Korean *No-Dong* programme. As yet, despite other use of CW in the region, CW has not been delivered by missile.

In many cases the Middle East range is not a problem. All of Israel and Kuwait are within 300km of potential hostile launch sites. In the Gulf, 300km-range SSM sited in Iran could reach Al Jubayl and Dharhan (in Saudi Arabia), Bahrain, Qatar, Abu Dhabi, Dubai and Muscat; San'a in Yemen is within 300km of the Saudi border. Amman, Damascus, Baghdad, Kirkuk and Basra can be struck by much shorter range missiles. Other countries with short-range missiles (*Scud*, SS-21 *Frog*) are Algeria, Egypt, Libya, the UAE and Yemen.

A number of ballistic and cruise missiles are being developed by India and Pakistan. At present only the Indian Army's *Privthi* (150km range with 1,000kg payload) and Pakistan's *Hatf* 1 (80km with 500kg payload) are known to be in service. Both countries have longer-range missiles probably in the final stages of development. The Air Force version of *Privthi* has a range of 250km with a 500kg payload. India's *Agni* is reported to have a planned range of up to 2,500km with a payload greater than 1,000kg: it has been successfully test fired to 1,450km. Pakistan's *Hatf* 2 could have a 280km range with a 500kg payload. While the *Agni* would reach all parts of Pakistan, and China's strategic missile sites in Qinghai, neither *Hatf* SSM version could target Delhi, nor could the Chinese M-11. It has been suggested that Pakistan is also developing a 600km range *Hatf* 3. While China has pledged to abide by the MTCR guidelines and so cannot sell its 600km range M-6 to Pakistan which would threaten Delhi, its long-term policy over missile control is uncertain. India also has a cruise-missile programme, the *Lakshya*, but this is more likely to be a reconnaissance UAV given its small, 200kg payload. However, the technology is being developed.

Table 2:   Ballistic Missiles Under Development

Range km	Missile Designation	Payload kgs	Country of Origin	In Service with
600	*Hatf* 3	1,000	Pakistan	Iran
1,000	*No-Dong*	1,000	N. Korea	Flight-tested
2,500	*Agni*	1,000	India	Flight-tested
	Taepo-Dong		N. Korea	
	Jericho 3		Israel	

North Korea causes the world the most concern. In addition to being strongly suspected of having a nuclear-weapons programme, it is known to have tested the *No-Dong* 1 SSM at a 500km range, and on 20 February 1995 carried out another test with a missile travelling some 1,500km. South Korea also has an active arms, including missile, export policy. The *No-Dong* 1 is considered to be a further development on the *Scud* design and could have a range of more than 1,000km. Most analysts consider the *No-Dong*, estimated to have a 1,000kg payload, to be relatively inaccurate with a circular error of probability (CEP) of 2,000–4,000 metres. There has been one report, as yet unconfirmed, that North Korea has up to six *No-Dong* mobile launchers operational. More worrying are reports released by the CIA and the US Department of Defense that North Korea is developing a new series of SSM, not based on *Scud* technology. These have been named *Taepo-Dong* 1 and 2; one with a 2,000km range, and the second with a 3,500km range. Such missiles would require a much higher degree of technology than *Scud* follow-ons, particularly regarding their engines, body strength (probably requiring an aluminium alloy) and guidance systems. There are some doubts as to whether North Korea can meet all these requirements and the *Taepo-Dong* series may still be some years away.

North Korean missile advances, and plans for new Chinese missiles reported in *The Military Balance 1994–1995*, could provoke other East Asian states into developing their own missiles as a counter-threat. Japan, South Korea and Taiwan all have the technical capability to do so, and indeed South Korea and Taiwan both have short-range missiles in service and Taiwan is believed to be developing a missile (the *Tien Ma*) with a range variously reported as between 600 and 950km. Japan has only a space-launch vehicle programme which it test-fired successfully in February 1994.

What can be done to halt missile proliferation? Obviously, global treaties banning weapons are the ideal, but may be unrealistic, with some countries claiming that their national-security situation precludes joining such a regime. Failing a global ban, a regional treaty could, in the first instance, help to limit missiles (as the START Treaty limits US and Russian strategic missiles), if not to ban them (on the lines of the INF Treaty). But it will certainly be necessary to solve the underlying security problem in any region before expecting to see a weapons ban or limitation regime agreed to. Greater transparency should also be sought through mechanisms such as the UN Conventional Arms Register. Supplier controls (i.e., controls on export) at present offer the best answer to proliferation, but even these are not a foolproof guarantee against proliferation.

Strategic Nuclear Forces: Russia, Belarus, Kazakhstan, Ukraine

Category	Missile	Current Situation: 1 June 1995 (Russia, Belarus, Kazakhstan, Ukraine) Using START II counting rules			Post-START I (a possible Russian deployment) Using START I counting rules					Post-START II (one possible Russian deployment) Using START II counting rules			
		Launchers deployed	Warheads/ launchers	Total warheads	Launchers deployed	Launcher limit	Warheads/ launchers	Total warheads	Warhead limit	Launchers deployed	Warheads/ launchers	Total warheads	Warhead limit
Heavy ICBM	SS-18	222	10	2,220	154	154	10	1,540	1,540				
Mobile ICBM	SS-24	36	10	360	36		10	360					
	SS-25	354	1	354	354		1	354		700[a]	1	700	
Subtotal mobile ICBM		*390*			*390*				*1,100*	*700*			
Other ICBM	SS-17	10	4	40									
	SS-19	230	6	1,380	160		6	960		105[b]	1	105	
	SS-24	56	10	560	10		10	100					
Total ICBM		*908*		*4,914*	*714*			*3,314*		*805*		*805*	
SLBM	SS-N-8	244	1	244									
	SS-N-18	208	3	624									
	SS-N-20	120	10	1,200	120		10	1,200		120	10	1,200	
	SS-N-23	112	4	448	112		4	448		112	4	448	
Subtotal SLBM		*684*		*2,516*	*232*			*1,648*		*232*		*1,648*	*1,750*
Total Ballistic Missiles		*1,592*		*7,430*	*946*			*4,962*	*4,900*	*1,037*		*2,453*	
Bombers ALCM-equipped	Tu-95H16	57	16	912	50		8	400		40	16	640	
	Tu-95H6	33	6	198	30		8	240		20	6	120	
	Tu-160	25	12	300	25		8	200		20	12	240	
Non-ALCM	Tu-95G	24	1/2	48	20		1/2	40					
Total Bombers		*139*		*1,458*	*125*			*880*		*80*		*1,000*	
GRAND TOTAL		**1,731**		**8,888**	**1,071**			**5,842**	**6,000**	**1,117**		**3,453**	**3,500**

[a] Not all SS-25 would be mobile, maybe 50% in silos.

[b] Downloaded to single warhead.

Nuclear-Capable Delivery Vehicles: NATO, Nuclear-Armed Republics of the Former Soviet Union, and China

Many delivery systems are dual-capable; the total number in service are shown, even though a high proportion may not be assigned a nuclear role. Maximum aircraft loadings are given, although often fewer weapons may be carried. Some loadings differ from those under SALT/START counting rules. All ground-launched tactical nuclear weapons (SSM and artillery) have been withdrawn to store in Russia and the US. Delivery systems of other states are no longer listed. All sea-launched weapons (incl SLCM) other than SLBM have been withdrawn from ships, and air-delivered weapons from ships and shore-based maritime air stations in the US, Russia and NATO. All former Soviet tactical nuclear weapons have been moved to Russia. No nuclear warheads remain in Kazakhstan.

Category and type	Year deployed	Range (km)[a]	Throw- weight[b]	CEP (m)[c]	Launcher total	Munition/ warhead	Yield per warhead[d]	Remarks
UNITED STATES								
LAND-BASED								
Strategic								
ICBM								
LGM-30F	1966	11,300	8.0	370	14	Mk 11C; W-56	1.2MT	Guidance and warheads removed.
Minuteman II								
LGM-30G	1980	12,900	11.5	220	531	3 x Mk 12A MIRV; W-78	335KT	
Minuteman III	1986	11,000	39.5	100	50	10 x Mk 21 MIRV; W-87	300 or 400KT	In mod *Minuteman* silos.
LGM-118								
Peacekeeper (MX)								
SEA-BASED								
Strategic								
SLBM								
UGM-93A *Trident* C-4	1980	7,400	15	450	192	8 x Mk 4 MIRV; W-76	100KT	Installed in 8 SSBN.
UGM-133A *Trident* D-5	1989	12,000	28	90	192	8 x Mk 5 MIRV; W-76/-88	300–475KT	Installed in 8 SSBN (W-88 production halted).
Tactical[e] (all nuclear warheads withdrawn from ships/submarines)								
SLCM								
BGM-109A *Tomahawk*[g]	1983	2,500	n.k.	80	–	TLAM-N; W-80	200KT	78 submarines, 66 surface combatants have launchers (350 warheads produced).

AIR
Strategic
Long-range bombers[e]

	Year deployed	Radius of action (km)[a]	Max speed (mach)	Weapon load (000 kg)	Launcher Total	Max ordnance load[f]	Remarks
B-52G	1959	4,600	0.95	29.5	0	Internal: 12 bombs (B-61/-83) or 8 Harpoon	148 ac awaiting conversion/elimination.
B-52H	1962	6,140	0.95	29.5	93	Attributed with 20 warheads: bombs, SRAM or ALCM (8 internal, 12 external)	Plus 1 test ac.
B-1B	1986	4,580	1.25	61.0	93	Internal: 16 SRAM or 16 B-61 bombs	Plus 2 test ac. Not equipped for ALCM, and to be re-roled as conventional bbrs.
B-2A	1993	5,840	1(-)	ε18	9	Internal: 16 SRAM; or 8 SRAM plus 8 B-61/-83 bombs; or 16 bombs	Plus 6 test ac.
Tactical[e]							
Land-based							
F-111E/F	1967	1,750	2.2/2.5	13.1	95	3 bombs (B-61)	Plus 3 in store.
F-4E	1969	840	2.4	5.9	20	3 bombs (B-61)	Plus some 216 in store.
F-16	1979	550/930	2+	5.4	1,253	1 bomb (B-61)	Plus 347 in store.
Carrier-borne							
A-6E	1963	1,250	0.9	8.1	127	3 bombs (B-61)	
F/A-18	1982	850	2.2	7.7	880	2 bombs (B-61)	Incl 262 USMC.

	Year deployed	Range (km)[a]	Max speed (mach)	Missile total	Munition/warhead	Yield per warhead[d]	Remarks
ALCM							
AGM-86B[c]	1982	2,400	0.66	-	1,200	W-80	170-200KT	
AGM-129 ACM	1991	3,000	n.k.	-	300	W-80	170-200KT	Production limited to 460.
ASM							
AGM-69A (SRAM)	1972	56 (low) 220 (high-altitude)	3.5	-	1,000	W-69	170KT	

For notes, see p. 293.

BOMBS[h]

Type	Yield per warhead[d]	Weapon stockpile	Remarks
B-61 (strategic)	100–500KT(s)	900	In-flight yield selection and fusing, hard target penetration.
B-61 (tac)	1–345KT	1,525	Replaced B-28, B-53.
B-83	1–2MT	650	

Category and type	Year deployed	Range (km)[a]	CEP (m)[c]	Launcher total	Munition/warhead	Yield per warhead[d]	Remarks
NATO (excluding US)[j]							
LAND-BASED							
Intermediate-range							
IRBM							
SSBS S-3D	1980	3,500	n.k.	18	TN-61	1MT	Fr.
Short-range							
Hadès	not deployed	480	n.k.	0	AN-51	15 or 25KT	Fr 15 in store.
SEA-BASED							
Strategic							
SLBM							
Polaris A-3 TK	1967	4,600	900	32	3 x MRV; W-58 (*Chevaline*)	200KT	UK. In 2 SSBN.
M-4	1985	5,000	n.k.	80	6 x MRV; TN-70/-71	150KT	Fr. In 5 SSBN.
Trident D-5 becomes op	1994	12,000	28	16	Up to 6 MIRV	<200KT	UK. 1 SSBN; a second SSBN early 1996.

Category and type	Year deployed	Radius of action (km)[a]	Max speed (mach)	Weapon load (000 kg)	Launcher total	Max ordnance load	Remarks
AIR[e]							
Tactical							
Land-based							
F-4E/F	1967–73	840	2.4	5.9	356	1 B-61 bomb	Ge (150), Gr (52 plus 19 in store), Tu (144)
F-16	1982	930	2+	5.4	612	1 B-61 bomb	Be (133 plus 43 in store), Dk[k] (66), Gr (35 plus 3 in store), Nl (183), No[k] (59), Tu (146)
Mirage IVP	1986	930	2.2	9.3	18	1 *ASMP*	Fr.
Mirage 2000N	1988	690	2.2	6.3	72	1 *ASMP*	Fr.

For notes, see p. 293.

Category and type	Year deployed	Radius of action (km)[a]	Max speed (mach)	Weapon load (000 kg)	Launcher total	Max ordnance load	Remarks
Jaguar A	1974	850	1.1	4.75	157	1 or 2 AN-52 bombs	Fr (93) (no longer in nuclear role), UK (54 plus 16 in store).
Tornado IDS	1981	1,390	0.92	6.8	394	n.k.	Ge (192), It (70 plus 21 in store), UK (167 plus 21 in store).
Carrier-borne							
Super Etendard	1980	650	0.98	2.1	38	ASMP	Fr, plus 19 in store.
Sea Harrier	1980	460–750	0.98	2.3	20	1 (or 2) WE-177 bombs	UK, plus 15 in store.

Category and type	Year deployed	Range (km)[a]	Max speed (mach)	Weapon load (000 kg)	Launcher total	Munition/ warhead	Yield per warhead[d]	Remarks
ASM								
ASMP	1986	80 (low) 250 (high)	2	0.2	ε100		300KT	Fr.
Bombs								
AN-22	–	–	–	–	–		15, 300KT	Fr.
WE-177	–	–	–	–	–		10, 200, 400KT	UK

NUCLEAR-ARMED FORMER SOVIET REPUBLICS

Category and type	Year deployed	Range (km)[a]	Throw-weight[b]	CEP (m)[c]	Launcher total	Munition/ warhead	Yield per warhead[d]	Remarks
LAND-BASED								
Strategic								
ICBM								
SS-17 (RS-16) mod 3 Spanker	1982	10,000	25.5	400	10	4 x MIRV	500KT	Russia.

	Year deployed	Range (km)[a]	Throw-weight[b]	CEP (m)[c]	Launcher total	Munition/warhead	Yield per warhead[d]	Remarks
SS-18 (RS-20) mod 4	1982	11,000	88	250	} 222	10 x MIRV	500KT	48 Kazakhstan, 174 Russia.
Satan mod 5	–	ε9,000	88	n.k.		10 x MIRV	750KT	
SS-19 (RS-18) mod 3 *Stiletto*	1982	10,000	43.5	300	250	6 x MIRV	550KT	160 Russia, 90 Ukraine.
SS-24 (RS-22) *Scalpel*	1987–8	10,000	40.5	ε200	92	10 x MIRV	100KT	36 rail-based, Russia; 56 silo-based; 10 Russia, 46 Ukraine.
SS-25 (RS-12M) *Sickle*	1985–6	10,500	10	ε200	354	single RV	750KT	Road-mobile. 336 Russia, 18 Belarus.
Short-range[e] (All warheads located in Russia)								
SSM								
FROG-7 (*Luna*)	1965	70	–	n.k.	} some 600	–	200KT	
SS-21 (*Tochka*) *Scarab*	1978	120	–	n.k.		–	100KT	
SS-1c (R-17) *Scud-D*[e]	1965	300	–	50		–	KT range	
GLCM								
SS-C-1b *Sepal*	1962	450	–	n.k.	40	–	350KT	Coastal defence; nuclear role doubtful.
Artillery[f]								
2A36 152mm towed	1978	27.0	–	n.k.	430	–	2–5KT	
2S5 152mm SP	1980	27.0	–	n.k.	398	–	2–5KT	
D-20 152mm towed	1955	17.4	–	n.k.	293	–	2KT	
2S3 152mm SP	1972	27.0	–	n.k.	980	–	under 5KT	
2S7 203mm SP	1975	18+	–	n.k.	105	–	2–5KT	
2S4 240mm SP mor	1975	12.7	–	n.k.	9	–	n.k.	
SAM								
SH-11 mod *Galosh*	1983–4	320	–	–	36	–	n.k.	
SH-08 *Gazelle*	1984	80	–	–	64	–	10KT	
SA-10 *Grumble*[e]	1981	100	–	–	1,750	–	n.k. }	Deployed Moscow Only
SA-5 *Gammon*[e]	1967	300	–	–	500	–	n.k.	

For notes, see p. 293.

Category and type	Year deployed	Range (km)[a]	Throw-weight[b]	CEP (m)[c]	Launcher total	Munition/warhead	Yield	Remarks
SEA-BASED								
Strategic								
SLBM								
SS-N-8 Sawfly mod 1	1972	7,800	11.0	1,500	} 224	single RV	800KT	In 19 SSBN.
mod 2	1973	9,100	11.0	900		2 MRV	800KT	In 16 SSBN.
SS-N-18 mod 1	1977	6,500	16.5	1,400		3 MIRV	20KT	
Stingray mod 2	1977	8,000	16.5	900	} 208	single RV	450KT	7 warheads originally attributed: in START, counted as 3.
mod 3	1978	6,500	16.5	900		7 MIRV	100KT	
SS-N-20 Sturgeon	1981	8,300	25.5	500	120	10 MIRV	100KT	In 6 SSBN.
SS-N-23 Skiff	1985	8,300	28.0	900	112	4 MIRV	100KT	In 7 SSBN.
Tactical (all warheads withdrawn from ships/submarines)								
SLCM								
SS-N-3 Shaddock[e]	1962	450	–	n.a.	4	–	350KT	In 1 CG.
SS-N-7 Starbright[e]	1968	n.a.	–	n.a.	16	–	200KT	In 2 SSGN.
SS-N-9 Siren[e]	1968-9	100	–	n.a.	186	–	200KT	In 31 corvettes.
SS-N-12 Sandbox[e]	1973	550	–	n.a.	56	–	350KT	In 1 SSGN, 3 CG.
SS-N-19 Shipwreck[e]	1980	550	–	n.a.	380	–	500KT	In 12 SSGN, 4 CGN, 1 CVV
SS-N-21 Sampson	1987	3,000	–	150	ε128	–	200KT	In 3 SSGN, 17 SSN (ε4 per SSN).
SS-N-22 Sunburn[e]	1981	400	–	n.k.	284	–	200KT	In 1 CG 17 DDG, 29 corvettes.
SS-NX-24	–		–	n.k.	ε12	–	n.k.	In trials SSGN.
ASW								
SS-N-14 Silex[e]	1974	55	–	n.a.	226	–	1 – 5KT	In 1 CGN, 15 CG, 26 frigates.
SS-N-15 Starfish	1982	45	–	n.k.	n.k.	–	about 5KT	In 26 SSN.
Type 53-68 HWT	1970	14	–	–	n.k.	torpedo	20KT	Usable from all 533mm TT.
Type 65 HWT	1981	50	–	–	n.k.	torpedo	20KT	Usable from all 650mm TT.
Mines	n.k.	–	–	n.k.	–	–	5–20KT	–

	Year deployed	Radius of action (km)[a]	Max speed (mach)	Weapon load (000 kg)	Launcher Total	Max ordnance load	Remarks
AIR							
Strategic							
Long-range bombers							
Tu-95 *Bear A/B*		5,690	0.9	11.3	2	4 bombs/1 and 2 AS-4 ASM	Ukraine in store.
Bear G	1956	5,690	0.9	11.3	45	6 AS-15 ALCM	Russia plus 8 test ac mark n.k.
Bear H6					33	16 AS-15 ALCM	28 Russia, 5 Ukraine.
Bear H16					57	12 AS-15 ALCM	37 Russia, 20 Ukraine.
Tu-160 *Blackjack*	1988	7,300	2.3	16.3	25		6 Russia, 19 Ukraine plus 6 test ac.
Medium-range bombers[c]							
Tu-22 *Blinder*	1962	1,500	1.4	10	10	1 AS-4 ALCM, 1 bomb	10 Navy (plus 60 in store).
Tu-22M *Backfire*	1974	4,430	1.92	12	220	1–2 AS-4/-16 ALCM, 2 bombs	Incl 90 Navy (plus 30 in store).
Tactical[c]							
Land-based							
MiG-27 *Flogger D/J*	1971	390/600	1.7	4.5	50	2 bombs	
Su-24 *Fencer*	1974	320/1,130	2.3	8	570	2 bombs	Incl 70 Navy.
Maritime ASW[e]							
Tu-142 *Bear F*	1972	1,510	0.83	10	50	2 bombs	8 hrs endurance at radius of action.
Il-38 *May*	1970	1,700	0.64	7	36	ε2 bombs	8 hrs endurance at radius of action; total endurance 15 hrs
Be-12 *Mail*	1965	600	0.5	10	65	2 bombs	8 hrs endurance at radius of action; total endurance 12 hrs

	Year deployed	Range (km)[a]	Max speed (mach)	Weapon load (000 kg)	Weapon total	Yield[d]	Remarks
ALCM							
AS-4 *Kitchen*	1962	300	3.3	n.k.	n.k.	1MT	
AS-6 *Kingfish*	1977	300	3	n.k.	n.k.	350KT–1MT	
AS-15 *Kent*	1984	1,600	0.6	n.k.	n.k.	250KT	
AS-16 *Kickback*	1989	200	n.k.	n.k.	n.k.	350KT	
Bombs	n.k.	–	–	–	n.k.	Strategic: 5, 20, 50MT Tactical: 250, 350KT	
Depth-charges	n.k.	–	–	–	n.k.	–	Known to exist; no details available.

For notes, see p. 293.

	Year deployed	Range (km)[a]	CEP (m)[c]	Launcher total	Munition/ warhead	Yield per warhead[a]	Remarks
CHINA							
LAND-BASED							
Strategic							
ICBM							
CSS-4 (DF-5)	1981	15,000	n.k.	7	single RV	5MT	
CSS-3 (DF-4)	1978/9	7,000	n.k.	10	single RV	3MT	
IRBM							
CSS-2 (DF-3)	1970	2,700	n.k.	60	single RV	2MT	
CSS-5 (DF-21)	1983	1,800	n.k.	ε10	single RV	250KT	
SEA-BASED							
Strategic							
SLBM							
CSS-N-3 (JL-1)	1983/4	2,200–3,000	n.k.	12	–	ε2MT	Installed in 1 SSBN.
		Radius of action (km)[a]	Max speed (mach)	Weapon load (000kg)	Maximum ordnance load		
AIR							
Strategic[g]							
Medium-range bombers							
H-6	1968–9	2,180	0.91	9 up to 145	ε2 bombs	n.k.	incl 25 Navy.

Chinese *tactical* nuclear weapons have been reported, but no details are available.

Sources: include Cochrane, Arkin and Hoenig, *Nuclear Weapons Databook*, vol. I (Cambridge, MA: Ballinger, 1984); Cochrane, Arkin, Norris and Hoenig, *Nuclear Weapons Databook*, vol. II (Cambridge, MA: Ballinger, 1987); Hansen, *US Nuclear Weapons, The Secret History* (New York: Orion, 1988); *Bulletin of the Atomic Scientists* (various issues); Treaty between the US and USSR on the Reduction and Limitation of Strategic Offensive Arms; Norris, Burrows and Fieldhouse, *Nuclear Weapons Databook*, vol. V (Boulder, CO: Westview, 1994).

Notes:

[a] Ranges and aircraft radii of action in km: for nautical miles, multiply by 0.54. A missile's range may be reduced by up to 25% if max payload is carried. Radii of action for ac are in normal configuration, at optimum altitude, with a standard warload, without in-flight refuelling. When two values are given, the first refers to a low–low–low mission profile and the second to a high–low–high profile.

[b] Throw-weight concerns the weight of post-boost vehicle (warhead(s), guidance systems, penetration aids and decoys). No definition of the term is given in the START Treaty document. Throw-weight is expressed in terms of kg (100s).

[c] CEP (circular error of probability) = the radius of a circle around a target within which there is a 50% probability that a weapon aimed at that target will fall.

[d] Yields vary greatly: figures given are estimated maxima. KT range = under 1MT: MT range = over 1MT. Yield, shown as 1–10KT, means the yield is between these limits. Yields shown as 1 or 10KT mean that either yield can be selected.

[e] Dual-capable.

[f] Numbers cited are totals of theoretically nuclear-capable pieces. Not all will be certified for nuclear use, and in practice relatively few are likely to be in a nuclear role at any one time. All artillery pieces listed are dual-capable.

[g] It is not possible to give launcher numbers as the vertical launch system (VLS) can mount a variety of missiles in any of its tubes.

[h] All bombs have five option fusing: freefall airburst or surface burst, parachute retarded airburst or surface burst, and retarded delayed surface burst.

[i] External loads are additional to internal loads.

[j] Except for French and UK national weapons, nuclear warheads held in US custody.

[k] No nuclear warheads held on Canadian, Danish, Norwegian, Spanish or Portuguese territory.

Other Arms-Control Developments

This section provides a brief update on all arms-control developments, other than those concerning nuclear, chemical and biological weapons and ballistic missiles for the period June 1994–July 1995.

Conventional Forces in Europe (CFE) Treaty

The CFE Treaty, signed in November 1990 before the dissolution of the Warsaw Pact and the break-up of the Soviet Union, was designed to reduce weapons holdings in Europe and to limit what are now known as the North Atlantic Treaty Group and the Budapest/Tashkent Group to equal numbers of certain armaments. The Treaty came into force on 17 July 1992 and the elimination of equipment above Treaty limits is due to be completed by 17 November 1995. The extent to which elimination has taken place will become known on 19 August (90 days before the end of the reduction period) when signatories must notify their total holding of each type of treaty-limited equipment (TLE). This notification comes just too late to be included in this edition of *The Military Balance*, but data showing the position at the end of 1994 is set out on **[page xx]**. By the end of 1994, all except two countries had completed the reduction of their combat aircraft and only one still had more attack helicopters than its quota. Rather more ground-force equipment remained to be eliminated although few countries had more than a couple of hundred of any one type of TLE still to be destroyed. However, Romania had just over 2,000 TLE still to be eliminated. Belarus had just over 1,000 TLE above its limit when President Aleksandr Lukashenka announced he was suspending elimination on economic grounds.

The only other major problem likely to frustrate the full implementation of the Treaty is Russia's stance on the flanks issue. This problem is discussed in detail on **[page xx]**.

The Treaty's first review conference is to be held in May 1996, and it is hoped that Russia's request for changes can be held over until then. New rules will have to be formulated to take account of NATO enlargement, but otherwise there appears to be no inclination to expand or alter the Treaty in any way.

'Open Skies' Treaty

The Treaty on 'Open Skies', which will create an aerial observation regime to allow specified observation flights over the whole territory of its signatories (i.e., all of Canada, Russia and the US), still requires ratifications by Russia and Ukraine before it can enter into force.

Organisation for Security and Cooperation in Europe

The Conference (now Organisation) for Security and Cooperation in Europe (OSCE) held a Review Summit meeting in Budapest on 5 and 6 December 1994. The decisions taken were:

- to provide a peacekeeping force for Nagorno-Karabakh;
- to begin discussions on a common and comprehensive security model for Europe;
- to direct the Forum for Security Cooperation to develop an agenda establishing new arms-control, confidence- and security- building measures with special emphasis on long-term stability in south-eastern Europe;
- to endorse the 1994 Vienna Document;
- to underscore its transformation from a negotiating body to a security institution by changing its name from Conference to Organisation and renaming other OSCE bodies.

The OSCE Senior Council (the renamed Committee of Senior Officials) met in Prague on 30 and 31 March 1995 to begin discussing a common and comprehensive security model which will lead to recommendations to be debated at the OSCE Ministerial Council (the renamed OSCE Council) at Budapest in December 1995. The 1996 OSCE Summit meeting will review progress.

Middle East Arms Control

One outcome of the October 1991 Madrid peace conference was the establishment of a multilateral peace conference involving other states in addition to those negotiating bilaterally. One working group is responsible for Arms Control and Regional Security. Information on progress made by the working group is difficult to acquire. There are several reasons for this sensitivity: the talks are still boycotted by Syria and Lebanon; implementation of any measures agreed to is optional; and open cooperation with Israel is still politically too sensitive for some countries to permit any publicity. This last is well demonstrated by the decision to postpone the Canadian-sponsored naval search-and-rescue demonstration and seminar when this was widely publicised and misinterpreted by some journalists as a joint naval exercise. The group is working on issues such as:

- exchange of military information;
- notification of future military activity;
- military contacts and visits;
- satellite cooperation;
- establishment of Regional Security Centres/Conflict Prevention Centres;
- maritime confidence-building measures;
- communications.

United Nations Register of Conventional Arms

The United Nations Register of Conventional Arms was introduced as an arms-control transparency measure in 1993. Reports detailing certain military imports and exports covering the previous calendar year (see *The Military Balance 1993–1994*, p. 248), are to be submitted to the UN Secretary-General by the end of April each year. The Register is now in its third year, but because of the late submission of many reports, data is only available for the first two years. The number of countries participating in the Register hardly changed between 1993 and 1994, but their regional make-up did. One more European country reported, as did three more Asian and three more Sub-Saharan African states. On the other hand, one less Latin American, one less former Soviet republic and four less Middle Eastern countries reported. As in 1993, there were significant absences from the list of major importers, mainly from the Middle East, including Saudi Arabia (3), Egypt (8), UAE (17), Kuwait (21) and also Taiwan (numbers in parentheses refer to the position in the list of importing countries by value). The only major exporter who did not report was North Korea. A list has been published of those countries which had reported to the UN Register by 5 July 1995, but it gives no further details. Of the 59 countries that reported, 32 reported imports and 18 exports. The remainder either reported no exports nor imports, or else purely submitted explanations.

The first review of the Register took place in 1994 and was carried out by a Group of Experts from mainly military or diplomatic backgrounds. The Group reported its findings in October 1994 and in November a draft resolution – 'Transparency in Armaments' – was submitted to the UN First Committee. The Group of Experts made three recommendations:

- that no adjustments to the definitions of the seven reporting categories should yet be made;
- that no new categories of conventional weapons, including anti-personnel land-mines, should yet be added;
- that expanding the Register to include military holdings and procurement from national production should be an early goal, but would need further consideration.

No changes were therefore made to the Register's scope. While this will disappoint many, it is still true that the most important aim must be to increase the number of states reporting rather than to improve the contents of reports.

Multilateral Export Controls

Progress will soon be made on establishing a follow-on body to the Coordinating Committee for Multilateral Export Controls (COCOM) which was disbanded in March 1994 before agreement could be reached on a successor. Delay has been caused by disagreement over whether Russia should be a founder-member, as France and the UK insist, or not. On 30 June 1995, the US and Russia reached agreement on the cessation of Russian arms exports to Iran and the US dropped its objection to Russia being a founder-member. In September in Paris, 23 nations will meet to begin establishing a new regime.

Anti-Ballistic Missile Treaty

The Anti-Ballistic Missile (ABM) Treaty signed by the US and the USSR in 1972 to restrict the deployment of ABMs includes a prohibition of 'space-based ABM systems and components'. The future of the ABM Treaty is becoming another point of disagreement between the US Administration and Congress. The most recent US–Russian statement on ABM was made at the Moscow summit in May 1995 when two new criteria for defining Theatre Missile Defences (TMD), which are allowed under ABM, were agreed. 'TMD will not pose a realistic threat to the strategic nuclear forces of the other side' and 'will not be tested to give such systems that capability'. While both sides reaffirmed their commitment to the ABM Treaty, the technical details defining the difference between TMD and strategic missile defence are far from agreed, and the US Congress fears this demarcation process will constrain eventual deployments of strategic missile defences to protect the US. The 1994 Defense Authorisation Bill (DAB) requires the US President to submit ABM Treaty-related agreements to the Senate for advice and consent. A number of Senators reminded President Clinton of the DAB and warned him of their objections to any strengthening of the ABM Treaty before he went to Moscow. On 14 June, the US House of Representatives added $628 million to the Administration's request for missile-defence funding and directed the Administration to deploy an anti-missile system at the earliest practical date.

Mines

The UN estimates that there could be as many as 100 million land-mines in 64 countries which kill or wound over 25,000 people a year. Many more mines are laid each year than international efforts are currently managing to lift. Attempts to cope with the problem focus on two separate objectives: demining; and negotiations to ban anti-personnel mines.

Demining

In December 1994, the UN General Assembly passed a resolution calling on member-states to assist in mine clearance. The UN is supporting programmes for mine clearance in Afghanistan, Cambodia, Mozambique and the former Yugoslavia, employing some 4,800. A major programme is under way in Angola, but the operation in Somalia had to be withdrawn. Mine clearance now features largely in the mandates for most new UN peacekeeping forces. The UN-sponsored a conference on demining in Geneva from 5 to 7 July 1995 with two aims. First, it aimed to keep the problems of demining in the public eye and called on governments to pledge money to the UN Demining Trust Fund. However, only $21.6m was pledged against the target of $75m. Second, it enabled demining experts from around the world to meet and discuss technical and organisational matters. During the last 12 months, the UN and other agencies lifted some 150,000 mines, but during the same period perhaps as many as 2 million were laid in Bosnia and the North Caucasus region of Russia.

Arms Control

At the moment, the use of land-mines is covered by the UN Convention on Prohibitions and Restrictions on the use of certain Conventional Weapons which may be deemed to be Excessively Injurious or to Have Indiscriminate Effect (UNWC).

Protocol 11 of the UNWC lays down that land-mines and booby-traps should not be used indiscriminately or against civilians (sadly, this is just how they are used most). Remote-delivered (i.e., sub-munitions weapons) mines must have a neutralising mechanism. After hostilities end, information must be exchanged on the location of land-mines. Only 42 states (out of 185 UN members) have ratified the UNWC. A UNWC review conference will be held in September 1995 at which land-mines will be given a high priority.

In December 1963, the UN General Assembly approved a resolution calling for a moratorium on exporting land-mines. The US declared a moratorium on exporting anti-personnel mines in 1992 and extended this for three more years on 30 November 1993. Moratoria, of differing lengths and conditions, have been introduced in the following countries: Argentina, Belgium, Canada, France, Germany, Greece, Israel, the Netherlands, South Africa, Spain and the UK.

Conventional Forces in Europe

Manpower and TLE: current holdings and CFE limits of the forces of the CFE signatories
(Current holdings are derived from data declared as at 15 December 1994 and so may differ from *The Military Balance* listing)

	Manpower		Tanks[a]		ACV[a]		Arty[a]		Attack Hel		Combat Aircraft[b]	
	Holding	Limit	Holding	Limit	Holding	Limit	Holding	Limit	Holding	Limit	Holding	Limit
Budapest/Tashkent Group												
Armenia	52,686	32,682	102	220	285	220	225	285	7	50	6	100
Azerbaijan	86,849	70,000	285	220	835	220	343	285	18	50	58	100
Belarus	98,525	100,000	2,348	1,800	3,046	2,600	1,579	1,615	78	80	348	260
Georgia[c]	–	40,000	39	220	49	220	27	285	1	50	2	100
Moldova	11,899	20,000	0	210	190	210	129	250	0	50	27	50
Russia[d]	998,811	1,450,000	6,696	6,400	11,806	11,480	6,240	6,415	872	890	3,283	3,450
Ukraine	475,822	450,000	4,768	4,080	5,187	5,050	3,407	4,040	270	330	1,276	1,090
Bulgaria	103,132	104,000	1,786	1,475	2,077	2,000	1,917	1,750	44	67	273	235
Czech Republic	67,702	93,333	1,011	957	1,451	1,367	893	767	36	50	215	230
Hungary	73,638	100,000	1,016	835	1,598	1,700	909	840	39	108	170	180
Poland	262,770	234,000	2,017	1,730	1,590	2,150	1,879	1,610	80	130	412	460
Romania	198,728	230,248	2,011	1,375	2,505	2,100	2,449	1,475	16	120	400	430
Slovakia	52,015	46,667	644	478	749	683	632	383	19	25	116	115
North Atlantic Treaty Group												
Belgium	50,479	70,000	334	334	756	1,099	316	320	46	46	196	232
Canada[e]	681	10,660	0	77	0	277	6	38	0	13	0	90
Denmark	30,158	39,000	401	353	273	316	553	533	12	12	90	106
France	323,433	325,000	1,313	1,306	3,595	3,820	1,141	1,292	350	352	678	800
Germany	291,340	345,000	4,116	4,166	4,042	3,446	2,488	2,705	306	306	592	900
Greece	161,332	158,621	2,139	1,735	2,283	2,534	2,079	1,878	0	18	511	650
Italy	280,674	315,000	1,319	1,348	3,031	3,339	1,946	1,955	157	142	511	650
Netherlands	44,250	80,000	736	743	955	1,080	563	607	0	69	174	230
Norway	23,000	32,000	208	170	187	225	402	527	0	0	78	100
Portugal	48,274	75,000	198	300	419	430	354	450	0	26	146	160
Spain	175,830	300,000	766	794	1,199	1,588	1,207	1,310	28	71	177	310
Turkey[d]	575,963	530,000	2,954	2,795	2,191	3,120	3,416	3,523	20	43	456	750
UK	179,707	260,000	905	1,015	3,005	3,176	537	636	355	384	661	900
US	116,472	250,000	1,357	4,006	2,497	5,372	1,266	2,492	225	518	216	784

Notes:
[a] Includes TLE with land-based maritime forces (Marines, Naval Infantry etc.).
[b] Does not include land-based maritime aircraft for which a separate limit has been set.
[c] Did not declare its manpower holding at 15 December 1994.
[d] Manpower and TLE is for that in ATTU zone only.
[e] Canada has now withdrawn all its TLE from the ATTU except for the prepositioned stockpile of 6 arty in Norway.

Peacekeeping Operations

UNITED NATIONS

If anything, the last 12 months have been even more depressing for UN peacekeepers than the previous year. During this period the mission in Somalia has been abandoned, and there are growing frustrations in – and serious consideration of withdrawal from – both Bosnia and Croatia. But two missions have been completed successfully – those to El Salvador and Mozambique. One new, though small, mission has been instituted to assist the peacekeepers of the Commonwealth of Independent States (CIS) in Tajikistan, and deployment has begun on a remandated mission to Angola. The UN has also assumed responsibility for the US-led multinational force in Haiti.

In January 1995, UN Secretary-General Boutros Boutros-Ghali presented the 'Supplement to an Agenda for Peace' to the UN General Assembly. The paper discussed preventive diplomacy and peacemaking; peacekeeping; post-conflict peace-building; disarmament; sanctions; and enforcement action. The Secretary-General complained that although 19 governments had troops on stand-by for UN operations, none were prepared to contribute to the mission in Rwanda. He therefore proposed that the UN consider establishing a rapid-reaction force as a strategic reserve for use in emergency situations (but pointed out that the value of such an arrangement would depend on whether contributing states made earmarked forces available for it).

In October 1994, the UN opened its first permanent logistics base in Brindisi, Italy. The main purpose of the base is to recover UN stores and equipment after the end of a UN mission (such as that in Somalia). Equipment would be refurbished and made available for issue to new or ongoing peacekeeping missions.

The UN Security Council (UNSC) decided on 4 November 1994 to end the mission in Somalia because of its limited impact on both the peace process and security. Withdrawal was to be completed by 31 March 1995. In the event, the final withdrawal took place on 2 March 1995 under the protection of the US Marines, who landed a proportion of their offshore force.

United Nations Truce Supervision Organisation (UNTSO)

Mission: Established in June 1948 to assist the Mediator and the Truce Commission in supervising the observance of the truce in Palestine called for by the Security Council. At present, UNTSO assists and cooperates with UNDOF and UNIFIL; Military Observers are stationed in Beirut, South Lebanon, Sinai, Jordan, Israel and Syria.
Strength: 220. **Cost 1994:** $30m.
Composition: Observers from Argentina, Australia, Austria, Belgium, Canada, Chile, China, Denmark, Finland, France, Ireland, Italy, Netherlands, New Zealand, Norway, Russia, Sweden, Switzerland, the US.

United Nations Military Observer Group in India and Pakistan (UNMOGIP)

Mission: To supervise the cease-fire between India and Pakistan along the Line of Control in the state of Jammu and Kashmir.
Strength: 40. **Cost 1994:** $8m.
Composition: Observers from Belgium, Chile, Denmark, Finland, Italy, South Korea, Sweden, Uruguay.

United Nations Peacekeeping Force in Cyprus (UNFICYP)

Mission: Established in 1964 to help prevent the recurrence of fighting and to contribute to the restoration and maintenance of law and order and a return to normal conditions. Since the hostilities of 1974, this has included supervising the cease-fire and maintaining a buffer zone between the lines of the Cyprus National Guard, and the Turkish and Turkish-Cypriot forces.

Strength: 1,173. **Cost 1994:** $47m.
Composition: Units from Argentina (inf), Austria (inf), UK (inf, hel, log); Staff Officers from Canada, Finland, Hungary, Ireland; civil police detachments from Australia, Ireland.

United Nations Disengagement Observer Force (UNDOF)

Mission: To supervise the cease-fire between Israel and Syria, and to establish an area of separation and verify troop levels, as provided in the 31 May 1974 Agreement on Disengagement between Israeli and Syrian Forces.
Strength: 1,036. **Cost 1994:** $35m.
Composition: Units from Austria (inf), Canada (log), Poland (log).

United Nations Interim Force in Lebanon (UNIFIL)

Mission: Established in 1978 to confirm the withdrawal of Israeli forces from southern Lebanon, to restore international peace and security, and to assist the government of Lebanon in ensuring the effective return of its authority in the area.
Strength: 4,963. **Cost 1994:** $138m.
Composition: Units from Fiji (inf), Finland (inf), France (log), Ghana (inf), Ireland (inf, admin), Italy (hel), Nepal (inf), Norway (inf, maint), Poland (medical).

United Nations Iraq/Kuwait Observer Mission (UNIKOM)

Mission: Established in April 1991 following the recapture of Kuwait from Iraq by Coalition Forces. Its mandate is to monitor the Khor Abdullah and a demilitarised zone extending 10km into Iraq and 5km into Kuwait from the agreed boundary between the two. It is to deter violations of the boundary and to observe hostile or potentially hostile actions. In a March 1995 report to the UNSC, the Secretary-General recommended that the mission be maintained.
Strength: 1,111. **Cost 1994:** $73m.
Composition: Units from Bangladesh (inf), Denmark (admin), Norway (medical); Observers from Argentina, Austria, Bangladesh, Canada, China, Denmark, Fiji, Finland, France, Ghana, Greece, Hungary, India, Indonesia, Ireland, Italy, Kenya, Malaysia, Nigeria, Pakistan, Poland, Romania, Russia, Senegal, Singapore, Sweden, Thailand, Turkey, UK, Uruguay, US, Venezuela.

United Nations Mission for the Referendum in Western Sahara (MINURSO)

Mission: Established in April 1991 to supervise a referendum to choose between independence and integration into Morocco. A transitional period would begin with a cease-fire and end when the referendum results were announced. Although a cease-fire came into effect on 6 September 1991, the transitional period did not begin as the UN had been unable to complete its registration of eligible voters. MINURSO is currently restricted to verifying the cease-fire. UNSC Resolution 973 adopted on 13 January 1995 authorised an expansion of MINURSO to allow a more timely completion of the referendum identification process. The transition period was expected to begin on 1 June and the referendum to be held in October. Morocco is still obstructing the identification process and by February 1995 only 11,000 eligible voters had been identified, leading to claims that it will be three more years before the referendum is held. In March, the UN Secretary-General announced that the earliest possible date for a referendum was January 1996.
Strength: 398 incl 112 police. **Cost 1994:** $40m.
Composition: Units from Canada (movement control), Switzerland (medical); Observers from Argentina, Austria, Bangladesh, Belgium, China, Egypt, El Salvador, France, Ghana, Greece, Guinea, Honduras, Ireland, Italy, Kenya, South Korea, Malaysia, Nigeria, Pakistan, Poland, Russia, Tunisia, Uruguay, US, Venezuela; police from Austria, Egypt, Germany, Hungary, Ireland, Nigeria, Norway, Uruguay.

United Nations Angola Verification Mission III (UNAVEM III)

Mission: Established by UNSC Resolution 976 of 8 February 1995, UNAVEM III replaced UNAVEM II with a more limited mandate. UNAVEM III's primary tasks are to assist in the disengagement of forces; set up verification mechanisms; establish communications links between the government, UNITA and UNAVEM; and to start the process of mine clearance. In this phase, military and police observers have been deployed along with UNAVEM logistic, communications and engineer units. Once the cease-fire has been proved effective, six infantry battalions are to deploy.
Strength: 1,969. **Cost 1994:** $25m.
Composition: Contingents from India (engr), Portugal (comms), Romania (medical), UK (log), Uruguay (inf); Observers from Algeria, Argentina, Bangladesh, Brazil, Bulgaria, Congo, Egypt, Fiji, France, Guinea-Bissau, Hungary, India, Jordan, Kenya, Malaysia, Mali, Morocco, Netherlands, New Zealand, Nigeria, Norway, Pakistan, Poland, Portugal, Russia, Senegal, Slovakia, Sweden, Uruguay, Zambia, Zimbabwe.

United Nations Assistance Mission for Rwanda (UNAMIR)

Mandate: Established on 5 October 1993 to monitor the Arusha agreement reached by the Rwandan government and the Rwanda Patriotic Front (RPF), to establish a demilitarised zone between the two sides in northern Rwanda and to assist in the integration of the two armies. UNAMIR had grown to about 2,500 when the civil war re-erupted and the genocidal attacks on the Tutsi minority forced the UN to withdraw, except for the Canadian commander and some 250 troops to keep Kigali airport open for aid flights. On 8 June 1994, the UNSC adopted Resolution 925 approving plans to deploy 5,500 peacekeepers to Rwanda. The new force's mandate is to continue to act as an intermediary between the parties and to achieve a cease-fire agreement. It is also to contribute to the protection of refugees and other civilians at risk and provide security and support for the distribution of humanitarian relief. UNSC Resolution 997 adopted on 9 June 1995 cut the strength of the force to 1,800 by 9 October. At the same time the mandate was extended to include assistance with demining and police training.
Strength: 5,951 plus 68 civil police. **Cost 1993:** $34m; **1994:** $98m.
Composition: Units from: Australia (inf), Canada (log), Ethiopia (inf), Ghana (inf), India (inf), Malawi (inf), Mali (inf), Nigeria (inf), Senegal (inf), Tunisia (inf), Zambia (inf); Observers from Argentina, Austria, Bangladesh, Canada, Congo, Fiji, Ghana, Guinea, Guinea-Bissau, India, Malawi, Mali, Nigeria, Poland, Russia, Senegal, Tunisia, Uruguay, Zambia, Zimbabwe. Civil Police from Chad, Djibouti, Germany, Ghana, Guinea-Bissau, Jordan, Mali, Nigeria, Zambia.

United Nations Observer Mission in Georgia (UNOMIG)

Mission: Established by UNSC Resolution 858 on 24 August 1993, its mandate is to verify compliance with the cease-fire agreement of 27 July 1993 between the Republic of Georgia and forces in Abkhazia; to investigate and attempt to resolve reports of violations; and to report to the Secretary-General on implementation of its mandate including violations of the agreement. UNSC Resolution 937 adopted on 21 July 1994 expanded the mandate to include:

- monitoring and verifying implementation by the parties to the Agreement on a Cease-fire and Separation of Forces signed in Moscow on 14 May 1994;
- observing the operation of the CIS peacekeeping force within the framework of the Agreement;
- verifying, through observation and patrol, that troops of the parties do not remain in or re-enter the security zone and that heavy military equipment does not remain in or is not reintroduced into the security zone or the restricted weapons zone;
- monitoring the storage areas for heavy military equipment withdrawn from the security zone and the restricted-weapons zone in cooperation with the CIS peacekeeping force, as appropriate;
- monitoring the withdrawal of Georgian troops from the Kodori valley to beyond the borders of Abkhazia, Republic of Georgia;

- patrolling regularly the Kodori valley;
- investigating, at the request of either party or the CIS peacekeeping force, or on its own initiative, reported or alleged violations of the Agreement and attempting to resolve or contribute to the resolution of such incidents;
- reporting regularly to the Secretary-General, in particular on the implementation of the Agreement, any violations and their investigation by UNOMIG, as well as other relevant developments;
- maintaining close contacts with both parties to the conflict and cooperating with the CIS peacekeeping force and, by its presence in the area, contributing to conditions conducive to the safe and orderly return of refugees and displaced persons.

Resolution 858 authorised an increase in strength to 136 observers.
Strength: 135. **Cost 1994:** $5m.
Composition: Observers from: Albania, Austria, Bangladesh, Cuba, Denmark, Egypt, France, Germany, Greece, Hungary, Indonesia, Jordan, South Korea, Pakistan, Poland, Russia, Sweden, Switzerland, Turkey, UK, Uruguay, US.

United Nations Observer Mission in Liberia (UNOMIL)

Mission: Established by UNSC Resolution 866 on 22 September 1993, its mandate is to investigate all reported violations of the cease-fire agreement and report to the Violations Committee; to monitor compliance or other elements of the peace agreement of 25 July 1993 signed by the three Liberian parties in Cotonou, Benin; to observe and verify the election process; to assist in coordination of humanitarian assistance activities; to develop a plan for the demobilisation of combatants; to train ECOMOG (Military Observer Group of the Economic Community of West African States) engineers in mine clearance; and to coordinate with ECOMOG in its separate responsibilities. Should the political stalemate continue, the UN Secretary-General has recommended that UNOMIL's mission be terminated on 30 September 1995 and converted into a small military liaison cell, subject to the consent of the Security Council.
Strength: 70 including military observers, medical staff and engineers. **Cost 1994:** $65m.
Composition: Troops from Bangladesh; Observers from Bangladesh, China, Czech Republic, Egypt, Guinea-Bissau, India, Jordan, Kenya, Malaysia, Pakistan, Uruguay.

United Nations Mission of Observers in Tajikistan (UNMOT)

Mission: The UNSC unanimously adopted Resolution 968 on 16 December 1994 which established an observer mission to monitor the cease-fire between the government and the Islamic opposition and to cooperate with the CIS peacekeeping force.
Strength: 39.
Composition: Observers from Austria, Bangladesh, Brazil, Denmark, Hungary, Jordan, Poland, Ukraine, Uruguay.

Former Yugoslavia

United Nations Peace Force HQ

A series of UNSC Resolutions (981–983) were adopted on 31 March 1995 which, in addition to extending the mandate for UN forces in the former Yugoslavia until 30 November 1995, altered the name of the force in Croatia to the United Nations Confidence Restoration Operation in Croatia (UNCRO) and of that in the FYROM to the United Nations Preventative Deployment Force (UNPREDEP). The headquarters controlling all three forces remains in Zagreb.
Strength: 7,506 plus 107 civil police (includes HQs at Zagreb and Pleso, Liaison Office in Belgrade and units supporting all UN operations in the former Yugoslavia).
Composition:
Pleso: Finnish guard unit, Swedish HQ coy, Canadian log bn, French log bn, Netherlands sigs

unit, Norwegian movement control, US coord gp for *Operation Provide Promise*.
Elsewhere: Belgian tpt coy, UK spt gp, French engr bn, French hel det, Indonesian medical unit, Netherlands tpt bn, Norwegian log bn, Slovak engr bn.

United Nations Confidence Restoration Operations in Croatia (UNCRO)

Mission: Established in March 1992 as UNPROFOR, UNCRO includes military, police and civilian components. It was originally deployed in three UN Protected Areas (UNPAs) (four sectors) in Croatia to create the conditions of peace and security required to permit negotiation of an overall political settlement of the Yugoslav crisis. UNCRO is responsible for ensuring that the UNPAs are demilitarised through the withdrawal or disbandment of all armed forces within them, and that all persons residing in them are protected from armed attack. To this end, UNCRO is authorised to control access to the UNPAs, to ensure that they remain demilitarised, and to monitor the functioning of the local police to help ensure non-discrimination and the protection of human rights. Outside the UNPAs, UNCRO military observers will verify the withdrawal of all Yugoslav Army (JA) and Serbian forces from Croatia, other than those disbanded and demobilised there.

When the UNSC renewed the mandate in October 1993, it also adopted Resolution 871 which authorises UNPROFOR, 'in carrying out its mandate in the Republic of Croatia, acting in self-defence, to take the necessary measures, including the use of force, to ensure its security and freedom of movement'.

UNSC Resolution 981, which established UNCRO, added to the UN's tasks in Croatia that of 'assisting in controlling, by monitoring and reporting the crossing of military personnel, equipment, supplies and weapons over international borders between Croatia and Bosnia Herzegovina and Croatia and the Federal Republic of Yugoslavia (Serbia and Montenegro)'. Adopted on 28 April 1995, UNSC Resolution 990 authorised the deployment of 8,750 troops in Croatia, some 5,000 fewer than were deployed at the time. By 1 June 1995, the forces had not been reduced, nor had monitors been stationed on Croatia's borders. Following the Croat recapture of western Slavonia and Krajina in August 1995, the UN began to withdraw some of its national contingents.

Strength: 12,146 plus 418 civil police.
Composition:
Sector North: 3,532, inf bn from Denmark, Jordan, Poland and Ukraine. **Sector South:** 3,915, inf bn from Canada, Czech Republic, Jordan, Kenya. **Sector East:** 1,731, inf bn from Belgium and Russia. **Sector West:** 2,804, inf bn from Argentina, Jordan and Nepal.

United Nations Protection Force (UNPROFOR): Bosnia-Herzegovina:

Mission: On 29 June 1992, the UN Security Council adopted Resolution 761 authorising the deployment of additional troops to ensure the security and functioning of Sarajevo airport and the delivery of humanitarian assistance. Initially, a Canadian battalion deployed to Sarajevo and was relieved by a small headquarters and three infantry battalions (from Egypt, France and Ukraine). On 13 August 1992, Security Council Resolution 770 was adopted calling on states to take all measures necessary to facilitate the delivery of humanitarian aid. Following the International Conference in London on 26–28 August 1992, NATO offered to provide a force and headquarters to protect aid convoys. Resolution 776 adopted on 14 September accepted and authorised the offer. UNPROFOR II commenced its deployment in October 1992 and four battalion groups were deployed. In November, UN Resolution 781 authorised 75 observers to monitor flights over Bosnia from airfields in Croatia, Bosnia and the Federal Republic of Yugoslavia (39 airfield observers are currently deployed).

Resolution 824, adopted on 6 May 1993 after Serbian attacks in eastern Bosnia had left a number of Muslim towns surrounded, declared that Sarajevo, Tuzla, Zepa, Gorazde, Bihac and Srebrenica would be treated as safe areas; and Bosnian Serb units were to cease armed attacks there immediately and withdraw to a distance from which they could no longer constitute a menace.

The Resolution also authorised the deployment of 50 additional military observers. When it was clear that UNPROFOR was not strong enough to deploy sufficient forces to the safe areas, the Security Council adopted Resolution 844 authorising a reinforcement of 7,600 troops for their protection. The Resolution reaffirmed the use of air power to protect UNPROFOR troops, if necessary.

On 9 February 1994, NATO, in compliance with a request from the UN Secretary-General, issued an ultimatum to the Bosnian-Serbs: all heavy weapons had either to be withdrawn 20km from Sarajevo or, if left within the area, placed under UN supervision. Any uncontrolled weapons found in the area after midnight on 20 February, or weapons found anywhere else that had fired on Sarajevo, would be subject to air attack. On the same day, the UN commander in Bosnia arranged a cease-fire in Sarajevo that also included the withdrawal or control of the heavy weapons of both sides and the interposition of UN troops between the two factions. On 18 March, the Bosnian government and Bosnian-Croat forces throughout Bosnia-Herzegovina reached a cease-fire agreement. UN troops were to patrol the cease-fire lines. On 31 March, UNSC Resolution 908 authorised a reinforcement of 3,500 UNPROFOR troops.

On 10 and 11 April 1994 at the height of Serbian attacks on Goradze, close air support was used to protect UN observers under fire in the area. Later, a cease-fire and a heavy-weapons exclusion zone 20 km around Goradze, similar to that around Sarajevo, were agreed. On 27 April, the Security Council authorised further reinforcements of 6,550 troops, 150 military observers and 275 civilian police monitors.

On 30 May 1995, the UN Secretary-General reported to the Security Council on the situation in Bosnia and Herzegovina. The report summarised events during the UN presence in Bosnia, and those since May 1995 in more detail. The report examined UNPROFOR's security and freedom of movement and the implications of the use of force. After debating UNPROFOR's future role, the Secretary-General presented four options for the Security Council's consideration:

- to withdraw UNPROFOR, leaving a small political mission, if wished by the parties;
- to retain UNPROFOR's existing tasks and the methods currently used to implement them;
- to change the existing mandate to permit UNPROFOR to use greater force;
- to revise the mandate to include only those tasks that a peacekeeping operation can realistically be expected to perform in the circumstances prevailing in Bosnia Herzegovina.

As yet, the Security Council has not formally responded.

Following the taking of numerous UN hostages by the Bosnian-Serbs in May 1995, France and the UK decided to send additional troops to Bosnia to form a rapid-reaction force. Resolution 998 of 16 June authorised the deployment of 12,500 troops. Following the London conference of 21 July, which decided that any move to attack Goradze would be met by immediate and substantial use of air power, the UN Secretary-General revised the rules for authorising the use of air-power and delegated responsibility for it to the military commander of the UNPF.

Strength: 19,040 plus 31 civil police (excluding rapid-reaction force reinforcements).

Composition: Danish HQ coy. **Sector Sarajevo:** 4,732, inf bn from Egypt, France (3), Russia and Ukraine (with elm in Zepa), French spt units. **Sector North-east:** 5,046, inf bn from Jordan, Netherlands (Srebrenica), Nordic countries, Pakistan (2). **Sector South-west:** 7,234, inf bn from Canada, Malaysia, Spain, Turkey, UK (2 plus armd recce sqn) (elm in Goradze), inf coy from New Zealand. **Bihac Area:** 1,284: Bangladeshi bn.

Rapid-Reaction Force: Additional troops have been deployed. France: sqn AMX-10RC, Scout coy, spt coy with 120mm mor, engr coy, hel bn (8 attack, 7 tpt hel) plus comd and log elm. Netherlands: marine coy. UK: bde HQ, inf bn, arty regt (18 105mm lt gun), armd engr sqn, hel regt (12 *Gazelle*, 24 *Lynx* hel), Air Force 6 *Puma*, 6 *Chinook* hel.

United Nations Preventative Deployment Force (UNPREDEP): Former Yugoslav Republic of Macedonia (FYROM):

Mission: In late 1992, President Gligorov requested a UN presence in the FYROM. A mission from UNPROFOR visited the former republic from 28 November–3 December 1992 and its

report was accepted. UN Resolution 795 authorised the deployment of an infantry battalion and observers to monitor the FYROM's borders with Albania and the Federal Republic of Yugoslavia, and also to act as a deterrent against attacks on the FYROM. On 18 June 1993, the Security Council authorised the reinforcement of the Macedonian Command by the United States.
Strength: 1,127 plus 23 civil police.
Composition: 1 Nordic bn (Denmark, Finland, Norway, Sweden), 1 US bn.

Note: Strength figures taken from UNPF Fact Sheet, June 1995.

NATO Operations in Support of the UN

Operation Provide Promise: The airlift of humanitarian aid into Sarajevo airport commenced in July 1992. During the three years to 8 April 1995 when Sarajevo airport was closed to aid flights, some 153,412 tons of stores had been delivered in 12,320 aircraft sorties, and over 900 sick and wounded had been flown out. Some 20 countries had contributed aircraft to the airlift. In February 1993, the operation was extended to include parachute drops of supplies, originally to the besieged Muslims in enclaves in eastern Bosnia (Gorazde, Srebenica, Zepa) and later to other towns that road convoys could not reach (Maglaij, Mostar, Tarcin, Tesanj). Aircraft from France, Germany and the US have flown 2,800 sorties dropping some 17,900 tons of stores.

Operation Deny Flight: UN Resolution 781 declared a no-fly zone over Bosnia-Herzegovina in October 1992 monitored by NATO early-warning aircraft. UNSC Resolution 816, adopted on 31 March 1993, authorised enforcement of the zone and action in the event of violations. NATO aircraft were deployed to Italy and the operation began on 12 April 1993. UNSC Resolution 836 of 10 June 1993 extended UNPROFOR's mandate to include monitoring cease-fires in the safe areas and authorised the use of air-power to support UNPROFOR in and around them, while NATO agreed to provide the necessary air support. Land-based and carrier-borne aircraft from France, the Netherlands, Spain, Turkey, the UK and the US, together with aircraft from NATO's multinational airborne early-warning force, have flown a total of 60,890 aircraft sorties between 12 April 1993 and 5 July 1995 consisting of 21,854 close air support; 21,334 air defence; and 19,942 reconnaissance, airborne early-warning, in-flight refuelling and other support sorties. The composition of the force is given under Italy on p. 55.

Operation Sharp Guard: UN resolutions established an embargo on the provision of weapons and military equipment to Yugoslavia (713 of 1991) and a general trade embargo, with the exception of medical and food supplies, on Serbia and Montenegro (757 of 1992). UNSC Resolutions 787 of 1992 and 820 of 1993 authorised implementation and enforcement of the embargo. Until June 1993, two separate naval forces, one under NATO control and the other under the Western European Union (WEU), enforced the embargo; now naval ships from 14 nations are operating in the Adriatic as part of Combined Task Force 440, formed in June 1993. From 22 November 1992–1 June 1995, 52,277 merchant vessels were challenged, 4,099 boarded and 1,137 diverted and inspected in port. The forces currently deployed on *Operation Sharp Guard* are shown under Italy on p. 55.

United Nations Special Commission (UNSCOM)

UNSCOM was established in 1991 to oversee the destruction of Iraq's stocks and capability to produce nuclear, chemical and biological weapons and ballistic missiles, and to monitor its continued compliance. The Executive Chairman of UNSCOM, Ralph Ekeus, submitted a report covering UNSCOM's activities during the first six months of 1995. The report concluded: 'The Commission is now confident that in the ballistic missile and chemical weapon areas that it has a good overall picture of the extent of Iraq's past programmes and that the essential elements of its proscribed capabilities have been disposed of'. On the question of biological weapons, Iraq has been less cooperative and the Commission has been unable to obtain a credible account of Iraq's past military biological activities. The Commission was able to report that the systems for monitoring and verification were in place and the system was operational. It also reported that Iraq had cooperated fully in setting up the monitoring systems. On 4 August 1995, Iraq handed over a 530-page document concerning its biological-weapons programme, which UNSCOM specialists are now examining.

The International Atomic Energy Agency (IAEA) is responsible for the nuclear aspects of Iraq's disarmament and, since August 1994, it has maintained a permanent presence in Iraq. In April 1995, the IAEA presented its seventh report on its monitoring and verification programme. In the period from November 1994–May 1995, over 160 inspections took place, many on a no-notice basis. Environmental monitoring is regularly conducted as well. The IAEA is confident that the essential elements of Iraq's nuclear-weapons programme have been eliminated.

Note: All composition of forces data are taken from *The UN Monthly Summary of Troop Contributions to Peacekeeping Operations* as of 31 May 1995 unless otherwise indicated.

OTHER MISSIONS

Peacekeeping missions not under UN control are listed under this heading. Available information on the mandates, strengths and compositions of ECOMOG in Liberia and the peacekeeping forces deployed by the Commonwealth of Independent States (CIS) is still too insufficient to list here, but known troop contributions are listed in the relevant countries' entries.

Organisation for Security and Cooperation in Europe (OSCE) Missions

Between August 1992 and February 1994, the OSCE established seven missions: Skopje (FYROM); Georgia; Estonia; Moldova; Latvia; Tajikistan; and the Federal Republic of Yugoslavia (FRY). This last, deployed to Kosovo, Sanjak and Vojvodina, was withdrawn in July 1993 when the FRY refused to extend the mandate further. Each mission has a specific mandate, though they all aim, in general, to act as impartial third-party observers ready to offer advice and promote stability, dialogue and understanding. Missions in Ukraine and Sarajevo were established in October and November 1994, respectively. The Mission to Ukraine's task is to support OSCE experts on constitutional and economic matters who are there to help defuse tensions and improve understanding between Ukraine and the Autonomous Republic of Crimea. The Mission in Sarajevo is to support the three OSCE ombudsmen (one for each faction). Most missions consist of six to eight members, while the mission to Georgia has 17 members.

OSCE Sanctions Assistance Missions (SAM)

Mission: Between October 1992 and April 1993, SAMs consisting of varying numbers of Customs Officers were established in Albania, Bulgaria, Croatia, Hungary, the FYROM, Romania and Ukraine. Their function is to provide advice to host-country authorities on the implementation of sanctions imposed by UNSC Resolutions 713 (arms embargo on all former-Yugoslav republics), 757 (trade sanctions against Serbia and Montenegro), and 787 and 820 (enforcement of sanctions). 165 customs officers are deployed under the coordination of a Brussels-based OSCE/EU official.

OSCE Mission to Nagorno-Karabakh

The OSCE established the Minsk Group, including representatives from Turkey, Russia and the US, to be responsible for OSCE efforts to hold a peace conference to settle Armenia and Azerbaijan's conflict over Nagorno-Karabakh. The Initial Operations Planning Group (IOPG) was set up in November 1992 as a secretariat to plan and administer a monitoring mission. When, in December 1994, it was decided that a full-scale peacekeeping force was more appropriate than a monitoring mission, the IOPG was expanded and renamed the High Level Planning Group (HLPG). The work of the HLPG has advanced well and a number of reconnaissance visits to Nagorno-Karabakh have taken place. There is a provisional outline plan to establish a minimum force of three battalions and three independent companies along the current line of contact including the Lachin Corridor, and then to supervise the withdrawal of troops to the agreed boundaries. No action has yet been taken to earmark forces for the mission, nor has a name for the force been chosen. The delay in implementing the plan is due to a lack of consensus among the parties on the future status of Nagorno-Karabakh.

Multinational Force and Observers (MFO)

Mission: Established in August 1981 following the peace treaty between Israel and Egypt and the subsequent withdrawal of Israeli forces from Sinai. Its task is to verify force levels in the zones in which forces are limited by the treaty, and to ensure freedom of navigation through the Strait of Tiran.
Strength: 1,950.
Composition: Units from Australia (HQ unit), Colombia (inf), Fiji (inf), France (FW avn), Hungary, Italy (naval coastal patrol), New Zealand (trg), Uruguay (engr and tpt), the US (inf and log). Staff Officers from Canada and Norway.

Neutral Nations' Supervisory Commission for Korea (NNSC)

Mission: Established by the Armistice Agreement in July 1953 at the end of the Korean War. The Commission is to supervise, observe, inspect and investigate the Armistice and to report on these activities to the Military Armistice Commission. Today its main role is to maintain and improve relations between the two sides and thus keep open a channel of communication.
Composition: Diplomats and military officers from Sweden, Switzerland.

European Community Monitor Mission (ECMM)

Mission: Established in July 1991 by the CSCE, it brought together the then 12 EC countries and five CSCE countries (Canada, Sweden, Czech Republic, Slovakia and Poland). Its first task was to monitor and assist with the withdrawal of the Yugoslav Army (JA) from Slovenia. Its mandate was later extended to Croatia and then to Bosnia-Herzegovina and the FYROM. The mission attempts to conduct preventive diplomacy, mediation and confidence-building between the parties. All ECMM monitors work unarmed. The Head of the Mission and the senior staff are appointed by the EC Presidency and rotate every six months. The ECMM provide monitors at airfields in Split and Pula in Croatia.
Strength: 200 monitors (mainly serving or retired military officers or diplomats) and 120 support staff. Italy provides three helicopters.

Ecuador–Peru Military Observers Mission (MOMEP)

Mission: MOMEP was formed by the four guarantor countries of the 1942 Rio de Janeiro Protocol to monitor the 13 February 1995 cease-fire agreed between Ecuador and Peru after fighting broke out in January.
Strength: 50 observers.
Composition: Argentina, Brazil, Chile, US.

Combat Aircraft: Key Characteristics

Notes:

[1] **Name:** NATO designators for aircraft of Russian/Chinese manufacture are given in quotation marks (e.g., *'Fishbed'*).

[2] **Payload:** For bomber and attack aircraft, weights are given for maximum warload, with stores on all external hard points. For air-defence aircraft, the numbers of air-to-air missiles which can be carried is shown.

[3] **Radius of action:** The figures given are aircraft in normal configuration, with a standard warload, without in-flight refuelling. When appropriate, data are given for performance at low altitude (less than 300 metres) and at high (more than 11,000 metres). For aircraft which are operated mainly in one or the other of these altitude bands, such as fighter aircraft (high altitude) or fighter ground attack (low altitude), the appropriate single value is shown. When two values are given, the 'low' radius refers to a low–low–low mission profile and the 'high' value to a high–low–high profile. The times in parentheses represent patrol capabilities at the radius of action.

Designator	Name	Role	Armament	Payload (kg)	Radius of Action (km) Low	Radius of Action (km) High
A-4	*Skyhawk*	FGA	ASM / BMB / RKT / CNN / AAM	4,500		1,230
A-6	*Intruder*	BBR	ASM / GBM / CBU / BMB / AAM	8,100		1,250
A-7	*Corsair* II	FGA	ASM / GBM / BMB / RKT / CNN / AAM	6,000		880
A-10	*Thunderbolt*	CAS	CNN / ASM / GBM / CBU / BMB	7,300	460	
AC-130	*Spectre*	CAS	CNN / RKT / GUN	1,400		2,100
Alphajet		CAS	BMB / RKT / CNN / AAM	2,000	390	580
AV-8	*Harrier* II	CAS	ASM / GBM / BMB / RKT / CNN / AAM	2,800	170	890
AMX		FGA	AAM / BMB / CNN / CBU / RKT / ASM	3,800	528	926
B-1	*Lancer*	STRAT BBR	ALCM / SRAM / NUC / BMB	61,000		4,580
B-2	*Spirit*	STRAT BBR	SRAM / NUC / BMB	16,919		5,830
B-52	*Stratofortress*	STRAT BBR	ALCM / SRAM / NUC / BMB	29,500		6,140
Ching-Kuo		FTR	AAM / CNN / ASM			
F-4	*Phantom*	MRCA	ASM / GBM / CBU / BMB / RKT / CNN / AAM	5,900		840
F-5	*Freedom Fighter*	FGA	ASM / CBU / BMB / RKT / CNN / AAM	3,200		310
F-7	(MiG-21)	FTR / CAS	AAM / CNN / BMB	4 AAM	370	600
F-8	*Crusader*	FTR	ASM / BMB / RKT / CNN / AAM	4 AAM		680
F-8	*'Finback'*	FTR / CAS	AAM / CNN / RKT	7 AAM		800
F-14	*Tomcat*	FTR	AAM / CNN / BMB	8 AAM		1,220
F-15	*Eagle*	MRCA	AAM / ASM / CBU / BMB / RKT / CNN	10,700		1,440
F-16	*Falcon*	MRCA	AAM / ASM / GBM / CBU / BMB / RKT / CNN	5,400	550	930
F/A-18	*Hornet*	MRCA	ASM / GBM / CBU / BMB / RKT / CNN / AAM	7,700		740
F-104	*Starfighter*	FTR / FGA	AAM / ASM / BMB / RKT / CNN	1,800		1,110
F-111		FGA	ASM / BMB / CNN	13,150		1,750
F-117	*Nighthawk*	BBR	AAM / ASM / GBM	2,268		1,056
G-4	*Super Galeb*	FGA / TRG	AAM / ASM / BMB / CBU / CNN	1,280		650
G-91		CAS	BMB / RKT / CNN	1,800		750
Harrier Mk-7		CAS	CBU / BMB / RKT / CNN / AAM	2,300	370	670
Sea Harrier		FTR / STRIKE	AAM / NUC / BMB / ASM / CBU / BMB / RKT	2,300	460	750
Hawk		FTR / CAS / TRG	AAM / CBU / BMB / RKT / CNN	2,950		185
IA-63		FGA / TRG	BMB / MG	1,700	440	750
IAR-93	*Orao*	CAS	CBU / BMB / RKT / SMN / CNN	2,800	260	530
J-7 (See F-7)						
J-8 (See F-8)						
Jaguar		STRIKE / FGA	NUC BMB / CBU / GBM / ASM / AAM	4,750		850
MB-339		LT ATTK	ASM / BMB / RKT / CNN / AAM	1,810	370	540
MiG-17	*'Fresco'*	FGA	BMB / RKT / CNN / AAM	500		560
MiG-21	*'Fishbed'*	FTR / FGA	AAM / BMB / RKT / CNN	1,500		480

Abbreviations:

Role:

BBR	Bomber (exclusively)
CAS	Close air support (battlefield operational)
FGA	Ground attack aircraft, interdiction, counter-air roles
FTR	Fighter, air defence/air superiority aircraft
LT ATTK	Weapons trainer, capable of employment in ground attack (normally in low-intensity operations)
MRCA	Multi-role combat aircraft
NUC	Nuclear
STRIKE	Aircraft with primary nuclear role
STRAT BBR	Deployed in strategic nuclear role

Armament:

AAM	Air-to-air missile
ALCM	Air-launched cruise missile
ASM	Air-to-surface missile
BMB	Free-fall bomb
CBU	Cluster bomb
CNN	Cannon
GBM	Guided bomb
GUN	Gun 40mm/105mm
MG	Machine gun
NUC BMB	Free-fall nuclear bomb
RKT	Rocket
SMN	Sea mines
SRAM	Short-range air-to-ground missile

Notes:

[4] **Cruising speed:** Values shown are *cruising* speed for maximum range. This reflects normal operational practice. In the low-level approach to a surface target, the speed selected (penetration speed) would represent a compromise between the demands of safe operation of the aircraft and the need to confound air-defence radar and missiles. As long as the pilot is directly controlling the aircraft, it is probable that penetration speed at heights of less than 61 metres will not greatly exceed 1,111 km/hr. Maximum speed would be used in emergency only. Speeds are shown for low- and high-level operation where appropriate.

[5] **Performance:** Entries under this heading indicate important aspects of the aircraft's capability. Examples are: the ability to refuel in flight; vertical take-off; and landing performance.

[6] **Equipment:** Broad indications are given of the nature of equipment fitted to the various aircraft. Only categories of equipment which are relevant to the performance of the primary task are shown.

Cruising Speed (km/hr)		Performance	Equipment	Origin	Designator
Low	High				
	810	CARRIER / FR	MMR / CWAS / ECM	US	A-4
	770	CARRIER / FR	MMR / TFR / CWAS / INS / IIR / LSR	US	A-6
	750	CARRIER / FR	MMR / CWAS / INS / ECM	US	A-7
510			LSR	US	A-10
410	480	FR	CWAS / INS / IIR / ATV / ECM	US	AC-130
740	710			Fr/FRG	*Alpha Jet*
850	820	CARRIER / STOVL	CWAS / INS / LSR / ESM	US	AV-8
		FR		Brazil/It	AMX
970	840	FR	MMR / CWAS / INS / ECM / ESM	US	B-1
		FR / ST	CWAS / ECM / ESM / TFR	US	B-2
670	820	FR	MMR / CWAS / IIR / INS	US	B-52
				Taiwan	*Ching-Kuo*
	920	FR	MMR / CWAS / INS / ECM / ESM	US	F-4
	860	FR	RDR / ESM	US	F-5
			PDR / ESM	China	F-7
	890	CARRIER	RDR / ESM	US	F-8
				China	F-8
980	960	CARRIER / FR / VG	PDR / CWAS / DLK	US	F-14
980	980	FR	PDR / CWAS / INS / ESM	US	F-15
	920	FR	PDR / CWAS / INS / ESM	US	F-16
	900	CARRIER / FR	PDS / CWAS / INS / ESM	US	F / A-18
	920		RDR / INS	US	F-104
	950	FR / VG	MMR	US	F-111
	1,000	ST	CWAS / ESM / IIR / LSR	US	F-117
	550			Yug	G-4
	750		IIR	It	G-91
920	810	STOVL / FR	ATV / CWAS / IIR / INS / ESM	UK	*Harrier* Mk-7
960	830	CARRIER / STOVL	MMR / INS / ESM	UK	*Sea Harrier*
920	780			UK	*Hawk*
440	550			Brazil	IA-63
920	800			Ro / Yug	IAR-93
960	880	FR	CWAS / INS / LSR / ESM	UK/Fr	*Jaguar*
810	750			It	MB-339
880	800			Russia	MiG-17
			RDR	Russia	MiG-21

Abbreviations:

Performance:

CARRIER	Capable of operation from aircraft carriers
FR	In-flight refuelling capability
ST	Stealth
STOL	Short take-off and landing
STOVL	Short take-off, vertical landing
Dash	Capable of supersonic flight for a relatively short ime
VG	Variable geometry ('swing-wing' aircraft)
hrs	Total Endurance, see note 3 above

Equipment:

ATV	All light television
CWAS	Computerised weapon-aiming system
DLK	Data-link equipment
ECM	Electronic countermeasures (active)
ESM	Electronic support measures (passive)
IIR	Imaging infra-red equipment
INS	Inertial navigation system
IR	Infra-Red radiation detecting equipment
LSR	Laser target-maker, or laser rangefinder
MMR	Multi-mode fighter radar; navigation and weapon-aiming functions
PDR	Pulse-doppler radar; effective against low-flying fast targets
RDR	Basic fighter radar, primarily for weapon-aiming
TFR	Terrain-following/terrain-avoidance radar

Notes:

[1] **Name:** NATO designators for aircraft of Russian/Chinese manufacture are given in quotation marks (e.g. *'Fishbed'*).

[2] **Payload:** For bomber and attack aircraft, weights are given for maximum warload, with stores on all external hard points. For air defence aircraft, the numbers of air-to-air missiles which can be carried is shown.

[3] **Radius of action:** The figures given are aircraft in normal configuration, with a standard warload, without in-flight refuelling. When appropriate, data are given for performance at low altitude (less than 300 metres) and at high (more than 11,000 metres). For aircraft which are operated mainly in one or the other of these altitude bands, such as fighter aircraft (high altitude) or fighter ground attack (low altitude), the appropriate single value is shown. When two values are given, the 'low' radius refers to a low–low–low mission profile and the 'high' value to a high–low–high profile. The times in parentheses represent patrol capability at the radius of action.

Designator	Name	Role	Armament	Payload (kg)	Radius of Action (km) Low	High
MiG-23	*'Flogger'*	FTR / FGA	AAM / ASM / CBU / BMB / RKT	3,000	450	950
MiG-25	*'Foxbat'*	FTR	AAM	4 AAM		750
MiG-27	*'Flogger D'*	FGA	ASM / NUC / GBM / BMB / RKT / AAM	4,500	390	600
MiG-29	*'Fulcrum'*	FTR	AAM / CNN	6 AAM		1,150
MiG-31	*'Foxhound'*	FTR	AAM	8 AAM		1,500
Mya-4	*'Bison'*	STRAT BBR / TKR	NUC BMB	15,000		5,100
Mirage F-1		FTR / FGA	AAM / ASM / BMB / RKT / CNN	4,000	640	
Mirage III		FTR / FGA	AAM / ASM / BMB / RKT / CNN	1,810	830	
Mirage IV		STRAT BBR	NUC ASM / BMB			930
Mirage 5/50		FGA	ASM / BMB / RKT / CNN	4,200	630	
Mirage 2000C		FTR	AAM / CNN / ASM / GBM / BMB / RKT	4 AAM		690
Mirage 2000N		STRIKE	NUC ASM / BMB / GBM / CBU / RKT	6,300		690
Q-5 (A-5 *Fantan*)		CAS / FGA	AAM / BMB / CBU / CNN / NUC BMB / RKT	2,000	400	600
Su-15	*'Flagon'*	FTR	AAM / CNN	1,300		720
Su-17/-20/-22	*'Fitter B-J'*	FGA	NUC BMB / ASM / RKT / AAM	4,000	430	680
Su-24	*'Fencer'*	STRIKE / FGA	NUC BMB / ASM / CNN / AAM	8,000	320	1,130
Su-25/28	*'Frogfoot'*	CAS	ASM / GBM / BMB / RKT / CNN / AAM	4,500	250	550
Su-27	*'Flanker'*	FTR	AAM / CNN	6 AAM		1,500
Su-30		MRCA	AAM / CNN			1,500
Super Etendard		STRIKE	NUC BMB / ASM / RKT / AAM	2,100	650	
Tornado IDS		STRIKE / FGA	NUC BMB / ASM / CBU / RKT / AAM	6,800		1,390
Tornado ADV		FTR	AAM / CNN	8 AAM		1,850
Tu-16	*'Badger'*	BBR / MR / EW / RECCE / TKR	NUC ASM / BMB	9,000		2,180
Tu-22	*'Blinder'*	BBR / MR / EW / RECCE	NUC ASM / BMB	10,000		1,500
Tu-22M	*'Backfire'*	STRAT BBR	ALCM / NUC ASM / BMB / SMN	12,000		4,430
Tu-28	*'Fiddler'*	FTR	AAM	4 AAM		1,250
Tu-95	*'Bear A-E'*	STRAT BBR / EW / RECCE	NUC ASM / BMB	11,300		5,690
Tu-160	*'Blackjack'*	STRAT BBR	ALCM / NUC / ASM	12,000	1,850	2,200
Yak-28	*'Firebar'*	FTR / EW	AAM	2 AAM		900
Yak-38	*'Forger'*	FTR / FGA	ASM / BMB / RKT / AAM	1,000	240	370

Abbreviations:

Role:			*Armament:*	
BBR	Bomber (exclusively)		AAM	Air-to-air missile
CAS	Close air support (battlefield operational)		ALCM	Air-launched cruise missile
FGA	Ground attack aircraft, interdiction, counter-air roles		ASM	Air-to-surface missile
			BMB	Free-fall bomb
FTR	Fighter, air defence/air superiority aircraft		CBU	Cluster bomb
LT ATTK	Weapons trainer, capable of employment in ground attack (normally in low-intensity operations)		CNN	Cannon
			GBM	Guided bomb
			GUN	40mm/105mm
MRCA	Multi-role combat aircraft		MG	Machine gun
NUC	Nuclear		NDC	Nuclear depth charge
STRIKE	Aircraft with primary nuclear role		NUC	Nuclear
STRAT BBR	Deployed in strategic nuclear role		NUC BMB	Free-fall nuclear bomb
			RKT	Rocket
			SMN	Sea mines
			SRAM	Short-range air-to-ground missile

Notes:

[4] **Cruising speed:** Values shown are *cruising* speed for maximum range. This reflects normal operational practice. In the low-level approach to a surface target, the speed selected (penetration speed) would represent a compromise between the demands of safe operation of the aircraft and the need to confound air defence radar and missiles. As long as the pilot is directly controlling the aircraft, it is probable that penetration speed at heights of less than 61 metres will not greatly exceed 1,111 km/hr. Maximum speed would be used in emergency only. Speeds are shown for low- and high-level operation, where appropriate.

[5] **Performance:** Entries under this heading indicate important aspects of the aircraft's capability. Examples are: the ability to refuel in flight; vertical take-off and landing performance.

[6] **Equipment:** Broad indications are given of the nature of equipments fitted to the various aircraft. Only categories of equipment which are relevant to the performance of the primary task are shown.

Cruising Speed (km/hr)		Performance	Equipment	Origin	Designator
Low	High				
960	950	VG	PDR / LSR / ECM / ESM	Russia	MiG-23
	980		RDR / ESM	Russia	MiG-25
960	890	VG	RDR / LSR / ECM	Russia	MiG-27
	960		PDR / CWAS / IR / ECM / ESM	Russia	MiG-29
	980	FR	PDR / CWAS / ESM	Russia	MiG-31
	780	FR	RDR ESM	Russia	Mya-4
980	980		MMR / CWAS	Fr	*Mirage* F-1
970	950		MMR / CWAS /INS	Fr	*Mirage* III
	950	FR	MMR / CWAS	Fr	*Migage* IV
970	950		RDR (-5) / MMR (-50)	Fr	*Mirage* 5/50
970	950	FR	PDR / CWAS / INS / ECM / ESM / LSR	Fr	*Mirage* 2000C
	950	FR	MMR / CWAS / INS / ECM / ESM / LSR	Fr	*Mirage* 2000N
			ECM / ESM / MMR	China	Q-5 (A-5 *Fantan*)
	920		RDR / ESM	Russia	Su-15
950	950	VG	RDR / ESM	Russia	Su-17/-20/-22
930	970	VG	MMR / TFR / ECM / ESM	Russia	Su-24
740	880		LSR / ECM / ESM	Russia	Su-25
	960		PDR / IR / ESM	Russia	Su-27
		FR	DLK / PDR / IR / ESM	Russia	Su-30
950	810	FR	MMR / CWAS / INS	Fr	*Super Etendard*
	820	FR	MMR / TFR / CWAS / INS / LSR / ESM	UK / FRG / It	*Tornado* IDS
	950	FR	PDR / CWAS / INS / ESM	UK / FRG / It	*Tornado* ADV
	750	FR	RCR / ECM / ESM	Russia	Tu-16
	860	Dash / FR	RDR / ECM / ESM	Russia	Tu-22
	920	VG / FR	MMR / ECM / ESM	Russia	Tu-22M
	900		RDR	Russia	Tu-28
	750	FR	RDR / ECM / ESM	Russia	Tu-95
		VG / FR	CWAS / ECM / ESM / RDR	Russia	Tu-160
	900		RDR / ECM / ESM	Russia	Yak-28
960	830	CARRIER / STOVL	RDR / ESM	Russia	Yak-38

Abbreviations

Performance:

CARRIER	Capable of operation from aircraft carriers
FR	In-flight refuelling capability
ST	Stealth
STOL	Short take-off and landing
STOVL	Short take-off, vertical landing
Dash	Capable of supersonic flight for a relatively short time
VG	Varianle geometry ('swing-wing' aircraft)
hrs	Total endurance, see note 3 above

Equipment:

ATV	All light television
CWAS	Computerised weapon-aiming system
DLK	Data-link equipment
ECM	Electronic countermeasures (active)
ESM	Electronic support measures (passive)
IIR	Imaging infra-red equipment
INS	Inertial navigation system
IR	Infra-red radiation detecting equipment
LSR	Laser target-maker, or laser rangefinder
MMR	Multi-mode fighter radar; navigation and weapon-aiming functions
PDR	Pulse-doppler radar; effective against low-flying fast targets
RDR	Basic fighter radar, primarily for weapon-aiming
TFR	Terrain-following/terrain-avoidance radar

Artillery and Multiple Rocket Launchers: Key Characteristics

Notes:

[1] This table does not aim to compare the capabilities of individual artillery pieces but is included to allow readers to estimate, in conjunction with the entries in country sections, the scale and capability of artillery which could be brought to support ground forces. However, artillery is purely the delivery means, whilst ammunition is the true weapon. Logistic support is therefore critical.

[2] **Calibre:** This is given in millimetres (mm). Only weapons with calibre of 105mm or above are included.

[3] **Type:** The abbreviations used to show the type of weapon are: AB = airborne; HOW = howitzer; MRL = multiple rocket launcher.

[4] **Mobility:** weapons are shown as either towed or self-propelled (SP). The latter are either wheeled (Wh), in which case the number of driven wheels is shown, or tracked. Mobility is highly important when counter-bombardment fire can be expected within 5–7 minutes.

[5] **Protection:** the abbreviations used are: AC for armoured chassis only (where the gun and, when firing, crew are not protected); T for turret-mounted gun, where protection equates more to that of an APC than a tank. Protection can also be derived from dispersion, which can be more easily achieved with the availability of automatic-data-processing-assisted fire control and autonomous navigation systems.

Calibre mm	Designation	Country of design	Type	Mobility	Protection	Max range km
105	Model 56	Italy	How	Pack (122kg)	–	14,600
105	L-118	UK	Gun	Towed	–	17,200
105	M-101	US	How	Towed	–	14,500
110	LARS	Germany	MRL	Wh 6 x 6	–	14,000
120	2S9	Russia	AB How	Track	AC + T	10,500
122	BM-21	Russia	MRL	Wh 4 x 4	–	20,500
122	RM-70	Czech Rep.	MRL	Wh 8 x 8	–	20,500
122	D-30	Russia	How	Towed	–	21,900+
122	2S1	Russia	How	Track	AC + T	21,900
122	APR-40	Romania	MRL	Wh 6 x 6	–	20,400
128	M-77	Yugoslavia	MRL	Wh 6 x 6	–	20,600
128	M-63	Yugoslavia	MRL	Towed	–	13,000
140	Teruel	Spain	MRL	Wh 6 x 6	–	28,000
152	D-20	Russia	Gun/How	Towed	–	24,000+
152	2A36	Russia	Gun	Towed	–	27–40,000
152	2A65	Russia	How	Towed	–	24,000
152	M-84	Yugoslavia	Gun/How	Towed	–	27,000
152	2S5	Russia	Gun	Track	AC	30–35,000
152	2S3	Russia	Gun/How	Track	AC + T	30,000
152	M-77 Dana	Czech Rep.	How	Wh 8 x 8	–	28,200
152	2S19	Russia	Gun/How	Track	AC + T	20,000
155	FH-70	Ge/UK/It	How	Towed	–	31,000
155	TR-F-1	France	Gun	Towed	–	32,500
155	M-114/39	Netherlands	How	Towed	–	30,000
155	M-114	US	How	Towed	–	19,300
155	M-198	US	How	Towed	–	30,000
155	FH-77A	Sweden	How	Towed	–	22,000
155	M-109A2	US	How	Track	AC + T	23,500
155	F-3	France	Gun	Track	AC	24,800
155	AS-90	UK	Gun	Track	AC + T	31,500
155	M-44	US	How	Track	AC	14,600
155	AU-F-1	France	Gun	Track	AC + T	31,500
155	G-5	S. Africa	Gun / How	Towed	–	39,000
155	G-6	S. Africa	Gun / How	Wh 6 x 6	AC + T	39,000
155	M-109A6	US	How	Track	AC + T	30,000
203	M-115	US	How	Towed	–	17–30,000
203	M-110	US	How	Track	AC	30,000
203	2S7	Russia	Gun	Track	AC	35,000+
220	9P140	Russia	MRL	Wh 8 x 8	–	35,000
227	MLRS	US	MRL	Track	AC crew	30,000
262	M-87	Yugoslavia	MRL	Wh 8 x 8	–	50,000
300	9A52	Russia	MRL	Wh 8 x 8	–	70,000

[6] **Maximum range:** This is given in metres and is the range achieved by the furthest-reaching projectile for that equipment, often an RAP. It should be noted that RAP are only used when essential, as they are far more expensive than normal HE rounds.

[7] **Rates of fire:** Two examples are given, in rounds per minute: one for sustained rates, which can be maintained for considerable periods of time; and one for maximum or burst rates, which can only be sustained for short periods at intervals. For MRL we have shown the number of tubes mounted and the time taken to reload after a complete salvo has been fired; this data is marked with an asterisk.

[8] **Ammunition natures:** The abbreviations used are:

NUC = nuclear; HE = high-explosive; RAP = rocket-assisted projectile; FRAG = fragmentation; AP GREN = anti-personnel grenade (sub-munition); AP MINE = anti-personnel mine (sub-munition); ATK MINE = anti-tank mine (sub-munition); ERBS = extended-range bomblet shell; CW = chemical warfare agent; HEAT = high-explosive anti-tank; HESH = high-explosive sqash-head; SMK = smoke; ILL = illuminating; MKR = marker; ICM = improved conventional munition.

[9] **Ammunition holdings:** Ammunition holdings are only given on the SP chassis or the towing vehicle. Where dedicated ammunition vehicles are provided for each gun, the relevant holding is shown in brackets. Holdings are often reinforced by 'dumping' particularly in defence and when a high rate of expenditure can accurately be anticipated.

Rates of fire		Ammunition natures	Ammo holding	Designations
Sustained	Max/burst			
4	8	HE / RAP / AP GREN / SMK/ILL	n.k.	Model 56
3	6	HE / HESH / SMK / ILL / MKR	n.k.	L-118
3	10	HE / RAP / AP GREN / SMK / ILL	n.k.	M-101
36*	15 min*	HE / ATK MINE / FRAG / SMK	36	*LARS*
8–10	n.k.	HE / HEAT / SMK / ILL / INC	60	2S9
40 in 20 sec*	n.k.*	HE / CW / SMK	40	BM-21
40 in 20 sec*	2–3 min*	HE	80	RM-70
7–8	n.k.	HW / RAP / CW / HEAT / SMK / ILL	n.k.	D-30
5	n.k.	HE / RAP / CW / HEAT / SMK / ILL	n.k.	2S1
40*	15 min*	HE / SMK	40	APR-40
32 in 25 sec*	5 min*	HE	n.k.	M-77
32*	5 min*	HE	n.k.	M-63
40 in 45 sec*	5 min*	HE / AP GREN / ATK MINE / SMK	40 (+80)	*Teruel*
4	5	NUC / HE / RAP / CW / HEAT / SMK / ILL		D-20
5-6	n.k.	NUC / HE / RAP / CW / ATK / SMK / FRAG	n.k.	2A36
n.k.	7	NUC / HE / HEAT / FRAG / RAP / SMK	n.k.	2A65
4	6	NUC / HE / HEAT / FRAG / RAP / CW / SMK / ILL	n.k.	M-84
4-5	n.k.	NUC / HE / RAP / CW / HEAT	40	2S5
4-5	6	NUC / HE / RAP / HEAT / SMK / ILL	40	2S3
4-5	n.k.	HE / RAP / SMK / ILL	n.k.	M-77 *Dana*
n.k.	8	NUC / HE / HEAT / FRAG / RAP / SMK	50	2S19
2	3 in 15 sec	HE / SMK / ILL / ICM	68	FH-70
6	3 in 18 sec	HE / RAP / SMK / ILL	48	TR-F-1
n.k.	4	HE / ERBS	n.k.	M-114/39
40 per hr	2	NUC / HE / AP GREN / CW / SMK / ILL	n.k.	M-114
4	n.k.	NUC / HE / RAP / AP GREN / ATK MINE / CW	n.k.	M-198
3 per 8 sec	n.k.	HE / SMK / ILL	n.k.	FH-77A
1	3	NUC / HE / RAP / AP GREN / ATK MINE / HEAT / SMK / ILL	34 (+93)	M-109A2
1	4	HE / RAP / SMK / ILL	(+25)	F-3
2	3 in 10 sec	HE / HEAT / RAP / AP GREN /SMK / ILL	48	AS-90
n.k.	n.k.	HE / AP GREN / CW / SMK / ILL	24	M-44
8	6 in 45 sec	HE / RAP / ATK MINE / SMK / ILL	42	AU-F-1
3 in15 min	3	HE / RAP / FRAG / AP GREN / SMK / ILL	n.k.	G-5
3 in 15 min	3	HE / RAP / FRAG / AP GREN / SMK / ILL	45	G-6
1	3 in 13 sec	NUC / HE / RAP / AP GREN / ATK MINE / HEAT / SMK / ILL	39	M-109A6
1 per 2 min	1	NUC / HE / RAP / CW	n.k.	M-115
1 per 2 min	2	NUC / RAP / HE / RAP / AP GREN / CW	2 (+98)	M-110
1	2	NUC / HE / RAP / CW	10	2S7
16 in 20 sec*	20–30 min*	HE / ATK MINE / AP MINE / CW	16 (+16)	9P140
12*	n.k.*	ICM (ATK) / ATK MINE	12	MLRS
12*	n.k.*	HE / HEAT (FRAG) / ATK MINE /AP	12 (+24)	M-87
12*	n.k.*	HE / FRAG / CW	12 (+12)	9A52

Designations of Aircraft and Helicopters listed
in *The Military Balance*

Notes:

[1] The use of [square brackets] shows the type from which a variant was derived. 'Q-5 . . . [MiG-19]' indicates that the design of the Q-5 was based on that of the MiG-19.

[2] (Parentheses) indicate an alternative name by which an aircraft is known – sometimes in another version. 'L-188 . . . *Electra* (P-3 *Orion*)' shows that in another version the Lockheed Type 188 *Electra* is known as the P-3 *Orion*.

[3] Names given in 'quotation marks' are NATO reporting names – e.g., 'Su-27 . . . *Flanker*".

[4] When no information is listed under 'Origin' or 'Maker', the primary reference given under 'Name/designation' should be looked up under 'Type'.

Type	Name/designation	Origin	Maker
AIRCRAFT			
A-3	*Skywarrior*	US	Douglas
A-4	*Skyhawk*	US	MD
A-5	*Fantan*	China	Nanchang
A-6	*Intruder*	US	Grumman
A-7	*Corsair* II	US	LTV
A-10	*Thunderbolt*	US	Fairchild
A-36	*Halcón* (C-101)		
A-37	*Dragonfly*	US	Cessna
AC-130	(C-130)		
AC-47	(C-47)		
Airtourer		NZ	Victa
AJ-37	(J-37)		
Ajeet	(Folland *Gnat*)	India/UK	HAL
Alizé		France	Breguet
Alpha Jet		France/Ge	Dassault/Breguet Dornier
AM-3	*Bosbok* (C-4M)	Italy	Aermacchi
An-2	'Colt'	Russia	Antonov
An-12	'Cub'	Russia	Antonov
An-14	'Clod'	Russia	Antonov
An-22	'Cock'	Russia	Antonov
An-24	'Coke'	Russia	Antonov
An-26	'Curl'	Russia	Antonov
An-30	'Clank'	Russia	Antonov
An-32	'Cline'	Russia	Antonov
An-124	'Condor' (*Ruslan*)	Russia	Antonov
Andover	[HS-748]		
Atlantic	(*Atlantique*)	France	Dassault/Breguet
AS-202	*Bravo*	Switz	FFA
AT-3		Taiwan	AIDC
AT-6	(T-6)		
AT-11		US	Beech
AT-26	EMB-326		
AT-33	(T-33)		
AU-23	*Peacemaker* [PC-6B]	US	Fairchild
AV-8	*Harrier* II	US/UK	MD/BAe
Aztec	PA-23	US	Piper
B-1		US	Rockwell
B-52	*Stratofortress*	US	Boeing
BAC-111		UK	BAe
BAC-167	*Strikemaster*	UK	BAe
BAe-146		UK	BAe
BAe-748	(HS-748)		

Type	Name/designation	Origin	Maker
Baron	(T-42)		
Be-6	'Madge'	Russia	Beriev
Be-12	'Mail' (*Tchaika*)	Russia	Beriev
Beech 50	*Twin Bonanza*	US	Beech
Beech 95	*Travel Air*	US	Beech
BN-2	*Islander, Defender, Trislander*	UK	Britten-Norman
Boeing 707		US	Boeing
Boeing 727		US	Boeing
Boeing 737		US	Boeing
Boeing 747		US	Boeing
Bonanza		US	Beech
Bronco	(OV-10)		
Bulldog		UK	BAe
C-1		Japan	Kawasaki
C-2	*Greyhound*	US	Grumman
C-4M	*Kudu* (AM-3)	S. Africa	Atlas
C-5	*Galaxy*	US	Lockheed
C-7	DHC-7		
C-9	*Nightingale* (DC-9)		
C-12	*Super King Air* (*Huron*)	US	Beech
C-17	*Globemaster* III	US	McDonnell Douglas
C-18	[Boeing 707]		
C-20	(*Gulfstream* III)		
C-21	(*Learjet*)		
C-22	(Boeing 727)		
C-23	(*Sherpa*)	UK	Short
C-42	(Neiva *Regente*)	Brazil	Embraer
C-45	*Expeditor*	US	Beech
C-46	*Commando*	US	Curtis
C-47	DC-3 (*Dakota*) (C-117 *Skytrain*)	US	Douglas
C-54	*Skymaster* (DC-4)	US	Douglas
C-91	HS-748		
C-93	HS-125		
C-95	EMB-110		
C-97	EMB-121		
C-101	*Aviojet*	Spain	CASA
C-115	DHC-5	Canada	De Havilland
C-117	(C-47)		
C-118	*Liftmaster* (DC-6)		
C-119	*Packet*	US	Fairchild
C-123	*Provider*	US	Fairchild
C-127	(Do-27)	Spain	CASA
C-130	*Hercules*	US	Lockheed

Type	Name/ designation	Origin	Maker
	(L-100)		
C-131	Convair 440	US	Convair
C-135	[Boeing 707]		
C-137	[Boeing 707]		
C-140	(Jetstar)	US	Lockheed
C-141	Starlifter	US	Lockheed
C-160		Fr/Ge	Transall
C-212	Aviocar	Spain	CASA
C-235		Spain	CASA
CA-25	Winjeel	Aust	Common-wealth
Canberra	(B-57)	UK	BAe
CAP-10		France	Mudry
CAP-20		France	Mudry
CAP-230		France	Mudry
Caravelle	SE-210	France	Aérospatiale
CC-109	(Convair 440)	US	Convair
CC-115	DHC-5		
CC-117	(Falcon 20)		
CC-132	(DHC-7)		
CC-137	(Boeing 707)		
CC-138	(DHC-6)		
CC-144	CL-600/-601	Canada	Canadair
CF-18	F/A-18		
CF-116	F-5		
Cheetah	[Mirage III]	S. Africa	Atlas
Cherokee	PA-28	US	Piper
Cheyenne	PA-31T [Navajo]	US	Piper
Chieftain	PA-31-350 [Navajo]	US	Piper
Ching-Kuo		Taiwan	AIDC
Chipmunk	DHC-1		
Citabria		US	Champion
Citation	(T-47)	US	Cessna
CJ-5	[Yak-18]	China	
CL-215		Canada	Canadair
CL-44		Canada	Canadair
CL-601	Challenger	Canada	Canadair
CM-170	Magister [Tzukit]	France	Aérospatiale
CM-175	Zéphyr	France	Aérospatiale
CN-235		Sp/Indon	CASA/ IPTN
Cochise	T-42		
Comanche	PA-24	US	Piper
Com-mander	Aero-/Turbo-Commander	US	Rockwell
Commod-dore	MS-893	France	Aérospatiale
Corvette	SN-601	France	Aérospatiale
CP-3	P-3 Orion		
CP-121	S-2		
CP-140 Lockheed	Aurora (P-3 Orion)	US	
	Acturas		
CT-4	Airtrainer	NZ	Victa
CT-39	Sabreliner	US	Rockwell
CT-114	CL-41 Tutor	Canada	Canadair
CT-133	Silver Star [T-33]	Canada	Canadair

Type	Name/ designation	Origin	Maker
CT-134	Musketeer		
Dagger	(Nesher)		
Dakota		US	Piper
Dakota	(C-47)		
DC-3	(C-47)	US	Douglas
DC-4	(C-54)	US	Douglas
DC-6	(C-118)	US	Douglas
DC-7		US	Douglas
DC-8		US	Douglas
DC-9		US	MD
Deepak	(HT-32)		
Defender	BN-2		
DH-100	Vampire	UK	De Havilland
DHC-1	Chipmunk	Canada	DHC
DHC-2	Beaver	Canada	DHC
DHC-3	Otter	Canada	DHC
DHC-4	Caribou	Canada	DHC
DHC-5	Buffalo	Canada	DHC
DHC-6	Twin Otter	Canada	DHC
DHC-7	Dash-7 (Ranger, CC-132)	Canada	DHC
DHC-8		Canada	DHC
Dimona	H-36	Ge	Hoffman
Do-27	(C-127)	Ge	Dornier
Do-28	Skyservant	Ge	Dornier
Do-128		Ge	Dornier
Do-228		Ge	Dornier
E-2	Hawkeye	US	Grumman
E-3	Sentry	US	Boeing
E-4	[Boeing 747]	US	Boeing
E-6	[Boeing 707]		
E-26	T-35A (Tamiz)	Chile	Enear
EA-3	[A-3]		
EA-6	Prowler [A-6]		
Electra	(L-188)		
EC-130	[C-130]		
EC-135	[Boeing 707]		
EMB-110	Bandeirante		
EMB-111	Maritime Bandeirante	Brazil	Embraer
EMB-120	Brasilia	Brazil	Embraer
EMB-121	Xingu	Brazil	Embraer
EMB-312	Tucano	Brazil	Embraer
EMB-326	Xavante (MB-326)	Brazil	Embraer
EMB-810	[Seneca]	Brazil	Embraer
EP-3	(P-3 Orion)		
Etendard		France	Dassault
EV-1	(OV-1)		
F-1	[T-2]	Japan	Mitsubishi
F-4	Phantom	US	MD
F-5	-A/-B: Freedom Fighter; -E/-F: Tiger II	US	Northrop
F-5T	JJ-5	China	Shenyang
F-6	J-6		
F-7	J-7		
F-8	J-8		
F-8	Crusader	US	Republic
F-14	Tomcat	US	Grumman
F-15	Eagle	US	MD
F-16	Fighting Falcon	US	GD

Type	Name/ designation	Origin	Maker	Type	Name/ designation	Origin	Maker
F-18	[F/A-18]			IAR-93	*Orao*	Yug/Ro	SOKO/IAR
F-21	*Kfir*	Israel	IAI	Il-14	'Crate'	Russia	Ilyushin
F-27	*Friendship*	Nl	Fokker	Il-18	'Coot'	Russia	Ilyushin
F-28	*Fellowship*	Nl	Fokker	Il-20	(Il-18)		
F-35	*Draken*	Sweden	SAAB	Il-28	'Beagle'	Russia	Ilyushin
F-84	*Thunderstreak*	US	Lockheed	Il-38	'May'	Russia	Ilyushin
F-86	*Sabre*	US	N. American	Il-62	'Classic'	Russia	Ilyushin
F-100	*Super Sabre*	US	N. American	Il-76	'Candid' (tpt),	Russia	Ilyushin
F-104	*Starfighter*	US	Lockheed		'Mainstay' (AEW),		
F-106	*Delta Dart*	US	Convair		'Midas' (tkr)		
F-111		US	GD	*Impala*	[MB-326]	S. Africa	Atlas
F-172	(Cessna 172)	France/ US	Reims- Cessna	*Islander*	BN-2		
				J-2	[MiG-15]	China	
F/A-18	*Hornet*	US	MD	J-5	[MiG-17F]	China	Shenyang
Falcon	*Mystère-Falcon*			J-6	[MiG-19]	China	Shenyang
FB-111	(F-111)			J-7	[MiG-21]	China	Xian
FH-227	(F-27)	US	Fairchild- Hiller	J-8	[Sov Ye-142]	China	Shenyang
				J-32	*Lansen*	Sweden	SAAB
Flamingo	MBB-233	Ge	MBB	J-35	*Draken*	Sweden	SAAB
FT-5	JJ-5	China	CAC	J-37	*Viggen*	Sweden	SAAB
FT-6	JJ-6			JA-37	(J-37)		
FTB-337	[Cessna 337]			*Jaguar*		Fr/UK	SEPECAT
G-91		Italy	Aeritalia	JAS-39	*Gripen*	Sweden	SAAB
G-222		Italy	Aeritalia	*Jastreb*		Yug	SOKO
Galaxy	C-5			*Jet Provost*		UK	BAe
Galeb		Yug	SOKO	*Jetstream*		UK	BAe
Gardian	(Falcon 20)			JJ-6	(J-6)		
Genet	SF-260W			JZ-6	(J-6)		
GU-25	(Falcon 20)			K-8		China/ Pak	NAMC/PAC
Guerrier	R-235						
Gulfstream Aviation		US	Gulfstream	KA-3	[A-3]		
				KA-6	[A-6]		
Gumhuria	(Bücker 181)	Egypt	Heliopolis	KC-10	*Extender* [DC-10]	US	MD
H-5	[Il-28]	China	Harbin	KC-130	[C-130]		
H-6	[Tu-16]	China	Xian	KC-135	[Boeing 707]		
H-36	*Dimona*			KE-3A	[Boeing 707]		
Halcón	[C-101]			*Kfir*		Israel	IAI
Harrier	(AV-8)	UK	BAe	*King Air*		US	Beech
Harvard	(T-6)			*Kiran*	HJT-16		
Hawk		UK	BAe	*Kraguj*		Yug	SOKO
HC-130	(C-130)			*Kudu*	C-4M		
HF-24	*Marut*	India	HAL	LAC52	YAK52	Russia	Aerostar
HFB-320	*Hansajet*	Ge	Hamburger FB	LIM-6	[MiG-17]	Poland	
				L-4	*Cub*		
HJ-5	(H-5)			L-18	*Super Cub*	US	Piper
HJT-16	*Kiran*	India	HAL	L-19	O-1		
HPT-32	*Deepak*	India	HAL	L-21	*Super Cub*	US	Piper
HS-125	(Dominie)	UK	BAe	L-29	*Delfin*	Cz	Aero
HS-748	[Andover]	UK	BAe	L-39	*Albatros*	Cz	Aero
HT-2		India	HAL	L-70	*Vinka*	Finland	Valmet
HU-16	*Albatross*	US	Grumman	L-90TP	*Redigo*	Finland	Valmet
HU-25	(Falcon 20)			L-100	C-130 (civil version)		
Hunter		UK	BAe				
HZ-5	(H-5)			L-188	*Electra* (P-3 *Orion*)	US	Lockheed
IA-35	*Huanquero*	Arg	FMA				
IA-50	*Guaraní*	Arg	FMA	L-410	*Turbolet*	Cz	LET
IA-58	*Pucará*	Arg	FMA	L-1011	*Tristar*	US	Lockheed
IA-63	*Pampa*	Arg	FMA	*Learjet*	(C-21)	US	Gates
IAI-201/-202	*Arava*	Israel	IAI	Li-2	[DC-3]	Russia	Lisunov
IAI-1124	*Westwind, Seascan*	Israel	IAI	LR-1	(MU-2)		
				Magister	CM-170		
IAR-28		Ro	IAR	*Marut*	HF-24		

Type	Name/designation	Origin	Maker	Type	Name/designation	Origin	Maker
Mashshaq	MFI-17	Pakistan/ Sweden	PAC/ SAAB	P-92		Italy	Teenam
				P-95	EMB-110		
Matador	(AV-8)			P-149		Italy	Piaggio
MB-326		Italy	Aermacchi	P-166		Italy	Piaggio
MB-339	(*Veltro*)	Italy	Aermacchi	PA-18	*Super Cub*	US	Piper
MBB-233	*Flamingo*			PA-23	*Aztec*		
MC-130	(C-130)			PA-24	*Comanche*	US	Piper
Mercurius	(HS-125)			PA-28	*Cherokee*	US	Piper
Merlin		US	Fairchild	PA-31	*Navajo*	US	Piper
Mescalero	T-41			PA-34	*Seneca*	US	Piper
Metro		US	Fairchild	PA-44	*Seminole*	US	Piper
MFI-15	*Safari*	Sweden	SAAB	PBY-5	*Catalina*	US	Consolidated
MFI-17	*Supporter* (T-17)	Sweden	SAAB	PC-6	*Porter*	Switz	Pilatus
MH-1521	*Broussard*	France	Max Holste	PC-6A/B	*Turbo Porter*	Switz	Pilatus
MiG-15	'Midget' trg	Russia	MiG	PC-7	*Turbo Trainer*	Switz	Pilatus
MiG-17	'Fresco'	Russia	MiG	PC-9		Switz	Pilatus
MiG-19	'Farmer'	Russia	MiG	PD-808		Italy	Piaggio
MiG-21	'Fishbed'	Russia	MiG	*Pembroke*		UK	BAe
MiG-23	'Flogger'	Russia	MiG	*Pillán*	T-35		
MiG-25	'Foxbat'	Russia	MiG	PL-1	*Chien Shou*	Taiwan	AIDC
MiG-27	'Flogger' D'	Russia	MiG	*Porter*	PC-6		
MiG-29	'Fulcrum'	Russia	MiG	PS-5	[SH-5]	China	HAMC
MiG-31	'Foxhound'	Russia	MiG	PZL-104	*Wilga*	Poland	PZL
Mirage		France	Dassault	PZL-130	*Orlik*	Poland	PZL
Mission-master	N-22			Q-5	'Fantan' [MiG-19]		China
					Nanchang		
Mohawk	OV-1			*Queen Air*	(U-8)		
MS-760	*Paris*	France	Aérospatiale	R-160		France	Socata
MS-893	*Commodore*			R-235	*Guerrier*	France	Socata
MU-2		Japan	Mitsubishi	RC-21	(C-21)		
Musketeer	*Beech* 24	US	Beech	RC-47	(C-47)		
Mya-4	'Bison'	Russia	Myasishchev	RC-95	(EMB-110)		
Mystère-Falcon		France	Dassault	RC-135	[Boeing 707]		
				RF-4	(F-4)		
N-22	*Floatmaster, Missionmaster*	Aust	GAF	RF-5	(F-5)		
				RF-35	(F-35)		
N-24	*Searchmaster B/L*	Aust	GAF	RF-84	(F-84)		
				RF-104	(F-104)		
N-262	*Frégate*	France	Aérospatiale	RF-172	(Cessna 172)	France	Reims-Cessna
N-2501	*Noratlas*	France	Aérospatiale				
Navajo	PA-31	US	Piper	RG-8A		US	Schweizer
NC-212	C-212	Sp/Indon	CASA/ Nurtanio	RT-26	(EMB-326)		
				RT-33	(T-33)		
NC-235	C-235	Sp/Indon	CASA/ Nurtanio	RU-21	(*King Air*)		
				RV-1	(OV-1)		
Nesher	[*Mirage* III]	Israel	IAI	S-2	*Tracker*	US	Grumman
NF-5	(F-5)			S-3	*Viking*	US	Lockheed
Nightingale	(DC-9)			S-208		Italy	SIAI
Nimrod		UK	BAe	S-211		Italy	SIAI
Nomad		Aust	GAF	*Sabreliner*	(CT-39)	US	Rockwell
O-1	*Bird Dog*	US	Cessna	*Safari*	MFI-15		
O-2	(Cessna 337, Skymaster)	US	Cessna	*Safir*	SAAB-91 (SK-50)	Sweden	SAAB
				SC-7	*Skyvan*	UK	Short
OA-4	(A-4)			SE-210	*Caravelle*		
OA-37	*Dragonfly*			*Sea Harrier*	(*Harrier*)		
Orao	IAR-93			*Seascan*	IAI-1124		
Ouragan		France	Dassault	*Search-master*	N-24 B/L		
OV-1	*Mohawk*	US	Rockwell	*Seneca*	PA-34	US	Piper
OV-10	*Bronco*	US	Rockwell		(EMB-810)		
P-2J	[SP-2]	Japan	Kawasaki	*Sentry*	(O-2)	US	Summit
P-3		Switz	Pilatus	SF-37	(J-37)		
P-3	*Orion*	US	Lockheed				

Type	Name/designation	Origin	Maker
SF-260	(SF-260W Warrior)	Italy	SIAI
SH-37	(J-37)		
Sherpa	Short 330, C-23		
Short 330		UK	Short
Sierra 200	(Musketeer)		
SK-35	(J-35)	Sweden	SAAB
SK-37	(J-37)		
SK-50	(Safir)		
SK-60	(SAAB-105)	Sweden	SAAB
SK-61	(Bulldog)		
Skyvan		UK	Short
SM-1019		Italy	SIAI
SN-601	Corvette		
SNJ	T-6 (Navy)		
SP-2H	Neptune	US	Lockheed
SR-71	Blackbird	US	Lockheed
Su-7	'Fitter A'	Russia	Sukhoi
Su-15	'Flagon'	Russia	Sukhoi
Su-17/-20/-22 Sukhoi	'Fitter'	Russia	
Su-24	'Fencer'	Russia	Sukhoi
Su-25	'Frogfoot'	Russia	Sukhoi
Su-27	'Flanker'	Russia	Sukhoi
Super		France	Dassault
Shrike Aero-commander		USA	Rockwell
Super Galeb		Yug	SOKO
Super Mystère		France	Dassault
T-1		Japan	Fuji
T-1A	Jayhawk	US	Beech
T-2	Buckeye	US	Rockwell
T-2		Japan	Mitsubishi
T-3		Japan	Fuji
T-6	Texan	US	N. American
T-17	(Supporter, MFI-17)	Sweden	SAAB
T-23	Uirapurú	Brazil	Aerotec
T-25	Neiva Universal	Brazil	Embraer
T-26	EMB-326		
T-27	Tucano	Brazil	Embraer
T-28	Trojan	US	N. American
T-33	Shooting Star	US	Lockheed
T-34	Mentor	US	Beech
T-35	Pillán [PA-28]	Chile	Enaer
T-36	(C-101)		
T-37	(A-37)		
T-38	Talon	US	Northrop
T-39	(Sabreliner)	US	Rockwell
T-41	Mescalero (Cessna 172)	US	Cessna
T-42	Cochise (Baron)	US	Beech
T-43	(Boeing 737)		
T-44	(King Air)		
T-47	(Citation)		
T-400	(T-1A)	US	Beech
TB-20	Trinidad	France	Aérospatiale
TB-30	Epsilon	France	Aérospatiale
TBM-700		France	Socata
TC-45	(C-45, trg)		
T-CH-1		Taiwan	AIDC
Texan	T-6		
TL-1	(KM-2)	Japan	Fuji
Tornado		UK/Ge/It	Panavia
TR-1	[U-2]	US	Lockheed
Travel Air	Beech 95		
Trident		UK	BAe
Trislander	BN-2		
Tristar	L-1011		
TS-8	Bies	Poland	PZL
TS-11	Iskra	Poland	PZL
Tu-16	'Badger'	Russia	Tupolev
Tu-22	'Blinder'	Russia	Tupolev
Tu-26	'Backfire' (Tu-22M)	Russia	Tupolev
Tu-28	'Fiddler'	Russia	Tupolev
Tu-95	'Bear'	Russia	Tupolev
Tu-126	'Moss'	Russia	Tupolev
Tu-134	'Crusty'	Russia	Tupolev
Tu-142	'Bear F'	Russia	Tupolev
Tu-154	'Careless'	Russia	Tupolev
Tu-160	'Blackjack'	Russia	Tupolev
Turbo Porter	PC-6A/B		
Twin Bonanza	Beech 50		
Twin Otter	DHC-6		
Tzukit	[CM-170]	Israel	IAI
U-2		US	Lockheed
U-3	(Cessna 310)	US	Cessna
U-7	(L-18)		
U-8	(Twin Bonanza/Queen Air)	US	Beech
U-9	(EMB-121)		
U-10	Super Courier	US	Helio
U-17	(Cessna 180, 185)	US	Cessna
U-21	(King Air)		
U-36	(Learjet)		
U-42	(C-42)		
U-93	(HS-125)		
UC-12	(King Air)		
UP-2J	(P-2J)		
US-1		Japan	Shin Meiwa
US-2A	(S-2A, tpt)		
US-3	(S-3, tpt)		
UTVA-66		Yug	UTVA
UTVA-75		Yug	UTVA
UV-18	(DHC-6)		
V-400	Fantrainer 400	Ge	VFW
V-600	Fantrainer 600	Ge	VFW
Vampire	DH-100		
VC-4	Gulfstream I		
VC-10		UK	BAe
VC-11	Gulfstream II		
VC-91	(HS-748)		
VC-93	(HS-125)		
VC-97	(EMB-120)		
VC-130	(C-130)		
VFW-614		Ge	VFW
Vinka	L-70		
VU-9	(EMB-121)		
VU-93	(HS-125)		
WC-130	[C-130]		
WC-135	[Boeing 707]	US	Boeing
Westwind	IAI-1124		
Winjeel	CA-25		

Type	Name/designation	Origin	Maker
Xavante	EMB-326		
Xingu	EMB-121		
Y-5	[An-2]	China	Hua Bei
Y-7	[An-24]	China	Xian
Y-8	[An-12]	China	Shaanxi
Y-12		China	Harbin
Yak-11	'Moose'	Russia	Yakovlev
Yak-18	'Max'	Russia	Yakovlev
Yak-28	'Firebar' ('Brewer')	Russia	Yakovlev
Yak-38	'Forger'	Russia	Yakovlev
Yak-40	'Codling'	Russia	Yakovlev
YS-11		Japan	Nihon
Z-43		Cz	Zlin
Z-226		Cz	Zlin
Z-326		Cz	Zlin
Z-526		Cz	Zlin
Zéphyr	CM-175		

HELICOPTERS

Type	Name/designation	Origin	Maker
A-109	*Hirundo*	Italy	Agusta
A-129	*Mangusta*	Italy	Agusta
AB-...	(Bell 204/205/206/212/214, etc.)	Italy/US	Agusta/Bell
AH-1	*Cobra/Sea Cobra*	US	Bell
AH-6	(Hughes 500/530)	US	MD
AH-64	*Apache*	US	Hughes
Alouette II	SE-3130, SA-318	France	Aérospatiale
Alouette III	SA-316, SA-319	France	Aérospatiale
AS-61	(SH-3)	US/Italy	Sikorsky/Agusta
AS-332	*Super Puma*	France	Aérospatiale
AS-350	*Ecureuil*	France	Aérospatiale
AS-355	*Ecureuil* II		
AS-365	*Dauphin*	France	Aérospatiale
AS-532	*Super Puma*	France	Aérospatiale
AS532 UL	*Cougar*	France	Eurocopter
AS-550	*Fennec*	France	Aérospatiale
ASH-3	(*Sea King*)	Italy/US	Agusta/Sikorsky
AUH-76	(S-76)		
Bell 47		US	Bell
Bell 204		US	Bell
Bell 205		US	Bell
Bell 206		US	Bell
Bell 212		US	Bell
Bell 214		US	Bell
Bell 406		US	Bell
Bell 412		US	Bell
Bo-105	(NBo-105)	Ge	MBB
CH-8	(SH-3)		
CH-34	*Choctaw*	US	Sikorsky
CH-46	*Sea Knight*	US	Boeing-Vertol
CH-47	*Chinook*	US	Boeing-Vertol
CH-53	*Stallion* (*Sea Stallion*)	US	Sikorsky
CH-54	*Tarhe*	US	Sikorsky
CH-113	(CH-46)		

Type	Name/designation	Origin	Maker
CH-124	SH-3		
CH-135	Bell 212		
CH-136	OH-58		
CH-139	Bell 206		
CH-146	Bell 412	Canada	Bell
CH-147	CH-47		
Cheetah	[SA-315]	India	HAL
Chetak	[SA-319]	India	HAL
Commando	(SH-3)	UK/US	Westland/Sikorsky
EH-60	(UH-60)		
EH-101		UK/Italy	Westland/Agusta
FH-1100	(OH-5)	US	Fairchild-Hiller
Gazela	(SA-342)	France/Yug	Aérospatiale/SOKO
Gazelle	SA-341/-342		
H-34	(S-58)		
H-76	S-76		
HA-15	Bo-105		
HB-315	*Gavião* (SA-315)	Brazil/France	Helibras/Aérospatiale
HB-350	*Esquilo* (AS-350)	Brazil/France	Helibras/Aérospatiale
HD-16	SA-319		
HH-3	(SH-3)		
HH-34	(CH-34)		
HH-53	(CH-53)		
Hkp-2	*Alouette* II/SE-3130		
Hkp-3	AB-204		
Hkp-4	KV-107		
Hkp-5	Hughes 300		
Hkp-6	AB-206		
Hkp-9	Bo-105		
Hkp-10	AS-332		
HR-12	OH-58		
HSS-1	(S-58)		
HSS-2	(SH-3)		
HT-17	CH-47		
HT-21	AS-332		
HU-1	(UH-1)	Japan/US	Fuji/Bell
HU-8	UH-1B		
HU-10	UH-1H		
HU-18	AB-212		
Hughes 269		US	MD
Hughes 300		US	MD
Hughes 369		US	MD
Hughes 500/520	*Defender*	US	MD
IAR-316/-330 IAR/	(SA-316/-330)	Ro/France	Aérospatiale
Ka-25	'Hormone'	Russia	Kamov
Ka-27	'Helix'	Russia	Kamov
Ka-50	*Hokum*	Russia	Kamov
KH-4	(Bell 47)	Japan/US	Kawasaki/Bell

Type	Name/designation	Origin	Maker
KH-300	(Hughes 269)	Japan/US	Kawasaki/MD
KH-500	(Hughes 369)	Japan/US	Kawasaki/MD
Kiowa	OH-58		
KV-107	[CH-46]	Japan/US	Kawasaki/Vertol
Lynx		UK	Westland
MD-500/530	*Defender*	US	McDonnell Douglas
MH-6	(AH-6)		
MH-53	(CH-53)		
Mi-1	'Hare'	Russia	Mil
Mi-2	'Hoplite'	Russia	Mil
Mi-4	'Hound'	Russia	Mil
Mi-6	'Hook'	Russia	Mil
Mi-8	'Hip'	Russia	Mil
Mi-14	'Haze'	Russia	Mil
Mi-17	'Hip'	Russia	Mil
Mi-24	'Hind'	Russia	Mil
Mi-25	'Hind'	Russia	Mil
Mi-26	'Halo'	Russia	Mil
Mi-28	'Havoc'	Russia	Mil
Mi-35	(Mi-25)		
NAS-332	AS-332	Indon/France	Nurtanio/Aérospatiale
NB-412	Bell 412	Indon/US	Nurtanio/Bell
NBo-105	Bo-105	Indon/Ge	Nurtanio/MBB
NH-300	(Hughes 300)	Italy/US	Nardi/MD
NSA-330	(SA-330)	Indon/France	Nurtanio/Aérospatiale
OH-6	*Cayuse* (Hughes 369)	US	MD
OH-13	(Bell 47G)		
OH-23	*Raven*	US	Hiller
OH-58	*Kiowa* (Bell 206)		
OH-58D	(Bell 406)		
PAH-1	(Bo-105)		
Partizan	(*Gazela*, armed)		
PZL-W3	*Sokol*	Poland	Swidnik
RH-53	(CH-53)		
S-55	(*Whirlwind*)	US	Sikorsky
S-58	(*Wessex*)	US	Sikorsky
S-61	SH-3		
S-65	CH-53		
S-70	UH-60	US	Sikorsky
S-76		US	Sikorsky
S-80	CH-53		
SA-315	*Lama* [*Alouette* II]	France	Aérospatiale
SA-316	*Alouette* III (SA-319)	France	Aérospatiale
SA-318	*Alouette* II (SE-3130)	France	Aérospatiale
SA-319	*Alouette* III (SA-316)	France	Aérospatiale
SA-321	*Super Frelon*	France	Aérospatiale
SA-330	*Puma*	France	Aérospatiale
SA-341/-342	*Gazelle*	France	Aérospatiale
SA-360	*Dauphin*	France	Aérospatiale
SA-365	*Dauphin* II (SA-360)		
Scout	(*Wasp*)	UK	Westland
SE-3130	(SA-318)		
SE-316	(SA-316)		
Sea King	[SH-3]	UK	Westland
SH-2	*Sea Sprite*	US	Kaman
SH-3	(*Sea King*)	US	Sikorsky
SH-34	(S-58)		
SH-57	Bell 206		
SH-60	*Sea Hawk* (UH-60)		
Sioux	(Bell 47)	UK	Westland
TH-50	Esquilo (AS550)		
TH-55	Hughes 269		
TH-57	*Sea Ranger* (Bell 206)		
TH-67	Creek (Bell 206B-3)	Canada	Bell
UH-1	*Iroquois* (Bell 204/205)		
UH-12	(OH-23)	US	Hiller
UH-13	(Bell 47J)		
UH-19	(S-55)		
UH-34T	(S-58T)		
UH-46	(CH-46)		
UH-60	*Black Hawk* (SH-60)	US	Sikorsky
VH-4	(Bell 206)		
VH-60	(S-70)		
Wasp	(*Scout*)	UK	Westland
Wessex	(S-58)	US/UK	Sikorsky/Westland
Whirlwind	(S-55)	US/UK	Sikorsky/Westland
Z-5	[Mi-4]	China	Harbin
Z-6	[Z-5]	China	Harbin
Z-8	[SA-321]	China	Changhe
Z-9	[SA-365]	China	Harbin

ABBREVIATIONS

⟨	under 100 tons
−	part of unit is detached/less than
+	unit reinforced/more than
*	training aircraft considered as combat capable
†	serviceability in doubt
ε	estimated
' '	unit with overstated title/ship class nickname
AA(A)	anti-aircraft (artillery)
AAM	air-to-air missile
AAV	amphibious armoured vehicle
AAW	anti-air warfare
AB	airborne
ABD	airborne division
ABM	anti-ballistic missile
about	the total could be higher
ac	aircraft
ACM	advanced cruise missile
ACV	air cushion vehicle/vessel armoured combat vehicle
AD	air defence
adj	adjusted
AE	auxiliary, ammunition carrier
AEF	auxiliary explosives and stores
AEW	airborne early warning
AF	stores ship with RAS capability
AFB/S	Air Force Base/Station
AGHS	hydrographic survey vessel
AGI	intelligence collection vessel
AGM	air-to-ground missile
AGOR	oceanographic research vessel
AGOS	ocean surveillance vessel
AH	hospital ship
A(I)FV	armoured (infantry) fighting vehicle
AIP	air-independent propulsion
AK	cargo ship
ALCM	air-launched cruise missile
amph	amphibious/amphibian
AMRAAM	advanced medium-range air-to-air missile
AO	tanker(s) with RAS capability
AOE	auxiliary, fuel and ammunition, RAS capability
AOT	tanker without RAS capability
AP	passenger ship
APC	armoured personnel carrier repair ship
AR	repair ship
Arg	Argentina
ARM	anti-radiation (anti-radar) missile
armd	armoured
arty	artillery
AS	submarine depot ship
aslt	assault
ASM	air-to-surface missile
ASTT	anti-submarine TT
ASUW	anti-surface-unit warfare

ASW	anti-submarine warfare
AT	tug
ATACMS	army tactical missile system
ATBM	anti-tactical ballistic missile
ATGW	anti-tank guided weapon
ATK	anti-tank
Aust	Australia
avn	aviation
AWACS	airborne warning and control system
BB	battleship
bbr	bomber
bde	brigade
bdgt	budget
Be	Belgium
BMD	ballistic missile defence
bn	battalion/billion
bty	battery
Bu	Bulgaria
cal	calibration
CAS	close air support
CASM	conventionally armed stand-off missiles
casevac	casualty evacuation
Cat	Category
cav	cavalry
cbt	combat
CBU	cluster bomb unit
CC	cruiser
Cdn	Canada
cdo	command
CEP	circular error of probability
CFE	Conventional Armed Forces in Europe
CG	SAM cruiser
CGH	CG with helicopters
CGN	nuclear-fuelled CG
cgo	freight aircraft
Ch	China (PRC)
civ pol	civilian police
COIN	counter-insurgency
comb	combined/combination
comd	command
comms	communications
CONUS	Continental United States
coy	company
CV	aircraft carrier
CVBG	carrier battle group
CVN	nuclear-fuelled CV
CVV	V/STOL and hel CV
CW	chemical warfare/weapons
Cz	Czech Republic
DD	destroyer
DDG	destroyer with area SAM
DDH	destroyer with hel
DDS	dry dock shelter
def	defence
defn	definition
det	detachment
div	division
Dk	Denmark
ECM	electronic countermeasures
ECR	electronic combat and reconnaissance
EDA	Emergency Drawdown Authorities

EEZ	exclusive economic zone
ELINT	electronic intelligence
elm	element
engr	engineer
EOD	explosive ordnance disposal
eqpt	equipment
ESM	electronic support measures
est	estimate(d)
EW	electronic warfare
excl	excludes/excluding
exp	expenditure
FAC	forward air control
fd	field
FF	frigate
FFG	frigate with area SAM
FFH	frigate with helicopter
FGA	fighter, ground-attack
flt	flight
FMA	foreign military assistance
FMF	foreign military financing
Fr	France
FRY	Federal Republic of Yugoslavia
FSU	former Soviet Union
ftr	fighter (aircraft)
FW	fixed-wing
FY	fiscal year
GDP	gross domestic product
Ge	Germany
GNP	gross national product
gp	group
Gr	Greece
GS	General Service (UK)
GW	guided weapon
HACV	heavy armoured combat vehicle
HARM	high-speed anti-radiation missile
hel	helicopter
HMMWV	high mobility multipurpose wheeled vehicle
HS	Home Service (UK)
HWT	heavy-weight torpedo
Hu	Hungary
hy	heavy
ICBM	intercontinental ballistic missile
IMET	international military education and training
imp	improved
incl	includes/including
indep	independent
Indon	Indonesia
inf	infantry
IRBM	intermediate-range ballistic missile
Is	Israel
It	Italy
JSTARS	joint strategic airborne reconnaissance system
KT	kiloton
LAMPS	light airborne multi-purpose system
LANTIRN	low-altitude navigation and targeting infra-red system night

LCA	landing craft, assault
LCAC	landing craft, air cushion
LCM	landing craft, mechanised
LCT	landing craft, tank
LCU	landing craft, utility
LCVP	landing craft, vehicles and personnel
LGB	laser-guided bomb
LHA	landing ship, assault
LKA	assault cargo ship
log	logistic
LPD	landing platform, dock
LPH	landing platform, helicopter
LSD	landing ship, dock
LSM	landing ship, medium
LST	landing ship, tank
lt	light
LWT	light-weight torpedo
maint	maintenance
MBT	main battle tank
MCC/I/O	mine countermeasures vessel, coastal/inshore/offshore
MCMV	mine countermeasures vessel
MD	Military District
mech	mechanised
med	medium
MEF/B/U	Marine Expeditionary Force/Brigade/Unit (US)
MG	machine gun
MHC/I/O	minehunter, coastal/inshore/offshore
MICV	mechanised infantry combat vehicle
mil	military
MIRV	multiple independently-targetable re-entry vehicle
misc	miscellaneous
Mk	mark (model number)
ML	minelayer
mob	mobilisation/mobile
mod	modified/modification
mor	mortar
mot	motorised/motor
MLRS	multiple launch rocket system
MP	Military Police
MPA	maritime patrol aircraft
MPS	marine prepositioning squadron
MR	maritime reconnaissance/motor rifle
MRBM	medium-range ballistic missile
MRD	motor rifle division
MRL	multiple rocket launcher
MRR	motor rifle regiment
MRV	multiple re-entry vehicle
MSC/I/O	minesweeper, coastal/inshore/offshore
msl	missile
MT	megaton
mtn	mountain
n.a.	not applicable
NBC	nuclear, biological and chemical

NCO	non-commissioned officer
n.k.	not known
Nl	Netherlands
nm	nautical mile
NMP	net material product
No	Norway
nuc	nuclear
obs	observation
OCU	operational conversion unit(s)
OECD	Organization for Economic Cooperation and Development
off	official
OOA	Out of Area
OOV	Objects of Verification
op/ops	operational/operations
org	organised/organisation
OTH	over-the-horizon
OTH-B	over-the-horizon backscatter(radar)
OTHR	over-the-horizon radar
OTHT	over-the-horizon targeting
para	parachute
pax	passenger/passenger transport aircraft
PCC/I/O/R	patrol craft, coastal/inshore/offshore/riverine
pdr	pounder
PFC/I/O	fast patrol craft, coastal/inshore/offshore
PFM	fast patrol craft, SSM
PFT	fast patrol craft, torpedo
PHM/T	hydrofoil, SSM/torpedo
pl	platoon
Pol	Poland
POMCUS	prepositioning of materiel configured to unit sets
Port	Portugal
PPP	purchasing-power parity
PSC	principal surface combatant
publ	public
RAS	replenishment at sea
RCL	recoilless launcher
R&D	research and development
recce	reconnaissance
regt	regiment
RL	rocket launcher
Ro	Romania
ROC	Republic of China (Taipei)
ro-ro	roll-on, roll-off
RPV	remotely piloted vehicle
Rus	Russia
RV	re-entry vehicle
SAM	surface-to-air missile
SAR	search and rescue
SEAL	Sea–Air–Land
SES	surface-effect ship
SEWS	satellite early-warning system
SF	Special Forces
SIGINT	signals intelligence
sigs	signals
SLAM	Stand-off Land Attack Missile
SLBM	submarine-launched ballistic missile

SLCM	sea-launched cruise missile
SLEP	service life extension programme
some	up to
Sov	Soviet
Sp	Spain
SP	self-propelled
spt	support
sqn	squadron
SRAM	short-range attack missile
SRBM	short-range ballistic missile
SS(C/I)	submarine (coastal/inshore)
SSB	ballistic-missile submarine
SSBN	nuclear-fuelled SSB
SSGN	SSN with dedicated non-ballistic missile launchers
SSM	surface-to-surface missile
SSN	nuclear-fuelled submarine
START	Strategic Arms Reduction Talks
STOL	short take-off and landing
STOVL	short take-off, vertical landing
SUGW	surface-to-underwater GW
SURV	surveillance
Sw	Sweden
SWATH	small waterplane area twin hulled (vessel)
Switz	Switzerland
sy	security
t	tonnes
TA	Territorial Army (UK)
tac	tactical
TASM	tactical air-to-surface missile
TD	tank division
tempy	temporary
tk	tank
tkr	tanker
TLE	treaty-limited equipment (CFE)
TMD	theater missile defence
tps	troop
tpt	transport
tr	trillion
trg	training
TT	torpedo tube
Tu	Turkey
UAV	unmanned aerial vehicle
UN	United Nations
(See pp. 253–60 for peacekeeping forces)	
URG	underway replenishment group
USGW	underwater-to-surface GW
utl	utility
UUGW	underwater-to-underwater GW
veh	vehicle
VIP	very important person
VLS	vertical launch system
V(/S)TOL	vertical(/short) take-off and landing
wg	wing
wpn	weapon
Yug	Yugoslavia

Desserts

Everyday recipes to enjoy

manhattan cheesecake

ingredients

SERVES 8–10

6 tbsp butter

200 g/7 oz digestive biscuits,
    crushed

sunflower oil, for brushing

400 g/14 oz cream cheese

2 large eggs

140 g/5 oz caster sugar

1½ tsp vanilla essence

450 ml/16 fl oz sour cream

blueberry topping

55 g/2 oz caster sugar

4 tbsp water

250 g/9 oz fresh blueberries

1 tsp arrowroot

method

1 Melt the butter in a pan over low heat. Stir in the biscuits, then spread in a 20-cm/8-inch springform tin brushed with oil. Place the cream cheese, eggs, 100 g/3½ oz of the sugar and ½ teaspoon of the vanilla essence in a food processor. Process until smooth. Pour over the biscuit base and smooth the top. Place on a baking sheet and bake in a preheated oven, 190°C/375°F/Gas Mark 5, for 20 minutes until set. Remove from the oven and set aside for 20 minutes. Leave the oven switched on.

2 Mix the sour cream with the remaining sugar and vanilla essence in a bowl. Spoon over the cheesecake. Return it to the oven for 10 minutes, cool, then chill in the refrigerator for 8 hours or overnight.

3 To make the topping, place the sugar in a pan with 2 tablespoons of the water over low heat and stir until the sugar has dissolved. Increase the heat, add the blueberries, cover and cook for a few minutes or until they begin to soften. Remove from the heat. Mix the arrowroot and remaining water in a bowl, add to the fruit and stir until smooth. Return to low heat. Cook until the juice thickens and turns translucent, then set aside to cool.

4 Remove the cheesecake from the tin 1 hour before serving. Spoon the fruit topping over and chill until ready to serve.

pecan pie

ingredients

SERVES 8

pastry

250 g/9 oz plain flour

pinch of salt

115 g/4 oz butter, cut into
    small pieces

1 tbsp lard or vegetable
    shortening, cut into
    small pieces

55 g/2 oz golden caster sugar

6 tbsp cold milk

filling

3 eggs

250 g/9 oz muscovado sugar

1 tsp vanilla essence

pinch of salt

85 g/3 oz butter, melted

3 tbsp golden syrup

3 tbsp molasses

350 g/12 oz pecan nuts,
    roughly chopped

pecan halves, to decorate

whipped cream or vanilla ice
    cream, to serve

method

1 To make the pastry, sift the flour and salt into a mixing bowl and rub in the butter and lard with the fingertips until the mixture resembles fine breadcrumbs. Work in the caster sugar and add the milk. Work the mixture into a soft dough. Wrap the pastry and chill in the refrigerator for 30 minutes.

2 Roll out the pastry and use it to line a 23–25-cm/9–10-inch tart tin. Trim off the excess by running the rolling pin over the top of the tart tin. Line with baking parchment and fill with baking beans. Bake in a preheated oven, 200°C/400°F/Gas Mark 6, for 20 minutes. Take out of the oven and remove the paper and beans. Reduce the oven temperature to 180°C/350°F/Gas Mark 4. Place a baking sheet in the oven.

3 To make the filling, place the eggs in a bowl and beat lightly. Beat in the muscovado sugar, vanilla essence and salt. Stir in the butter, golden syrup, molasses and chopped nuts. Pour into the pastry case and decorate with the pecan halves.

4 Place on the heated baking sheet and bake in the oven for 35-40 minutes until the filling is set. Serve warm or at room temperature with whipped cream or vanilla ice cream.

banoffee pie

ingredients

SERVES 4

filling

3 x 400 g/14 oz cans
    sweetened condensed
    milk
4 ripe bananas
juice of 1/2 lemon
1 tsp vanilla essence
75 g/2³/4 oz plain chocolate,
    grated
475 ml/16 fl oz double
    cream, whipped

biscuit crust

85 g/3 oz butter, melted,
    plus extra for greasing
150 g/5¹/2 oz digestive
    biscuits, crushed into
    crumbs
25 g/1 oz almonds,
    toasted and ground
25 g/1 oz hazelnuts,
    toasted and ground

method

1 Place the unopened cans of condensed milk in a large saucepan and add enough water to cover them. Bring to the boil, then reduce the heat and simmer for 2 hours, topping up the water level to keep the cans covered. Carefully lift out the hot cans from the pan and cool.

2 To make the crust, place the butter in a bowl and add the crushed digestive biscuits and ground nuts. Mix together well, then press the mixture evenly into the base and sides of a greased 23-cm/9-inch tart tin. Bake in a preheated oven, 180°C/350°F/Gas Mark 4, for 10–12 minutes, then remove from the oven and cool.

3 Peel and slice the bananas and place in a bowl. Squeeze over the juice from the lemon, add the vanilla essence and mix together. Spread the banana mixture over the biscuit crust in the pan, then spoon over the contents of the cooled cans of condensed milk.

4 Sprinkle over 50 g/1³/4 oz of the chocolate, then top with a layer of whipped cream. Sprinkle over the remaining grated chocolate and serve the pie at room temperature.

lemon meringue pie

ingredients

SERVES 4

pastry

185 g/6¹/₂ oz plain flour, plus
    extra for dusting
85 g/3 oz butter, cut into
    small pieces, plus extra
    for greasing
55 g/2 oz icing sugar, sifted
finely grated rind of ¹/₂ lemon
¹/₂ egg yolk, beaten
1¹/₂ tbsp milk

filling

3 tbsp cornflour
300 ml/10 fl oz water
juice and grated
    rind of 2 lemons
185 g/6¹/₂ oz caster sugar
2 eggs, separated

method

1 To make the pastry, sift the flour into a bowl. Rub in the butter with the fingertips until the mixture resembles fine breadcrumbs. Mix in the remaining ingredients. Knead briefly on a lightly floured work surface. Chill in the refrigerator for 30 minutes.

2 Grease a 20-cm/8-inch pie dish with butter. Roll out the pastry to a thickness of 5 mm/¹/₄ inch; use it to line the base and sides of the dish. Prick all over with a fork, line with baking parchment and fill with baking beans. Bake for in a preheated oven, 180°C/350°F/Gas Mark 4, for 15 minutes. Remove from the oven and take out the paper and beans. Reduce the temperature to 150°C/300°F/Gas Mark 2.

3 To make the filling, mix the cornflour with a little of the water. Place the remaining water in a saucepan. Stir in the lemon juice and rind and cornflour paste. Bring to the boil, stirring. Cook for 2 minutes, then cool a little. Stir in 5 tablespoons of the sugar and the egg yolks and pour into the pastry case.

4 Whisk the egg whites in a clean, grease-free bowl until stiff. Whisk in the remaining sugar and spread over the pie. Bake for another 40 minutes. Remove from the oven, cool and serve.

plum & almond tart

ingredients

SERVES 8

butter, for greasing

plain flour, for dusting

400 g/14 oz ready-made
    sweet pastry

filling

1 egg

1 egg yolk

140 g/5 oz golden caster
    sugar

55 g/2 oz butter, melted

100 g/3^1/$_2$ oz ground almonds

1 tbsp brandy

900 g/2 lb plums, halved
    and stoned

whipped cream, to serve
    (optional)

method

1 Grease a 23-cm/9-inch tart tin. On a lightly floured work surface, roll out the pastry and use it to line the tart tin. Line with baking parchment and fill with baking beans, then bake in a preheated oven, 200°C/400°F/Gas Mark 6, for 15 minutes. Remove the paper and beans and return to the oven for a further 5 minutes. Place a baking sheet in the oven.

2 To make the filling, place the egg, egg yolk, 100g/3^1/$_2$ oz of the caster sugar, melted butter, ground almonds and brandy in a bowl and mix together to form a paste. Spread the paste in the pastry case.

3 Arrange the plum halves, cut-side up, on top of the almond paste, fitting them together tightly. Sprinkle with the remaining caster sugar. Place the tart tin on the preheated baking sheet and bake for 35–40 minutes or until the filling is set and the pastry case is brown. Serve warm with whipped cream, if you like.

summer fruit tartlets

ingredients

MAKES 12

pastry

200 g/7 oz plain flour, plus
    extra for dusting
85 g/3 oz icing sugar
55 g/2 oz ground almonds
115 g/4 oz butter
1 egg yolk
1 tbsp milk

filling

225 g/8 oz cream cheese
icing sugar, to taste, plus
    extra for dusting
250 g/9 oz fresh summer
    fruits, such as red and
    whitecurrants, blueberries,
    raspberries and
    small strawberries

method

1 To make the pastry, sift the flour and icing sugar into a bowl. Stir in the ground almonds. Add the butter and rub in until the mixture resembles breadcrumbs. Add the egg yolk and milk and work in with a spatula, then mix with your fingers until the pastry binds together. Wrap the pastry in clingfilm and chill in the refrigerator for 30 minutes.

2 On a floured work surface, roll out the pastry and use to line 12 deep tartlet or individual brioche pans. Prick the bottoms. Press a piece of foil into each tartlet, covering the edges and bake in a preheated oven, 200°C/400°F/Gas Mark 6, for 10–15 minutes or until light golden brown. Remove the foil and bake for a further 2–3 minutes. Transfer to a wire rack to cool.

3 To make the filling, place the cream cheese and icing sugar in a bowl and mix together. Place a spoonful of filling in each pastry case and arrange the fruit on top. Dust with sifted icing sugar and serve.

upside-down pudding

ingredients

SERVES 6–8

225 g/8 oz unsalted butter,
　　plus extra for greasing
55 g/2 oz light brown sugar
14–16 hazelnuts
600 g/1 lb 5 oz canned
　　apricot halves, drained
175 g/6 oz demerara sugar
3 eggs, beaten
175 g/6 oz self-raising flour
55 g/2 oz ground hazelnuts
2 tbsp milk
cream or custard, to serve

method

1 Beat 55 g/2 oz of the butter with the light brown sugar and spread over the base of a greased and base-lined 25-cm/10-inch cake tin. Place a hazelnut in each apricot half and invert onto the base. The apricots should cover the whole surface.

2 Beat the demerara sugar together with the remaining butter until pale and fluffy, then gradually beat in the eggs. Fold in the flour, the ground hazelnuts and the milk and spread the mixture over the apricots.

3 Bake in the centre of a preheated oven, 180°C/350°F/Gas Mark 4, for about 45 minutes or until the pudding is golden brown and well risen. Run a knife around the edge of the pudding and invert onto a warm serving plate. Serve warm with cream or custard.

sticky coffee & walnut sponges

ingredients

SERVES 6

1 tbsp instant coffee powder

150 g/5$\frac{1}{2}$ oz self-raising flour

1 tsp ground cinnamon

55 g/2 oz butter, softened,
plus extra for greasing

55 g/2 oz brown sugar, sifted

2 large eggs, beaten

55 g/2 oz finely chopped
walnuts

butterscotch sauce

25 g/1 oz roughly chopped
walnuts

55 g/2 oz butter

55 g/2 oz brown sugar

150 ml/5 fl oz double cream

method

1 Dissolve the coffee powder in 2 tablespoons of boiling water and set aside. Sift the flour and cinnamon into a bowl. Place the butter and sugar in a separate bowl and beat together until light and fluffy. Gradually beat in the eggs. Add a little flour if the mixture shows signs of curdling. Fold in half the flour and cinnamon mixture, then fold in the remaining flour and cinnamon, alternately with the coffee. Stir in the walnuts.

2 Divide the batter between 6 greased individual metal pudding bowls. Place a piece of buttered foil over each bowl and secure with an elastic band. Stand the bowls in a roasting tin and pour in enough boiling water to reach halfway up the sides of the bowls. Cover the roasting tin with a tent of foil, folding it under the rim.

3 Bake the sponges in a preheated oven, 190°C/375°F/Gas Mark 5, for 30–40 minutes or until well risen and firm to the touch.

4 Meanwhile, make the sauce. Place all the ingredients in a saucepan over low heat and stir until melted and blended. Bring to a simmer, then remove from the heat. Turn the sponges out on to a serving plate, spoon over the hot sauce and serve.

cappuccino soufflé puddings

ingredients

SERVES 6

6 tbsp whipping cream

2 tsp instant espresso
   coffee granules

2 tbsp Kahlua

butter, for greasing

2 tbsp golden caster sugar,
   plus extra for coating

3 large eggs, separated,
   plus 1 extra egg white

150 g/5½ oz plain chocolate,
   melted and cooled

cocoa powder, for dusting

vanilla ice cream, to serve

method

1 Place the cream in a small, heavy-based saucepan and heat gently. Stir in the coffee until it has dissolved, then stir in the Kahlua. Divide the coffee mixture between 6 lightly greased 175-ml/6-fl oz ramekins coated with caster sugar.

2 Place the egg whites in a clean, grease-free bowl and whisk until soft peaks form, then gradually whisk in the sugar until stiff but not dry. Stir the egg yolks and melted chocolate together in a separate bowl, then stir in a little of the whisked egg whites. Gradually fold in the remaining egg whites.

3 Divide the mixture between the ramekins. Place the ramekins on a baking sheet and bake in a preheated oven, 190°C/375°F/Gas Mark 5, for 15 minutes or until just set. Dust with sifted cocoa powder and serve immediately with vanilla ice cream.

chocolate mousse

ingredients

SERVES 4–6

225 g/8 oz plain chocolate,
  chopped

2 tbsp brandy, Grand Marnier
  or Cointreau

4 tbsp water

30 g/1 oz unsalted
  butter, diced

3 large eggs, separated

1/4 tsp cream of tartar

55 g/2 oz sugar

125 ml/4 fl oz double cream

method

1 Place the chocolate, brandy and water in a small saucepan over low heat and melt, stirring, until smooth. Remove the pan from the heat and beat in the butter. Beat the egg yolks into the chocolate mixture, one after another, until blended, then cool slightly.

2 Meanwhile, using an electric mixer on low speed, beat the egg whites in a spotlessly clean bowl until frothy, then gradually increase the mixer's speed and beat until soft peaks form. Sprinkle the cream of tartar over the surface, then add the sugar, tablespoon by tablespoon, and continue beating until stiff peaks form. Beat several tablespoons of the egg white mixture into the chocolate mixture to loosen.

3 In another bowl, whip the cream until soft peaks form. Spoon the cream over the chocolate mixture, then spoon the remaining whites over the cream. Use a large metal spoon or rubber spatula to fold the chocolate into the cream and egg whites.

4 Either spoon the chocolate mousse into a large serving bowl or divide between 4 or 6 individual bowls. Cover with clingfilm and chill the mousse for at least 3 hours before serving.

coffee panna cotta with chocolate sauce

ingredients

SERVES 6

oil, for brushing

600 ml/1 pint double cream

1 vanilla pod

55 g/2 oz golden caster sugar

2 tsp instant espresso coffee
    granules, dissolved in
    4 tbsp water

2 tsp powdered gelatine

chocolate-covered coffee
    beans, to serve

chocolate sauce

150 ml/5 fl oz single cream

55 g/2 oz plain chocolate,
    melted

method

1 Lightly brush 6 x 150-ml/5-fl oz moulds with oil. Place the cream in a saucepan. Split the vanilla pod and scrape the black seeds into the cream. Add the vanilla pod and the sugar, then heat gently until almost boiling. Sieve the cream into a heatproof bowl and reserve. Place the coffee in a small heatproof bowl, sprinkle on the gelatine and leave for 5 minutes or until spongy. Set the bowl over a saucepan of gently simmering water until the gelatine has dissolved.

2 Stir a little of the reserved cream into the gelatine mixture, then stir the gelatine mixture into the remainder of the cream. Divide the mixture between the prepared moulds and cool, then chill in the refrigerator for 8 hours, or overnight.

3 To make the sauce, place a quarter of the cream in a bowl and stir in the melted chocolate. Gradually stir in the remaining cream, reserving 1 tablespoon. To serve the panna cotta, dip the base of the moulds briefly into hot water and turn out onto 6 dessert plates. Pour the chocolate sauce around. Dot drops of the reserved cream onto the sauce and feather it with a skewer. Decorate with chocolate-covered coffee beans and serve.

mixed fruit salad

ingredients

SERVES 4

1 papaya, halved, peeled
and deseeded

2 bananas, sliced thickly

1 small pineapple, peeled,
halved, cored and sliced

12 lychees, peeled if fresh

1 small melon, deseeded and
cut into thin wedges

2 oranges

grated rind and juice of 1 lime

2 tbsp caster sugar

method

1 Arrange the papaya, bananas, pineapple, lychees and melon on a serving platter. Cut off the rind and pith from the oranges. Cut the orange segments out from between the membranes and add to the fruit platter. Grate a small quantity of the discarded orange rind and add to the platter.

2 Combine the lime rind, juice and sugar. Pour over the salad and serve.

peaches with raspberry sauce

ingredients

SERVES 4–6

450 g/1 lb fresh raspberries

finely grated rind of 1 orange

2 tbsp freshly squeezed
   orange juice

2 tbsp Grand Marnier,
   Cointreau, or other
   orange-flavoured liqueur

2–3 tbsp caster sugar

6 ripe fresh peaches

vanilla ice cream, to serve

langues de chats, to serve
   (optional)

method

1 Purée the raspberries in a food processor or blender, then press through a fine non-metallic sieve into a mixing bowl to remove the seeds.

2 Stir the orange rind and juice and liqueur into the raspberry purée. Add sugar to taste, stirring until the sugar dissolves. Cover and chill in the refrigerator until required.

3 Meanwhile, bring a large saucepan of water to the boil over high heat. Add the peaches, 1 or 2 at a time, and let them stand in the water for 10–20 seconds, then remove with a slotted spoon. When the peaches are cool enough to handle, peel off the skins, then cut them in half and remove the stones.

4 Cut each peach half into two and stir into the raspberry sauce. Cover and chill in the refrigerator until required.

5 When ready to serve, put a scoop or two of ice cream into individual glasses or bowls, then top with the peaches and spoon some extra sauce over. Serve with the langues de chats on the side, if using.

rich vanilla ice cream

ingredients

SERVES 4–6

300 ml/10 fl oz single cream
    and 300 ml/10 fl oz
    double cream or 600 ml/
    1 pint whipping cream
1 vanilla pod
4 large egg yolks
100 g/3^1/$_2$ oz caster sugar

method

1 Pour the single and double creams or whipping cream into a large heavy-based saucepan. Split open the vanilla pod and scrape out the seeds into the cream, then add the whole vanilla pod, too. Bring almost to the boil, then remove from the heat and infuse for 30 minutes.

2 Put the egg yolks and sugar in a large bowl and whisk together until pale and the mixture leaves a trail when the whisk is lifted. Remove the vanilla pod from the cream, then slowly add the cream to the egg mixture, stirring all the time with a wooden spoon. Strain the mixture into the rinsed-out pan or a double boiler and cook over low heat for 10–15 minutes, stirring all the time, until the mixture thickens enough to coat the back of the spoon. Do not let the mixture boil or it will curdle. Remove from the heat and cool for at least 1 hour, stirring from time to time to prevent a skin forming.

3 Churn the custard in an ice cream maker, following the manufacturer's instructions. Serve immediately if wished, or transfer to a freezerproof container, cover with a lid and store in the freezer.

berry yogurt ice

ingredients

SERVES 4

125 g/4¹/₂ oz raspberries

125 g/4¹/₂ oz blackberries

125 g/4¹/₂ oz strawberries

1 large egg

175 ml/6 fl oz thick natural
    yogurt

125 ml/4 fl oz red wine

2¹/₄ tsp powdered gelatine

fresh berries, to decorate

method

1 Place the raspberries, blackberries and strawberries in a blender or food processor and process until a smooth purée forms. Rub the purée through a sieve into a bowl to remove the seeds.

2 Break the egg and separate the yolk and white into separate bowls. Stir the egg yolk and yogurt into the berry purée and set the egg white aside.

3 Pour the wine into a heatproof bowl set over a saucepan of water. Sprinkle the gelatine on the surface of the wine and stand for 5 minutes to soften. Heat the pan of water and simmer until the gelatine has dissolved. Pour the mixture into the berry purée in a steady stream, whisking constantly. Transfer the mixture to a freezerproof container and freeze for 2 hours or until slushy.

4 Whisk the egg white in a spotlessly clean, grease-free bowl until very stiff. Remove the berry mixture from the freezer and fold in the egg white. Return to the freezer and freeze for 2 hours or until firm.

5 To serve, scoop the berry yogurt ice into glass dishes and decorate with fresh berries of your choice.

This edition published in 2013
LOVE FOOD is an imprint of Parragon Books Ltd

Parragon
Chartist House
15–17 Trim Street
Bath, BA1 1HA, UK

ISBN: 978-1-4723-0572-5

Printed in China

Notes for the Reader

This book uses both metric and imperial measurements. Follow the same units of measurement throughout; do not mix metric and imperial. All spoon measurements are level: teaspoons are assumed to be 5 ml, and tablespoons are assumed to be 15 ml. Unless otherwise stated, milk is assumed to be full fat, eggs and individual vegetables are medium, and pepper is freshly ground black pepper. Unless otherwise stated, all root vegetables should be washed in plain water and peeled prior to using.

Garnishes, decorations and serving suggestions are all optional and not necessarily included in the recipe ingredients or method.

The times given are an approximate guide only. Preparation times differ according to the techniques used by different people and the cooking times may also vary from those given. Optional ingredients, variations or serving suggestions have not been included in the time calculations.

Recipes using raw or very lightly cooked eggs should be avoided by infants, the elderly, pregnant women, convalescents and anyone suffering from an illness. Pregnant and breastfeeding women are advised to avoid eating peanuts and peanut products. Sufferers from nut allergies should be aware that some of the ready-made ingredients used in the recipes in this book may contain nuts. Always check the packaging before use.